AFRICA IN GLOBAL HISTORY

WITH SOURCES

W. W. Norton & Company has been independent since its founding in 1923, when William Warder Norton and Mary D. Herter Norton first published lectures delivered at the People's Institute, the adult education division of New York City's Cooper Union. The firm soon expanded its program beyond the Institute, publishing books by celebrated academics from America and abroad. By midcentury, the two major pillars of Norton's publishing program—trade books and college texts—were firmly established. In the 1950s, the Norton family transferred control of the company to its employees, and today—with a staff of four hundred and a comparable number of trade, college, and professional titles published each year—W. W. Norton & Company stands as the largest and oldest publishing house owned wholly by its employees.

Printed in Canada
First Edition

Editor: Jon Durbin
Project Editor: Jennifer Barnhardt
Editorial Assistants: Kelly Rafey and Lily Sivitz Gellman
Managing Editor, College: Marian Johnson
Managing Editor, College Digital Media: Kim Yi
Production Manager: Sean Mintus
Media Editor: Laura Wilk
Associate Media Editor: Sarah Rose Aquilina
Media Project Editor: Rachel Mayer
Media Editorial Assistant: Alexandra Malakhoff
Ebook Production Manager: Mateus Manço Teixeira
Ebook Production Coordinator: Lizz Thabet
Marketing Manager, History: Sarah England Bartley
Design Director: Hope Miller Goodell
Designers: Chin-Yee Lai and Debby Dutton
Photo Editor: Trish Marx
Permissions Manager: Megan Schindel
Permissions Associate: Elizabeth Trammell
Composition: Jouve
Illustrations: Mapping Specialists, Ltd.
Manufacturing: Transcontinental

Permission to use copyrighted material is included in the credits section of this book, which begins on page C-1.

ISBN: 978-0-393-92757-3 (pbk.)

W. W. Norton & Company, Inc., 500 Fifth Avenue, New York, NY 10110
wwnorton.com

W. W. Norton & Company Ltd., 15 Carlisle Street, London W1D 3BS

1 2 3 4 5 6 7 8 9 0

AFRICA IN GLOBAL HISTORY

WITH SOURCES

ROBERT HARMS

W. W. NORTON AND COMPANY
NEW YORK • LONDON

BRIEF CONTENTS

CONTENTS

PART 6 AFRICA IN THE AGE OF THE GREAT CONVERGENCE, 1990–2017 630

MAPS

PERSPECTIVES (Primary Sources)

PREFACE

Ever since the first modern humans strode out of Africa some 50–80 thousand years ago to populate the rest of the world, Africa has been an integral part of global history. The history of the world cannot be adequately understood without taking African contributions and developments into account, and the history of Africa cannot be understood without an awareness of its relationship to larger currents of global history. By taking a fresh look at Africa's past in a global perspective, we can gain a greater awareness of both the diversity and the unity of the planet we all live on.

I wrote this book with three goals in mind. The first is to present histories that reflect the ecological, economic, cultural, religious, and political diversity of the African continent. The interaction among African peoples having different cultural traditions and ways of life has been a major driver of historical change. The second is to explore the complex ways in which Africans have blended local interests and outside influences in specific historical contexts. Throughout their history, Africans have been very adept at picking and choosing among the new ideas and belief systems that infiltrated their continent and adapting them to their needs. The third goal is to provide compelling narratives that shed light on specific aspects of Africa's past. By situating each narrative in its cultural and historical context, we can better understand the diversity of historical experiences that made the people of Africa who they are today.

The book opens with an introductory chapter that provides an overview of Africa's interactions with wider global histories, gives a tour of Africa's ecosystems, and dives into the deep history of human origins and the peopling of the globe by Africans. The rest of the book is divided into six parts, each of which explores developments in Africa during a particular era in global history. Nearly half the book is devoted to the period after 1870 because that is when life for ordinary Africans began to change at an accelerated pace due to colonial occupation, the expansion of world religions, and the spread of modern technology.

Part 1 (chapters 2–4) focuses on early African innovations and historical interactions with other regions of the Old World. Chapter 2 shows how a revolution in food production in the Nile valley paved the way for the spectacular civilizations in Egypt and Nubia, and how farming and herding gradually displaced hunting and gathering throughout the African continent. Chapter 3 looks at the long history of commercial and cultural interactions in the Mediterranean world that facilitated the spread of Christianity and Islam across North Africa. Chapter 4 explores the rise of powerful empires in the West African Sahel and splendid city-states along the East African coast, developments facilitated by long-distance trade in gold and the expansion of Islam.

Part 2 (chapters 5–7) focuses on Africa during the age of global war capitalism, a time when the nations of Atlantic Europe used armed ships and violent seizures of ports, territory, and human labor to dominate the international economy. Chapter 5 looks at the creation of the Atlantic world and its repercussions in Africa during the early centuries of the trans-Atlantic slave trade. Chapter 6 examines the functioning and impact of the slave trade during the violent eighteenth century, when nearly 7 million captives were forcibly extracted from Africa. Chapter 7 explores the variant forms of war capitalism in the Mediterranean and Indian Ocean worlds that accompanied the expansion of the Ottoman Empire into North Africa and the founding of Portuguese and Dutch settler colonies in southern Africa.

Part 3 (chapters 8–9) looks at Africa during the age of Europe's Industrial Revolution, a period when the trans-Atlantic slave trade was gradually replaced by an expanded trade in commodities needed by an industrializing Europe. Chapter 8 explores the political and social changes that accompanied the rise of indigenous plantation agriculture in areas near Africa's Atlantic and Indian Ocean coasts and the penetration of the interior by armed African caravans seeking ivory. Chapter 9 examines a series of indigenous religious and political innovations that restructured many of the major states in nineteenth-century Africa.

Up until the late nineteenth century, Africa was one of the few remaining regions of the world that had largely escaped occupation by the imperialist nations of Atlantic Europe. Part 4 (chapters 10–12) explores how all that changed when those nations partitioned, conquered, and colonized the African continent. Chapter 10 explores the causes of these developments and traces the trajectories of European conquests and African resistance. Chapter 11 examines the political and economic policies imposed by Europeans after World War I, while chapter 12 traces social and cultural changes in African life during the high colonial era.

Part 5 (chapters 13–15) looks at developments in Africa under the influence of two global wars: World War II and the Cold War. Chapter 13 examines the impact of World War II and the renewed emphasis on colonial economic development that emerged in the postwar era. Chapter 14 looks at the political struggles that led to independence in many African countries by 1965, while chapter 15 explores the influence of Cold War politics on those newly independent countries and traces the wars of liberation that engulfed the southern third of Africa. Part 6 consists of a single chapter (chapter 16) that examines the diverse paths toward sustainable governance and economic development that different African countries have followed since the end of the Cold War.

The narratives in the text are supplemented by a set of tools to help bring them to life. Full-color maps, antique paintings, and rare photographs add a visual dimension to the text. The Perspectives sections at the end of each chapter introduce students to a sample of the primary sources on which histories of Africa have been built. Students can read the words of kings and captives, soldiers and farmers, saints and sinners, and imperialists and rebels—all of whom played their respective roles in shaping the course of Africa's past. It is my hope that the narratives, illustrations, and primary texts will work together to give students and instructors alike a new understanding and appreciation of the struggles and triumphs of the people of Africa throughout their incredibly long and varied past.

It is in the nature of writing a broad survey like this one that I relied heavily on books and articles written by my colleagues in the field of African history. Information on Africa's past has increased exponentially in recent decades, and reading or rereading the excellent work of my colleagues was one of the most rewarding aspects of this project. Limitations of space have prevented me from acknowledging all of the sources that I used, but I am grateful for all the primary research and thoughtful analysis by my fellow historians of Africa that made this book possible. Many of my colleagues will recognize the influence of their scholarship on the narratives I have written.

I was aided in this endeavor by Samuel Severson, a Yale graduate student in African history, who tracked down many of the images and primary texts used in this book. In addition, I want to thank all of the instructors who reviewed this project and offered their valuable thoughts, including: Jessie Ruth Gaston, California State University, Sacramento; Meredith McKittrick, Georgetown University; Osaak Amukambwa Olumwullah, Miami University; Scopas S. Poggo, Ohio State University; Jean Muteba Rahier, Florida International University; Melissa M. Soto-Schwartz, Cuyahoga Community College; Tim Stapleton, University of Calgary; Christian Strother, Southern New Hampshire University; Ezekiel Walker, University of Central Florida.

Finally, I want to thank my partners at W. W. Norton, who have played an instrumental role in creating the first edition of my new book, especially Jon Durbin, Karl Bakeman, Kelly Rafey, Jennifer Barnhardt, Lily Gellman, Laura Wilk, Sarah Rose Aquilina, Sean Mintus, Tiani Kennedy, Norma Sims Roche, Bob Byrne, Trish Marx, Hope Miller Goodell, Chin-Yee Lai, Debby Dutton, Megan Schindel, and Elizabeth Trammel.

ABOUT THE AUTHOR

Robert Harms is the Henry J. Heinz Professor of History and African Studies at Yale University. A multiple award–winning author, he has written books and articles on topics such as African environmental history, oral traditions, the ivory trade, the Congo Red Rubber atrocities, the trans-Atlantic and Indian Ocean slave trades, and the impact of colonialism. His much-celebrated book *The Diligent: A Voyage through the Worlds of the Slave Trade* (2001) is based on the extraordinary journal of French lieutenant Robert Durand, who participated in the slave trade. He has taught in Africa at the high school and university levels and has conducted extensive research in the Democratic Republic of the Congo, Guinea, and Zanzibar.

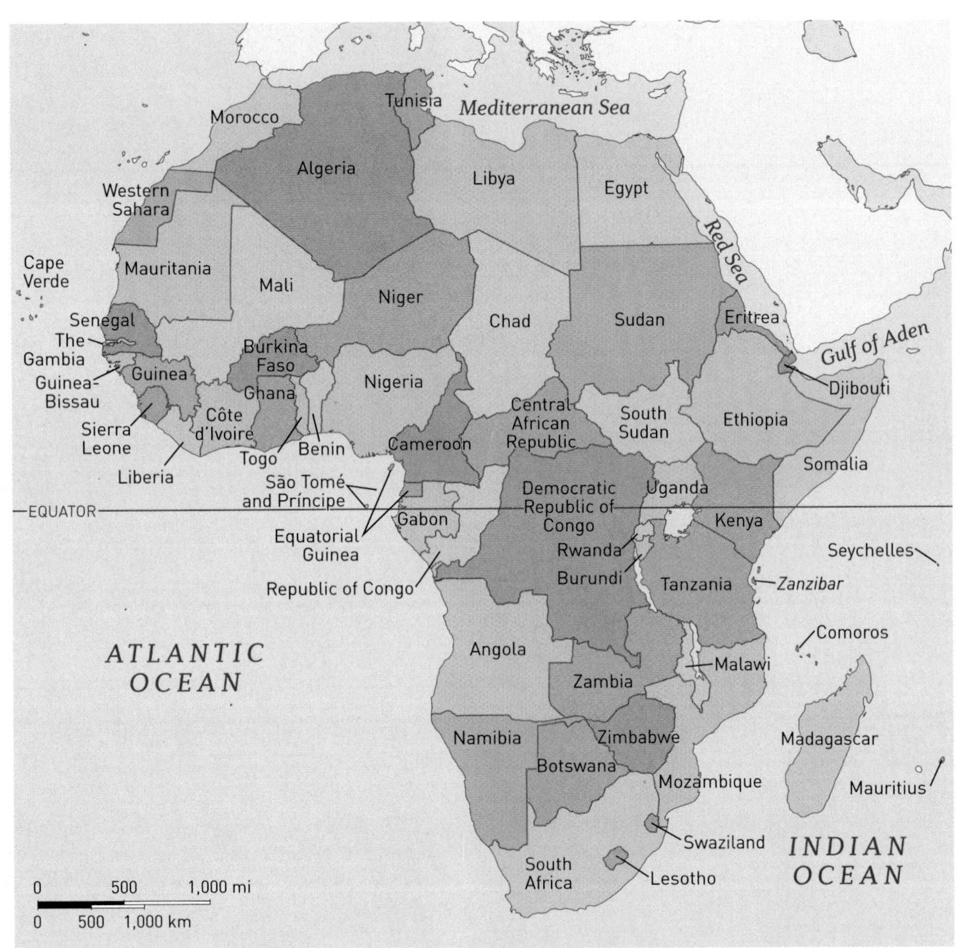

THE COUNTRIES OF AFRICA IN 2017 The United Nations lists 54 independent countries in Africa, including 6 island nations. Algeria is the largest African country by area, while the smallest is the Seychelles, a string of 115 tiny islands along Africa's east coast. The most populous country in Africa is Nigeria, while the least populous is the Seychelles.

AFRICA

IN

GLOBAL HISTORY

WITH SOURCES

THE HUNTING PARTY Rock art by early hunter-gatherers often depicted scenes from everyday life. This painting from the Drakensberg escarpment in South Africa shows a large hunting party that is breaking camp and going out to hunt a large animal. More than 20,000 rock art paintings have been cataloged on the outcroppings and caves of the Drakensberg escarpment.

6 million years ago	**3.2 million years ago**	**1.6 million years ago**
Millennium Man	Lucy	Turkana Boy

1

OUT OF AFRICA

When the African country of South Sudan gained its independence on July 9, 2011, it became the 54th fully independent country in Africa and the 193rd member of the United Nations. Although only four African countries were among the members when the United Nations was founded in 1945, over a quarter of the countries that currently sit in its General Assembly are located in Africa. The sudden burst of new African countries onto the world stage during the 1960s and 1970s caused some people in Europe and America to imagine that the history of Africa was just beginning, but that impression ignores the thousands of years of history that have made the people of Africa who they are today. Although the countries themselves are new, the societies and civilizations they represent have long histories.

For thousands of years, most Africans lived under independent political systems of their own creation. Then, in the late nineteenth century, the British, French, Portuguese, Germans, Italians, and Spanish—flush with the technology and weaponry generated by Europe's Industrial Revolution—carved up the African continent into colonies, which they ruled as overlords. When Africans regained their independence starting in the 1950s, the colonies became newly independent countries that were still saddled with their colonial borders, their colonial languages, and in many cases, their colonial names. It was almost as if centuries of history had been erased by a single century of colonial rule.

This chapter offers a first look at the long-term history of Africa in order to establish the broad context for the more detailed histories that follow. We begin

200,000–100,000 years ago
Genetic "Adam and Eve"

80,000–50,000 years ago
Humans migrate out of Africa

with a brief overview of Africa's interactions with the wider world across different historical periods to preview some of the themes in the coming chapters and to provide a global context for later discussions of indigenous African developments. The second part of the chapter focuses on the African continent itself, exploring the variety of natural environments that produced the modes of livelihood, social systems, and civilizations that animated Africa's history. The third part dives into Africa's deep history to explore recent scientific findings regarding the evolution of modern humans in Africa and their migrations across the globe. Bolstered by DNA studies, scientists are nearing a consensus in favor of the **Out of Africa hypothesis**, which holds that all modern humans on the planet stem from a single group of *Homo sapiens* who migrated out of Africa more than 2,000 generations ago.

AFRICA IN GLOBAL HISTORY

Africa is characterized by geographers as a continent, but a view from outer space would show it as part of the Afro-Eurasian landmass that historians call the Old World. Africa's ancient land and sea connections to Europe and Asia facilitated a long history of exchanges of people, crops, products, and ideas among inhabitants of the three Old World continents.

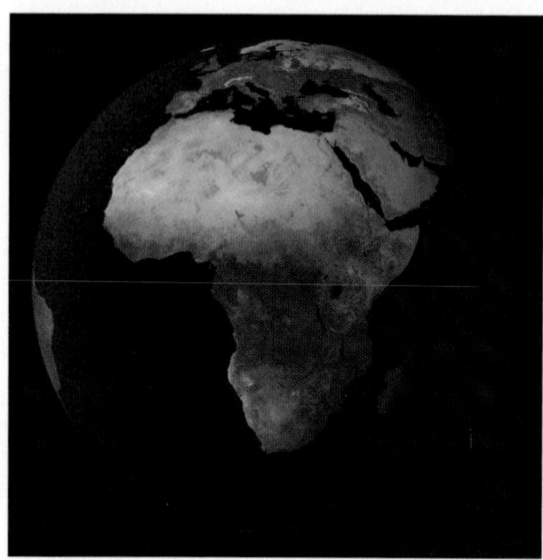

AFRICA IN GLOBAL PERSPECTIVE This composite satellite image shows that the Isthmus of Suez (at the northeastern corner of Africa) provides a land bridge between Africa and Asia, while only 9 miles of sea separates Africa's northwestern corner from Europe at the Strait of Gibraltar. Africa has long been in communication with other parts of the world.

The Early Stages of African History

In the earliest stage, successive migrations of early and modern humans out of Africa led to the peopling of the entire globe. Recent studies of human genomes in hundreds of indigenous populations around the world suggest that many of those early migratory populations eventually died out, and that a single migration from Africa between 50,000 and 80,000 years ago accounts for all of the non-Africans living in the world today. In the next stage, the arrival of Fertile

Crescent crops from Southwest Asia led to surplus production of wheat, barley, and flax that supported powerful states and original civilizations in the Nile River valley and the coastal plain of North Africa. Meanwhile, Africans farther south were domesticating crops such as millet, sorghum, coffee, rice, and yams, which were more suited to the majority of African environments. The arrival of plantains and sweet bananas from Southeast Asia greatly aided the settlement of the equatorial parts of Africa. Christianity and Islam, two of the world's great religions, originated in Jerusalem and Mecca, respectively, less than 300 miles from the northeastern corner of Africa, and both implanted themselves in Africa within a century of their founding. Gold from sub-Saharan Africa undergirded the monetary systems of the Christian and Muslim worlds, leading to the formation of large empires in the West African Sahel and splendid cities along the East African coast.

The Expansion of Atlantic Europe into Africa

Throughout that long history of Old World interactions and exchanges, the Atlantic Ocean was seen as an insurmountable barrier by Africans and Europeans alike. Not only was the Afro-Eurasian landmass isolated from the Americas, but a thousand miles of barren Sahara Desert coastline discouraged maritime traffic between Europe and sub-Saharan Africa. That situation changed dramatically after 1400, when Portuguese ships pushed southward along the desert coastline until they reached the land they called Guinea—"the land of the Blacks"—and Christopher Columbus sailed westward from Spain to reach the Caribbean island of Hispaniola. Those voyages marked the beginning of new patterns of world trade and migration that expanded farther after 1498, when the Portuguese rounded the southern tip of Africa and crossed the Indian Ocean.

Over the next four centuries, ships from the nations along Europe's Atlantic Seaboard dominated the maritime trade routes to create worldwide commercial networks. They seized North and South America, the Caribbean Islands, India, Australia, the Philippines, Indonesia, and the southern tip of Africa, among other places. The historian Sven Beckert has called this time the era of war capitalism because it was characterized by armed trade and the violent expropriation of land and labor. National governments sponsored military expeditions and laid claim to colonies, while large chartered trading companies such as the Dutch East India Company and the British East India Company operated as quasi-governmental corporations with the power to wage war, sign treaties, and establish colonies. Four centuries of war capitalism resulted in a massive rearrangement of the global patterns of trade, forced and voluntary migration, and political domination.

The expansion of Atlantic Europe had a devastating effect on both the New World and Atlantic Africa. Europeans carried deadly diseases to the New World that ravaged the indigenous populations and brought about a demographic collapse that some scholars have referred to as genocide (which was often the effect, though not necessarily the intention). Soon thereafter, European ships started coming to Africa in search of war captives to be carried to the New World as slave laborers. In 1525, the Portuguese ship *Santa Maria de Bogoña* carried 359 captive Africans across the Atlantic to Hispaniola. Only 287 of them survived the voyage. That was the beginning of the trans-Atlantic slave trade that would carry more than 12.5 million people out of Africa and land 10.7 million of them in the New World, leaving nearly 2 million who didn't survive the crossing.

The trans-Atlantic slave trade became an integral part of the newly interconnected world economy. European ships arrived in Africa carrying trade goods from Asia, which they exchanged for African war captives to be taken to the Americas. Soon Africa, Asia, Europe, and the Americas were all enmeshed in a global system of exchanges built on the violence, exploitation, and human misery of the slave trade. In West Africa, the slave trade fostered the growth of expansionist states such as Fuuta Jaloo, Asante, and Dahomey, which built up powerful armies to the detriment of their neighbors. South of the equator, the Kongo Kingdom disintegrated under pressure from competing slave trade networks, and Angola became engulfed in a century of warfare unleashed by Portuguese depredations. Throughout Atlantic Africa, ordinary people altered their weaponry, their residence patterns, the architecture of their towns and villages, their choices of crops, and their systems of production in order to protect themselves.

Prior to 1830, three-quarters of all the people who landed in the New World were enslaved Africans who crossed the Atlantic on slave ships, in chains and against their will. Those who survived the deplorable conditions of the Middle Passage were sold at auction and taken to farms, mines, and plantations, where they worked grueling hours without pay under brutal conditions. They were vulnerable to being beaten, raped, ill-housed, undernourished, and sold at the whim of their masters. As victims of the largest forced migration in world history, they were indispensable to building up the white settler economies of the New World, even though they themselves did not benefit from the fruits of their labor.

Although the captives were viewed by their white masters primarily as units of labor, they carried valuable African knowledge and ideas with them to the New World. Enslaved miners from the Gold Coast taught Brazilian miners how to extract gold from ore; enslaved rice growers from Sierra Leone brought innovations in wet-rice farming to South Carolina; enslaved cattle herders from West Africa kept the ox-powered sugar mills running in the Caribbean; and enslaved African farmers introduced intercropping techniques on New World farms. The captives also brought elements of African cultures and cosmologies, carrying religions such as Vodun and Santeria to the Americas along with Africanized forms of Islam and Christianity, thereby creating new trans-Atlantic religious traditions. In addition, they brought knowledge of African herbal medicines and healing practices, and they introduced a variety of cultural innovations in music, dance, oratory, storytelling, and cuisine.

Impact of Industrial Capitalism on Africa

The global order shifted in the nineteenth century, when a new economic system based on industrial capitalism was developing in Atlantic Europe. Machines powered by water wheels or coal-fired steam engines were increasingly used in manufacturing; large factories replaced cottage industries; steam-powered trains and ships revolutionized transportation; and telegraph lines facilitated long-distance communication. The profits from industrial capitalism made some of the Atlantic European countries the wealthiest nations on earth and financed their economic, military, scientific, and educational development. The historian Kenneth Pomeranz has characterized this process as the Great Divergence because the nations of Atlantic Europe were emerging for the first time in their history as the world's dominant economic and military powers. Industrial capitalism shaped a new global economic order in which other regions of the world played roles as suppliers of raw materials for European industries, as markets for European-made goods, or both.

As industrial capitalism gathered steam, the nations of Atlantic Europe no longer needed African captives to labor on their New World plantations as much as they needed African raw materials for their factories and African luxury products for their growing middle class. Egyptian cotton kept the textile factories of Europe running when slave-produced American cotton was embargoed during the Civil War; African palm oil and peanut oil became key ingredients in making European soap; spices from Zanzibar enhanced European cuisine; and African ivory provided piano keys and billiard balls for the parlors of the American and European middle class. In response to the rise in European demand, cotton-growing estates owned by large landowners sprang up in Egypt's Nile River delta; peasant farmers increased their peanut production in Senegal; African plantations using slave labor produced cloves in Zanzibar and palm oil in Dahomey and the Niger delta; and African ivory caravans traveled hundreds of miles into the interior as the elephants retreated from the coasts.

The Colonial Conquests of Africa

Europe's increasing dependence on African raw materials led to the colonial conquest of Africa in the late nineteenth century. It's no accident that some of the earliest decrees of the colonial powers called for increased production of rubber and cotton, two products that could not be produced in the cooler climate of Europe. As colonial control became consolidated in Africa in the early twentieth century, the colonizers realized that Africa could not become a reliable supplier of raw materials for European factories or of agricultural products for European consumers without better transportation networks to bring the products to market, so roads and railroads were built using forced African labor. Because the colonial state needed skilled workers and civil servants, schools were built to fill that need. All of those improvements were paid for by taxing the colonies themselves. Because salubrious climates, natural resources, and fertile soils were not evenly distributed across the continent, Africa became divided into three types of production zones: regions where African farmers produced cash crops needed by Europe, often under imposed production quotas; regions where European settlers seized the best land for large farms and plantations to be worked by African laborers; and regions of African subsistence production that served as labor reserves. Men in labor-reserve regions often traveled hundreds of miles to work in European-owned mines, plantations, and farms to earn money to pay their colonial taxes, usually leaving the women at home to produce the food, market the crops, and care for the young and the elderly.

As Africans became increasingly integrated into globalized networks of colonial power, commodities, and ideas, many of them sought new frameworks of thought for interpreting their new circumstances. One result was the expansion of both Islam and Christianity during the colonial period. Many African converts saw world religions such as Islam and Christianity, with their holy books and belief in a universal God, as better suited to the conditions of the twentieth century than were their local African religions, but other converts followed a world religion and a local religion simultaneously in order to cover all their bases. Tensions between the universal and the local fueled the rise of independent Islamic and Christian movements that sought to adapt universal beliefs to local needs.

Decolonization in Africa

World War II reconfigured global power relations, leaving Europe temporarily devastated as the United States and the Soviet Union emerged as the world's dominant military powers. When the European colonizers assessed the progress of their African colonies in the aftermath of the war, it became clear to them that although their colonial policies had brought about some improvement in transportation and education, mostly paid for by the colonies themselves, agricultural products were still produced mainly with a hoe and a machete, and there was no manufacturing to speak of outside of white settler areas. If Africa was to meet European demand, there would need to be substantial investments in education, health care, equipment, and transportation. Those were investments that the

European colonizers, still trying to rebuild from the ravages of World War II, were either unwilling or unable to make.

At the same time, there was a growing class of educated Africans who saw clearly that colonial rule contradicted European ideals regarding democracy, and who began to agitate for independence. They gained support from urban laborers, who had organized for better working conditions and higher wages, and from rural people who resented colonial taxes, migratory labor, and forced cash-crop production, which often took valuable time and land away from the production of food. Faced with resistance on multiple fronts, the British, French, and Belgians agreed to grant independence to their colonies, beginning with Ghana in 1957. In less than a decade, all the British and French colonies became independent countries. The Portuguese, in contrast, held on to their African colonies, even in the face of armed rebellions, because the Portuguese dictator António Salazar believed that colonies were essential to maintaining Portugal's status as a world power. It was not until the Salazar regime was overthrown in 1974 that the Portuguese colonies gained their independence.

Post-Colonial Africa

Independence brought new faces to African governments but did not fundamentally reorient the relationship between African producers of raw materials and European companies that purchased them. If Africans breathed a sigh of relief at the departure of colonial forces and administrators, European governments felt relief that they could now profit from African products without bearing any responsibility for making the investments required for further economic development. The narrative of African history becomes more complex at this point because each country charted its own course in response to its own internal and external pressures. Some countries adopted grand experiments in socialism—complete with Soviet-style collective agriculture—that were ultimately abandoned. Others retained close ties with their former colonizers, as when France's former West African colonies adopted a common currency tied to the French franc. Independence gave African countries opportunities to develop new international partnerships with countries such as the United States, the Soviet Union, and China.

By the 1990s, the nations of Atlantic Europe that had previously led the world in economic growth were being outpaced by some of their former colonies as industrial technology spread around the globe and the information revolution facilitated the movement of capital, information, and educational resources. The once-stark inequality between the former colonial powers and their former colonies was diminishing. If the nineteenth century could be characterized as the time of the Great Divergence, when Western European economic growth leapt ahead of that in other parts of the world, then the period after 1980 could be characterized as the Great Convergence, as other parts of the world began catching up. Asian countries led the way, but the process also provided encouragement for the African countries, which emerged from colonialism later than the others and had more catching up to do. Annual economic growth for Africa as a whole was about 2 percent during the 1980s and 1990s, but between 2001 and 2014 it was above 5 percent, which beat the worldwide average. Africa experienced extraordinary growth in many spheres: the population quadrupled during the second half of the twentieth century; urban areas expanded rapidly; and every African country developed a class of wealthy people who lived in grand cosmopolitan style. But for many ordinary Africans in both rural and urban areas, poverty remained. The challenge for African nations in the twenty-first century has been to find new ways to leverage their participation in an increasingly globalized world for the benefit of their growing populations.

AFRICA'S VEGETATION ZONES This composite satellite image shows Africa's deserts (yellow and orange), tropical rainforest (dark green), and the woodland and grassland savannas (lighter shades of green). Although the green areas are the most favorable to human habitation, people have historically devised ways to wrest a living from even the harshest environments.

AFRICAN ENVIRONMENTS

Throughout Africa's long history, the majority of Africans have made their living from the land as farmers, nomadic herders, or hunter-gatherers. The ways of life they developed were admirably adapted to their natural environments. Prior to the twentieth century, the overwhelming majority of Africans lived in rural areas and depended on the land to make their living. Today, however, 40 percent of Africans live in urban areas, and Africa has two cities—Lagos, Nigeria and Cairo, Egypt—with populations that surpass 20 million. In subsequent chapters, we'll look at the many ways people lived in their different environments, but first, it's important to take a look at the African environments themselves.

With 11.6 million square miles of land, Africa is the world's second-largest continent (after Asia). It's big enough to contain the United States (including Alaska and Hawaii), Europe, and China with room left over. An alternative calculation shows that Africa could hold the continental United States, China, India, Japan, and all of Europe. The population of Africa surpassed a billion people by 2010, making it the second most populous continent (after Asia) on earth.

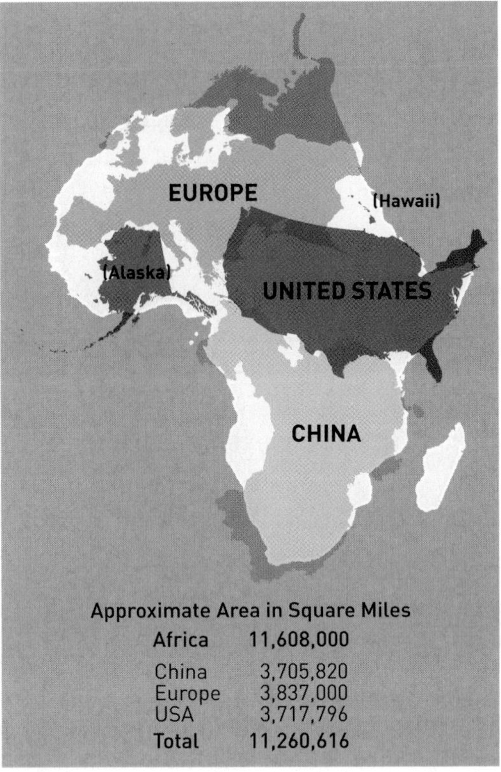

THE SIZE OF AFRICA This map illustrates how Europe, the United States, and China could fit into the African continent with space left over. The great size of the continent, along with its environmental and cultural diversity, helps to explain why Africa has such a complex history.

Adrienne and Amari Travel to the Northern and Southern Extremities of Africa

The city of Mbandaka in the Democratic Republic of Congo lies at the spot where the Congo River crosses the equator. Its latitude is 0°. The days and nights are of roughly equal length all year long, with sunrise at about 6:00 a.m. and sunset at about 6:00 p.m. The average daytime high temperature year round is 99°F, and the nighttime lows average 55°F. Because Africa enjoys warm temperatures all year round, the concepts of winter, summer, spring, and fall are meaningless. Instead, seasons are defined in terms of rainy and dry seasons. Lying on the equator, Mbandaka sits in one of the rainiest regions of Africa. It rains an average of one day out of three year round, with the heaviest rains falling in October, November, and December, and at least 3 inches of rain falling in each of the driest months. In all, Mbandaka receives about 64 inches of rain per year.

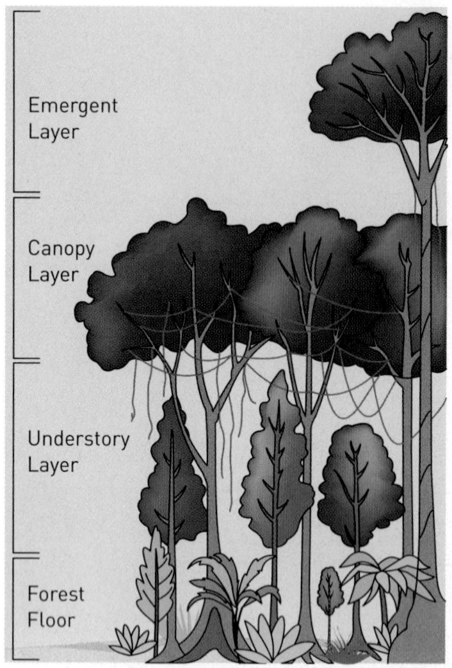

TRIPLE-CANOPY RAINFOREST The canopy layer in a typical tropical rainforest is made up of trees 100–150 feet tall. Below it is the understory layer, and above it is the emergent layer, which reaches heights of up to 200 feet. Very little light or rain penetrates the triple canopy, leaving the forest floor almost devoid of grasses or vegetation.

With its warm and humid climate, the city of Mbandaka is surrounded by the **tropical rainforest**. To a person flying over the rainforest in a small airplane, the forest canopy appears impenetrable, like a plush green carpet composed of trees between 100 and 150 feet tall. The canopy is occasionally pierced by emergent trees that have broken through to reach the sunlight and rise to heights of 200 feet or taller. Below the canopy is a layer of smaller trees that make up the understory. They have large leaves to absorb whatever sunlight reaches them through the canopy. The forest floor is relatively dark and cool because very little sunlight reaches it through the three layers of trees. A raindrop that falls on the dense canopy can take up to 10 minutes to reach the ground. The diversity of animal and plant life in the rainforest is astonishing—a patch of forest only 4 miles square can contain up to 400 bird species and 60 species of amphibians. Over 8,000 species of rainforest plants have been identified, of which over a thousand live exclusively in the tropical African rainforest.

Let's imagine that two travelers—Adrienne and Amari—are in Mbandaka preparing to set out on long journeys across Africa. Adrienne will travel north until she reaches Tunis, on the shore of the Mediterranean Sea, the northernmost city in Africa. Amari, for his part, will travel south to Cape Town, at the southern tip of Africa. Adrienne and Amari will travel mostly through the rural countryside where people make their living from the land. Amazingly, their treks will be roughly equal in length. If they both travel in a straight line, Adrienne will travel 2,594 miles, and Amari will travel 2,350 miles. That's because the equator bisects Africa, dividing the northern half from the southern half. Together, Adrienne and Amari will travel nearly 5,000 miles.

Let's follow Adrienne's journey to the north. Traveling through the rainforest, she occasionally comes across clearings that contain fields of root crops such as yams and cassava, along with oil palm trees and stands of plantains and bananas. At other times, she passes through former clearings that have been left alone to regenerate for up to 20 years before they will be used again. Forestry experts estimate that all patches of the tropical African rainforest have been cut down at least once in the past, some of them many times.

As Adrienne moves north through the rainforest, she notices that the rainfall gradually diminishes and an annual dry season appears. By the time she gets about 300 miles north of her starting point, the dry season is a full 2 months long. As she travels, the trees get progressively smaller, and the canopy gets thinner. By the time she gets about 500 miles from her starting point, the annual dry season is 3 months long. At this point, she is leaving the rainforest and entering the woodland **savanna**. As Adrienne continues her journey northward, the dry season will get longer and the rainy season will get shorter until the rains stop altogether when she enters the Sahara Desert.

Geographers picture the region between the tropical rainforest and the Sahara Desert as consisting of three successive bands that run in an east–west direction: the woodland savanna, the grassland savanna, and the Sahel. Adrienne, however, will experience them as a gradual continuum of progressively drier weather and progressively sparser vegetation. As she travels north, she moves through the woodland savanna for about 400 miles. The landscape is covered with tall grasses, scattered trees, and gallery forests along streams and rivers. With plenty of rain, farmers cultivate yams and oil palm trees. Continuing north, she leaves the woodland savanna and travels through the grassland savanna for the next 200 miles. Here the grasses are shorter, the trees are more scattered, and the gallery forests have disappeared. The dry season is 6 months long or longer, with rains falling mostly between May and October. The southern edge of the grassland savanna gets about 48 inches of rain per year, but rainfall diminishes progressively to 24 inches at the northern edge of the zone. The weather is hot, with an average daytime high of 95°F and an average overnight low of 70°F.

Leaving the grassland savanna, Adrienne continues north into the region known as the Sahel, through which she will travel for about 300 miles before reaching the Sahara Desert. In the Sahel, the dry season is 9 months long, and rains fall mostly in July, August, and September. The southern part of the Sahel gets about 20 inches of rain per year, while the northern edge gets only 10. That's not enough precipitation to support rain-fed agriculture, so rural people in the Sahel make their living by herding livestock or by irrigated farming in river floodplains. Because of the limited rainfall, the landscape is covered with short grasses and spiny plants. Thorny, shrub-like acacia trees with small green leaves dot the

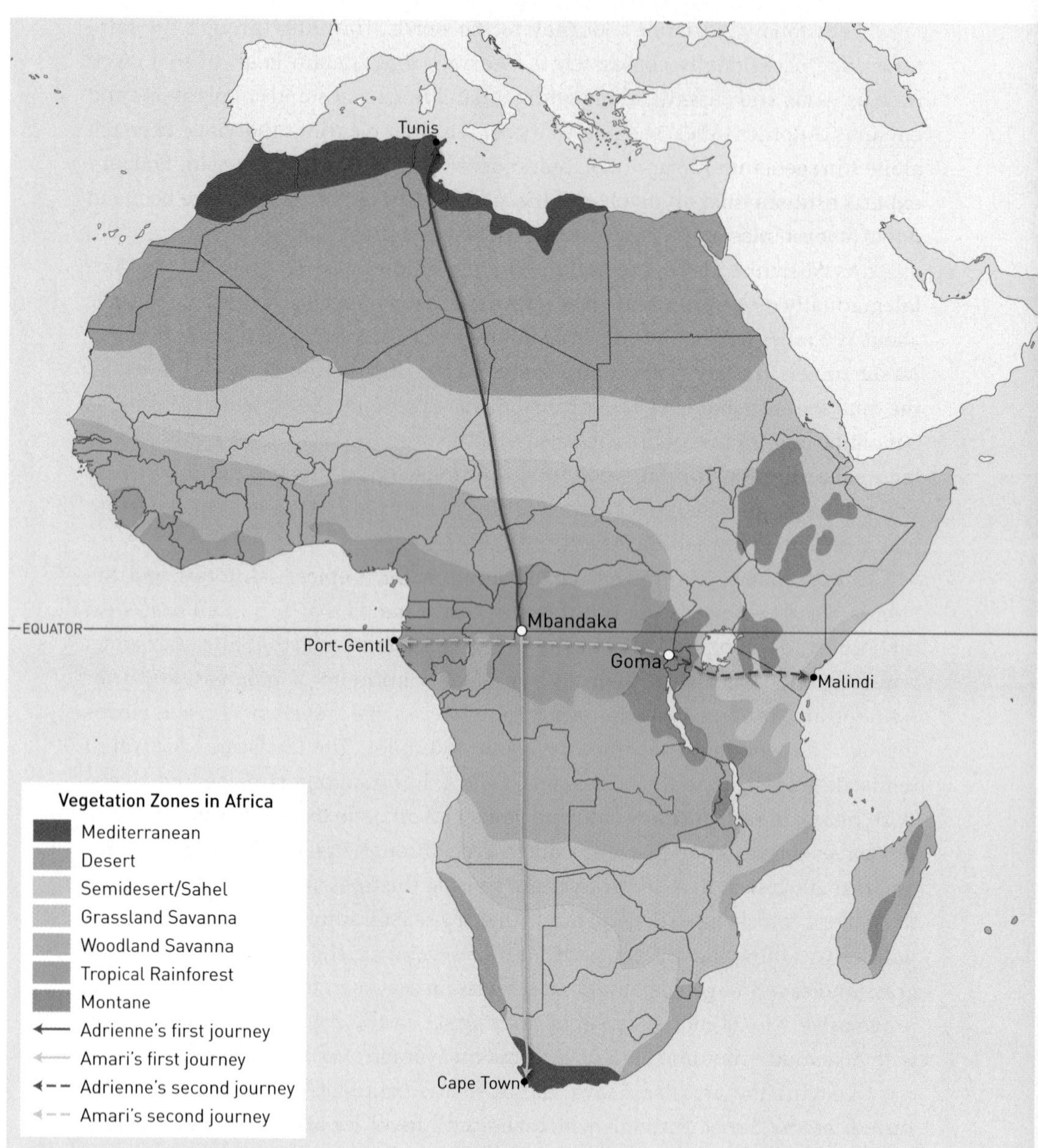

ADRIENNE'S AND AMARI'S JOURNEYS ACROSS AFRICA When Adrienne and Amari travel north and south from Mbandaka (on the equator), they each pass through a similar sequence of vegetation zones, but when they travel east and west from Goma (on the western rift), each one travels through a unique environment.

landscape. The temperature gets hotter as Adrienne approaches the Sahara Desert, with average daily highs around 98°F. Despite the daytime heat, the temperature drops rapidly when the sun goes down. Average nighttime lows are around 70°F.

After traveling north through the Sahel for about 300 miles, Adrienne arrives in the Sahara Desert, the largest desert in the world. Average annual precipitation is less than an inch, with some places going decades without rain and a few favored places getting up to 4 inches per year. Because there is little cloud cover or humidity, temperatures are hot during the day and cool at night. The average daytime high is 99°F, but temperatures can reach 120°F in April, May, and June. Average nighttime lows are 68°F, but temperatures can dip as low as 37°F in December and January. The few plants that can survive in the desert environment are found mostly in dry riverbeds, where water collects during the rare rains.

It's tempting to picture the Sahara Desert as an endless sandy beach, but in fact it contains a variety of landforms such as regs, ergs, mountains, and oases. Seventy percent of the Sahara's surface is covered by regs, which are plains of sand and gravel that are the remains of prehistoric sea- and riverbeds. Ergs, which are sand dunes up to 1,000 feet high, stretch for hundreds of miles and cover 20 percent of the desert's surface. There are also three mountain ranges in the Sahara, with peaks reaching as high as 11,000 feet. Oases form around underground water sources that reach the surface via springs and wells. Oases provide water for growing date palms and watering the flocks of nomadic camel and sheep herders. All the oases in the Sahara put together take up only 800 square miles, which is only about 0.02 percent of the desert's total surface. Yet 75 percent of all the inhabitants of the Sahara live in those oases; the rest are camel-herding nomads who move from place to place with their herds in search of water and pastures.

After crossing the Sahara Desert, Adrienne arrives at a spot about 200 miles south of her destination. Keeping the Atlas Mountains on her left, she enters a fertile coastal plain that receives about 20 inches of rainfall annually from the Mediterranean Sea. She is now in a Mediterranean climate zone characterized by rains that fall mostly between October and April. The coastal plain is dotted with olive trees and vineyards, and it also produces cereals and citrus fruits. The temperature is pleasant, with average daily highs of 77°F and average nightly lows of 60°F. Reaching the city of Tunis after traversing the coastal plain, she sips a glass of Tunisian wine at a restaurant that overlooks the Mediterranean Sea while reflecting on her trip. She has started out in the middle of the tropical rainforest and has subsequently traversed the woodland savanna, the grassland savanna, the Sahel, the Sahara Desert, and the North African coastal plain. The environmental diversity of Africa never ceases to amaze her.

Amari, for his part, leaves Mbandaka the same day as Adrienne, but he heads south toward Cape Town, at the southern tip of Africa. Even though he is traveling in the opposite direction, his trip will be remarkably similar to Adrienne's. For the first 300 miles, he travels through the rainforest, which thins out as he moves south and the dry season gets longer. Leaving the rainforest, he enters the woodland savanna and travels through it for a thousand miles. Then he passes through about 400 miles of grassland savanna before reaching a dry, semidesert country known as the Kalahari, which is the southern African equivalent of the Sahel. His route does not force him to cross a true desert, but the Namib Desert will be to his west throughout his entire trip through the Kalahari.

When Amari arrives at a spot about 300 miles from his destination, he enters a Mediterranean climate zone animated by rains coming from the South Atlantic Ocean. Like the region near Tunis, where Adrienne will soon arrive, this region gets about 20 inches of rainfall per year. There are few olive trees at the southern tip of Africa, but there are vineyards that thrive in the Mediterranean climate. Arriving in Cape Town, Africa's southernmost city, Amari finds the weather pleasant. Average daily highs are 71°F and average nighttime lows are 52°F. He finds a restaurant overlooking the South Atlantic, orders a glass of South African wine, and raises it in a salute to Adrienne. Like Adrienne, he has traveled through the tropical rainforest, the woodland savanna, the grassland savanna, a semidesert region similar to the Sahel, and the Mediterranean zone. If he had shifted his path just 200 miles to the west, he would have traveled through 300 miles of true desert.

The travels of Adrienne and Amari show that Africa's environments can be perceived as a series of east–west climate bands that determine the unique vegetation in each region and influence how people make a living from the land. Rainfall is heaviest near the equator, and it diminishes progressively as one leaves the equator and travels north or south until it finally stops altogether in the Sahara and Namib Deserts. Beyond the deserts, however, are bands of Mediterranean climate at the extreme north and south of the continent.

The East African Rift System

A notable exception to the climate-band scheme is found in eastern and northeastern Africa, where the climate and vegetation are totally different from what that scheme would predict. The reason for that region's uniqueness can be found in the highlands and mountain ranges that border the **East African Rift System**, a series of geological trenches 20–50 miles wide that form a shallow arc running from north to south and roughly paralleling the Indian Ocean coast. The same geological processes that pushed up the mountains some 75 million years ago also caused cracks in the African tectonic plate; these cracks make up the East African Rift System. Even today, the cracks continue to widen a few millimeters each year,

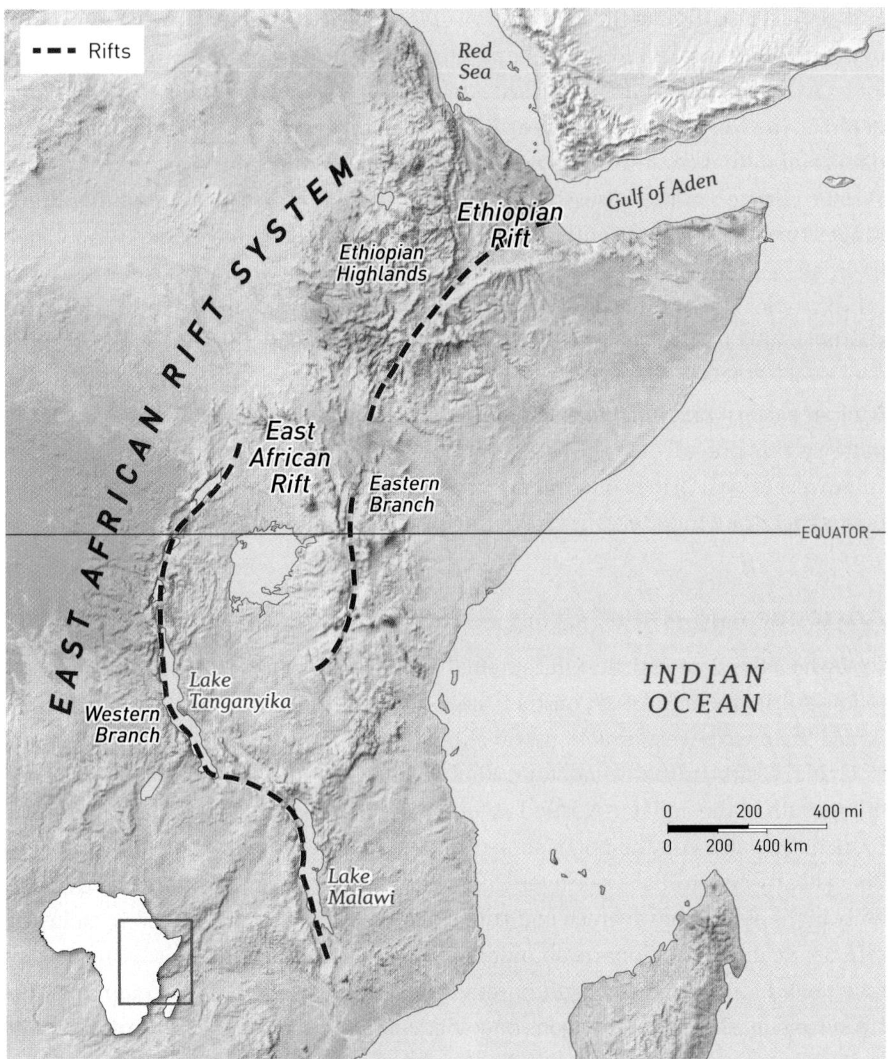

WHERE AFRICA SPLITS APART The Ethiopian rift, the western rift, and long, narrow lakes form an arc that defines East Africa as a distinct geological and environmental zone. Some scientists are predicting that millions of years from now, East Africa will split off from the rest of the continent.

and geologists estimate that the eastern side of Africa will break away within the next 50 million years and form a separate continent.

At the northern end of the East African Rift System, the Ethiopian Rift is bordered on the west by the Ethiopian highlands, a fertile agricultural area with abundant rainfall that contains many of Africa's highest mountains. Farther south, the Western Branch of the East African Rift is bordered by a succession of mountain ranges running north to south. Portions of the trench itself have filled with water to create some of the largest and deepest lakes in the world. Lake Tanganyika, for example, is 420 miles long and nearly a mile deep, while Lake Malawi, the southernmost lake in the East African Rift System, is 580 miles long and reaches depths of 2,300 feet. The Ethiopian highlands and the mountain ranges effectively wall off eastern and northeastern Africa from the Atlantic Ocean–based weather patterns that prevail over the rest of the continent. Crossing over those mountains from west to east brings one into a very different series of climates and environments that draw their weather from the Indian Ocean monsoons.

Adrienne and Amari Cross Africa by Traveling East and West

To see how the East African Rift System divides Africa between east and west, let's follow Adrienne and Amari on their next adventure. On this trip, they will cross Africa in an east–west direction, traveling parallel to the equator. They will begin in Goma, a city in the Democratic Republic of Congo that lies about a hundred miles south of the equator. Nestled among the mountains and lakes of the Western Branch, Goma sits on the north shore of Lake Kivu, which is over 1,500 feet deep. Being nearly a mile above sea level, Goma has a pleasant temperature, with average daily highs of 78°F and average nighttime lows of 58°F. The city receives 47 inches of rain per year, which supports abundant agriculture on the volcanic soils of the terraced mountainsides. The volcanic activity that accompanied the formation of the rift system millions of years ago is ongoing; when the Nyiragongo volcano erupted in 2002, lava flowed into Goma and destroyed nearly 5,000 houses and buildings.

Amari plans to head west to Port-Gentil, Gabon, on Africa's Atlantic coast, while Adrienne plans to travel east to Malindi, Kenya, on the Indian Ocean coast. Both will travel parallel to the equator, about 100 miles to its south. Amari will travel 1,416 miles. Adrienne, on the other hand, will travel only 759 miles, roughly half as far as Amari. As Amari treks westward, descending from the Virunga Mountains, the temperature gets warmer, and the vegetation changes from heather and alpine tundra at the higher elevations to bamboo and montane forest at the lower elevations. After traveling about 200 miles, he is out of the mountains and enters the tropical rainforest. For the next 1,200 miles, he travels through the rainforest until he arrives at Port-Gentil. He treks through triple-canopy forest interrupted by occasional clearings, regenerating fields, and villages. Despite its astonishing biodiversity, the rainforest starts to seem monotonous to him after the first few days.

Adrienne's journey to the Indian Ocean coast, though roughly half as long as Amari's, will be very different. After traveling east through the mountains for less than 200 miles, she arrives at the shore of Lake Victoria, the largest of Africa's Great Lakes and the second-largest freshwater lake in the world. Because it lies in between two branches of the East African Rift, but not in the rift itself, the lake is relatively shallow, with a maximum depth of 272 feet. Lake Victoria is the source of the Nile River, the longest river in the world, which flows north for over 4,000 miles to the Mediterranean Sea.

Soon after leaving the lake, Adrienne enters the ecosystem known as the **Serengeti**—the endless plain. At first, she passes through a savanna with medium-high grasses and thorny acacia trees, but she gradually moves into treeless grasslands with short grasses. The Serengeti grasslands receive a massive migration of wild animals from January to March; 1.3 million blue wildebeest, 200,000 zebras, and 400,000 gazelles pass through each year. Nomadic cattle herders formerly shared those plains with the wildlife, but now cattle grazing is prohibited because the land is part of Tanzania's Serengeti National Park and Kenya's Masai Mara National Reserve. Continuing eastward, Adrienne enters a semidesert grassland region that contains Tsavo National Park, home to wild animals such as lions, elephants, rhinoceroses, and giraffes. While traveling through those dry environments, Adrienne is at nearly the same latitude as Amari, who is traveling through the tropical rainforest. After passing through those varied environments, she arrives at Malindi, on the Indian Ocean coast.

The reason that Adrienne's trip is so different from Amari's is that the rain clouds that move east from the Atlantic Ocean and keep the tropical rainforest green cannot pass over the mountains that border the Western Branch. Instead, the rains in eastern and northeastern Africa come from the Indian Ocean, creating weather patterns that are entirely different from those found elsewhere in Africa. Climatologists are at a loss to explain the deficiency of rainfall in tropical East Africa. Some say it is because the wind systems run parallel to the coast rather than blowing onshore; others say it is because the rain-bearing equatorial low-pressure system passes through the region too rapidly.

Adrienne's and Amari's travels across Africa from north to south and from east to west have revealed the diversity of environments in Africa. People who historically made their living from the land did so in ways that were adapted to their unique environments, contributing to the complex mosaic of languages, cultures, social systems, and political systems that Africans developed over the millennia.

THE EVOLUTION OF HUMANS IN AFRICA

The story of humans on Planet Earth begins in Africa. In recent years, scientists who study human origins have been approaching a general consensus around three major conclusions. The first is that the ancestors of modern humans evolved in Africa starting about 6 million years ago. The second is that modern humans first emerged in Africa about 200,000 years ago. And the third is that all people now living on earth are descended from modern humans who migrated out of Africa between 50,000 and 80,000 years ago.

The evidence that underpins those conclusions comes from new fossil discoveries in Africa, new techniques for analyzing the fossil record, and dramatic developments in genetics. As a result, the narrative that historians construct about the early African past cannot be separated from a discussion of the methods used to recover that evidence. As new fossils are discovered and new analytical techniques are developed, the narrative is likely to change further. This section focuses on relatively recent scientific developments in research into human origins and their implications for how we understand the early history of Africa.

The greatest scientific advance of the early twenty-first century was produced by the **Human Genome Project**: an international collaborative research program that spent 13 years mapping the human genome (the totality of all our genes) by analyzing human DNA. The results, published in 2003, provided the first complete genetic blueprint for building a human being. Two years after the Human Genome Project published its findings, another international team of scientists completed the mapping of the genome of a chimpanzee named Clint that lived at the National Primate Research Center in Atlanta, Georgia. After adjusting for duplication of certain segments of the genetic code, they found that the human and chimpanzee genomes differed by only 1.2 percent.

The findings confirmed the long-held notion—elaborated by Charles Darwin in 1871—that chimpanzees and humans have a common ancestor. By looking at the degree of genetic difference between the two species in the light of known rates of genetic mutation, scientists have calculated that the ancestors of modern humans diverged from the ancestors of modern chimpanzees about 6 million years ago. If the genetically based calculations are roughly correct, then scientists would expect to find fossilized remains of creatures that were neither apes nor humans dating back to 6 million years ago.

Early Hominins

Scientists use the term **hominin** as a broad biological category that includes humans and their immediate ancestors, but not apes. Here we make a distinction between early hominins (who were not human) and humans (or late hominins). The fossil evidence for early hominins has been found exclusively in Africa. Paleoanthropologists (scientists who excavate and analyze fossilized bones of humans and their ancestors) have uncovered a variety of early hominin fossils in parts of the continent as widespread as South Africa, Tanzania, Kenya, Ethiopia, and Chad. They distinguish early hominin fossils from those of apes by two main criteria: the first is bipedalism (walking upright on two feet), and the second is having smaller canine teeth. In recent years, the analysis of fossilized remains has been revolutionized by the use of new tools such as electron microscopes, for finding markings that are invisible to the naked eye, and CT scans, which use X-rays and computer imaging to peer beneath the surface of a bone, erase rock or other encrustations, reconstruct incomplete fossils, or even create solid replicas using a 3-D printer.

A key challenge in reconstructing the fossil history of Africa is to determine the dates of bones, which often requires dating of the layers of volcanic and sedimentary rock in which they are found. The most common methods for dating use radiometric analysis to measure the amount of decay of certain unstable (radioactive) chemical elements such as potassium-40 or carbon-14, then calculate the age of the material on the basis of known rates of radioactive decay. Other dating tools include thermoluminescence, optically stimulated luminescence, and electronic spin analysis, all of which measure the quantity of electrons absorbed by a tooth or a rock over time. Geneticists can compute the time span since two organisms diverged by looking at the degree of genetic difference between them and comparing it with known rates of genetic mutation, in effect using the genetic difference as a molecular clock. As these and other methods get more refined, scientists are growing increasingly confident of their dates.

The oldest hominin fossil ever discovered is a skull that has been named Toumai (*Sahelanthropus tchadensis*), found near Lake Chad in 2001. Dated to between 6 million and 7 million years ago, Toumai had an ape-sized braincase with a volume of 360–370 cubic centimeters (cc), but he had small canine teeth, which differentiated him from the apes. Moreover, the hole where the spinal cord exited his brain was located underneath the braincase, indicating that the skull sat on top of a vertical spine. It seems likely that Toumai walked upright, but without finding his leg or pelvic bones, it is difficult to say more.

A more complete early hominin fossil, named **Millennium Man** (*Orrorin tugenesis*), was discovered in northern Kenya in 2000. His bones have been dated to about 6 million years ago. His legs appear to be adapted to upright walking, but his arms seem more adapted to climbing trees and grasping branches, all of which indicates that he could function in a mixed environment of trees and open spaces. He was more ape-like than human-like, which is why the early hominins have sometimes been referred to as "bipedal apes." The fossilized remains of Toumai and Millennium Man demonstrate that

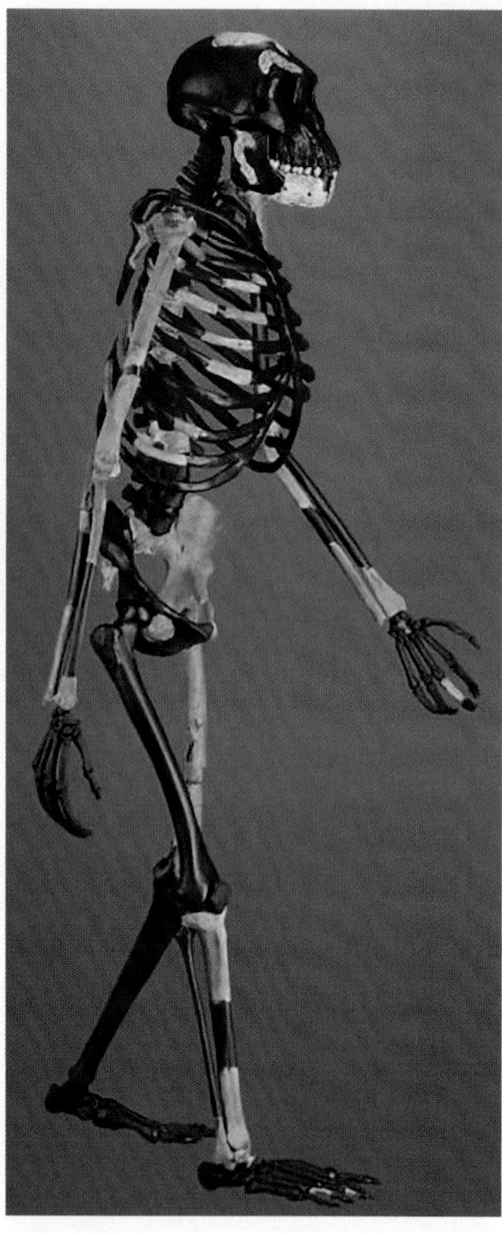

about 6 million years ago, creatures that were neither apes nor humans, but occupied an intermediate category between the two, were living in Africa.

One of the best-preserved early hominin skeletons is that of a female called **Lucy** (*Australopithecus afarensis*), who lived 3.2 million years ago. The team of American and French paleoanthropologists who uncovered her fossilized bones near Ethiopia's Awash River in 1974 celebrated their discovery while listening to the Beatles' hit song "Lucy in the Sky with Diamonds," which explains her name. Lucy was only 3 feet 6 inches tall and weighed about 60 pounds. She had a chimpanzee-sized braincase that was about 450 cc in volume. The appearance of her skeleton, with its short legs and elongated arms, was ape-like. Her curved fingers were well suited to climbing trees, but her knees and pelvis were completely adapted to walking upright.

LUCY The discovery of Lucy's fossilized skeleton in Ethiopia in 1974 revolutionized the study of humankind's ancestors. She had a grapefruit-sized brain and long arms for climbing trees, but she could also walk upright. Neither an ape nor a human, Lucy was an early hominin who lived about 3.2 million years ago.

Other fossil finds from the immediate region provide a glimpse into some aspects of Lucy's life. The remains of 13 individuals found nearby suggest that creatures like Lucy lived in social groups. At a site across the Awash River, paleoanthropologists discovered the bones of large animals dated at 3.4 million years ago. When examined under an electron microscope, they showed cutting and scraping marks that appear to have been made by a stone tool, most likely a sharp rock. The marks indicate that Lucy and her fellow creatures cut up large animals and scraped the meat off their bones. The remains of other early hominins roughly similar to Lucy (known as *australopithecines*) have been found at scattered sites in eastern Africa from South Africa up to Ethiopia.

About 700,000 years after Lucy (i.e., 2.5 million years ago), an early hominin that paleoanthropologists called *Australopithecus garhi*, but that we can simply call Gary, lived at another site along Ethiopia's Awash River. In many ways, Gary resembled Lucy, but there was an important difference between them: Gary had proportionally longer legs, which meant that he could walk with longer strides. Moreover, the site where he was found contained animal bones that showed cut marks made by stone tools, and crudely made stone tools were found nearby. In contrast to Lucy's group, who used naturally broken sharp rocks as tools, Gary and his friends were making their own crude tools by banging rocks together to break off sharp flakes!

Evidence of other makers of primitive tools who emerged between 2 million and 2.5 million years ago has been found at scattered sites in eastern and southern Africa. These hominins have been called Handyman (*Homo habilis*) because their bones have often been found near collections of primitive stone tools. They were somewhat larger than Lucy and Gary, had larger braincases (600–700 cc), and their feet had nicely sprung arches. Nevertheless, their teeth and jaws had the same proportions as Lucy's and Gary's, and their limbs were adapted to climbing trees. Tools found near Handyman bones have been dated between 1.5 million and 1.8 million years ago. They include some relatively crude tools, such as pebble hammer stones, as well as more sophisticated ones, such as double-edged flakes, scrapers with sharp edges, and pointed awls. Such tools were mainly used to strip meat from animal carcasses, as evidenced by cut marks found on animal bones.

In order to create a coherent narrative of early hominin development in Africa over the past 6 million years, it is tempting to imagine a single line of evolution and to say, for example, that Toumai was the direct ancestor of Millennium Man, who was the direct ancestor of Lucy, and so on down the line. But recent fossil finds in Africa have displayed such a variety of archaic forms and features that it is hard to make the case that a certain earlier creature was the direct ancestor of a certain later one. Most of them probably represent evolutionary lines that

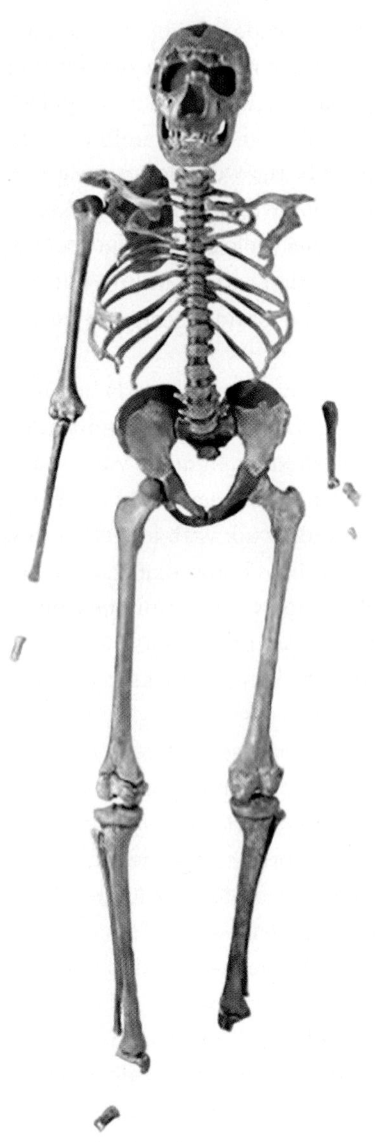

died out. All we can say for certain is that between 6 million and 2 million years ago, there lived in Africa a variety of creatures that were neither apes nor humans. The earlier ones could be seen as bipedal apes, but the later ones had more human-like features. All of those intermediate creatures lived in Africa and nowhere else on the planet.

Humans

A skeleton known as **Turkana Boy** (*Homo ergaster*), discovered in northern Kenya in 1984, gives a clear indication of being more human than ape-like. Turkana Boy died some 1.6 million years ago on the shores of Lake Turkana. His nearly complete skeleton provides a striking contrast to Lucy, who died 1.6 million years earlier. Whereas Lucy was 3 feet 6 inches tall, Turkana Boy was 5 feet 3 inches. Whereas Lucy had apelike proportions with short legs and long arms, Turkana Boy had long legs, which gave him body proportions close to those of modern humans. Whereas Lucy's brain had a volume of 450 cc, Turkana Boy's brain was nearly 900 cc; whereas Lucy could live either on the ground or in trees, Turkana Boy was clearly built for striding across the open plains; and whereas Lucy could be thought of as a bipedal ape, Turkana Boy had the anatomy of an early human. Other skulls similar to Turkana Boy's have been found near Lake Turkana and date back to

TURKANA BOY This fossilized skeleton was discovered near Lake Turkana in Kenya in 1984. Its most striking feature is the long legs that allowed Turkana Boy to walk and run in an upright posture. He could abandon the trees altogether and live in the grasslands. Here was an early human who lived about 1.6 million years ago.

1.8 million years ago. Turkana Boy was the earliest fossil to be undisputedly classified by paleoanthropologists as an early human.

Turkana Boy's striking differences from Lucy and Gary raise the question of why no clear transitional forms between those earlier hominins and Turkana Boy have been found. It may simply be that those bones were not preserved or have not yet been found, but there is another possible explanation as well. Recent advances in our understanding of genetics show that biological evolution need not be a gradual sequence of small changes leading step by step from creature A to creature B, but can progress in biological leaps because small genetic modifications can produce large changes in morphology. If such a leap occurred among Turkana Boy's ancestors, then there may be no "missing link" to be found.

All of the world's hominin fossils that are more than 2 million years old have been found exclusively in Africa, a clear indication that Africa was the home of the ancestors of humans. Then, sometime about 2 million years ago, early humans began to migrate out of Africa. Fossils roughly similar to Turkana Boy and dating to as early as 1.8 million years ago have been found in central Asia, China, and Indonesia. It is generally accepted that the ancestors of those creatures came from Africa because none of those regions have a fossil record of early hominins. The details of those early migrations, however, remain murky.

We have more detailed evidence of a migration of early humans from Africa into Europe that took place half a million years ago. The first such evidence was a skull belonging to a type of early human known as Heidelberg Man (*Homo heidelbergensis*), dated to 500,000 years ago, that was discovered in a quarry near Heidelberg, Germany, in 1907. Similar skulls, dated to about 400,000 years ago, have been found in Britain, Spain, France, and Greece. In all those places, no remains of early hominins have been found, so it seems likely that the ancestors of Heidelberg Man came from Africa. That hypothesis was confirmed in 1976 and again in 1997 when researchers in Ethiopia and Eritrea found fossilized remains similar to Heidelberg Man dated to 600,000 years ago and possibly earlier. Most Heidelberg Man fossils consist of skulls without skeletal bones. Their main feature is a braincase between 1,166 cc and 1,325 cc, which puts its volume close to the range of modern humans (which average 1,350–1,400 cc).

The era of the Heidelberg Men in Europe came to an end with the rise of the Neanderthals (*Homo neanderthalensis*) sometime after 250,000 years ago. We know that the two species coexisted in Europe for a time, but there is no conclusive evidence that Heidelberg Man was the direct ancestor of the Neanderthals. In the subsequent competition for resources and territory, the Neanderthals won out and the Heidelberg Men disappeared. Because most of the known Neanderthal bones were found in caves, the Neanderthals formed the basis of our popular-culture images of "cavemen." Neanderthals had braincases with a volume of 1,475 cc, slightly larger than those of modern humans. They spoke, hunted large animals, cared for their sick, and buried their dead. They were the dominant early human species in Europe and western Asia for 200,000 years. Then, about 25,000 years ago, they died out. In recent years, scientists have extracted enough DNA from Neanderthal bones to map the complete Neanderthal genome. Their findings confirm that the Neanderthals were a distinct species and were not the direct ancestors of modern humans.

At about the same time that the Neanderthals were emerging in Europe, modern humans (*Homo sapiens*) were emerging in Africa. Evidence of their origin has been collected by three different methods. The first is examination of the fossil record. Several skulls that can be identified as modern humans have been found in Ethiopia and dated to 190,000–160,000 years ago. We don't have any transitional fossils that link archaic humans such as Heidelberg Man to the first modern humans, so we cannot trace their direct ancestry. Scientists are still debating whether the emergence of *Homo sapiens* was the result of a gradual, continuous evolutionary process or episodes of sudden morphological change.

The second method is the comparison of DNA samples from living humans around the world in order to measure genetic diversity. A variety of studies have confirmed that the genetic diversity within Africa is far greater than the genetic diversity in other parts of the world, which indicates that humans have been living in Africa much longer than anywhere else. The studies have also found that the human populations outside of Africa all appear to be derived from a single genetic subset of the African population. Geneticists have calculated that an ancestral population consisting of as few as 1,000 people who migrated out of Africa could have contributed the genetic material that makes up the rest of the world's populations. Although there is evidence of multiple dispersals of modern humans out of Africa beginning about 120,000 years ago, the genetic lines of those early migrants apparently died out. Three separate DNA studies published in 2016 concluded that all the people now living on earth are descended from a single Great Migration of *Homo sapiens* out of Africa that took place between 80,000 and 50,000 years ago.

The third method also relies on DNA collected from a range of living populations around the globe. Using this DNA, researchers work down the family tree in order to reconstruct genetic lineages going back to a hypothetical common female or male ancestor. Such studies use either mitochondrial DNA (which is passed down only in the female line) or Y chromosome DNA (which is passed down in the male line). A variety of studies published since 1987 have shown that DNA from people in different regions of the globe can be traced back to a single male genetic lineage and a single female genetic lineage that existed in Africa between 100,000 and 200,000 years ago. No one claims that the hypothetical "genetic Adam" and "genetic Eve" represent the first man and woman on earth, but rather that they represent early genetic lineages that have survived unbroken to the present day.

Although it is relatively straightforward to compare the bones of modern humans with those of the earlier hominins and to measure the volumes of their braincases, it is much more difficult to determine the mental abilities that functioned inside those brains or to identify the intangible factors that separate modern humans from all other creatures on earth. The Australian psychologist Thomas Suddendorf reviewed the various studies comparing the mental abilities of humans with those of our closest animal relatives and concluded that there are two fundamental abilities that make us unique: "our open-ended ability to imagine and reflect on different situations and our deep-seated drive to link our scenario-building minds together." Those two qualities, wrote Suddendorf, allowed humans to transform "animal communication into open-ended human language, memory into mental time travel, social cognition into theory of mind, problem solving into abstract reasoning, social traditions into cumulative culture, and empathy into morality."

Putting the fossil and genetic evidence together, we can say that modern humans emerged in Africa roughly 200,000 years ago. That historical depth is reflected in the high amount of genetic diversity both within and between African population groups. Then, sometime around 120,000 years ago, small groups of modern humans left Africa and began to spread out. The early migrant groups eventually died out, but the Great Migration that took place between 80,000 and 50,000 years ago succeeded in populating the entire world. It is estimated that modern humans began living in China as early as 60,000 years ago and in Europe about 45,000 years ago, where they coexisted for a time with the Neanderthals. They came to the Americas about 15,000 years ago by crossing the Bering land bridge from Siberia to Alaska. No matter what our nationality, race, or ethnicity, we are all Africans.

Race and Races

All modern humans in the world belong to a single species—*Homo sapiens*—but there are observable regional differences in their skin color, hair color, eye shape, nose shape, lip thickness, and so on. In the eighteenth century, biologists used those superficial features to classify people into different "races," a vaguely defined term that meant different things to different people. In the nineteenth century, some biologists began to attribute cultural and intellectual characteristics to each race and to establish a hierarchy of what they deemed to be superior and inferior races. Because the people who proposed those schemes were Europeans

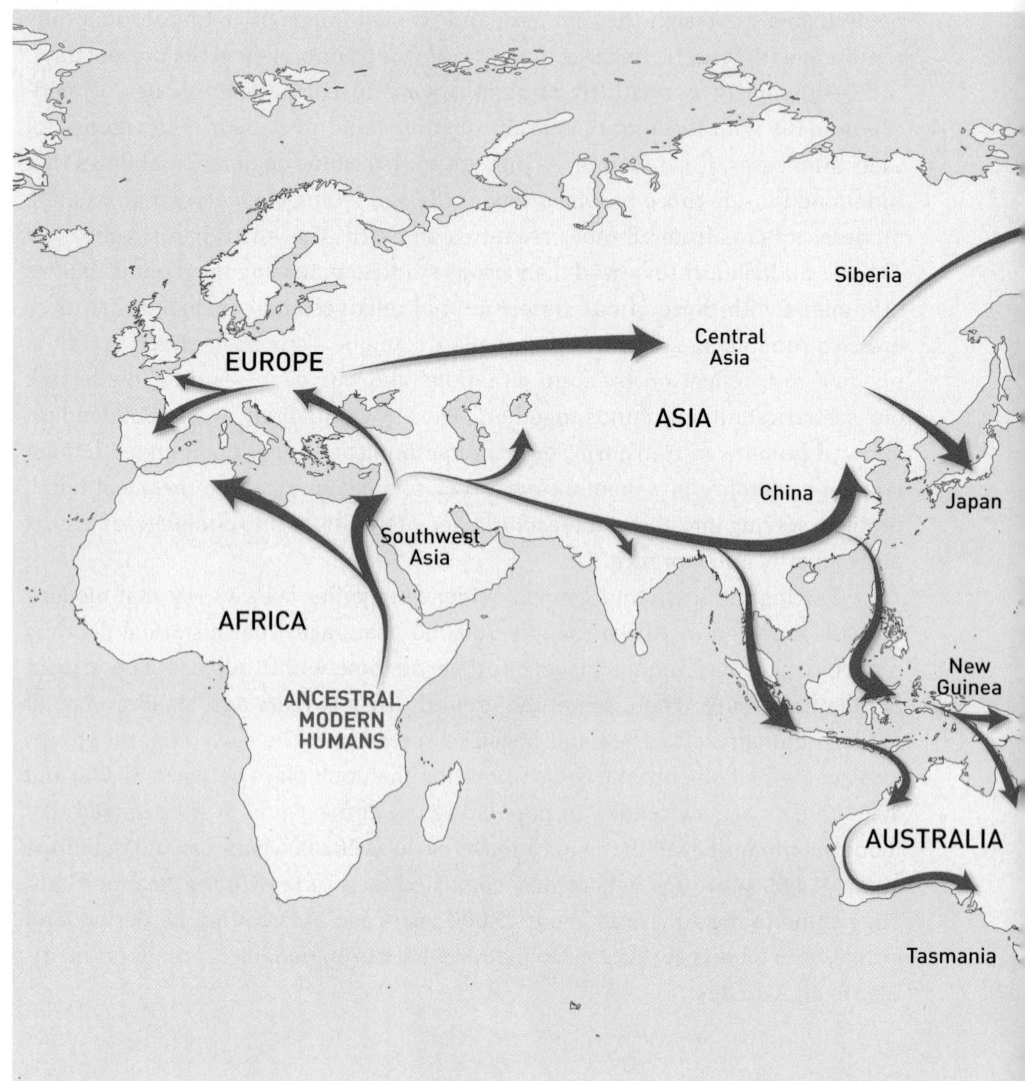

POPULATING THE PLANET This map shows possible routes by which modern humans left Africa and populated the rest of the world. The movements of humans toward Australia and North America were facilitated by climatic periods of low sea levels that led to the emergence of land bridges.

and Euro-Americans, it was not surprising that light-skinned Europeans always came out on top. Such classification schemes formed the basis for the racism that reached its peak in the twentieth century, when European colonialism dominated

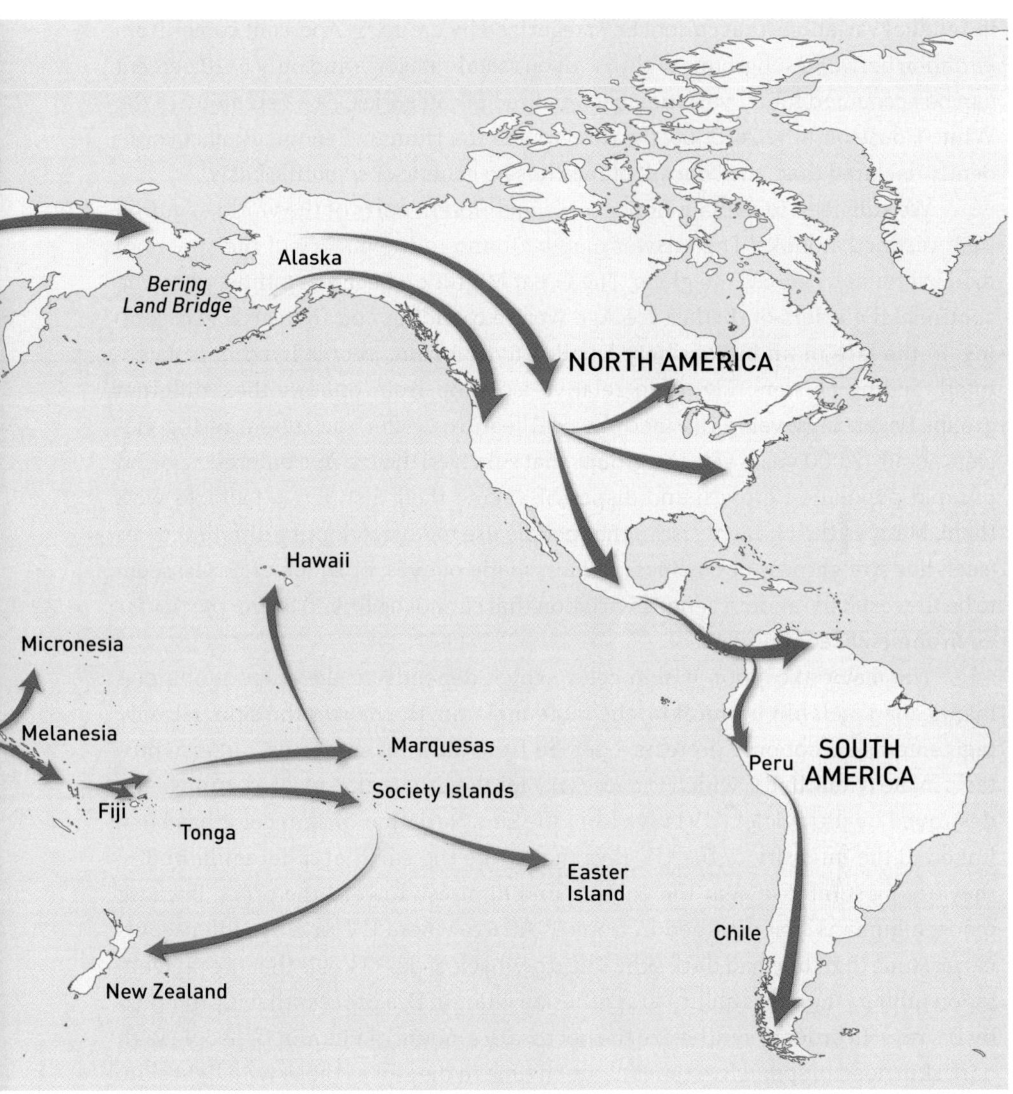

the international order and legalized racial segregation was the rule in many parts of the United States. The different races were talked about almost as if they were different species.

Racial classification schemes have been undercut by recent advances in genetics. By the time the first draft of the Human Genome Project was released in 2000, it had been established that there is no "race gene" and that all human beings are 99.9 percent the same in their genetic makeup. Several studies have shown that of the 0.1 percent of the genome that is variable, 90–94 percent consists of random individual variations that cannot be categorized by group, 5–7 percent comes from variation between subgroups within a given racial category, and only 6–10 percent can be accounted for by variation between racial categories. At a ceremony in the White House on June 26, 2000, the directors of the Human Genome Project confidently declared that "the concept of race has no genetic or scientific basis."

We still need to explain how people in different parts of the world acquired their distinctive looks. The answer may be found in the history of the spread of modern humans across the globe. The Great Migration began at a time when the continental glaciers of the last Ice Age were expanding and the earth was cooling. In the face of an increasingly hostile environment, people lived in isolated, interbreeding clusters. Living in relative isolation from one another, different groups began to develop distinct physical features. After the retreat of the glaciers about 12,000 years ago, the groups that survived the Ice Age entered a period of rapid population growth and dispersal, taking their distinctive features with them. Many of the characteristics that people use today to identify different races (such has straightness or curliness of hair, shape of eyes, or shape of noses) seem to be the result of random genetic variation that cannot be linked to any particular environmental adaptations.

The major exception is skin color, which depends on the amount of a pigment called melanin in the skin: the more melanin, the darker the skin. Heavily pigmented skin not only protects a person from harmful sunburns, but also protects folate (vitamin B_9), which is necessary for the production of DNA, from being destroyed by ultraviolet (UV) rays from the sun. Variation in skin color has been linked to the intensity of the UV rays that strike the earth at different latitudes: they are most intense near the equator and diminish toward the poles. Because modern humans first emerged in tropical Africa, where UV rays are intense, we can assume that they had dark skin. The drawback of dark skin is that the pigmentation inhibits the skin's ability to synthesize vitamin D, a process that is promoted by UV rays. In order to synthesize the necessary amount of vitamin D, people with dark skin need to spend five times as much time in the sun as those with light skin. Because sunlight is so abundant in the tropics, making enough vitamin D was not a problem there. However, as people moved to higher latitudes to the north and the south, where UV rays are less intense, inadequate vitamin D synthesis promoted strong natural selection for lighter skin pigmentation.

The results of this process can be seen today if one travels through Europe and Africa along a longitudinal meridian from north to south. In Lapland, which is north of the Arctic Circle, one encounters the light-skinned Sami people. Traveling south, one passes through the lands of the light-skinned Scandinavians, and pigmentation gradually increases as one approaches the Mediterranean coast of Europe. The people of North Africa and the nomads of the Sahara Desert have moderately pigmented skins that are darker than those of the southern Europeans. South of the desert, one encounters people with heavily pigmented skin that is commonly described as "black," even though there is a great deal of individual and regional variation in skin tones. Heavy pigmentation dominates from about 20° north latitude, through equatorial Africa, and on to 20° south latitude. In southern Africa, the San hunters have moderately pigmented skin similar to that of the people of North Africa. The north–south gradient along which melanin levels in human skin correspond to latitude and UV intensity is not as clear-cut in other parts of the world, such as the Americas, where human populations have arrived more recently, but it is clearly observed in Africa, where natural selection has been going on for a much longer time.

Populating Africa

DNA studies of modern African populations show that their genetic lineages began to diverge from one another about 150,000 years ago. The result was at least 14 distinct ancestral population clusters, each of which went on to produce its own genetic variations over time. The deep history revealed by genetic studies is also reflected in Africa's linguistic diversity. Languages, like human populations, can be grouped into families. Linguists construct language family trees showing how modern languages grew out of ancient ones (as Italian, Spanish, Portuguese, and French grew out of Latin in medieval Europe). Using this technique, they have grouped the more than 2,000 languages spoken in Africa today into 16 language families.

The 14 ancestral population clusters identified by the geneticists show a high correlation with the 16 African language families that have been identified by linguists. Because language is the main carrier of culture, linguistic diversification is also a mark of cultural diversification. Taken together, the genetic evidence and the linguistic evidence testify to a long history of invention and innovation in which people branched out from their ancestral homelands, settled in new places, and developed new languages and cultures. The result was the populating of the African continent with people representing a variety of languages, cultures, and phenotypes. It was this diversity that animated much of the subsequent history of Africa.

The modern humans that populated the African continent made and used stone tools, which became more efficient and refined with the passage of millennia. A major innovation was to blunt one edge of the blade (a technique known as backing) so that it did not cut the user's hand. Seventy-two thousand years ago, people living at Pinnacle Point, near the southern tip of Africa, had learned to make stone blades from silcrete that they hardened by a complex series of steps involving heating and cooling the stone. Soon they began to produce smaller blades known as microliths (literally, "small rocks"). These blades could be attached to handles using resin from trees as glue in order to make knives, scrapers, spears, and arrows. Microliths dating from 70,000 years ago have been found in South Africa, and others dating from 50,000 years ago have been found in Kenya.

These early African people fed themselves by hunting and fishing and by gathering fruits, berries, nuts, wild grains, tubers, and other edible plants. They had fire, and they cooked their food when required. Their diets varied according to region and season, but on average, about 30 percent of their daily calories came from protein and 35 percent from fats (but only 7.5 percent of their calories came from saturated fats). Carbohydrates made up about 35 percent of their calories (as opposed to 50 percent for modern Americans). The fruits and vegetables that supplied those carbohydrates were high in fiber and had low glycemic indexes. Honey was their only source of added sugar, and it made up only 2–3 percent of their carbohydrate intake. Some evolutionary nutritionists believe that the diets of these hunter-gatherers were healthier than those eaten by most Americans today.

Food was abundant for those who knew how to look for it. A group could feed itself if the able-bodied adults worked at food production for an average of 3–5 hours per day. In practice, however, they were more likely to alternate long days of hunting or foraging with days off until the food was eaten. There was no need to store extra food because fresh food was readily available. If a hunter killed a large animal, the meat would be shared with other members of the group, thus ensuring that the hunter would receive a share when somebody else killed a large animal. On the whole, it seems that the early hunter-gatherers ate well and had considerable leisure time. One anthropologist has referred to them as "the original affluent society."

The major drawback of the hunting and gathering way of life was defined by the law of diminishing returns: the longer a group stayed in one place, the more difficult it became to find abundant food. Soon they had to move on, make a new camp, and exploit a new territory. That general pattern of life has been confirmed by recent archaeological studies of hunter-gatherer sites in southern Africa, which found little evidence of food storage or status differentiation, but high levels of terrestrial mobility. Necessity sometimes forced people to move away from their original homelands and thus brought about the peopling of large areas of Africa. The fact that the San hunters who now live in southern Africa and the Baka and Bakola (pygmy) hunters of the Congo rainforest are close genetic cousins testifies to the long-range movements of early hunting and gathering populations. Because groups had to move frequently, maintaining mobility was a high social priority, and having too many old people or too many young children around made it harder to move on. In order to maintain the low population densities optimal for hunting and gathering, groups would split up when they became too big. They would also limit their population size and enhance their mobility by engaging in infanticide, senilicide, and birth control (mainly by periods of sexual abstinence).

One thing those early people did in their leisure time was create art. At Blombos Cave in southern Africa, archaeologists found plaques made of ochre (an iron-rich mineral) dated to 72,000 years ago that had been engraved with geometric designs. At some point after that, hunter-gatherers in southern Africa began creating paintings on rock outcroppings and on the walls of caves, using pigments made of finely ground iron oxides mixed with animal fat or blood. Rock paintings have been found at sites scattered throughout southern Africa. Most of them are very hard to date, but some paint fragments found in datable archaeological deposits go back as far as 28,000 years ago. The paintings show a variety of animals: antelopes, giraffes, elands, rheboks, elephants, rhinos, lions, and leopards. They also depict men in hunting parties and groups of female foragers, as if to emphasize the social nature of food production. In depicting humans, the paintings highlight the essential social roles in a hunting and gathering society: father/hunter, mother/forager, and provider/protector. Some art historians have attributed religious and cosmological significance to the paintings, but that remains a matter of interpretation. We can never know exactly what was in the minds of those early artists, but it is clear that they were leaving a record of a way of life that has long since disappeared.

By 10,000 years ago (8000 BCE), modern humans were living in all parts of Africa (with the possible exception of the tropical rainforest), and microlithic stone tools were ubiquitous. They had learned to exploit the available flora and fauna, organized social groups, developed languages and cultures, and even established artistic traditions. In response to the law of diminishing returns and the need for mobility, they kept their populations small, which left them thinly scattered on the ground. There is no way to estimate the population of Africa in 8000 BCE, but it was undoubtedly very small compared with that of more recent times. That situation would change with the advent of herding and farming.

CONCLUSION

African history presents us with the paradox of peoples with ancient societies and civilizations living in recently minted countries. This chapter sets out the larger context for tracing Africa's long history by looking at three themes. The first of those themes is Africa's interactions with other parts of the world over a series of historical periods. The brief overview presented here suggests that these interactions were beneficial for Africans during certain periods of history, but detrimental in others. The second theme is the variety of natural environments that make up the African continent. Human adaptation to different environments helps to explain the incredible diversity of languages, ways of life, cultures, and civilizations that developed over Africa's long history.

The third theme concerns the Out of Africa hypothesis, which holds that all modern humans on Planet Earth are descended from ancestors who migrated out of Africa. In this sense, Africa's interactions with the wider world began about 2 million years ago, when early humans similar to Turkana Boy strode out of Africa with their bipedal gait and founded new populations from central Asia to China. The fossil record shows that all early hominin fossils that are more than 2 million years old have been found in Africa, and that no such early fossils have been found anywhere else. The second phase began about 500,000 years ago, when early humans similar to Heidelberg Man moved out of Africa into Europe and spread from Greece to Spain and Britain. The most important development of all came some 200,000 years ago, when modern humans first developed in Africa. Sometime around 120,000 years ago, they began to spread out beyond Africa. Most of those migratory populations died out over time, but between 50,000 and 80,000 years ago came the Great Migration that eventually populated the rest of the planet. The fossil evidence and the DNA evidence demonstrate that all people throughout the world have African ancestors. In effect, we are all Africans.

At the same time that modern humans were spreading across the globe, they were also spreading across the African continent and learning to live in its diverse environments, which ranged from rainforests to deserts. DNA studies show that there is far more genetic diversity among different African population groups than is found in the rest of the world. The DNA evidence testifies to a long process of genetic divergence and remixing that has been going on longer in Africa than anywhere else. We know very little about the lives of early Africans, but archaeological evidence shows that they used fire, produced increasingly sophisticated stone tools, and made paintings on rocks. By about 10,000 years ago, variations of the hunting and gathering way of life had been established in all parts of Africa.

CHAPTER REVIEW

KEY TERMS AND VOCABULARY

- Out of Africa hypothesis
- tropical rainforest
- savanna
- East African Rift System
- Serengeti
- Human Genome Project
- hominin
- Millennium Man
- Lucy
- Turkana Boy

STUDY QUESTIONS

1. How would you assess the impact of Africa's long history of interaction with the wider world? On balance, were they mainly beneficial to Africa or destructive?
2. How would you explain the extreme diversity of natural environments in Africa?
3. Why does East Africa have a unique ecosystem that does not fit into the regular pattern of African vegetation zones?
4. In what ways did different environments engender different ways of life?
5. Why is there a growing consensus among scientists that all people on planet Earth are descended from ancestors who lived in Africa?
6. Do DNA studies complement or contradict the fossil and bone evidence in the search for human origins?
7. How do you explain the development of physically and linguistically distinct population groups in early Africa?

THE EAST AFRICAN SUPERPLUME

The mountains and high plateaus of the East African Rift System define the boundaries of the distinctive climates and ecosystems of eastern and northeastern Africa. By exploring volcanoes, depressions, and geothermal vents, scientists are discovering the natural forces behind this unique geological formation that may someday split Africa in two. This article from Scientific American *outlines the nature and significance of their findings.*

A Superplume Is the Reason Africa Is Splitting Apart

Africa is splitting in two. The reason: a geologic rift runs along the eastern side of the continent that one day, many millions of years in the future, will be replaced with an ocean. Scientists have argued for decades about what is causing this separation of tectonic plates. Geophysicists thought it was a superplume, a giant section of the earth's mantle that carries heat from near the core up to the crust. As evidence, they pointed to two large plateaus (one in Ethiopia and one in Kenya) that they said were created when a superplume pushed up the mantle. Geochemists were not able to confirm that theory. Instead they thought there might be two small, unrelated plumes pushing up the plateaus individually. The theories did not align, says David Hilton, a geochemist at the Scripps Institution of Oceanography in La Jolla, Calif. "There was a mismatch between the chemistry and the physics."

So in 2006 and 2011 Hilton headed to East Africa to see whether he could lay the argument to rest. He and his team decided to use gases emanating from the rift to determine how it was created. Donning gas masks, they hiked to the tops of volcanoes in Tanzania and Ethiopia and climbed into *mazuku* (the Swahili word for "evil wind")—geothermal vents and depressions where deadly gases accumulate and often kill animals. At these locations, the team collected samples of rocks deposited during eruptions, including olivines, crystals that trap volcanic gases like a bottle.

Back home in California, Hilton crushed the rocks inside a vacuum to release their gases. He was looking for helium 3, an isotope of helium present when the planet was forming that was trapped in the earth's core. Hilton figured that if rocks around both the Ethiopian and Kenyan plateaus contained this primordial gas, that would at least confirm that underground mantle plumes created them. The readings showed that, indeed, both plateaus contained helium 3. But Hilton and his group still had to wonder: Was one superplume behind it all? Or were there a couple of lesser plumes?

To answer this question, they turned to another primordial gas trapped in the mantle: neon 22. They found that neon 22 existed in both plateaus and that the ratios of helium to neon in those locations matched results published in April in *Geophysical Research Letters*. That meant that the plume underneath both plateaus was of the same material and of the same age. Hence, there was one common superplume. The geophysicists, it turns out, had been right all along.

1. *How does the superplume hypothesis help to explain why eastern and northeastern Africa has a distinctive ecosystem?*
2. *How great is the danger that the African continent will split in two?*

Source: Erin Biba, "A Superplume Is the Reason Africa Is Splitting Apart," *Scientific American*, July 15, 2014.

DISCOVERING LUCY

The 1974 discovery of the fossilized skeleton known to scientists as AL 288-1, but popularly known as Lucy, marked a major step forward in the scientific understanding of human origins. The bones were found in the Awash Valley in the Afar region of Ethiopia. Paleoanthropologist Donald Johanson tells the story of the discovery and naming of the most famous hominin fossil ever found. At the time, he was working with Tom Gray, his graduate student assistant.

With my gaze still glued to the ground, I cut across the midportion of the plateau toward the Land Rover. Then a glint caught my eye, and when I turned my head I saw a two-inch-long, light brownish gray fossil fragment shaped like a wrench, which my knowledge of osteology told me instantly was part of an elbow. I knelt and picked it up for closer inspection. As I examined it, an image clicked into my brain and a subconscious template announced hominid. . . . The only other thing it could have been was monkey, but it lacked the telltale flare on the back that characterizes monkey elbows. Without a doubt, this was the elbow end of a hominid ulna, the larger of the two bones in the forearm. Raising my eyes, I scanned the immediate surroundings and spotted other bone fragments of similar color—a piece of thighbone, rib fragments, segments of the backbone, and, most important, a shard of skull vault.

"Tom, look!" I showed him the ulna, then pointed at the fragments. Like me, he dropped to a crouch. With his jaw hanging open, he picked up a chunk of mandible that he wordlessly held out for me to see. "Hominid!" I gushed. "All hominid!" Our excitement mounted as we examined every splinter of bone. "I don't believe this! Do you believe this?" we shouted over and over. Drenched in sweat, we hugged each other and whooped like madmen.

"I'm going to bring the ulna to camp," I said. "We'll come back for the others." I wanted to mark the exact location of each bone fragment scattered on the landscape, but there were too many pieces and time was short.

"Good idea. Don't lose it," Tom joked, as I carefully wrapped the ulna in my bandanna. I decided to take a fragment of lower jaw, too, for good measure. I marked the exact spots where the bones had lain, scribbled a few words in my field notebook, and then got back into the Land Rover. . . .

We celebrated the discovery with a delicious dinner of roasted goat and pan fried potatoes washed down with a case of Bati beer my students had somehow managed to smuggle into camp. . . .

While we were all talking, *Sgt. Pepper's Lonely Hearts Club Band* was playing on a small Sony tape deck. When "Lucy in the Sky with Diamonds" came on, my girlfriend Pamela Alderman, who had come to spend some time in the field with me, said, "Why don't you call her Lucy?" I smiled politely at the suggestion, but I didn't like it because I thought it was frivolous to refer to such an important find simply as Lucy.

1. *To what extent are pathbreaking archaeological finds the result of luck versus skill?*
2. *Why did the name Lucy catch on, even though Donald Johanson thought it was too trivial a name for such an important discovery?*

Source: Donald C. Johanson and Kate Wong, *Lucy's Legacy: The Quest for Human Origins* (New York: Three Rivers Press, 2010), pp. 5–8.

TURKANA BOY

The fossilized bones of Turkana Boy (1.6 million years old) are approximately half the age of Lucy's (3.2 million years old). Ian Tattersall, the former curator of the Spitzer Hall of Human Origins at the American Museum of Natural History in New York, describes the skeleton and explains its significance for tracing the development of early humans.

Here, though, was the almost entire skeleton of an unfortunate individual who had died prematurely, face down in lakeside swampy mud, some 1.6 million years ago. Fortunately for us, his remains had been covered by soft protective sediments before they could attract the attention of scavengers. . . .

What is most remarkable about the Boy is that his skeleton presents a striking contrast to that of Lucy and other bipedal apes. The Boy was tall, with long legs that contributed importantly to basic body proportions that are close to our own. Some echoes of the past remain; but in all the essentials we see a creature not too dissimilar from ourselves, at least below the neck. Here, at last, is a hominid adapted to striding out across the open savanna, far from the shelter of trees. Gone are the "have your cake and eat it" ambiguities of the bipedal ape skeleton. The Boy's body is that of an obligate biped, rather than simply a facultative one: it is the body of a creature that was committed to upright bipedality as a way of life, rather than one that simply had this way of getting around as an option.

To put the situation another way, the Boy and others like him had adopted the savanna as their home. By 1.6 million years ago, grasslands had already become widespread in Africa, although those open, Serengeti-style savannas where the view goes on forever were still several hundred thousand years in the future. The environments through which *Homo ergaster* moved still largely resembled the mosaic of the past, with larger or smaller patches of grassland interspersed with clumped or scattered trees, true forest in hollows and along watercourses, and swamplands along lake margins such as the one on which the Turkana Boy died. But the new body form certainly reflects—or permitted, or even mandated—a novel way of exploiting the environment, with an emphasis on the resources available in the more open areas.

The definitive abandonment of the trees is reflected throughout the Turkana Boy's skeleton. For example, the extravagantly broad pelvis of Lucy had disappeared, apparently in concert with a lengthening of the leg. For while Lucy had needed a wide pelvis whose horizontal rotation could counteract excessive dropping of her center of gravity as she swung each leg forward, the Boy's long legs provided an alternate means of achieving the same thing.

1. *Assess the relative importance of the fossil discoveries of Lucy versus Turkana Boy.*
2. *Why is it significant that Turkana Boy lived in the grasslands and not in the trees?*

Source: Ian Tattersall, *Masters of the Planet: The Search for Our Human Origins* (New York: Palgrave Macmillan, 2012), pp. 91–94.

THE GREAT DISPERSAL

Although it has been established by scientists that early humans evolved in Africa, there is less certainty about how and when they dispersed throughout the world. This article from Science *summarizes three DNA studies that trace the dispersal of humans to a single migration out of Africa. This finding does not preclude other migrations from Africa, but rather concludes that the genetic lines of those migrations eventually died out.*

Australian Aborigines have long been cast as a people apart. Although Australia is halfway around the world from our species's accepted birthplace in Africa, the continent is nevertheless home to some of the earliest undisputed signs of modern humans outside Africa. . . . A trio of genomic studies, the first to analyze many full genomes from Australia and New Guinea . . . conclude that, like most other living Eurasians, Aborigines descend from a single group of modern humans who swept out of Africa 50,000 to 60,000 years ago and then spread in different directions. The papers "are really important," says population geneticist Joshua Akey of the University of Washington, Seattle, offering powerful testimony that "the vast majority of non-Africans [alive today] trace their ancestry back to a single out-of-Africa event."

Three large groups of geneticists independently set out to fill the gaps, adding hundreds of fully sequenced genomes from Africa, Australia, and Papua New Guinea to existing databases. . . .

A team led by evolutionary geneticist Eske Willerslev of the University of Copenhagen zeroed in on Australia and New Guinea in what Akey calls a "landmark" paper detailing the colonization of Australia. By comparing Aboriginal genomes to other groups, they conclude that Aborigines diverged from Eurasians between 50,000 and 70,000 years ago, after the whole group had already split from Africans. That means Aborigines and all other non-African people descend from the same out-of-Africa sweep, and that Australia was initially settled only once, rather than twice as some earlier evidence had suggested. Patterns in the Aboriginal DNA also point to a genetic bottleneck about 50,000 years ago: the lasting legacy of the small group that first colonized the ancient continent.

In another paper, a team led by population geneticist David Reich of Harvard University comes to a similar conclusion. . . . "The take-home message is that modern human people today outside of Africa are descended from a single founding population almost completely," Reich says. "You can exclude and rule out an earlier migration; the southern route."

But the third paper, by a team led by Mait Metspalu of the Estonian Biocentre in Tartu, makes a different claim. . . . The group concludes that at least 2% of the genomes of people from Papua New Guinea comes from an early dispersal of modern humans, who left Africa perhaps 120,000 years ago. Their paper proposes that *Homo sapiens* left Africa in at least two waves.

Reich questions that result, but says that his and Willerslev's studies can't rule out a contribution of only 1% or 2% from an earlier *H. sapiens* migration. Akey says: "As population geneticists, we could spend the next decade arguing about that 2%, but in practical terms it doesn't matter." The most recent migration "explains more than 90% of the ancestry of living people."

---

1. *How convincing is the evidence that all humans on earth are descended from a single migration out of Africa?*
2. *How does the Out of Africa hypothesis affect the way we think about racial and ethnic diversity in the world today?*

Source: Elizabeth Culotta and Ann Gibbons, "Almost all living people outside of Africa trace back to a single migration more than 50,000 years ago," *Science*, September 21, 2016.

PART 1

AFRICA IN THE OLD WORLD, EARLY TIMES TO 1500 CE

Africa has never been isolated from the rest of the world. At its northwestern corner along the Strait of Gibraltar, Africa is only 9 miles from Europe; at its northeastern corner, it is connected to Southwest Asia by the Isthmus of Suez; and at the southern end of the Red Sea, it is only 20 miles from the Arabian Peninsula. A view from outer space would show Africa, Asia, and Europe as one enormous landmass, partially interrupted by the Mediterranean and Red Seas. That reality was recognized already in the fourth century CE when the North African theologian Augustine of Hippo (later known as Saint Augustine) observed that the global landmass was divided into three parts—Asia, Africa, and Europe—with Asia equal in size to Europe and Africa combined. That formula became the basis for the medieval ***orbis terrarum*** (circle of the lands), a type of schematic map that portrayed the landmass as a circle divided into three continents by two perpendicular lines that formed a T. Geographers have used the term Afro-Eurasia to describe that landmass, but historians simply refer to it as the Old World.

The 75-mile-wide land bridge that connects northeastern Africa to Southwest Asia, which allowed early humans to migrate out of Africa and populate the rest of the world, also facilitated the spread of African languages beyond the African continent. The prime example is the Semitic language family, which includes Arabic, Hebrew, Phoenician, Acadian (the language of the ancient Assyrians and Babylonians), and several languages spoken in Ethiopia. The Semitic languages are a branch of a much larger language family that includes ancient Egyptian and the Berber languages spoken by nomads in the Sahara Desert. Linguistic reconstructions indicate that the Semitic, Egyptian, and Berber languages were all derived from a common ancestral language that was spoken in the region between the Nile River delta and

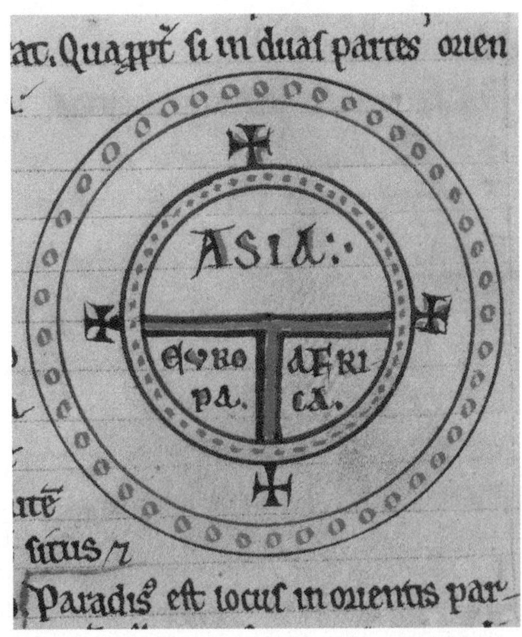

MAP OF THE KNOWN WORLD This schematic *mappa mundi* (map of the known world) first appeared in Isidore of Seville's *Etymologiae*, written in 623 CE. It corresponds to Augustine of Hippo's description of the world as divided into Asia, Africa, and Europe, with Asia being equal to the sum of Africa and Europe.

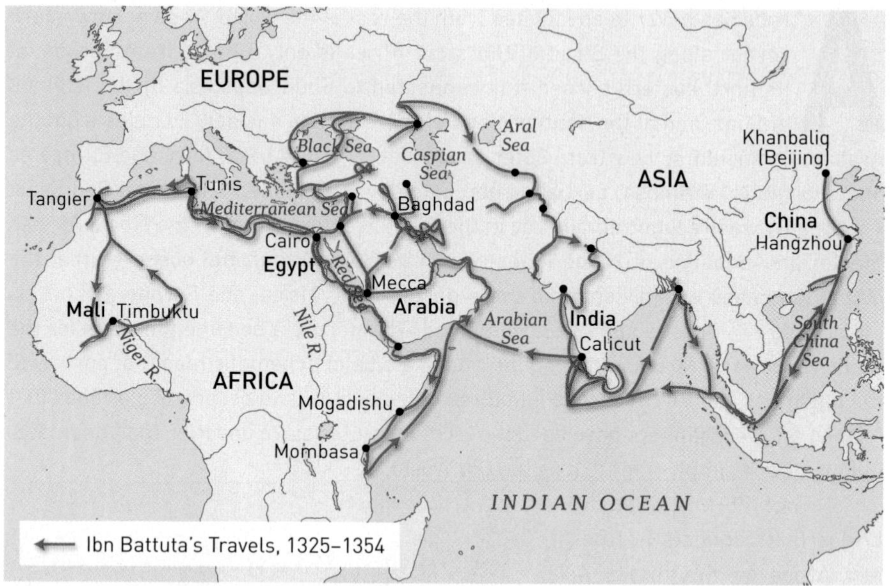

IBN BATTUTA'S TRAVELS The travels of Ibn Battuta between 1325 and 1354 illustrate the interconnectedness of the Old World. Traveling by land and sea from his home in Tangier, at the northwestern corner of Africa, he visited Europe, sub-Saharan Africa, the East African coast, India, and China, among other places.

the Isthmus of Suez. From there, the Semitic languages dispersed across a broad region of Southwest Asia, including the Arabian Peninsula.

From early times, Africa has been connected to distant parts of the Old World by ship traffic. From the Mediterranean coast of North Africa, a ship could travel to Italy or Greece using the islands of Malta, Sicily, and Crete as stopovers. Even the vast Indian Ocean was not a barrier to travel. Pushed along by the monsoon winds, ships could sail from the coast of East Africa to the Arabian Peninsula, the Persian Gulf, and India, from where they could set sail to Southeast Asia or China. The winds reversed their direction every 6 months, making it possible for a ship to make a round trip between Africa and India in a year with the wind always at its back.

The many ways in which Africa was connected to Asia and Europe can be illustrated by the journey of Ibn Battuta in the fourteenth century. Beginning in Tangier, the city of his birth in northwestern Africa, he traveled by land to Cairo, Jerusalem, and Mecca. He then took a ship down the Red Sea and along the East African coast to Kilwa, at the southern limit of the monsoon winds, and returned to the Arabian Peninsula when the winds reversed their direction. From there he traveled by land through central Asia before arriving in India, where he set out for China by ship. After returning to his home city of Tangier, he took a boat across the Strait of Gibraltar for a brief visit to Moorish Spain, then journeyed across the Sahara Desert by camel caravan to visit the African kingdom of Mali before finally returning home to Tangier to write a book about his travels. In all, he had traveled about 75,000 miles in 29 years.

Africa's land and sea connections to Europe and Asia facilitated a long history of exchanges of people, animals, crops, and ideas. Domesticated animals such as sheep, goats, horses, and camels spread from Europe and Southwest Asia to supplement the domestic cattle, pigs, and donkeys that were indigenous to Africa. Crops such as wheat, barley, and flax from Southwest Asia facilitated surplus production in the Nile River valley and North Africa, while plantains and sweet bananas from Southeast Asia aided the settlement of equatorial Africa. At the same time, Africans were domesticating crops such as millet, sorghum, coffee, rice, and yams that were well adapted to African environments. The development of herding and settled agriculture led to two different types of political organizations: tribal organizations, in which authority was based on a hierarchy of genealogical ties among groups of nomadic herders, and state systems, in which the ruler controlled a certain bounded territory.

The Mediterranean world, with its easy communication by water, was an incubator of cultural and commercial exchanges between Africa, Europe, and Southwest Asia. The history of Christianity is generally associated with Palestine, but Jesus, its founder, spent his early years in Egypt, and the Egyptian city of Alexandria later became a leading intellectual center for the development of Christian doctrines. In a similar way, the history of Islam is generally associated with Mecca, on the Arabian Peninsula, but within a century of the Prophet Muhammad's death, Islam had spread all along the coast of North Africa, and nomads from North Africa went on to found Islamic empires that spanned the Sahara and extended into Spain. Commercial exchanges in the Mediterranean world during the Middle Ages were facilitated by gold from sub-Saharan Africa, which was transported by camel across the desert and by ship along the East African coast. The gold trade undergirded powerful states in the West African Sahel and on the Zimbabwe Plateau and prosperous cities along the East African coast. Indeed, the history of Africa prior to 1500 is a story of repeated innovations and adaptations carried out in the context of wider relations with other parts of the Old World.

THE PYRAMIDS AT GIZA The pyramids of Menkaure (left), Khafre, and Khufu were built over three generations during the Fourth Dynasty. Despite its appearance in the photo, Khufu's pyramid (right) is the largest of the three. The three small pyramids at the lower left were for queens. The pyramids were built using forced labor by Egyptian peasants.

7000 BCE	**2950 BCE**	**1450 BCE**
Settlement at Nabta Playa, Egypt	King Narmer unites Egypt	Egypt gains control of Kush

2

FOOD REVOLUTIONS AND FRONTIER SOCIETIES, 8000 BCE–1000 CE

Up until about 10,000 years ago, all people throughout the world obtained their food by hunting and foraging. People could eat well by those methods, provided that they spread themselves thinly over the land. The key to success was in maintaining their mobility so that they could follow the migratory wanderings of the wild game and gather seasonal berries and nuts as they went. People organized themselves in small, mobile groups that lived in temporary camps, not permanent towns. Leaders of hunting groups focused on moving to the right place at the right time. Successful leaders gained followers, and those who failed at the hunt soon found themselves without a following. Authority did not have geographical boundaries.

This chapter assesses the changes that took place in Africa when food-producing plants became domesticated and animals began to be kept as livestock. It looks at the rise of floodplain agriculture in the Nile River valley and the Middle Niger floodplain in order to explore its relationship to early urbanism and state building. It also examines the effects of shifting cultivation techniques in areas with rain-fed agriculture. Finally, it explores the migrations of the Bantu-speaking farmers who settled the southern half of Africa. By 1000 CE, every region in Africa that had a sustainable environment for farming or herding had been occupied.

750–664 BCE Nubian pharaohs rule Egypt	**500 BCE** Settlements develop near the Niger bend	**500 BCE** Bantu speakers migrate into the rainforest

THE AGRICULTURAL REVOLUTION

Of the roughly 200,000 species of flowering plants in the world, only about a dozen of them provide 80 percent of the food that feeds the world today. The "Big Twelve" include wheat, corn, rice, barley, sorghum, soybeans, potatoes, cassava, sweet potatoes, sugarcane, sugar beets, and bananas. Because the wild precursors of those plants were found only in certain places in the world, we can identify a limited number of domestication centers that account for most of the crops grown in the modern world.

The earliest known center of crop domestication was the **Fertile Crescent** region of Southwest Asia: the crescent-shaped highlands that include parts of modern Turkey, Iraq, Syria, Jordan, and Israel. Southwest Asia enjoyed a moderate Mediterranean climate, but more important, it was home to wild forms of wheat, barley, and rye, as well as lentils, peas, and chickpeas, all of which were plants with large seeds that were not only edible but also nutritious. Even with those advantages, however, the domestication of crops in the Fertile Crescent was a slow and haphazard process. Archaeological sites containing traces of grains in both their wild and domesticated forms show that it took over a thousand years to make the transition. There seems to have been a lot of trial and error throughout the region, and many attempts at domestication failed.

We often think of agriculture as more "advanced" than hunting and gathering because of its association with state building, literacy, and urbanism. Research has shown, however, that early farmers actually labored longer than hunter-gatherers to produce the same number of calories, and that the farmers' grain-based diet was less healthy and less varied than the diets of hunter-gatherers. Agriculture and foraging were competing strategies of food production that coexisted for thousands of years. Many people experimented with a combination of both systems, planting and harvesting short-season crops in favorable locations before moving on.

HERDING AND FARMING IN THE SAHARA

An intermediate lifestyle that fell somewhere in between foraging and farming was the herding of cattle, sheep, and goats. Herders were nomads who lived in camps and moved seasonally in search of new pastures and watering holes, but they differed from hunters and gatherers in that their herds represented substantial possessions that needed to be cared for and defended. Herding societies often developed great military prowess. Because they were mobile, they could swoop down on agricultural settlements in times of war, and they could retreat into the wilderness when confronted by more powerful forces.

SAHARAN ROCK ART This rock painting from Tadrart Acacus shows hunters and cattle herders in the Sahara Desert during the pastoral period 4,000–7,500 years ago, when the Sahara was much wetter than it is today. The Tadrart Acacus mountain range in western Libya has thousands of rock and cave paintings dating from 12,000 BCE to 100 CE.

The earliest evidence of cattle herding in Africa comes from the region that is now the **Sahara Desert**. Twelve thousand years ago, during the last Ice Age, the region was dry, much as it is today. Then the glaciers retreated, and the monsoon rains moved northward into the southern Sahara, bringing seasonal summer rains that caused lakes and ponds to develop in natural depressions. The region became covered with grasslands and acacia forests and teemed with wildlife. Rock paintings in widely scattered regions of what is now desert show cattle herding from about 7,500 years ago. The paintings also show giraffes tethered to a stake or restrained by a halter, indicating that people were experimenting with domesticating various animals.

The best-documented example of life in the Sahara during the wet period comes from **Nabta Playa**, in Egypt's western desert near the modern border with Sudan. The summer rains created seasonal lakes and ponds, which brought nomadic cattle herders to the area about 10,000 years ago. The early visitors to Nabta Playa lived by a combination of herding, hunting, and gathering wild plants. Beginning 9,000 years ago, people dug deep wells that provided a reliable water source, and they began to stay at Nabta Playa year round, supplementing their diet with grains such as wild millet and wild sorghum. Each house had one or more large, bell-shaped storage pits for the grain. Sheep and goats, which had originally been domesticated in Southwest Asia, were introduced in the millennium that followed. Then, about 5,000 years ago, the Sahara once again turned dry, and Nabta Playa was abandoned as the people moved toward the Nile River valley.

Perhaps the most striking feature of Nabta Playa was its role as a ceremonial center. In the valley that brought water to the lake when the rains fell, there was a series of megaliths (monument stones) that stretched on for nearly 3,000 yards. The stones were aligned with the rising positions of four prominent stars—Sirius, Alpha Centauri, Arcturus, and the Belt of Orion—and therefore show continuity with later developments in pharaonic Egypt, as those same stars were prominent in its cosmology. Burial mounds, such as one containing a carved stone cow and another, built 7,400 years ago, containing the bones of a young cow in an elaborate burial chamber, are evidence of a cattle cult at Nabta Playa. Later, cattle would

CALENDAR CIRCLE AT NABTA PLAYA Built at least 7,000 years ago, this structure in Egypt's western desert predates Stonehenge by thousands of years. Archaeologists believe it was an archaeoastronomical device to mark the summer solstice, which signaled the onset of the summer rains, and to chart the most prominent stars in the night sky.

become a central symbol in the belief system of pharaonic Egypt. The valley at Nabta Playa also contained a stone "calendar circle" with two lines of stone sights aimed at the position of the sunrise at the summer solstice, which marked the beginning of the rainy season. Nabta Playa is the earliest ceremonial center ever found in Africa, and its remains provide important clues to some of the roots of ancient Egyptian culture.

THE NILE RIVER VALLEY

When the Greek historian Herodotus, who visited Egypt in the fifth century BCE, wrote that "Egypt is the gift of the Nile," he was merely stating the obvious. The Nile River runs through Egypt from south to north, where it empties into the Mediterranean Sea. It has its origin in Lake Victoria, which straddles the equator some 4,000 miles south of the river's mouth. As the White Nile, as this part of the river is called, approaches Egypt, it is joined by the Blue Nile, which flows down from the highlands of Ethiopia. Swollen by the monsoon rains that fell in the Ethiopian highlands, the Nile would rise in Egypt from June to October in an annual flood, even though Egypt itself received almost no rain at all. When the waters receded after October, they left behind rich black alluvial silt. This fertile black earth was truly a gift of the Nile. It washed down from the Ethiopian highlands and gave the waters of the Blue Nile their bluish-gray hue. The ancient Egyptians referred to their land as *kmt*—literally, "the black land"—because Egypt was the land of the black earth (as opposed to the

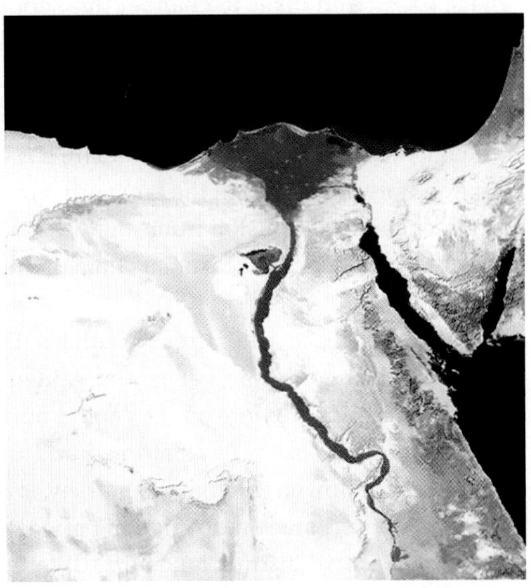

SATELLITE VIEW OF EGYPT The green vegetation visible in the triangular Nile delta and along the Nile valley floodplain indicates areas of human settlement. The rest is desert. The Nile delta (northern Egypt) and the Nile valley (southern Egypt) were the "two lands" united by the pharaoh Narmer. With the exception of a few desert nomads, all the ancient Egyptians lived within the green zone.

reddish earth of the surrounding deserts). So important was the Nile to Egyptians' lives that they divided their year into three seasons based on its annual rise and fall: *Akhet* (the period of inundation), *Peret* (growth of the crops), and *Shemu* (harvest). Agriculture in Egypt depended completely upon water and soil that came from elsewhere.

About 7,000 years ago, the domesticated barley and wheat that would later make Egypt the breadbasket of the Mediterranean world were already being grown in the **Nile River valley**, along with other Fertile Crescent crops such as lentils, peas, and flax for making cloth. The settlements were impermanent so that the people could migrate with their herds, and their communities were relatively egalitarian, as shown by the funerary goods in their graves. Then the Sahara started to dry out, and people began to crowd into the Nile valley. By 5,500 years ago, there is evidence of a more stratified society dominated by exploitative elites, who were buried in elaborate tombs. By 5,200 years ago, people were constructing canals, levies, and dikes to channel the floodwaters into storage basins for later release, and a complex administrative organization was developing to oversee the building and maintenance of these irrigation works. At that time, most of southern Egypt came under the control of a king who ruled from the city of Abydos. Although the details of this period remain hazy, it's clear that the precursors of the Egyptian state developed in the far south, not the Mediterranean north. A similar pattern of cultural diffusion from south to north can be seen in the spread of the ancient Egyptian language from its homeland in the far south to the Nile delta in the north.

In 2950 BCE, a ruler from southern Egypt named Narmer brought his army north along the Nile valley and gained control of the land all the way to the Mediterranean. He moved his capital northward to **Memphis** (near modern Cairo), where the Nile valley flattened and the river fanned out into numerous tributaries that flowed through the marshy, low-lying lands of the **Nile delta**. The ancient Egyptians made a distinction between the Nile delta and the Nile valley, seeing them as two distinct lands that differed from each other in terms of their shape, size, and character. In the Nile valley, the river flowed northward uninterrupted for 660 miles from the first cataract (set of rapids) at Aswan to the beginning of the delta. The fertile floodplain of the Nile valley was incredibly narrow, ranging from 1.25 miles wide at Aswan to 11 miles wide farther north. The Nile delta, in contrast, formed a triangle that measured 100 miles from its apex to the sea and occupied 155 miles of Mediterranean coastline. The triangle-shaped Nile delta had twice as much arable land as the Nile valley (8,500 square miles vs. 4,250). Historians customarily refer to the Nile valley as "Upper Egypt" because it occupied the upriver stretch of the Nile River, and to the Nile delta as "Lower

Egypt" because it was situated near the downriver outlets. To avoid confusion, this chapter will use the terms "Southern Egypt" for the Nile valley and "Northern Egypt" for the Nile delta.

It was no accident that the new capital of Memphis was located at the meeting point of the valley and the delta, in the region known as "the balance of the Two Lands." As the ruler of the Two Lands, the pharaoh had a double crown that combined the red crown of the delta and the white crown of the Nile valley, and he used a royal title that was written using the symbols of the cobra, which represented the Nile delta, and the vulture, which represented the Nile valley.

The Egyptian state that King Narmer created by uniting the Two Lands in 2950 BCE would last for over 2,600 years before it was conquered by Alexander the Great in 331 BCE. During that long stretch of time, more than 177 pharaohs, as the kings of Egypt were called, ruled over the state. Most of them were men, but women ruled as queens or regents on at least 10 occasions. Historians have grouped the rulers of Egypt into 30 successive royal **dynasties**. The longest-running dynasty (the Eighteenth) ruled Egypt for 247 years, while the shortest (the Twenty-Eighth) ruled for only 5 years. A typical dynastic reign was about a hundred years long. Throughout the long history of ancient Egypt, periods of administrative unity alternated with periods of chaos and disorder. The periods of unity have been named the Old Kingdom, the Middle Kingdom, the New Kingdom, and the Late Period. The periods of disorder are known as the Intermediate Periods.

The discussion that follows looks first at the political culture and institutions created during the Old Kingdom, which remained remarkably durable throughout three millennia of Egyptian history. It then shifts its focus to Egypt's relations with its southern neighbors in order to explore the history of Kush and Meroe, two kingdoms located up the Nile between the first and the sixth cataracts, in a region that the Egyptians called Nubia. Egyptian and Nubian civilizations were often intertwined, but remained very different from each other as they competed for control of territory and trade routes. Nubia has been characterized as Egypt's rival in Africa.

THE EGYPTIAN STATE

King Narmer and his successors created the world's first nation-state: a form of political organization in which the various peoples in a ruler's territory speak a common language and develop a common political and cultural identity. The key to creating that common identity was the pharaoh, who was portrayed as a god who mediated between the human and the divine. As befits a god, the pharaoh had several titles. The main one was Horus, the supreme celestial deity. Because Horus was popularly depicted as a falcon, the king's seal showed a falcon perched atop the gate of the royal palace. The pharaoh in his palace was thus seen as the god incarnate, and he was worshipped and obeyed as Horus himself. The deification of the pharaoh reached a peak during the Fourth Dynasty when King Sneferu took the title *neb maat*, literally "the keeper of the divine order of the universe." As such, he could claim a cosmic mandate to regulate order, enforce proper behavior, and generally maintain the Egyptian way of doing things. To make sure that everybody got the message, he also adopted the title *netjer nefer*, which meant "the perfect god."

The pharaoh was perceived not only as the embodiment of a god, but also as the embodiment of Egypt. One of the earliest Egyptian creation myths holds that in the beginning, there was nothing but watery chaos. When the waters receded, they revealed a mound of earth on which sat the creator god Atum, whose name meant both "everything" and "nothing." The annual flood of the Nile River and its recession were thus seen as a continuous reenactment of the original act of creation. The god Atum was often depicted in Egyptian paintings wearing the double crown of the Two Lands, representing him as the creator of the Egyptian state as well as the creator of the universe. The story thus portrays the Nile floods, the cosmic order, and the political order as inseparable.

A number of institutions and administrative structures were developed to uphold the image and power of the pharaoh. One of them was the cadre of literate bureaucrats and administrators that served the state. The *idea* of writing seems to have been developed by the Sumerians in the Fertile Crescent, but the Egyptian system of characters known as hieroglyphs was entirely original and reflected the unique language and environment of Egypt. The earliest sample of hieroglyphic writing in Egypt comes from the tomb of a local ruler who lived 150 years before King Narmer. Hieroglyphic writing was a system of symbols that could either be used as pictographs or be combined phonetically to form words and sentences. It was so complex that only a tiny minority of the population ever attained literacy. Those who mastered this skill, however, could earn a good living. Originally, writing was used mainly for keeping administrative records, but later it was used to produce religious texts, mythological narratives, historical chronicles, and even satirical poetry. The literate elite of Egypt included architects, engineers, astronomers, and medical specialists, all of whom were supported by the pharaohs.

Artists and craftsmen were also mobilized to uphold the power of the pharaoh. The Egyptian state was the main patron of the artwork that adorned palaces, temples, and burial chambers. Artistic production was not limited to painting and sculpture, but also included ceramics, jewelry, gold work, and woodwork. Artists and craftsmen worked under a strict set of rules that defined stylistic conventions for depicting people, gods, and pharaohs, which explains why there was so little variation in artistic styles over the centuries. The art was not created for purposes of individual expression, but was instead produced by the state bureaucracy to serve specific purposes, the most important being the glorification of the pharaohs.

The army of scribes, intellectuals, administrators, artists, and priests that upheld the power and glory of the pharaoh was expensive to maintain and depended on the pharaoh's capacity to extract resources and labor from the common people. Egypt had a centrally controlled command economy, which was presided over by the pharaoh and administered by bureaucrats. The essential requirement for maintaining the power of the pharaoh was to collect taxes and build up the resources of the Egyptian state. The successor to King Narmer (who had originally united the Two Lands) created an event called "the following of Horus" that took place every 2 years, in which the king and his court traveled in boats along the Nile valley and made a formal census of the country's agricultural wealth. In every village and town, the king made his presence felt, dispensed justice, and levied taxes. The biannual procession was later abandoned when the pharaohs divided the Nile valley into 22 provinces and the Nile delta into 20. Governors who reported to the pharaoh were headquartered in provincial capitals with their scribes and administrators. With each governor responsible for a relatively small territory, the governors could keep the agricultural census up to date and oversee the collection of taxes.

In addition to keeping a census of the country's agricultural wealth, the government began measuring and recording the level of the annual Nile flood. They knew that the height of the floodwaters was directly related to the agricultural yield. If the flood was too low, the farmland would not be adequately watered, but if it was too high, it could destroy the irrigation dams and delay the planting season until it was too late. The measurement of the Nile flood allowed the government to set the appropriate level of taxation on the harvest. Because money did not exist in ancient Egypt, taxes were collected as a portion of the harvest, which was put in storage in government granaries. Some of the grain was used to finance government activities, but a significant portion was set aside as an emergency food bank to be distributed in case of a poor harvest. To make agricultural production more efficient, the government reorganized the agricultural land in the delta, sometimes relocating entire communities to make room for crown lands and royal estates.

In contrast to the opulence of the pharaohs and the luxurious lifestyles of high government officials, the average farmer was very poor, often eking out a bare subsistence. Like serfs in medieval Europe, the peasants were regarded

THE POWER OF THE PHARAOH The base of this statue of King Djoser (Third Dynasty) shows the pharaoh trampling on his foreign enemies (symbolized by bows) and on his Egyptian subjects (symbolized by lapwing birds). The statue that once stood on the base has disappeared, but the message that the pharaoh crushes both his enemies and his subjects is clear.

almost as part of the land and were not allowed to leave it. Men were the primary cultivators, although women and children worked in the fields at harvest time to winnow and sieve the grain. In return for food security in famine years, male farmers were subject to compulsory labor on the irrigation works or the king's special projects. They could also be drafted into the army in times of war. An idea of how the pharaohs regarded the common people can be gleaned from how they were portrayed in art. Some images depicted the pharaoh holding a shepherd's crook in one hand and a whip in the other, indicating that he (or she) was the keeper of the people, but also their master. On the other hand, the base of a statue of King Djoser (Third Dynasty) was decorated with lapwings—birds that symbolized the common people in hieroglyphics—suggesting that the pharaoh trampled the common people underfoot.

Building the Pyramids

The most extravagant symbols of the power and wealth of the pharaohs were the pyramids constructed during the Fourth Dynasty (2575–2450). Each pyramid was built to be the tomb of a particular pharaoh and was thought to be his residence in the afterlife. King Djoser of the Third Dynasty had presided over the construction of a step pyramid that rose upward in a stairstep fashion, but the classic pyramid with smooth sides was first achieved under the direction of King Sneferu during the Fourth Dynasty. His first attempt was the pyramid at Meidum, which he built as a step pyramid with the idea of adding a smooth façade later. At some point in the process, however, the outer layer collapsed under its own weight, leaving a heap of rubble around a central tower. His second attempt resulted in the Bent Pyramid, so called because halfway up the sides, the angle of the incline shifted from 55 degrees to 43 degrees. King Sneferu's engineers and architects finally achieved the smooth, straight sides that became the classic pyramid shape on their third attempt, when they built the Northern Pyramid, using a relatively low incline of 43 degrees.

It was during the reign of Sneferu's son Khufu that the art and science of pyramid building reached its greatest perfection. The Great Pyramid of Khufu is a marvel of engineering and craftsmanship that astonishes people even today. Its proportions were gigantic: its base measured 250 yards on each side, and it was 481 feet high. Its sides rose up toward the peak at an eye-pleasing angle of 51 degrees and 50 minutes. Until the Eiffel Tower was completed in 1889, it was the tallest structure in the world. It contained 2.3 million blocks of stone that weighed an average of 2.5 tons; the stones near the top were much smaller than the average, while those at the base weighed as much as 15 tons each. Despite the massive materials involved, the construction was so precise that the variation in length between sides is less than 2 inches, and the pyramid's expansive base—the size of 12 football fields—is level to within an inch. The pyramid was aligned according to the cardinal directions, with an average deviation of just 3 minutes and 6 seconds of arc. All that precision was accomplished using simple wooden squares, measuring sticks, and plumb lines.

A major challenge in constructing such a massive structure was obtaining the building materials. The main limestone blocks for the Great Pyramid came from a quarry just 300 yards away, but the fine white limestone for the outer façade came from across the Nile valley, and the massive granite blocks for the king's burial chamber came from Aswan, nearly 600 miles to the south. The granite blocks were apparently carried down the Nile on barges and then hauled to the site on sledges that traveled on special hauling tracks made with wooden beams, limestone chips, and mortar to create a hard surface that was lubricated with water to reduce friction (the wheel was unknown at the time). At the construction site, ramps were built to allow the stone to be hauled up to its final resting place. Iron was unknown in Egypt at the time, so people worked with wooden levers to pry out blocks of stone from the bedrock. Workers had narrow copper chisels less than one-third of an inch wide, and they used copper saws and drills together with a slurry of quartz sand that did the actual cutting.

It took two decades to build the Great Pyramid, though the number of workers involved at any one time has been debated by historians for centuries. The Greek historian and traveler Herodotus, writing 2,000 years after the completion of the Great Pyramid, claimed that 100,000 workers labored 20 years to build it, but that was surely an exaggeration because there was not enough space at the work site to accommodate that many people. More recently, a team from *NOVA* went to Egypt to build a small pyramid using the ancient technology. They calculated that the pyramids could have been built with 20,000–25,000 workers at any given time. The majority of the laborers were peasant conscripts who worked in 3-month shifts. The pharaoh's representatives scoured the countryside for able-bodied recruits, and few dared to refuse. Herodotus was told that the great age of pyramid building was remembered by the people as a "terrible period" in Egyptian history, and that the Egyptians loathed King Khufu so much that they had ever since avoided mentioning his name.

After King Khufu's death, his son Khafre built a pyramid almost as large as his father's, but 10 feet shorter. After that, the building of massive pyramids stopped, perhaps because it put too much strain on the country's resources. Khafre's successor Menkaure built a pyramid near those of Khufu and Khafre, but it was a tenth of the size of the other two. Although pyramids continued to be constructed up through the Thirteenth Dynasty, most of those pyramids, too, were less than a tenth as large as Khufu's Great Pyramid. The last Egyptian pyramid, which was built by King Khendjer around 1745 BCE, was tiny, less than 2 percent of the volume of Khufu's pyramid. When pyramid building later resumed in northeastern Africa after a hiatus of 800 years, it would not be in Egypt, but in Nubia, far to the south.

The awesome power projected by the pyramid builders of the Fourth Dynasty could not last forever, and by the end of the Sixth Dynasty, cracks were appearing in the royal edifice. The devolution of power to provincial officials, undertaken near the end of the Fifth Dynasty, was creating local administrators who acted like independent rulers. They gave themselves an ever-expanding repertory of honorific titles and built themselves elaborate burial chambers while neglecting their duties to the state. Over time, more and more land was given to temples and nobles, who could keep the taxes from their lands for themselves, which significantly shrunk the tax base. The royal treasury was in poor shape, and it was put under additional strain when a series of disastrously low floods crippled the agricultural economy and depleted the royal granaries. The inability of the pharaohs to feed the people in times of famine further undermined their central authority. Eventually, Egypt fragmented along regional lines, and local administrators set themselves up as independent rulers.

By 2125 BCE, the period known as the Old Kingdom was over. It had lasted 450 years. By then, however, the basic features of Egypt's political system, economic system, science, culture, and religion were firmly established, and despite occasional periods of political disorder, they would remain remarkably stable for the next 1,800 years.

Interpreting Ancient Egypt

Although much of what we know about ancient Egypt is set in stone, so to speak, there are issues of historical interpretation that have been the subject of lively debate. One issue concerns whether Egyptian culture was primarily African or primarily Asian. Living at the intersection of two continents, Egyptians could borrow ideas and practices from their neighbors on either side or develop innovations of their own. Some basic Egyptian practices, such as grain farming, probably came from the Fertile Crescent, a region that was blessed with ideal conditions for the early domestication of plants and animals, whereas certain cultural practices were adopted from African groups that had developed an early interest in cattle cults, astronomy, and cosmology. The Egyptians adapted all of these ideas and innovations that came from elsewhere and integrated them into a unique cultural configuration. Innovations related to state building, hieroglyphic writing, pyramid building, mummification of the dead, and management of the annual floods were unique to Egypt itself. The astonishing achievements of the ancient Egyptians owe much to the power of the state to mobilize the intellectual resources of the country and channel them in support of the pharaohs and their projects. That power, in turn, depended upon the wealth that was extracted from the grain production of Egyptian peasants.

Another debate concerns the racial identity of the ancient Egyptians. This controversy has stemmed in part from an older notion that the human population consisted of "pure races," with perhaps some mixing at the margins. Thus, in 1844, the American natural scientist Samuel George Morton classified the ancient Egyptians as "Caucasians" of European or Near Eastern origin, whereas the Senegalese historian and anthropologist Cheikh Anta Diop declared in 1974 that "the ancient Egyptians were Negroes." Current biological anthropologists have rejected such outmoded categories in favor of looking for biological affinities between a certain population and its neighbors. Studies of crania from southern Egypt dating between 4000 and 3100 BCE show them to be more similar to the crania of ancient Nubians and Kushites (Egypt's African neighbors to the south) than to those of ancient southern Europeans. In a similar way, studies of the limb proportions of skeletons, which vary between tropical and colder climates, show tropical proportions, even though Egypt itself was not in the tropics. The conclusion is that the southern Egyptians, who created the Egyptian state, were Africans with measurable biological affinities to their African neighbors.

The Nile valley is the only place in Africa where human settlement stretches across the Sahara without a break, and the people who lived there formed a continuum of biological and physical variation. Their skin tones were light brown near the Mediterranean Sea and chocolate brown or black in the south, and their hair was more wavy in the north and more curly or kinky in the south. The change was imperceptible from village to village, although it was recognizable over longer distances. All of these people were Africans who had biological affinities with other African peoples.

Despite this unbroken continuum of physical variation along the Nile valley, ancient Egyptian art sometimes used stylized representations to portray Egyptians as a physically distinct population. Tomb paintings from the New Kingdom depicted Egyptians with a russet or medium-brown hue, while Assyrians from Southwest Asia had a pale yellowish color, and Nubians, who lived south of Egypt, were shown as chocolate brown or black. Indeed, the Egyptian word for the Nubians was *Nehesy*, which meant "bronzed" or "burnt," a clear reference to their dark skin. A hymn to the sun god that compared Egyptians, Assyrians, and Nubians stated that the god "has set every man in his place" and went on to say that "their colors are different, since thou hast made foreigners different." The hymn made it clear that *both* the light-skinned Assyrians and the dark-skinned Nubians were considered foreigners. The ancient Egyptians preferred to think of themselves as a unique people with an original civilization.

EGYPT AND NUBIA

Egypt's field of vision was oriented toward its African neighbors to the south. The "forward part of the earth" was said to be located far up the Nile, and south would have been "up" on a pharaonic map. During the Old Kingdom, Egyptian control of the Nile valley ended at the first cataract at Aswan, which marked the terminus of boat traffic along the river. South of the first cataract, the landscape changed. Instead of a broad, fertile valley, the Nile River was flanked by low, barren hills that reduced the size of the floodplain and restricted farming. Settlements were isolated and small, and the people were poor. The semidesert surrounding the river supported only nomadic populations. The second cataract, over 200 miles south of the first, consisted of a 40-mile stretch of rapids where the Nile cut through

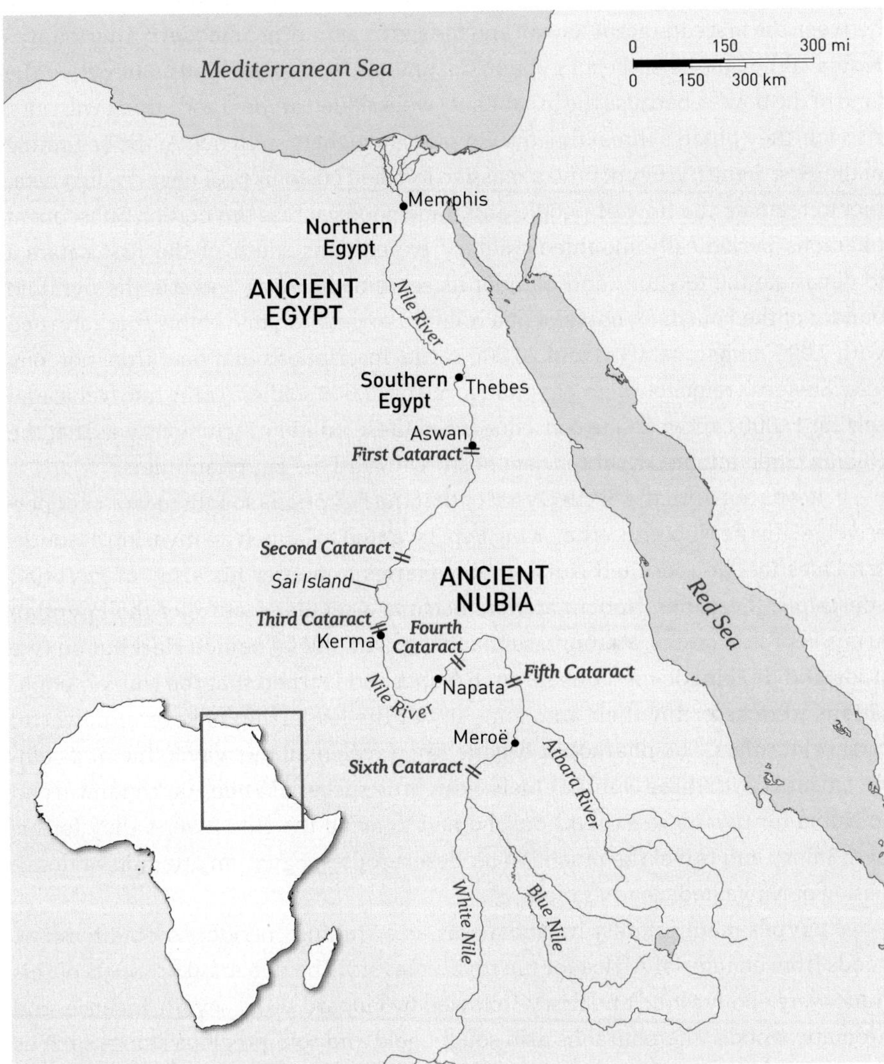

THE NILE RIVER, 2,950 BCE–100 CE Egypt occupied the Nile valley from the Mediterranean Sea to the first cataract, while the region between the first and sixth cataracts was known as Nubia or Kush. The centers of Kushitic civilization moved southward over time from Kerma, to Napata, and finally to Meroe.

a desolate region populated by small bands of nomads. It was only when travelers arrived at Sai Island, nearly 350 miles south of the first cataract, that they once again encountered low, well-watered banks with a fertile floodplain and prosperous agricultural settlements.

Historians refer to the land defined by the 1,100-mile stretch of the Nile between the first cataract at Aswan and the sixth cataract near modern Khartoum as **Nubia**, although the earliest Egyptian documents refer to the land as *Ta-Seti*—"the land of the bow"—because the inhabitants were skilled archers and strong warriors. As such, they posed a threat that the Egyptians sought to snuff out. At the beginning of the First Dynasty, Egypt built a massive fortified customs post near the first cataract to regulate the flow of people and trade goods across the border. Subsequent pharaohs periodically mounted military expeditions south of the first cataract to devastate the territory and plunder its settlements. King Sneferu, the pyramid builder of the Fourth Dynasty, sent a military expedition into Nubia that returned with 7,000 human captives and 20,000 cattle. Inscriptions that date from not long after Sneferu's reign tell of an Egyptian army of 20,000 soldiers going into Nubia and seizing 17,000 captives. One consequence of these military incursions was that the Nubian chiefs adopted a subservient posture toward the Egyptian rulers.

It was not until the Sixth Dynasty that the Egyptians sought to work cooperatively with the Nubians. When King Pepi I wanted to launch an invasion of southern Palestine, he recruited Nubian mercenaries to bolster his army of Egyptian conscripts; thereafter, Nubian archers became a regular feature of the Egyptian army. Pepi's successor, Merenra, sent an Egyptian official named Harkhuf on two trade and diplomatic missions through Nubia and learned that the Nubian populations were asserting their autonomy under the leadership of several powerful territorial rulers. The pharaoh subsequently traveled all the way to the first cataract to meet with three Nubian chiefs, with little success. When Harkhuf returned to Nubia for two more expeditions, he had to avoid the Nile River valley for his own safety and travel the much longer desert routes. Egyptian attempts at domination of Nubia had clearly failed.

Egypt's main interest in Nubia was as a trading corridor to obtain exotic goods from equatorial Africa for the royal treasury. The two main products of this trade were ebony wood and ivory, followed by leopard skins, myrrh, incense, and aromatic woods. The pharaohs also sought gold and semiprecious stones such as jasper, ochre, and malachite. On Harkhuf's third trading expedition, he returned with 300 donkey loads of "incense, ebony, precious oil, grain, panther skins, elephant tusks, and throw sticks." On his fourth trip, he brought back a pygmy from the "land of the horizon dwellers," his reference to equatorial Africa. His expeditions made it clear that the pharaohs placed a high value on luxury goods from Nubia and equatorial Africa.

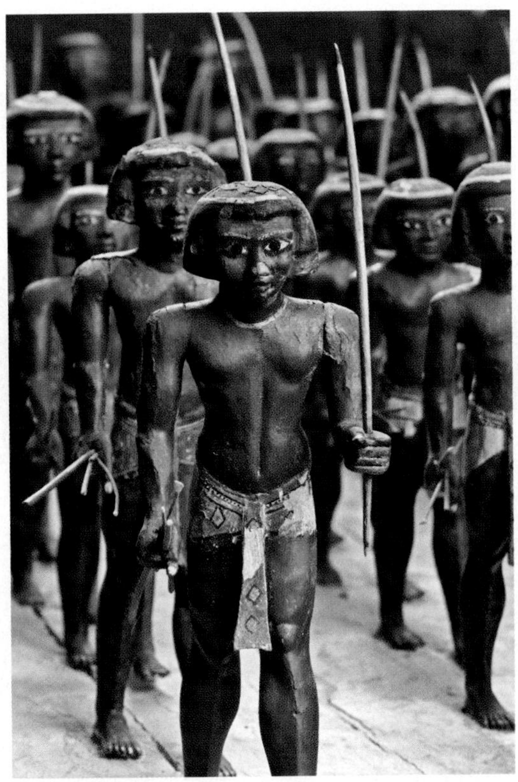

NUBIAN ARCHERS These wooden figures of black-skinned Nubian archers came from an Eleventh Dynasty tomb. Each carries a bow in one hand and arrows in the other. King Mentuhotep II, who may have been of Nubian descent himself, depended on hired Nubian archers in his battles to unify Egypt and establish the Eleventh Dynasty.

Following the collapse of the Old Kingdom and a chaotic Intermediate Period that lasted more than a hundred years, Egypt was reunited under the rule of King Mentuhotep II, who inaugurated the period known as the Middle Kingdom. His interest in Nubia was different from that of his predecessors because he had relied on hired Nubian archers in his battles to become the sovereign ruler of Egypt, and he had taken several Nubian wives. His successors, who were partly of Nubian ancestry, embarked on an energetic program to expand Egyptian influence in Nubia all the way to the second cataract. At the north end of the rapids, they built a massive fort with dry moats and walls up to 30 feet high. This was followed by nine more forts at strategic points along the rapids. The last two forts faced each other across the Nile at the southern end of the rapids, marking the new southern boundary of Egypt. The inscription on the boundary marker read in part, "I have carried off their women and brought away their dependents, burst forth to poison their wells, driven off their bulls, ripped up their barley and set fire to it." The inscription leaves no doubt that the Egyptian conquest of northern Nubia was brutal and had a devastating impact on the local populations.

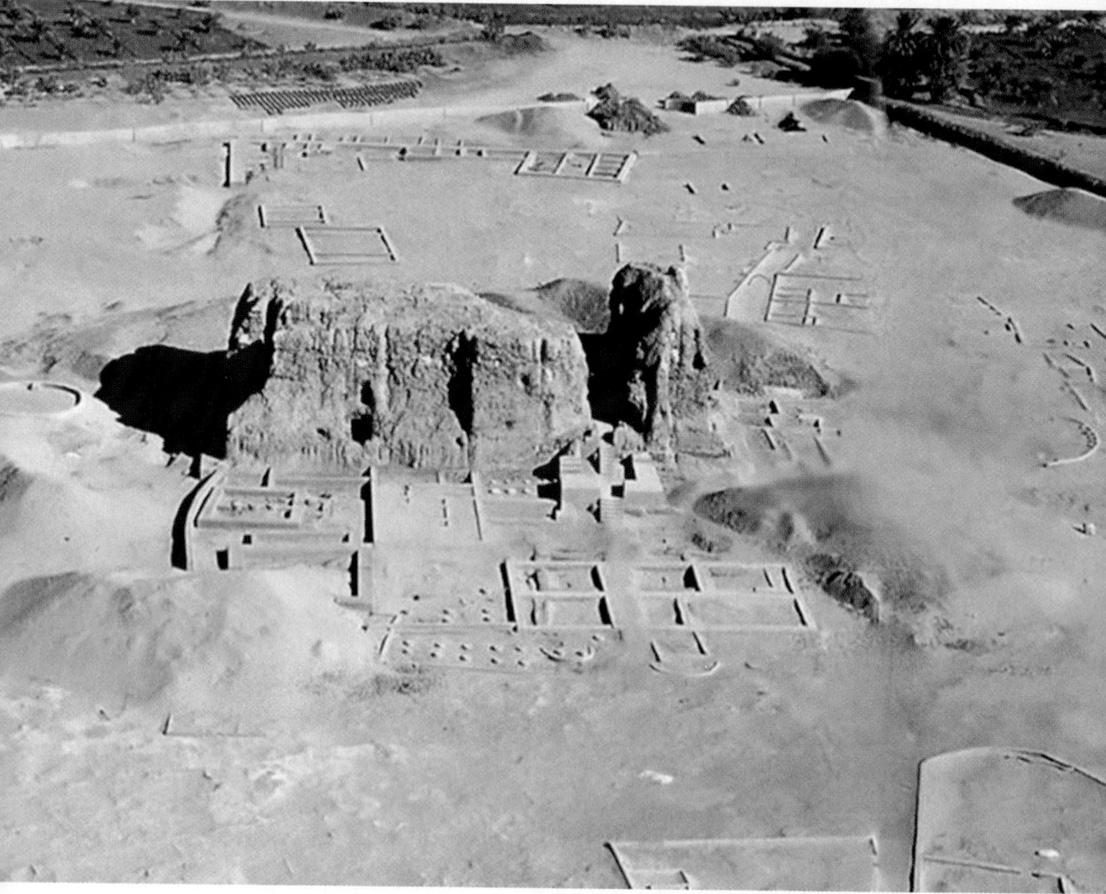

THE RUINS OF KERMA This photo shows the ruins of the temple precinct in Kerma, the ancient capital of Kush. Located on the east bank of the Nile, Kerma sat on a floodplain south of the third cataract. In addition to its agricultural advantages, Kerma was linked to the Red Sea and Central Africa by trade routes, which facilitated regular contact with a variety of cultures and peoples.

Kerma and the Kingdom of Kush

When Egypt extended its southern border from the first cataract to the second, it obtained better access to the Nile valley trade, but it gained very little agricultural land. Between the third and fourth cataracts, however, was a low-lying floodplain in a region where the land received brief summer rains that allowed people to pasture cattle. In this lush environment lay the Nubian city of Kerma. Inscriptions at Kerma written in Egyptian hieroglyphs show that two Egyptian riverboat captains had visited the city during the Sixth Dynasty, and it is likely that the traveler Harkhuf visited as well. During the Twelfth Dynasty, when Egypt was expanding southward to the second cataract, there was an increase in the number of Egyptian trade goods that made their way to Kerma. During the chaotic Thirteenth Dynasty, an 85-year period during which at least 50 different pharaohs ruled, Egypt was too financially strained to keep up the forts below the first cataract, and they were abandoned. Freed from the Egyptian threat, Kerma reached the peak of its prosperity, carrying on trade and producing luxury items such as wooden furniture, cut stone jewelry, cast bronze weapons, and stone statues. Although some of those objects reflected Egyptian influence, the majority were produced by local artisans using styles that were unique to Kerma.

Ever since the Twelfth Dynasty, Egyptian inscriptions had mentioned a kingdom called Kush located beyond the second cataract. After the Egyptians withdrew from their Nubian forts during the Thirteenth Dynasty, Egyptian military officers wrote inscriptions pledging their loyalty to the King of Kush, who had apparently taken over the forts. Archaeologists are now convinced that Kerma was the capital of Kush. After the unity of the Egyptian state was restored with the rise of the New Kingdom, King Thutmose I was determined to conquer Kush and reestablish Egyptian rule in Nubia. He personally accompanied his war fleet up the Nile. They dredged out an old channel through the first cataract so that the ships could pass, and they forced the ships over the "place of capsizing" at the second cataract. The pharaoh then ordered his soldiers to drag their boats around the third cataract in order to launch an attack on Kerma from the river. In the ensuing onslaught, Kerma was sacked and burned, and its temple was desecrated. King Thutmose I left a chilling inscription at the edge of the city to celebrate the carnage. It says in part, "There is not one of them left. The Nubian bowmen have fallen to the slaughter, and are laid low throughout their lands." The boasts of Thutmose I notwithstanding, the Kushites continued to fight the Egyptians during the reigns of Thutmose II and his successor, Queen Hatshepsut. It was not until 1450 BCE, when Thutmose III built a temple to the god Amun at Napata, just below the fourth cataract, that Egypt finally consolidated its domination of Nubia.

For the next 400 years, the kingdom of Kush was an Egyptian province ruled by an Egyptian viceroy known as "the king's son of Kush." The territory was divided into "princedoms," each governed by a local ruler who was seen as simultaneously the ruler of his own people and an official of the Egyptian government. Egypt levied taxes on the harvest, collected tribute in cattle, mined gold in the eastern desert, and sent back ships filled with exotic products from equatorial Africa. At the annual "presentation of the tribute," a ceremony held in the Egyptian capital that was designed to portray the pharaoh as a world ruler, Nubian representatives were present along with conquered peoples from western Asia. Nubia thus had some characteristics of an Egyptian province and some characteristics of a conquered foreign territory.

The cultural impact of Egyptian rule in Nubia was enormous. Egyptian towns and temples were built to encourage Egyptians to settle in Nubia, and over time, more and more Nubians moved into the Egyptian towns. The Nubian upper classes embraced the Egyptian language, hieroglyphic writing, and Egyptian funerary goods. But the Nubians also exerted an influence on Egyptian culture. After the pharaohs of the Eighteenth Dynasty made **Thebes** the capital of Egypt, they made the cult of the Theban god Amun the dominant religious cult. The temple of Amun, near Thebes, employed the finest craftsmen in the land, and it controlled extensive landholdings and cattle herds throughout Egypt, as well as mines in the eastern desert and in Nubia. In Egypt, Amun was depicted wearing a flat-topped crown, but in Nubia he was pictured as a ram-headed man wearing a sun disk on his head in accordance with ancient Nubian images of sacrificial rams with spherical crowns. The Nubians had, in effect, created a Nubian version of Egypt's dominant god that fit better into their system of religious symbols.

Napata and the Nubian Pharaohs

At the end of the Twentieth Dynasty, around 1069 BCE, Egypt again fragmented into rival political domains, ushering in what has been called the Third Intermediate Period, a turbulent period that lasted over 400 years. During much of that time, Egypt was once again divided into "the Two Lands," with the northern part ruled from the Nile delta city of Tanis, and the southern part governed by the high priests of Amun from their temple near Thebes. Egyptian administrators and military personnel withdrew from Nubia, which faded from the historical record for 350 years. By the eighth century BCE, the former kingdom of Kush reemerged in the historical record, ruled by a new dynasty located at Napata. During the period of Egyptian occupation, Napata had marked the southern limit of Egyptian control, and it was the place where the Egyptians had built the temple to the god Amun. Now it emerged as the new capital of Kush.

In the Egyptian pantheon of gods, Amun was the creator god at Thebes (different regions of Egypt had their own creator gods), and he was credited as the source of the original Egyptian kingship. There were only two temples to Amun: one at Thebes in Egypt and one at Napata in Nubia. When the pharaoh Thutmose III built the temple at Napata, his priests declared it to be the southern home of Amun and the birthplace of the Egyptian monarchy. In effect, Thutmose III had used the temple to justify Egypt's annexation of Nubia by claiming that Nubia had been an essential part of Egypt from the beginning, but later Kushite rulers in Napata used the old Egyptian texts from the temple to reverse the situation and claim to be the true rulers of Egypt. Sometime around 780 BCE, King Kashta of Kush (known as "Kashta the Kushite") left an inscription below the first cataract stating his claim to be the legitimate ruler of the Two Lands of ancient Egypt, but it is uncertain how far north his authority extended.

It was Kashta's son Piye, who became the ruler of Kush in 750 BCE, who backed up his father's claims by invading Egypt. Moving down the Nile from Napata, he was able to capture Thebes, the capital of southern Egypt almost without a fight. A devoutly religious man, Piye had reunited all the lands between the two temples of the god Amun. After returning home to Napata, he wrote an inscription claiming that "Amun in Thebes has made me king of Egypt, but Amun in Napata has made me the ruler of all lands." Both temples to Amun were essential to his kingship. Soon after his return to Napata, Piye learned that an Egyptian army from the Nile delta was marching toward Thebes. He sent out his army in the name of the god Amun, and told his soldiers that when they arrived at Thebes, they should go to the temple and make offerings before moving north. He was, in effect, waging a holy war. When the soldiers reached the ancient capital of Memphis, at the "balance of the Two Lands," Piye personally led the assault that gave them the victory. After receiving submission from the various rulers in the Nile delta, he returned to Napata and never set foot in Egypt again. Egypt was now a single nation, ruled from Napata, that stretched from the sixth cataract in the south to the Mediterranean Sea in the north. To celebrate his rule, Piye built a pyramid at Napata near the temple of Amun—the first pyramid that had been built in 800 years.

The Egyptian Twenty-Fifth Dynasty inaugurated by Piye is known as the dynasty of the **Nubian pharaohs** (also known as the black pharaohs). It included five pharaohs who ruled for a total of 71 years from 728 to 657 BCE. Although the successors to Piye ruled mostly from Thebes and Memphis, they never forgot their Nubian roots, and they were all buried in pyramids they built near Napata. Even though they were regarded by many Egyptians as foreign rulers, the Nubian pharaohs sought to restore the ancient Egyptian culture and the glory of the Old Kingdom. Archaic forms of the written language were reinstated, and statues using Old Kingdom proportions were produced. The Nubian pharaohs ordered renovations in temples throughout the country and constructed new temples in Nubia and elsewhere. They also introduced Nubian elements such as African facial features, large earrings, and ram's-head pendants into the repertory of official royal art.

The efforts of the Nubian pharaohs to restore Egypt's ancient culture to its former glory were cut short by the Assyrian Empire, which was asserting control over large parts of western Asia. Assyria invaded Egypt four times in a period of 10 years. In the last invasion, in 664 BCE, they captured Memphis and continued up the Nile to Thebes, where they ransacked the temples and carried away their treasures. King Tanutamun, the last of the Nubian pharaohs, retreated to Nubia, never to return.

Seventy years later, with the Assyrians gone and a new dynasty ruling Egypt, the ruler at Napata assembled an army to invade Egypt and restore Nubian rule. Learning of the impending invasion, the new Egyptian pharaoh sent an army bolstered by Greek and Judean mercenaries to invade Nubia. They destroyed Kerma and continued upriver to Napata, where they sacked the royal palace and destroyed the king's statues. They did not, however, seek to colonize Nubia again. After the army returned to Egypt, the pharaoh ordered that the names of the Nubian pharaohs be chiseled off all statues of those rulers; their noses were broken to prevent them from breathing, and the double-cobra symbols, which represented their authority over both Egypt and Nubia, were smashed. He tried to make it look as if the black pharaohs had never existed.

Although the rulers of Napata never again tried to conquer Egypt, they did not reject Egyptian pharaonic culture. They maintained the royal title of "pharaoh" for their kings, wrote inscriptions in hieroglyphs, and constructed pyramids for their burials. The 25 rulers of Kush who succeeded Piye were all buried in pyramids near Napata. They continued to worship Egyptian gods, the chief one being Amun, and their temples resembled those in Egypt. Although the ruling classes embraced and preserved many elements of Egyptian culture, the common people maintained a substantial continuity with the ancient culture of Nubia, as is reflected in their pottery styles, housing styles, and burial arrangements.

The Rise of Meroe

The fall of the Nubian pharaohs inaugurated what historians refer to as the Late Period of Egyptian history. Punctuated by occasional invasions by the Persians, the Late Period came to an end in 332 BCE, when the Greek conqueror Alexander the Great invaded Egypt and introduced a new dynasty of Greek-speaking rulers who oriented themselves toward the greater Mediterranean world. They staffed their administration with Greek officials and built an army of Greek mercenaries. That invasion marked the end of pharaonic Egypt, which had existed as a nation-state for over 2,600 years. It also marked a reversal of Egypt's field of vision: henceforth, Egypt would look north toward Greece instead of south toward Nubia.

With the culture of Egypt under attack by its Greek conquerors, elements of pharaonic culture continued to flourish in Nubia. After 300 BCE, there were no more royal burials near Napata because the center of political and economic power had shifted southward to Meroe, between the fifth and sixth cataracts. In contrast to Napata, which was built on a narrow strip of low-lying land sandwiched between the Nile and its desert hinterland, Meroe was far enough south to receive regular seasonal rainfall, which made it possible to grow crops not only on the irrigated riverbanks, but also in valleys that received runoff from the adjacent plateau. The rains also created good grazing land for cattle.

The city of Meroe became the center of a powerful state that controlled the Nile valley from the first cataract to the confluence of the Blue Nile and White Nile. Meroe was the largest urban agglomeration in Nubia, containing palaces, temples, houses, and cemeteries, which included more than a hundred pyramids. Meroe's largest temple was dedicated to Amun, as was the temple at Napata, but there were

PYRAMIDS AT MEROE The royal cemetery at Meroe contains burial pyramids for 30 kings, 8 ruling queens, and 3 crown princes. The two other cemeteries at Meroe contain 105 additional pyramids. Much smaller than the famous pyramids of Giza, the tallest pyramid at Meroe is 96 feet high. Nevertheless, more pyramids were built at Meroe than were ever built in Egypt.

also temples to Nubian gods, such as the lion-headed Apedemek. A major industry in Meroe was the smelting of iron, which began in the sixth or seventh century BCE and reached a massive scale in the final centuries before the Common Era. A writing system that adapted Egyptian hieroglyphs to record the Meroitic language was invented, and gradually Meroitic replaced Egyptian in inscriptions on monuments. Unfortunately, these inscriptions have yet to be deciphered by modern scholars, and much of Meroe's history remains unknown.

OTHER EARLY CENTERS OF AGRICULTURE AND URBANIZATION

Aksum

Herodotus's famous statement that "Egypt is the gift of the Nile" could be made more precise by saying that "Egypt is a gift from Ethiopia." The Nile floods had their source in the annual monsoon rains that fell on the Ethiopian highlands, and those highlands were the source of the rich volcanic soil that was washed into the Nile and deposited in Egypt during the annual floods. The monsoon rains and the volcanic soil in the Ethiopian highlands also supported an ancient tradition of farming and plant domestication in the highlands themselves. Among the crops first domesticated in the Ethiopian highlands were teff, a tiny-grained cereal; enset, a banana-like plant that could be made into bread-like loaves; coffee (a stimulant); chat (a narcotic); and cotton. To those crops were added plants brought in from elsewhere. Finger millet came from what is now northern Uganda. Wheat and barley originally came from the Fertile Crescent, but the Ethiopians developed local varieties unknown elsewhere—evidence of agriculture's great antiquity in Ethiopia. Cattle, sheep, and goats were not indigenous to the region, but were adopted from early on, as can be seen in the rock art of the region. Donkeys, which were apparently indigenous to northeastern Africa, were domesticated, and they were joined as beasts of burden by camels from the Arabian Peninsula. Together, these crops and animals provided the elements for prosperous farming communities. Because the fertile volcanic soils could sustain deeper tillage than the tropical soils found elsewhere in sub-Saharan Africa, the Ethiopian highlands developed a unique tradition of ox-plow agriculture, evidenced by a cave painting from 500 BCE depicting a plow pulled by two oxen.

Sometime around 500 BCE, the Ethiopian highlands established strong trade and diplomatic connections with southern Arabia, just across the Red Sea, which led to the introduction of writing, sculpture, and monumental architecture into Ethiopia. The temple of the moon god at Yeha contained square monolithic pillars similar to those found at a moon god temple in Yemen. It attracted pilgrims from

THE LARGEST MONOLITHIC STELA IN THE WORLD The monolithic stelae in Aksum's burial ground mark the tombs of rulers or other important persons. Stela no. 1, which once stood 97 feet tall, lies broken on the ground. It was designed to represent a 13-story tower. Weighing 520 tons, it is the largest monument ever carved from a single block of stone. The center upright stela in the background is 69 feet tall.

as far away as the Arabian Peninsula, showing that Ethiopia was participating in a wider regional culture as well as in regional trade.

The first century CE saw the rise of the kingdom of **Aksum** in the Ethiopian highlands. The Aksumite kings could support their state by taxing the agricultural production of the highlands and by controlling the trade route between the Red Sea, to the east, and the Nile valley, to the west. They saw themselves as part of a wider cultural and economic region. Beginning in the third century CE, they issued coins in gold, silver, and copper, inscribed with the names of the kings. Aksum expanded eastward, gaining control of southern Arabia between 200 and 500 CE, and westward, briefly occupying Meroe in the Nile valley. In the third century CE, the Persian prophet Mani listed Aksum as the third kingdom of the world, after Rome and Persia.

With access to both the Red Sea and the Nile valley, Aksum imported goods from Egypt, Nubia, the Mediterranean, the Persian Gulf, and India. The kings of Aksum constructed huge monolithic monuments (stelae) for their grave sites. The largest one stood 97 feet high and weighed 520 tons. Even today, it remains the largest monument ever carved from a single stone. Archaeological excavations of elite residences show that there was a substantial upper class that included government officials and merchants. The wealth of the area began to decline in the sixth century CE, when the Persians captured the southern entrance to the Red Sea, and the Arabs took it over shortly thereafter. Deprived of its access to the Red Sea trade, the capital city of Aksum gradually lost its prosperity and was abandoned. After 650 CE, no more coins were issued by the kings of Aksum.

The Middle Niger Floodplain

The Niger River in West Africa played a role in the development of agriculture somewhat similar to that of the Nile in Egypt. The headwaters of the Niger are located in the rainy Fuuta Jaloo highlands near the Atlantic coast. From there, the river flows northeast, where it becomes shallow and overflows to form the **Middle Niger floodplain**. Beyond the floodplain, it makes a huge bend and then flows southeast. Although in modern times the floodplain and the Niger bend get very little rain, they profit from the annual floodwaters coming from the Fuuta Jaloo, nearly 800 miles away. As in Egypt, the floodwaters permit dense settlement in a region of little rain.

About 8,500 years ago, when the Sahara was much wetter than it is today, the Azawad region north of the Niger bend contained a huge lake and marshes. The waters of the annual flood spread out along natural channels that continued for over a hundred miles. Wild grasses that were the ancestors of sorghum, millet, fonio (a small-grained cereal), and West African rice grew in seasonally inundated depressions. The surrounding grasslands were home to elephants, giraffes, antelopes, and wild cattle. By 7,000 years ago, there were small human communities living in the area, and cattle had been domesticated.

The Sahara began to dry out around 4,500 years ago, prompting people to move farther south, toward the Middle Niger floodplain. It was during that period that rice and cereals became domesticated, as shown by imprints of millet grains in potsherds from about 4,000 years ago. By 300 BCE, urban agglomerations started to appear. One of these settlements was Jenne-Jeno, which was situated at the intersection of four ecological zones: floodplain agricultural land, pastureland, wooded areas, and the river. The inhabitants ate rice, pearl millet, two forms of sorghum, and fonio. In an area of uncertain climate, they were keeping all their food options open. Near Jenne-Jeno were small satellite villages that specialized in fishing, metalwork, weaving, or agriculture. Thus the inhabitants practiced a kind of decentralized urbanism, with the city at the center of a cluster of specialized economic zones.

A somewhat different settlement pattern developed farther down the river along the Niger bend itself, where dense settlements appeared around 500 BCE. Excavations at Tombouze (near modern Timbuktu) have revealed a kind of low-density urbanism that fluctuated on a seasonal basis depending on the level of the flood. People crowded onto a series of large mounds covering a total of as 250 acres during the high-water season, but radiated out to temporary seasonal camps on the dry floodplain during the low-water seasons. Like the satellite villages at Jenne-Jeno, the seasonal camps were economically specialized for farmers, fishermen, potters, weavers, or metalworkers. This was a West African type of urbanism, with settlement patterns that remained flexible to accommodate the changing conditions of the different seasons.

The Spread of Ironworking

The Egyptians in the Old Kingdom, for all their technological sophistication, had not yet discovered ironworking, and constructed their huge pyramids using tools of wood, stone, and copper. The process of extracting iron from ore-bearing soil and chemically fusing it with the carbon found in charcoal requires temperatures within the narrow range of 1,100°F–1,400°F (just below the melting point of iron ore) and is so counterintuitive that it was probably discovered only once in world history. Its place of origin would most likely have been a region with a long tradition of copper metallurgy, which archaeologists generally locate in Anatolia (modern Turkey). Once ironworking was discovered, the technology was closely guarded, and iron objects remained rare until about 850 BCE.

In the eighth century BCE, the secrets of ironworking spread to Egypt and were simultaneously carried by the Phoenicians to Carthage and other colonies in North Africa. Ironworking began at Meroe within 100–200 years after its arrival in Egypt. Meroe was far enough south that wood for the smelting furnaces was plentiful, whereas in Egypt it was scarce. By the final centuries before the Common Era, Meroe was producing iron on a substantial scale. The bulk of the iron was probably exported to Egypt and Aksum, as archaeologists have found few iron objects in Meroe itself.

From points along the Mediterranean coast, iron smelting spread southward across the Sahara Desert by 500 BCE. Two centuries later, iron was being smelted at

Nok, in modern Nigeria, and it reached Begho, in modern Ghana, a century later. Although our knowledge of the historical trajectory of ironworking in West Africa remains incomplete, it is certain that there was a great deal of technological innovation, as shown by the great variety in blast furnaces, tubes, and bellows found there, many with no known counterparts on other continents. One early ironworking site contains four different blast-furnace designs. An important African innovation was the tall natural-draft furnace, which could produce high-carbon steel. Archaeologists agree that steel was widely manufactured in Africa from early times.

In places like the floodplain of the Middle Niger, iron tools were important because they made it easier to work the heavy soils there. Blacksmiths, whose skills could turn iron-rich soil into iron tools and weapons, were both revered and feared. From early on, they clustered in economically specialized communities and developed special rituals to complement their technical knowledge. Over time, they became a closed caste in which only the son of a smith could become a smith, thus ensuring that their trade secrets did not get out.

The Diffusion of Rain-Fed Agriculture

Our discussion so far has focused mostly on regions of floodplain agriculture, in part because those regions had concentrated populations who lived in urban agglomerations, which left traces that can be excavated by archaeologists. But in the aftermath of the drying out of the Sahara Desert, farmers spread out in the grassland savanna, where they kept cattle and grew cereal crops such as millet and sorghum. Because cattle herds needed to move periodically to find new pasture, economic specialization developed in which nomadic cattle herders exchanged their products with sedentary farmers. Farther south, in the woodland savanna, cattle herding was not possible because the cattle died of trypanosomiasis, carried by tsetse flies. Near the edges of the tropical rainforest, the inhabitants domesticated and cultivated yams and oil palm trees.

As rain-fed agriculture spread across the grassland and woodland savannas, the farmers had to deal with the problem of poor soils that still plagues African agriculture to this day. The most fertile soils in the world are the postglacial soils found in the plains of America, Europe, and Asia, the alluvial soils found in river floodplains and deltas, and the volcanic soils found in mountainous highlands. Those soils can maintain their fertility for hundreds or even thousands of years if properly managed. Although Africa had volcanic soils in the highlands surrounding the East African Rift System and alluvial soils in the floodplains and deltas of the Nile and the Niger, those areas made up only a tiny fraction of the continent's arable land. The overwhelming majority of Africa's farmland lay in the woodland and grassland savannas, where it had all the deficiencies of tropical soils.

Soil fertility depends on an adequate level of soil organic matter (SOM), which gives the soil bulk density and helps it to retain water and nutrients. Tropical soils have a very low level of SOM to begin with, and it breaks down quickly when the land is under cultivation. In contrast to the prairie soils of the American Midwest, which a century ago had 5–10 percent SOM and still retain nearly half that amount after a century of constant overuse, African tropical soils often have less than 3 percent SOM to begin with, and half of it is lost in the first few years of cultivation. If the field continues to be cultivated, the SOM level dwindles to almost nothing.

African farmers developed various methods to cope with poor soils. They used manure and compost as fertilizer for their household gardens, but did not have enough for the large fields where the staple crops grew. A second technique was intercropping, in which several different crops were interspersed in a single field. The right mixture of intercropped plants improves productivity by taking advantage of the fact that different crops have different nutritional requirements and different root-system depths. A third approach was crop rotation, in which farmers planted successive crops that pulled different nutrients from the soil. In the woodland savanna, for example, the yams planted one year might be followed the next year by sorghum, and the next year by millet, before the field was abandoned. Such techniques delayed the exhaustion of the soil, but did not prevent it.

To cope with the rapid depletion of tropical soils, African farmers developed a system known as **shifting cultivation**. Starting with a virgin plot covered with grasses, shrubs, or trees, the farmers would cut down the vegetation, allow it to dry out, and then burn it, leaving a layer of mineral-rich ashes on the ground. They then worked the ashes into the soil using short-handled hoes, leaving the nutrients from the ashes near the surface. This is precisely the sort of "minimal tillage" that modern soil experts advocate using on African tropical soils today. Boosted by the infusion of nutrients from the ashes, the field would produce a good crop in its first year, but by the second year the farmer would see diminishing returns. By the third or fourth year, the harvest would be so meager that the field had to be abandoned and left fallow for up to 20 years to regenerate. The farmer would then cut a new field and start the process all over again. When the cultivable fields near a village were exhausted, the farmers had to relocate to a completely new area. The result was a kind of itinerant agriculture in which entire villages moved every few years in search of fresh land. This process scattered early farmers across the landscape. For these farmers, ownership of land was not an important issue because they knew they would soon be moving on.

A variant of the shifting cultivation system was land rotation agriculture, in which villages had no need to move because the farmers returned to their former fields after the fertility of the soil had been restored. In such a system, each family needed to claim 5–10 times as much land as it could cultivate in any given year in order to give their fields enough time to regenerate. In order to make sure that every family in the community had adequate land for farming, land rights were usually allocated by village chiefs or councils of elders. Individual families could receive permanent user rights to certain plots of cultivated and fallow land, but individual ownership of land in the Western sense was rare. Farming areas were sparsely populated because at any given time, the majority of the farmland would lie fallow or be held in reserve for future needs. When all the usable land near a village was claimed, young people had to migrate to find fresh land. Shifting cultivation and land rotation agriculture thus encouraged farming populations to spread out over the grassland and woodland savannas. At the same time, these systems discouraged the kinds of population concentrations that would have led to the rise of urban centers such as those found in the Nile Valley, Aksum, the Niger floodplain, and the Niger bend.

THE BANTU MIGRATIONS

The region between the southern tip of Africa and a line 6 degrees north of the equator (which encompasses roughly the southern half of Africa) is populated today by people who speak a variety of closely related languages, which use a common sound system and share many root words and grammatical features. Linguists refer to this group of languages as the **Bantu languages**, using a name borrowed from the common Bantu term for "people." There are 440–680 Bantu languages spoken in Africa today, depending on where the line is drawn between a language and a dialect, and one-third of all Africans speak a Bantu language. Linguists have reconstructed the Bantu languages' family tree by identifying the major linguistic branches and working backward to find the common trunk. By combining linguistic analysis with archaeological and botanical evidence, historians are reconstructing the spread of the Bantu speakers throughout the southern half of Africa.

Five thousand years ago, the speakers of the ancestral Bantu language (known to linguists as "Proto-Bantu") lived in the woodland savanna near the present-day border between Nigeria and Cameroon. They cultivated yams and pearl millet using stone tools, and they extracted oil from palm and canarium trees. Just south of them lay the great tropical rainforest, which occupied an area as large as the United States east of the Mississippi River. Despite the luxuriant vegetation and amazing biodiversity of the rainforest, the reddish and yellowish soils of the rainforest floor are actually nutrient poor. The nutrients that sustain the towering trees come from a process known as nutrient cycling, in which the nutrients released from fallen leaves and branches percolate into the soil, where they are picked up by shallow roots and sent back up into the trees. The nutrients live in the vegetation itself, not in the soil.

Between 2000 and 1500 BCE, cooler ocean temperatures and decreased rainfall caused the rainforest to recede from parts of the Atlantic coastal plain, a development that allowed Bantu speakers to expand southward into what are now the central Cameroonian lowlands. Then, around 500 BCE, rainfall became increasingly seasonal, which created patches of open forests and savannas. Over time, those open patches merged to form a 200-mile-wide grassland corridor (known to scientists as the Sangha River Interval) that ran through the rainforest from north to south. Centuries later, the rainfall increased and the forest recovered, but pollen samples collected by scientists have revealed the former grassland corridor, which allowed the early Bantu speakers to move southward through the once-impenetrable rainforest.

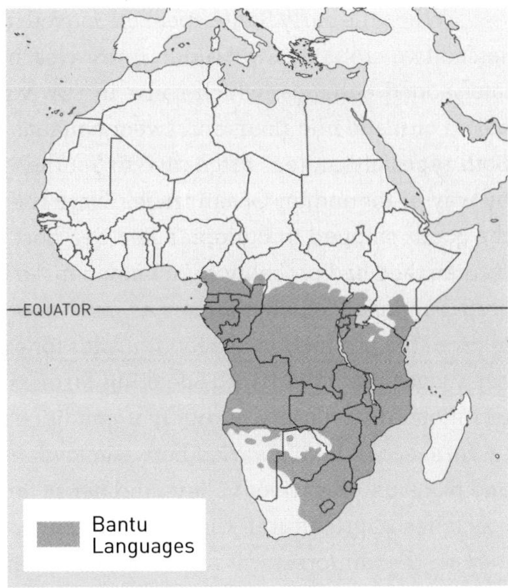

BANTU LANGUAGES Map showing the distribution of Bantu languages today. Between 440 and 680 Bantu languages are currently spoken in Africa, depending on how one divides languages from dialects. The distribution shown on this map is the result of the Bantu migrations, a long process that began around 3000 BCE and resulted in the dispersion of Bantu speakers throughout the agriculturally viable parts of equatorial, eastern, and southern Africa.

The introduction of iron smelting in equatorial Africa around 500 BCE made it possible for Bantu speakers to leave the grassland corridor and move into the rainforest itself. Iron knives, hoes, axes, spears, and arrowheads made it easier to cut down trees, hunt large animals, and wage war. Not every community had the iron ore or the knowledge needed to produce its own iron, so certain centers of iron production emerged and traded their products over long distances. Because the process required to make even a small quantity of iron was so labor-intensive, iron objects remained rare and expensive. Those characteristics made them a socially useful currency for marriage payments, tribute, and fines.

When the early Bantu speakers moved into the rainforest, they already possessed two crops that thrived in forest clearings: yams and oil palm trees. They later added bananas, which came in two varieties: plantains, which could be baked or made into flour, and sweet bananas, which could be peeled and eaten. Both types of bananas are native to Southeast Asia and were brought to Africa by way of the Indian Ocean trade. There is evidence that bananas were among the goods shipped to Ethiopia's Red Sea port of Adulis around 500 CE, although by then they had probably been known in Africa for hundreds of years. As a food crop, bananas yielded 10 times as much food value per acre as yams and thus allowed the production of a food surplus for exchange.

Over time, the Bantu-speaking farmers learned to adapt their cultivation techniques to a variety of different conditions. The tropical rainforest was not a uniform ecosystem: it varied between lowlands and highlands, swampy regions and plateaus, open river valleys and dense forest canopies, all of which required specialized agricultural knowledge to cultivate. The gradual occupation of all parts of the rainforest was a process of constant experimentation and innovation to adapt to the local conditions. By 500 CE, all parts of the vast tropical rainforest had been settled by Bantu-speaking farming communities.

When the first Bantu-speaking farmers arrived in the rainforest, it was sparsely settled by people who made their living by hunting and foraging. Averaging about 7 inches shorter in stature than their Bantu-speaking neighbors, these people are collectively known today as pygmies, although the different pygmy groups are known by their ethnic group names, such as Aka, Koya, Mbuti, Twa, and so forth. Genome studies suggest that the different pygmy groups that live in the African rainforest today are all descended from a common ancestral population that survived intact until the arrival of Bantu-speaking farmers caused it to scatter into separate groups. As the farmers cleared land and settled in villages, they entered into trading relationships with the pygmy hunter-gatherers, who brought them meat, nuts, berries, and other forest products in exchange for food from the farmers' fields and gardens. Oral traditions of the Bantu-speaking immigrants frequently praise the pygmies for teaching them how to survive in the rainforest environment. Over time, the pygmies adopted the languages of the Bantu-speaking groups with whom they traded, and the original pygmy language disappeared. The only remaining traces are found in the pygmy botanical terminology that was adopted by the Bantu speakers and integrated into their languages.

The Bantu-speaking groups who continued to drift southward along the grassland corridor eventually emerged from the rainforest into the southern savanna, where environmental conditions were roughly similar to those found north of the rainforest. The southern third of Africa at that time was lightly populated by San hunters and gatherers, leaving large areas available for the

Bantu-speaking farmers to settle. These farmers moved to the existing frontier in search of new land, and their successors repeated the process a few generations later. Thus their movement was more of a slow drift of the population than a purposeful migration. The dispersal of Bantu speakers south of the rainforest initially proceeded in an easterly direction and skirted the southern and eastern edges of the rainforest. As they arrived in the region of Lake Victoria, they acquired cattle. They then began to disperse into eastern and southern Africa.

The spread of Bantu languages across eastern and southern Africa corresponds with the spread of a cluster of innovations in crops, animal husbandry, and village settlements, as well as a distinctive style of pottery that some archaeologists refer to as "Chifumbazi complex." By tracing the spread of the pottery, archaeologists have concluded that sometime after 100 CE, there was an extremely rapid movement of Bantu speakers from the area of modern Tanzania all the way to South Africa—a distance of over 1,500 miles—in less than two centuries. The Bantu-speaking farmers grew pearl millet, finger millet, sorghum, cowpeas, squash, and beans—crops that had been previously cultivated in the regions north of the tropical forest. A late addition was plantains and sweet bananas, which were grown in the better-watered areas, especially the mountains. The farmers used iron tools and weapons, and they made jewelry out of copper and gold. As the farmers took over more and more of the well-watered lands for fields and pastures, the hunter-gatherers were pushed into marginal lands with inadequate rainfall.

Whereas iron and copper objects were the major repositories of wealth in the tropical rainforest, cattle became the major form of wealth in southern Africa. Villages in southern Africa were often built with the houses arranged around a central corral, indicating that the herds were the focal point of the settlement. By the tenth century CE, there is evidence that people in southeastern Africa relied on cattle not only as a source of milk and meat, but also as a symbol and depository of wealth. As a consequence, ownership of cattle was monopolized by men, while women were responsible for farming. Cattle, like iron and copper in the north, could be used as currency and were typically included in a bride-price, which a young man had to pay the family of his prospective wife before he could marry. A wealthy man could marry several wives and build up a large family, whereas a poor man with no source of material wealth might not be able to get married at all. Material wealth provided a way of rationing social investment and maintaining the power of the elders over their offspring.

By 1000 CE, the agricultural revolution had spread to all the regions of Africa that had adequate rainfall. Throughout the continent, farming was predominantly done by women, who prepared the soil, planted the seeds, weeded the fields, harvested the crops, and processed the harvest. Men's roles in the agricultural cycle varied according to local environments and cultures: they were generally

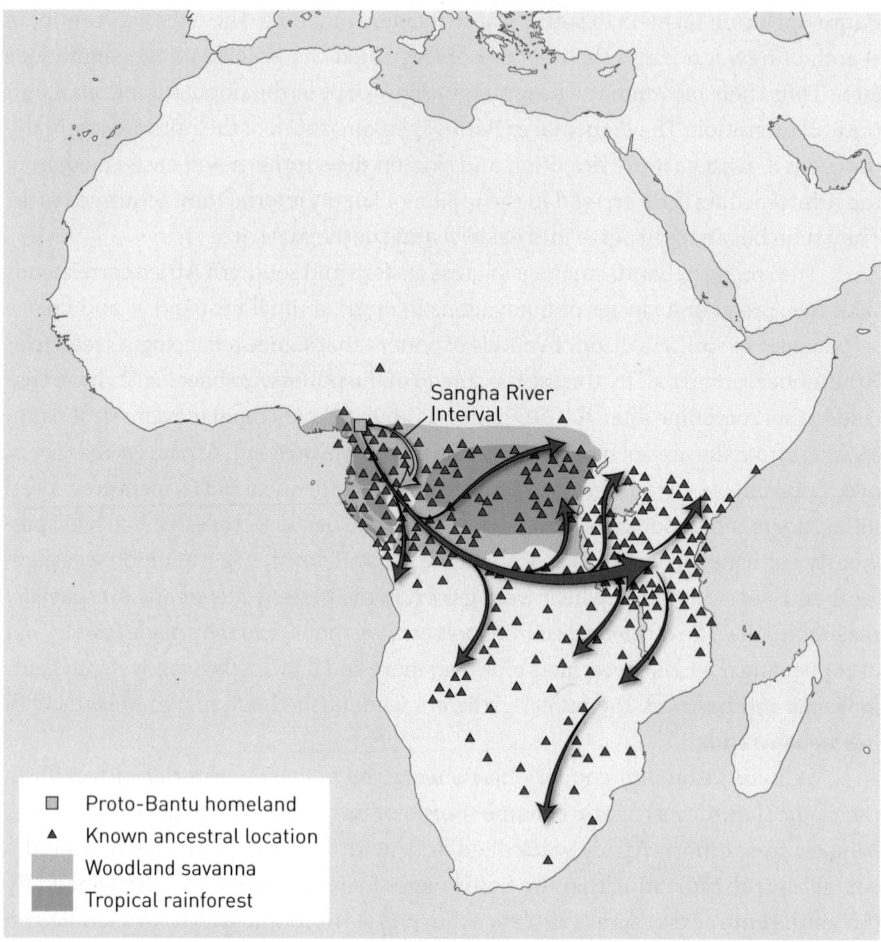

BANTU EXPANSION Map showing the original expansion of Bantu speakers into the tropical rainforest and their later dispersion throughout southern and eastern Africa. The arrows indicate general directions of migration, and the triangles indicate known ancestral locations. The Sangha River Interval was a grassland corridor that opened in the tropical rainforest during an epoch of diminished rainfall.

responsible for cutting down trees in wooded areas to clear a field and for doing the rough hoeing, and they sometimes claimed exclusive rights to cultivate certain prestigious crops such as yams, bananas, or fruit trees. In the grassland savannas of East and West Africa, men often participated in all phases of the agricultural cycle, although women remained the primary cultivators. Because the main purpose of farming was to produce food for the family, men and women divided up the harvest, especially in polygynous households (those in which a man had several wives), because each wife needed enough food to feed herself and her children. In a survey of women's roles in agriculture worldwide, the noted agricultural economist and historian Ester Boserup observed that "Africa is the region of female farming *par excellence*!" The frontier phase of Africa's history was closing, and people began to focus less on strategies for survival and more on developing their social structures, political systems, and cultural traditions.

CONCLUSION

Starting about 10,000 years ago, the plants and animals that made Africa's agricultural revolution possible were domesticated in the Nile valley, the Middle Niger floodplain, and the Ethiopian highlands, as well as in the Fertile Crescent of Southwest Asia. Crops from Southeast Asia, such as plantains and sweet bananas, arrived much later. Even in that early period of Africa's history, Africans did not live in isolation from the wider world. Change came about as a result of both local innovation and the adaptation and integration of ideas and objects from elsewhere.

The switch from foraging to agriculture brought major changes to every society involved, but the impact was most dramatic in regions of floodplain agriculture, such as the Nile valley and the Middle Niger. In floodplains, the annual infusion of fresh silt kept the soil productive. Because farmers could settle in one place for life and build permanent villages, floodplain agriculture concentrated people in densely populated river valleys, creating the conditions for urban life. Memphis and Thebes were among the largest cities in the world during Egypt's New Kingdom. The situation was somewhat different in the Middle Niger region, where the floodplains were more expansive and the populations were less concentrated. There, urbanism took the form of multifunctional urban centers surrounded by suburban villages with specialized economies.

In contrast, the shifting cultivation that predominated in the rain-fed regions of Africa that had nutrient-poor soils encouraged people to spread out in a continuous search for fresh land to clear. The fact that farmers needed to claim 5–10 times as much land as they could cultivate in any given year created land shortages even when the local population was relatively small. The special conditions of shifting cultivation help to explain how early farmers spread over the African continent and why the system discouraged the dense settlement of urban centers. Shifting cultivation has sometimes been derided by historians and anthropologists as "slash and burn" agriculture that was less sophisticated than the floodplain agriculture of the Nile and Niger valleys or the ox-plow agriculture of the fertile Ethiopian highlands. In the end, however, it was the shifting cultivators who colonized and settled most of the arable parts of the African continent.

Five thousand years ago, Africa could be divided into two economic zones. North of the equator, most people made their living by farming and herding. Foraging as a way of life had largely disappeared and had been replaced by the growth of professional hunters' associations and the part-time gathering of useful plants. The regions south of the equator, in contrast, were populated by full-time hunter-gatherers such as the pygmies of the tropical rainforest and the San of southern Africa. That situation was transformed by the migration of Bantu speakers, a long-term historical process that took almost four thousand years to complete. During that time, Bantu speakers gradually occupied all parts of the tropical rainforest. Knowledge of iron smelting, introduced after 500 BCE, greatly aided their progress. The Bantu speakers who followed the north–south grassland corridor through the rainforest emerged into the southern savanna. After picking up knowledge of cattle herding in the Lake Victoria region, they rapidly dispersed throughout vast regions of Africa south of the rainforest. By about 1000 CE, most of the ecologically viable parts of Africa were populated by farmers and cattle herders, while the hunter-gatherers were pushed into marginal lands.

CHAPTER REVIEW

KEY TERMS AND VOCABULARY

Fertile Crescent
Sahara Desert
Nabta Playa
Nile River valley
Memphis
Nile delta
dynasty
Nubia
Thebes
Nubian pharaohs
Aksum
Middle Niger floodplain
shifting cultivation
Bantu languages

STUDY QUESTIONS

1. What was the impact of the drying out of the Sahara Desert on where people lived and how they made their living?
2. Why was the Nile River so important to the Egyptian people and the Egyptian State?
3. Why is the era of the great pyramid builders remembered as a terrible time in Egyptian history?
4. What factors explain why the Egyptian state endured for over 2,600 years despite periodic intervals of disintegration and disorder?
5. How did the Nubians relate to ancient Egyptian culture when they controlled Egypt throughout the 25th dynasty?
6. What are the advantages of shifting cultivation for regions of rain-fed agriculture? How would shifting cultivation affect settlement patterns and political power?
7. How were the speakers of Bantu languages able to become the dominant population in the southern half of Africa?

PERSPECTIVES

HYMN TO THE NILE

The Nile flood was the central event in the Egyptian agricultural year. In a land where rainfall was sparse (less than 2 inches per year), agriculture would have been impossible without the annual floods, which brought water that irrigated the land and deposited the fine silt that fertilized the fields. The Hymn to the Nile was composed around 2100 BCE, during the Middle Kingdom, and dedicated to the scribe of the treasury. There were annual festivals celebrating the flood, at which this hymn might have been performed.

Hail to thee, O Nile! Who manifests yourself over this land, and comes to give life to Egypt! Mysterious is your issuing forth from the darkness, on this day whereon it is celebrated! Watering the orchards created by Ra, to cause all the cattle to live, you give the earth to drink, inexhaustible one! Path that descends from the sky, loving the bread of Seb and the first-fruits of Nepera, you cause the workshops of Ptah to prosper!

Lord of the fish, during the inundation, no bird alights on the crops. You create the grain, you bring forth the barley, assuring perpetuity to the temples. If you cease your toil and your work, then all that exists is in anguish. If the gods suffer in heaven, then the faces of men waste away.

Then he torments the flocks of Egypt, and great and small are in agony. But all is changed for mankind when he comes; he is endowed with the qualities of Num. If he shines, the earth is joyous, every stomach is full of rejoicing, every spine is happy, every jaw-bone crushes (its food).

He brings the offerings, as chief of provisioning; he is the creator of all good things, as master of energy, full of sweetness in his choice. If offerings are made it is thanks to him. He brings forth the herbage for the flocks, and sees that each god receives his sacrifices. All that depends on him is a precious incense. He spreads himself over Egypt, filling the granaries, renewing the marts, watching over the goods of the unhappy. . . .

The night remains silent, but all is changed by the inundation; it is a healing-balm for all mankind. Establisher of justice! Mankind desires you, supplicating you to answer their prayers; you answer them by the inundation! Men offer the first-fruits of corn; all the gods adore you! The birds descend not on the soil. It is believed that with your hand of gold you make bricks of silver! But we are not nourished on lapis-lazuli; corn alone gives vigor. . . .

O inundation of the Nile, offerings are made unto you, oxen are immolated to you, great festivals are instituted for you. Birds are sacrificed to you, gazelles are taken for you in the mountain, pure flames are prepared for you. Sacrifice is made to every god as it is made to the Nile. The Nile has made its retreats in Southern Egypt, its name is not known beyond the Tuau. The god manifests not his forms, he baffles all conception.

1. *Why was the Nile so important to the people and the state of Egypt?*
2. *Does the Hymn portray the Nile as a god? Or as greater than the gods?*

Source: *The Library of Original Sources*, edited by Oliver J. Thatcher (Milwaukee: University Research Extension, 1907), vol. 1, pp. 79–80, 82–83.

BUILDING THE PYRAMIDS

The Greek scholar Herodotus (485–425 BCE) has often been called the father of history because he collected information systematically and arranged it into historical narratives. He traveled widely in the Mediterranean world and spent time in Egypt, where he had conversations with priests and government officials. Because he collected the story of the great pyramid of Khufu (Cheops) more than 2,000 years after it was built, his account probably tells us more about later Egyptian attitudes toward the pyramids than about the construction itself.

The priests said that up to the reign of King Rhampsinitus Egyptian society was stable and the country was very prosperous, but that under their next king, Cheops [Khufu], it was reduced to a completely awful condition. He closed down all the sanctuaries, stopped people performing sacrifices, and also commanded all the Egyptians to work for him. Some had the job of hauling blocks of stone from the quarries in the Arabian mountain range as far as the Nile, where they were transported across the river in boats and then passed on to others, whom he assigned to haul them from there to the Libyan mountains. They worked in gangs of 100,000 men for three months at a time. They said that it took ten years of hard labor for the people to construct the causeway along which they hauled the blocks of stone. . . . The actual pyramid took twenty years to build. Each of its sides, which form a square, is eight *plethra* long [1 plethron = 32.28 yards] and the pyramid is eight *plethra* high as well. It is made of polished blocks of stone, fitted together perfectly; none of the blocks is less than thirty feet long. . . .

The Egyptians said that after a reign of fifty years Cheops died and the kingdom passed to his brother Chephren [Khafra]. He carried on in the same manner as his brother, and not least in the sense that he too built a pyramid, although it did not reach the size of his brother's. I know because in fact I measured them both myself. There are no underground chambers in Chephren's pyramid, nor does a channel come flowing into it from the Nile, as in the case of the other one, where a conduit was built so that the Nile would encircle an island on which, they say, Cheops himself is buried. The bottom layer of Chephren's pyramid was made out of patterned Ethiopian stone and the whole thing is the same size as the other pyramid, but forty feet less tall. Both of them stand on the same hill, which is about a hundred feet high. They said that Chephren's reign lasted fifty-six years.

So by their own reckoning, this terrible period in Egypt lasted 106 years, and the sanctuaries, locked for all these years, were never opened. The Egyptians loathe Chephren and Cheops so much that they really do not like to mention their names. Instead, they say the pyramids belonged to a shepherd called Philitis, who at this time used to graze his flocks on the same land.

1. *What do the pyramids tell us about the capacity of the pharaohs to command the labor of the Egyptian peasants?*
2. *Why was the period of pyramid building remembered as a terrible period in Egypt's history?*

Source: Herodotus, *The Histories* (New York: Oxford University Press, 2008), pp. 144–146.

PERSPECTIVES

THE TRAVELS OF HARKHUF

Harkhuf was a nobleman from Aswan, at the southern border of Egypt. His titles included governor of the south, sole companion, ritual priest, and caravan conductor. A caravan trader by profession, he made four journeys to the Nubian country of Yam and its neighboring regions. The accounts of the first three journeys, which he made for King Merenra [Mernere], were inscribed in his tomb. Our knowledge of his fourth journey comes from a royal decree of King Pepi II, which was also inscribed in Harkhuf's tomb.

The majesty of Mernere my lord, sent me, together with my father, the sole companion, and ritual priest, Iry, to Yam, in order to explore a road to this country. I did it in only seven months, and I brought all kinds of gifts from it. I was very greatly praised for it.

His majesty sent me a second time alone; I went forth upon the Elephantine road, and I descended from Irthet, Mekher, Tereres, Irtheth, being an affair of eight months. When I descended I brought gifts from this country in very great quantity. Never before was the like brought to this land. I descended from the dwelling of the chief of Sethu and Irthet after I had explored these countries. Never had any companion or caravan-conductor who went forth to Yam before this, done so.

His majesty now sent me a third time to Yam; I went forth upon the Uhet road, and I found the chief of Yam going to the land of Temeh to smite Temeh as far as the western corner of heaven. I went forth after him to the land of Temeh, and I pacified him, until he praised all the gods for the king's sake....

I descended with three hundred asses laden with incense, ebony, heknu, grain, panthers, ivory, throw-sticks, and every good product. Now when the chief of Irthet, Sethu, and Wawat saw how strong and numerous was the troop of Yam, which descended with me to the court, and the soldiers who had been with me, then this chief brought and gave me bulls and small cattle, and conducted me to the roads of the highlands of Irthet, because I was more excellent, vigilant, and . . . than any count, companion, or caravan-conductor, who had been sent to Yam before. . . . [Signed] The count, wearer of the royal seal, sole companion, ritual priest, treasurer of the god, privy councilor of decrees, the revered, Harkhuf.

Royal decree to the sole companion, the ritual priest and caravan-conductor Harkhuf

I have noted the matter of this thy letter, which thou hast sent to the king, to the palace, in order that one might know that thou hast descended in safety from Yam with the army which was with thee. Thou hast said in this thy letter, that thou hast brought all great and beautiful gifts. . . . Thou hast said in this thy letter, that thou hast brought a dancing dwarf of the god from the land of spirits, like the dwarf which the treasurer of the god Burded brought from Punt in the time of Isesi. Thou hast said to my majesty: "Never before has one like him been brought by any other who has visited Yam."

1. *Why were kings Mernere and Pepi II interested in Nubia?*
2. *Assess the capacity of the Nubian chiefs to defend themselves against domination by the Egyptians.*

Source: *Ancient Records of Egypt: Historical Documents*, compiled and edited by James Henry Breasted (Chicago: University of Chicago Press, 1906), pp. 150–160.

BANTU EXPANSION

The dispersal of speakers of Bantu languages over the southern half of Africa is one of the most significant cultural transformations in Africa's history. Yet we know very little about it because the early Bantu speakers did not leave accounts or records of their movements. Historians, linguists, archaeologists, and climate scientists are using indirect and circumstantial evidence to reconstruct this history. This article is the result of the collaboration of six scholars working to provide a new synthesis of the Bantu dispersion.

The Bantu expansion that swept out of West Central Africa beginning ~5,000 years ago is one of the most influential cultural events of its kind, eventually spreading over a vast geographical area a new way of life in which farming played an increasingly important role. We use a new dated phylogeny of ~400 Bantu languages to show that migrating Bantu-speaking populations did not expand from their ancestral homeland in a "random walk" but, rather, followed emerging savannah corridors, with rainforest habitats repeatedly imposing temporal barriers to movement. When populations did move from savannah into rainforest, rates of migration were slowed, delaying the occupation of the rainforest by on average 300 years, compared with similar migratory movements exclusively within savannah or within rainforest by established rainforest populations. Despite unmatched abilities to produce innovations culturally, unfamiliar habitats significantly alter the route and pace of human dispersals. . . .

Bantu migrations swept out of West Central Africa beginning ~5,000 years ago (B.P.) and eventually moved all the way down to the southern tip of the African continent. It was one of the most influential cultural events of its kind, spreading over a vast geographical area a new, more sedentary way of life that was fundamentally different from that of indigenous forest foragers—ancestral Bantu speakers had mixed-subsistence economies, in which farming gradually gained in importance.

Two major events in the recent paleoenvironmental history of Central Africa might have influenced the route of the Bantu expansion. The first was a contraction at ~4000 B.P. of the Congo rainforest at its periphery, for instance along the coasts of South Cameroon, Gabon, and Congo. A second event at ~2500 B.P. affected amongst others the western part of the Congo Basin, creating patches of more or less open forests and wooded or grassland savannahs. These areas eventually merged into a corridor known as the "Sangha River Interval" that repeatedly facilitated the north–south spread of certain typical savannah plant and animal species.

The Sangha River Interval may also have been a crucial passageway for the initial north–south migration of Bantu speech communities across the Equator. The archaeological evidence is not yet detailed enough on its own to test this idea. However, the geographical expansion of the Bantu linguistic family, coupled with phylogenetic trees that make use of archaeological evidence, provides an opportunity to reconstruct how and when this cultural expansion moved through the varying habitats of West Central Africa.

1. *Why did the rainforest present such a barrier to southward Bantu expansion?*
2. *How did changing climatic conditions affect the Bantu dispersion through the rainforest?*

Source: Rebecca Grollemund, Simon Branford, Koen Bostoen, Andrew Meade, Chris Venditti, and Mark Pagel, "Bantu Expansion Shows That Habitat Alters the Route and Pace of Human Dispersal," *PNAS* [Proceedings of the National Academy of Sciences], vol. 112, no. 43, October 27, 2015, pp. 13296–13301.

THE KAABA AT MECCA The Kaaba is a former pagan shrine that contained 360 idols representing various gods. When the Prophet Muhammad and his followers gained control of Mecca in 630 CE, they smashed the idols and declared the Kaaba to be a house of God. The Great Mosque of Mecca was later built around it. The Kaaba is the most sacred shrine in Islam.

814 BCE	**146 BCE**	**43–48 CE**
Carthage founded by Phoenicians	Roman conquest of Carthage	Christianity arrives in Egypt

3

IMPERIAL POWER AND RELIGIOUS REVOLUTIONS IN THE MEDITERRANEAN WORLD, 800 BCE–1500 CE

Africa, Europe, and western Asia are all connected by the Mediterranean Sea. Since ancient times, ships have sailed along its shores and crossed its waters. Because of the advantages of maritime travel, many cities on the coast of North Africa were effectively closer to ports in southern Europe or western Asia than they were to more distant cities in North Africa. As a result, the Mediterranean world was a melting pot of peoples, commodities, and ideas; an event on one shore could have major repercussions across the sea, and religious ideas could spread rapidly. In many ways, the peoples of the Mediterranean world have a shared history.

This chapter looks at the ancient commercial ties, expanding empires, and religious affiliations that linked North Africa to Europe and Southwest Asia. The towns and cities of coastal North Africa were successively part of the Phoenician commercial network, the Hellenistic (Greek) empire of Alexander the Great, the Roman Empire, the Byzantine (Eastern Roman) Empire, and the Islamic Caliphate, all of which encompassed large parts of the Mediterranean world. It also explores

642	969	1214
Muslim conquest of Egypt	Fatimid conquest of North Africa	Maximum extension of Almohad Empire

the relationship between powerful empires and the spread of universal religions such as Christianity and Islam. **Christianity** could spread across the Mediterranean world in the early centuries of the Common Era because the Roman Empire had created political unity and the dispersal of the Greek language had created a common literate culture. When Christianity became the official religion of the Roman Empire, the merger of religion and state was complete. **Islam**, in contrast, developed among the nomadic tribes in the Arabian Desert and used Arabic—the language of the desert—for its prayers and sacred texts. During the Arab conquests of the seventh century, the expansion of the **Islamic Caliphate** (a powerful state led by successors of the Prophet Muhammad) and the spread of Arabic language and culture outpaced religious conversion. It was almost as if the state had to expand in order to prepare an environment for Islamic conversion. In the aftermath of the Arab conquests, dissident Islamic sects tried to replicate the process, forming new states by conquest that were more hospitable to their particular interpretation of Islam. That is why doctrinal disputes were often settled on the battlefield.

NORTH AFRICA AND ITS INVADERS

The Mediterranean coast of North Africa can be divided into two roughly equal parts. The eastern half, which is mostly barren desert, was interrupted occasionally by coastal settlements. Most of the population was concentrated in Egypt's densely populated Nile River valley, where the annual floods allowed for irrigated agriculture. The western half, in contrast, is characterized by a strip of coastal plain less than 200 miles wide, running from east to west, that enjoys a Mediterranean climate similar to that of southern Europe. Even though the soils are relatively poor, they were nevertheless adequate for growing grain and olive trees. South of the coastal plain are the Atlas Mountains, which were inhabited mostly by sheep and goat herders who migrated seasonally to exploit different pastures. Beyond the mountains stretches the vast, barren Sahara Desert, which was inhabited by nomads. Because of its unique landscape and ecology, the western half of Africa's Mediterranean coast has long been identified as a single geographical region known as the **Maghreb**, an Arabic term signifying "land of the sunset."

Carthage in the Maghreb

The earliest known commercial network that unified the Mediterranean world was established by the Phoenicians, who lived on the eastern coast of the Mediterranean (in present-day Lebanon). Beginning around 900 BCE, they began to establish trading colonies around the Mediterranean coast. In 814 BCE, they built the trading city of **Carthage** on a headland overlooking the Gulf of Tunis

THE MEDITERRANEAN WORLD This satellite photo shows the unity of the Mediterranean world, with Europe to the north, Africa to the south, and Asia to the east. The green areas represent forests or farmland. Note that North Africa has farmland mostly along the coastal plain of the Maghreb and in the Nile valley of Egypt. The rest is desert or dry plains.

(in present-day Tunisia) and brought in settlers who spoke Punic, the language of the ancient Phoenicians. Located at the eastern end of the Maghreb, Carthage was ideally situated to dominate the trade of the western Mediterranean.

The city-state of Carthage was originally governed by a monarch, but by 396 BCE, it had developed a republican form of government. The Greek philosopher Aristotle considered the political system of Carthage to be the ideal combination of the three great political systems of the ancient Mediterranean world: monarchy (as embodied by the magistrates), aristocracy (as seen in the senate), and democracy (as seen in the citizens' assembly). By 480 BCE, Carthage had become the dominant military power in the western Mediterranean, and by 250 BCE it controlled a series of trading towns along the North African coast for a thousand miles to the east and the west.

At the time Carthage was founded, the population of the Maghreb consisted of people who spoke Berber languages (which are part of the larger Afro-Asiatic language family that includes ancient Egyptian and Arabic). The lifestyles of the **Berbers** reflected the tripartite division of the landscape described in the previous section: those who lived on the coastal plain were mostly settled farmers, while those in the Atlas Mountains were seminomadic pastoralists, and those in the Sahara Desert were nomads. With the vast majority living nomadic or seminomadic lives, the Berbers had developed a segmented form of political organization in which small, kin-based political units called clans operated more or less independently under their own leaders. In times of war or crisis, however, the clans would coalesce into **tribes** by uniting with other clans on the basis of real or fictitious claims of descent from a common ancestor (the term *tribe*, as used here, is restricted to nomadic societies and their offshoots). Tribes, in turn, would occasionally unite in confederations. The clans, tribes, and confederations were continually merging and separating according to the needs of the moment. Although a number of tribes and tribal confederations could be identified at any given time, the cohesion of the component groups over the long term was largely ephemeral. Because of its flexibility and adaptability, the tribal form of political organization was admirably suited to the pastoral and nomadic ways of life.

An analogous system reigned among the settled Berbers on the coastal plain, who lived in permanent villages but roamed occasionally with their flocks in search of pastures. A number of kin groups lived together in a village that was governed by a village council. A group of 2–5 villages formed a tribe, which in turn belonged to a tribal confederation. In times of trouble or stress, each tribe would send representatives to a meeting of the confederation council. Like the nomads, the plains dwellers distrusted centralized authority, as shown by their reliance on village and confederation councils. The council system shows how a tribal form of political organization borrowed from the nomadic Berbers could be adapted to a more settled way of life.

The founding of the city-state of Carthage by settlers from the eastern Mediterranean created a challenge to the Berber tribes. A **state**, in contrast to a tribe, is a form of political organization associated with centralized control over a certain territory and the exercise of political authority by rulers who levy taxes, enforce laws, and employ armed forces to defend their domains. In the early centuries, Carthage paid tribute to its Berber neighbors to forestall potential attacks and facilitate good relations, but after 480 BCE it stopped paying tribute and began subjugating the Berbers instead, eventually conquering nearly half of present-day Tunisia. From this region, Carthage collected taxes and conscripted soldiers. Taxes sometimes reached oppressive levels—as much as 50 percent of the harvest—triggering frequent Berber rebellions during the fourth century BCE.

Although the coastal towns were dominated by Punic-speaking elites of Carthaginian origin, the towns farther inland were inhabited by Berbers who spoke their own language along with Punic and occasionally Greek. It is not surprising that some members of the urban elite in those towns would emulate Carthage and found states just inland from the narrow strip of shoreline Carthage controlled. Beginning in the third century BCE, Berber kingdoms were formed to the west of Carthage in Numidia and Mauretania. The cosmopolitan nature of the new Berber royalty can be illustrated by King Masinissa of Numidia, who dressed like a Roman, spoke Punic like a Carthaginian, and sent his sons to be educated in Greece. Unlike tribal or confederation leaders, the Berber kings had royal courts, standing armies, and a hereditary aristocracy. One royal tomb from the third century BCE was built with thousands of blocks cut from stone and 29 tons of lead from local mines, thus demonstrating the king's command over resources and labor.

The Punic Wars

The power of Carthage in the western Mediterranean was challenged in the third century BCE by the growing power of the Roman Republic. This rivalry led to three long and exhaustive wars between Carthage and Rome, known as the Punic Wars, that stretched from 264 to 146 BCE. During the Second Punic War (218–201 BCE), the Carthaginian general Hannibal took his army (which included three dozen trained war elephants from the Atlas Mountains) across Spain and over the Alps to attack the Romans. Hannibal's invasion of Italy turned into a 15-year siege, during which his army pillaged the countryside for food and supplies, but was unable to capture the city of Rome itself. With the war in a stalemate, the Romans sent an army across the Mediterranean to attack Carthage, sending Hannibal scurrying back to defend his city. In the ensuing battle, the Romans blew horns and trumpets to frighten and confuse Hannibal's charging elephants, a tactic that helped them to gain the upper hand. After imposing a heavy indemnity on Carthage, the Romans withdrew.

Although Carthage was defeated, it is nevertheless noteworthy that the greatest external threat ever faced by the Romans came from North Africa in the form of conscripted Berber soldiers and African elephants. Two centuries later, the Roman historian Titus Livius wrote that it was "the most memorable of all wars that were ever waged. . . . So various was the fortune of the conflict, and so doubtful the victory, that they who conquered were more exposed to danger. The hatred with which they fought also was almost greater than their resources." In 149 BCE, the Romans began the Third Punic War, in which they finally destroyed the city of Carthage. Over a century would pass before the Romans built a new city over the ruins of the old Carthage and declared it the capital of the new Roman province they called Africa. Many centuries later, the name Africa would be applied by others to the whole continent.

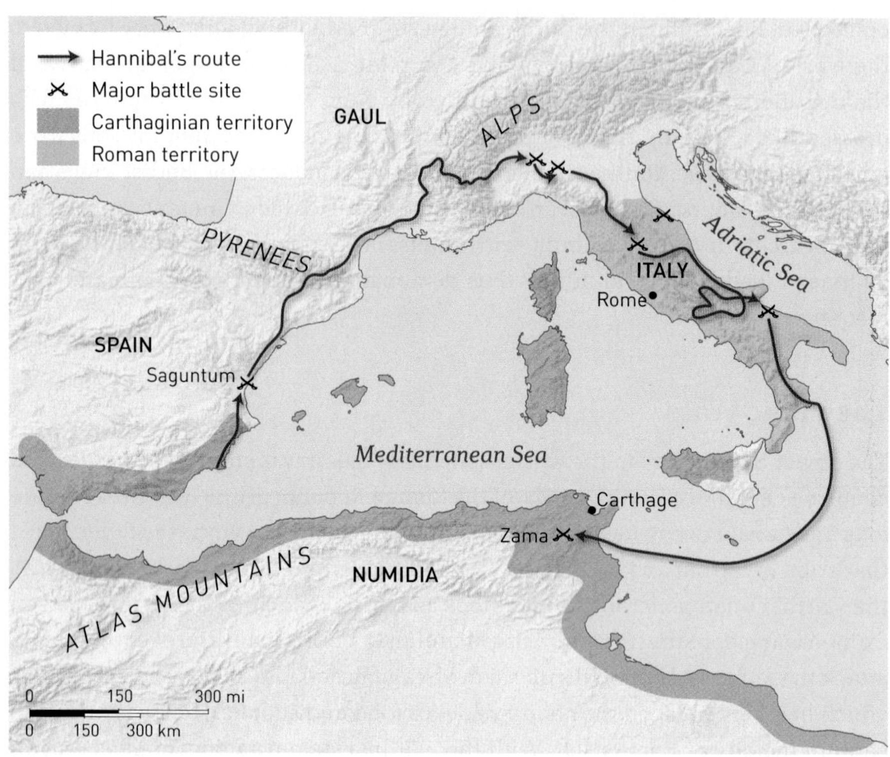

HANNIBAL'S INVASION OF ITALY In 219 BCE, the Carthaginian general Hannibal attacked the independent city of Saguntum, an ally of Rome on the eastern coast of Spain, and then he marched his army, along with his war elephants, across the Pyrenees and the Alps to invade Italy. Over the next 15 years, he controlled parts of southern Italy, but refrained from attacking Rome. When the Romans sent an army to invade North Africa, Hannibal returned to defend Carthage. In 202 BCE, he was defeated by the Romans at Zama some 75 miles southwest of Carthage, thus ending the Second Punic War.

The Roman Province of Africa

The incorporation of the province of Africa into the Roman Empire had a profound impact on the Berbers. Carthage had been a trading center that needed only enough food to feed its own population, which was supplied by large estates located in the immediate vicinity. The empire, however, needed grain and olive oil to feed the burgeoning urban population of Rome. By about 50 BCE, the dry plains east of Carthage were exporting a million liters (265,000 gallons) of olive oil per year, and a century later, the province of Africa was exporting half a million tons of wheat per year, which was two-thirds of the amount needed to feed the population of Rome. That is why North Africa (including Egypt) was called the "granary of Rome." The first century CE was a golden age of agriculture, when all suitable land on the coastal plain was planted in grain; during the next century, olive trees were planted on land that was too dry or too infertile to grow grain.

The intensification of agriculture had far-reaching consequences. One was a slow evolution of land tenure from village to individual ownership, as the Romans were eager to give land titles to anyone who would open up new fields. More important was its effect on the nomads, who came to the coastal plain each year to work in the grain harvest, after which their livestock grazed on the stubble and left manure that fertilized the fields. The result was a huge seasonal migration of people, cattle, and sheep between the mountains and the coastal plain.

To control this annual migration, the Romans constructed *limes*, or lines of fortified frontier posts, which were often reinforced with long ditches. Although the Romans constructed limes in many of their frontier territories, the Maghreb was unusual in that it had two sets of limes running parallel to each other. The exterior limes, which marked the southern limit of Roman territory, divided the region of seminomadic farming from the Sahara Desert, while the interior limes protected the grain-growing region near the Mediterranean coast. In between the two was the "waiting zone," where herds and flocks that had wintered in the desert were allowed to pass the exterior limes, but were then kept from entering the farming territory until the grain had been harvested. For many years, historians believed that the limes had been built to keep the nomads out, but it now appears that their purpose was to regulate the seasonal movements of people and their flocks.

The increasing agricultural production led to the growth of cities. The old Phoenician cities on the coast became commercial centers for shipping agricultural products and livestock to Rome, while new cities populated by Roman veterans grew up around the frontier posts. The most noteworthy urban expansion, however, was the growth of Berber market towns with populations of 10,000–15,000, built of stone and scattered across the agricultural regions. The farmlands in what is now northern Tunisia had 200 such towns, often located only 6 to 8 miles apart. In all, nearly 600 stone cities dotted the landscape of Roman North Africa, supported by numerous aqueducts to bring water from the mountains and over 12,000 miles of roads. With the expansion of agricultural production stimulating the growth of stone cities, Roman North Africa has been characterized by one scholar as a "landscape of opportunity" that was exploited by Romans and Berbers alike.

Greeks and Romans in Egypt

In the eastern part of North Africa, Egypt fell to the army of Alexander the Great, who had been tutored as a boy by the Greek philosopher Aristotle, and who had later united the Greek states and built up a powerful army. Before Alexander left Egypt in 331 BCE to continue his conquest of western Asia, he founded the city of Alexandria at the point where the western edge of the Nile River delta meets the Mediterranean. Following Alexander's death a decade later, his generals divided up his empire. Egypt went to General Ptolemy, who founded a dynasty that would rule Egypt for nearly 300 years. Although the Ptolemaic rulers styled themselves as latter-day Egyptian pharaohs (they are sometimes referred to as the Greek pharaohs), they encouraged large-scale immigration of Greeks from around the Mediterranean and Jews from Palestine, making Alexandria a very cosmopolitan city. They staffed the Egyptian government with Greek officials who spoke to the Egyptians through interpreters, and they created an Egyptian army of Greek mercenaries who were given grants of land and became a new rural elite. Over time, some native Egyptians who learned Greek made their way into the administration and the army, but they never attained the highest ranks.

The focal point of Greek culture in Egypt was the Museum and Library of Alexandria, which contained nearly 700,000 scrolls that served as a compendium of all the knowledge of the Mediterranean world. It had laboratories for studying anatomy and astronomy and a zoo for the study of exotic animals. Intellectuals from all over the Greek-speaking world came to study there. Scholars living in Alexandria made great strides in developing an understanding of the solar system, anatomy, geometry, physics, and geography. Eratosthenes, for example, calculated the circumference of the earth accurately within 50 miles, while Hero built the first recorded steam engine. With such a store of intellectual resources, Alexandria became the intellectual center of the Mediterranean world.

In order to gain acceptance as legitimate pharaohs, the Ptolemies turned to religion. When the body of Alexander the Great was being carried from Babylon to Macedonia for burial in 323 BCE, General Ptolemy hijacked the funeral cortege and took the body to Memphis, the traditional capital of the pharaohs. Building on Egyptian beliefs about divine kingship, he declared Alexander a national god and elevated the high priest of Alexander to be the most powerful religious figure in Egypt. Ptolemy also built a temple in Alexandria dedicated to a new god called Serapis, who represented an amalgamation of the Egyptian gods Osiris and Apis with the Greek gods Zeus and Helios. Even though the new god was supposed to represent a fusion of Egyptian and Greek divinities, the statue of Serapis created by the Greek master sculptor Bryaxis looked remarkably like Zeus. At the same time, the Ptolemies carried out the religious duties of traditional pharaohs by visiting Egypt's most important shrines and constructing spectacular new temples to Egyptian gods that were bastions of traditional pharaonic religion and culture. Like the older temples, the new ones were major landowners and centers of economic activity.

The main preoccupation of the Ptolemies was exploiting the agricultural potential of Egypt. They launched ambitious engineering projects to reclaim large tracts of land from the western desert through irrigation, but mostly they put pressure on the Egyptian peasants to maximize their yields. Every February, the scribes from the rural villages were summoned by the provincial governors to prepare the annual survey of agricultural production, and they traveled to Alexandria in the summer to report on the harvest. The Ptolemies imposed a heavy land tax in northern Egypt and a harvest tax in southern Egypt. Their punitive economic policies led to periodic peasant rebellions under Ptolemy III and Ptolemy IV.

The last of the Ptolemaic rulers—and the last pharaoh of Egypt—was **Cleopatra**, a woman of great intelligence and strong character who spoke about a dozen different languages. As the only Ptolemaic ruler who could speak to Egyptians in their own language, she declared herself to be the reincarnation of the goddess Isis, thus transforming herself into a distinctly Egyptian figure who was accepted by at least some of her subjects as a legitimate pharaoh. According to the Greek chronicler Plutarch, she had irresistible charm, persuasive speech, and a stimulating character. She also had political ambitions. In the waning days of the Roman Republic, she married the Roman ruler Julius Caesar and had a child with him. After Caesar was assassinated in the Roman Senate in 44 BCE, a power struggle broke out between two Roman generals—Mark Antony and Octavian—that became a Roman civil war. Antony, who

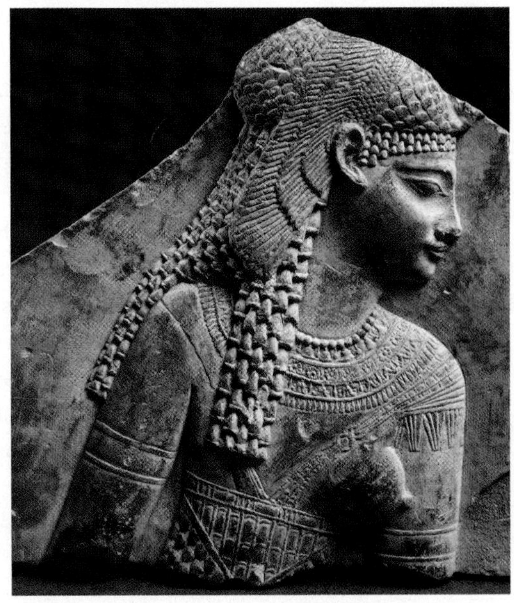

THE LAST PHARAOH This bas-relief from Alexandria depicts Cleopatra, the last active ruler of Ptolemaic Egypt. Although the Ptolemies were of Macedonian Greek descent, they saw themselves as latter-day pharaohs. Cleopatra's involvement in a Roman civil war led to the Roman conquest of Egypt. After her death by suicide, Egypt ceased to be an independent state and became a Roman province.

had earlier been romantically involved with Cleopatra, moved to Alexandria in 36 BCE and married her, hoping to use her money and military support to defeat his rival Octavian. When Octavian's army successfully invaded Egypt in 30 BCE, Antony killed himself, and Cleopatra, it was said, committed suicide with the aid of a venomous snake. After that, Egypt became a Roman province, and the autonomous Egyptian state that had endured for nearly three millennia ceased to exist.

The Roman conquest added an extra layer of complexity to Egyptian society. The Roman governors and top administrators stationed in Alexandria spoke Latin, but Greek remained the normal language of government because the middle and lower levels of the administration were filled by Greeks and Greek-speaking Egyptians (as they had been under the Ptolemies). The four largest Egyptian cities were cosmopolitan spaces inhabited largely by Romans, Greeks, Jews, and assimilated Egyptians. The great mass of the Egyptian population, however, lived in roughly 2,500 rural villages scattered throughout the Nile delta and the Nile valley, where they produced the grain that supplied one-third of the population of Rome. The Roman administration gave tax reductions to large landowners in order to stimulate economic growth, while the peasants who farmed on government land continued to pay high taxes. So great was the burden on the peasantry that many fled their farms and took up lives of rural brigandage.

By the beginning of the Common Era, the Mediterranean Sea could accurately be characterized as a "Roman lake" because a person could travel around its perimeter on foot or horseback and always be in a Roman province or client state. In the wake of the bloody conquests by Alexander the Great and the Roman generals, the arrival of two centuries of relative peace (known as the *pax romana*) must have come as a relief, even to those who felt oppressed by the Roman Empire. That period of political unity in the Mediterranean world provided a unique environment for the expansion of a new religion.

CHRISTIANITY IN NORTH AFRICA

The Christian religion was founded in Jerusalem in the early years of the Common Era by the followers of a Jewish preacher named Jesus. They believed that Jesus was the son of God, that he had been crucified by the Romans, and that he had risen from the dead 3 days later and ascended to heaven. They also believed that he would soon return to establish the Kingdom of God on earth. Although the life of Jesus is mostly associated with the land of Palestine, the New Testament recounts that he spent time in Egypt as a baby. Traditions of the Egyptian Coptic Church that elaborate on this theme hold that the baby Jesus spent over 3 years in Egypt with his family and visited many places that have since become pilgrimage sites. In a similar way, traditions of the Ethiopian Orthodox Church hold that during his time in Egypt, Jesus and his mother made a visit to Lake Tana in Ethiopia, which later became a site of churches and monasteries and a destination for pilgrims. In this way, both Egyptian and Ethiopian Christians have laid claim to Jesus's African connections.

Early Christianity in Egypt

Christian tradition holds that the evangelist Mark brought Christianity to Egypt between 43 and 48 CE, roughly 10–20 years after Jesus's death. The earliest Christian community in Egypt was composed primarily of Jews living in Alexandria, but it became more Greek in nature after the Jewish community was nearly annihilated by the Romans in 117 CE. A major controversy was stirred up when Christian thinkers known as Gnostics tried to integrate Christian beliefs with ideas drawn from Greek philosophy and the cosmic science of the Ptolemaic astronomers. Christian scholars established the School of Alexandria in 180, in part to attack the Gnostics and defend a more orthodox version of Christianity. Its faculty included a variety of intellectual luminaries, including Origen, the greatest theologian in the early Church.

Beyond Alexandria, Christianity was spreading up the Nile valley, where Christian texts written in Greek had been circulating since 130. Around the year 200, Christian writings began to appear in Coptic, the ancient language of the Egyptians, but they were written using a modified Greek alphabet instead of Egyptian hieroglyphs. By the year 300, 72 orthodox Christian communities in Egypt were large enough to have a bishop, and there is evidence of Gnostic Christians living in southern Egypt as well. What we know of those Gnostic communities comes from 13 leather-bound books unearthed by an Arab farmer in 1945. Written on papyrus in Coptic between 350 and 400 CE, the books contain over 50 separate Gnostic texts translated from earlier writings in Greek. Apparently both Gnostic and orthodox Christianity flourished along the Nile.

Throughout the third century CE, the Roman emperors ordered periodic bouts of religious persecution. Some Egyptian Christians sought refuge in desert settlements where people lived communally; others chose to live in solitude as hermits, rejecting worldly pleasures in their search for the essence of spirituality. Around 305 CE, a hermit known as Antony of the Desert abandoned his solitary life and began to accept disciples to share his teachings. Other hermits followed his example, and soon monasteries were being constructed across the desert. By 400 CE, three different monastic styles could be found in Egypt, each in a different region. The desert of northern Egypt was home to many hermits. Although some

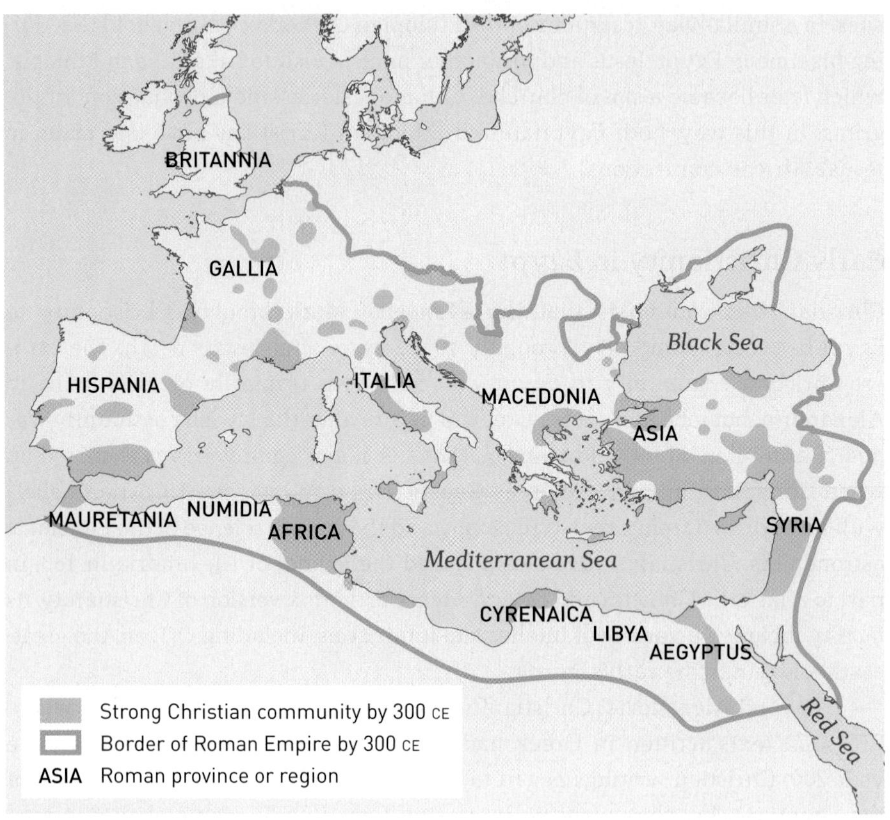

THE SPREAD OF CHRISTIANITY BY 300 CE As this map shows, all the strong Christian communities in 300 CE were located within the borders of the Roman Empire. The major Christian regions in Africa were in the Roman provinces of Aegyptus, Cyrenaica, and Africa.

of them took on disciples, they retained their solitary life and chose not to live together in communities. In southern Egypt, communities of "brothers" lived and worked together in a situation of equality. The fullest development of the monastic system was west of the Nile delta, where several monks would live together as disciples of an *abba* (father). In all cases, the monastic spirituality of the Egyptian desert was less a religious doctrine or fixed set of practices than it was a complete way of life that was absorbed through the daily practice of work and prayer. The monks (from the Greek word *monachos*, meaning "celibate") followed a daily routine that alternated work with prayer, solitude with community. Although most of the monks mentioned in the historical record were men, there is evidence that women also entered monasteries and attained positions of authority. One of the most famous was Amma (Mother) Sarah, who was said to have been so focused on her spiritual life that she lived for 60 years beside a river and never lifted her eyes to look at it. From the desert of Egypt came the monastic way of life that would later be replicated in Europe and around the Christian world.

The growth of Christianity signaled the end of the ancient Egyptian religious cults. The famous Serapeum in Alexandria, a temple dedicated to the god Serapis, was destroyed by a Christian mob in 391 on the orders of the patriarch Theophilus. It was converted into a church dedicated to Saint John the Baptist. Farther up the Nile, the cults of the ancient Egyptian gods were also under attack by Christians. The last known inscription in Egyptian hieroglyphs was written in 294 at a temple in Aswan. After that, hieroglyphic writing fell into disuse and was forgotten. The pyramids, monuments, and temples built by the ancient pharaohs stood as silent witnesses to the religious cults that had once thrived, but until their inscriptions were deciphered in the nineteenth century, there was no one who could read them.

Early Christianity in the Maghreb

The Christian community in the Maghreb, which was concentrated in Carthage, was also persecuted by the Romans. The earliest evidence of Christianity in the region comes from 180 CE, when five women and seven men from a small town near Carthage were put to death by the Romans for their religious beliefs. Other prominent martyrs soon followed. Perpetua, a 22-year-old mother imprisoned with her infant and servant, kept a diary in which she recorded the events leading up to her death, leaving a moving account of her suffering and her faith. Cyprian, a wealthy lawyer who sold his estates and donated the money to the poor, became the bishop of Carthage in 248. He worked to hold the church together in the face of doctrinal disputes and breakaway sects and to assert the authority of the bishops. After only 10 years as bishop of Carthage, he was executed by the Romans.

Major changes came to the Roman Empire during the fourth century. The persecution of Christians came to an end in 313, when the Edict of Milan permitted Christians to worship openly and recover their confiscated Church property. In 380, Christianity became the official religion of the Roman Empire: the old Roman religious cults were banned, and the pagan temples were torn down. When the emperor Theodosius I died in 395, the Roman Empire was divided between his two sons. The Western Roman Empire had its capital at Rome, and the Eastern Roman Empire had its capital at Constantinople (present-day Istanbul), a city built on the site of an earlier city called Byzantium; that is why the Eastern Roman Empire is often referred to as the Byzantine Empire.

With Christians freed from the threat of persecution and violence, the churches in North Africa flourished. The patriarch of Alexandria, who led more than a hundred bishops, was the most powerful person in Egypt, and his religious authority in the larger Christian world was second only to that of the pope in Rome. The importance of the North African churches in the development of Christian theology can be illustrated by the discussion about which Christian texts should be included in the New Testament. It was the patriarch of Alexandria who proclaimed the final list in 367, and his list was later confirmed by a council of bishops meeting at Hippo (in present-day Algeria).

The Monophysite Schism

The influence of Alexandria within the wider Christian world would fade after the Council of Chalcedon, held near Constantinople in 451. Over five hundred bishops from across the Christian world met to debate whether Jesus's humanity was inseparable from his divinity (the monophysite position), or whether he had two separate natures, one fully human and one fully divine (the dyophysite position). The monophysite position had been championed by Cyril, the recently deceased patriarch of Alexandria. The Council of Chalcedon condemned Cyril's position and voted instead for the idea that Jesus had a dual nature. That decision provoked bitter opposition in Egypt, where the new patriarch of Alexandria was lynched for supporting the council's position, and monks displaying dyophysite tendencies were driven out of the desert monasteries. After that, the Egyptian church became more independent and more isolated from the wider Christian world. It became known as the **Coptic Church** because Coptic was becoming the major literary and liturgical language of Egypt during the fifth century. Coptic antipathy toward the Byzantine emperors in Constantinople was so strong that when representatives of the emperor Justinian (who ruled 527–565) visited a monastery in southern Egypt, the monks washed the room with water to purify it after its pollution by the emperor's men.

The dissident doctrines of the Coptic Church in Egypt found support farther up the Nile valley. In the sixth century, Nubia was divided among three different kingdoms, two of which converted to monophysite Christianity and one of which chose dyophysite Christianity. By the eighth century, however, all the Nubian churches had unified around the monophysite position under the authority of the patriarch of Alexandria.

In the kingdom of Aksum (in present-day Ethiopia), King Ezana converted to Christianity around 350 CE. One can trace his religious evolution from the coins he issued, which show a shift over time from a pagan motif of a sun disk and crescent moon to a Christian cross. He also wrote an inscription on a large stone tablet

A CHURCH CARVED FROM SOLID ROCK The Church of Saint George at Roha (present-day Lalibela, Ethiopia) was carved out of the bedrock in the shape of a Greek cross. It was one of 11 rock-hewn churches built on orders from Ethiopian King Lalibela in the early thirteenth century. Altogether, more than 150 rock-hewn churches were carved in the Ethiopian countryside.

in which he referred to himself as "Ezana, King of the Aksumites and servant of Christ." The spread of Christianity among the common people of Aksum is attributed to the "Nine Saints," who arrived around 500 CE from Syria, a major center of monophysite Christianity. They are credited with translating the Bible into Geez (the language of Aksum) and founding monasteries that became centers for teaching, learning, and the spread of Christianity.

After the dissolution of the kingdom of Aksum in the seventh century, Christianity endured in scattered churches and monasteries until the twelfth century, when the Zagwe dynasty established a new kingdom with its capital at Roha (present-day Lalibela), some 150 miles to the south of the abandoned capital of

Aksum. King Lalibela set out to make his capital a pilgrimage center for Christians. Accordingly, he named the stream that flowed through his capital the River Jordan to emphasize the idea that Roha was the "new Jerusalem," and he built a series of 11 churches carved out of solid rock. These carved churches inspired the construction of over 150 rock-hewn churches in the Ethiopian countryside. The churches in Ethiopia, like those in Nubia, operated under the religious authority of the patriarch of Alexandria in Egypt. The northeastern corner of Africa had become the last bastion of monophysite Christianity.

AUGUSTINE OF HIPPO Born into a Romanized Berber family in North Africa, Augustine served as the bishop of Hippo (in present-day Algeria). He later became known as Saint Augustine. As the author of more than 300 works on Christian doctrine, he was by many accounts the most influential theologian in the history of the Catholic Church. This iconic image, made centuries after his death, accurately depicts him as a dark-skinned Berber.

Augustine of Hippo

While Christians in Egypt, Nubia, and Ethiopia were becoming isolated from the larger Christian world, the opposite trend could be seen in the Maghreb, which was becoming closely tied to the popes in Rome. Perhaps the most influential of all the early Christian thinkers was Augustine of Hippo, later known as Saint Augustine. Born to a Romanized Berber family in a mountainous region about 150 miles west of Carthage, he traveled to Carthage to study at the age of 17 and went on to teach rhetoric at the Roman imperial court in Milan. While in Italy, he converted to Christianity after reading an account of the life of Antony of the Desert, the famous Egyptian hermit. Returning to North Africa in 388, he sold his family's estate and founded a small monastery in his hometown. In 395, he was appointed bishop of Hippo. Writing some 300 works on Christian doctrine at a time when Christianity had recently become the official religion of the Roman Empire, Augustine sought to define what it meant to be a Christian in a larger Christian world. He is perhaps best known for his formulation of the doctrine of original sin, which holds that all humanity is tainted by the sins of the first man and woman, Adam and Eve, and is therefore in need of redemption.

After the city of Rome was sacked by the Visigoths (a Germanic tribe) in 410, sending shock waves throughout the Mediterranean world, Augustine began writing *The City of God*, his longest work. *The City of God* presented human history as a conflict between human kingdoms and the Kingdom of God, which he defined as a spiritual kingdom composed of all people who embraced the Christian faith. Human kingdoms, he argued, could be destroyed, but the Kingdom of God was indestructible. He was, in effect, assuring his readers that the Christian society that had emerged in the late Roman Empire would endure long after the fall of Rome itself. Thus did Augustine, a Berber from the mountains of North Africa, create the intellectual bridge that would ease Europe's transition from the dying ancient world to the emerging Middle Ages.

THE RISE AND EXPANSION OF ISLAM

The Muslim religion began in the Arabian Peninsula, a region of desert and semi-desert lands inhabited by camel- and sheep-herding nomads who spoke Arabic. So isolated was the area from the major centers of power in the Mediterranean world that the Romans had never attempted to conquer it. In the seventh century, a caravan trader named Muhammad, who was based in the trading town of Mecca, said that he had been visited by the invisible presence of God. In 613, he proclaimed the profession of faith that defines Muslims to this day: "There is no god but God, and Muhammad is God's messenger." In his preaching, Muhammad repeatedly made reference to Jewish and Christian prophets who had come before him, and he placed himself firmly in that tradition (Judaism, Christianity, and Islam are sometimes referred to as the Abrahamic religions because they all trace their history back to the Jewish patriarch Abraham). After being driven out of Mecca in 622, Muhammad established a community of his followers in Medina, some 250 miles to the northwest. In 630, he and his followers occupied Mecca by force; they smashed all the idols in the pagan temple known as the Kaaba and declared it to be a house of God. That act made Mecca the spiritual center of the Muslim world.

Establishing the Islamic Caliphate

At the time of Muhammad's death in 632, Islam was far from being a fully formed system of religious beliefs and practices. After a meeting of Muhammad's closest companions, it was decided that Abu Bakr would lead the community and hold the title of caliph, or successor of the Prophet Muhammad. As a secular and military leader who did not have any religious authority, his main goal was to create a state that would consolidate control over the nomadic tribes of the Arabian Peninsula. Abu Bakr died after 2 years and was succeeded by Umar (634–644), Uthman (644–656), and Ali (656–661). Those four companions of Muhammad—later known as the four patriarchs—were responsible for the initial expansion of the Islamic Caliphate.

The early military expeditions sent out by the caliphs were designed more to gain booty than to create an empire, but their very success led inexorably to an

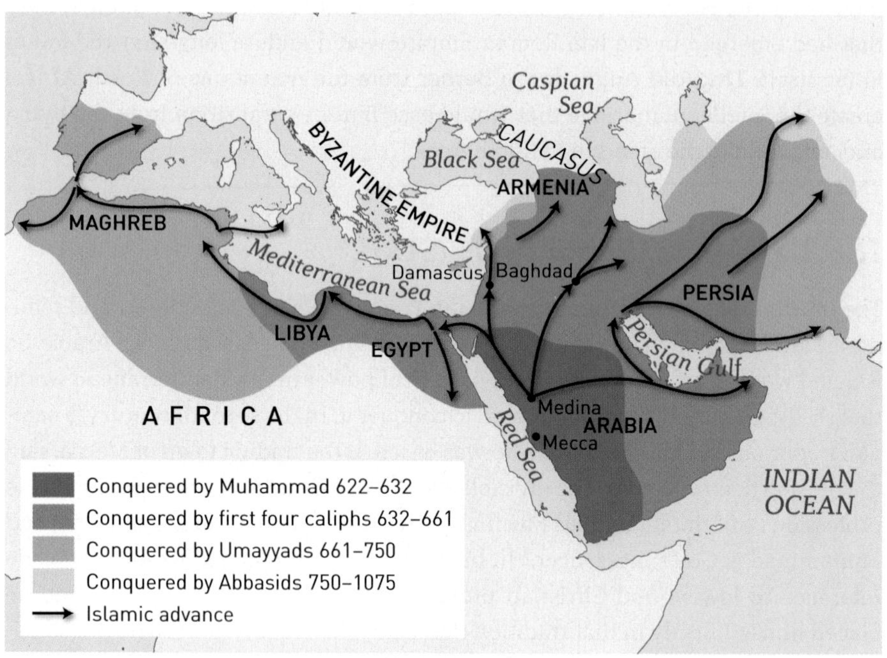

EXPANSION OF THE ISLAMIC CALIPHATE This map shows the four stages of the expansion of the Islamic Caliphate by conquest between 622 and 1075. The Muslim armies advancing across North Africa reached Tangier, at the strait of Gibraltar, in 710, giving them complete control of Africa's Mediterranean coast.

expansion of the Caliphate. Following a victory over the forces of the Byzantine Empire near the Sea of Galilee in 636, the Muslims moved north to occupy most of Syria. By 642, they had conquered Egypt, which gave them a base for moving westward along the coast of North Africa. To the east, they occupied the whole of Iran and began moving into central Asia and northwestern India by 652. Once the Muslim armies had advanced too far from Medina to return home after an expedition, they established military camps in the conquered territories. Over time, those camps became the centers of provincial administration in the rapidly expanding Caliphate.

Contrary to certain popular notions, the military expansion of the Islamic Caliphate was not accompanied by forced conversions to Islam. The conquerors were far more interested in domination than in conversion. In the early years of their dominion, there was very little conversion to Islam in the conquered territories, but the process would accelerate over time as Islamic doctrine became more developed and mosques and schools were built. "People of the Book," as Christians and Jews were called, received the status of "protected minorities," which made them second-class citizens who had to pay a poll tax to the Muslim governors. The early governors did not encourage mass conversion to Islam because it would have reduced their tax revenue. When people in Khurasan (present-day Iran) began to convert to Islam, its Muslim governor was skeptical. "I have learned that the people of As-Sughd and their likes have not become Muslims sincerely," he wrote. "They have accepted Islam only to escape the poll tax. Investigate this matter and discover who is circumcised, performs the required acts of devotion, is sincere in his conversion to Islam, and can read a verse of the *Quran*."

After the assassination of Caliph Ali—the last of the four patriarchs—in 661, the Caliphate passed into the hands of the Umayya family from Mecca, who moved the capital to Damascus, Syria, and transformed the position of caliph into one more like that of a king in a secular monarchy. No longer would caliphs be selected from among the companions of the Prophet Muhammad; instead, there would be dynastic succession from father to son. The military expansion of the Caliphate continued under the Umayyad dynasty, especially to the west, where it conquered the Mediterranean coast of North Africa all the way to the Atlantic Ocean. In 711, an Arab army crossed the Strait of Gibraltar into Spain. Soon it had occupied all the major towns on the Iberian Peninsula and advanced as far as the French city of Narbonne. Less than a century after the death of Muhammad, Arab armies had conquered a region that stretched all the way from Spain to northwestern India and created one of the largest empires in world history. After the Umayyad dynasty fell in 750, a family from Mecca known as the Abbasids took control of the Islamic Caliphate. They moved the capital to Baghdad, from where they would rule for the next 500 years.

Defining Islamic Belief and Practice

As the Arab armies moved from victory to victory, the teachings of Muhammad were being organized and codified into a coherent set of religious beliefs and practices. The most important step was to collect those teachings, which Muhammad had recited orally to a group of followers known as the *Qurra*. Muhammad was illiterate, but his recitations were memorized and often written down by his followers. After Muhammad's death, the Qurra began to spread Muhammad's teachings, which were collectively known as the *Quran*. Over the years, discrepancies among different texts began to be noticed. In 650, Caliph Uthman commissioned a group of scholars to prepare a single authoritative text of the Quran, then ordered all the variant texts to be brought to Medina and burned.

If the Qurra were responsible for preserving and broadcasting the recitations of the Prophet Muhammad, it was the *ulama*—a class of Islamic scholars and jurists—who codified Islamic practice and law. As the Caliphate expanded and encompassed people of diverse cultures and languages, the ulama struggled to formulate a uniform way for Muslims to express their faith through ritual practice. The result was the Five Pillars of Islam. The first pillar was a simple statement of belief: "There is no god but God, and Muhammad is God's messenger." The second pillar was a ritual prayer, performed five times a day, either individually or in a group, while the worshippers faced toward Mecca. The third pillar was the payment of the *zakat*, a tax that was originally collected by the community and distributed to the poor. As the Caliphate developed, it became a state tax levied on all Muslims. The fourth pillar was the month-long period of fasting known as Ramadan, during which Muslims were not allowed to eat or drink from sunup to sundown. As the practice developed, the days of fasting were often followed by great feasts at night. The fifth pillar was participation in the annual pilgrimage to Mecca and in the rituals held at the Kaaba at least once in a lifetime. Mecca was accessible to almost everyone in the days when most Muslims lived in the Arabian Peninsula, but when Islam spread to faraway lands, the pilgrimage became the preserve of a privileged few. Those Muslims who lacked the means to make the trip were exempt from this requirement.

The second major accomplishment of the ulama was the development of a body of Islamic law, the sharia. In the beginning, Muslims simply followed traditional Arab customs, but as Islam spread to other regions it became necessary to specify which actions were obligatory, which were simply desirable, and which were forbidden. The laws covered every aspect of life, from personal hygiene to legal matters. They were based on the thousands of anecdotes, known as *hadiths*, about what the Prophet Muhammad had reportedly said or done. Major areas of law were marriage, inheritance, food, drink, usury, and slavery. During the eighth century, four different schools of thought on Islamic jurisprudence arose, opening heated debates among Muslim jurists. Law and jurisprudence, rather than doctrine and theology, were the major pursuits of Muslim scholars.

Sectarian Divisions Emerge

Even though Islamic thought did not place its primary emphasis on theology, sectarian divisions nevertheless developed in the expanding Muslim world. Mainstream Islam under the Caliphate became known as Sunni Islam, and two of the most important variant groups were the Shias and the Sufis. The Shias developed as partisans of Ali, the last of the four patriarchs. During his embattled 5-year reign, Ali tried to reorient the role of caliph toward the religious piety embodied by the Prophet Muhammad, but this effort ended when he was assassinated in 661. When the ruler who succeeded Ali transformed the role of caliph into a hereditary position controlled by the Umayya family, Ali's son Hussein led a failed revolt, in which he was killed. To the Shias, Ali was the first *Imam* (proof of God on earth), and Hussein was a martyr whose death embodied a new theology of atonement through sacrifice, a notion that is absent in mainstream (Sunni) Islam. The Shia profession of faith is, "There is no god but God, Muhammad is God's messenger, and Ali is God's interpreter." Shia Islam would become important in North Africa with the rise of the Fatimids in the tenth century.

Sufism, in contrast, stressed the mystical elements of religious practice, focusing on meditation and asceticism. Because many of these mystics dressed in wool (*suf* in Arabic), they were called Sufis. The Sufis did not reject the laws and ritual practices of Sunni and Shia Islam, but rather sought to transcend them to gain a more direct experience of God. Sufi mystics often withdrew from the community to pursue purification and inner enlightenment. They would attract disciples, who would in turn attract their own disciples, thus passing their accumulated knowledge and wisdom to new generations. This process led to the development of Sufi religious orders beginning in the thirteenth century. Although some of the Sufi orders were considered heretical, most of them gained acceptance within the Sunni or Shia tradition.

The rise of the Islamic Caliphate was a complex process involving three distinct elements: the military and political expansion of the state, the spread of Arabic language and culture, and the spread of Islam as a religion. Under the four patriarchs (632–661) and the Umayyad dynasty (661–750), the expansion of the

Caliphate was simultaneously an expansion of Arab military power, while the expansion of the Islamic faith lagged behind. After the Abbasids gained control of the Caliphate and moved its capital to Baghdad, they allowed non-Arab Muslims to hold high positions, and their new capital in Baghdad showed significant influences of Persian culture. In short, the Caliphate under the Abbasids became less of an Arab state and more of a multicultural Muslim one.

The Arab Conquest of North Africa

At the time of Muhammad's death in 632, the Mediterranean coast of North Africa from Egypt to Carthage was under the control of the Byzantine Empire, ruled from Constantinople. By 642, the Arabs had driven the Byzantine overlords out of Egypt and established a capital in the region of present-day Cairo. Throughout the seventh century, the Arab government of Egypt retained the pre-existing administrative structure, using Greek as the official language of state. Christians were granted the status of a protected minority as long as they paid the poll tax called the *jizya*. Christian monks were exempted from the tax, and the Coptic Church hierarchy remained in place.

Things changed in the eighth century, when Arabic became the language of administration and the administrators sent out by the Abbasid caliphs in Baghdad began to raise taxes. Christian farmers in the agriculturally rich Nile delta carried out a series of revolts beginning in the 770s, escalating to an all-out revolt against the tax collectors in 829. That revolt was so massive that the Abbasid caliph in Baghdad marched all the way to Egypt at the head of a large army to suppress it. In the wake of the revolt, thousands of Egyptian Christians were deported to Baghdad or sold as slaves; laws were passed prohibiting Christians from holding processions or erecting a cross in public; and the monks lost their tax exemption. Arabic was spreading, and many people found converting to Islam religiously, economically, or socially advantageous. Even so, Muslims remained a minority in Egypt through the tenth century.

After Egypt was conquered in 642, Muslim expansion in North Africa was temporarily stalled because a thousand miles of desert lay between the Nile delta and the coastal plain of the Maghreb. It was not until 669 that the Arab armies established a permanent presence in the region of Tripolitania (now northwestern Libya). After capturing Carthage in 698, they destroyed it and replaced it with nearby Tunis. By 710, they had reached Tangier (at the Strait of Gibraltar), and they crossed over into Spain the following year. By then, all of North Africa was under the control of the Umayyad caliphs in Damascus. As the Arab armies swept across North Africa, their ranks swelled with Berber soldiers, many of whom were conscripts (as illustrated by an oral tradition about a Berber tribe that was obligated to supply 12,000 horsemen as the terms of its surrender), while others joined the Arab army voluntarily in hopes of amassing booty during the invasion of Spain.

THE RISE OF BERBER EMPIRES

In the wake of the Arab conquests, the Berbers of the Maghreb found themselves in a contradictory position: many of them had served in the armies of the conquerors and converted to Islam, but they were also tribute-paying subjects in conquered provinces who sometimes saw their daughters sent to slave markets in the east and their sheep slaughtered to provide lambskins to Persia. Believing that the Arab rulers had become corrupt and had abandoned the true faith, many Berbers saw themselves as the true Muslims. Oppressive rulers, they proclaimed, should be put to death and replaced by the most devout individuals regardless of race or ethnicity. The result was a series of Berber revolts that began in Tangier in 740 and spread across the Maghreb, destroying the political unity of the Islamic Caliphate and leaving the region splintered among competing Islamic sects and ruling dynasties. North Africa would not be united again until 969, and its new rulers would be Shia Muslims known as Fatimids who did not recognize the authority of the caliphs in Baghdad.

The Fatimids

The Fatimids were a branch of Shia Islam that claimed descent from Fatima, the daughter of the Prophet Muhammad and the wife of Ali, the founder of Shia Islam. Fatimids had long been active in southern Iraq and Syria before a Fatimid missionary converted a Berber tribe in eastern Algeria and organized a revolt against the existing Muslim rulers. In 909, the Fatimids captured the Muslim stronghold of Qayrawan (in present-day Tunisia) and gradually extended their control over the Maghreb. By 969, the Berber army of the Fatimids had conquered Egypt and moved into western Asia, where they captured Palestine, Syria, and the parts of the Arabian Peninsula that contained the Islamic holy sites of Mecca and Medina. They set up a **Fatimid caliphate**, with its capital in Cairo, that followed Shia Islam and rivaled the Abbasid Caliphate in Baghdad (which practiced Sunni Islam). Their dream was to capture Baghdad and create a Shia caliphate that would rule the entire Muslim world.

Although the founder of the Fatimid caliphate, Abdullah al-Mahdi Billah, was an Arab who claimed direct descent from the Prophet Muhammad, he had relied on Berber soldiers in the conquest of North Africa. When those soldiers moved into Syria, however, they often found themselves outmatched by the Turkish soldiers of the Abbasid Caliphate, many of whom were slaves. As a result, the Fatimids diversified their army by adding units of free and enslaved Turkish soldiers along with units of enslaved black African soldiers, transforming it from a Berber tribal army into a multiethnic army in which at least a third of the troops were slaves. Rivalry for military and political influence among the ethnically constituted units led to a civil war in Egypt in the 1060s, in which the Turkish soldiers briefly held Cairo. After that, the influence of the Berber units began a slow but steady decline.

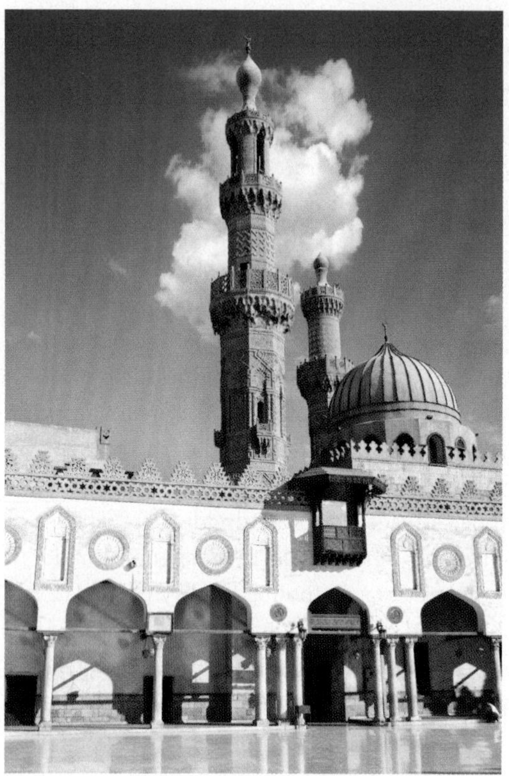

THE AL-AZHAR MOSQUE AND UNIVERSITY The al-Azhar mosque opened in Cairo in 972 under the rule of the Fatimids. Seventeen years later, it engaged 35 Islamic scholars to form a university. Originally founded as an institution of Shia Islam, the university became a Sunni institution after the fall of the Fatimid rulers. In the fourteenth century under the Mamluk rulers, it became the preeminent university in the Muslim world.

As a religious group that had long experience as a persecuted minority in the Muslim world, the Fatimids did not try to force conversion on the Sunni Muslims, Christians, and Jews living in Egypt. Coptic Christians continued to dominate financial affairs and to serve in high government posts. The Fatimid rulers encouraged the spread of Shia Islam by building mosques and *madrasas* (religious secondary schools), and they built the al-Azhar Mosque and University in Cairo, where students could study Islamic law and jurisprudence, Arabic grammar, Islamic astronomy, Islamic philosophy, and logic. These actions were effective in propagating Shia Islam, and by the end of the tenth century, Muslims formed the majority in Egypt for the first time.

Because of the distance separating Egypt from the populated centers in the Maghreb, the Fatimids did not try to rule the Maghreb directly from Cairo, but instead appointed emirs (governors) from among the Zirid family of Berbers, who followed Shia Islam. At first, the Zirid family held power in the name of the Fatimid caliph in Cairo, but over time they began to view themselves as an independent ruling dynasty. In 1048, the Zirid emir declared independence from Cairo and pledged loyalty to the (Sunni) Abbasid Caliphate in Baghdad. In response, the Fatimid ruler in Cairo persuaded some nomadic Arab tribes to migrate westward into the Maghreb. Fifty thousand Arab warriors, in addition to women and children, invaded the Maghreb in 1052 and settled mostly in the region that is now Libya and Tunisia. They pillaged the countryside and turned farmland into sheep pastures, causing a sharp decline in wheat production. The Arab historian Ibn Khaldun, writing in the late fourteenth century, referred to the invaders as a "swarm of locusts" that brought destruction to the country. As a result of this invasion, Arabic, which had previously been spoken mostly in the coastal cities, spread into the countryside, and intermarriage between Arabs and Berbers accelerated the spread of Arab culture and customs.

For all the destruction it wrought, the influx of Arab nomads failed to reestablish Fatimid control over the Maghreb. The Fatimids also faced trouble in Palestine, where Christians from Europe captured Jerusalem in 1099 during the First Crusade. The Fatimid caliphate gradually shrank until it consisted only of Egypt. In the 1160s, a conflict erupted between two rival Fatimid contenders for power. One of them sought help from a Christian crusader army, a move that briefly made Egypt a protectorate of the crusaders. The other contender sought help from a Sunni Muslim army loyal to the Abbasid Caliphate. By 1169, the crusaders had been expelled, and Egypt was under the control of the Kurdish general known as Saladin. Two years later, Saladin pledged allegiance to the Abbasid caliph in Baghdad. After two centuries of Shia domination, Egypt rejoined the Islamic Caliphate and made the religious transition back to Sunni Islam.

Egypt after the Fatimids

As a person of Kurdish descent born in Tikrit (in present-day Iraq), Saladin was oriented more toward the Islamic heartland of western Asia than toward North Africa. The Berber soldiers who had powered the original Fatimid conquests had gradually departed, often to be replaced by Turkish slave soldiers. By Saladin's time, professional armies made up of slave soldiers had became common in the Muslim world because it was widely believed that, as outsiders, they had no divided loyalties. The slave soldiers were called **Mamluks**, a term derived from a

Turkish word meaning "owned." By the 1240s, Turkish Mamluks had become the core of the Egyptian army. During a power struggle in Egypt in 1260, a Turkish Mamluk army commander assassinated the reigning Egyptian strongman and gained the support of the Mamluk regiments. The Mamluks would rule Egypt for the next two centuries.

The Mamluk army of Egypt was made up of enslaved Turks from southern Russia and Ukraine until 1382, when it switched to Circassian slave recruits from the Caucasus Mountains. In both cases the recruits were young men who had been seized by raiders, captured in war, or sold by their parents. They were purchased by Italian slave traders from Genoa at slave markets bordering on the Black Sea and taken to Egypt. Once in Egypt, each boy was assigned to a Mamluk regiment, converted to Islam, and trained in horseback riding, archery, and other military skills. Upon successfully completing his training, he would be granted his freedom by his commander and permitted to join the regiment as a free man. This process created a lifelong bond between a soldier and the commander who had set him free. The continued recruitment of new soldiers from the Black Sea slave markets was a major feature of the Mamluk army because ordinary Egyptians and the children of Mamluk soldiers were discouraged from joining. The Mamluk army was thus continually renewed by the importation of new enslaved boys. It was also continually foreign to the Egyptian population.

The rise of Mamluk power in Egypt coincided with the decline of the Abbasid Caliphate in Baghdad. The caliphs of the Abbasid dynasty had once been both the political and the spiritual rulers of the Muslim world, but centuries of competition from dissident Islamic groups such as the Fatimids of Egypt had eroded their influence. In 1258, a Mongol army from central Asia sacked Baghdad, and the Abbasid caliph was killed. Three years later, a member of the Abbasid family asked the Mamluk ruler in Cairo to grant him refuge. From then on, the Abbasid caliphs were based in Cairo and claimed religious authority, but not political authority. The Abbasid caliphs who had ruled in Baghdad for 500 years had lost their power, and with that the former Islamic Caliphate was no more. Cairo was now the religious center of Sunni Islam. Both the diminished caliphs and the Mamluk rulers would continue to exercise authority in Egypt until their reigns were ended by the Ottoman Turks in 1517.

The Almoravid Empire

In the eleventh century, the Maghreb was in turmoil following the invasion by nomadic Arab tribes and the retreat of Fatimid authority. In the face of political weakness along the coastal plain, the center of Berber power shifted south of the

Atlas Mountains to the western portion of the Sahara Desert. This region was occupied by Sanhaja Berbers, who were themselves subdivided into a number of distinct tribes. Writing in 1068, the Muslim geographer Al-Bakri described these desert nomads as follows: "They know nothing about tilling the land or cultivating crops, nor do they know bread. Their wealth consists only of herds, and their food of meat and milk. One of them might spend his whole life without eating or seeing bread if the merchants who pass through their country from the land of Islam or Sudan did not give him bread or present him with flour." He added that "all the tribes of the desert preserve the custom of wearing a veil which screens their foreheads, above the other veil which covers the lower part of the face, so that only their eyes are visible. They do not remove these veils under any circumstances. A man cannot recognize his relative or friend unless he is wearing the veil."

Although Sunni Islam had spread among the Sanhaja Berbers since the ninth century, their knowledge of Islam remained rudimentary. The leader of one of the Sanhaja tribes looked for a person of learning and piety to teach the nomads about Islam. After being turned down by a number of Muslim scholars, he finally found a young man from southern Morocco named Ibn Yasin, a jurist who followed the Maliki school of Islamic law. The Malikites, as they were called, advocated a strict interpretation of Islamic law based on a literal reading of the Quran and the *Sunna* (the actions and sayings of the Prophet Muhammad). The intellectual center of Malikite teaching was Qayrawan, but Malikite scholars had also established themselves in Morocco.

When Ibn Yasin arrived among the desert nomads, he was shocked to discover that men married six, seven, or ten wives as they desired (Islam allowed only four), that most of them did not pray, and that they knew nothing of Islam other than the basic declaration of faith: "There is no god but God, and Muhammad is God's messenger." Ibn Yasin demanded strict observance of Islamic law and imposed severe punishments for those who fell short: 100 lashes for adultery, 80 lashes for drunkenness or slander, 20 lashes for failing to attend the Friday mosque, and 5 lashes for failing to genuflect when repeating a prayer. As might be expected, his efforts provoked strong opposition, and he was soon sent packing. Ibn Yasin went into exile with a small number of disciples, but soon he was joined by a steady stream of new followers from various Sanhaja tribes. Referring to his followers as Almoravids, he subjected them to rigorous discipline and molded them into a militant reform movement. Emerging from exile in 1042, he found an ally in the leader of one of the Sanhaja tribes, and together they spent the next 10 years subjecting the other Sanhaja tribes of the western Sahara Desert. In the process they built up a formidable fighting force.

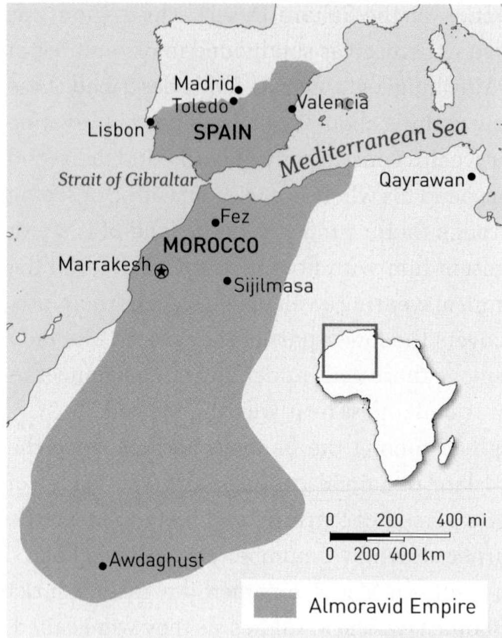

THE ALMORAVID EMPIRE This map shows the Almoravid Empire at its greatest extension in 1117. The Almoravid movement began among the nomadic tribes in the Sahara Desert and expanded northward across the Atlas Mountains and into Spain. The oasis town of Awdaghust, which was a key node on the trans-Saharan trade routes, marked the southern limit of the Almoravid conquests.

The early goal of the Almoravids was to capture the trans-Saharan trade route that ran from the town of Sijilmasa in the north to Awdaghust in the south. By 1054, both towns had been captured, and the caravan route was under Almoravid control. After Ibn Yasin was killed in battle in 1059, his allies continued the movement. Moving north, they gained control of Fez (in present-day Morocco) in 1069, and in the following year, they began construction of their new capital city, Marrakesh. After consolidating their control over Morocco, they crossed the Strait of Gibraltar and annexed the Islamic states in Spain. It was at this point that the Almoravids encountered Christian armies that were trying to drive the Muslims out of Spain. Although the Almoravids managed to capture Madrid, Valencia, and Lisbon from the Christians, their two attempts on Toledo failed. In the end, the Almoravid expansion in Spain was stopped by the Christian forces.

By 1110, the **Almoravid Empire** stretched from Awdaghust, in the southern reaches of the Sahara Desert, to the middle of Spain. The Sanhaja Berbers, who continued to wear their veils, formed the empire's military and social aristocracy. Within the religious establishment, the jurists held the primary positions. The study of the Quran and the prophetic traditions were ignored, while the legal manuals of the Maliki school were avidly studied. Almoravid leaders showed their contempt for more mystical interpretations of Islam by burning the works of the renowned theologian and mystic Abu Hamid al-Ghazali. The Almoravids had less success in imposing their views on the Muslims of southern Spain, where the rough desert nomads seemed to be seduced by the more refined aspects of Spanish Muslim culture.

The Almohad Empire

The reaction against the Almoravids came quickly and was led by Ibn Tumart, a Masmuda Berber from the Atlas Mountains in Morocco. In contrast to the legal rigidity of Ibn Yasin, he had gained a more cosmopolitan outlook after studying in Muslim Spain, Egypt, and Baghdad. He challenged the scriptural literalism of the Almoravids (who believed that God literally had hands, eyes, and ears) and instead emphasized the transcendental unity of God. Seeking to recapture the original purity of the Muslim faith, he refused to acknowledge the authority of any of the recognized schools of Islamic law, which he denounced as heretical human elaborations on the original teachings of the Prophet. His followers described themselves as Almohads, meaning "those of the oneness." Despite his doctrinal differences with the Almoravids, Ibn Tumart was equally strict about enforcing his ideas of proper Islamic practice. He once threw his sister off her horse for riding without a veil. In 1121, he went to the Almoravid capital, Marrakesh, where he mocked the emir to his face for wearing a veil just like a woman and denounced him for finding pleasure in music. Although Ibn Tumart was subsequently banned from Marrakesh and threatened with death, his teachings found an enthusiastic reception among the Masmuda Berbers.

Because the mounted armies of the Almoravids could not fight effectively on the steep, narrow trails of the Atlas Mountains, the Masmuda Berbers had been pretty much left alone by the Almoravid rulers in Marrakesh. Ibn Tumart settled among them and began to unite the various Masmuda tribes into a larger tribal confederacy, creating a Council of Fifty that contained representatives of all the affiliated tribes. He also sent out military expeditions to impose his authority on those tribes that were reluctant to join. Once the alliance was solidified, he launched an unsuccessful assault on Marrakesh in 1130. Ibn Tumart died a few months later and was replaced by his trusted lieutenant Abd al-Mumin, a brilliant military strategist. Under the leadership of al-Mumin, the Almohads captured Marrakesh in 1147. Not wishing to be defiled by praying in the Almoravid mosque, which they judged to be decadent, they demolished it and built a new one in its place. By 1160, they had conquered the coastal plain of the Maghreb eastward as far as Tripoli. By 1200, the **Almohad Empire** had captured all of Muslim Spain. As Berbers from the Atlas Mountains, they had no interest in conquering the Sahara

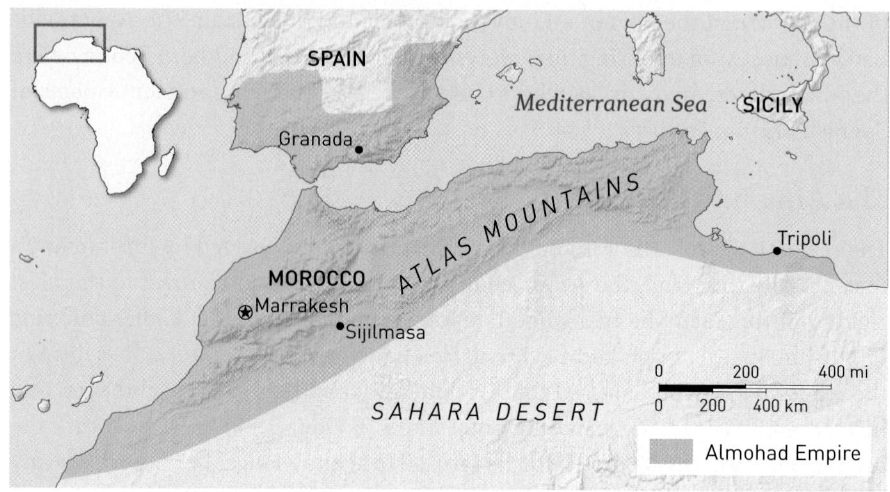

THE ALMOHAD EMPIRE This map shows the Almohad Empire at its greatest extension in 1172, before it started to shrink in the 1200s because of internal rebellions and attacks by Christian armies. The Almohad movement began among the Masmuda Berbers in the Atlas Mountains and expanded northward into Spain and eastward toward Tripoli. Because the Masmuda Berbers had no experience operating in a desert environment, they never attempted to move southward to capture the trading centers in the Sahara.

Desert and were content with seizing Sijilmasa, the northern terminus of the trans-Saharan caravan route.

Just as the Sanhaja Berbers had formed the aristocracy of the Almoravid Empire, the Masmuda Berbers dominated the military and administrative system of the Almohads. The Council of Fifty, which contained representatives of the founding Masmuda tribes, continued to operate throughout the Almohad period. The Malikite legal manuals that had guided administrators during Almoravid rule were banned and later burned. Instead, provincial administrators were required to memorize the writings of Ibn Tumart. Like the Almoravids before them, the Almohads made no effort to integrate the peoples they had conquered into their system of government.

No sooner had the Almohad Empire reached the peak of its power, around 1200, than it started to disintegrate. By 1250, the Spanish Christians had conquered most of Muslim Spain, with the exception of Granada, which held out as an Islamic state for another 250 years. Rebellions against the Almohads broke out in different parts of the Maghreb. The rebels sacked Marrakesh in 1269 and defeated the last remnant of the Almohad army in 1275. From start to finish, the Almohad Empire had lasted a little over a hundred years.

Taken together, the Almoravid and Almohad empires dominated the Maghreb for two centuries. Although rivals, they had much in common. Both movements were ignited by militant Islamic reformers from southern Morocco who died just as their conquests were gaining momentum, leaving their disciples and successors to build the empires. Both were authentically Berber and operated independently of the Arabs, the Fatimid rulers in Egypt, and the caliphs in Baghdad. Both remained true to their tribal roots: the Almoravid emirs continued to wear their desert veils, and the Almohads never abandoned their tribal Council of Fifty. As a result, neither movement made a serious attempt to integrate conquered peoples into its government, which may have been a fatal flaw for them both.

There were significant differences between the two empires as well. The Sanhaja Berbers of the Almoravid Empire were historically bitter enemies of the Masmuda Berbers of the Almohad Empire. As for their religious beliefs, the Malikite legalism of Ibn Yasin stood in sharp contrast with the mystical "oneness" of Ibn Tumart. Although both the Almoravid and Almohad empires disintegrated almost as quickly as they expanded, they left a lasting legacy in the spread of Islam and Arabic to regions of the Maghreb far from the Mediterranean coast.

CONCLUSION

We normally think of Africa, western Asia, and Europe as separate continents with separate histories, but they all came together in the ancient Mediterranean world. The straight-line distance from Carthage to Rome, for example, was only about one-third of the distance from Carthage to Alexandria. Because of the efficiency of sea transportation, people, goods, and ideas could travel with relative ease from any point in the Mediterranean world to any other point. It was the wide diffusion of Greek and Roman culture throughout the Mediterranean world that created the medium for the spread of Christianity, which relied heavily on religious texts written in Greek and Latin. After Christianity became the official religion of the Roman and Byzantine Empires, the fate of the Christian churches became intertwined with the political and military fortunes of the empires. It was Augustine of Hippo, a Berber from the Atlas Mountains of the Maghreb, who created the conceptual framework for separating the religious from the political in Christian thought.

The initial expansion of Islam is more difficult to conceptualize, as it hinged on the seemingly unrelated project of transforming a tribally organized society into a unified Arab state. The Islamic Caliphate was simultaneously a political empire and a religious authority, and the two roles often came into conflict. Conversion did not come until well after conquest, and the early caliphs sometimes discouraged their subjects from converting to Islam for fear of losing tax revenue. The Abbasid Caliphs transcended their Arab ethnicity when they moved their capital to Baghdad and allowed non-Arabs into their administration. After the Mongols sacked Baghdad in 1258, the Caliphate moved to Cairo, where political authority was taken up by the Mamluk rulers of Egypt and the caliphs were stripped of all but religious authority.

In the Maghreb, the Berbers demonstrated once again the capacity of tribally organized societies to create powerful empires. Like the Islamic Caliphate, those empires were simultaneously religious and political. Berber armies were responsible for the military expansion of the Fatimid caliphate, but they were never in control of the political state, and they were ultimately shunted aside. The Almoravid and Almohad empires, in contrast, were under the complete control of the Sanhaja Berbers and the Masmuda Berbers, respectively. It was their political failure to convert their tribally organized movements into stable territorial states that ultimately sealed their doom.

CHAPTER REVIEW

KEY TERMS AND VOCABULARY

Christianity
Islam
Islamic Caliphate
Maghreb
Carthage
Berber
tribe
state
Cleopatra
Coptic Church
Fatimid caliphate
Mamluk
Almoravid Empire
Almohad Empire

STUDY QUESTIONS

1. How does the inter-connectedness of the Mediterranean world blur the distinctions between Africa, Southwest Asia, and Europe?
2. In the Maghreb, why did states form mainly on the coastal plains, whereas tribal forms of political organization dominated in the mountains and the Sahara Desert?
3. In what ways did the existence of the Roman Empire aid or hinder the spread of Christianity in the Mediterranean world?
4. Why did the churches in Egypt and northeast Africa become isolated from the wider Christian world?
5. Why did Islam initially expand by conquest? Can you distinguish between the expansion of Arab power and the spread of Islam?
6. Why did the Fatimid rulers of Muslim Egypt adopt a tolerant attitude toward Christians and Jews?
7. How do you account for the rapid growth and the equally rapid demise of the Almoravid and Almohad empires?

PERSPECTIVES

ANTONY OF THE DESERT

Antony of the Desert (251–356 CE) has been called the father of monasticism. He was not the first Egyptian Christian to retreat into the desert to live as a hermit, but over the course of his long life he attracted many visitors and inspired others to follow his example. Athanasius, the patriarch of Alexandria, wrote the Life of Antony *shortly after the hermit's death in 356. In the ensuing decades, Greek and Latin versions of the biography circulated widely in the Mediterranean world.*

Antony was an Egyptian by race. His parents were well born and prosperous, and since they were Christians, he also was reared in a Christian manner. . . .

He went into the church, . . . and just then it happened that the Gospel was being read, and he heard the Lord saying to the rich man, *If you would be perfect, go, sell what you possess and give to the poor, and you will have treasure in heaven*. . . . Immediately Antony went out from the Lord's house and gave to the townspeople the possessions he had from his forebears. . . . And selling all the rest that was portable, when he collected sufficient money, he donated it to the poor, keeping a few things for his sister.

But when, entering the Lord's house once more, he heard in the Gospel the Lord saying, *Do not be anxious about tomorrow*, he could not remain any longer, but going out he gave those remaining possessions also to the needy. Placing his sister in the charge of respected and trusted virgins, and giving her over to the convent for rearing, he devoted himself from then on to the discipline rather than the household, giving heed to himself and patiently training himself. There were not yet many monasteries in Egypt, and no monk knew at all the great desert, but each of those wishing to give attention to his life disciplined himself in isolation, not far from his own village.

Now at that time in the neighboring village there was an old man who had practiced from his youth the solitary life. When Antony saw him, he emulated him in goodness. At first he also began by remaining in places proximate to his village. And going forth from there, if he heard of some zealous person anywhere, he searched him out like the wise bee. He did not go back to his own place unless he had seen him, and as though receiving from him certain supplies for traveling the road to virtue, he returned. Spending the beginning stages of his discipline in that place, then, he weighed in his thoughts how he would not look back on things of his parents, nor call his relatives to memory. All the desire and all the energy he possessed concerned the exertion of the discipline. He worked with his hands, though, having heard that he who is idle, *let him not eat*. And he spent what he made partly for bread, and partly on those in need. He prayed constantly, since he learned that it is necessary to pray unceasingly in private.

---

1. *Why was Antony attracted to the lifestyle of a hermit?*
2. *Why was Anthony's example emulated by others?*

Source: Athanasius, Saint, Patriarch of Alexandria, *The Life of Antony and the Letter to Marcellinus*, translated and introduced by Robert C. Gregg (New York: Paulist Press, 1980), pp. 30–32.

THE CITY OF GOD

Augustine of Hippo (354–430 CE) was born into a Berber family in what is now Algeria, but was then the Roman province of Africa, and spent the last 34 years of his life as the bishop of Hippo (in present-day Algeria). He was perhaps the most influential Christian theologian in the history of the Catholic Church. In his book The City of God, *he drew a contrast between the earthly city of Rome, which had recently been sacked by the Visigoths, and the heavenly City of God that endures forever. He sketched out a vision of a universal Christian society that would not be dependent on any particular political or military power.*

MY DEAR MARCELLINUS: This work which I have begun makes good my promise to you. In it I am undertaking nothing less than the task of defending the glorious City of God against those who prefer their own gods to its Founder. I shall consider it both in its temporal stage here below (where it journeys as a pilgrim among sinners and lives by faith) and as solidly established in its eternal abode—that blessed goal for which we patiently hope "until justice be turned into judgment," but which, one day, is to be the reward of excellence in a final victory and a perfect peace. The task, I realize, is a high and hard one, but God will help me. . . .

Hence, in so far as the general plan of the treatise demands and my ability permits, I must speak also of the earthly city—of that city which lusts to dominate the world and which, though nations bend to its yoke, is itself dominated by its passion for dominion.

From this earthly city issue the enemies against whom the City of God must be defended. Some of them, it is true, abjure their worldly error and become worthy members in God's City. But many others, alas, break out in blazing hatred against it and are utterly ungrateful, notwithstanding its Redeemer's signal gifts. For, they would no longer have a voice to raise against it, had not its sanctuaries given them asylum as they fled before the invaders' swords, and made it possible for them to save that life of which they are so proud.

Have not even those very Romans whom the barbarians spared for the sake of Christ assailed His Name? To this both the shrines of the martyrs and the basilicas of the Apostles bear witness: amid the city's devastation, these buildings gave refuge not only to the faithful but even to infidels. Up to the sacred threshold raged the murderous enemy, but the slayers' fury went no farther. The merciful among the enemy conducted to the churches those whom they had spared even outside the holy precincts, to save them from others who lacked such mercy.

1. *What did Augustine mean by the eternal "City of God" and the "earthly city"?*
2. *What was the relationship between the two cities?*

Source: Saint Augustine, *The City of God*, translated by Demetrius B. Zema and Gerald G. Walsh (Washington, DC: Catholic University of America Press, 1950), pp. 17–19.

JIHAD IN ISLAMIC LAW

The Islamic Caliphate spread primarily by military conquest. As a consequence, Muslim jurists adhering to different schools of Islamic law debated and clarified the laws of war. This treatise on jihad (holy war) was written in 1167 by Averroes, who was both a judge and the personal physician of the Almohad ruler Abu Yaqub. Although his writings maintain a neutral posture, Averroes was influenced by the Malikite school of Islamic jurisprudence. The numbers in brackets refer to verses in the Quran. The references to the People of the Book refer to Christians and Jews.

Scholars agree that the jihad is a collective not a personal obligation. Only 'Abd Allāh Ibn al-Hasan professed it to be a recommendable act. According to the majority of scholars, the compulsory nature of the jihad is founded on [Q2:216]: "*Fighting is prescribed for you, though it is distasteful to you.*" That this obligation is a collective and not a personal one, i.e. that the obligation, when it can be properly carried out by a limited number of individuals, is cancelled for the remaining Moslems, is founded on [Q9:112]: "*It is not for the believers to march out all together,*" on [Q4:95]: "*Though to all, Allah hath promised the good (reward),*" and, lastly, on the fact that the Prophet never went to battle without leaving some people behind. All this together implies that this activity is a collective obligation. The obligation to participate in the jihad applies to adult free men who have the means at their disposal to go to war and who are healthy. . . .

According to all scholars, the prerequisite for warfare is that the enemy must have heard the summons to Islam. This implies that it is not allowed to attack them before the summons has reached them. All Moslems are agreed about this because of [Q17:15]: "*We have not been accustomed to punish until We have sent a messenger.*" However, there is controversy about the question of whether the summons should be repeated when the war is resumed. Some hold that this is obligatory, others consider it merely recommendable. . . .

The Moslems are agreed that the aim of warfare against the People of the Book . . . is twofold: either conversion to Islam, or payment of poll-tax (*jizya*). This is based on [Q9:29]: "*Fight against those who do not believe in Allah nor in the last Day, and do not make forbidden what Allah and His messenger have made forbidden, and do not practice the religion of truth, of those who have been given the Book, until they pay the jizya off-hand, being subdued.*" Most lawyers likewise agree that poll-tax may also be collected from Zoroastrians on the strength of the words of the Prophet: "*Treat them like the People of the Book.*" There is, however, controversy with regard to polytheists who are not People of the Book: is it allowed to accept poll-tax from them or not? Some, like Mālik, have taught that it may be collected from any polytheist. Others make an exception for the polytheist Arabs. Shāfi'ī, Abū Thawr and a few others maintain that poll-tax may only be accepted from People of the Book and Zoroastrians.

1. *What was the nature of the obligation for jihad?*
2. *On which issues did the scholars disagree?*

Source: *Jihad in Mediaeval and Modern Islam*, translated from the Arabic and annotated by Rudolph Peters (Leiden: Brill, 1977), pp. 9–10, 19–20, 23–24.

ISLAM AND THE SCIENCES

Born in Tunis in 1332 into a family with roots in southern Arabia, Ibn Khaldun was a forerunner of modern historiography and social science. He wrote a definitive history of Muslim North Africa in which he explored the dynamics of the relationship between Arabs and Berbers, but his most celebrated work was The Muqaddimah: An Introduction to History, *written in Algeria in 1377. In this excerpt from* The Muqaddimah, *he explains the difference between the philosophical sciences and the traditional (or handed-down) sciences in order to define the place of Islamic thought in Muslim intellectual life.*

It should be known that the sciences with which people concern themselves in cities and which they acquire and pass on through instruction, are of two kinds: one that is natural to man and to which he is guided by his own ability to think, and a traditional kind that he learns from those who invented it.

The first kind comprises the philosophical sciences. They are the ones with which man can become acquainted through the very nature of his ability to think and to whose objects, problems, arguments, and methods of instruction he is guided by his human perceptions, so that he is made aware of the distinction between what is correct and what is wrong in them by his own speculation and research, in as much as he is a thinking human being.

The second kind comprises the traditional, conventional sciences. All of them depend upon information based on the authority of the given religious law. There is no place for the intellect in them, save that the intellect may be used in connection with them to relate problems of detail with basic principles. Particulars that constantly come into being are not included in the general tradition by the mere fact of its existence. Therefore, they need to be related (to the general principles) by some kind of analogical reasoning. However, such analogical reasoning is derived from the (traditional) information, while the character of the basic principle, which is traditional, remains valid (unchanged). Thus, analogical reasoning of this type reverts to being tradition (itself), because it is derived from it.

The basis of all the traditional sciences is the legal material of the Qur'ân and the Sunnah [customary behavior of the Prophet], which is the law given us by God and His messenger, as well as the sciences connected with that material, by means of which we are enabled to utilize it. This, further, requires as auxiliary sciences the sciences of the Arabic language [that is, grammar, rhetoric, lexicography, etc.]. Arabic is the language of Islam, and the Qur'ân was revealed in it. . . .

Furthermore, the duties of the Muslim may concern either the body or the heart. The duties of the heart are concerned with faith and the distinction between what is to be believed and what is not to be believed. This concerns the articles of faith which deal with the essence and the attributes of God, the events of the Resurrection, Paradise, punishment, and predestination, and entails discussion and defense of these subjects with the help of intellectual arguments. This is speculative theology.

1. *How did Ibn Khaldun define the Muslim attitude toward science?*
2. *What was the difference between the philosophical and traditional sciences?*

Source: Ibn Khaldun, *The Muqaddimah: An Introduction to History*, 2nd ed., translated by Franz Rosenthal (Princeton: Princeton University Press, 1967), vol. 2, pp. 436–438.

A CARAVAN IN THE SAHARA DESERT A camel caravan carrying slabs of salt approaches a modern desert town in Mali, much as caravans have done for over a thousand years. Because camels could travel up to 10 days without water, the caravans crossed the Sahara by going from oasis to oasis. They often traveled at night to avoid the searing heat.

1068	1324	1331
Ghana Empire at the height of its prosperity	Mansa Musa of Mali makes a pilgrimage to Mecca	Ibn Battuta visits Kilwa

4

CITIES OF GOLD: THE WEST AFRICAN SAHEL AND THE EAST AFRICAN COAST, 800–1600

"They travel over the sands like seas," wrote Abu Hamid al-Gharnati in the twelfth century, "led by guides who direct themselves over the wastes according to the stars and the mountains." The Spanish-born Muslim traveler was describing the camel caravans crossing the Sahara Desert, likening them to ships on the Mediterranean Sea. We can identify two further parallels between the desert and the sea: caravans crossed the sands by going from oasis to oasis, just as ships cross waters by traveling from island to island; and just like the sea, the desert has a shore. The Arabic term for the east-west belt of semiarid grassland that borders the Sahara on the south is *sāhil*, which means "shore, coast, or borderland." Today, geographers refer to that region as the **Sahel** (see chapter 1), a name derived from that Arabic term.

This chapter focuses on two "coastal" or "borderland" regions whose histories were shaped in large part by their location in geographical transition zones. The first is the West African Sahel, which borders the Sahara Desert. The second is the Indian Ocean coast of East Africa, where people spoke a language called

1469	1490	1591
Songhay ruler Sunni Ali conquers Timbuktu	Great Zimbabwe is deserted	Morocco invades the Songhay Empire

Swahili, another name derived from the Arabic word *sāhil*. In the most literal sense, Swahili was the "language of the coast," and so the region where the Swahili speakers lived became known as the Swahili Coast. Geographers have noted that borderlands can be either barriers or bridges, depending upon how they are used. In that sense, both of these regions became bridges that facilitated commercial and cultural exchanges between Africa and the wider world.

Being located in geographical transition zones, the inhabitants of the Sahel and the Swahili Coast were well placed to maximize their economic, cultural, and political opportunities. When the Islamic Caliphate adopted the gold dinar as its official currency in the eighth century, it created an unlimited demand for gold that kept its value high. Because both West Africa and East Africa had rich gold deposits, the profits from the gold trade could be used to subsidize trade in a variety of less lucrative commodities as well. Equally important was Islam's religious and cultural influence. Islam flourished at the royal courts in both the Sahel and the Swahili Coast, and Islamic scholars and jurists were held in esteem in both regions. Despite the economic and cultural similarities between the two regions, however, their political systems developed in very different ways. The Sahel saw the formation of the powerful Ghana, Mali, and Songhay empires, whereas the Swahili Coast gave rise to a series of independent trading towns that did not try to establish territorial empires. With trade relations and cultural exchanges flourishing in both regions, as well as along the Mediterranean coast (see chapter 3), the only African shoreline that failed to generate long-distance commercial activity prior to 1450 was the Atlantic coast.

THE WEST AFRICAN SAHEL

It may seem odd that the precarious and unforgiving grasslands of the Sahel could be the incubator of vast empires and renowned centers of commerce and learning. The explanation lies, at least partially, in the uneven distribution of two mineral resources. The West African Sahel was poor in a mineral that every family needed: salt. Salt came mostly from mines deep in the Sahara Desert, from where it was transported in large blocks fastened to the backs of camels. Salt was an ideal product for long-distance trade because a single ounce could be sold for a high price. The Muslim traveler al-Gharnati was perhaps exaggerating in the twelfth century when he claimed that an ounce of salt was worth an ounce of gold, but he was correct in depicting salt as a valuable commodity. People in the Sahel would buy it, even at high prices, because every family needed a little, but no family needed a lot.

The wealth of the Sahel, on the other hand, came from its gold, which was found mainly in the Bambuk and Buré regions near the southern edge of the Sahelian zone. The problem, historically, had been how to transport the gold

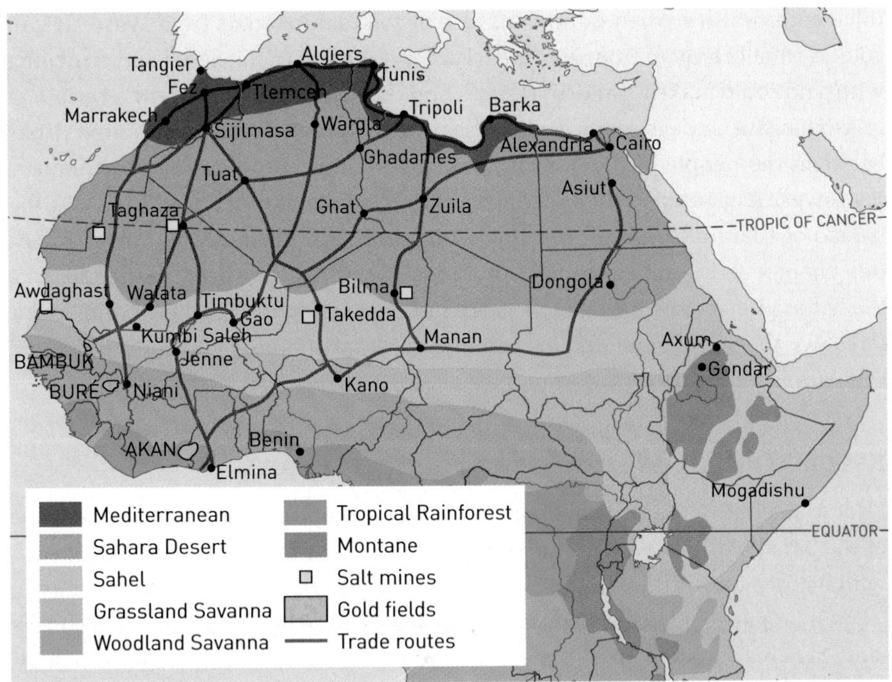

TRADE ROUTES IN THE DESERT The main trade routes discussed in this chapter were used to transport gold from Bambuk and Bure to destinations in North Africa. Because camel caravans crossed the Sahara Desert by going from oasis to oasis, the trade routes across the desert were fixed according to the locations of the water sources. Gold from the Akan goldfields in the south was sent north to Jenne and on to Timbuktu to join the trans-Saharan trade routes.

across the desert to the markets in Mediterranean North Africa. After the climate of the Sahara, which had once been lush and green (see chapter 2), reached its driest point between 2000 and 1600 BCE, long-distance journeys across the desert became virtually impossible until the spread of domesticated camels from the Arabian Peninsula around the beginning of the Common Era. During the first and second centuries CE, the Berber nomads in the southern portions of the Sahara became experts at breeding camels for transportation. A camel could go 10 days without water, and a camel caravan could cross the desert by traveling from oasis to oasis, provided that the route was carefully chosen. By the fourth century CE, a small, irregular supply of gold from the Sahel was making its way to North Africa.

Gold from the Sahel had long been desired in the Mediterranean world for jewelry, ornamentation, and the coins minted in Carthage for the Byzantine Empire. Its value rose in the eighth century when Muslim rulers in North Africa and Southwest Asia needed it for their currencies, and it increased further in the thirteenth century when Europeans also began to mint coins from West African gold. A camel caravan from North Africa carrying salt to the Sahel and returning with gold could make a handsome profit and could thus afford to carry a variety of less expensive trade items as well. These caravans created lasting, if indirect, links between the people of the West African Sahel and the people of North Africa, Southwest Asia, and southern Europe. One result of those connections was the spread of Islam in the centuries following the Muslim conquest of North Africa (see chapter 3). Islam had spread slowly southward among the Berber nomads of the Sahara Desert according to the seasonal movements of their herds and flocks, but it was the trade routes and the camel caravans that brought Muslim clerics and scholars to settle and form communities in the trading cities of the Sahel.

Reconstructing West African Political History

Prior to the rise of the Ghana, Mali, and Songhay empires, the political landscape of the Sahel was dotted with independent chiefdoms and small kingdoms, each with its own political institutions and its accompanying political terminology in its own language. In order to discuss this variety of political systems in a consistent way, this book will use a simple hierarchical model and English terminology. In this model, a *chiefdom*, ruled by a chief, encompassed a group of villages and towns. A *kingdom*, ruled by a king or a queen, encompassed a group of chiefdoms. An *empire*, by extension, encompassed a group of formerly independent kingdoms and chiefdoms, and its ruler—following the English terminology used in the British Empire—was also known as a king or a queen. To distinguish between the ruler of an empire and the ruler of a kingdom, subordinate kings will be referred to as *vassals* or *vassal kings*, and their kingdoms as *vassal states*.

An empire grew by conquering and annexing weaker kingdoms whose rulers agreed to pay tribute and accept a subordinate status. When a formerly independent kingdom was incorporated into a larger empire, it did not lose its identity or its internal political structure; it merely added a new layer of bureaucracy on top of the existing one. The Arab writer al-Ya'qubi captured the essence of the system in 872, when he wrote of a certain West African ruler, "There are a number of kingdoms whose rulers pay allegiance to him and acknowledge his sovereignty, although they are kings in their own lands." During times when an empire was weak, the vassal states would break away and reclaim their independence, only to be brought back under imperial authority when the empire was stronger and more prosperous. That is why the boundaries of empires varied widely from decade to decade. When an empire declined, it did not leave anarchy in its wake. Instead, the formerly independent kingdoms and chiefdoms reverted to their previous, autonomous state.

The reconstruction of the history of the three empires described in this chapter is based on both written documents and oral traditions (stories and narratives that were passed down orally from generation to generation). Although written documents have long been the bread and butter of historians, in recent years scholars have begun to acknowledge the value of oral traditions. In order to use oral traditions properly, it is important to take two considerations into account. First, oral traditions often employed vivid imagery and stories of magical events to make their point—in part because boring stories were unlikely to get retold from generation to generation, and also because the storytellers and their audiences held a worldview that allowed for the possibility of miraculous occurrences. Second, oral traditions are more focused on capturing the meaning of historical events than on recounting factually accurate details. It is best to think of these narratives as interpretations of events, more suited to the editorial page of a newspaper than to its front page. Oral traditions about the founding of a kingdom, for example, often focus on the founder's relation to otherworldly forces in order to explain why he should be seen as a legitimate ruler. In interpreting oral traditions, the symbolism of the stories can be as important as the events themselves. By combining concrete details from written documents with the interpretive power of oral traditions, one gets a more complete picture of the historical events and their meanings.

ISLAMIC GOLD DINAR Containing 4.25 grams of gold, the dinar was the official gold coin of the Islamic Caliphate. Dinars made from West African gold were minted in North Africa as early as 703 CE. This coin was minted in Tripoli in 1072–1073 under the authority of the Fatimid caliphate. The use of gold dinars in the Muslim world created a strong and steady demand for West African gold.

The Ghana Empire

When the Arabs conquered Morocco at the beginning of the eighth century, they heard about the gold from a kingdom south of the Sahara known as Ghana (not to be confused with the modern African nation of Ghana). Gold had gained great political and economic importance after a gold coin called the *dinar*, first minted in Damascus in 691, became the official currency of the Muslim world. The governor of Morocco sent a military expedition into the desert to conquer Ghana and capture the sources of the gold; it returned with gold and captives, but utterly failed in its original objectives. This failure convinced the governor to concentrate on peaceful trade, and accordingly, he ordered wells to be dug along the trade route to aid the camel caravans. By the year 804, Arab rulers in North Africa were minting their own coins using gold purchased from Ghana.

The Founding of the Ghana Empire

The **Ghana Empire** had been founded by speakers of the Soninke language, who referred to their kingdom by the name Wagadu. Soninke oral traditions speak of a wanderer named Dinga who acquired occult knowledge in the course of his travels, which gave him the ability to control rain and to vanquish the water genies that controlled the ponds and wells. At one well, in what would later become the Ghana heartland, he defeated a female water genie after a long ritual battle, thus gaining the right to marry her three beautiful daughters and father sons who became the ancestors of several important Soninke families. The symbolism of the story emphasizes the crucial importance of controlling water resources in the parched landscape. In the Sahel, water was power, and control of water was the basis for political legitimacy.

According to Soninke oral traditions, the Ghana Empire was founded by Diabe Cissé, one of Dinga's sons (historians put the date of its founding sometime between 500 and 700 CE). The traditions recount that Diabe Cissé received support from four cavalry troops who came from the four corners of the wilderness and recognized him as their leader. The cavalry commanders later became the governors of the four central provinces of the kingdom, which then expanded by conquest. The early history of Ghana can be seen as a slow process of incorporating a variety of existing chiefdoms and kingdoms into a larger imperial framework. The four central provinces established by Diabe Cissé formed the empire's heartland, with vassal states forming the periphery. Some of the vassal states remained largely autonomous and paid nominal tribute, while others were partially or fully administered from the capital. The cavalry-based army was supplemented with soldiers from the various provinces and vassal states, and its size varied widely over time. In 1068, when Ghana's power was at its height, the Arab geographer Al-Bakri estimated that the king could field an army of 200,000 soldiers.

Descriptions by Muslim writers confirm this view of Ghana as an amalgamation of previously independent kingdoms. "Then there is the kingdom of Ghana," wrote the historian al-Ya'qubi in 872. "Its king is also very powerful. Under his authority are several kingdoms." Two centuries later, Al-Bakri noted that when the king held an audience, the sons of the vassal kings of the empire stood to the king's right, "wearing splendid garments, and their hair plaited with gold." This scene provides insights into the personalized nature of the relationships between the kings of Ghana and their vassals. As long as relations were cordial, the sons of the vassals were honored guests, but they could easily become hostages if relations turned sour.

Gold in Ghana's Economy

Arab writers and Soninke oral traditions both emphasized the importance of gold in Ghana's economy. "The most productive gold mine in all the world is that of Ghana," wrote the Arab scholar Al-Hamdani in the tenth century, and his contemporary, a traveler from the Fertile Crescent named Ibn Hawqal, reported that the king of Ghana "is the wealthiest king on the face of the earth because of the treasures and stocks of gold extracted in olden times." Soninke oral traditions, for their part, recount that when Diabe Cissé, the founder of Ghana, set out to establish a capital for his kingdom, he chose a place that was guarded by a mythical black snake named Bida. The snake gave him permission to settle and promised him abundant rain and gold. In return, Diabe was required to sacrifice a beautiful young virgin each year to the snake. Once a year, representatives of the four central provinces assembled to sacrifice a virgin to Bida in order to ensure continuing prosperity in the form of rain and gold, two of the most precious resources in the Sahel. The purpose of the story is clearly to establish the legitimacy of the rulers of Ghana by giving them credit for ensuring the prosperity of the empire.

Despite stories that celebrate Ghana as the land of gold, the truth was that the kings of Ghana had only tenuous control over that all-important resource. The Bambuk goldfields were located far to the south, just beyond the town of Ghiyaru, which was the southernmost trading outpost of Ghana. The chief of the village nearest to a mining area had local authority over it, and local earth priests conducted annual rituals so that the land would continue to yield its precious metal. During the dry season, local farmers would dig vertical shafts up to 60 feet deep into the soil and then carve out horizontal shafts as far as they could without the ground caving in. All gold nuggets weighing over an ounce were reserved for the king, and ordinary people were allowed to trade only in gold dust. Itinerant African merchants purchased gold at the trading outpost of Ghiyaru and carried it to the capital of Ghana, some 18 days' travel to the north. Miners were so distrustful of the merchants that they would not meet with them face to face. Instead, they worked through a neutral arbitrator who guaranteed the fairness of the exchange.

Another major source of the wealth of the kings of Ghana came from their control of the north–south trade routes. With each load of salt that came in from the north, the king received one gold dinar in taxes; he collected two more dinars when it left. The king also levied various customs duties on loads of copper, which were brought to Ghana from southern Morocco, and on all other goods besides. The trade in those products operated alongside a trade in captives. Often, they would be taken in the course of ordinary warfare, but Ghana's armies also engaged in slave raids. The Moroccan geographer Al-Idrisi, writing in 1154, described a town in Ghana whose inhabitants would travel to a land he called Lamlam to take captives, who were sold to the merchants of Ghana, and the Arab writer Al-Zuhri mentioned that Ghana had a tradition of raiding the lands of Barbara and Amima to capture people for the same purpose. During the reign of the Ghana Empire, approximately 5,000 captives made the brutal trip across the Sahara to slave markets in North Africa each year, although it is likely that fewer than half of them came from Ghana.

Religion and Culture in Ghana

The capital of Ghana, Kumbi-Saleh, consisted of a pair of twin towns designed to mitigate the ethnic and religious tensions inherent in a geographical and cultural borderland. On the desert side was the Muslim trading town, which possessed 12 mosques that supported salaried clerics as well as Muslim jurists and scholars. The wealth generated by trade supported their activities. In this parched land, the town had wells that provided water for drinking and growing vegetables. Six miles to the south, in an area called "The Forest," was the town where the king of Ghana resided. That town was bordered on three sides by ponds that held water collected during the brief rainy season. The king's palace consisted of a number of domed buildings surrounded by a wall, and the rest of the inhabitants lived in houses built of stone and acacia wood.

Although the king's town contained a mosque where Muslim visitors could go to pray, its very layout showed support for Soninke religious cults. Surrounding the town were sacred groves, thickets, and domed buildings where priests of indigenous religious cults performed their duties. The people of the king's town wore robes of cotton, silk, or brocade according to their means, but they did not wear Muslim-style sewn clothes. All of the men shaved their beards, and the women shaved their heads, which once again distinguished them from the inhabitants of the Muslim trading town. The twin towns demonstrated that Islam and indigenous religions could exist side by side without one of them yielding to the other. Religious tolerance also extended to the pageantry of the king's audiences. When the king's subjects approached him, they fell on their knees and sprinkled dust on their heads as a sign of respect. Muslim visitors, on the other hand, were allowed to greet him by simply clapping their hands.

The religious tolerance of Kumbi-Saleh was challenged in the mid-eleventh century by the militant Islamic Almoravid movement among the nomadic Berbers of the southern Sahara (see chapter 3). In 1055, the Almoravids captured the oasis trading town of Awdaghust, which had come under the control of Ghana earlier in the century. With the Almoravids firmly in control of the trade routes, and with sectarian warfare spreading instability throughout the region, the rulers of Ghana converted to Islam in 1076. Soon thereafter, Ghana began to produce Islamic scholars, lawyers, and Quran readers, many of whom gained preeminent positions in their fields. Some of the scholars visited centers of learning in Muslim Spain or made the pilgrimage to Mecca. It was also reported that Ghana spent large sums of money on wars against its pagan neighbors, in which it took captives for export to Morocco.

The Decline of the Ghana Empire

During the eleventh century, new goldfields began to be developed at Buré, which was located far to the south and east of Bambuk, well out of the commercial reach of Ghana. Itinerant Soninke traders known as *wangara* transported gold from Buré to the Middle Niger region instead of carrying it to Kumbi-Saleh. Over time, the annual production of the Buré goldfields would exceed that of Bambuk by 800 percent. The flow of gold toward the Middle Niger encouraged the development of a new trade route across the Sahara that bypassed Kumbi Saleh and brought the caravans from North Africa to the desert trading town of Walata, which gave them access to the trading towns of the Middle Niger. Ghana's resulting economic problems were exacerbated by a series of severe droughts after 1200 that made it even harder than usual to sustain a major commercial city in an area of low and increasingly uncertain rainfall.

By the thirteenth century, Ghana's political and economic power was clearly in decline. References to Ghana in Arabic sources were becoming infrequent and vague. Oral traditions recount that Bida, the mythical snake who brought prosperity to the kingdom, was killed by the suitor of a virgin who was about to be sacrificed. Because the suitor had a Muslim name, the story has been interpreted as a reference to the abandonment of the royal Soninke rituals when the rulers converted to Islam. The oral traditions further state that when Bida was killed, his bleeding head bounced seven times and finally landed in Buré, which had become the most prolific source of gold in the Sahel. As oral traditions make clear, the prosperity of Ghana was based on gold and rain, but after the death of Bida, both resources became scarce. Ghana had been originally formed as an amalgam of smaller kingdoms held together by the wealth and might of the royal court. As the resources dried up, the component parts of the empire broke away one by one.

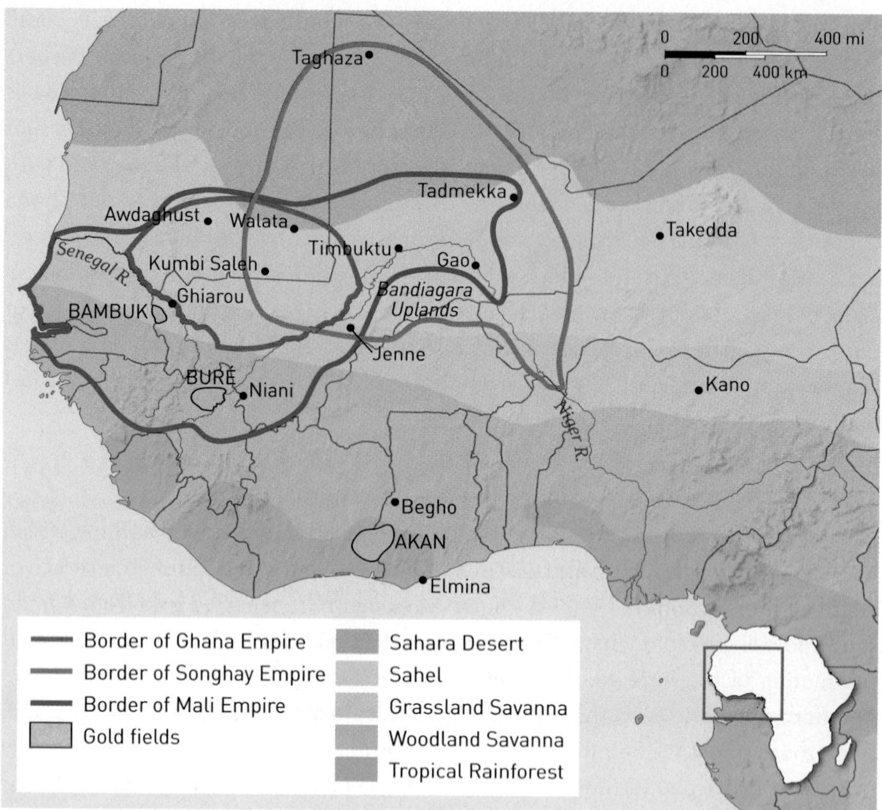

EMPIRES OF THE SAHEL This map shows the territory covered, successively, by the Ghana, Mali, and Songhai empires. Although their territories overlapped, they were not identical. The Mali Empire extended farther south than the other two, and the Songhay Empire, which controlled the salt mines of Taghaza, stretched into the Sahara. Not all of the territory within those borders was under the continuous control of the imperial governments. The gold-bearing regions, for example, remained autonomous.

The Mali Empire

Nestled between the upper reaches of the Senegal and Niger Rivers, some 350 miles to the southeast of the Ghana heartland, lies the region where the **Mali Empire** was formed. Unlike the Ghana Empire, with its proximity to the desert and its legendary obsession with water, the Mali Empire began in the better-watered southern grasslands near the Buré goldfields. The region was occupied by speakers of Mande languages who had developed a unique Mande social system in which the people were divided into exclusive categories: nobles, commoners, slaves, and members of hereditary occupational guilds. There were four guilds: blacksmiths, wood-carvers, leatherworkers, and bards (the keepers of the oral traditions, who functioned as historians, genealogists, and epic poets). Members of an occupational guild did not intermarry with families outside of their own guild.

The Founding of the Mali Empire

Before the Mali Empire existed, the small kingdoms in the region were headed by hunter-kings who were said to use their specialized occult hunting knowledge to communicate with the spirits of the bush. Professional hunters were organized into associations whose members went through extensive training to learn the secrets and rituals of their craft. In contrast to the hereditary occupational guilds, the hunting associations were open to anybody who successfully completed the training. Because hunters were skilled in the use of weapons, they could defend their villages or serve as an attack force. Sometime around 1200, this prosperous region was subjugated by the king of Sosso, one of the breakaway successor states of the failing Ghana Empire. In the subsequent struggle to regain their independence, the small Mande kingdoms united under the charismatic leadership of a hunter-warrior, **Sunjata**.

The legend of Sunjata has been told and retold by Mande bards over the centuries. According to the legend, Sunjata overcame childhood physical handicaps to become a great hunter and warrior, attracting a local following. He was driven into exile by his half-brother, who was jealous of Sunjata's power and growing influence. After an urgent plea that he return and save his people from the devastation of the Sosso army, Sunjata was provided with troops by the king of Mema, another successor state of Ghana, and blessed as the legitimate successor to the ancient kings of Ghana. He returned home with his troops, combined them with the hunters' associations to form an elite fighting force, and won a series of victories against the Sosso army.

The legend portrays the epic battle in which Sunjata finally defeated the despotic invaders as a contest of occult powers and skills between Sumanguru, the blacksmith king of Sosso, and Sunjata, the hunter-warrior of the Mande people. The symbolism of the story is important here: hunters' associations were more inclusive than blacksmith guilds, and hunters, unlike blacksmiths, could bridge the gap between the domesticated life of the towns and the unruly spirits of the wilderness. Sunjata based his political legitimacy on the authority and inclusiveness of the hunters' associations. He also claimed the legacy of the old Ghana Empire because he had secured the blessing and support of the king of Mema, a former province of Ghana. In short, he developed an inclusive political ideology that made it easy to incorporate a variety of peoples and ideas as the kingdom of Mali expanded into an empire.

The Expansion of the Mali Empire

After consolidating its authority over the Mande heartland, the kingdom of Mali expanded by conquest, and it incorporated the conquered areas under various arrangements. Beyond the core of the kingdom were partially autonomous provinces that paid tribute, and beyond them were nominally independent vassal states such as Mema and Wagadu (both successor states to the defunct Ghana Empire). At the far fringes were vassal states such as Takrur, on the western edge of the empire, and Songhay, on the eastern edge, that chafed under the rule of local puppet dynasties and waited for a chance to break away. Mali employed a system of indirect rule that largely left local authorities in place as long as they recognized the authority of the kings of Mali.

The prizes sought by the conquering armies of Mali were not the numerous small kingdoms and chiefdoms in the grasslands, but the trading towns in the Sahel. The commercial center of Walata, on the southern fringes of the Sahara, had replaced Awdaghust as the primary gateway to the trans-Saharan trade in the thirteenth century, just as the Mali Empire was forming. The caravan route from North Africa to Walata passed the salt pans of Taghaza, providing an opportunity for the camels to be loaded up with salt. Despite this commercial advantage, Walata was a high-risk trading center because it was too far away from the last desert oasis for a caravan to reach it without running out of water. Before leaving the oasis, the caravan would send a scout to Walata to announce that the caravan was on the way. People from Walata then traveled 4 days into the desert with an extra water supply to meet the caravan. If the scout failed to reach Walata, the whole caravan could perish. By 1352, Walata was the northwesternmost province of Mali, headed by an appointed governor. When caravans arrived from the north, the traders first called on the governor and then paid a visit to the overseer of the market, who also served as the king of Mali's commercial agent. In addition to salt, the caravans brought various wares from North Africa and Europe to exchange for hides, ivory, kola nuts, and gold from the Sahel.

The greatest prize of all was the city of Jenne. Located in the agriculturally rich Middle Niger floodplain, Jenne was surrounded by water during the annual flood. The prosperity of Jenne at this time came in part from its position along the trade routes between Walata and the Mali heartland. Some archaeologists believe that the Arab geographer Al-Idrisi was referring to Jenne in his statement that "its inhabitants are rich, for they possess gold in abundance, and many good things are imported to them from the outermost parts of the earth." Whether or not Mali ever succeeded in capturing Jenne is in dispute. It seems likely that Jenne sometimes paid tribute to Mali to ensure its autonomy, but the *Tarikh al-Sudan*, a chronicle written in Timbuktu by an Islamic scholar, reports that Mali repeatedly failed to conquer Jenne, even after 99 attempts, and when Al-Umari listed the provinces of Mali in the early fourteenth century, Jenne was not on the list.

The other key prizes were the desert-edge cities of Timbuktu and Gao, both located on the Niger bend, where the Niger River flows northeast, deep into the driest part of the Sahel, before making a slow U-turn toward the southwest. Their locations made these cities vital transition points between the overland trade routes across the desert and boat traffic along the Niger River. **Timbuktu** had once been used by desert nomads as a place to store grain that had been shipped along the Niger from the Middle Niger floodplain, but after 1100 it began to develop as a market town and attract trans-Saharan traders who had formerly gone to Walata. Timbuktu came under the control of Mali at the end of the thirteenth century, and by the end of the fourteenth century it had replaced Walata as the major southern terminus of the trans-Saharan trade. The shift in trade routes can be gleaned from maps made on the Mediterranean island of Majorca: a map made by Angelino Dulcert in 1339 shows the trans-Saharan route going to Walata, whereas the *Catalan Atlas*, made in 1375 by Abraham Cresques, shows the route going to Timbuktu and doesn't show Walata at all. The other important desert-edge city was Gao, the easternmost trading town in Mali, which provided access to the trade route that went to Egypt. When Mali's King **Mansa Musa** made his famous pilgrimage to Egypt and Mecca in 1324, he left Mali via Walata, but he returned via Gao and Timbuktu.

The wealth of the Mali Empire came more from control of the trade routes than from direct control of the goldfields. When a king of Mali conquered the gold-producing areas and tried to propagate Islam, gold production stopped. So the gold areas remained quasi-independent vassal states as long as they paid tribute. In some cases, gold-producing areas paid no tribute at all as long as they kept supplying gold to itinerant traders. In its pursuit of the gold trade, Mali benefited from developments both to the north and to the south of the grasslands. In the north, Europe was emerging from the depression of the early Middle Ages, and Europeans began to mint gold coins once again. The rising demand for gold in Europe stimulated traders from Italy, Marseille, and Majorca to purchase the gold of Mali from merchants in North Africa. The other development was that the *wangara* pioneered new trade routes that went hundreds of miles south to the goldfields of the Akan forest, from which they brought gold to the trading towns of the Middle Niger. With new sources of both supply and demand, the trans-Saharan gold trade reached its peak in the fourteenth century.

The Golden Age of the Mali Empire: The Reign of Mansa Musa

The golden age of the Mali Empire is epitomized by the pilgrimage that King Mansa Musa made to Egypt and Mecca in 1324. He was not the first king of Mali to make the pilgrimage, but he was certainly the most memorable. By one account, he was accompanied by 60,000 soldiers and 500 slaves, each of whom carried a gold wand weighing nearly 5 pounds. Another account holds that he set out with one hundred camel-loads of gold. It was reliably reported in Cairo in 1336 that Mansa Musa gave out such lavish gifts of gold in Egypt that its value was depressed for the next 12 years. Although Mansa Musa insisted that the trip was undertaken for purely religious purposes, he certainly captured the attention of people from Spain to Syria. The *Catalan Atlas*, made in 1375, featured an image of Mansa Musa wearing a gold crown, holding a gold scepter in one hand and a large gold nugget in the other. The caption explained, "This black lord is named Mussa Melly, lord of the Blacks of Guinea. This king is the richest and most noble lord of all this country by reason of the abundance of gold taken out of his land."

By that time, Mali was widely recognized as an integral part of the Muslim world, and Mansa Musa was viewed as a devout and pious Muslim. He brought Islamic clerics and scholars back to Mali with him, built mosques and minarets, and instituted public prayer in the Mali capital. He and his successors celebrated Islamic holidays, but the pageantry of the celebrations included traditional Mande ceremonial elements and lavish praise for the king, who was clearly trying to satisfy both his Muslim constituents and those who favored more traditional ceremonies. Islamic law, on the other hand, was often ignored. Rather than create a new synthesis of Islamic and local religious practices, the kings of Mali were content to allow them to exist side by side, occasionally intermingling at the royal court. Although Islam was practiced by government officials and traders, it remained largely a religion of the urban centers, while rural villages and towns throughout the empire continued to follow customary ways.

Twelve years after Mansa Musa's pilgrimage, the Syrian writer Al-Umari wrote a description of the Mali Empire based on the account of an Arab merchant who had lived in Mali for 35 years. Mali's capital city, he reported, was located in the central province, which occupied the old Mali heartland. The capital was very extensive and not enclosed by a wall. The king maintained several palaces surrounded by circular walls. Beyond the central province of Mali were 13 outlying provinces. The empire extended from the Atlantic Ocean in the west to the town of Muli, east of the Niger bend, a distance that required more than 4 months of travel. The empire covered a similar distance from north to south. Different provinces and vassal states had different relationships with the central court. Al-Umari noted that none of the vassal rulers could claim the title of "king" except for the king of Ghana, suggesting that Ghana still commanded respect even though it no longer had power. The Mali army numbered about 100,000 soldiers, of whom 10,000 rode Arabian horses that the king had imported from the desert nomads at great cost.

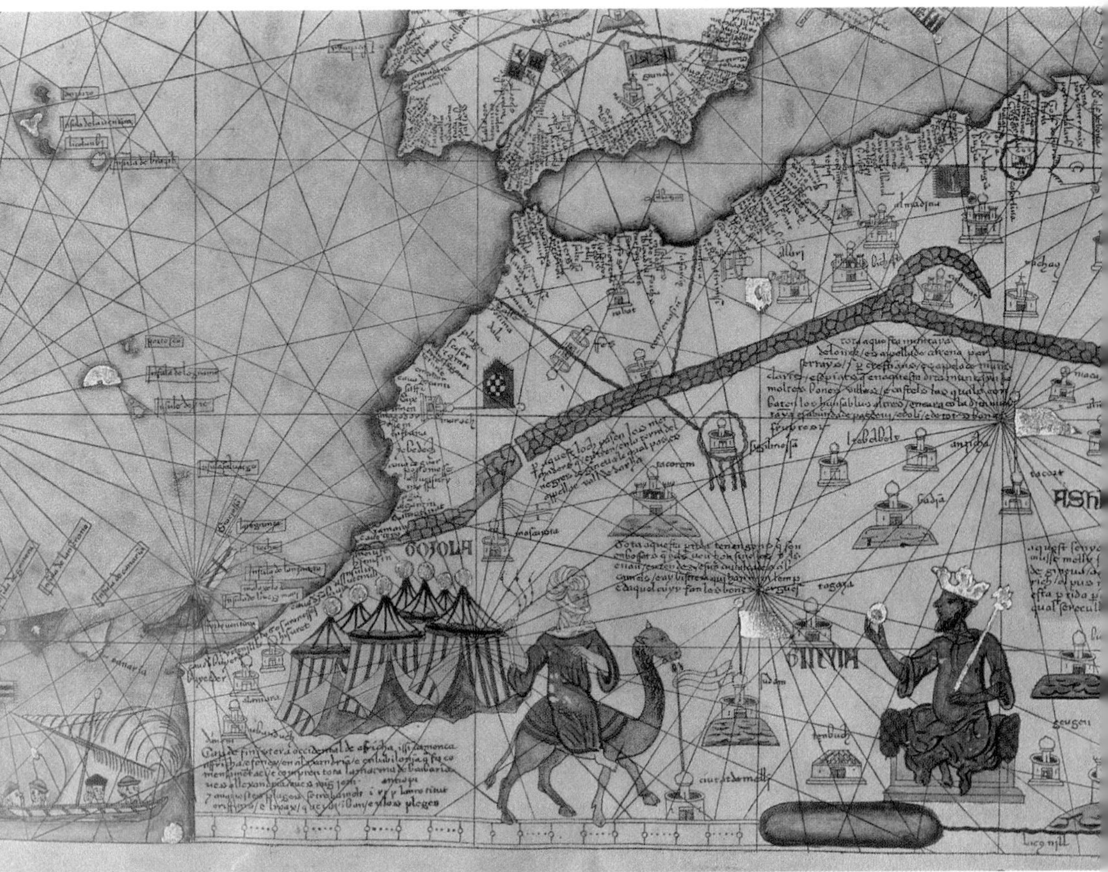

THE RICHEST KING The 1375 *Catalan Atlas* shows King Mansa Musa of Mali (right) holding a gold nugget in his right hand and a golden scepter in his left. The caption says, "This king is the richest and most noble lord of all this country by reason of the abundance of gold taken out of his land." The mapmaker, Abraham Cresques, lived on the Mediterranean island of Majorca.

At the beginning of the fifteenth century, the economic prosperity of Mali was heavily dependent on its control of the trade routes that ran from the Middle Niger floodplain to the desert termini at the Niger bend, but this control was soon challenged. Attacks from the Mossi who lived to the south of the Niger bend, the aggressive actions of the Tuareg nomads who lived north of the Niger bend, and periodic rebellions in the city of Gao forced Mali to withdraw from Gao and Timbuktu by 1438. The northern vassal kingdom of Mema, which had supplied soldiers to aid Sunjata at the time of Mali's founding, regained its independence at about the same time. The trading town of Jenne, which had always maintained a combative relationship with the Mali Empire, reasserted its independence in the early fifteenth century and gained control of large portions of the Middle Niger floodplain. The diminished kingdom of Mali would continue to dominate its old Mande heartland and the adjoining areas in the southern grasslands, but the desert trade was being lost to the rising Songhay Empire.

The Songhay Empire

With the retreat of Mali from the Niger bend, a ruler of the **Songhay Empire**, named Sunni Ali, stepped into the vacuum. The heart of his kingdom was the Songhay-speaking region south of the trading city of Gao at the eastern edge of the Niger bend. From his capital at Gao, he used his large army, his cavalry, and his fleet of war canoes on the Niger to capture Timbuktu, the Middle Niger floodplain, Jenne, and the Bandiagara uplands. His goal was to control the gold and salt trade of the Middle Niger. Although he was a Muslim, Sunni Ali was neither strict nor devout, and he preserved traditional Songhay royal symbols such as the sacred drum and the sacred fire. He had little use for the Islamic scholars from various parts of the world who had been visiting or settling in Timbuktu ever since the time of Mansa Musa's pilgrimage. The *Tarikh al-Sudan* characterized Sunni Ali as "a great oppressor and a notorious evil doer," and reported that "he tyrannized the scholars and holy men, killing them, insulting them, and humiliating them." As a result, many scholars fled to Walata.

The Reign of the Askia Dynasty

The death of Sunni Ali in 1492 led to a successional dispute in which his son was defeated in battle by a provincial governor, who ascended to the throne as Askia Muhammad. His rule marked the beginning of the Askia dynasty that would rule the Songhay Empire until its demise. Askia Muhammad was not ethnically Songhay, and thus he could not base his authority on the traditional rituals and royal regalia of the Songhay people. Instead, he based his legitimacy on Islam, and he quickly set out to establish Songhay as a Muslim kingdom. Just 4 years after taking power, he made a pilgrimage to Mecca and returned with the authority to rule over the Muslims of the Sahel in the name of the caliph in Cairo. Askia Muhammad expanded the empire, adding tributary lands to the east and the west and moving up into the desert to capture the salt pans of Taghaza. His objective was to control access to the major trade routes across the Sahara. By 1512, it was reported that even the king of Mali was paying tribute to the Askia. After Askia

Muhammad was deposed by his own sons in 1528, there was no further expansion of the Songhay Empire. There began the now-familiar cycle of central power waxing and waning over time as vassal states broke away or became reintegrated into the empire.

The Trading City of Gao

Even during the heyday of the old Mali empire, Gao had been described by the Muslim traveler Ibn Battuta as "one of the finest and biggest cities of the Blacks, and the best supplied with provisions." In the sixteenth century, as the capital of the Songhay Empire, Gao had a population of between 38,000 and 76,000, not counting the nomads who camped around its edges. Feeding such a large population in the semiarid grasslands was not easy. Vegetables and melons could be grown in the wetlands left by the annual flood of the Niger, but grain had to be grown elsewhere and shipped in by large boats that could carry as much as 20 tons. To feed the royal court, the Askias maintained plantations in the flooded rice lands farther up the Niger, which were worked by royal slaves and supervised by slave officials.

A major economic development in the sixteenth century was the strengthening of the Jenne-Timbuktu trade axis. Early in the century, it was reported that salt arriving by camel in Timbuktu was transported by boat along the Niger River to Jenne, where the large blocks were divided into smaller pieces to be sold by the itinerant merchants. The salt was exchanged for gold that traders brought up from the Akan forest, far to the south, and then shipped to Timbuktu by boat. It was said that Timbuktu owed its prominence as a terminus for caravans to its symbiotic relationship with Jenne. From its location in the Middle Niger floodplain, Jenne could ship large quantities of rice and other foodstuffs to the desert-edge towns of Timbuktu and Gao.

The revenues of the Songhay Empire came from several sources. Given the agricultural abundance of the Middle Niger floodplain, it is not surprising that Songhay imposed direct taxes on the agricultural populations there. The traveler Leo Africanus reported in 1513 that the Askias taxed the rural populations so heavily that they barely had enough left to live on. There was also a tax on every slab of rock salt that came from Taghaza. The king had representatives in Jenne and Timbuktu to collect taxes on the trans-Saharan trade, while the harbormaster in Gao taxed the trade that came in on the Niger River. From the more distant parts of the empire, the Askias collected annual tribute, and they also profited from the booty taken in wars, especially captives who could be sold as slaves. It was reported that Askia Ismael (1536–1539) once returned from a military campaign with so many captives that the price on the Gao slave market fell to a mere 300 cowrie shells.

TIMBUKTU Located where the Niger River bend approaches the Sahara Desert, Timbuktu was a major gateway to the trans-Saharan trade. It became a renowned center for Islamic learning and scholarship in the fifteenth and sixteenth centuries under the patronage of the Songhay rulers. This sketch from the 1850s shows travelers arriving in Timbuktu. Note how the skyline is dominated by the three major mosques.

Timbuktu

The Askias used some of their income to support scholars and holy men in Timbuktu and to pay for upkeep and repairs of the mosques. Between 1350 and 1500, a variety of scholars from North Africa, desert oasis towns, and the Middle Niger region had visited or settled in Timbuktu. The Great Mosque of Timbuktu had been built in the fourteenth century by Mansa Musa under the supervision of a Spanish Muslim scholar and poet who accompanied him on his return from his pilgrimage to Mecca. Soon thereafter, a larger mosque was built in the Sankore quarter in the northern part of the city, paid for by a wealthy Tuareg woman who had made a small fortune in the trans-Saharan trade. The Sankore section of Timbuktu became the city's major center of Islamic teaching and learning. A third mosque, the Sidi Yahya Mosque, was built in the early fifteenth century.

In contrast to Sunni Ali, who had killed many of the scholars and driven others into exile when he conquered Timbuktu in 1468, his successor, Askia Muhammad, lured scholars back with gifts in cash and kind, as well as exemption from taxes. By 1526, Leo Africanus reported that "in Timbuktu there are numerous judges, scholars, and priests, all well paid by the king. Many manuscript books coming from Barbary are sold. Such sales are more profitable than any other goods." Askia Dawud (1549–1582) established public libraries and hired scribes and calligraphers to copy books. The public and private libraries of Timbuktu contained handwritten books on a wide range of subjects, including calculus, geometry, geography, philosophy, botany, medicine, and astronomy. One prominent scholar had a personal library of 1,600 volumes. In such a supportive atmosphere, Islamic scholarship flourished in Timbuktu during the sixteenth century.

Higher learning in Timbuktu operated through a tutorial system, in which a student would study a particular text with a single teacher. Students would first render their own copy of the text, after which they would engage in commentary

THE TREASURES OF TIMBUKTU Handwritten illuminated books were the intellectual and artistic treasures of Timbuktu, and manuscripts such as this one (which is adorned with gold) were quite expensive. Thousands of books were held in Timbuktu's private libraries, and one prominent scholar owned more than 1,600 volumes.

and interpretative discussions with the teacher. A student who demonstrated mastery over a given text was given a license by the teacher to teach it to others. Many students studied under six or seven different teachers to master a range of subjects. In addition to Islamic commentaries and law, students could study rhetoric, logic, poetry, astronomy, and Arabic grammar. Lessons were usually held in the teacher's house, but larger classes could also be held at one of the three main mosques. Recitations and commentaries that were aimed at public audiences were often held at the Sankore mosque.

The Moroccan Invasion of Songhay

The prosperity of the Songhay empire was threatened in the late sixteenth century when the ruler of Morocco, Al-Mansur, sought to gain control of the trans-Saharan trade routes. In the 1580s, he sent an army into the desert to capture the salt mines of Taghaza, but it arrived only to find that the population had fled, leaving no one to work in the mines. Al-Mansur then began to plan an extraordinary expedition across the Sahara Desert to capture Timbuktu, Gao, and Jenne. The attack force would use 8,000 camels and 1,000 pack horses to make the desert crossing. The army he raised consisted of 2,000 foot soldiers armed with muskets, 500 mounted musketeers, and a spear-wielding cavalry of 1,500. When his Moroccan advisers expressed skepticism about the venture, Al-Mansur replied that the Songhay army had "only spears and swords, weapons that will be useless against modern arms."

After a 20-week desert crossing, the army reached the Niger bend at a point halfway between Gao and Timbuktu. The Songhay commanders were aware of the approaching Moroccan army, but they had been so confident that it would founder in the desert that they were caught unprepared when it arrived. Using the familiar military tactics of Sahel warfare, the Songhay cavalry charged the Moroccans from both flanks, but they had no chance against the blazing muskets. The Songhay army retreated across the Niger and left the Moroccans free to enter Gao unopposed. After seizing whatever booty they could find, the Moroccans abandoned Gao and marched 29 days to Timbuktu, which they entered without opposition. Although many inhabitants of Timbuktu had fled, most of its merchants and scholars remained in place, feeling that they had nothing to fear from their fellow Muslims. The quick capitulation of Timbuktu and the exhaustion of the Moroccan soldiers saved the city from being plundered, at least for the moment.

After building a fort on land confiscated from wealthy merchants and leaving behind a garrison, the Moroccan forces left Timbuktu for further conquests. While they were away, an insurrection broke out in Timbuktu that would not be subdued until 300 Moroccan musketeers rushed back from the war front to save the garrison. Although Tuareg nomads were apparently behind the insurrection, the Moroccan commander, Mahmud Pasha, blamed it on the scholars and jurists. When he returned from his conquests in 1593, he executed a carefully laid plan to loot Timbuktu and arrest the leading scholars and jurists.

According to the *Tarikh al-Sudan*, written some 60 years after the events, "Pasha Mahmud entered their houses and removed all the valuables, household goods, and furnishings in quantities that none but God could measure. His followers plundered whatever they could lay their hands on, and brought dishonor upon the scholars, stripping their womenfolk and committing acts of indecency. Then they took the women to the fort and imprisoned them there with the men for six months." Then Mahmud sent the scholars, their books, and their families across the Sahara to Morocco, along with a paltry 100,000 *mithqals* of looted gold. After his initial expectations of finding fabulous wealth in Timbuktu had evaporated, Mahmud had apparently concluded that the scholars and their books were the true treasures of the city. Although some of the scholars eventually found their way back to Timbuktu, its golden age of learning and scholarship was over.

The Moroccans had come with ambitious plans to capture the goldfields, but they soon realized that such a goal was unrealistic given the vast distances involved and their own diminishing numbers. So they focused instead on controlling the Middle Niger from Gao to Jenne. They established their capital at Timbuktu, where they ruled through a pasha appointed from Morocco. Many of the surviving Moroccan soldiers married Songhay women from noble families and began to form a new ruling elite known as the Arma. In 1612, the Arma deposed the Moroccan-appointed pasha and seized power as an independent authority. Over subsequent generations, they gradually lost their foreignness and were slowly absorbed into the local population, but they never gained political legitimacy in the eyes of the populations they ruled. Although the Arma maintained tenuous control of the key trade routes of the Middle Niger into the eighteenth century, the desert trade was diminishing, in part because Portuguese and Dutch merchants were siphoning off increasing quantities of gold to the Atlantic coast.

Imperial Legacies

The histories of Ghana, Mali, and Songhay form a sequence that reflects the discoveries of new sources of gold and the consequent eastward displacements of the trans-Saharan trade routes. Cobbled together out of preexisting kingdoms and chiefdoms, these empires did not seek to impose a uniform political culture on their distinct populations or to institute a centrally administered bureaucracy. Instead, they used a strategy of indirect rule that left most of the local chiefs and smaller kings in place, much as the European colonizers would attempt to do in the twentieth century. As long as they controlled the trade routes and the trading towns, the three empires prospered, but as soon as they lost that control, they went into decline.

Ghana, Mali, and Songhay were medieval empires that differed in significant ways from the modern states that populate the world today. Whereas border control is a hallmark of the modern state, the boundaries of medieval empires were only vaguely defined, and they expanded and contracted with the waxing and waning of power at the center. The kings sought to control their vassals through webs of personal relationships and economic ties rather than through legal or constitutional frameworks. Relationships with their vassals, allies, and enemies defined the empires more accurately than did notions of territorial integrity. In the sparsely populated Sahel, control of trading towns and agriculturally rich floodplains was far more important than dominion over vast expanses of semiarid land.

In all three empires, the rulers staked their claim to legitimacy on their access to occult powers or divine blessings, which were believed to give them the power to bring good fortune or harm to the societies they ruled. The oral traditions of Ghana stressed the ability of the founder to vanquish the water spirits, whereas the oral traditions of Mali emphasized Sunjata's ability to tame the spirits of the bush. Both Ghana and Mali eventually adopted Islam, adding a new layer of divine blessing without abandoning the traditional rituals and beliefs. In the Songhay Empire, however, Askia Muhammad was a usurper and a foreigner. Because he could not make a traditional claim to power, he and his successors in the Askia dynasty clung to Islam as their key to legitimacy, even while retaining the traditional Songhay symbols of kingship.

The legacies of the three empires varied considerably. After the dissolution of the Ghana Empire, its successor states derived their legitimacy from their claimed connections to that once-great empire. Even after Ghana was reduced to a mere province of the Mali Empire, its king retained a title of respect.

The Songhay Empire, in contrast, developed as an extended attempt to control trade routes and access points to the Sahara. Because the ruling ideology of the Songhay Empire was largely Islamic, it nurtured a golden age of Islamic scholarship and produced thousands of hand-written books that have been preserved to this day, but it had little lasting effect on the vast majority of its subjects, who continued to follow local beliefs and practices. When the Songhay army was defeated in 1591, the vast empire quickly disintegrated as the outlying provinces and vassal states broke away one by one.

The greatest legacy of all was left by the Mali Empire, which held on in the Mande heartland long after it had lost control of the Middle Niger region. In 1599, 8 years after the defeat of the Songhay Empire by the Moroccans, the king of Mali took advantage of the chaotic situation to make yet another attempt to capture the trading town of Jenne. The attack was a failure, in part because he could not convince the rulers of his former vassal states to join his cause. After that defeat, Mali was no longer mentioned in the Arabic language records. Its major legacy was in the spread of the Mande languages and social system throughout the lands of the empire and beyond, in part because of the prestige of the Mali kings and the power of the occupational guilds. Some scholars now speak of a common Mande cultural zone in the West African grasslands, which would be the Mali Empire's most enduring legacy.

THE EAST AFRICAN COAST

Just as camels and oases made it possible to cross the forbidding Sahara Desert, ships and islands facilitated the crossing of the Indian Ocean. The trading network of the western Indian Ocean was a child of the **monsoon winds**. From October to April, the northeast monsoon blew from India to the Swahili Coast, passing over the Persian Gulf and the southern part of the Arabian Peninsula, and continuing as far south as the port of Kilwa, at the entrance to the Mozambique Channel. Ships would set out for the east coast of Africa soon after the monsoon set in. Dhows (Indian Ocean Sailing vessels) from India could reach the East African ports of Zanzibar and Mombasa in 20–30 days, whereas dhows from the Persian Gulf averaged 30–40 days owing to the lighter winds on the edge of the monsoon. Beginning in April, the winds reversed themselves and blew from the southwest. With favorable winds and currents, a dhow could make the 2,400-mile trip from a port on the east coast of Africa to the western corner of Arabia in as little as 10–12 days, though a normal trip took 17–20 days. The dhow crossings ceased during the months of June and July, when the winds died down and could leave a dhow stranded, but they picked up again in August.

Swahili Settlements and Trade

The earliest mention of seafaring trade along the eastern coast of Africa was in the *Periplus of the Erithrean Sea*, a travelers' guide written in Alexandria, Egypt, around 100 CE. The *Periplus* speaks of a trading port called Rhapta (located south of the equator near the modern city of Dar es Salaam) and other market towns where ships from Egypt went to purchase ivory, tortoiseshell, rhinoceros horn, and coconut oil. Rhapta was also mentioned in Ptolemy's *Geographia*, published in

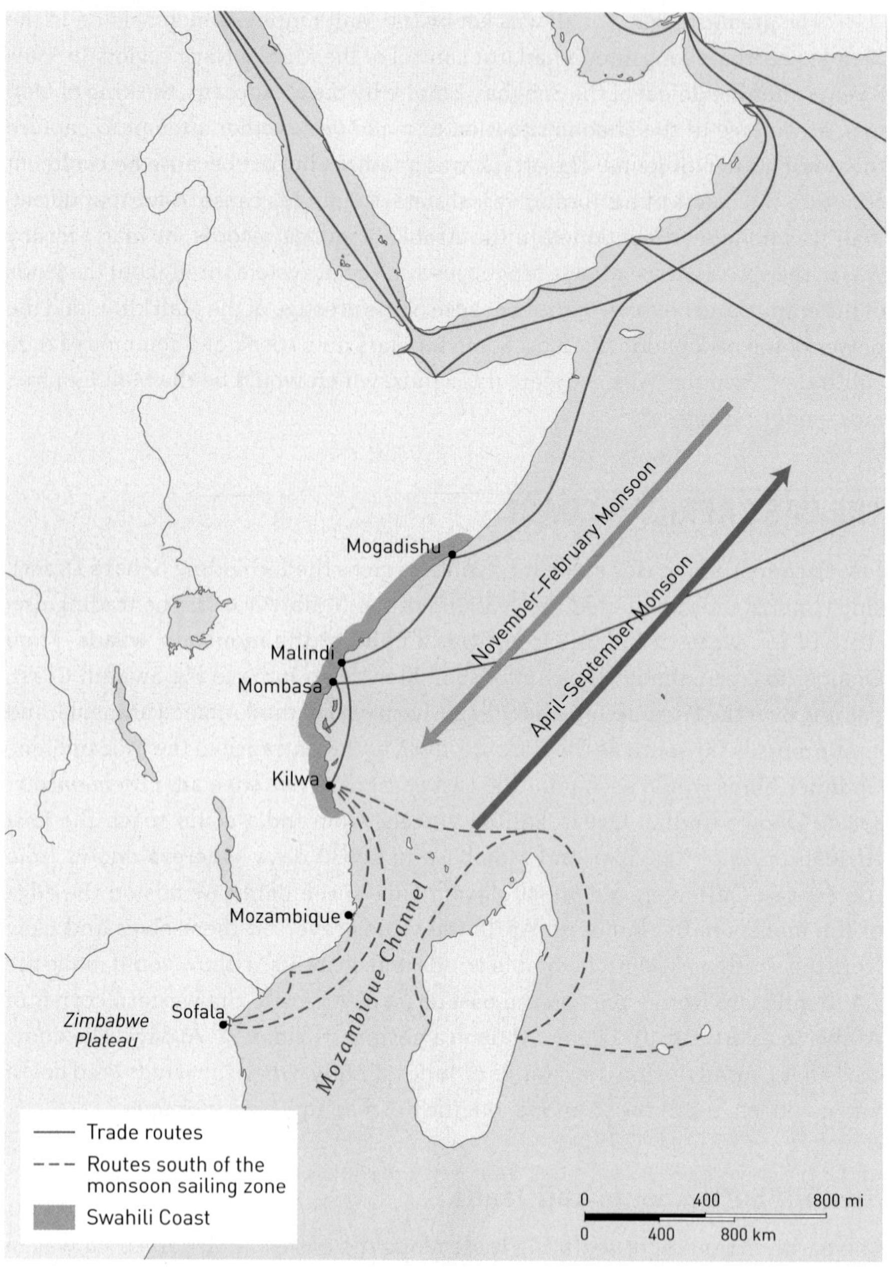

INDIAN OCEAN WINDS The coastal region between Mogadishu (in the north) and Kilwa (in the south) is known as the Swahili Coast because it was the home of seafaring people who spoke Swahili. Blown by the monsoon winds, ships could sail along the Swahili Coast from East Africa to the Arabian Peninsula, the Persian Gulf, and India from November to February, and could return from April to September when the winds blew in the opposite direction. Kilwa marked the southern limit of the monsoon sailing zone.

Byzantium around 400. There appears to have been an upswing in Indian Ocean trade after 800. A Chinese compendium of knowledge published in the ninth century reported that eastern Africa exported ivory, ambergris (from whales), and captives. In 869, there was a prolonged and bloody rebellion of slaves from the Nile valley and eastern Africa who labored to drain the marshes of southern Iraq and mine the salt pans of Basra. When the Arab traveler Al-Masudi visited the east African coast in the early tenth century, he listed trade in ambergris, leopard skins, tortoiseshell, ivory, and gold, but made no mention of captives. In return for their exports, the coastal towns received glass vessels, Islamic pottery, and stone bowls.

It was during this period of expanding trade that Swahili-speaking merchants from the northern part of the east African coast began to move southward to establish trading outposts on coastal islands or promontories. Swahili oral traditions tell of a seafaring stranger from the north who settled in a southern coastal town and agreed to pay tribute to the local inhabitants. Soon, however, the stranger married a local woman, gained rights to land, and made inroads into the local society. Eventually, he made a bargain with the locals, who granted him the right to rule in exchange for providing them with trade goods, yet he was still considered an outsider. It was not until the stranger's son, the child of a local mother, succeeded him that the community could come together.

The story suggests that Swahili settlements along the east African coast were undergoing fundamental changes, both economically and socially. Archaeological studies confirm that analysis and suggest that maritime trade grew more important toward the year 1000 as the coastal settlements oriented themselves toward the sea and away from their hinterlands. During this transition period, numerous small coastal fishing villages gave way to a handful of larger settlements, and new styles in pottery and architecture developed that were distinct from those in the east African interior. At the same time, stone mosques were constructed at key places along the coast, testifying to the widespread adoption of Islam. By the thirteenth century, the defining elements of Swahili society—urbanism, a maritime orientation, and Islam—were all in place, and a common Swahili culture dominated the port towns along the east African coast from Mogadishu in the north to Kilwa in the south. All of them were in the monsoon sailing zone and thus had direct access to the trans-Indian Ocean trade. By then, this stretch of Indian Ocean coastline could appropriately be referred to as the Swahili Coast.

The Gold Trade from the Zimbabwe Plateau

Ships sailing south from the Swahili Coast entered the Mozambique Channel (an arm of the Indian Ocean nearly 1,000 miles long and 250 miles wide), which ran between the east African coast and the large island of Madagascar. Once there, they encountered the strong, south-flowing Mozambique Current, which was formed when the waters of the South Equatorial Current were funneled into the channel. The problems of sailing in the Mozambique Channel help to explain why the Swahili-speaking peoples did not seek to settle south of Kilwa, even though the channel was on the maritime route to the sources of the gold trade.

The gold that was traded along the east African coast was found on the Zimbabwe plateau (in present-day Zimbabwe), nearly 1,000 miles southwest of Kilwa and about 250 miles inland from the coast. The gold-bearing veins within the granite core of the plateau were fractured and fissured, making gold mining difficult and its results unreliable. During the lean months of July, August, and September, after the harvest was complete and the rains had ceased, people would pan for gold in drying riverbeds and sink shafts as deep as 80 feet. The gold was then sold to traders at markets or fairs that were established on the plateau, often near the towns of local political authorities. Although the authorities did not control the markets, all nuggets were considered the property of the ruler, while gold dust or impure gold could be freely traded. One of the earliest markets was located near the settlement of Great Zimbabwe, which now exists only as a remarkable set of ruins.

Great Zimbabwe was not built on one of the gold belts, but rather on the southeastern edge of the plateau, which received the moist southeast trade winds from the coastal plain and was more favorable for agriculture. It was also in a favorable position for travel to the coast via the Sabi River valley. The city was laid out in a labyrinth-like pattern, with curved stone walls defining domestic spaces that were filled in with clay houses. In the local language known as Shona, the word *Zimbabwe*, which means "venerated house," refers to the dwelling of a chief or king. The ruler's palace was an enormous elliptical building with an outer wall 35 feet high and 17 feet thick. The grandiose architecture of the stone enclosures reveals their function as political symbols that embodied the control of the ruling elite over its subjects. For all their grandeur, the stone enclosures of Great Zimbabwe housed a modest population that numbered only in the hundreds. The inhabitants included the ruler, his relatives, government officials, and priests. Beyond the stone enclosures were mud houses inhabited by farmers, artisans, and craftsmen.

Permanent settlement at Great Zimbabwe began in the eleventh century. Construction of walls continued into the late fourteenth and early fifteenth centuries, which marked the period of Great Zimbabwe's greatest prosperity. It was a center of crafts and industry, where gold, copper, and iron were worked. Archaeological excavations show that it was at the center of a regional trading

GREAT ZIMBABWE The palace at Great Zimbabwe was an elliptical building with walls 35 feet high and up to 17 feet thick. During the period of its greatest prosperity in the fifteenth century, Great Zimbabwe was a trading hub, profiting off of gold from the Zimbabwe Plateau and goods from abroad transported along the Indian Ocean trading system.

network that was connected to the Indian Ocean trading system, and that it received trade goods from as far away as China. Its wealth came from trade rather than direct control of the gold veins.

Gold from the Zimbabwe Plateau was carried by traders to the coastal port of Sofala, a town that was mentioned by the Arab traveler Al-Masudi in 915 as being in "a land which produces gold and many other wonderful things." The disadvantage of Sofala for maritime trade was its location on the Mozambique Channel, south of the prevailing monsoon winds, where the south-flowing current made sailing difficult. Seafaring traders who wanted reliable monsoon winds ended their journey at Kilwa, north of the Mozambique Channel.

Trading Towns of the Swahili Coast

Although the trading towns along the Swahili Coast shared a common language, culture, and religion, each one of them was politically and economically independent. It follows that each of them had a unique and separate history, which was influenced in part by their location within the Indian Ocean trading networks and their relationship with the people in their hinterlands.

KILWA

The southernmost of the Swahili trading town was **Kilwa**, located at the southern edge of the monsoon zone. It was built on an island in a sunken estuary that provided security and a sheltered harbor. Its trading relations with the Muslim world were already evident by the eleventh century, when a modest stone mosque was built to serve the Muslim community. During the thirteenth century, Kilwa gained a monopoly on the gold trade and reduced Sofala to tributary status. Small coasting vessels would bring gold and ivory from Sofala to Kilwa, where the products would be transferred to oceangoing dhows. The fourteenth century was a time of growth for Kilwa, when the mosque was enlarged to four times its original size and the magnificent Husuni Kubwa palace was constructed by the king. Located on the tip of a headland a mile out of town, the palace outshone all others along the Swahili Coast in size and splendor. Within its ornate arcades, pavilions,

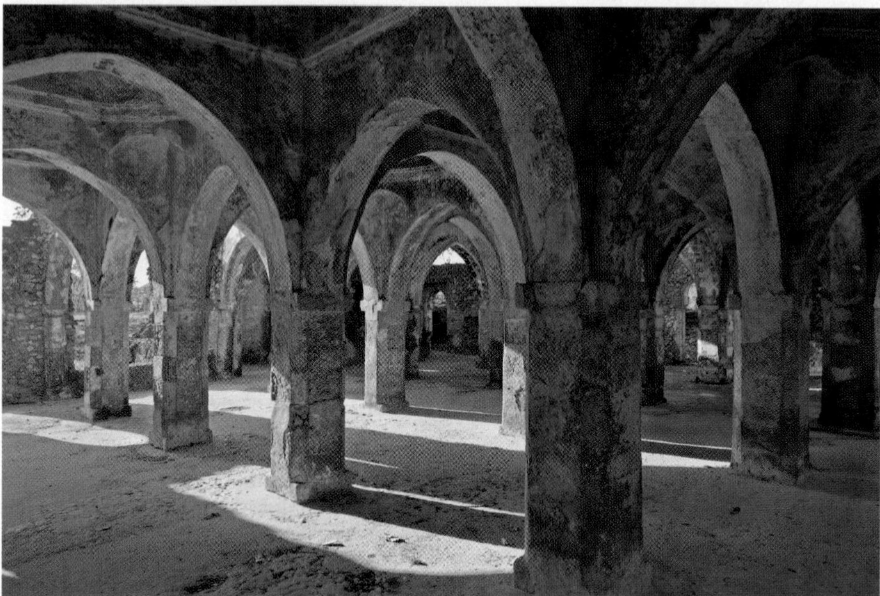

THE GREAT MOSQUE AT KILWA Kilwa was the southernmost Swahili port for ships that caught the monsoon winds to sail to the Persian Gulf and India, and was the major outlet for the gold trade from the Zimbabwe Plateau. Kilwa's mosque was built in the tenth and eleventh centuries and was enlarged in the fourteenth century, when a dome was added. At the time, it was the largest mosque in sub-Saharan Africa.

vaulted ceilings, and domes, the palace contained the apartments of the ruler and his family, courts for holding audiences, reception rooms, domestic quarters, and a bathing pool. The importance of commerce was indicated by its warehouses for import and export merchandise and the sketches of square-rigged dhows that were scratched into its plaster walls as graffiti.

When the Arab traveler Ibn Battuta visited Kilwa in 1331, he noted that it was one of the most beautiful towns in the world and was elegantly built. He was informed that the port of Sofala was a month's journey away by boat, and from there it was another month's journey inland to the goldfields. The inhabitants of Kilwa, whom he described as having extremely black skin, were devout Muslims. Because the king was known far and wide for his generosity to *sharifs* (direct descendants of the Prophet Muhammad), itinerant sharifs would come to him from as far away as Arabia and Iraq. Ibn Battuta also noted that the king was devoted to waging jihad against the unbelievers on the mainland, bringing back booty that most likely included ivory and captives.

By the mid-fifteenth century, Kilwa's fortunes were declining, and the ruling king abandoned the splendid Husuni Kubwa palace for a more modest dwelling at the edge of the city. The decline was a result of a larger economic downturn in the northern Indian Ocean, but it was also affected by events on the Zimbabwe Plateau. The golden age of Kilwa in the fourteenth century had coincided with the golden age of Great Zimbabwe, illustrating the powerful commercial symbiosis between the two states. When, for reasons that remain unclear to historians, Great Zimbabwe fell into economic decline and was abandoned during the fifteenth century, two new kingdoms arose to succeed it. In the northern part of the Zimbabwe Plateau arose the Monomotapa kingdom, founded by emigrants from the region of Great Zimbabwe who moved north and conquered the Zambezi River valley and the Shona peoples living between the Zimbabwe Plateau and the coast. At the southwestern end of the plateau arose the Torwa kingdom, which continued the tradition of stone-walled capitals and built its economy on the gold and cattle resources of the southwestern plateau. This disunity ushered in a period of warfare and uncertainty that severely disrupted the gold trade in the region, which in turn contributed to Kilwa's commercial decline. As an island whose prosperity depended on trade, Kilwa reflected economic conditions in both the wider Indian Ocean and the Zimbabwe Plateau.

The Northern Swahili Trading Towns

Although Kilwa, with its location at the southern end of the monsoon zone and its monopoly over the gold trade, was the most prosperous of the Swahili trading towns, other Swahili towns located farther north also flourished. These northern towns developed trading partnerships with the Arab world, Persia, India, and China. Tortoiseshell, ivory, rhinoceros horn, and animal skins were the main exports, along with mangrove poles, which were much in demand as building material for roofs and ceilings in the treeless plains of southern Arabia and the Persian Gulf. Perhaps the most exotic product was the live giraffe shipped to the emperor of China in the early fifteenth century. Because these products could be obtained on or near the coast, the Swahili maritime trade north of Kilwa did not lead to the development of long-distance trade routes into the East African interior.

The most important northern Swahili trading town was Mogadishu, which had once controlled Sofala and the southern gold trade. Even after losing the gold trade to Kilwa in the late thirteenth century, it remained a vibrant commercial center. When Ibn Battuta visited Mogadishu in 1331, he reported that the town contained powerful merchants who made a fine living off the export of locally woven cotton cloth. At this time, Mogadishu was becoming something of an Islamic center. Its ruler was a pious Muslim who hosted Islamic scholars and jurists at his court. Both the Great Mosque and the Mosque of Fakhr al Din were built in the early fourteenth century, but no more large edifices were constructed after that. By the early sixteenth century, Mogadishu could still be described as "a large town with houses of several stories, big palaces at its center, and four towers around it."

Other important Swahili trading towns were described by the Portuguese around 1500. Malindi had stone and mortar houses of many stories, with many windows and flat roofs. Its merchants dealt in cloth, gold, ivory, wax, and other products. The island of Pate manufactured fine silk cloth, and ships arrived from as far away as India to buy it. Mombasa was described as a very large town with two- and three-story houses of the same type as those of Kilwa. It was a major supplier of cotton cloth for the entire Swahili Coast as far south as Sofala, and its inhabitants possessed luxury items such as gold, silver, pearls, silk, gold-embroidered clothes, and fine carpets.

Although each town was enmeshed in a unique web of cultural relations with its mainland neighbors and its overseas trading partners, the far-flung Swahili trading towns nevertheless shared elements of a common Swahili culture. In addition to the Swahili language, they shared a social system that divided society into categories of patricians and commoners. The patricians were generally from wealthy merchant families, whereas commoners were mostly fishermen and farmers. Patricians used strict genealogical rules of descent through male lines to create exclusive clans, which were subdivided into ranked subclans and lineages. Aristocratic clans asserted cultural hegemony over the commoners and manipulated their genealogies to claim ancestral origins stretching back to Arabia or Persia. They did not seek to become landed aristocrats, but instead invested their wealth in conspicuous consumption, Islamic piety, and charity. This consumption pattern, along with certain aristocratic manners and dress, made it easy to distinguish the patricians from the commoners. Just as wealthy Swahili merchants did not seek to acquire land, Swahili kings and queens did not seek to acquire territory. Most of them lived in sumptuous palaces, but ruled over little more than their own towns.

The Swahili trading towns had gained wealth and power as intermediaries in the trade between the coastal interior and the Indian Ocean trading network. Some of them, such as Malindi, were situated on the coast; others, such as Kilwa and Mombasa, were located on islands that almost touched the mainland; while still others, such as Pate, were on offshore islands located within a few miles of the coast. In no case did a Swahili trading town try to turn its commercial advantage into a large territorial empire. The only territorial empires that arose around the gold trade were the inland polities on the Zimbabwe Plateau.

CONCLUSION

This chapter has looked at two borderland areas of Africa where politics and statecraft were intermingled with the effort to dominate long-distance trade. Both regions possessed goldfields, and both sought to profit from the rising demand for gold coins in the Mediterranean world. In the fourteenth century, it was said that two-thirds of the gold flowing into the Muslim and Christian lands came from West Africa, while an unknown amount came via the east African coast. In both cases, the trade in gold stimulated trade in other products because even a small fortune in gold took up only a portion of a sailing ship or a camel caravan, leaving plenty of room for other items.

People crossed the Sahara Desert and the Indian Ocean along with commodities. Some of them were merchants, travelers, and religious pilgrims, but many of them were captives who were sent out against their will. Documents from the Islamic period give evidence of an export trade in captives that carried 4.8 million sub-Saharan Africans across the Sahara Desert from 650 to 1600 CE, and of a parallel trade that carried 2.4 million captives from eastern Africa across the Indian Ocean to the Red Sea, the Persian Gulf, and India between 800 and 1600 CE. That slave trade was a uniquely Old World phenomenon in which captives were transported from one region of the Old World to another.

The trade routes also facilitated the transmission of ideas and belief systems. The most dynamic intellectual force of the age was Islam, and it's no surprise that Islam spread across the Sahara Desert and down the coast of east Africa. Prosperous trading towns became centers of Islamic learning that attracted scholars, jurists, and itinerant sharifs from far and wide. But Islam made little headway in the countryside, where people relied on long-standing religious practices to ensure the fertility of the earth, the coming of the rains, and the protection of their domestic spaces. In the royal courts of the West African Sahel, Islamic and traditional symbols lived side by side. In a similar way, the Swahili trading towns fully embraced Islam, but they did not try to spread it to their inland neighbors. On the contrary, they used their Islamic piety and their manipulated genealogies as markers of a distinct and exclusive Swahili identity.

Despite the many similarities between the West African Sahel and the Swahili Coast, the political systems that supported and profited from long-distance trade were very different in the two regions. The West African Sahel became the home of large empires, whereas the independent Swahili trading towns of the coast of east Africa had no interest in establishing or maintaining territorial control. How do we account for the difference? One reason is cultural. The empires of the West African Sahel developed as extensions of preexisting territorial kingdoms, whereas the Swahili trading towns developed a maritime and mercantile culture that placed little value on owning land or controlling territory. Another reason is geographical. The large empires of the West African grasslands needed to control the gateways to the trans-Saharan trade routes in order to maximize their revenues, whereas the Swahili trading towns along the coast of east Africa had direct access to the Indian Ocean world and saw little need to conquer territory in search of wealth. Although the West African Sahel and the Swahili Coast were both responding to the demand for gold in the Mediterranean world and the growing influence of Islam, they did so in very different ways that were shaped by their unique cultural roots and geographical locations.

CHAPTER REVIEW

KEY TERMS AND VOCABULARY

Sahel
Swahili
Ghana Empire
Mali Empire
Sunjata
Timbuktu
Mansa Musa
Songhay Empire
monsoon winds
Great Zimbabwe
Kilwa

STUDY QUESTIONS

1. How did the semi-barren West African Sahel become the home of rich and powerful empires?
2. How do oral traditions enrich our understanding of West African history?
3. How did Ghana, Mali, and Songhay become wealthy and powerful empires even though they failed to gain control of the gold-mining regions?
4. Why was the capital of each successive Sahelian empire located farther east than the previous one?
5. List the factors that made Timbuktu a major center of higher learning. Why did it decline?
6. Why did the gold trade on the East African coast foster independent trading towns instead of large empires?
7. Were the Swahili trading towns oriented mainly toward the Indian Ocean world or toward the African mainland?

PERSPECTIVES

THE GHANA EMPIRE IN 1068

This description of the Ghana Empire was written by the geographer Al-Bakri in 1068. He never left his home region in Muslim Spain, but he collected information from merchants and other travelers who crossed the Sahara Desert on the caravan routes. The geographical term Sudan *comes from the Arabic* Bilad al-Sudan, *which means "the land of the blacks."*

The city of Ghana consists of two towns situated on a plain. One of these towns, which is inhabited by Muslims, is large and possesses twelve mosques, in one of which they assemble for the Friday prayer. There are salaried imams and muezzins, as well as jurists and scholars. In the environs are wells with sweet water, from which they drink and with which they grow vegetables. The king's town is six miles distant from this one and bears the name of Al-Ghaba [The Forest]. Between these two towns there are continuous habitations. The houses of the inhabitants are of stone and acacia wood. The king has a palace and a number of domed dwellings all surrounded with an enclosure like a city wall. In the king's town, and not far from his court of justice, is a mosque where the Muslims who arrive at his court pray. Around the king's town are domed buildings and groves and thickets where the sorcerers of these people, men in charge of the religious cult, live. In them too are their idols and the tombs of their kings. These woods are guarded and none may enter them and know what is there. . . .

On every donkey-load of salt when it is brought into the country their king levies one golden dinar, and two dinars when it is sent out. From a load of copper the king's due is five mithqals, and from a load of other goods ten mithqals. The best gold found in his land comes from the town of Ghiyaru, which is eighteen days' travelling distant from the king's town over a country inhabited by tribes of the Sudan whose dwellings are contiguous.

The nuggets found in all the mines of his country are reserved for the king, only this gold dust being left for the people. But for this the people would accumulate gold until it lost its value. The nuggets may weigh from an ounce to a pound. It is related that the king owns a nugget as large as a big stone. . . .

The king of Ghana, when he calls up his army, can put 200,000 men into the field, more than 40,000 of them archers. The horses in Ghana are very small.

1. *Why was the capital of Ghana arranged in the form of two separate towns?*
2. *What arrangements facilitated the coexistence of Ghanaian religious cults and Islam?*

Source: *Corpus of Early Arabic Sources for West African History*, translated by J. F. P. Hopkins, edited and annotated by N. Levtzion and J. F. P. Hopkins (Cambridge: Cambridge University Press, 1981), pp. 79–81.

THE MALI EMPIRE

Al-Umari was born in Damascus in 1301, but spent many years in Cairo as an official of the Mamluk sultanate. He was in Damascus at the time of Mansa Musa's visit to Cairo, but upon his return to Cairo he obtained information about the Mali Empire from Egyptian officials and merchants. As in the previous reading, the geographical term Sudan, *as used here, means "the land of the blacks."*

This kingdom [of Mali] lies to the south of the extreme west and adjoins the Atlantic Ocean. The king's capital there is the town of BYTY. This country is very hot. The means of subsistence are exiguous, the varieties of food few. The people are tall, with jet black complexion and crinkly hair.

This king is the greatest of the Muslim kings of the Sudan. He rules the most extensive territory, has the most numerous army, is the bravest, the richest, the most fortunate, the most victorious over his enemies, and the best able to distribute benefits.

The truthful and trustworthy *shaykh* Abu Uthman Sa'id al-Dukkali, who lived at BYTY for 35 years and went to and fro in this kingdom, related to me that it is square, its length being four or more months' journey and its width likewise. It lies to the south of Marrakech and the interior of Morocco and is not far from the Atlantic Ocean. It extends in longitude from Muli to Tura on the ocean. It is all inhabited with few exceptions. Under the authority of the sultan of this kingdom is the land of Mafazat al-Tibr. They bring gold dust (*tibr*) to him each year. They are uncouth infidels. If the sultan wished he could extend his authority over them, but the kings of this kingdom have learned by experience that as soon as one of them conquers one of the gold towns and Islam spreads and the muezzin calls to prayer, there the gold there begins to decrease and then disappears, while it increases in the neighboring heathen countries. When they had learned the truth of this by experience they left the gold countries under the control of the heathen people and were content with their vassalage and the tribute imposed on them.

On Mansa Musa's visit to Cairo in 1324.

Gold was at a high price in Egypt until they came in that year. The mithqal did not go below 25 *dirhams* and was generally above, but from that time its value fell and it cheapened in price and has remained cheap till now. The mithqal does not exceed 22 *dirhams* or less. This has been the state of affairs for about twelve years until this day by reason of the large amount of gold which they brought into Egypt and spent there.

The king of this country imports Arab horses and pays high prices for them. His army numbers about 100,000, of whom about 10,000 are cavalry mounted on horses and the remainder infantry without horses or other mounts.

1. *Why did the kings of Mali fail to establish direct control over the goldfields?*
2. *Why did the price of gold in Cairo diminish after 1324?*

Source: *Corpus of Early Arabic Sources for West African History*, translated by J. F. P. Hopkins, edited and annotated by N. Levtzion and J. F. P. Hopkins (Cambridge: Cambridge University Press, 1981), pp. 261–271.

PERSPECTIVES

TIMBUKTU AND THE SONGHAY EMPIRE

Al-Hasan ibn Muhammad al-Wazzan al-Zayyati was a Berber who was educated in Fez, Morocco. Sometime between 1506 and 1510, he accompanied his uncle on a diplomatic mission to the Songhay Empire. In 1518, while returning from a pilgrimage to Mecca, he was captured by Sicilian pirates and presented to Pope Leo X. The following year he was baptized and became known as Leo Africanus. His Description of Africa, *written in 1526, was published in Italian in 1550 and subsequently translated into Latin, French, and English. In this excerpt, he describes Timbuktu.*

The houses of Timbuktu are huts made of stakes daubed with clay, and with straw roofs. In the middle of the town there is a temple built with masoned stones and limestone mortar by an architect of the Béticos [a mountain range in southern Spain], a native of the town of al-Mana, and a large palace built by the same master builder, where the king stays. There are numerous artisans' work-shops, merchants, and in particular, weavers of cotton cloths. The cloths of Europe reach Timbuktu, brought by Barbary merchants.

The women of the town still have the custom of veiling their faces, except for the slaves, who sell all the foodstuffs. The inhabitants are very rich, especially the resident strangers, to the extent that the present king has given two of his daughters in marriage to two merchant brothers, because of their wealth. There are several sweet water wells in Timbuktu. In addition, during the flood season of the Niger, water reaches the town by canals. There is great abundance of cereals and livestock, and hence the consumption of milk and butter is considerable. But salt is in short supply because it is brought from Taghaza, which is about five hundred miles distant from Timbuktu. . . . The king possesses great treasure in coin and gold ingots. One of these ingots weighs 1,300 pounds.

The royal court is very well organized and magnificent. When the king goes from one town to another with his courtiers, he rides a camel, and the horses are led by grooms. . . . When anyone wants to address the king, he kneels before him, takes a handful of dust and sprinkles it over his head and shoulders. . . . The king has some three thousand cavalry, and a huge number of infantry armed with bows made of wild fennel. They fire poisoned arrows. This king only makes war on those neighbors of his who are enemies, and on those who refuse to pay him tribute. When victorious, he has those captured in combat sold in Timbuktu, even the children. . . .

In Timbuktu there are numerous judges, scholars and priests, all well paid by the king. Many manuscript books coming from Barbary are sold. Such sales are more profitable than any other goods.

Instead of coined money they use pieces of pure gold, and for small purchases cowries, that is to say shells brought from Persia, of which four hundred are worth one ducat. . . .

The people of Timbuktu have a light-hearted nature. It is their habit to wander in the town at night between 10 p.m. and 1 a.m., playing musical instruments and dancing. The citizens have many slaves to serve them, both male and female.

1. *What were the main industries in Timbuktu?*
2. *Explain why Timbuktu became a major center for Islamic learning and scholarship.*

Source: Giovan Leoni Africano, *Della discrittione dell'Africa*, in G. B. Ramusio, *Delle navigationi e viaggi* (Venice, 1550), reprinted in *Timbuktu and the Songhay Empire*, translated and edited by John O. Hunwick (Boston: Brill, 1999), pp. 279–282.

IBN BATTUTA SAILS TO KILWA

The Moroccan-born traveler Ibn Battuta visited the East African coast in 1330–1332 after spending 3 years as a Muslim pilgrim in Mecca and Medina. In this excerpt, he describes his trip down the coast to the port of Kilwa, which marked the southernmost reach of the monsoon winds. He noted that Kilwa was a major emporium for the gold trade and also that sharifs (descendants of the Prophet Muhammad) came to Kilwa from as far away as Iraq to enjoy the sultan's largess.

Then I set off by sea from the town of Mogadishu for the land of the Swahili and the town of Kilwa, which is in the land of Zanj. We arrived at Mombasa, a large island two days' journey from the land of the Swahili. The island is quite separate from the mainland. It grows bananas, lemons, and oranges. The people also gather a fruit which they call *jammun*, which looks like an olive. It has a nut like an olive, but its taste is very sweet. The people do not engage in agriculture, but import grain from the Swahili. The greater part of their diet is bananas and fish. They follow the Shafi'i rite, and are devout, chaste, and virtuous. Their mosques are very strongly constructed of wood.

We spent a night on the island and then set sail for Kilwa, the principal town on the coast, the greater part of whose inhabitants are Zanj of very black complexion. Their faces are scarred, like the Limiin at Janada. A merchant told me that Sofala is half a month's march from Kilwa, and that between Sofala and Yufi in the country of the Limiin is a month's march. Powdered gold is brought from Yufi to Sofala.

Kilwa is one of the most beautiful and well-constructed towns in the world. The whole of it is elegantly built. The roofs are built with mangrove poles. There is very much rain. The people are engaged in a holy war, for their country lies beside that of pagan Zanj. The chief qualities are devotion and piety: they follow the Shafi'i rite.

When I arrived, the Sultan was Abu al-Muzaffar Hasan surnamed Abu al-Mawahib [the Father of Gifts] on account of his numerous charitable gifts. He frequently makes raids into the Zanj country, attacks them and carries off booty, of which he reserves a fifth, using it in the manner prescribed by the Quran. That reserved for the kinsfolk of the Prophet is kept separate in the Treasury, and, when Sharifs come to visit him, he gives it them. They come to him from Iraq, the Hijaz, and other countries.

1. *Explain the relationship between the towns of Kilwa and Sofala.*
2. *Why did pilgrims come to Kilwa from distant countries?*

Source: *The East African Coast: Select Documents from the First to the Earlier Nineteenth Century*, compiled by G. S. P. Freeman-Grenville (Oxford: Clarendon Press, 1962), pp. 31–32.

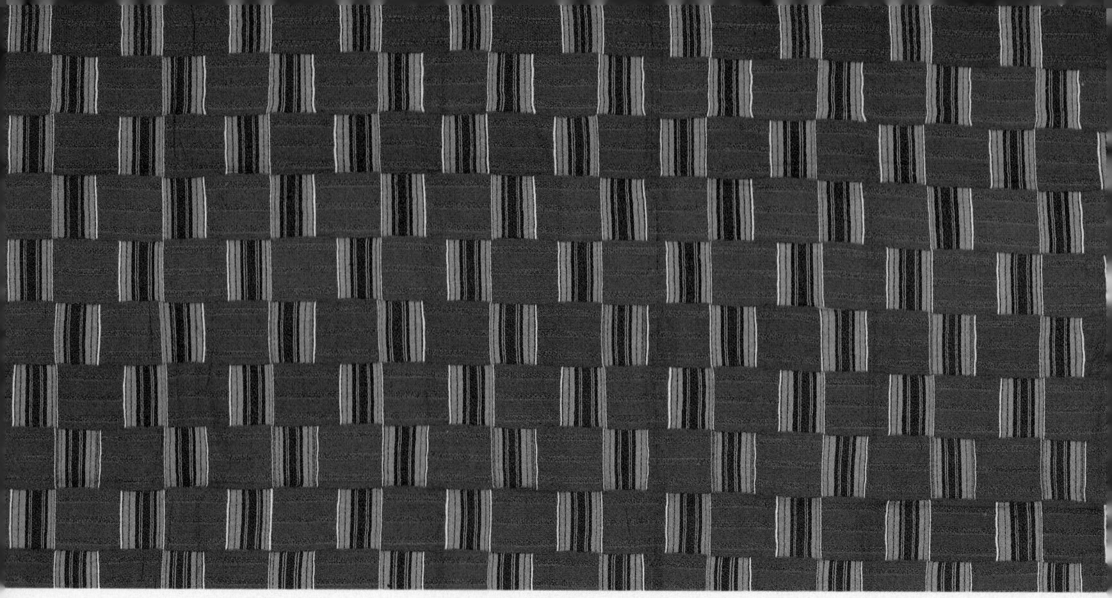

PART 2

AFRICA IN THE AGE OF GLOBAL WAR CAPITALISM, 1400–1800

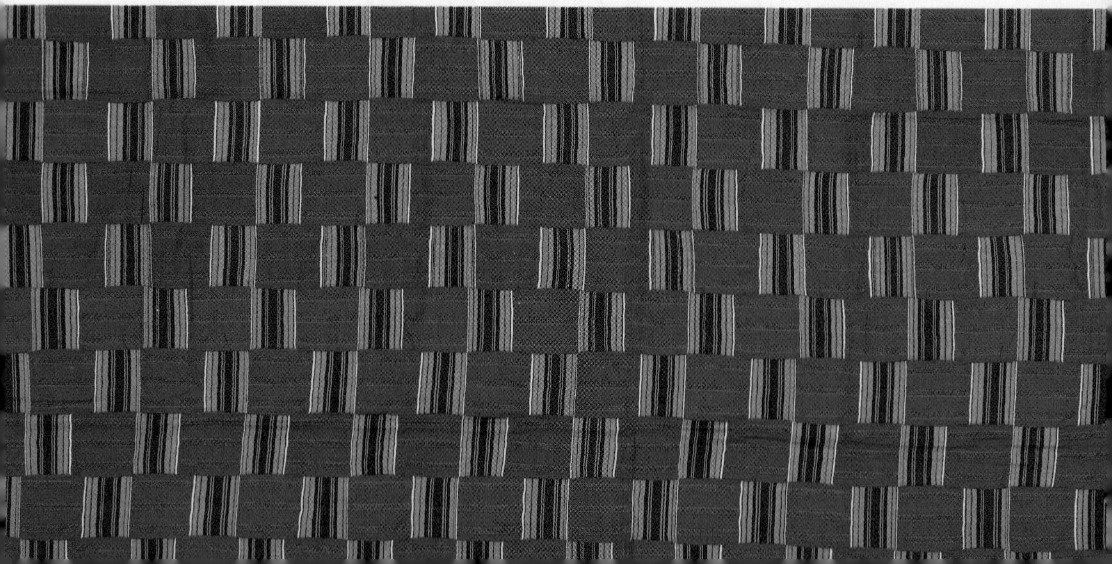

Between 1400 and 1800, the countries on Europe's Atlantic Seaboard created maritime empires that spanned the globe. They sent out warships to seize control of shipping lanes and embarked on military expeditions to conquer territory. In the Indian Ocean, they captured key ports and choke points in order to dominate the trade routes, and they seized control of the spice- and cotton-producing regions. In the Atlantic, they established trading enclaves along the African coast and claimed vast territories in the Americas, where they produced sugar, tobacco, and cotton on plantations worked by enslaved Africans. Because the period between 1400 and 1800 was characterized by armed trade and the violent expropriation of land and labor, the historian Sven Beckert has characterized it as the age of war capitalism.

EARLY WAR CAPITALISM IN THE MEDITERRANEAN WORLD

War capitalism has existed since antiquity, but the immediate precursor to the war capitalism of Atlantic Europe can be found in the Mediterranean world during the Middle Ages. Beginning around 1100, the independent trading cities of Venice and Genoa (in modern Italy) created empires that controlled maritime trade networks rather than land-based territories. Their expansion began during the First Crusade, when they attacked Muslim ports on the eastern shore of the Mediterranean and helped the crusaders establish the Latin Kingdom of Jerusalem, thus gaining privileged access to the spice markets of Southwest Asia. Over the next three centuries, they seized coastal enclaves; trafficked in slaves; engaged in piracy; established plantations on Mediterranean islands; and fought wars against Muslims, Christians, and each other. By 1300, Venice was the most prosperous city in Europe, with Genoa not far behind. Between them, the two city-states dominated commerce in the Mediterranean world.

The prosperity of Venice and Genoa was based on their trade in spices, gold, and captives. Spices from Asia were valued not only for their culinary and aromatic properties, but also because many of them had psychoactive effects when taken in large quantities. The merchants of Venice and Genoa bought spices from Muslim merchants in Egypt and Syria at high prices and were often forced to pay in gold because they lacked products of equivalent value. The spice trade caused a drain on European gold supplies. In 1411 alone, merchants from Venice paid out more than 2 tons of gold ducats to buy spices. Because Europe produced very little gold, the merchants of Venice and Genoa purchased West African gold that arrived at North African ports via the trans-Saharan trade routes, paying as much as nine weights of European silver for one weight of gold. Europeans were well aware that the African gold mines lay south of the Sahara Desert because the mapmakers on the Mediterranean island of Majorca made maps that depicted camel caravans in the desert, the gold of the West African Sahel, King Mansa Musa of Mali holding up a gold nugget, and even a "River of Gold" flowing into the Atlantic at roughly the location of the Senegal River.

MARCO POLO LEAVES VENICE The city-state of Venice used its domination of Mediterranean trade networks to become the most prosperous city in Europe. In 1271, the Venetian merchant Marco Polo left Venice with his father and uncle on a trip to Asia that lasted 24 years. His book describing his travels by land and sea was instrumental in disseminating information about the peoples and commerce of Asia. This picture is from a fifteenth-century illuminated manuscript of Marco Polo's travels.

Venice and Genoa also carried on a lively slave trade in the eastern Mediterranean by purchasing captive Slavs, Tartars, and Turks in ports on the Black Sea. Some of the captives were taken to Egypt, where they were trained to be Mamluk soldiers (see chapter 3); others were taken to Venice and Genoa to work as domestic servants and urban laborers; while the majority labored on sugar plantations that Venetians and Genoese had established on the islands of Cyprus, Crete, and Sicily. Those captive laborers were called *sklabos*, the Latin word for "Slav," which became the basis for the English word *slave*. When the Ottoman Turks captured the Black Sea slaving ports in the 1470s and caused the supply of white captives to dry up, slave traders from Venice and Genoa traveled to the North African ports of Tripoli and Tunis to purchase enslaved Africans who had been brought to North Africa along the trans-Saharan trade routes. The new captives were called *sklavi negri*—"black Slavs." By the 1490s, the "black Slavs" in Sicily outnumbered the "white Slavs."

WAR CAPITALISM GOES GLOBAL

Beginning in the fifteenth century, the style of war capitalism developed in the Mediterranean by Venice and Genoa was replicated in the Atlantic Ocean by Portugal and Spain, and expanded on a worldwide scale. Like the rise of Venice and Genoa, the initial Portuguese expansion was related to the Crusades. In 1415, Prince Henry of Portugal (later known as Prince Henry the Navigator) helped to lead an invasion of Ceuta, a Moroccan port city that looked out on the Strait of Gibraltar. Although his primary goal was to gain a Christian foothold in the Muslim lands of the western Mediterranean, Prince Henry was aware that Ceuta was a major terminus of the trans-Saharan gold trade and a transit point for sending gold across the Strait of Gibraltar to the Spanish Muslim emirate of Granada. After Ceuta fell into Christian hands, however, the Muslim merchants diverted their caravans to Tangier, on Morocco's Atlantic coast. Prince Henry's subsequent assault on Tangier ended in a crushing defeat.

With no hope of tapping into the trans-Saharan caravan routes, Prince Henry encouraged his mariners to push southward beyond the settled parts of the Moroccan coast in order to find a sea route to the gold and other products of the West African Sahel. But they could not sail beyond Cape Bojador, which was seen as a "point of no return" because those mariners who had done so could not overcome the south-flowing Canary Current and the northeast trade winds in order to return home. That problem was solved in the 1430s, when Portuguese mariners learned to escape the Canary Current by sailing far out to sea, beyond the Canary Islands, and picking up the southeasterly winds that would take them back to Portugal. They called that maneuver *volta do mar,* which meant "the turn of the sea." The Portuguese also lacked ships that were maneuverable enough to tack into the fickle winds and small enough to explore

VENETIAN GOLD DUCAT Europe had not minted any gold coins since the seventh century, but in the thirteenth century, both Venice and Genoa began minting coins from West African gold that had been carried across the Sahara by camel caravans. By the fifteenth century, the Venetian gold ducat had become the international trade currency in the eastern Mediterranean.

THE BLACK SEA SLAVE TRADE Between 1250 and 1450, the Black Sea port of Kaffa (now Feodosia in Crimea) was the largest slave market in the Mediterranean world. Genoese ships carried enslaved Tartars, Slavs, and Turks to labor on sugar plantations on Cypress, Crete, and Sicily, and furnished enslaved military recruits to Mamluk Egypt. The Genoese fort at Kaffa, where the captives embarked, now lies in ruins.

coastal inlets and rivers. They solved that problem by modifying a highly maneuverable type of fishing boat known as a *caravel*. Caravels were small ships (40–60 feet in length) powered by lateen rigging (triangular sails mounted on long, movable crossbars). By the 1440s, Portuguese expeditions were using caravels exclusively.

Prince Henry's efforts to circumvent the trans-Saharan caravan routes were very successful. In 1456, Portuguese ships traveled up the Gambia River and purchased sufficient gold to allow the Portuguese Crown to issue a type of gold coin, called the *cruzado*, the following year. Fifteen years later, Portuguese ships reached the Gold Coast, where they purchased gold in such great quantities that the king of Portugal proclaimed a royal monopoly over the gold trade. In 1498, a Portuguese fleet commanded by Vasco da Gama rounded the southern tip of Africa and sailed all the way to India, landing on the pepper-rich Malabar Coast. The peppers they brought back to Portugal were worth six times the cost of the expedition. The Portuguese had not only gained direct access to African gold and Indian spices, but had also developed the capacity to reach any part of the Old World by sea.

Five years before Vasco da Gama left Portugal to sail to India, Christopher Columbus left a Spanish port and sailed west into the Atlantic Ocean to seek a shortcut to the spice islands of Asia. Columbus was born and raised in Genoa and was well acquainted with its tradition of war capitalism. After his search for a royal sponsor had been rebuffed in Genoa, Venice, and Portugal, he finally gained the backing of the Spanish Crown. Between 1492 and 1503, he made four voyages that visited a number of Caribbean islands as well as the coasts of Central America and Venezuela. When he died in Spain in 1506, he still believed that he had discovered a new route to Asia, even though he had failed to find any of the common Asian spices.

After 1500, Spain and Portugal expanded their commercial reach to all parts of the globe and developed a system of global war capitalism that claimed sovereignty over vast areas of land and sea. The Netherlands, England, France, and

Denmark soon joined them as the hub of European maritime commerce shifted from the Mediterranean world to the Atlantic Seaboard. There were significant differences among the operations of global war capitalism in different parts of the world. In the Americas, countries such as Spain, Portugal, France, and England claimed vast inland territories, where they encouraged the production of mood-altering commodities such as sugar and tobacco by providing cheap land and slave labor for European settlers who wished to establish plantations. In Asia, global war capitalism was largely about monopolizing existing production and trade using chartered companies that had quasi-governmental authority to wage war, sign treaties, establish colonies, and administer territories. In Africa, European ships came mostly to trade, not to claim territory or create plantation economies. Even though European trading companies built trading forts on islands or the seashore, they generally refrained from seizing land from African kings and chiefs. That pattern can be partially explained by the nefarious nature of the trade that the Europeans conducted: human trafficking in enslaved Africans.

The trans-Atlantic slave trade provided captive African labor for the New World's plantations in the aftermath of the demographic collapse of its indigenous peoples, who lacked immunity to the diseases introduced by Europeans. As such, the slave trade was an integral component of global war capitalism. Although it has frequently been pictured as a triangle in which ships moved between Europe, Africa, and the New World, a more complete picture would show that the supply chains that fed into the slave trade extended all the way to India and beyond. The cotton cloth that Europeans exchanged for African captives was imported from India because cotton did not grow in the cool climate of Europe, and the cowrie shells that served as a currency along the West African coast were imported from the Maldives in the Indian Ocean. The trans-Atlantic slave trade enriched Indian cloth merchants, New World sugar planters, and European slave traders, but its impact on Africa was devastating. Africans paid a high price in lives, bondage, and forced labor in a system of global war capitalism that enhanced economic growth in some parts of the world at the expense of others.

CASTLE OF THE MINE The castle called St. George of the Mine (later known as Elmina) was built by the Portuguese to facilitate the gold trade. This illustration shows the castle in 1574, with the African town on the left. The inscription reads: "The town of St. George, called Mina, was built on the orders of King John II of Portugal, in Guinea in 1482. The Moorish merchants bring bullion, for which they receive from the Christians red and yellow linen and similarly sought-after goods." Note the two Portuguese caravels in the foreground.

1482	**1507**	**1650s**
Portuguese build Elmina Castle	Afonso seizes Kongo throne	Expansion of Denkyira

5

ATLANTIC AFRICA AND THE CREATION OF THE ATLANTIC WORLD, 1400–1700

If the Mediterranean, Saharan, and Indian Ocean shores of Africa were the major zones of Africa's commercial and cultural interaction with the wider world prior to 1400, then the Atlantic coast was Africa's backwater. African mariners in Atlantic coastal villages and towns had seafaring canoes that they used for fishing and coastal trade, but they didn't venture very far out to sea, in part because of the strong currents that ran parallel to the coast. That is why Atlantic islands such as São Tomé, Principe, and the Cape Verde Islands were uninhabited before 1450. Like Europeans prior to Christopher Columbus, Africans could only speculate as to what lay beyond the ocean. The people of the Kongo Kingdom, for example, believed that beyond the waters lay the Land of the Dead.

This chapter explores what happened when European war capitalism came into contact with the kingdoms and chiefdoms on Africa's Atlantic coast. Although Europeans purchased commodities such as gold, ivory, spices, resins, and hides, their main interest was in obtaining African captives whom they could exploit as slave laborers on the plantations of the New World. In the face of strong African resistance, they quickly abandoned their initial tactic of raiding coastal villages. Instead, they began to create fortified trading enclaves in order to engage

1656	1669	1672–1677
Queen Njinga's treaty with Portuguese	Soyo sacks the capital of Kongo	War of the Marabouts in Senegambia

in sustained human trafficking. Their switch in tactics from raiding to trading put pressure on coastal African rulers to meet or resist their ever-increasing demand for captives, causing turmoil, rebellions, and civil wars within the African kingdoms themselves.

The repercussions were devastating for millions of Africans. The *Trans-Atlantic Slave Trade Database*, which contains information on over 35,000 separate slaving voyages and uses statistical projections to fill in the gaps in the data, shows that over 12.5 million captives were taken out of Africa between 1501 and 1866, and that over 1.8 million of them died tragically during the Atlantic crossing. Of the 10.7 million Africans who were landed in the New World to spend their lives toiling as slaves, only about 400,000 were brought to North America; the rest went mostly to the sugar-producing regions in the Caribbean and Brazil.

The trans-Atlantic slave trade took a terrible toll on its victims: enslavement deprived them of their birthright in their families and communities, and slave trading turned them into commodities that could be bought and sold. Much historical writing about the trans-Atlantic slave trade has rightly focused on the terrible physical sufferings of the captives, but the psychological displacement of being stripped of one's identity and having no way to reclaim it was perhaps equally devastating. That is why the historical sociologist Orlando Patterson has described enslavement as "social death."

In order to discuss slavery as a *process* rather than a fixed status, this chapter employs a model by which a person who was enslaved through warfare, kidnapping, or judicial condemnation is referred to as a "captive" throughout the period of displacement via overland slave caravans and slave ships. It was only after the captive arrived at his or her ultimate destination (either in Africa or the Americas), was purchased by a master, and settled into a slave community that the person is referred to as a "slave." If enslavement resulted in "social death," then purchase by a master gave the person a new identity and community, albeit ones that were totally determined by the needs and desires of the master.

THE BEGINNING OF THE TRANS-ATLANTIC SLAVE TRADE

In 1443, Prince Henry of Portugal gained direct access to West African gold when he received a royal monopoly on Portuguese trade along the Atlantic coast of Africa south of Cape Bojador. His first commercial venture was organized by Lançarote de Freitas, a tax collector who had grown up in Prince Henry's household. Sailing south along the coast of the Sahara Desert with a fleet of six caravels, Lançarote found no gold, but instead brought back 235 Muslim Berbers he had captured in a surprise attack on the small coastal island of Tidra. Forty-six of them (the royal fifth) were claimed by Prince Henry, while the others were sold at auction and dispersed throughout Portugal. As a reward for his plunder, Lançarote was knighted. The prince then dispatched a caravel commanded by Gonçallo de Sintra to obtain more captives, but this time the Portuguese were met by 300 armed defenders, who killed de Sintra and six members of his raiding party. The ship returned to Portugal with only two captives.

African resistance to the Portuguese attacks was even stronger when the expeditions passed the Senegal River and reached the region that the Portuguese called Guinea—the land of the blacks (from *aguinaou*, the Berber word for a black person). When a fleet of five caravels sailed south along the coast from the Senegal River to Cape Verde in 1445, they were afraid to land because they feared the poisoned iron arrowheads used by the Africans. It was said that even a slight scratch from these arrows could result in death a day or two later. African defenses were equally effective at the mouth of the Gambia River in 1446, when a Portuguese knight named Nuno Tristam anchored his caravel and set out in two longboats with 22 armed men to attack a riverside village. Suddenly they were challenged by 12 African war canoes containing 70–80 men armed with bows and poisoned arrows. Twenty of the Portuguese raiders were killed, including Nuno Tristam. The seven crew members who had remained behind on the ship were so eager to escape that they didn't even bother to hoist up the anchor and the longboats. They simply cut the ropes and sailed away.

Reviewing the mixed record of Portuguese successes and disasters in the early 1450s, Prince Henry decided that it would be more profitable and considerably less dangerous to engage in peaceful trade with the Africans. He dispatched three ships under the command of Diogo Gomes in 1456 to negotiate trade agreements with African rulers. By recruiting African interpreters who could explain that his mission was peaceful, and by giving generous gifts, Gomes made peace with several African

REPLICA OF A PORTUGUESE CARAVEL
Caravels were small, highly maneuverable ships with lateen rigging (triangular sails mounted on long, movable crossbars) that allowed the ships to sail close to the wind. Prince Henry's decision to use caravels for the exploration of the Atlantic coast of Africa helps to explain why the missions he sent out succeeded although others before them had failed.

rulers who had previously attacked Portuguese ships. Near the mouth of the Gambia River, he purchased gold in exchange for cloth and thick brass bracelets. A few months later, Alvise Cadamosto sailed up the Gambia River and successfully bartered European trade goods for gold and captives. Those expeditions set the pattern of trading for the next four centuries, by which Europeans bartered for gold, ivory, and captives with African rulers and merchants.

The Growth of the Trans-Atlantic Slave Trade

During the 50 years after Lançarote de Freitas delivered his first load of African captives to Portugal, the Portuguese made contact with Africans all along the Atlantic coast, reaching the Gold Coast (modern Ghana) in 1471 and the mouth of the Congo River in 1482. This coastal region would quickly change from a commercial backwater to the major zone of interaction between Africa and the wider Atlantic world. The number of captives being taken from Africa was still relatively small—about a thousand per year in the 1480s, climbing to 2,500 per year in 1490. While many of the captives were taken to Lisbon and Seville to work as household servants or urban laborers, an increasing number were purchased to work on sugar plantations that Portuguese settlers had started on the Atlantic islands of Madeira and São Tomé or on Spanish sugar plantations in the Canary Islands.

A major expansion of the slave trade came in the wake of Christopher Columbus's second voyage to the New World in 1493, when he brought sugarcane to the island of Hispaniola (now Haiti and the Dominican Republic). The Spanish settlers there planned to enslave the indigenous Tainu people to work on their sugar plantations, but the Tainu were rapidly decimated by smallpox and other European diseases to which they had no immunity, as well as by the harsh conditions of enslavement by the Spanish colonists. The Tainu population plummeted from over 300,000 in 1492 to roughly 10,000 by 1515. A Spanish report written in 1542 stated that there were no native people left in the Bahamas, Jamaica, Cuba, or Puerto Rico. In response to this complete demographic collapse (which has been called genocide), King Ferdinand of Spain authorized the transportation of 4,000 captives directly from Africa to Spain's New World colonies. Because a Spanish-Portuguese treaty signed in 1479 had forbidden Spain to trade in Africa, the captives were carried on Portuguese ships. That was the beginning of the trans-Atlantic slave trade.

During the sixteenth century, the Portuguese exercised a near monopoly on the trans-Atlantic slave trade as sugar production in the Portuguese colony of Brazil expanded rapidly after 1550. The Dutch challenged Portuguese dominance in the seventeenth century by driving them from their trading forts on the Gold Coast and in Angola. English involvement in the slave trade also developed in the seventeenth century, driven mostly by the demand for labor on the sugar plantations of Barbados and later Jamaica. French demand for African captives arose after 1640, when sugar production began in France's Caribbean colonies: Guadeloupe, Martinique, and Saint-Domingue. Because the Spanish were forbidden by treaty from trading in Africa, they contracted with other European nations to bring captives to the Spanish colonies in the New World. That contract, known as the *asiento*, would be held successively by the Portuguese, the Dutch, the French, and the English. All of the European trading nations initially conducted their trans-Atlantic slave trade through government-chartered companies. Private slave traders were considered interlopers; if caught, they could be arrested, and their cargoes could be confiscated.

Justifying the Slave Trade

One reason why the trans-Atlantic slave trade was able to implant itself in Africa at this time was a considerable body of thought among Christians, Muslims, and Africans that accepted the existence of slavery as part of the normal order of things. Instead of condemning slavery, they sought to limit its damage by focusing on the issues of who could legitimately be enslaved and who was exempt from enslavement. In Europe, according to ancient practice, all prisoners of war could be enslaved, but by 1300, most Europeans had accepted the Catholic Church's policy that Christians could enslave only infidels who had been taken in a just war. In 1452, when the Portuguese were still in the early stages of their exploration of Africa's Atlantic coast, Pope Nicholas V issued a papal bull (*Dum Diversas*) to King Afonso V that allowed the Portuguese to "invade, search out, capture, and subjugate the Saracens [Muslims] and pagans and any other unbelievers and enemies of Christ . . . and to reduce their persons to perpetual slavery." That pronouncement was based on the idea that any war against Muslims was an extension of the Crusades, and was therefore a just war.

After the Portuguese started to purchase black African captives who were not Muslims, the just war argument no longer applied. A subsequent papal bull (*Romanus Pontifex*) issued jointly to King Afonso V and Prince Henry the Navigator in 1455 permitted enslavement by purchase: "Many Guineamen and other negroes taken by force, and some by barter of non-prohibited articles, or by other lawful contract of purchase, have been sent to the said kingdoms [Portugal and Algarve]. A large number of these have been converted to the Catholic faith." The pope seemed to imply that the possibility of converting Africans to Christianity justified exploiting them as slaves, but the Portuguese military theoretician Fernando Oliviera pointed out the contradiction in that argument. He noted that if the goal of enslavement was religious conversion, then slaves who converted to Christianity should be freed, and their children, who were born and baptized as Christians in Portugal, should never be slaves at all.

Islamic law forbade Muslims to enslave other Muslims, but they were free to enslave pagans or infidels captured in war. The Islamic scholar Ahmad Baba, who lived in Timbuktu, insisted that it was permissible for Muslims to enslave unbelievers. In a treatise on slavery that he wrote in the early seventeenth century, he stated that "the reason for slavery is unbelief, and the unbelievers of the Sudan [black Africa] are like any other unbelievers in this regard—Jews, Christians, Persians, Berbers, or any others who persist in unbelief and do not embrace Islam. Whoever is enslaved in a state of unbelief may rightly be owned, whoever he is." Concerned that the wars between Muslim kingdoms in the West African Sahel often resulted in the enslavement of Muslims by other Muslims, he drew up a list of which populations were fair game for enslavement and which were off limits.

The idea that human beings could be bought and sold under certain circumstances was not alien to African thought. Most African societies practiced some form of domestic slavery by which prisoners of war or convicted criminals were forcibly removed from their home communities and sold into alien communities, where they lived as socially marginal outsiders under the control of a master. Lacking kinsmen to support and protect them, they were vulnerable to being exploited for economic, political, or social purposes. The majority of slaves in sub-Saharan Africa were women, in part because women and children predominated among those enslaved through warfare. Female slaves filled major roles in agricultural production (just as they did in their home communities), and they also served as domestic servants or as concubines who bore children that enlarged their masters' households. In the internal slave markets, women generally brought higher prices than men.

African societies had a variety of civil laws and customary practices that regulated who could or could not be enslaved. There seemed to be a general consensus, for example, that kings should not enslave or export their own subjects. King Afonso of the Kongo Kingdom believed so strongly that no Kongo subjects should be enslaved that he established a special board to inspect all captives being exported. Some kings in the Senegambia region, in contrast, enslaved some of their own subjects, but that practice provoked a series of popular rebellions. Even politically decentralized societies had rules about who could be enslaved. The Igbo writer Olaudah Equiano wrote in the eighteenth century that the politically decentralized Igbo sold only "prisoners of war, or such among us who had been convicted of kidnapping, or adultery, and some other crimes which we esteemed heinous." He also noted that when African slave merchants brought slaves through Igbo territory, "the strictest account is exacted of their manner of procuring them before they are suffered to pass."

Trading Regions of Atlantic Africa

Five major trading regions emerged along Africa's Atlantic coast during the first 250 years of the slave trade era. These regions, in order from north to south along the coast, are: Senegambia, where the depredations of the kings resulted in a series of popular revolts; the Sierra Leone coast, where European traders integrated themselves into African communities; the Gold Coast, where the Portuguese initially brought captives *into* the area and traded them for gold; the Kongo Kingdom, which became recognized by the pope as one of the world's Christian kingdoms; and Angola, where the Portuguese established a settler colony that waged a century of war against its African neighbors. Each trade region serves as a different case study, demonstrating that the trans-Atlantic slave trade had very different consequences for different parts of Africa's Atlantic coast.

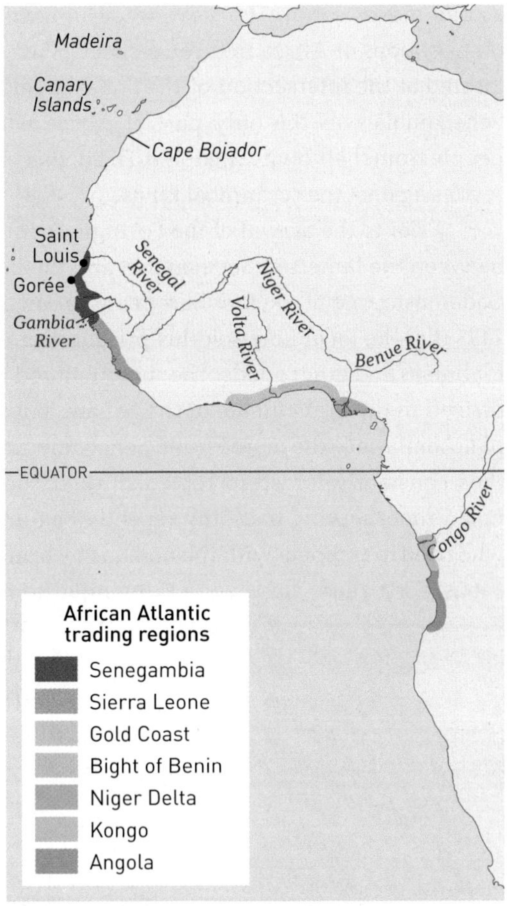

ATLANTIC COAST TRADING REGIONS This map shows the major trading regions along the Atlantic coast of Africa between 1500 and 1800. Five of them—Senegambia, Sierra Leone, Gold Coast, Kongo, and Angola—are discussed in this chapter. The Bight of Benin and the Niger Delta, which were most heavily affected by the slave trade after 1700, are discussed in chapter 6.

SENEGAMBIA

The geographical region referred to as **Senegambia** is outlined by the Senegal River to the north and the Gambia River to the south. The land north of the Senegal River is semidesert occupied by Berber nomads, whereas the land between the two rivers is mostly grassland savanna that is sparse in the north and grows lusher as one moves south. The slave trade in Senegambia differed from that in most other regions of Africa in three respects. First, the kingdoms in Senegambia were located at the intersection of the Saharan and Atlantic trading systems. Second, Senegambia was the only part of Africa where kings would enslave and sell people from their own kingdoms. Third, this practice triggered a series of popular revolts against the tyrannical kings.

Prior to the arrival of the Portuguese in 1446, there had been a robust trade between the famers of Senegambia and the Berber nomads in the Sahara. Alvise Cadamosto, one of the first Europeans to sail along the Senegal River, reported in 1455 that the local king sold his prisoners of war to the desert nomads in return for horses and other goods. The thoroughbred Barbary horses used by the nomads thrived in the arid climate of the Sahara, but were vulnerable to dying from trypanosomiasis in the more humid Senegambian Sahel. Armies in Senegambia were thus constantly forced to replenish their supply of cavalry horses. Cadamosto noted that the king had only recently begun to sell captives to the Portuguese, who tried to compete with the nomads by bringing in Spanish horses. By the early 1460s, Portuguese ships were bringing in so many Spanish horses that the price dropped from twelve captives per horse to six. The influx of cavalry horses sparked an uptick in slaving and other military activity.

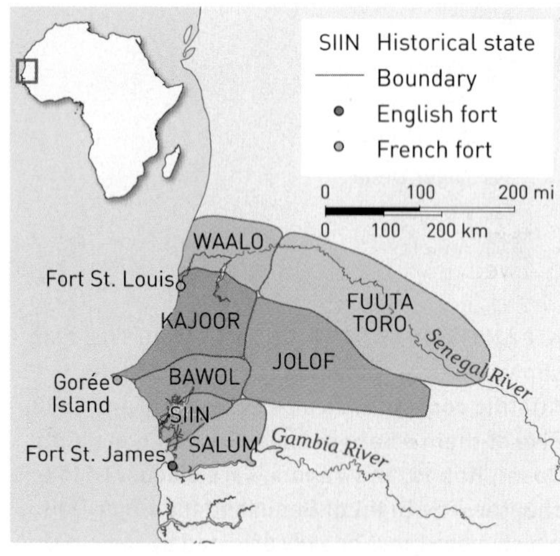

KINGDOMS OF SENEGAMBIA This map shows the major kingdoms in the region between the Senegal and Gambia rivers between 1550 and 1700. The coastal kingdoms of Kajoor and Bawol were very powerful because they were often ruled by the same king. All of the kingdoms shown here were affected by Nasir al-Din's revolution.

When the Portuguese first arrived, all of coastal Senegambia was under the control of the powerful Jolof Kingdom. The Portuguese geographer Valentim Fernandes reported in 1507 that the Jolof king had a cavalry of 8,000 horsemen, who rode mostly thoroughbred Barbary horses, along with a much smaller number of Spanish horses. Under the authority of the king were a series of noble titleholders, corresponding roughly, Fernandez claimed, to Portuguese dukes and counts. The political unity of the Jolof

Kingdom would be challenged after 1549, when the coastal provinces of Kajoor, Bawol, and Waalo broke away and become independent kingdoms, while the remainder of the Jolof Kingdom hung on in the hinterland as a much diminished state. One reason for the breakup was that the coastal provinces could get cavalry horses directly from the Portuguese slave traders and used them to build up armies that were independent of the Jolof rulers.

The nature of Senegambia's Atlantic commerce changed in the seventeenth century as other European nations began to challenge Portuguese dominance. In 1651, the English built Fort St. James on an island in the mouth of the Gambia River, which gave them a monopoly on the trade in gold and captives along the Gambia. In 1659, the French built Fort St. Louis on an island in the mouth of the Senegal River, where they traded for cattle hides, ivory, gum arabic (used in dyeing cloth), and captives. In 1677, they captured Gorée Island (a mile off the coast of Cape Verde), which had previously changed hands several times as it had been fought over by the Dutch, the Portuguese, and the English. In addition to protecting their monopolies, the forts allowed the European trading companies to store commodities and hold captives until a company ship arrived to pick them up. It is significant that the Europeans built their forts on offshore islands so as not to encroach on the lands of the local kings.

Nasir al-Din and the War of the Marabouts

Up to 1675, about a thousand African captives per year were taken away from the Senegambia region by European slave ships. Many of the captives had been taken prisoner in the wars that broke out between the various kingdoms in the region, but others had been enslaved by their own kings. Cadamosto reported in 1455 that the Jolof king "supports himself by raids, which result in many slaves from his own as well as neighboring countries." He later observed that the governor of Kajoor "exacts obedience and fear from the people by selling their wives and children." Half a century later, Valentim Fernandes noted that the Sereer people near the Gambia River maintained a decentralized political system with no kings or lords because they feared that a sovereign ruler would "sell their wives and children, as was done in other places."

It was that method of enslavement that lay behind the series of rebellions that broke out in the 1670s. Those rebellions have come to be known by historians as the **War of the Marabouts**. They were led by a young Mauritanian *marabout* (itinerant Muslim preacher/teacher) named Nasir al-Din. During the 1660s, he preached Islamic religious reform among the Berbers of the desert and gained authority as a religious leader. In 1672, when he was not yet 30 years old, he sent a delegation to the kingdom of Fuuta Toro, along the middle Senegal River, with the

MARABOUT The term *marabout* referred to a Muslim cleric and teacher in the West African Sahel. Like Nasir al-Din, many marabouts were itinerant evangelists. This painting of a marabout who lived near the Senegal River was made by Abbé David Boilat in the 1840s. It shows the marabout wearing a full robe with a shawl over his shoulders. Nasir al-Din, in contrast, shunned elaborate vestments.

message that the kings should be more diligent in their prayers, limit themselves to three or four wives, and get rid of their bards and minstrels. If they did not change their ways, he would declare them enemies of God, take up the sword, and throw them out of their kingdoms to be replaced by rulers of his own choosing.

After the king of Fuuta Toro had rejected seven successive delegations, Nasir al-Din entered the kingdom with a group of armed followers. He traveled through the countryside from village to village. Rejecting the elaborate robes worn by most marabouts, he appeared almost naked and with a shaved head. He told the villagers that God would not permit the king to pillage, kill, or enslave the common people. The kings, he said, existed to serve the people, not the other way around. Converts to his movement tore off their clothes and shaved their heads as signs of submission, and the marabout's armed following grew larger with each village he visited. As the reformers approached the capital, the king fled into exile, leaving Nasir al-Din free to appoint Muslim reformers to govern the kingdom.

Having secured a base south of the Senegal River, Nasir al-Din turned his attention to the kingdoms nearer to the coast. His army of reformers conquered the Jolof Kingdom, replaced the king with a Muslim cleric, and put Muslim clerics in charge of every village. The coastal kingdom of Waalo, near the mouth of the Senegal River, put up strong resistance, but finally succumbed to the Muslim reformers. In Kajoor, the most powerful of the coastal kingdoms, the reformers were aided by the ex–Queen Mother, who formed an alliance with a local Muslim cleric to rally support for Nasir al-Din's invading army.

As the Islamic reform movement advanced from success to success, it began to pick up millenarian overtones: some of its followers came to believe that God would make the crops grow without being planted. Only 2 years after the beginning of his reform movement, Nasir al-Din was killed in a battle against a Berber group north of the Senegal River. His movement soon fractured as his followers squabbled over who would replace him, and many farmers who had expected their crops to grow by themselves became disillusioned and turned against the reformers. Seeing their chance, the deposed royal families began plotting their comeback and sought military aid from the French in Fort St. Louis. By the end of 1677, the reformers had been driven out of all the kingdoms south of the Senegal River.

Latsukaabe Faal's Reforms

During the quarter century following the death of Nasir al-Din, the number of captives coming out of the Senegambian region doubled to over 2,000 per year. A partial explanation comes from the French traveler Le Maire, who reported in 1685 that the king of Waalo "often makes people slaves for the least shadow of offense." Three years later, a French priest named Jean-Baptiste Gaby observed that "the kings have no right to impose any tribute on their people. All their revenues are in the form of captives and livestock. They often go to pillage their subjects on the pretext that they have defamed them, committed theft, or been found guilty of murder. As a result, no one is secure in his possessions or his freedom because their kings take them off as captives. This was the cause of the revolution in their kingdoms." Only a decade after the expulsion of the Muslim reformers, the abuses that they had fought against were as rampant as ever.

In the 1690s, however, that situation began to change when a usurper named Latsukaabe Faal gained power in the coastal kingdoms of Kajoor and Bawol and instituted the very reforms that the War of the Marabouts had failed to achieve. Even though his father was the king of Bawol, Latsukaabe was not eligible to succeed to the throne because his mother was not of noble lineage. After his father's death, he defeated his rival half-brothers in battle and took the throne of Bawol in 1692. He then moved with his army into neighboring Kajoor, where he won support from the common people by promising to protect them from oppression by the nobility. By 1695, Latsukaabe was in control of both Bawol and Kajoor. He ended the practice of raiding villages within the borders of his kingdom and instituted a tax by which each family supplied one animal from its herd and one granary full of millet each year. The Islamic revolutions in Senegambia in the 1670s had demonstrated that the common people would not tolerate being pillaged and enslaved by their kings. Although those revolutions ultimately failed to restrain the power of the kings, Latsukaabe's reforms finally achieved that purpose.

THE SIERRA LEONE COAST

The Atlantic coast south of the Gambia River was referred to by Portuguese mariners as **Sierra Leone** because it contained a mountain that looked like the head of a lion. The Sierra Leone coast encompassed the modern nations of Guinea-Bissau, Guinea, and Sierra Leone. As a trading region, the Sierra Leone coast differed from Senegambia in two respects. First, trade in Senegambia was concentrated along the Senegal and Gambia Rivers, making it easy for a European trading company to build a fort near a river's mouth and claim a monopoly. Sierra Leone, in contrast, had a variety of inlets and small rivers where small Portuguese ships could land, thus negating the monopolistic advantages of trading forts. The second difference was that Sierra Leone was organized politically into small chiefdoms that maintained their independence even as large, powerful states arose in their hinterlands. Because of the fragmented political landscape, Portuguese traders needed to develop trading relationships with a variety of local chiefs instead of negotiating with just a few kings, as the English and French did in Senegambia.

Lançados and Their Descendants

The trading system that developed along the Sierra Leone coast was run by Portuguese traders who left the Cape Verde Islands and settled permanently on the African mainland. They were generally referred to as ***lançados***, meaning "those who were thrown out," or, alternatively, "those who threw themselves onto African soil." The reasons why certain individuals chose to become lançados are largely unknown, but we know that many of them were so-called New Christians—that is, Jews who had fled from the Spanish Inquisition of the 1480s to Portugal, where they were forced to convert to Christianity. Fearing religious persecution in Portugal, the New Christians scattered in all directions, from Amsterdam to the Ottoman Empire, and some settled in the Cape Verde Islands and in trading settlements along the Sierra Leone coast.

In order to be successful traders, the lançados had to accommodate themselves to the cultural norms of the majority African population, thus creating a hybrid or multiethnic culture. As outsiders, the lançados placed themselves under the protection of African chiefs and community leaders who guaranteed their personal safety and the security of their trade goods in return for an annual payment of rent. African chiefs would not sell land to the lançados, but rented them only enough for a house and a warehouse. Once established as traders, they purchased gold, cloth, ivory, hides, and captives in exchange for European trade goods that arrived via the Cape Verde Islands.

Lançados usually came to the Sierra Leone coast as single men who sought African wives in order to start a family and establish a social presence. In a region where local customs allowed a man to have more than one wife, lançados sought to marry the daughters of important chiefs or women who had gained wealth and status through trade. The wives were valuable interpreters of the local language and culture and were often skilled traders themselves. The children of those marriages, called *filhos da terra* (children of the soil) by the Portuguese, often inherited their mother's social rank and the right to cultivate land. Raised by their African mothers to speak African languages as well as Portuguese, they could take advantage of their dual identity to negotiate trade deals with Africans and Portuguese alike.

As several generations passed, the descendants of the original lançados became progressively more African in appearance and culture, yet they retained their Portuguese names, professed Catholicism, and spoke Crioulo (a mixture of African languages and Portuguese) along with one or more African languages. No longer called lançados, these people, who can be referred to as Eurafricans (Africans with varying degrees of European ancestry), combined elements of European and African culture into a new synthesis. The director of the French Senegal Company described the Eurafricans living along the Gambia River in 1685 as a class of blacks and mulattos who spoke Crioulo and identified as Portuguese. Living in earthen-walled houses built in the Portuguese style, they wore hats, shirts, and breeches like a European, and frequently carried a gun. They always wore a large crucifix around the neck and bore the name of a saint, even though for the most part they were neither baptized nor showed any evidence of practicing the Christian religion. When they were among Africans, they prayed Muslim prayers, but when they were in the company of European Catholics, they took out their rosary beads to pray. Using African-style dugout canoes that could carry more than 10 tons, they controlled the commerce along the Gambia River.

Signares and Other Women Traders

From the beginning, women were important figures in Eurafrican trade networks, and the French and English slave traders who arrived on the Sierra Leone coast after 1650 valued Eurafrican women as wives or domestic partners. Such women were addressed by titles such as *nhara*, *senora*, and *signare*, terms that denoted

SIGNARE The signares were the accomplished and elegant African wives of French Senegal Company employees who lived on the islands of St. Louis and Gorée. Many of the signares owned houses and operated businesses, and they often established independent households when their husbands died or returned to France. This signare was painted in the 1840s by Abbé David Boilat, who was himself the son of a signare.

a woman of property and high social standing. Those women generally possessed their own houses and domestic slaves, along with gold and silver jewelry and elegant clothes. The best-known Eurafrican women were the signares who lived on the small islands of Gorée and St. Louis along the coast of Senegambia, which contained trading forts owned by the French Senegal Company. Because women traders controlled the local commerce on those islands, partnerships developed between them and the French men who worked for the company. By 1690, the company reported that all of the French men were cohabitating with African women. When the company refused to permit the men to marry African women in Catholic marriages, they began to marry the women according to African marriage customs, which usually included paying a bride-price to the wife's family, financing a wedding feast, and providing her with a house. If the husband died or was recalled to France (both of which happened frequently), the wife was free to remarry. Some women accumulated great wealth in slaves, houses, and other possessions as a result of successive marriages.

In addition to managing their households and domestic slaves, signares were active in the local trade in cattle hides, millet, salt, and cotton cloth. Many of them had as many as 30–40 slaves, whom they sent on an annual voyage up the Senegal River to buy gold from Bambuk in exchange for salt. Some signares were very wealthy. The signare known as Princess Pinetica was both the wife of the French commander of Gorée Island and the niece of the king of Waalo. Her house on Gorée Island was described as a "sort of palace," where she was served by numerous slaves. Of the thirteen private properties on Gorée Island in 1749, nine belonged to signares. While French employees of the French Senegal Company came and went, the signares stayed in Senegal, where they combined certain features of African and European society to create an attractive and elegant lifestyle.

The signares of Senegal were not personally involved in the trans-Atlantic slave trade (although their French husbands were), but some Eurafrican women living farther south along the Sierra Leone coast were major participants in the slave trade. They included Betsy Heard, who owned the principal wharf at the trading port of Bereira and operated trading vessels along the coast; Elizabeth Frazer, who built a trading establishment called Victoria that facilitated the transport of captives between the Rio Pongo and Bissau; and Mary Faber, who used her private slave army to dominate trade along the upper Rio Pongo. The fragmented trading networks along the Sierra Leone coast provided openings for Eurafrican women as well as men.

THE GOLD COAST

The region that came to be called the **Gold Coast** was characterized by a rocky coastline punctuated by headlands and cliffs. Along the coast was a narrow strip of coastal grassland 10–30 miles wide. Behind that lay a belt of tropical rainforest (sometimes referred to as the Akan forest) that extended inland for 150–200 miles before yielding to the drier woodland savanna in the north. Gold was found mainly in the rainforest area. The Gold Coast presents an interesting contrast to Senegambia because, for the first hundred years after their arrival, Europeans brought captives *into* the region instead of taking them out. Why that was so, and why it changed in the seventeenth century, are key issues in Gold Coast history.

Prior to the arrival of the Portuguese, the gold mined in the Akan forest had been carried north for hundreds of miles through the Mali heartland to Jenne, on the Niger bend (see chapter 4). From there, it was carried by boat along the Niger River to Timbuktu, where it was transferred to camels for the trek across the Sahara Desert. When the Portuguese arrived on the Gold Coast in 1471, they discovered that the Africans weighed their gold using the Arabic unit of weight, the *mithqal*, which reflected their commercial orientation toward the Arab world. But the Africans were eager to sell gold to the Portuguese because the seafaring trade diminished transportation costs and eliminated most of the middlemen, making it possible for them to charge higher prices.

In 1474, the Portuguese king made trade with the Gold Coast a royal monopoly because its gold was becoming a major source of revenue for the Portuguese Crown. In response, the Spanish began to attack Portuguese merchant ships in hopes of seizing gold, and in 1478, they sent a fleet of 35 ships to the Gold Coast to procure gold for themselves. Fearing the loss of his monopoly over the gold trade, the Portuguese king decided to establish a permanent fortress on the Gold Coast to protect the gold supply. In 1481, he dispatched a fleet of 10 caravels carrying soldiers, carpenters, and stonemasons. After selecting a site for a fort, the Portuguese captain arranged for a meeting with the local chief, Caramansa. The chief appeared with his arms and legs covered with gold bracelets and wearing a collar adorned with golden bells. The Portuguese did not seek to purchase the land, but rather requested permission to build on land that would remain under Chief Caramansa's control. After some negotiations, the chief agreed, and work began on the stone castle called St. George of the Mine, which would come to be known simply as Elmina, "the mine." This treaty set the pattern for future Portuguese-African relations on the West African coast: the Portuguese would establish settlements on uninhabited islands off the coast, but would respect the rights of local African rulers on the continent itself.

Having a fort allowed the Portuguese to purchase gold a little at a time throughout the year and hold it there until the annual arrival of the treasure fleet that would carry it away. By 1540, the Portuguese were trading with all the coastal kingdoms and villages along the Gold Coast, and they had built a satellite fort at Axim to handle some of the trade. The Portuguese would simply wait for African merchant caravans to arrive at the forts with gold, which they purchased in exchange for cloth, copper, brass, and captives. Unlike merchant caravans in the Senegambia region, which used donkeys as pack animals, caravans in this region relied on human porters because the trade routes went through dense forests inhabited by tsetse flies that carried trypanosomiasis, a disease that killed horses and donkeys. Thus there was a steady demand for slaves to work as porters in merchant caravans and as laborers in the inland goldfields. To supply captives to the Gold Coast, Portuguese ships purchased them in the kingdom of Benin and the Niger delta and carried them to the Portuguese island of São Tomé, where they were held before being shipped to Elmina. During the sixteenth century, captives constituted 10–13 percent of the total value of Portuguese imports into the Gold Coast.

The Portuguese monopoly on trade with the Gold Coast came to an end when the Dutch ousted them from Elmina in 1637 and from Axim in 1642. Soon the English, Swedes, and Danes were building trading forts on the Gold Coast, and the Dutch were expanding their holdings by building new ones. Following the precedent set by the Portuguese, the Europeans sought permission from local rulers to build and paid an annual rent on the land; they did not try to claim territory on the Gold Coast for themselves. During the 1660s, many forts changed hands as the English and Dutch fought a series of wars in a futile attempt to oust each other from the Gold Coast. By the end of the seventeenth century, there were 25 trading forts along this 200-mile stretch of coastline, some of them within cannon shot of one another. There was a greater concentration of fortresses along the Gold Coast at that time than in any other place on earth.

Industrial and Agricultural Revolutions on the Gold Coast

As trading forts were multiplying along the coast, two revolutions were transforming economic and political life in the inland rainforest belt. First, the rising European demand for gold led to a major increase in African gold mining in the hinterland, which can be thought of as an industrial revolution. Gold was mined by sinking pits up to 100 feet deep into the earth, and the richest goldfields had up to 100 pits per acre. Gold mining required large amounts of labor because a mining team needed diggers, fillers, carriers, and washers. It could take up to a hundred workers to dig and work one 100-foot-deep pit. The skilled jobs were filled by professional gold miners, while the more mundane tasks were done by slaves or hired free laborers. The second revolution was an agricultural one that resulted from the massive clearing of dense forest to create farmland. This revolution was powered by entrepreneurs who used slave labor to clear unclaimed forest land, attract settlers, and become landlords. Over time, their original landed estates grew into tiny kingdoms. The descendants of the original landlords became the nobility, and the descendants of the original settlers became the commoners. The descendants of the slave laborers who had first cleared the forests were absorbed into the society as servants attached to noble families.

The industrial and agricultural revolutions on the Gold Coast produced a proliferation of tiny kingdoms. A Dutch map drawn in 1629 shows 43 kingdoms, most of which were less than 30 miles across. At the heart of each kingdom was a town of 5,000–20,000 inhabitants, which served as the administrative center. In order to make sure that the farmers in the countryside produced enough surplus food to feed the urban dwellers, the kings required that taxes be paid in gold. Thus the farmers had to bring their produce to the town markets to obtain the gold to pay their taxes. The king was considered the primary owner of all the land in the kingdom, which gave him not only the right to collect an annual land tax from the farmers, but also first claim on any gold found in his territory. In some cases, the king's administrators exploited the goldfields directly, using both slave labor and free hired miners. In other cases, private individuals would locate a gold vein and get a mining concession from the king by agreeing to give him 50 percent of the gold.

There were several merchant networks that purchased gold in the inland regions, brought it to the European forts on the coast, and traded it for European goods, which they carried back to the inland markets. In the seventeenth century, the dominant merchant group was the **Akani** commercial organization, which was said to supply two-thirds of the gold to the European trading companies on the coast. The Akani organization was made up of three different groups: First, there were investors who financed the trading operations. Second, there were traders who organized caravans, which might consist of a number of private merchants and up to 300 slave porters. Third, there were brokers who lived in the coastal ports and negotiated deals on behalf of the merchants in the caravans.

Up until 1650, the map of the kingdoms of the Gold Coast remained relatively stable. The tiny kingdoms fought frequent wars with one another, but these were fights to resolve disputes, not to conquer territory. The Dutch reported that these wars were usually of short duration and were followed by treaties in which the parties pledged to live in peace. The wars were mainly fought using spears and arrows, but even in 1602, the Dutch reported that the people near the coast were becoming quite expert at firing matchlock muskets.

The Rise of Denkyira

The political equilibrium of the Gold Coast would be shattered by the expansion of the small inland kingdom of **Denkyira**. One reason why Denkyira was able to dominate its neighbors was its rich supplies of gold. Its king pushed the population hard to increase gold production, and he used the gold to purchase large quantities of firearms. Denkyira's initial expansion after 1650 was to the north, but in the 1680s, the kingdom sent its army toward the coast, where it conquered rich goldfields and gained control of the westernmost trade route to the coast. Recognizing the rise of Denkyira as a powerful inland state, the Dutch, English, and Prussians sent representatives with gifts to the king, who in turn appointed a special trade representative to facilitate relations with the Europeans in their trading forts.

In the final phase of Denkyira's campaign to dominate the gold trade, it attacked the homeland of the Akani commercial organization. The Akani had always maintained a commercial empire instead of a military one, and they were devastated by the Denkyira invasion. Towns and villages were plundered, markets were destroyed, heavy tribute payments were imposed, and the Akani organization was shattered. Its end was accompanied by a decline in gold production and shrinking populations in many of the inland towns. The prosperity of those towns had rested on a robust trading economy, and when that was in decline, many urban dwellers returned to the countryside, where they could grow their own food. The rise of Denkyira thus marked a major shift in the political configuration of the Gold Coast. Denkyira had replaced a series of small kingdoms that maintained a rough balance of power with a large and powerful kingdom surrounded by smaller and weaker states. The former balance of power was forever broken.

This change in the political landscape was accompanied by another that was even more consequential. From 1481, when the Portuguese began building Elmina, until 1600, no captives were carried away from the Gold Coast. Between 1600 and 1650, a period during which the Portuguese were expelled and other European nations were building forts, fewer than 3,000 captives were carried away, an average of only 60 per year. But during the second half of the seventeenth century, over 100,000 captives were carried away by the Europeans. This abrupt and steep rise in the export of captives can be partially explained by the arrival of the English, who carried away 72,000 captives during this period, but it can also be attributed to the taking of captives in the wars of conquest that accompanied the expansion of Denkyira. By 1700, the political and economic landscape of the Gold Coast had been irrevocably changed.

THE KONGO KINGDOM

The **Kongo Kingdom** provides an example of a kingdom whose king and nobles embraced Christianity and certain aspects of European culture while at the same time participating in the trans-Atlantic slave trade. The kingdom's first encounter with Europeans came in 1482, when the Portuguese maritime explorer Diogo Cão landed his caravels in the estuary of the Congo River and discovered he had reached the lands of a powerful king. He sent messengers with greetings and gifts to the Kongo capital, located some 120 miles inland in the hill country beyond the coastal plain. The Kongolese had never seen white people before, and they regarded the Portuguese as water spirits because they had white skin and came from the sea. The Portuguese took several African hostages with them when they departed, and when Cão returned to the Congo River in 1485, he brought back the hostages, who had learned to speak Portuguese and could thus serve as translators and report on what they had seen in Portugal. He also brought along Catholic priests, stonemasons, and carpenters.

When Cão and his delegation arrived at the capital of Kongo on his second voyage, they were welcomed with an elaborate ceremony. The Portuguese received permission to build a church, and the stonemasons set to work. Before the church was finished, the king agreed to be baptized. He did not see himself as abandoning the local religious beliefs, but as merely adding a new cult to the existing configuration of earth spirits, water spirits, and sky spirits. In baptism, he took the Christian name João, after the reigning king of Portugal. Six members of the nobility who also requested baptism took Christian names after members of the Portuguese king's household. That was the beginning of the practice of Kongolese nobles bearing Portuguese names in order to distinguish themselves from the lesser nobility and the commoners.

The Portuguese were prudent in seeking good relations with the king of Kongo because he exercised tight control over commerce. Unlike the kings of Ghana, Mali, and Songhay, who taxed the gold trade but did not control the gold mines themselves, the kings of Kongo exploited the resources of several ecological zones directly. The governor of each province collected the key resources available there, such as salt, shell money, copper, and raffia cloth (woven from the fibers of the raffia palm tree), and sent them to the capital, where the king redistributed them to other provinces. Agricultural products and small craft items were traded freely in local markets, but the king and the governors controlled the long-distance trade in key resources.

The death of King João in 1506 created a crisis of succession in the Kongo Kingdom. Kongolese custom held that his successor should be chosen from among the sons of the king's lesser wives, so that the kingship could rotate among the 12 royal families that formed the historical core of the kingdom. But the Portuguese priests, applying European notions of primogeniture (succession by the eldest son of the father), insisted that the only legitimate heir was Afonso, the eldest son of the king's principal wife. At the time, Afonso was serving as governor of the province of Nsundi, which was rich in copper. With the encouragement of the Portuguese priests, he invaded the capital and seized the throne. Since he was not considered a legitimate heir according to Kongolese custom, Afonso sought legitimacy by establishing Christianity as the official religion of the kingdom and by using the European doctrine of the "divine right of kings" to give his reign legitimacy. He gradually gained the support of the high nobility, in part because he held the monopoly on overseas trade. Having gained control of the copper mines during his time as governor of Nsundi, he sold copper to the Portuguese in exchange for European goods, which he distributed as political patronage to the nobles and provincial governors.

Kongo as a Christian Kingdom

In contrast to his father, King Afonso was a zealous advocate of Christianity and an avid reader of theology. His Portuguese theological adviser reported that "he knows the prophets and the preaching of our Lord Jesus Christ and all the lives of the saints, and all things of the Holy Mother Church better than we ourselves

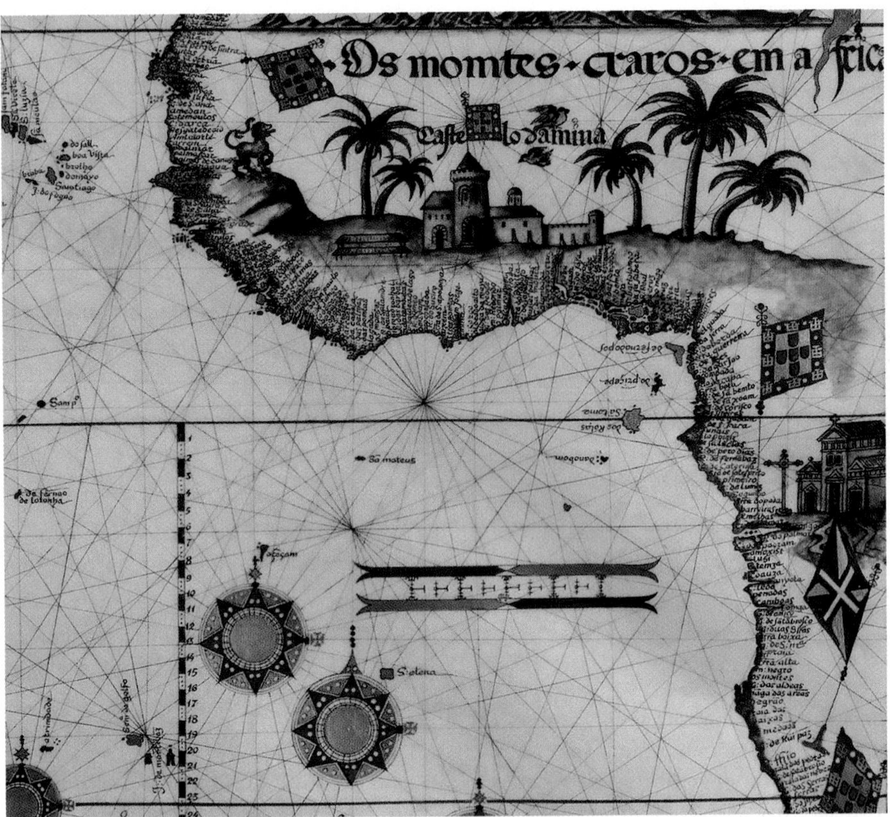

A CHRISTIAN KINGDOM This 1558 Portuguese map of the Atlantic world by Sebestião Lopes uses a Christian cross and a church to identify the Kongo Kingdom. The flag displays the emblem of the Military Order of Christ, an organization that was formerly headed by Prince Henry of Portugal. The map provides visual evidence that the Portuguese considered Kongo to be one of the Christian kingdoms of the Atlantic world.

do." Afonso built several new churches in the Kongolese capital and renamed it São Salvador. He also built churches in all the provincial capitals and ordered the governors to be baptized. More than 30 of his sons and kinsmen were sent to study in Portugal and be ordained as priests, and his son Henrique was ordained by the pope as the bishop of Kongo. From that time on, the Vatican considered Kongo to be one of the world's Christian kingdoms.

By 1531, it was reported that there were churches in "all the kingdoms, lordships, and provinces" of Kongo. A school staffed by Portuguese priests was established in São Salvador to teach literacy in Portuguese, Christian doctrine,

AMBASSADOR TO THE VATICAN In an attempt to break the religious monopoly of the Portuguese priests, the Kongo Kingdom sent Antonio Manuel ne Vunda to be its ambassador to the Vatican. He arrived in Rome in January 1608, but took ill and died a short while later. The engraving was made in 1608, one year after his death.

and some Latin to the children of the Kongolese nobility. Some of the graduates became teachers and catechists who created a uniquely Kongolese interpretation of Christianity. Others became government administrators who communicated with one another by letters written in Portuguese. By the late sixteenth century, the Kongo king felt restricted by the influence of Portuguese priests in the affairs of the Kongo Church and wanted direct relations with the Vatican. In 1607, the king dispatched a Kongolese ambassador named Antonio Manuel ne Vunda directly to the Vatican, but he died shortly after arriving in Rome. In 1613, King Alvaro II of Kongo complained to Pope Paul V that "the foreign priests who come to Kongo have no preoccupation other than enriching themselves and returning to their countries. They take no interest in gaining souls for heaven." After years of delicate negotiations with the Portuguese Crown, the pope replaced the Portuguese priests in 1645 with Capuchin priests from Italy.

The Slave Trade in Kongo

A more ominous aspect of Kongo's relationship with the Portuguese surfaced shortly after King Afonso took power in 1507. Sugar production was expanding on the nearby Portuguese island of São Tomé, and the Portuguese asked King Afonso to provide slave laborers for the plantations. In an effort to maintain his monopoly on trade with the Portuguese, Afonso demanded that they buy captives only from him. Although slavery had existed in Kongo since the earliest days of the kingdom, it was a relatively minor institution in the early sixteenth century, and there were customary prohibitions against selling free Kongolese. Afonso therefore ordered raids on the neighboring kingdom of Ndongo, but lacking a large standing army, he was unable to supply the Portuguese with as many captives as they wanted. His monopoly soon frayed as Portuguese traders began to purchase captives directly from individual chiefs and governors in the provinces.

The actions of the Portuguese traders created two problems for King Afonso. First, they were violating the customary principle that free Kongolese should not be sold. Writing to the king of Portugal in 1526, Afonso complained that free citizens and nobles were being sold surreptitiously to satisfy an illicit appetite for Portuguese merchandise. To combat these losses, he set up a special board to regulate the slave trade and make sure that no free Kongolese were taken away by the Portuguese slave traders. The principle of protecting free Kongolese would also be honored by Afonso's successors, some of them going so far as to negotiate the return of illegally enslaved Kongo subjects from as far away as Brazil. The second problem was that King Afonso was losing his monopoly on overseas trade. "Our kingdom is being lost," he wrote to the king of Portugal. "This is caused by the excessive freedom given to your factors and merchants, who are allowed to come to this kingdom to set up shops with goods and many things which have been prohibited by us." In 1530, King Afonso regained his monopoly over the slave trade when a new trade route opened up by which captives could be brought from the interior of the Congo River basin. Because the new trade route allowed him to supply as many captives as the Portuguese required, they stopped trading with provincial officials.

During the seventeenth century, however, the royal monopoly on trade was further weakened as the balance of power began to shift from the royal court to the provinces. Gun ownership had been a royal monopoly in the sixteenth century, but the seventeenth century witnessed a rise of gun ownership in all the provinces. The province of **Soyo**, on the Atlantic coast, had an ample supply of muskets and some 50 artillery pieces. Furthermore, slave ownership by the Kongolese nobility, which had once been concentrated in the region around São Salvador, became common among the nobles in the provinces. By the 1660s, the number of slaves in Kongo was almost equal to the number of free people.

The province of Soyo, nestled against both the Atlantic coast and the south bank of the Congo River estuary, had long been a challenge to the monopolistic ambitions of the Kongolese kings because its merchants and nobles had direct access to European ships that anchored in the estuary. In the early seventeenth century, Dutch and English ships began to visit the estuary to purchase ivory, redwood, and raffia cloth. The governor of Soyo used the profits from this trade to reduce his dependence on the king, making the province quasi-independent. In the 1640s, the governor began to sell captives to the English, Dutch, and Portuguese.

The Kongolese Civil Wars

By the 1660s, there were two rival power centers in the Kongo Kingdom: one in the capital city of São Salvador and the other in the province of Soyo. In 1666, during a successional dispute in São Salvador, an army from Soyo sacked the capital and installed its own candidate as king. The imposed king, however, was unable to garner enough support from the nobility to consolidate his rule. So Soyo sacked the capital again in 1669 and installed another king, who simply ruled by right of conquest. In response to the imposition of this unwanted king, the noble families in São Salvador fled with their slaves to reestablish themselves in the countryside. The population of São Salvador dropped from 50,000 in 1650 to 3,000 in 1672, and thereafter the city was virtually abandoned. The grand public squares, churches, and palaces were soon overgrown by lush tropical vegetation. The banana trees that had once graced the compounds now attracted herds of elephants that knocked down the flimsy houses of the commoners and trampled on their mud walls. For the rest of the century, Kongo was involved in almost continuous civil war as rival groups of nobles fought one another for control of the kingdom.

The collapse of centralized power in São Salvador unleashed a variety of social and political changes. With almost continuous warfare among competing factions, the long-standing principle that free citizens of the Kongo Kingdom could not be sold into the trans-Atlantic slave trade was abandoned. Even baptized Catholics were now being sold to European slave traders. The Capuchin priest Lorenzo da Lucca was bothered by this development, mainly because the prince of Soyo was selling captives of the civil wars to the English, who were Protestants. "It is not right," he wrote in 1702, "that Christians baptized in the Catholic faith should be sold to people who are enemies of their faith." He accordingly urged the prince to sell captives only to Catholic slave traders.

Dona Beatriz Seeks to Restore the Kongo Kingdom

During the long years of conflict, the idea of Kongo as a unified Christian kingdom and the importance of São Salvador as a symbol of national unity remained powerful in the minds of many people. These ideals were resurrected by a remarkable young woman known as **Dona Beatriz Kimpa Vita**. As her Portuguese title "Dona" indicates, she was born into a family of the Kongolese high nobility, and "Beatriz" was the name of a Catholic saint. As a young woman, she received instruction in the Christian faith and also underwent training as a traditional Kongolese religious practitioner. Like most Kongolese, she maintained an inclusive attitude toward religion, embracing Christianity without giving up the traditional cults.

In August 1704, when she was 20 years old, Dona Beatriz became ill. A few days later, she got up from her bed and informed her family that Saint Anthony (the patron saint of Portugal) had entered her body, and that she had been commanded by God to end the civil wars and reunite the Kongo Kingdom. After her message was rejected by the nobles in her home region, she traveled through the villages and towns preaching that she was the reincarnation of Saint Anthony, thus claiming for herself the prestige and authority that had once belonged to the Portuguese. She wrote a prayer to Saint Anthony modeled after the well-known liturgical prayer *Salve Regina*, which was addressed to the Virgin Mary. The *Salve Antoniana*, as her prayer was called, said in part: "Saint Anthony is our remedy. Saint Anthony is the restorer of the Kingdom of Kongo. Saint Anthony is the comforter of the Kingdom of Heaven." She preached that Jesus was born in São Salvador and that he was baptized in the Kongo province of Nsundi. The Virgin Mary, she told her followers, was Kongolese, as was Jesus, the offspring of Mary's womb.

By the time Dona Beatriz began preaching, Kongo had been a Christian kingdom for nearly two centuries. Although Christianity no longer seemed like a foreign religion, it still contained many foreign elements. Dona Beatriz was reinterpreting those foreign elements in order to create a version of Christianity that seemed more authentically Kongolese. She preached direct communication with God, and she urged her followers to burn their traditional Kongolese charms and their Christian crosses, both of which, she believed, smacked of idolatry. In the political realm, she ordered the warring nobles to come together at the abandoned capital of São Salvador to recognize her as their spiritual leader. She would then select a new king to rule over a united and restored Kongo Kingdom. As she preached, her following grew, and rumors spread that she had performed miracles—healing the sick, curing infertility, and even turning her enemies into wild animals.

Dona Beatriz Reoccupies São Salvador

In November 1704—just 3 months after Dona Beatriz had had her vision of Saint Anthony—she and her followers entered the abandoned capital of São Salvador, and she called on the people of Kongo to come in from the countryside and

CHAMPION OF THE PEOPLE Dona Beatriz Kimpa Vita rallied the Kongolese peasants to reoccupy the Kongo Kingdom's abandoned capital. Captured by her enemies, she was accused of heresy and burned at the stake. This image of Dona Beatriz wearing a crown was painted by Father Bernardo da Gallo, an Italian Capuchin missionary who was her avowed enemy and was present at her execution.

repopulate the city. Her call was heeded. The Italian priest Bernardo da Gallo, an avowed enemy of Dona Beatriz who believed that she was possessed by the devil, nevertheless acknowledged that "São Salvador was rapidly repopulated. In this way the false Saint Anthony became the restorer, ruler, and lord of Kongo, and was acclaimed, adored, and esteemed as such by everyone."

Having become pregnant, she left São Salvador to have her baby in the bush, as was customary in Kongo. On the way back to São Salvador in the company of only one other person, she was seized by her enemies and taken to the mountaintop court of Pedro IV, the leader of one of the warring factions. After several months of vacillation, Pedro IV and his council sentenced her to be burned to death as a heretic. In July 1706, a huge crowd attended the public burning. Despite the efforts of two Italian priests to make her confess, she refused to recant any of her claims about herself or her movement. Then the fire was lit. Fearing that her followers would sift through her ashes to find bits of bone that they could preserve as sacred relics, the executioners burned the ashes a second time.

After executing Dona Beatriz, Pedro IV successfully captured São Salvador in February 1709 and set himself up as king of Kongo. In the ensuing decade, the various rival factions, exhausted from decades of fighting, came forward to recognize Pedro IV's sovereignty. Kongo finally achieved a fragile and precarious unity, but four decades of civil war had taken a heavy toll in terms of lives lost, populations displaced, and captives sold. Exports of captives from Kongolese ports during the final quarter of the seventeenth century had been seven times as high as they had been in the previous 25 years. Many of those captives were Kongolese Christians who had Portuguese names. Furthermore, the political unification of the kingdom failed to bring a return to the centralized control that had characterized Kongo prior to the civil wars. Political and economic power in Kongo had devolved to the provincial capitals, and it remained there throughout the eighteenth century. The kingdom survived more as an idea and a symbol than as a political and economic force.

ANGOLA

The history of **Angola** (located within the modern nation of Angola) differs significantly from those of the other four regions we have examined because here the Portuguese established a settler colony, which they used as a base to fight wars against the inland kingdoms and obtain captives whom they could sell as slaves. Portuguese activity in Angola began in 1520, when a Portuguese delegation sought to establish ties with the kingdom of Ndongo, located some 200 miles south of the Kongo capital. The Portuguese considered Ndongo to be the second most powerful kingdom in West Central Africa (after Kongo). Their diplomatic mission ended in failure, and they did not try again until 1557, when a representative of the king of Ndongo arrived in Portugal to ask the Portuguese to send out a new delegation. Led by Paulo Dias, the delegation included a Jesuit priest who went to convert the king to Christianity. The negotiations began smoothly, but relations soon broke down. The delegation was expelled from the kingdom, except for Dias and the priest, who were kept as hostages. Not until 1565 was Dias allowed to return to Portugal. The priest died in captivity.

Up until this time, the Portuguese had been scrupulous about respecting the sovereignty of African rulers. The major Portuguese settlements had been built on uninhabited islands, and the Portuguese fort on the Gold Coast had been constructed with the permission of the local chief. But when Paulo Dias returned to Portugal after spending 7 years as a hostage in Ndongo, he became a forceful advocate for establishing a Portuguese colony on African soil. Dias received a royal charter that allowed him to establish an administration, collect taxes, build forts, and bring in settlers. In a sharp departure from all previous Portuguese policy in Africa, the charter permitted him to "subjugate and conquer" the kingdom of Ndongo. The establishment of a Portuguese settler colony on African soil would make the subsequent history of Angola very different from Portuguese ventures in other parts of Africa.

The Portuguese Settler Colony at Luanda

In 1575, Paulo Dias and his group settled on a coastal spit of land known as Luanda, where local fishermen and a few private Portuguese slave traders were already established. From his settlement at Luanda, Dias initially tried to establish cordial relations with the kingdom of Ndongo, whose capital was over 100 miles inland. But when he built a small fort some 30 miles inland from Luanda, the king of Ndongo interpreted it as a threat and attacked it with 12,000 soldiers. For the next decade, Paulo Dias was at war with Ndongo. He recruited thousands of Kongolese Christians to his army, and he offered protection to the chiefdoms just beyond the coastal plain if they would become his vassals, supply soldiers for his wars, and pay tribute in captives. Although many of the vassal chiefs submitted to Portuguese sovereignty under duress, others did so voluntarily in order to gain protection from the cruelty of the king of Ndongo. As a result of the wars and the tribute captives, some 52,000 captives were exported from Luanda between 1579 and 1592.

In 1590, the army of Ndongo inflicted a crushing defeat on a Portuguese army that consisted of 15,000 African archers, 125 Portuguese musketeers, and 3 Portuguese horsemen. After that, the Portuguese Crown revoked Dias's private charter and took direct control of the colony, which consisted of the port town of Luanda and a loose network of vassal chiefdoms just beyond the coastal plain. The new governor of the colony sought to obtain captives exclusively through peaceful trade, relying on itinerant traders known as *pombeiros*, who were often the children of Portuguese fathers and African mothers. Like the Eurafricans on the Sierra Leone coast, pombeiros were conversant with both African and Portuguese culture. They traveled to local markets scattered throughout the inland plateau to purchase captives in exchange for raffia cloth. In a complex series of exchanges, the pombeiros took coastal salt, shells, and European trade goods to a region northeast of the Kongo Kingdom, called Kongo de Batta, to buy raffia cloth, which was woven there. The cloth was produced in 2-foot squares that could be used as currency or sewn together to make garments. The pombeiros then used the raffia squares to purchase captives on the Angolan plateau. African-made raffia cloth was clearly preferred over European cloth.

When Bento Cardoso became governor of Angola in 1611, he was determined to reinstate the policy of obtaining captives through warfare. His chances of winning on the battlefield were greatly enhanced when he made an alliance with several bands of Imbangala warriors who had recently entered the area. The **Imbangala** were a highly mobile people who had abandoned the agricultural way of life and the lineage form of social organization. Instead, they organized themselves into military bands that were constantly on the move. So committed were they to their militaristic lifestyle that many of them practiced infanticide so that small children would not hamper their mobility. Instead, they kept captured boys and girls 13–14 years of age and raised them as their own children. The boys were forced to wear a special collar until they had proved their worth in battle by killing an enemy. The Imbangala population grew more by incorporating war captives than by natural reproduction.

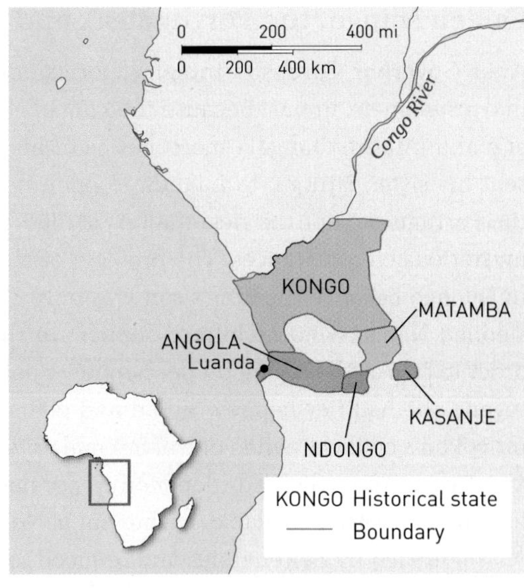

MAJOR STATES IN WEST-CENTRAL AFRICA
This map shows major states in West-Central Africa between 1526 and 1641. The Kongo Kingdom was located just south of the Congo River. Angola was a Portuguese settler colony that waged war on the African states in the region. Ndongo and Matamba were conquered and ruled by Queen Njinga. Kasanje, in the far interior, was founded by an Imbangala war band led by Jaga Kasanje, Njinga's former husband.

Governor Cardoso ordered a series of attacks on the kingdom of Ndongo, using the pretext that he was merely bringing recalcitrant vassals back under Portuguese control and opening up some blocked trade routes. With the aid of the Imbangala bands, his victorious army captured numerous prisoners, who were sold, and brought 80 small chiefdoms under Portuguese control, imposing annual tribute payments in the form of captives. His successor, Mendez de Vasconcelos, believed that "in order for the trade to be satisfactory, it is necessary to have an army in the field." He launched a major war against Ndongo in 1618, and even constructed a fortress at Ambaka, located 150 miles from the coast and within striking distance of Ndongo's capital. His slaving expeditions alarmed the bishop in Luanda, who complained to the Portuguese king that the capturing of innocent people in war was "not only against the law of God and nature, but even against the expressed instructions of Your Majesty." Although pombeiros continued to visit inland markets during lulls in the fighting, the Portuguese policy of relying on peaceful trade was finished.

Queen Njinga, the Portuguese, and the Imbangala

After Governor Cardoso's initial victories against Ndongo, the warfare settled into a stalemate, in part because the king of Ndongo copied the Portuguese strategy and hired Imbangala mercenaries of his own. In 1622, the king of Ndongo sent his sister, **Njinga**, to Luanda to open negotiations on a peace treaty with the Portuguese, but the negotiations stalled in 1624 when the king died under mysterious circumstances. The problem of choosing a successor created a crisis in Ndongo because the king's son was only 8 years old. Into the power vacuum stepped Njinga, who mobilized support in the royal court and the military in order to rule as the regent on her nephew's behalf. Dissatisfied with being a mere regent, she had her nephew killed and claimed the throne for herself. That act provoked a civil war when one of her male rivals took up arms to contest her rule. The Portuguese, who had reopened treaty negotiations with Njinga, abandoned her and helped her rival to drive her out of Ndongo.

Pursued by her enemies and reduced to a few hundred followers who had narrowly escaped death by descending a cliff on ropes, Njinga sought refuge with an Imbangala band that had formerly fought for the Portuguese. In return for marrying the Imbangala war leader, she was appointed to an Imbangala office that carried considerable political and military authority. By training her followers in the lifestyle, rituals, and military tactics of the Imbangala, she developed a formidable private army. But Njinga's alliance with the Imbangala proved to be as short-lived as her previous alliance with the Portuguese. Her Imbangala husband defected to the Portuguese, abandoning her on the specious grounds that she lacked Imbangala ancestry.

The next stage of Njinga's career began when she moved with her private army and a band of Imbangala warriors into Matamba, on the northeastern fringe of Ndongo. Matamba had once been an independent kingdom, but the king of Ndongo had annexed it during the sixteenth century, leaving only vassal rulers on the throne. The vassal king of Matamba had recently died, and his daughter, a potential heir to the throne, had been captured and enslaved by Njinga. By 1635, Njinga had conquered Matamba and installed herself as queen. Then her armies moved south and west into the lands of Ndongo, her former kingdom. Despite her military victories, Njinga had difficulty gaining acceptance as a legitimate ruler because of her sex. Her first solution was to marry weak and dependent men who held the title of king while she exercised the real power. When this arrangement proved unsatisfactory, she decided to rule as a man. She forced her successive husbands to wear women's clothing and sleep in the quarters of the maids-in-waiting, ordering them to avoid sexual contact with the maids upon penalty of death. She organized a battalion of female soldiers, who also served as her royal guard. As a war leader, she personally led her troops into battle.

During her brief sojourn with the Imbangala band, Njinga had come to appreciate the Imbangala tactic of integrating prisoners of war into the conquering army. The ranks of her army swelled with each victory, and the surplus captives were sold to finance her expanding kingdom. Needing revenue from the sale of captives, but being a bitter enemy of the Portuguese, Njinga began trading with

THE WARRIOR QUEEN Queen Njinga leads her army into battle in this watercolor painting from the 1660s. A successful military leader, she conquered the kingdoms of Ndongo and Matamba before signing a treaty with the Portuguese. The painting was made by Giovanni Antonio Cavazzi, an Italian Capuchin missionary who knew her personally and later presided over her funeral.

Dutch slave traders who were visiting the inlets and bays north of Luanda. When the Dutch captured the port of Luanda in 1641, Njinga became their main supplier, providing them with up to 13,000 captives a year. When the Portuguese drove out the Dutch and regained control of Luanda in 1648, Njinga realized that she would have to come to terms with them. After several years of negotiations, she concluded a formal treaty with them in 1656. In return for agreeing to trade with the Portuguese in Luanda, she received a royal monopoly on the supply of captives from Matamba. She also agreed to make Matamba a Christian kingdom, pay an annual tribute in captives to the Portuguese, and provide military assistance to them when needed. Perhaps more importantly for Njinga, the Portuguese agreed to stop supporting the claims of her rival to the throne of Ndongo. The lands over which she ruled became known as the Combined Kingdom of Matamba and Ndongo. Her rule paved the way for other female rulers: during the century after her death, five women and only three men sat on the throne of the Combined Kingdom of Matamba and Ndongo.

The End of the Angolan Wars

A century of nearly continuous warfare between the Portuguese colony on the Angola coast and the African kingdoms in the interior came to an end when the Portuguese signed peace treaties in 1683 with Matamba (ruled by a successor to Njinga) and the Imbangala state of Kasanje. Prior to 1683, the Portuguese governors in Luanda had sent out military expeditions nearly every year to collect tribute, open trade routes, defend African allies, or advance Portuguese interests. Whatever the pretext, those expeditions were little more than thinly disguised slave raids. After 1683, Portuguese military expeditions became much less frequent, and some governors served out their entire terms without a single military action. The end of the wars did not bring an end to the slave trade, however, because the captives were now coming via trade routes from the far interior. Under those circumstances, peaceful relations between the Portuguese and the African states near the coast facilitated the flow of captives into Luanda.

CONCLUSION

The arrival of Portuguese caravels along Africa's Atlantic coast around 1450 marked the beginning of war capitalism as a global system. Unlike the Europeans who arrived in the New World, where Spain, Portugal, France, the Netherlands, and England annexed vast territories and infected large populations with previously unknown diseases, those who came to Africa were more interested in establishing small enclaves to facilitate trade with independent African rulers and merchants. Yet they were practicing war capitalism nonetheless, because they were purchasing human beings who had been enslaved by violence and carrying them across the Atlantic Ocean chained in the holds of armed ships. By providing weapons and making warfare in Africa profitable, the trans-Atlantic slave trade was embroiled in the local wars that fed into the Atlantic-wide system of enslavement and plantation labor. The most direct application of war capitalism, however, was in Angola, where the Portuguese sent armies into the interior to enslave farmers and villagers.

During the years 1450–1700, the impact of Atlantic commerce on African societies was felt mainly within 250 miles of the coast. The five coastal regions examined in this chapter show that the nature and effects of this commerce varied from region to region. One set of differences can be seen in the actions of the Europeans regarding settlements on African land. In Senegambia and on the Sierra Leone coast, they restricted themselves to trading forts on offshore islands. On the Gold Coast, European establishments were limited to forts pressed hard against the seashore, which were built with the permission of the local rulers. The Portuguese did not build a fort in Kongo, in part because the Kongolese kings upheld the Portuguese trade monopoly. The glaring exception to this pattern was in Angola, where Paulo Dias established a Portuguese settler colony in 1575 and constructed a fort 30 miles inland from the coast, thus inaugurating a century of warfare between the Portuguese on the coast and the African kingdoms in the interior. It was not until 1683 that the warfare ended and regular trading networks could emerge in the interior of Angola.

Other differences among the regions are connected with the actions of African rulers and merchants. The Gold Coast, for example, sold mostly gold prior to 1650, whereas the other regions sold captives from the very beginning. It was the rise of the kingdom of Denkyira that started the transition to slave trading on the Gold Coast. In Senegambia, kings often sold people living within their own borders until the War of the Marabouts and the decree of Latsukaabe ended that practice. The Kongo Kingdom, in contrast, established a special inspection board to make sure that no Kongolese citizens were taken away by slave traders.

Religion also played different roles in different regions. In Senegambia, the common people used Islam as a basis for revolting against tyrannical rulers. When the Kongo Kingdom was torn apart by civil wars in the late seventeenth century, the common people united behind Dona Beatriz Kimpa Vita, a young woman who performed miracles and claimed the authority of the patron saint of Portugal. In Angola, Queen Njinga fought the Portuguese for many years before reaching an accommodation with them in which she agreed to make Matamba a Christian kingdom in return for getting a monopoly on the slave trade.

By 1700, the basic infrastructure of the slave trade was in place along Africa's Atlantic coast. Forts had been built, trade agreements had been negotiated, and new trade routes had been opened. As a result, over 2 million captives were taken out of Africa between 1450 and 1700. However, the flow of captives in these first 250 years of the slave trade was a mere trickle compared with the flood that would sweep the Atlantic world when the sugar plantations in the New World geared up to full production in the eighteenth century.

CHAPTER REVIEW

KEY TERMS AND VOCABULARY

Senegambia
War of the Marabouts
Sierra Leone
lançados
Gold Coast
Akani
Denkyira
Kongo Kingdom
Soyo
Dona Beatriz Kimpa Vita
Angola
Imbangala
Njinga

STUDY QUESTIONS

1. Discuss the ways that Christians and Muslims sought to justify the enslavement of captured or purchased people.
2. Why did Nasir al-Din's Islamic reforms in Senegambia attract so much popular support? Why did the movement ultimately fail?
3. How did the lançados and Eurafrican traders combine aspects of African and European culture?
4. How did Dona Beatriz Kimpa Vita succeed in uniting the people of the Kongo Kingdom after it had been torn apart by years of civil war?
5. Why did Paulo Dias seek the Portuguese Crown's permission to subjugate and conquer the Kingdom of Ndongo?
6. Why were Portuguese slaving operations in Angola so different from Portuguese practices on the Gold Coast and the Sierra Leone coast?
7. How do you explain the differing effects of the trans-Atlantic slave trade on different parts of the African coast?

PERSPECTIVES

POPE NICHOLAS V AUTHORIZES PORTUGUESE SLAVING

In 1455, Pope Nicholas V issued a papal bull entitled Romanus Pontifex *to King Afonso V of Portugal and Prince Henry (the Navigator), which granted Portugal exclusive rights to trade and colonize along the Atlantic coast of Africa south of Cape Bojador. In these excerpts from the bull, the second paragraph reiterates the earlier permission to enslave Muslims that had already been given in the 1452 papal bull* Dum Diversas*; the third paragraph recounts recent Portuguese activities south of the Senegal River; and the fourth paragraph authorizes the Portuguese to enslave or purchase black Africans in Guinea.*

The Roman pontiff, successor of the key-bearer of the heavenly kingdom and vicar of Jesus Christ, contemplating with a father's mind all the several climes of the world and the characteristics of all the nations dwelling in them and seeking and desiring the salvation of all, wholesomely ordains and disposes upon careful deliberation those things which he sees will be agreeable to the Divine Majesty, and by which he may bring the sheep entrusted to him by God into the single divine fold, and may acquire for them the reward of eternal felicity, and obtain pardon for their souls. . . .

We had formerly, by letters of ours, granted among other things free and ample faculty to the aforesaid King Afonso—to invade, search out, capture, vanquish, and subdue all Saracens [Muslims] and pagans whatsoever, and other enemies of Christ wheresoever placed, and the kingdoms, dukedoms, principalities, dominions, possessions, and all movable and immovable goods whatsoever held and possessed by them and to reduce their persons to perpetual slavery, and to apply and appropriate to himself and his successors the kingdoms, dukedoms, counties, principalities, dominions, possessions, and goods, and to convert them to his and their use and profit. . . .

And so it came to pass that when a number of ships of this kind had explored and taken possession of very many harbors, islands, and seas, they at length came to the province of Guinea, and having taken possession of some islands and harbors and the sea adjacent to that province, sailing farther they came to the mouth of a certain great river [the Senegal River] commonly supposed to be the Nile, and war was waged for some years against the peoples of those parts in the name of the said King Afonso and of the *infante* [Prince Henry], and in it very many islands in that neighborhood were subdued and peacefully possessed, as they are still possessed together with the adjacent sea.

Thence also many Guinea men and other negroes, taken by force, and some by barter of unprohibited articles, or by other lawful contract of purchase, have been sent to the said kingdoms. A large number of these have been converted to the Catholic faith, and it is hoped, by the help of divine mercy, that if such progress be continued with them, either those peoples will be converted to the faith or at least the souls of many of them will be gained for Christ.

1. *How did the pope seek to justify the enslavement of Africans in his prior papal bull, which he summarizes in paragraph 2?*
2. *Why did the pope need a new justification for the purchase of Africans in the region south of the Senegal River, as he outlines in paragraph 4?*

Source: *European Treaties bearing on the History of the United States and Its Dependencies to 1648*, edited by Francis Gardiner Davenport (Washington, DC: Carnegie Institution, 1917), pp. 20–26.

CAN MUSLIM STATES ENSLAVE MUSLIMS?

Ahmad Baba (1556–1627) was a Berber from Arawan, a small village in present-day Mali that was on the trans-Saharan caravan route. At a young age, he moved to Timbuktu with his father and later became Timbuktu's greatest legal scholar, writing more than 40 books on Islamic jurisprudence. In 1594, after the Moroccan army occupied Timbuktu, he was arrested and carried away to Morocco, where he was detained until 1608. Because of his own experiences in captivity, he explored the legal questions surrounding the enslavement of Muslims by Muslim states. The treatise below was written in 1614, after his return to Timbuktu. It uses a question-and-answer format.

You asked: "What have you to say concerning slaves imported from lands whose people have been established to be Muslims, such as Bornu, Afnu, Kano, Gao, and Katsina, and others among whose adherence to Islam is widely acknowledged? Is it permissible to own them or not?"

[The Reply]: "Be it known . . . that the people of these lands are Muslims, except for Afnu, whose location I do not know, nor have I heard of it. However, close to each of these is a land in which there are unbelievers whom the Muslim people of these lands make raids on. Some of them, as is well known, are under their protection and pay *kharaj* [tribute] according to what has come to our ears. Sometimes the sultans of these lands are in a state of discord the one with the other, and the sultan of one land attacks the other and takes whatever captives he can, they being Muslims. These captives, free Muslims, are then sold—to God we belong and to Him shall we return! This is commonplace among them in their lands. The people of Katsina attack Kano, and others do likewise, though they speak one tongue and their languages are united and their way of life similar. The only thing that distinguishes them is that some are born Muslims and others are born unbelievers. This is what confuses the situation concerning those who are brought to them, so that they do not know the true situation of the one imported."

You said: "It is known that according to the *sharia* the sole reason for being owned is unbelief. Thus whoever purchases an unbeliever is allowed to own him. In the contrary case he is not. Conversion to Islam subsequent to the existence of the aforementioned condition has no effect on continued ownership." The Reply is that this is so, provided he is not one with whom a pact has been made, or who possesses [a contract of] protection. There is no way round that.

You asked: "Were these aforementioned lands belonging to the Muslims of the Sudan conquered and their people enslaved in a state of unbelief, while their conversion to Islam occurred subsequently, so there is no harm [in owning them], or not?" The Reply is that they converted to Islam without anyone conquering them, like the people of Kano, Katsina, Bornu and Songhay. We never heard that anyone conquered them before their conversion to Islam. Among them are some who have long been Muslims, like the people of Bornu and Songhay.

---

1. *Explain how some Muslims became enslaved by Muslim rulers?*
2. *What, according to Ahmad Baba, was the sole justification for owning another person?*

Source: Ahmad Baba, *Mi'raj Al-Su'ud: Ahmad Baba's Replies on Slavery*, translated and annotated by John Hunwick and Fatima Harrak (Rabat, Morocco: Institute of African Studies, 2000), pp. 22–23.

AFRICANS FIGHT OFF PORTUGUESE SLAVERS

Nuno Tristam was a Portuguese knight by virtue of being a member of the Military Order of the Knights of Christ, an organization headed by Prince Henry (the Navigator). When he tried to launch a slave raid on an African village along the Gambia River, the inhabitants defended themselves and killed all but two of the raiders. This account was written by Gomes Eannes de Azurara, who was employed by King Afonso V to write a chronicle of the Portuguese explorations in Guinea. Azurara does not give a date for these events, but it was most likely 1446.

Of how Nuno Tristam was slain in the land of Guinea, and of those who died with him.

And passing by Cape Verde, he went sixty leagues further on and came unto a river, in which it seemed to him that there ought to be some inhabited places. Wherefore he caused to be launched two small boats he was carrying, and in them there entered twenty-two men, to wit, ten in one and twelve in the other. And as they began to take their way up the river, the tide was rising with which they entered, and they made for some habitations that they spied on the right hand. And it came to pass that before they went on shore, there appeared from the other side twelve boats, in which there would be as many as seventy or eighty Guineas, all Negroes, with bows in their hands. And because the water was rising, one of the boats of the Guineas crossed to the other side and put on shore those it was carrying, and thence they began to shoot arrows at our men in the boats. And the others who remained in the boats bestirred themselves as much as they could to get at our men, and as soon as they perceived themselves to be within reach, they discharged that accursed ammunition of theirs all full of poison upon the bodies of our countrymen.

And so they held on in pursuit of them until they had reached the caravel which was lying outside the river in the open sea; and they were all hit by those poisoned arrows, in such wise that before they came on board four of them died in the boats. And so, wounded as they were, they made fast their small boats to the ship, and commenced to make ready for their voyage, seeing their case, how perilous it was; but they were not able to lift their anchors for the multitude of arrows with which they were attacked, and they were constrained to cut the cables so that not one remained. And so they began to make sail, leaving the boats behind, for they could not hoist them up. And it came to pass that of the twenty-two men that left the ship only two escaped, to wit, one André Diaz and another Alvaro da Costa, both esquires of the *Infante* [Prince Henry] and natives of the city of Evora; and the remaining nineteen died, for that poison was so artfully composed that a slight wound, if it only let blood, brought men to their last end. And there died that noble Knight Nuno Tristam.

1. *Why did the Portuguese fear the arrows of the Africans?*
2. *What does this incident tell us about the capacity of the Africans to defend themselves against Portuguese slave raiders?*

Source: Gomes Eannes de Azurara, *The Chronicle of the Discovery and Conquest of Guinea* (London: Hakluyt Society, 1899), vol. 2, pp. 252–254.

THE KONGO KING'S COMPLAINT

King Afonso I of the Kongo Kingdom was literate in Portuguese and well versed in Catholic theology. In a letter to King John III of Portugal written on October 18, 1526, he proposed a way to reduce the devastation being caused by Portuguese slave traders. He had earlier threatened to cut off all trade, but was now seeking a compromise. Because the Kongo Kingdom under Afonso was officially a Christian kingdom, high Kongolese officials such as the three mentioned in the letter had Christian names. The mention of the king of Portugal's participation in the slave trade refers to Portugal's decree in 1519 establishing a royal monopoly on the trade in slaves.

There is a great obstacle to the service of God in our kingdoms. Many of our subjects keenly covet the Portuguese merchandise that your subjects bring to our kingdoms. To satisfy that illicit appetite, they abduct our free or liberated citizens, and even nobles, sons of nobles, and even our own relatives. They sell them to the white men who are in our kingdoms after transporting them [to the port of Mpinda] in secret or during the night so that they will not be recognized. As soon as the captives are in the power of the whites, they are marked with a red-hot branding iron. When they embark, they are spotted by our guards. The white men then claim that they had purchased them, but cannot say from whom. It is up to us to render justice and liberate those prisoners as they require.

To mitigate such damage, we decree that all the white men in our kingdoms who buy slaves in any manner must notify the three nobles and officers of our court whom we have put in charge of regulating the trade. They are Dom Pedro Manipunzo and Dom Manuel Manisaba, our chief justice, as well as Gonçalo Pires, our chief outfitter [of ships]. They must verify if the captives are free men or not. If they are certified to be slaves, they may be freely embarked, but if not, we will confiscate the captives of the white men.

We are giving you this favor and facilitation because of Your Highness's participation in this trade. We know, in effect, that it is for your service that the captives are abducted from our kingdoms. Otherwise, for the reasons cited earlier, we would not consent.

1. *Why were the Portuguese slave merchants able to purchase Kongolese captives?*
2. *What was the Kongolese king's remedy for the problem?*

Source: *Correspondance de Dom Afonso, Roi du Congo*, edited and annotated by Louis Jadin and Mireille Diccorato (Brussels: Academie Royale des Sciences d'Outre-Mer, n.s., vol. 41, no. 3, 1974), pp. 166–168. Translated into English by Robert Harms.

SLAVE CARAVAN FROM FUUTA JALOO This sketch of a slave caravan traveling from Fuuta Jaloo to the Sierra Leone coast was made by Samuel Gamble, captain of the British slave ship *Sandown*, in 1793. The caption reads, "A lot of Fulanis [Fulbe] bringing their slaves for sale to the Europeans." Gamble claimed that caravans came from as far as a thousand miles in the interior.

1701	1712	1727
Osei Tutu defeats Denkyira	Founding of Segu Kingdom	Dahomey invades Whydah

6

EXPANSIONIST STATES AND DECENTRALIZED POWER IN ATLANTIC AFRICA, 1700–1800

By the beginning of the eighteenth century, an economy built on war capitalism and slave labor had been firmly implanted in the Americas. The sugar plantations in Brazil, the Caribbean, and southern Mexico relied on slave labor, as did the gold mines in Brazil, the silver mines in northern Mexico, and the tobacco and rice estates in the United States; and slaves were commonplace in the urban and rural households of the European settlers. As a consequence, the trans-Atlantic slave trade was reaching its peak. The *Trans-Atlantic Slave Trade Database* shows that whereas nearly 2 million captives were taken out of Africa during the seventeenth century, close to 7 million were carried away during the eighteenth century. Nearly 60 percent of them were taken to the British, French, Dutch, and Danish sugar-producing colonies in the Caribbean, while approximately one-third went to the Portuguese colony of Brazil. Although slave shipments to North America experienced a dramatic rise, from 20,000 captives during the seventeenth century to nearly 360,000 during the eighteenth century, North America remained a minor destination for slave ships.

1737	**1756**
Islamic State of Fuuta Jaloo formed	Lunda slave caravans at Kasanje

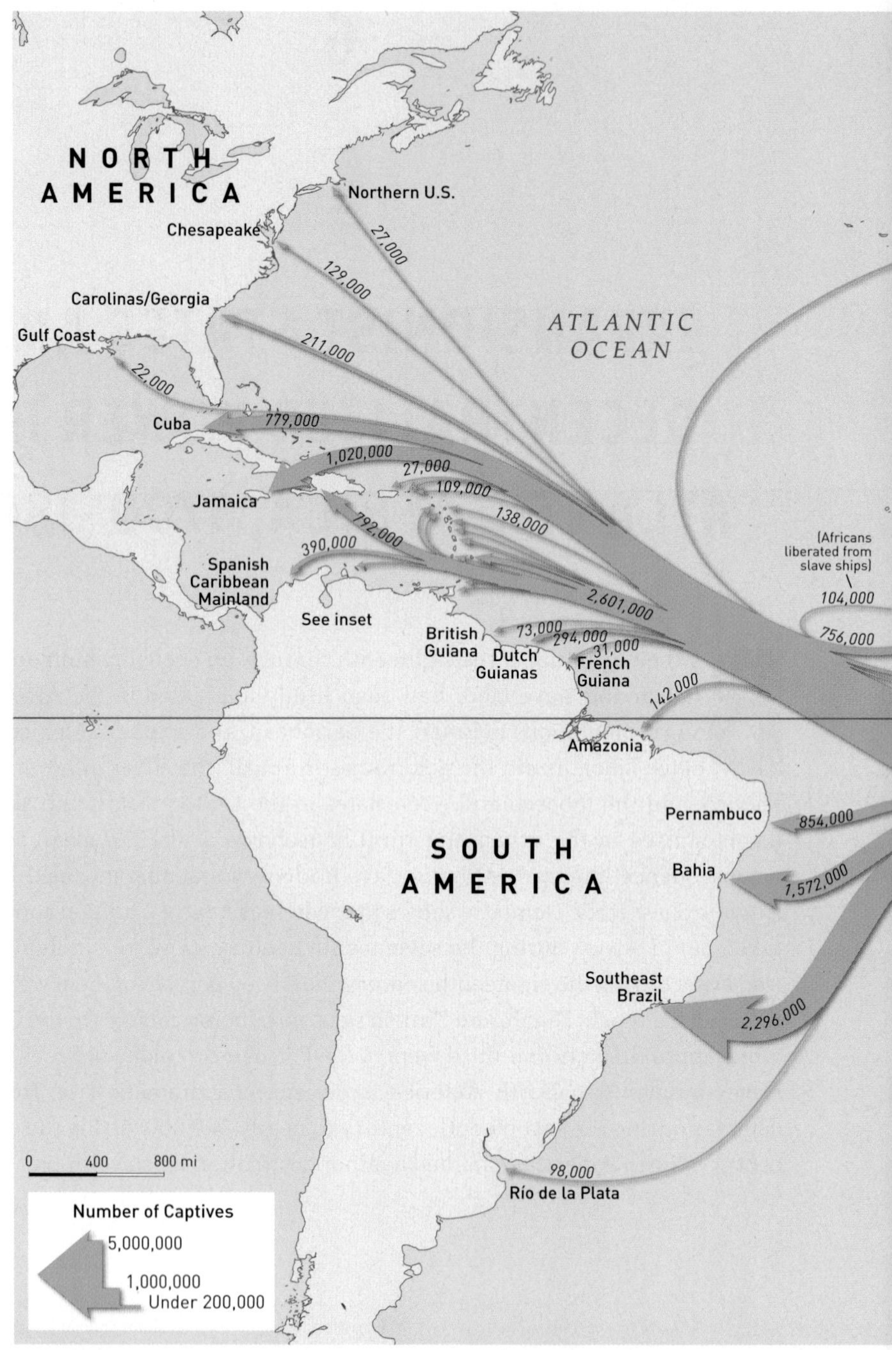

OVERVIEW OF THE TRANS-ATLANTIC SLAVE TRADE, 1501–1807 This map shows the routes across the Atlantic which brought the victims of the trans-Atlantic slave trade to the New World. The thickness of the arrows is in proportion to the number

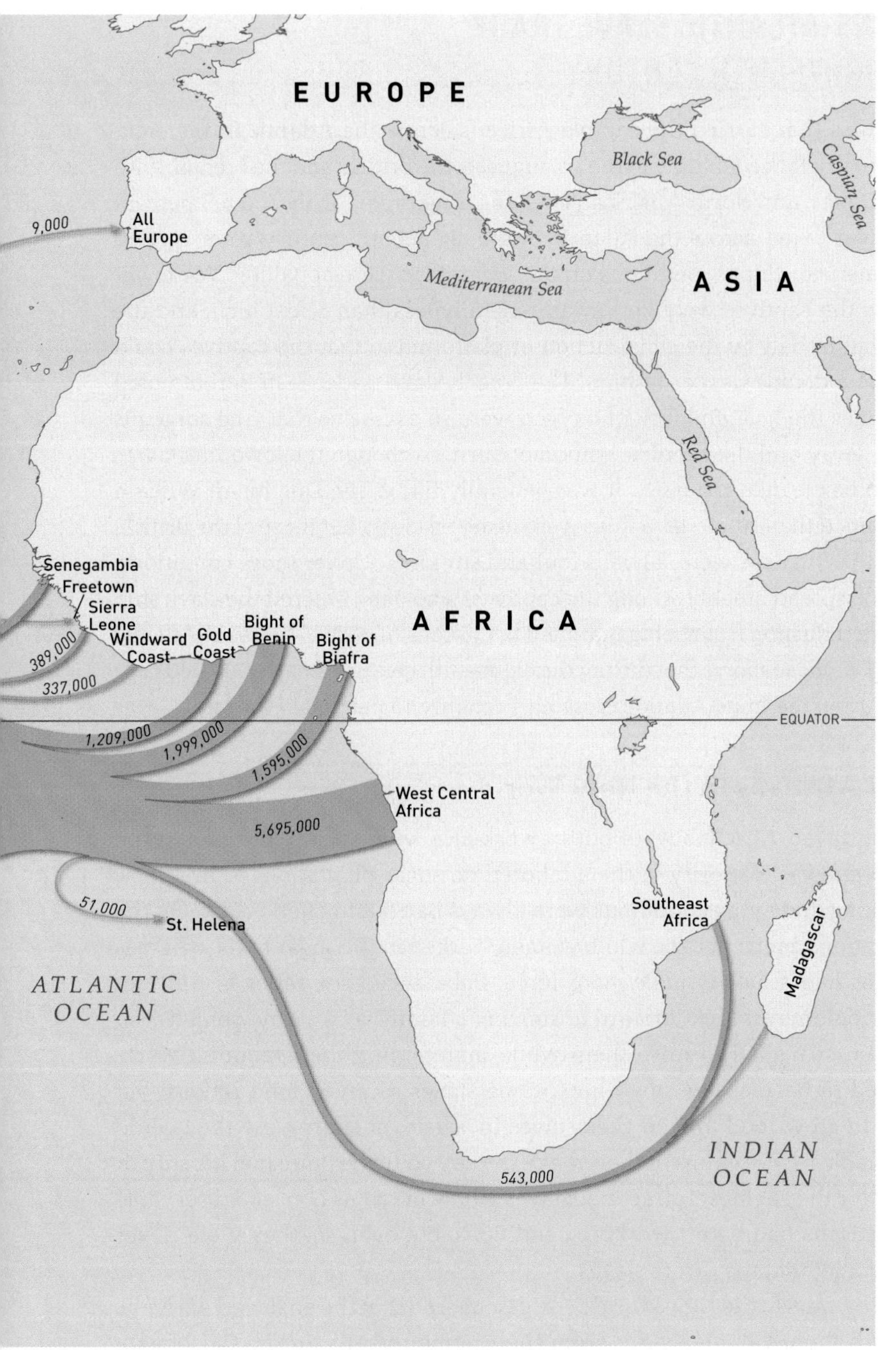

of captives carried on each route. In total, 12,521,000 Africans were carried away on slave ships. 10,703,000 were landed, mostly at New World destinations, leaving 1,818,000 who perished during the crossing.

THE TRANS-ATLANTIC SLAVE TRADE IN THE EIGHTEENTH CENTURY

The slave ships that carried the captive Africans across the Atlantic in the eighteenth century belonged mainly to the Portuguese, the British, and the French, with the Dutch, Danes, and North Americans playing minor roles. Only about 3 percent of the captives taken across the Atlantic in the eighteenth century were carried in North American ships. Conditions on the slave ships were appalling. The lower deck, where the captives were kept, was generally less than 5 feet high, and the space was cut in half by the construction of platforms so that the captives could be packed in a double-decker fashion. The French slave trader Jean Barbot noted that sometimes the heat and lack of oxygen were so excessive that "the surgeons would faint away and the candles would not burn." Although the lower deck was supposed to be cleaned regularly, it was generally filthy. The Dutchman William Bosman claimed that Dutch slave ships were neat and clean, but those of the British, French, and Portuguese were "always foul and stinking." Under those conditions, disease could spread quickly among the captives, who often entered the slave ship in a state of exhaustion from being marched to the coastal ports. The *Trans-Atlantic Slave Trade Database* shows that during the eighteenth century, nearly 900,000 captives died during the trans-Atlantic crossing—roughly 15 percent of the total.

Enslaved Africans in the New World

Although enslaved Africans were put to work at a wide variety of tasks in the New World, the vast majority of them labored on sugar plantations or in mines, where working and living conditions were always harsh and often brutal. On the sugar plantations, men cut cane while women worked in the sugar mills, whereas mining areas had a mostly male labor force. Imbalanced sex ratios meant that many men could never look forward to starting a family, and many women who bore children struggled to raise them while maintaining their required workload. Housed in barracks or small huts, some slaves received food rations, but others had to grow food to feed themselves in whatever spare time they could find. Vulnerable to the whims of their masters, they could be punished harshly or even killed for the slightest infraction. Slaves who worked as household servants or urban artisans had better working conditions, but even so, they were never allowed to forget that they were slaves.

Slave owners in the New World soon discovered that the enslaved Africans brought with them valuable skills from their home regions. In the Caribbean, where sugar mills were often powered by teams of horses or oxen, slaves from Senegambia were prized because they knew how to handle horses and cattle.

In the gold-mining region of Brazil, Africans from the Gold Coast were valued for their knowledge of gold mining. An eighteenth-century Brazilian document reveals that it was Africans who first taught the Portuguese how to remove the gold from the ore. Rice growers in Georgia and South Carolina sought Africans from the Sierra Leone coast because they had expertise in growing rice. Certain techniques used for controlling the flow of water in the irrigated rice fields of South Carolina can be traced directly to West Africa. Captive Africans also introduced a variety of new crops and edible plants that crossed the Atlantic with them on slave ships. White plantation owners in the New World would discover those plants by observing what the slaves were growing in their subsistence plots. In this way, plants such as yams, okra, sesame, pigeon peas, taro, bananas, millet, sorghum, and West African rice entered the cuisine of the Americas.

Although enslavement had stripped the captives of their African birthright and social identity, they did not easily forget their cultural roots. A variety of African healing rituals from Kongo, Angola, and the Gold Coast involving divination and spirit possession were popular and widespread in Brazil. Even white slave owners sought out *calundeiros* (practitioners of African healing rituals) to cure sick slaves, and by 1685, Catholic priests in Brazil were complaining that many white people were seeking cures from the *calundeiros* instead of asking the Catholic priests to perform prayers or exorcisms. Apparently, the *calundeiros* were considered more effective.

Many African religious beliefs and practices were carried to the New World by enslaved Africans. One of the best known was Voodoo, a religion that came from the West African kingdom of Dahomey, where it was known as Vodun, a name that meant "god" in the largest sense of the word. Encompassing the broad realm of the mysterious that revealed the divine, Vodun provided the context for a pantheon of celestial and terrestrial deities, each with their own priests and cults and their associated music, dances, ceremonies, and spirit-possession rituals. Vodun took root on the island of Hispaniola (now Haiti and the Dominican Republic) as well as in Cuba, Louisiana, and Brazil. In a similar way, Candomblé, an Afro-Brazilian religion of divination, healing, and spirit possession, had its origins among the Yoruba people in what is now southwestern Nigeria. Other African religions implanted in the New World included Umbanda, Xango, and Batuque in Brazil and Santeria and Palo Mayombe in Cuba.

Some of the captives were followers of world religions such as Islam and Christianity prior to being enslaved. Muslim captives from the Sahel region of West Africa were sometimes pressured to convert to Christianity, but they were also valued because many of them were literate in Arabic. African Catholics from the Kongo Kingdom joined Catholic lay brotherhoods in Brazil, whereas those arriving in North America often felt uncomfortable living under the authority of Protestant masters. During the Stono slave rebellion in South Carolina in 1739, many rebels of Kongolese ancestry tried to escape to Spanish-controlled Florida in order to live in a Catholic country.

Certain aspects of African political culture were also preserved in the New World, especially among slaves who came from the Kongo Kingdom. In Brazil, where slaves and free blacks of Kongolese ancestry predominated among the members of the Brotherhood of the Rosary (a Catholic organization for laymen), each local chapter organized an annual Festival of the Crowning of Our Lady of the Rosary that lasted 3–8 days and was presided over by an elected king and queen. The ceremonies, processions, and pageantry of the festival helped to keep memories of Kongolese royalty and nobility alive. A similar effort occurred during the Haitian Revolution in 1791, when rebels of Kongolese ancestry gave themselves titles of nobility and elected kings in an attempt to replicate the political structure of the Kongo Kingdom. During the Stono slave rebellion, the enslaved rebels stopped in an open field and began singing, dancing, and drumming to attract people to join their cause, a common way of rallying the population for war in the Kongo Kingdom. They were trying to reclaim their African culture as well as their freedom.

Economic Determinants of the Trans-Atlantic Slave Trade

Even after the New World plantation system stabilized, the demand for captive laborers did not diminish. Nearly two enslaved men were brought across the Atlantic for every woman, a ratio that made it nearly impossible to establish a self-sustaining slave population in the New World. Many New World planters believed that it was cheaper to replace aged or deceased slave laborers with new captives than to encourage childbearing and pay the costs of feeding children until they were old enough to work in the fields. A second reason for the continuing high demand for slaves was that sugar production in the Caribbean, Brazil, and Louisiana took a brutal toll on the lives and health of the workers. During harvest time, the sugar mills ran 24 hours a day to keep up with the incoming cartloads of sugarcane. And in the tropical climates of the Caribbean and Brazil, different cane fields were planted in different months to ensure a nearly continuous harvest over much of the year. The administrator of Martinique reported in 1735 that the high mortality rate among slaves "appears to be caused by the heavy labor that the planters make them perform without adequate nourishment."

After 1680, the demand for captive laborers in the New World outstripped the capacity of the European chartered companies to supply them. By 1730, the

Dutch West India Company, the British Royal African Company, and the French East India Company had been forced by their respective governments to open up the slave trade to private traders. As a result, the number of European ships seeking captives at African coastal ports increased by nearly 250 percent between the 1690s and the 1730s. The increasing demand was also reflected in the prices that the Europeans paid for captives on the African coast. Data from Senegambia show that between 1680 and 1830, the price of a captive increased over a thousand percent.

European slave ships brought a variety of trade goods to exchange for African captives. In deciding which goods to carry on a slaving voyage, the captains tried to keep up to date on which items were in demand at each African port. Some popular generalizations about the commodities involved in the slave trade have been called into question by recent research. First, the popular notion of a "gun-slave cycle," in which Europeans supplied guns that aided African rulers in obtaining more captives, has been overstated. While certain large African states that were gearing up for war sometimes imported huge quantities of guns and powder over a short period, arms made up only about 10 percent of imports into Senegambia in the eighteenth century and only about 5 percent in Angola. Alternatively, some historians have posited a "rum-slave cycle" because American slave ships often left New England loaded with rum. In reality, however, these ships met up with British ships on the coast of Africa and exchanged the bulk of their rum for cloth, beads, iron bars, and other commodities before attempting to purchase captives. Overall, the major commodity exchanged for African captives was cloth. In Senegambia, cloth rose from 30 percent of imports in the 1730s to 60 percent a century later, whereas it made up over 20 percent of imports into Angola in the late eighteenth century.

The bulk of the cloth carried on slave ships was cotton cloth, which was brought in from India because cotton did not grow in the cool climate of Europe. Lacking cotton, Europeans generally wore clothing made from wool or from linen (which was made from flax). Although a modest quantity of European wool and linen cloth entered the slave trade, it was dwarfed by Indian cottons. The trans-Atlantic slave trade has frequently been pictured as a triangle in which ships moved between Europe, Africa, and the New World, but a more complete picture would show that the supply chains that fed the slave trade extended all the way to India and beyond. Thus the trans-Atlantic slave trade had a global reach that went beyond the Atlantic.

As the prices that Europeans paid for slaves on the African coast rose during the eighteenth century, it became profitable for African caravan merchants to bring in captives from the far interior, causing the slaving frontier to move inland as the century progressed. The movement of the slaving frontier connected the

Atlantic coast to inland regions that had previously been isolated from the Atlantic world, and it encouraged the rise of new kingdoms and empires in the hinterlands that earned their revenues from the slave trade. The first part of this chapter will focus on five such expansionist kingdoms that arose during the era of the trans-Atlantic slave trade: Segu, Fuuta Jaloo, Asante, Dahomey, and the Lunda Empire. The second part of the chapter will look at regions inhabited by people who favored decentralized political systems that recognized no authorities higher than a village headman or a lineage elder. Complex networks of traders who could operate in a politically decentralized landscape supplied large numbers of captives to the Atlantic slave trade. The methods of slave trading and commercial organization in these societies were very different from those in the expansionist states. For their victims, however, the results were disturbingly similar.

EXPANSIONIST STATES IN THE AFRICAN HINTERLANDS

Many of the largest states in sub-Saharan Africa in the eighteenth century were of recent origin, having expanded by military conquest using weapons they had obtained by selling their prisoners of war to Europeans. In the process, their rulers had become dependent on European slave traders for weapons, as well as for the cloth and other luxury goods that they distributed to their followers. King Agaja of Dahomey sent a letter to King George I of England in 1726, saying that he had to keep a large quantity of gunpowder on hand to repel periodic attacks from his neighbors, and that he was required by his subjects to go out several times a year and distribute imported luxury goods among the common people. Other African kings, however, made it clear that the initiative behind their slaving activities was coming from the European slave traders. King Glele of Dahomey told British abolitionists that he did not send away captives in his own ships, but that white men came to him for them. If they did not come, he would not sell. In a similar manner, the ruler of Fuuta Jaloo told a British visitor that if he could get all the guns and powder he wanted by selling ivory, rice, and cattle, then he would immediately drive all the slave dealers out of his country. These examples illustrate how the economic effects of global war capitalism had penetrated the very structure of those kingdoms.

The growth of these expansionist states had contradictory effects. The people within their borders were safe from being sold to European slave traders, and thus the expanding state created an expanding zone of safety. At the same time, the state created a zone of death, destruction, and chaos on its periphery. People living in the vicinity of an expansionist state developed a variety of strategies for safeguarding their freedom. They would sometimes relocate to safer areas, such as mountains, swamplands, or islands in lakes. They would construct high walls around their villages, build houses with escape passages, or carve villages out of the sides of cliffs. And some of them even changed their agricultural systems in order to concentrate the fields for greater safety. Thus, even many people who escaped enslavement found their lives altered by the trans-Atlantic slave trade.

The Warlord Kingdom of Segu

During the eighteenth century, the frontier of the slave trade moved far inland from the coastal kingdoms of Senegambia. Slave caravans coming from the Middle Niger region, over 700 miles from the mouth of the Senegal River, were bringing captives to the navigable portions of the Senegal and Gambia Rivers to sell them to French and British slave traders. Two-thirds of the captives carried off from Senegambia during the eighteenth century came from the far interior. The major source of captives during this time was the kingdom of **Segu** on the Middle Niger. It is referred to here as a warlord kingdom because its rulers were not drawn from the local nobility, but were outsiders who had seized power by force.

The kingdom of Segu was founded in 1712 by **Mamari Kulubali**, a stranger and a hunter, whose personal history and lifestyle often clashed with the agrarian culture of the Bamana people who lived in the region. Mamari got himself elected head of the local young men's association because of his strength and leadership qualities, but young men from noble families resented his growing influence, so they expelled him, causing the young men's association to split in two. Mamari increased the membership of his faction by redeeming slaves, debtors, and criminals, and also by recruiting various disreputable elements of Bamana society, while transforming his group from a social organization into a military one. From its base near the city of Segu, his group raided the surrounding countryside and incorporated the young men they captured into its military organization. The oral traditions make it clear that Mamari and his followers had rejected the twin pillars of authority in Bamana society—the nobility and the elders—and had constructed a new kind of state based on raw military power exercised by commoners and outcasts.

The Segu Kingdom was supported by warfare. Even though Bamana society was based on agriculture, the slave soldiers who followed Mamari Kulubali had an aversion to farming. Instead of producing grain, they produced prisoners of war. The strongest captives were inducted into the army and given military training. The slave soldiers of Segu rejected the Islamic religion and consumed large quantities of alcohol, a practice forbidden by Islam. Under the leadership of Mamari, the army

BAMANA MAN AND BAMANA WOMAN The Bamana people were farmers in the West African Sahel who grew mostly millet. In the eighteenth century, their territory became dominated by a warrior caste that founded the kingdom of Segu. These pictures of a typical Bamana man and woman were painted by Abbé Boilat in the 1840s.

of Segu ranged widely throughout the Middle Niger and the Niger bend, collecting tribute from the trading center of Jenne (see chapter 3) and briefly occupying Timbuktu. To administer his growing kingdom, Mamari appointed slave soldiers as commanders of military regiments and administrators of the conquered territories.

The weak link in the system was that the slave soldiers remained loyal only as long as the king rewarded them with booty from their conquests. After Mamari's death in 1755, the war bands asserted their independence, and the kingdom splintered into regions controlled by different warring factions. Complete collapse was averted by a former slave soldier named Ngolo Jara, who was the official guardian of the traditional religious cults, a post that carried great ritual authority. In 1765, he called a meeting of all the warring factions at the central religious shrine. As tradition dictated, the soldiers entered the shrine unarmed. After some elaborate ceremonies, Ngolo Jara surrounded them with a cavalry troop and forced them to acknowledge his authority.

A former slave was now the ruler of Segu. "I have no doubts about the future," Ngolo Jara told the assembled soldiers. "We will live from pillage." He reorganized the army to bring it under his control, and he reconquered the areas that had broken away during the interregnum. Then he began new military campaigns to further expand the Segu Kingdom to the south and the east. During the reign of Ngolo Jara's son Monzon, the British traveler Mungo Park discovered the geographical reach of the king's authority. "The road is open for you everywhere," King Monzon told Park, "as far as this land extends. If you wish to go east, no one shall harm you from Segu until you pass Timbuktu. If you go west, you may travel through Faladoo and Manding, through Kassan and Bundu." The straight-line distance from Timbuktu to Bundu was over 600 miles!

Prisoners captured in those wars and raids faced one of four potential fates. Strong young men were likely to be incorporated into the Segu military. Other captives were brought to Segu to do agricultural labor for the military elites. It was

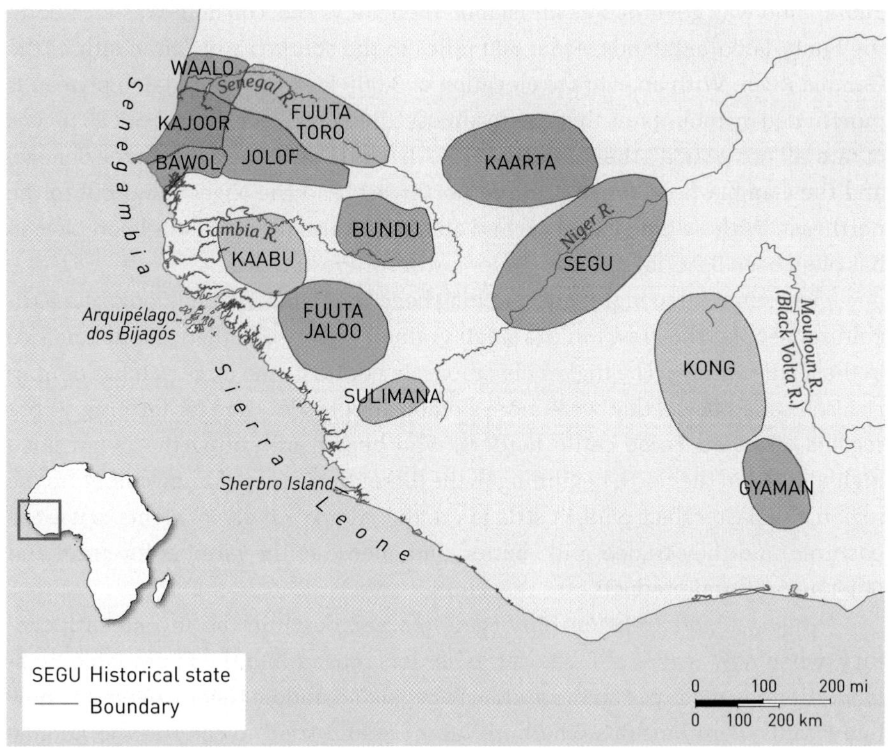

MAJOR STATES IN THE SENEGAMBIA AND SIERRA LEONE REGIONS AROUND 1750
Although the states in coastal Senegambia remained much the same as in the seventeenth century, the new expansionist states that arose in the interior during the eighteenth century included Kaarta, Segu, and Fuuta Jaloo, all of which expanded by warfare that produced captives, many of whom were sold into the trans-Atlantic slave trade.

agricultural production by slaves at home that left the military free to roam so widely. Third, the captives could be taken northward and sold to desert nomads in exchange for horses, which were essential equipment for an army that relied on a spear-wielding cavalry far more than on guns. Finally, they could be sold to itinerant merchants who traveled the caravan routes toward the European trading establishments along the Senegal and Gambia Rivers. During the eighteenth century, those trading establishments shipped nearly 400,000 captives to the New World.

The Jihadist Kingdom of Fuuta Jaloo

The kingdom of **Fuuta Jaloo** forms a sharp contrast with Segu because it was dominated by a landholding aristocracy and its army was manned by free citizens mobilized in time of war. In contrast to the proud paganism of the Segu soldiers, Fuuta Jaloo was governed as an Islamic theocracy. The kingdom was located in the Fuuta Jaloo highlands, some 300 miles to the southeast of the mouth of the Gambia River. With an average elevation of 3,000 feet, the Fuuta Jaloo plateau is punctuated by mountains that rise to almost 5,000 feet. Receiving about 80 inches of rainfall per year, it's the source of West Africa's three largest rivers: the Senegal and the Gambia flow out of it to the northwest, and the Niger flows out to the northeast. With its high elevation and abundant rainfall, the Fuuta Jaloo plateau has often been described as the "water tower" of West Africa.

The Fuuta Jaloo highlands had long been inhabited by the Jalonke, an agricultural people who grew fonio (a small-grained variety of millet) and upland rice in the fertile valleys. The higher elevations, in contrast, had large patches of iron-rich soil called *bowal* that were more suitable for pasture than for farming. Those regions attracted Fulbe cattle herders, who began infiltrating the Fuuta Jaloo highlands from the north beginning in the fifteenth century. As newcomers to the region, the pastoralists paid a cattle tax to the Jalonke chiefs for rights to use the pastures, and they traded milk, butter, and cheese to the farmers for grain and other agricultural products.

This symbiotic relationship began to break down in the seventeenth century, when new waves of Fulbe cattle herders moved into the Fuuta Jaloo highlands. Coming mostly from the middle Senegal and middle Niger valleys, the new immigrants were Muslims who built mosques and tried to convert the Jalonke to Islam. The Jalonke chiefs resisted this religious proselytism and attempted to forbid the Fulbe from constructing mosques and performing public prayers. In response, Fulbe groups from all parts of the Fuuta Jaloo plateau formed an alliance in 1727 to wage a jihad (holy war) against the Jalonke. Their swift victories soon gained them control of all parts of the plateau, causing many of the Jalonke to abandon their farms and flee westward toward the coast.

In 1737, the nine Fulbe regional leaders of the jihad formed a governing council and created a theocratic Islamic state divided into nine provinces. They elected Karamoko Alfa, a pious Muslim with leanings toward mysticism, as the king. For the first time in its history, the Fuuta Jaloo plateau was united under a single authority. To ensure stability and continuity, it was decided that future rulers would be chosen by the council from among the extended family and descendants of Karamoko Alfa. The political system thus combined elements of a monarchy with elements of a federated republic.

Agricultural land that had been vacated by fleeing Jalonke during the jihad was given to the important Fulbe families in each locality, as were the lands of Jalonke farmers who refused to convert to Islam. The cattle-herding Fulbe, who saw the agricultural way of life as degrading, reduced the Jalonke farmers to a servile status. The Fulbe aristocrats lived in towns called *misiide*, built on the high ground overlooking the valleys. At the center of each town was a mosque. The Jalonke farmers, in contrast, lived in slave villages called *runde* that were situated in the fertile valleys, where they produced grain and other agricultural products for their Fulbe overlords.

In contrast to the great empires of the Sahel, which had lively marketplaces and professional merchant organizations, the exchange of products in Fuuta Jaloo took place largely through socially constructed networks of kinsmen, patrons, and clients. The servile agriculturalists provided grain to their Fulbe masters, who redistributed it within their kin groups. Members of the artisanal castes provided objects made from leather, wood, and iron to their Fulbe patrons in return for gifts of grain and dairy products. The Fulbe aristocrats, in turn, paid land and cattle taxes in kind to the king. Some of the cattle and other goods received by the king were sent to the Atlantic coast in large annual trade caravans that were under the control of the king himself. When the caravans returned carrying goods from Europe and Asia, the king distributed those goods as gifts to favored government officials and aristocratic families. The economic system in Fuuta Jaloo was, in short, a closed one that operated largely without currencies, prices, or markets.

As an Islamic state surrounded by hostile people whom it regarded as pagans, Fuuta Jaloo waged jihad on its non-Muslim neighbors to expand the kingdom and keep enemies at bay. While some of the captives of its early wars may have been sold to British slave traders who visited the Sierra Leone coast, many others were settled on recently vacated land in Fuuta Jaloo, where they lived in slave villages and did agricultural labor. The British traveler James Watt, who was the first European to visit the region, was told by the prime minister of Fuuta Jaloo in 1794 that slaves outnumbered free people five to one. So worried was the Fulbe population about slave revolts that the kingdom passed a law requiring all Fulbe to carry weapons, while forbidding the servile population from doing the same.

Even so, there was a major slave revolt in 1756, during which many slaves escaped to the northeast, and another in 1785, during which a great number of slaves fled to a region outside the western border, where they obtained guns and built fortified villages. They maintained their independence for 10 years before their rebellion was finally crushed.

When Karamoko Alfa died in 1751, the governing council voted to replace him with his cousin Ibrahim Sori, who was the head of the army. Unlike his pious and mystical predecessor, Sori was a career soldier with a streak of ruthlessness and a fondness for worldly goods. Soon after taking power, he launched a series of attacks on neighboring regions that yielded a great many captives, most of whom were sold to European slave traders that visited the rivers and inlets along the Sierra Leone coast. Sori grew so wealthy from this trade that the Muslim scholars and holy men in Fuuta Jaloo became critical of his worldly ways. In 1761, the governing council stripped him of his title and replaced him with the 15-year-old son of Karamoko Alfa. Sori retired to his estate on Mount Helaya, but 2 years later, when the kingdom of Wasulu invaded Fuuta Jaloo and destroyed the capital city of Timbo, representatives of all nine provinces went to his estate to beg him to return and reclaim his title as king.

The next 15 years saw almost continuous warfare against external foes under the leadership of Ibrahim Sori. But even after Fuuta Jaloo's decisive victory in 1778, which effectively ended any external threats to the kingdom, the warfare continued. The wars were spoken of as jihads because they were waged against non-Muslims, but they had long ago lost any religious significance. In 1794, the deputy king of Fuuta Jaloo told James Watt that "the sole object of the wars was to procure slaves, as they could not get any European articles they were in want of without slaves, and they could not get slaves without fighting for them." The deputy king explained that the army needed guns, gunpowder, and artillery, which could be obtained only from the Europeans.

With agricultural labor done mostly by slaves, many Fulbe aristocrats devoted themselves to Islamic education and learning. All Muslim girls and boys over the age of 7 were required by law to attend elementary schools directed by marabouts, where they learned to read the Quran in Arabic and write Koranic texts. There were also secondary schools that taught students to translate and interpret the Quran and books on Islamic law. Higher education, in which students developed a deeper knowledge of the Quran and specialized in one or more Islamic sciences, was available in most provinces, but thrived especially in the central province of Labé. Students from across the Senegambian region came to Fuuta Jaloo to study with its most respected scholars. Fuuta Jaloo not only dominated its region militarily, but culturally as well.

The Expansionist Asante Empire

The **Asante Empire** that arose in the hinterland of the Gold Coast during the eighteenth century differed from both Segu and Fuuta Jaloo in that its wars were fought primarily to expand the empire and create a centralized bureaucratic state. Although many prisoners were captured in Asante's wars and sold to Europeans, these wars must be seen in the context of empire building rather than slave raiding. The Asante Empire was founded by **Osei Tutu**, who was born in a small kingdom called Kumasi, located 150 miles from the coast, where his maternal uncle was the king. After Kumasi was conquered by Denkyira in the 1660s (see chapter 5), Osei Tutu was taken as a hostage to reside at the court of Denkyira's king, Boamponsem. He married a Denkyira woman and lived a relatively peaceful life until he learned that the king had seduced his wife. Furious, Osei Tutu forced the king at knifepoint to swear an oath. Then he fled and lived in exile throughout the 1670s. In the early 1680s, he came out of hiding to succeed his uncle as the king of Kumasi.

When King Boamponsem died in 1694, there was suspicion that he had been poisoned or killed by occult magic. The main suspect fled from Denkyira and took refuge in Kumasi under the protection of Osei Tutu. When envoys from Denkyira arrived to demand that "the king and each of the leading men of Kumasi must send one of their wives whom they most love and one of their children whom they most love" to be hostages at the royal court of Denkyira, Osei Tutu refused, and he began to put together a coalition of five kingdoms to fight Denkyira. By November 1701, Dutch merchants on the coast reported that Osei Tutu's coalition forces had won a "very complete victory" over Denkyira. As the Dutchman William Bosman wrote, "The towering pride of Denkyira in ashes, they are forced to fly before those whom they not long ago thought no better than their slaves." The Dutch began to refer to the victorious coalition by the name "Asante."

The major task facing Osei Tutu was to transform his military coalition into a political union that saw itself as a single nation. This process undoubtedly involved much negotiation and compromise, but it was aided by the development of the Golden Stool as the symbol of the Asante nation. According to oral traditions, Osei Tutu called a great gathering of people in Kumasi. During the gathering, a wooden stool, partly covered with gold leaf, descended slowly from the sky and alighted on Osei Tutu's knees. The high priest told the people that the stool contained the soul of the Asante nation, and that their power, their health, their bravery, and their welfare were embodied in the stool. Another pillar of Asante unity was the annual Yam Harvest Festival, when the king would bless the nation: "May the nation prosper.

THE GOLDEN STOOL Asante chiefs sat on stools instead of thrones. Asante tradition holds that Osei Tutu, the founder of the Asante Empire, created the symbolic unity of the new state by burying all of the existing stools and replacing them with the Golden Stool, which he called down from the sky. Made of wood and covered with gold leaf, the Golden Stool was said to embody the spirit of the nation. It was never sat upon, but was displayed under a large umbrella during the annual Yam Harvest Festival.

Grant that fertile women bear children. Grant that our farms yield abundantly. Grant that the hunters kill meat. Let those who dig for gold find much gold to dig so that I get some to uphold my kingship." The next day, in a private ceremony, the king would vow to destroy any vassal king who was disloyal. Both the generosity and the vengeance of the king were considered necessary to preserve the unity of the nation.

The collapse of Denkyira allowed its southern tributary states to break away and reassert their control over the trade routes to the coast. Asante therefore launched a series of wars to gain control of the routes, especially the central trade routes that led to the Dutch traders at Elmina Castle and the British traders at the nearby Cape Coast Castle. The increase in warfare was reflected in the rising sales of guns and ammunition in the region. The demand for guns had increased after flintlock rifles replaced the unreliable matchlocks in the 1690s. By 1700, the Dutch were selling 20,000 tons of gunpowder annually along the Gold Coast, and by 1730, about 180,000 guns per year were coming into the Gold Coast and the neighboring Bight of Benin.

Asante was acquiring captives during its wars of expansion, but initially they were used for agriculture and gold mining. By the 1720s, however, Asante had built up such a large slave population that it began to experience massive slave desertions, and the Asante ruler began sending captives to the coastal forts in large numbers. The Asante trade caravans brought very little gold with them, in part because gold was now in great demand within Asante itself. Instead, they brought mostly ivory and captives from their wars. Shipments of captives from the Gold Coast jumped threefold, from 75,000 in the final quarter of the seventeenth century to 229,000 in the first quarter of the eighteenth century, and the number continued to rise throughout the eighteenth century as the Asante army continued to expand the empire and put down rebellions. In all, over a million captives would be shipped out of the Gold Coast during the eighteenth century.

As the Asante Empire grew, new administrative structures were needed to oversee the growing economy. King Osei Kwadwo (1764–1777) reduced the power of the hereditary nobility and replaced them with a new class of government officials controlled by the king. He created a treasury department staffed by literate Muslims, and he established ministries in charge of different sectors of the economy, such as the ivory trade, the kola trade, and the gold-producing regions. He also created a network of regional and district administrators who represented the interests of the government in the outlying regions. This was the beginning of an ongoing process that would enlarge state power and concentrate it in the monarchy, a process that would reach its zenith in the mid-nineteenth century.

ASANTE YAM HARVEST FESTIVAL The annual Yam Harvest Festival was the major Asante national celebration, in which the king would bless the people and curse his enemies. Held in the autumn right after the yam harvest, the festival lasted 5 days. This picture of the first day of the festival, first published in 1819, is based on sketches by British traveler and writer Thomas Edward Bowdich, who observed the festival in 1817.

From Trading State to Royal Monopoly in the Bight of Benin

A similar process unfolded in the Bight of Benin, where the coastal trading kingdom of Whydah was supplanted by the powerful, militaristic kingdom of Dahomey. The Bight of Benin is a shallow bend in the West African coastline that forms an open bay approximately 400 miles from one end to the other. Because it had a treacherous surf and a swampy, disease-ridden coastline, European ships normally sailed right past it without stopping during the fifteenth and sixteenth centuries. An English sea chantey gave voice to their fears: "Beware and take care of the Bight of Benin / There's one that comes out for forty goes in." It is therefore astonishing to discover that during the first half of the eighteenth century, nearly one in three captives taken out of Africa came from the Bight of Benin. So extensive was the expansion of the slave trade that the Bight of Benin became known to eighteenth-century Europeans as the "Slave Coast." This development came about as the result of two political transformations. The first, which began around 1650, was the rise of the trading state of Whydah, which became a preferred destination for African slave caravans traveling toward the Atlantic coast, and the second, after 1700, was the rise of the expansionist kingdom of Dahomey, which shut down the long-distance trade routes and instead produced captives from its own wars.

The Trading State of Whydah

The growth of the slave trade in the Bight of Benin was partly the result of a quirk of geography by which the grassland savanna normally found north of the rainforest belt descended all the way down to the sea, creating a grassland corridor known as the Dahomey Gap. The gap allowed slave caravans coming from the north to reach the coast without traveling through the dense forest. As more caravans followed the trade routes through the gap, the slave trade in the Bight of Benin grew steadily from about 1,000 captives per year in the 1650s to over 10,000 per year in the 1690s, when that stretch of the coast exported more captives than any other region in West Africa. Although a number of small kingdoms occupied the coastal region, the slave trade became more and more concentrated in the small kingdom of Whydah. After 1700, the British, French, and Portuguese received permission from the kings of Whydah to build trading forts at the coastal town of Glewe, and the Dutch built a trading lodge in Whydah's capital city of Savi. Between 1700 and 1725, some 378,000 captive Africans were taken out of Whydah, accounting for over a third of all the captives coming out of Africa.

The kingdom of Whydah was tiny, covering about 20 miles of coastline and extending inland for about 15 miles. The wooded grassland vegetation of the Dahomey Gap and the abundant rainfall provided ideal conditions for agriculture. European observers who had encountered sparse populations elsewhere in West

Africa were surprised by the density of the kingdom's population. One of them noted that the population was so dense that the kingdom could almost be said to comprise a single large village. The British surveyor and draftsman William Smith declared that Whydah was "one of the most beautiful countries in the world" because of the neatly cultivated fields and the well-ordered groves of trees. He described the inhabitants of Whydah as "gentlemanly people who abounded in good manners and ceremony to one another. All here are naturally industrious, and find constant employment, the men in agriculture and the women in spinning and weaving cotton to make cloth."

The captives that the Europeans purchased did not come from the kingdom of Whydah itself, and the kings of Whydah did not engage in wars to enslave their neighbors. Whydah was simply the southern terminus for trade routes from the heartland of the former Mali Empire and the grassland kingdom of Oyo. Some of the captives arriving at Whydah wore Muslim robes and were called "Malis," indicating that they had come from the old Mali heartland. They had been on the road for 3 months by the time they arrived at the coast. The revenue of Whydah came mostly from taxing the African caravan merchants and the European slave traders. The king appointed special officials who spoke the appropriate European languages to deal with the French, Dutch, British, and Portuguese traders who arrived in increasing numbers.

The kings of Whydah struggled to maintain order amid the brutal and chaotic conditions of the slave trade. In 1704, when quarrels between rival European traders threatened to disrupt the trade, the king summoned the heads of the European trading companies to his palace and forced them to sign a treaty promising to live in peace with one another. The preamble read: "The King of Whydah, having ordered the chiefs of the nations of Europe who have forts and posts in his kingdom and all the great men of the country to assemble at his palace, declares that irrespective of the wars that rage in Europe, or that they may have one against the other, they convene together in his presence a firm and durable peace in his harbor and even within sight of his harbor." In 1715, the king expelled the director of the French fort after learning that the French had contravened Whydah's monopoly by sending two ships to trade at the neighboring kingdom of Allada. But all seemed to be forgiven in 1725, when a new king of Whydah was enthroned. Representatives of the French, Dutch, British, and Portuguese trading companies all occupied places of honor at the ceremonies.

The Rise of Dahomey

While the kings of Whydah were busy managing the contentious relationships among European slave traders, political changes were brewing in the kingdom of **Dahomey**—located just inland from Whydah—that would forever alter the nature of the slave trade in the Bight of Benin. Small coastal kingdoms such as Whydah were organized on a family model. The king was called "father," and the kingdom was seen as an extended family writ large. No one could be a citizen unless they were born in the kingdom, and no native-born citizen could opt out. Blood relationships, not common interests, held the kingdom together. Dahomey, in contrast, depicted the state as a water pot perforated with holes. The king was the water, and the idea was that the state could not function unless each citizen put a finger in one of the holes to keep the water from leaking out. In other words, anyone who was willing to serve could be a citizen, and all citizens had to do their part to support the king. Whereas the family model used by Whydah encouraged the kingdom to stay small and familial, the water-pot model used by Dahomey provided a conceptual framework for state expansion and authoritarian rule.

Dahomey had remained relatively small until King **Agaja** assumed the throne in 1718, having previously been the commander of the Dahomian army. His first project was to create a professional army to replace the poorly trained farmers drafted to fight during the dry season after the harvest was in. He put his professional soldiers through extensive training and drills, and he replaced the longbows they had been using with flintlock muskets. Each musketeer was given a young apprentice who served as his shield carrier. When a battle began, the soldiers would fire their muskets. Then they would hand them to the shield carriers and take up swords and shields for close combat. Apprentices who performed bravely in battle would get a chance to become soldiers themselves. William Snelgrave, a British visitor who observed some of the army's drills and war games, described the soldiers as "elite troops, brave and well disciplined, supported by a staff of experienced officers."

During his years as commander of the Dahomian army, King Agaja had fought numerous battles that had produced prisoners of war, who were sent down the trade routes to Whydah to be sold to the Europeans. The trading system changed in 1718, when the king of Whydah decreed that all traders from the hinterlands were required to sell their captives to a royal agent of Whydah, who would then resell them at a profit to the Europeans. King Agaja wanted to sell his captives directly to the Europeans, without going through middlemen. In 1724, he invaded and conquered Allada, which gave him direct access to the Atlantic Ocean, but not to the European trading forts, which were located in Whydah. The following year, he sent an ambassador to the king of Whydah requesting open traffic through Whydah to the coast and offering to pay the usual customs on exports of captives. The request was denied. Two years later, the forces of Dahomey invaded and conquered Whydah, extending their kingdom down to the sea.

With his access to the coastal forts secured, King Agaja embarked on a series of battles to further expand his kingdom. After a battle, all the prisoners of war would be presented to the king in an elaborate ceremony. Some of the prisoners would be put to work as laborers on the king's farms or as servants in his palaces. Once a captive was claimed by the king, he or she could never again be sold. Other prisoners were distributed to army officers or royal officials as patronage. The rest were sent to the European forts to be sold in exchange for guns, gunpowder, cloth, and cowrie-shell currency. By shifting his army from longbows to flintlock muskets, King Agaja had made himself dependent on the European traders for a steady supply of gunpowder.

With Dahomey's conquest of the coast, the nature of the slave trade changed dramatically. Whydah had been a mercantile kingdom where the slave trade was conducted by private African merchants who paid customs and taxes to the king. Dahomey, on the other hand, was a militarized kingdom that produced captives

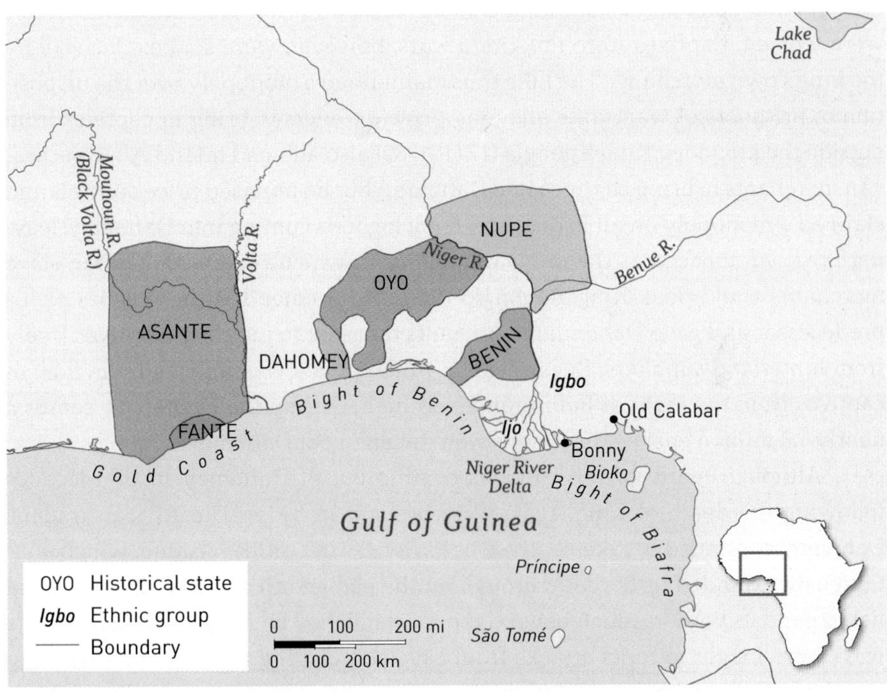

MAJOR STATES ALONG THE GOLD COAST AND THE BIGHT OF BENIN IN 1750 The expansion of Asante and Dahomey took place mostly after 1700 and became a major source of captives for the trans-Atlantic slave trade. The Niger River Delta ports of Bonny and Old Calabar made it a major slave trading destination in a region characterized by decentralized political systems.

from its own wars. King Agaja closed the trade routes to private African traders, making the slave trade a royal monopoly that was totally under his control. When he learned in 1732 that the ruler of the coastal port of Jakin was surreptitiously selling Yoruba captives who had been brought in by private African merchants, he destroyed the city, taking over 4,000 prisoners, most of whom were sold to European slave traders.

Dahomey after King Agaja

Subsequent kings of Dahomey modified the royal slave trade monopoly in various ways. King Tegbesu (1740–1774) proclaimed a policy of free trade, but African slave traders from inland regions were not allowed to travel through Dahomey and sell their slaves directly to Europeans. Instead, they had to sell their captives to Dahomian middlemen, a policy that led to the development of a powerful Dahomian merchant community. Some of the biggest private slave merchants were women. Captives from the king's wars, however, were sold exclusively by the king's own merchants. The king thus maintained a monopoly over the disposition of prisoners of war while allowing private traders to bring in captives from outside the kingdom. King Kpengla (1774–1789) also allowed inland African caravan merchants to bring captives into Dahomey, but he imposed price controls and claimed a monopoly on all British and French goods coming into Dahomey, leaving Brazilian tobacco as the only commodity in which private Dahomian slave merchants could deal. King Angonglo (1790–1818) amended the policies of his predecessor and gave Dahomian merchants the right to purchase captives freely from hinterland suppliers. Regardless of which policy was followed, the flow of captives from the Bight of Benin remained high. During the eighteenth century, nearly 1.3 million enslaved Africans were taken out of Dahomey.

Although many of the captives coming out of Dahomey in the decades following the death of King Agaja were brought in by private African traders, Dahomey continued to take captives in its own wars. Unlike Asante, which continuously extended its borders throughout the eighteenth century, Dahomey did not expand its borders much beyond those established by King Agaja. Some of its wars were fought to repel attacks from cavalries coming through the Dahomey Gap from the northeast, and others were fought to put down rebellions. But a substantial portion of Dahomey's military activity seems to have been devoted to slave raids conducted to fill the coffers of the king.

A major military innovation in Dahomey during the eighteenth century was the use of female soldiers, many of whom were slaves, as elite troops. King Agaja had used armed women as palace guards and as his personal bodyguards, but his successor, King Tegbesu, used female soldiers in battle when Dahomey repulsed an attack by Asante in 1764. A few years later, over 800 female troops were on display in a parade in the royal capital. In 1781, after the regular male army returned in defeat from a slave raid into the neighboring country of Aguna, King Kpengla immediately set out for Aguna with an army of 800 women, who successfully routed the enemy. By then the elite force of female soldiers, commanded by a female general, had become an indispensable part of Dahomey's military arsenal.

THE AMAZONS OF DAHOMEY The elite female soldiers of Dahomey were referred to as "Amazons" by Europeans (after the female warriors of Greek mythology). They often served as the shock troops who led the attack, and they fired their guns from the shoulder, while the men shot from the hip. This picture, first published in 1851, is based on a description by Frederick Forbes, who lived in Dahomey during 1849–1850.

The Lunda Empire

In Angola, nearly a century of warfare between the Portuguese in Luanda and the African kingdoms near the coast had come to an end in the 1680s with the signing of treaties between the Portuguese and the inland kingdoms of Matamba and Kasanje (see chapter 5). Further efforts to curb Portuguese violence in the interior followed. In 1703, the Portuguese banned whites and mulattoes from traveling into the interior, except for those who were stationed at the Portuguese forts; and in 1721, the Portuguese governors in Luanda were prohibited from running their own personal slave trading enterprises on the side. The slave trade continued at a brisk pace, but after 1700, the great majority of enslaved people came from the far interior. In contrast to the seventeenth century, when a substantial portion of the captives shipped out of Luanda had been directly enslaved by armies under

Portuguese control, the eighteenth century saw a division of labor in which most of the enslavement was done by African kings and chiefs in the far interior, while militarized caravans under African control moved captives from major market centers in the interior kingdoms to the Atlantic coast. The most important of these interior kingdoms was the Lunda Empire.

The **Lunda Empire** had a lot in common with the Asante Empire in that it fought wars primarily to expand the state. Captives were a product of those wars, but not the main reason for fighting them. A major difference was that Asante imported vast quantities of guns and ammunition, whereas Lunda imported fewer guns and a lot of cloth and beads. The Lunda Kingdom arose in the grasslands south of the tropical rainforest, over 600 miles inland from the Atlantic coast. Prior to the rise of the kingdom, the people in the Lunda heartland had developed a kinship system that recognized a person's kin along both male and female lines. That system created a web of kinship ties that was too complex

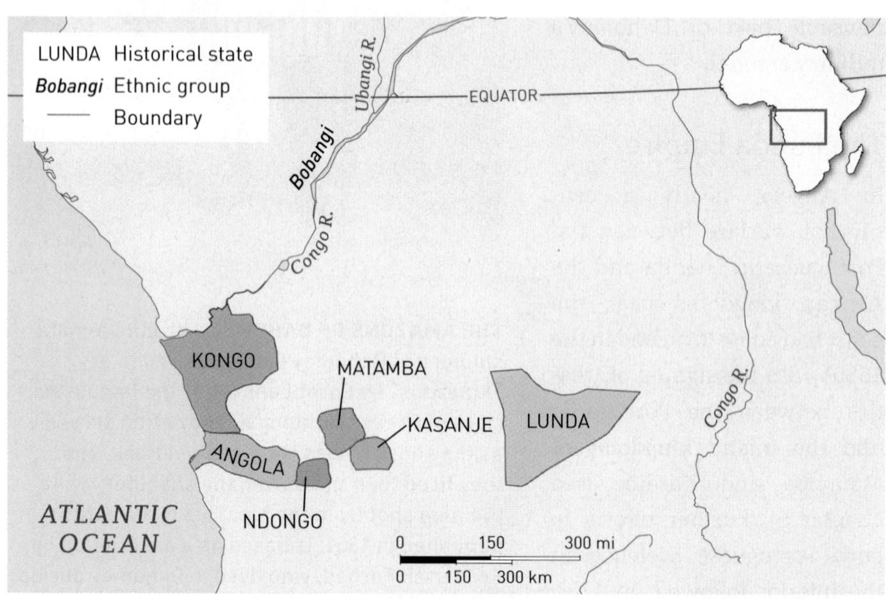

MAJOR STATES OF WEST CENTRAL AFRICA, 1642–1807 This map shows the Kongo Kingdom, the Portuguese colony of Angola, the kingdoms of Ndongo and Matamba (which were conquered and ruled by Queen Njinga), and the Imbangala state of Kasanje. The major new addition is the Lunda Empire, which began trading with Kasanje and Kongo during the eighteenth century. Also shown is the general location of the Bobangi trading towns along the Congo River—even though the Bobangi did not form a state, they dominated the trade in a decentralized region.

and amorphous to be the basis for social organization because it gave each person several options about whom to live with and whom to show solidarity with. Instead, the main social unit was the "house," which included whatever kinfolk from both sides of the family its headman could attract, and whatever strangers, clients, and slaves the headman could collect. Houses competed with one another for members, and the strength of a house was often directly related to the success of the headman. Over time, the most successful headmen became chiefs who ruled over several houses. In the next stage of political development, the most successful chiefdoms absorbed smaller chiefdoms, thus creating a distinction between great chiefs and petty chiefs. By this dynamic, the Lunda Kingdom emerged in the seventeenth century, when it consolidated a number of small chiefdoms under a single ruler.

As the Lunda Kingdom expanded in the seventeenth century, the king appointed tax collectors and trade officials who helped him gain control of the long-distance trade in coveted "noble goods," such as copper crosses, leopard skins, lion skins, and parrot feathers, which bestowed great prestige on their owners. Such items were collected by the king's tax collectors in each region and sent to the royal court. The king then redistributed them to territorial officials, who in turn gave them out as patronage to loyal subordinates. War captives were also considered to be luxuries who served the political elites, and they were distributed to subordinates in the same way as lion skins and copper crosses. Lunda traders traveled all the way to the major market in the Imbangala kingdom of **Kasanje** in the 1660s and 1680s, bringing raffia cloth mats that they had collected as tribute to trade for salt, which was scarce in the Lunda heartland. At that time, they did not bring captives to sell.

In the eighteenth century, the Lunda Kingdom was growing into the Lunda Empire through territorial conquest and expansion. These activities produced captives, many of whom were sold at the slave market in Kasanje. When the Portuguese slave trader Leitão visited Kasanje in 1756, he wrote that the Lunda king "is very powerful, and captains sent by him to the west, to the north, to the south, and to other parts with great numbers of troops come forth from his principalities and dominions to capture slaves, which they sell to the region which is closest to where they take them." Leitão added, "It is certain that were it not for them, we would not have so many slaves, because they are moved by their ambition and renown to conquer and circulate in lands very far removed from their fatherland, turned into terrestrial eagles, merely to become the masters of other peoples." By this time, Lunda was the largest supplier of captives to the market at Kasanje.

The Lunda king integrated the slave trade into his overall administrative structure. He sent large slave caravans manned by Lunda soldiers to the market at Kasanje to exchange his captives for guns, powder, cloth, mirrors, and beads. He kept the guns and powder for his army and distributed the other items to his tax collectors, who in turn distributed them to lesser titleholders. The beads and cloth became a necessary part of the wardrobes of well-dressed Lunda nobles, who stitched the beads into their caps and wrapped 5 or 6 yards of imported cloth around their waists, tucked over their belts in bulky pleats. To show that they owned more than one piece of imported cloth, they sewed contrasting borders onto different pieces. The Lunda Empire's blend of taxation and patronage was a key ingredient that held the administration of the expanding empire together.

JAGA KASANJE AND QUEEN NJINGA This painting shows the Imbangala war leader Jaga Kasanje and his wife Njinga during the brief period when they were married. After their divorce, Njinga and her followers conquered the kingdoms of Ndongo and Matamba, while Jaga Kasanje founded the Kingdom of Kasanje. The picture was painted in the 1660s by Giovanni Antonio Cavazzi, an Italian Capuchin missionary who knew both of them personally.

Between 1750 and 1800, the Lunda Empire launched a series of invasions of Kasanje in hopes of gaining control of the salt pans near the coast and of selling its war captives directly to the Portuguese. It complained that the Imbangala of Kasanje were buying Lunda's captives and then turning around and selling them to the Portuguese for three times the price. Failing to dislodge the Imbangala from Kasanje, Lunda diversified its market by sending some of its slave caravans toward the ports north of the Congo estuary and sending others toward the southern Angolan port of Benguela.

Recognizing that a number of inland states were sending their captives to ports other than Luanda, the Portuguese governor lamented in the 1760s that it was "an illusion to suppose that Europeans could impose terms on the trade and bully African merchants into disadvantageous bargains. Since marching slaves was a comparatively cheap form of transport, the [African] middlemen were willing to send them long distances to find the highest prices and seek the goods currently in greatest demand." By admitting that Europeans had only limited control over the Angolan slave trade, the governor revealed just how much the structure and practice of the slave trade in Angola had changed since the Portuguese wars of the seventeenth century.

COMMERCIAL NETWORKS IN POLITICALLY DECENTRALIZED REGIONS

Despite the existence of powerful kingdoms and large empires in Africa, there were many regions where people maintained decentralized political systems with no authority higher than a lineage headman or a village chief. Such systems gave people maximum control over the circumstances of their own lives. The advantages of decentralized systems were recognized as early as 1507, when Valentim Fernandes wrote that the people near the mouth of the Gambia River "have neither a king nor a particular lord, honoring one person among them more than another according to his qualities. They will not consent to accept a lord." These politically decentralized regions were not economic backwaters. They were often bristling with marketplaces and crisscrossed by itinerant traders. In the absence of a king to regulate the trade or ensure the security of the trade routes, the traders themselves formed networks and organizations to carry out these functions. This section will focus on two decentralized regions that were heavily involved in the trans-Atlantic slave trade.

The Niger Delta

A ship heading eastward along the African coast from the Gold Coast or the Bight of Benin would encounter nearly 300 miles of flooded mangrove swamp punctuated by numerous inlets, rivers, and creeks: the Niger River delta. From its source in the distant Fuuta Jaloo highlands, the Niger River flowed northeast to the edge of the Sahara Desert, passing the trading towns of Timbuktu and Gao, and then turned sharply southeast to make the long journey from the Sahara Desert to the Gulf of Guinea. As it neared the coast, the river disappeared into a labyrinth of creeks, lagoons, and waterways that threaded their way through the third-largest mangrove swamp in the world. So dense and extensive was the network

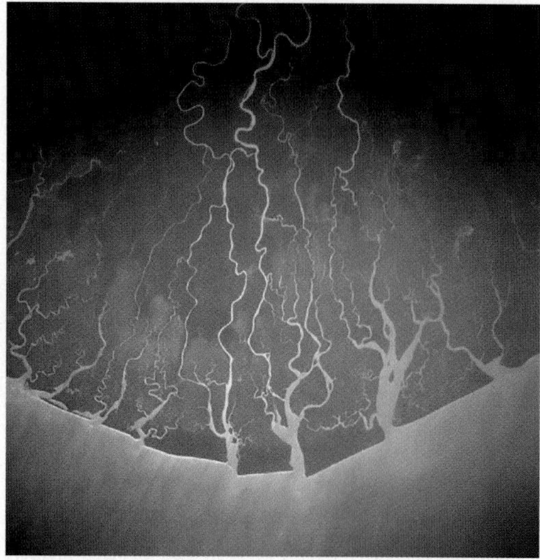

THE NIGER RIVER DELTA This photo taken from the space shuttle shows how the Niger River fans out into a series of creeks and streams to form the Niger delta. The Niger delta is twice the size of the state of Maryland. In the eighteenth century, it was populated by people who made their living by fishing and trading.

of waterways that it was possible to go by canoe from the western end of the delta to the eastern end without ever traveling on open sea. Because the Niger River did not have an identifiable mouth, European ships visited the area for over 300 years before they realized that this waterlogged wonderland was the delta of the Niger River.

Prior to the arrival of Europeans, the Ijo and Efik inhabitants of the Niger delta made their living mainly by fishing and making salt, which they exchanged for agricultural products, cloth, and tools with the people who lived farther inland. Because good settlement sites were scarce, they often congregated in towns, which were subdivided into wards. A ward was made up by a group of kinfolk related to one another through the male line. It was governed collectively by the heads of the component households, who selected a ward headman based on considerations of leadership qualities, wealth, and age, as well as genealogy. The headmen of the different wards formed a town council that made decisions for the town as a whole. Social solidarity among members of different wards was advanced through intermarriage, as well as by secret societies that offered membership to successful men. Some of the secret societies were responsible for performing the rituals needed to maintain good relations with the spirits of the rivers and the estuaries. Each town operated as an independent unit, and there were no kingdoms or empires in the Niger delta.

Portuguese ships began to visit the Niger delta in the sixteenth century to purchase captives, whom they took to Elmina, on the Gold Coast, to trade for gold. In the seventeenth century, they began exporting captives from the Niger delta to Brazil and the Spanish colonies of South America. After 1650, English, French, and Dutch ships began to visit the Niger delta in search of captives. Ships would stop at several towns in hopes of putting together a full cargo, but after 1730, they concentrated their commerce on two major ports: Bonny, in the western part of the delta, and Old Calabar, on the Cross River, just beyond the eastern edge of the delta. During the eighteenth century, the slave trade in the Niger delta came to be dominated by British ships sailing out of Liverpool.

The European traders who came in the eighteenth century were not permitted by the local town authorities to build forts or even warehouses in the Niger delta. Instead, a slave ship would arrive at a delta port and advance trade goods on credit to one or more African traders. The Africans would then go off in their large dugout canoes to purchase captives at markets in the interior, while the ship waited at anchor. To make sure that the African traders didn't abscond with the goods, the European captain would often require them to leave a son or a daughter on the ship as a pawn until all debts were paid. The captains of slave ships maintained long-term relationships with African traders by exchanges of letters, by bringing gifts for the traders' children, and even by taking children of African traders to be educated in Britain. This last practice created a group of African traders who were literate in English and regularly sent letters to their trading partners in Britain informing them of the state of the markets.

During the eighteenth century, the nature of the delta trading towns themselves was changing to accommodate the new emphasis on commerce. Wards were organizing themselves into trading firms that would send their members to the hinterlands in enormous dugout canoes to purchase people who had been enslaved. These trading firms were known as **canoe houses** because the head of the firm had to be capable of manning and maintaining at least one 50-person canoe that was armed to defend itself on expeditions up the Niger River. Successful firms would keep the strongest captives for themselves to serve as canoe paddlers. Since there was no king or army to prevent the enslaved paddlers from running away during a trading trip, they were often allowed to trade on their own account as an incentive to remain loyal to the firm. Successful traders, even those of slave origin, would use their profits to buy their own slave paddlers. When a subordinate member of the firm had acquired enough slaves to "fill his canoe," as it was called, he was allowed to trade entirely on his own, as long as he shared his profits with the head of the firm. The trading towns thus grew stronger and wealthier through the expansion and proliferation of canoe houses as these artificial socioeconomic entities replaced lineages as the basic unit of social organization. In the new system, several interconnected canoe houses made up a ward, and several wards made up a town.

After 1750, the Niger delta surpassed all other regions of West Africa in exports of captives, with Bonny and Old Calabar as the leading slave ports. The great majority of the captives came from the Igbo region, situated in the rainforest just inland from the coastal mangrove swamp. The Igbo people cultivated yams and other food crops in forest clearings, and they processed palm oil. The Igbo had a decentralized political system by which authority was exercised primarily within the patrilineage. A village council made up of the heads of the major lineages decided matters that involved the village as a whole, but the Igbo were too leery of authority to have village chiefs. The nineteenth-century writer James Africanus Horton, whose father was Igbo, wrote of the Igbo spirit: "They would not, as a rule, allow anyone to act the superior over them; nor sway their conscience by coercion to the performance of any act, whether good or bad, when they have not the inclination to do so; hence there is not that unity among them that is found among other tribes; in fact everyone likes to be his own master."

Even though the Igbo people had neither kings nor large armies, people in Igbo country could become enslaved by various means. They could be sentenced to slavery for a crime; they could be sold to pay a debt; or they could be kidnapped. Small-scale wars were fought between rival villages or groups of villages, but warfare was not the major cause of enslavement in this region. Instead, people became enslaved singly or in small groups in scattered locations throughout Igbo country. It took a vast trading system to gather them together for delivery to the European slave ships. The absence of centralized authority in Igbo country did not in any way discourage trade. The countryside was dotted with marketplaces that met every 4 days, with different markets meeting on different days of the week to avoid overlap. Certain Igbo market towns hosted periodic fairs that met once a month for 4 days at a time. Goods could travel from one end of Igbo country to the other by going from market to market, carried by short-distance traders who seldom traveled more than 15–20 miles from home.

Even in the absence of centralized political authority, it was possible to develop a centralized trade network. The dominant trade network in Igbo country during the eighteenth century was the Aro network, based in the town of Arochukwu, located on an escarpment overlooking the Cross River. The town was the home of the famous Arochukwu oracle, whose reputation for sage advice attracted pilgrims and inquirers from across Igbo country. Moving out from their base in Arochukwu, the Aro traders settled throughout the region to buy and sell captives and a variety of commodities. Their association with the oracle gained them respect and protection as they traveled around the countryside, but there were several additional reasons for their success, one of which was their easy access to firearms and gunpowder. Another was their extensive network. They made blood pacts with thousands of local leaders and married the daughters of prominent men in all the areas where they traded. Still another reason for their success was their effort to build up the commercial infrastructure in Igbo country. They promoted and maintained regional fairs, and they facilitated transportation through the rainforest by constructing a series of trails, bridges, and rest stops.

The expansion of the Aro network in the early eighteenth century provided the commercial infrastructure for a major increase in exports of captives from Bonny and Old Calabar, which tripled between 1730 and 1750, then doubled again by the 1780s. Traders from Old Calabar could get a load of captives by going up the Cross River to Arochukwu, the headquarters of the Aro network. Traders from Bonny, on the other hand, went up the Imo River through the mangrove swamps to river towns that were connected by overland routes to the Aro-dominated fair at Bende, in the heart of Igbo country. We can get a good sense of how the system operated from a description written in the 1780s by Alexander Falconbridge, a doctor on a slave ship that visited Bonny. "The preparations made by the black traders upon setting out for the fairs which are held upcountry are very considerable," he wrote. "From twenty to thirty canoes, capable of containing thirty or forty Negroes each, are assembled for the purpose; and such goods are put on board them as they expect will be wanted for the purchase of the number of slaves they intend to buy. When their loading is completed, they commence their voyage with colors flying and music playing. In about ten or eleven days, they generally return to Bonny with full cargoes." By this process, repeated over and over again, nearly a million enslaved Africans were taken out of the Niger Delta during the eighteenth century.

The Middle Congo River

A European ship entering the mouth of the Congo River could sail up the estuary for about 100 miles before running into impassable rapids. There was no point in trying to get around them, because the river for the next 200 miles was little more than an endless series of waterfalls and rapids. Those rapids were so formidable that the course of the Congo River above them remained a mystery to Europeans until 1877. Africans, however, knew that at the other end of the rapids, the river widened out into a calm lake known as Malebo Pool. From there, the Congo River was navigable upstream for over 1,000 miles as it flowed through the tropical rainforest and received water from a series of major tributaries. Given the difficulty of overland transportation in the dense rainforest, the middle Congo

A LARGE DUGOUT CANOE Carved from the trunk of a single tree, Congo River dugout canoes were up to 85 feet long and could carry up to 80 paddlers. Their thick, flattened bottoms and thin sides gave them a low center of gravity. They were so stable that the canoemen paddled standing up.

River and its tributaries provided a commercial lifeline that facilitated the transportation of people and trade goods by dugout canoe. Because the rainforest contained some very large trees, it was possible to carve out enormous canoes, which might be powered by up to 80 paddlers.

The people of the rainforest did not organize themselves into kingdoms or chiefdoms. Instead, the basic social and political unit was the house, which consisted of an extended family group who occupied a village or a portion of a village, plus any strangers, clients, or slaves that they had acquired to increase the size and power of their group. A house grew or shrank according to the economic fortunes of its headman. If he was wealthy, he used his wealth to marry several wives and purchase captives to augment the size and prestige of his house. Large houses attracted strangers and clients who joined voluntarily. In hard times, however, the clients deserted and the domestic slaves were sold, thus creating a spiral of decline. Although most houses in the rainforest neither enjoyed great wealth nor suffered great poverty, the people who controlled the trade along the rivers were susceptible to cycles of boom and bust.

The people who lived along the middle Congo River and its tributaries made their living through a combination of agriculture and fishing. While agriculture rooted them in one place, fishing forced them to range widely in their dugout canoes because the fish congregated in different places at different times of the year according to the rising and falling of the water. They were also forced to work out cooperative arrangements with neighboring fishing peoples, and thus they became knowledgeable about the course of the river far beyond their villages. As they traveled in their canoes, fishermen often carried on trade in local goods such as salt, pottery, camwood powder, and iron, as these resources were distributed unevenly throughout the forest. They also transported people who had become enslaved because of a local war, as punishment for a crime, or as payment for a debt. As in Igbo country, people of this region were usually enslaved singly or in small groups.

One key group of fishermen/traders in the forest region lived in Bobangi Esanga, a town composed of several independent wards nestled side by side along the lower Ubangi River, about 30 miles from the spot where the Ubangi flows into the Congo. Each of the component wards constituted a house with its own headman, and there was no single person who was the chief of the whole town. In the early eighteenth century, the fishermen of Bobangi Esanga began to purchase captives from the villages they visited in their travels. They took them down the Ubangi, and then down the Congo as far as the mouth of the Alima River, where they sold them to other canoe-based traders, who took them up the Alima and then sold them to yet another set of traders, who organized overland caravans to the Loango coast, just north of the mouth of the Congo River.

As the eighteenth century progressed, the **Bobangi**, as these traders had come to be called, took their captives farther down the Congo River until they emerged from the rainforest into the wooded grasslands, where they sold them to the Tio king at Mbe. The king, in turn, organized overland caravans to take them to the Atlantic coast. In an effort to gain a larger segment of the trade, Bobangi traders went all the way to Malebo Pool, where the rapids began. There were Tio chiefs installed at the pool, who would buy the captives from the Bobangi and resell them for a profit to the caravan merchants who took them overland to the coast. Desiring to sell their captives directly to the caravan merchants, the Bobangi made three different attempts to drive out the Tio and take over the trade at Malebo Pool, but they failed each time. The Bobangi traders eventually reached a trade agreement with the Tio chiefs.

At some point during this process of Bobangi expansion (the dates are far from certain), traders from Bobangi Esanga began to establish trading towns along the 300-mile stretch between the lower Ubangi and Malebo Pool. Because the Congo River was nearly 10 miles wide at some spots, and at other spots was dotted with chains of islands that prevented a person from seeing from one bank to the other, the Bobangi built their towns at places where the river narrowed, so that river traffic was easy to monitor and control. They also allowed other trading groups that did not come from Bobangi Esanga to join their commercial alliance and construct towns along the river. In this way, the Bobangi became a formidable trading alliance and gained a monopoly on trade along a 300-mile stretch of the Congo River.

In keeping with the decentralized nature of the forest societies, a typical Bobangi trading town consisted of a series of independent wards built side by side along the riverbank. Each ward was essentially an independent trading firm populated by the head trader, his wives, and his slaves. Enslaved women were purchased to grow food for the trading expeditions, while enslaved men were purchased to paddle the large trading canoes. To keep the slave paddlers from deserting on the long trading trips, which could last up to 6 months, their masters often gave them some trade goods so that they could make a profit by trading on their own. Slaves who proved to be talented traders were promoted to canoe captains and were eventually allowed to conduct their own trading missions. Successful captains invested their profits in buying captives. When a captain had enough slaves to man his own canoe, he established his own trading firm that was subordinate to the firm he had come from. In this way, successful firms grew and divided and grew some more, while less successful firms shrank and might disappear. The major consequence of this system was that most of the traders living in the Bobangi trading towns had begun their careers as captives.

Although the Bobangi controlled the key portion of the middle Congo River between the mouth of the Ubangi and Malebo Pool, they were only a part of a larger system. Upstream from the Bobangi stretch of the Congo, the trade was controlled by a similar trading alliance known as Bangala, and trade along each major tributary of the Congo was controlled by a separate waterborne trading group. In this way, anybody in the middle Congo region who was enslaved would be taken to the nearest river and sold to river traders, who would eventually sell him or her to the Bobangi for transportation to Malebo Pool. From there, the captive would be taken in an overland caravan to the coast. The vast tropical forest did not contain expansionist states or large armies, but it had nonetheless developed a devastatingly efficient system to gather up enslaved individuals from remote parts of the forest and deliver them to the Atlantic coast.

CONCLUSION

During the eighteenth century, nearly 7 million enslaved people were taken out of Africa to labor in the New World. Because of the voracious demand for slave labor in the Americas, the prices that European and American slave ships paid for captives on the African coast rose steadily throughout the century. This economic trend made it profitable for African caravan merchants to seek captives farther and farther inland, thus bringing new regions into the orbit of this brutal human traffic. In the seventeenth century, most captives had come from within 250 miles of the Atlantic coast. By the end of the 1750s, however, it was not unusual for captives to come from regions 600 or more miles from the coast, and many of the coastal states had become little more than corridors through which slave caravans from the deep interior passed. This process varied widely from region to region. In Senegambia after 1750, the vast majority of the captives were coming from inland kingdoms such as Segu. The Gold Coast presented a very different picture: the

Asante Empire arose in 1701 in the near interior, and its subsequent conquests were directed both southward toward the coast and northward toward the grasslands. A similar situation obtained in the kingdom of Dahomey, which continued to fight wars in the coastal zone but also received captives from the far interior via the trade routes. In West Central Africa, by contrast, most of the captives after 1750 came from such faraway places as the tropical rainforest and the Lunda Empire.

The rise of expansionist states that financed their conquests and wars through the sale of captives was a direct consequence of global war capitalism. The rulers of these states used their connections to the trans-Atlantic slave trade to monopolize imports of firearms, and they distributed imported luxury goods as patronage to their supporters. Yet there were significant differences among individual states. Segu was a warlord state that continually absorbed captives into its expanding armies and placed slave administrators in charge of conquered territory. Asante and Lunda, on the other hand, were expanding empires that created new administrative and ideological structures to integrate conquered peoples. Fuuta Jaloo and Dahomey fought numerous wars throughout the eighteenth century, but their boundaries did not expand accordingly. It seems likely that many of those wars were simply raids to gain captives.

Both expansionist states and corridor states retained a great many of the enslaved people who came into their possession to serve as laborers, soldiers, farmers, and concubines. Reports from Kongo, Segu, and Fuuta Jaloo estimated the local slave populations to be equal to or greater than the populations of free people. In the trading towns of the Niger delta and the middle Congo River, slaves outnumbered free people by a wide margin. It was only by rapidly assimilating them into the trading houses that rebellions or massive desertions were avoided. An important and somewhat novel use of enslaved persons was in the military. The army of Segu was composed primarily of slave soldiers, and the kingdom of Dahomey developed an elite force of female soldiers, many of whom were slaves.

Because of the growing internal use of slaves in the expansionist states, a person living in the far interior who was captured in a war was not necessarily fated to end up on a slave ship. Gender was one of the factors that tipped the balance. European slaving captains in the eighteenth century sought two or three men for every woman, so enslaved men were at far greater risk of being sold to Europeans than were captured women. Culturally constructed gender divisions of labor influenced the selection of captives because Europeans saw plantation agriculture as primarily men's work, whereas Africans saw many forms of agriculture as primarily women's work. As a result, two-thirds of the captives who were carried across the Atlantic during the eighteenth century were men, while many of the enslaved women remained in Africa as agricultural laborers for African slaveholders. Because African social systems generally allowed a man to have more than one wife, the surplus women could be absorbed into the host society and bear children. That gender imbalance among exported captives may have helped to prevent demographic collapse in the parts of Africa most affected by the trans-Atlantic slave trade.

Although much of the historical literature focuses on the role of African kingdoms and empires in the slave trade, politically decentralized societies developed equally efficient systems for collecting enslaved persons and delivering them to the coast. In the Niger delta, the politically decentralized Ijo and Efik people developed the canoe house system to ferry large numbers of captives over long distances. In the forest region inland from the Niger delta, the Igbo people maintained a decentralized political system while accommodating the development of a highly centralized commercial network run by the Aro traders. A very similar trading system developed along the middle Congo, even though the two regions were not in contact with each other. Because the societies of the tropical rainforest were politically decentralized, they were fertile ground for the establishment of commercial networks to integrate the region economically. When the Bobangi traders gained control of the middle Congo between the Ubangi and Malebo Pool, they became the dominant middlemen in a vast trading network.

Direct European influence waned in parts of Africa during the eighteenth century even as the slave trade grew. The Portuguese governor in Luanda was correct in the 1760s when he noted that the Europeans could not bully Africans into accepting low prices or shoddy trade goods. Despite the economic weakness of individual European slave traders, however, the economic power of European slave traders as a group was enormous because they were the gatekeepers to the global economy. Kingdoms such as Asante and Dahomey relied on the Europeans for continuing supplies of firearms and gunpowder, and African rulers regularly distributed European and Asian luxury goods that came in via the slave trade to ensure the loyalty of their subordinates, who prized the imported items as status symbols and displayed them conspicuously. King Agaja of Dahomey, for example, periodically distributed cowrie shells and brandy among the common people; the rulers of Fuuta Jaloo inserted European luxury goods into their closed economic circuit of taxation and patronage; and the Lunda kings distributed imported cloth and beads to the territorial officials. The ideology of kingship in some parts of Africa required the king to be both ruthless and generous. Both of those characteristics were in evidence in the expansionist kingdoms.

CHAPTER REVIEW

KEY TERMS AND VOCABULARY

Segu

Mamari Kulubali

Fuuta Jaloo

Asante Empire

Osei Tutu

Dahomey

Agaja

Lunda Empire

Kasanje

canoe house

Bobangi

STUDY QUESTIONS

1. Discuss the relative danger or security of living in an expansionist state in the eighteenth century versus living in the vicinity of an expansionist state.
2. What were the advantages and disadvantages of having an army made up of soldiers of slave origin, such as the Segu army in the eighteenth century?
3. Can you identify the major motivations for the wars waged by Fuuta Jaloo and Asante? Were they fought to take captives or to expand the state?
4. Why is the kingdom of Whydah characterized in this chapter as a corridor state?
5. How would you differentiate between the slaving operations of the different expansionist states described in this chapter?
6. Describe the differences between the trading systems of centralized states and those of the decentralized trading societies along the Niger and Congo Rivers.
7. How did the Oracle of Arochukwu become such a powerful figure?

PERSPECTIVES

FORMING A SLAVE CARAVAN IN SENEGAMBIA

Mungo Park was a Scottish traveler and adventurer who visited the kingdoms of Segu and Kaarta in 1795–1797. In the town of Kamalia, in the Middle Niger region, he met a Juula merchant named Karfa, who was organizing a caravan to take captives to sell to the British on the Gambia River. Eager to get back to the Atlantic coast, Park joined the caravan and traveled with it for nearly 2 months. He provided a rare account of the operations of a slave caravan in the interior of West Africa.

On the 24th January [1797], Karfa returned to Kamalia with a number of people, and thirteen slaves which he had purchased. . . . The slaves which Karfa had brought with him were all of them prisoners of war; they had been taken by the Bambarran army in the kingdoms of Wassela and Kaarta, and carried to Segu, where some of them had remained three years in irons. From Segu they were sent, in company with a number of other captives, up the Niger in two large canoes and offered for sale at Yamina, Bamako, and Kancaba; at which places the greater number of the captives were bartered for gold-dust, and the remainder sent forward to Kankaree.

They viewed me at first with a look of horror, and repeatedly asked if my countrymen were cannibals. They were very desirous to know what became of slaves after they had crossed the salt water. I told them that they would be employed in cultivating the land, but they would not believe me. A deeply rooted idea, that the whites purchase Negroes for the purpose of devouring them, or of selling them to others that they may be devoured hereafter, naturally makes the slaves contemplate the journey towards the coast with great terror; insomuch as the Slatees [African caravan merchants] are forced to keep them constantly in irons and watch them very closely to prevent their escape. . . .

April 19th. The long wished-for day of our departure was at length arrived, and the Slatees, having taken the irons from their slaves, assembled them at the door of Karfa's house, where the bundles were all tied up and everyone had his load assigned to him. The coffle [slave caravan] on its departure from Kamalia consisted of twenty-seven slaves for sale, the property of Karfa and four other Slatees; but we were afterwards joined by five at Maraboo and three at Bala, making in all thirty-five slaves. The free men were fourteen in number, but most of them had one or two wives and some domestic slaves, and the schoolmaster, who was now upon his return for Worakoo, the place of his nativity, took with him eight scholars; so that the number of free people and domestic slaves amounted to thirty-eight, and the whole amount of the coffle was seventy-three. Among the free men were six *Jillakeas* (singing men) whose musical talents were frequently exerted, either to divert our fatigue or to obtain us a welcome from strangers.

1. *How did the captives view white people?*
2. *Explain how Juula merchants, students, musicians, captives, and an Englishman could coexist in the same caravan.*

Source: Mungo Park, *Travels in the Interior Districts of Africa Performed under the Direction and Patronage of the African Association in the Years 1795, 1796, and 1797* (London: W. Bulmer and Co., 1799), pp. 318–319, 323–324.

THE PRINCELY SLAVE

Abdul Rahahman was the son of the ruler of Fuuta Jaloo. A colonel in his father's army, he was sent to put down a rebellion near the Atlantic coast. He was captured by the rebels and sold to a British slave ship that took him to Natchez, Mississippi. After 40 years as a slave, he was freed with help from President John Quincy Adams and given passage to Liberia. He contracted a disease in Liberia and died before he could reach his homeland of Fuuta Jaloo. Before leaving the United States, he told his story to a "gentleman from Natchez," who wrote it down.

I was born in the city of Timbuktu. My father had been living in Timbuktu, but removed to be King in Timbo, in Fuuta Jaloo. His name was Almami Abraham. I was five years old when my father carried me from Timbuktu. I lived in Timbo, mostly, until I was twenty-one, and followed the horsemen. I was made Captain when I was twenty-one; after they put me to that, and found that I had a very good head, at twenty-four they made me Colonel.

At the age of twenty-six, they sent me to fight the Hebohs, because they destroyed the vessels that came to the coast, and prevented our trade. When we fought, I defeated them. But they went back one hundred miles into the country, and hid themselves in the mountain. We could not see them, and did not expect there was any enemy. When we got there, we dismounted and led our horses, until we were half way up the mountain. Then they fired upon us. We saw the smoke, we heard the guns, we saw the people drop down. I told everyone to run until we reached the top of the hill, then to wait for each other until all came there, and we would fight them.

After I had arrived at the summit, I could see no one except my guard. They followed us, and we ran and fought. I saw this would not do. I told everyone to run who wished to do so. Everyone who wished to run, fled. I said, "I will not run for an African." I got down from my horse and sat down. One came behind and shot me in the shoulder. One came before and pointed his gun to shoot me, but seeing my clothes (ornamented with gold), he cried out, "that! the King." Then everyone turned down their guns, and came and took me. When they came to take me, I had a sword under me, but they did not see it. The first one that came, I sprang forward and killed. Then one came behind and knocked me down with a gun, and I fainted.

After they took me to their own country, they kept me one week. As soon as my people got home, my father missed me. He raised a troop and came after me; and as soon as the Hebohs knew he was coming, they carried me into the wilderness. After my father came and burnt the country, they carried me to the Mandingo country, on the Gambia. They sold me directly, with fifty others, to an English ship.

1. *Explain the circumstances of Abdul Rahahman's capture.*
2. *Why did his captors take him north to the Gambia River?*

Source: "Abduhl Rahahman, the Unfortunate Moorish Prince," *African Repository and Colonial Journal*, May 1828.

PERSPECTIVES

CAPTURING VENTURE SMITH

Venture Smith was born in the gold-mining country inland from the Gold Coast. His father was the ruler of a small kingdom. After being captured by an army of a neighboring country, he was sold to a slave ship from Rhode Island and taken to Connecticut to labor as a slave. He gradually earned enough money to buy his freedom and purchase a small farm. His autobiography was published in New London, Connecticut, in 1798.

I was born at Dukandarra, in Guinea, about the year 1729. My father's name was Saungm Furro, Prince of the Tribe of Dukandarra. My father had three wives. Polygamy was not uncommon in that country, especially among the rich, as every man was allowed to keep as many wives as he could maintain. . . .

A message was brought by an inhabitant of the place where I lived the preceding year that that place had been invaded by a numerous army, from a nation not far distant, furnished with musical instruments, and all kinds of arms then in use; that they were instigated by some white nation who equipped and sent them to subdue and possess the country. . . .

The same night which was fixed upon to retreat, my father and his family set off about break of day. But we presently found that our retreat was not secure. For having struck up a little fire for the purpose of cooking victuals, the enemy, who happened to be encamped a little distance off, had sent out a scouting party who discovered us by the smoke of the fire. Being unable to make any resistance, [we] immediately betook ourselves to the tall thick reeds not far off. They then came to us in the reeds, and the very first salute I had from them was a violent blow on the head with the fore part of a gun, and at the same time a grasp round the neck. I then had a rope put about my neck, as had all the women in the thicket with me. . . .

The army of the enemy was large, I should suppose consisting of about six thousand men. Their leader was called Baukurre. They decamped and immediately marched towards the sea, lying to the west, taking with them myself and the women prisoners. In the march a scouting party was detached from the main army. To the leader of this party I was made waiter, having to carry his gun. . . .

They then went on to the next district which was contiguous to the sea, called in Africa, Anamaboo. All of us were then put into the castle and kept for market. On a certain time I and other prisoners were put on board a canoe, under our master, and rowed away to a vessel belonging to Rhode-Island, commanded by Capt. Collingwood. I was bought on board by one Robertson Mumford, steward of said vessel, for four gallons of rum, and a piece of calico, and called VENTURE, on account of his having purchased me with his own private venture. Thus I came by my name.

1. *How did the army that captured Venture Smith get its weapons?*
2. *How much did Robertson Mumford pay to purchase Venture Smith?*

Source: Venture Smith, *A narrative of the Life and Adventures of Venture, a native of Africa: But Resident above Sixty Years in the United States of America. Related by Himself* (New London, CT: C. Holt, 1798), pp. 5–13.

AN AFRICAN SLAVE TRADER'S DIARY

Antera Duke was an Efik merchant who lived in Old Calabar, in the region of the Niger River delta. Like many African merchants in Old Calabar, he taught himself to speak and write English in order to communicate with the British captains and sailors who came to purchase captives. His diary from the years 1785–1788, which he wrote in "trade English," has been preserved, giving insights into the life and labors of an African merchant in a major slave trading port. The text has been translated from trade English into modern English.

January 22, 1786

At 5 a.m. at Aqua Landing, a little morning fog. I went down to the landing. Misimbo goes to Guinea Company to ask them to come make [an agreement] with Ephraim Ofiong about war coppers, and at 1 o'clock [Captain] Tom Cooper's tender [vessel that supplies other vessels] went away with 383 slaves and 4 tons [of produce].

January 23, 1786

About 6 a.m. at Aqua Landing. I went down to the landing. After 8 o'clock my brother Egbo Young and Apandam came home from Boostam with slaves and ivory, and we saw Tom Cooper and Captain Fairweather come up. They had taken the tender down to Aqua river.

January 29, 1786

At 5 a.m. at Aqua Landing, a fine morning. We all walked up to King Ekpe to work at the palaver house. Soon afterwards we heard that King Egbo Sam Ambo had stopped [seized] 3 Egbosherry men at the river because they had killed one of his men, and after 1 o'clock we heard that Egbo Young's dear wife had given birth to a young girl at Aqua Town.

February 8, 1786

At 5 a.m. in Akwa Bakasi Creek, a fine morning, and I got from [out of] Akwa Bakasi Creek at 1 o'clock. I found Archibong Duke and went alongside his canoe. I took a bottle of beer to drink with him and we called first at New Town and stayed at the landing. We came away, then went to town at 3 o'clock. We walked up to the palaver house at the same time to put Grand Ekpe in the house and "played" all night. [Captain Peter] Comberbach went away with 639 slaves and ivory tusks.

February 11, 1786

About 5 a.m. in Aqua Town. Archibong desired me to walk up to Cameroon with him. I did and we passed 3 little Cameroon towns on the way. We walked [about 40 minutes] up to 1 o'clock . . . to arrive at Big Town. There they killed a goat and "dashed" me 1 iron and 2 rods. We had a long discussion with them about Archibong's trading goods. They paid a boy slave and begged us to "drink doctor" with them. Archibong made one of his father's sons named Ebetim "drink doctor" with him too. They dashed us one male cow to be killed and 8 rods for that chop for us, so we came down at 6 o'clock at night.

March 2, 1786

Captain Potter went away with 284 slaves.

March 20, 1786

Soon I saw Tom Cooper come up river and he said that Captain Fairweather was going away to the bar with 440 slaves.

1. *What insights does the diary give us into Antera Duke's daily activities?*
2. *What does the diary reveal about Antera Duke's views on the slave trade?*

Source: *The Diary of Antera Duke, an Eighteenth Century African Slave Trader*, edited and annotated by Stephen Behrendt, A. J. H. Latham, and David Northrup (Oxford: Oxford University Press, 2010), pp. 175–177.

THE SHORES OF TRIPOLI After an Ottoman corsair known as Dragut captured the North African port city of Tripoli in 1551, the region became a province of the Ottoman Empire and became known as the Tripoli Regency. This painting from the mid-seventeenth century shows the seaside fortress that protected the city and a number of Dutch ships in the harbor. Along with Algiers and Tunis, Tripoli was a major haven for corsairs.

1505	**1517**	**1525**
Portuguese attack Swahili trading towns	Ottomans invade Egypt	Barbarossa takes Algiers

7

THE INDIAN OCEAN AND MEDITERRANEAN SHORES, 1500–1800

During the three centuries from 1500 to 1800, when the Atlantic Seaboard of Africa and its hinterlands were reeling under the impact of the Atlantic slave trade, the regions of Africa that bordered the Indian Ocean and the Mediterranean Sea were also being challenged by new maritime powers. In the Indian Ocean, the arrival of the Portuguese around 1500, followed by that of the Dutch, English, and French a century later, brought European-style war capitalism into the region as the newcomers employed naval power to compete with the existing trade networks and with one another. In the Mediterranean, the Ottoman Turks ousted the Genoese from the Black Sea, expelled the Venetians from Crete and Cyprus, and established hegemony over most of North Africa. They also gained a monopoly over the Red Sea trade, which gave them a gateway to the spice trade of the Indian Ocean. Unlike the Venetians and Genoese before them, the Ottomans were a power in both the Mediterranean and the Indian Ocean.

This chapter looks at the Indian Ocean and Mediterranean regions of Africa as they encountered the new varieties of war capitalism that emerged after 1500. Unlike the Atlantic world, where the nations of Atlantic Europe created a whole new system of plantation economies in the Americas that depended on captive

1551	1652	1698
Dragut captures Tripoli	Dutch establish the Cape Colony	Omanis eject Portuguese from Mombasa

labor brought in from Africa, the Indian Ocean and Mediterranean worlds possessed ancient trade routes and long-standing commercial relationships. The new maritime powers from Atlantic Europe and Ottoman Turkey were more focused on capturing existing nodes of production and trade than on creating new systems of production.

WAR CAPITALISM IN THE INDIAN OCEAN WORLD

When the Portuguese explorer Vasco da Gama rounded the southern tip of Africa and sailed up the eastern coast of Africa in 1498, he was not heading into unknown territory: the Venetian traveler Marco Polo had described the east African coast in 1295, and the Moroccan traveler Ibn Battuta, whose writings were known in Muslim Spain, had visited the city-states of the Swahili Coast (the portion of the east African coast extending from Kilwa northward to Mogadishu) in 1331. The Portuguese knew the general location of the spice and pepper markets of Asia, thanks to Marco Polo and other medieval travelers, but they needed a route to India that allowed them to bypass the Red Sea, which was under Muslim control. After leaving the Swahili Coast, Vasco da Gama caught the monsoon winds that took him to India. He spent 3 months on India's west coast, but his stay was unproductive because the Arab and Indian spice merchants there were unimpressed with his trade goods. They wanted gold, but he could offer only woolen cloth, hats, and some iron tools. The best he could do was to purchase small samples of spices and a few precious stones.

In 1500, after da Gama's return to Portugal, another Portuguese explorer, Pedro Alvares Cabral, left Portugal for India with a fleet of 13 vessels to negotiate rights to the lucrative spice trade. Instead of sailing south down the West African coast, he sailed southwest across the Atlantic and made landfall in Brazil, which he claimed for the Portuguese Crown. Leaving the coast of Brazil, he caught the south equatorial trade winds, which propelled him around the southern tip of Africa and into the Indian Ocean. Arriving at Calicut on the west coast of India, he was prevented from purchasing a load of spices by local Arab traders, so he sailed south along the coast to Cochin, where he had more success. Cabral returned to Portugal in 1501, carrying spices that were worth eight times the original investment in the voyage.

Realizing that the Arab traders would not easily relinquish their monopoly on the Indian Ocean spice trade, the Portuguese opted for war, moving with astonishing speed and ruthlessness to capture strategic harbors that would serve as naval bases and commercial hubs. They built forts at Sofala (the main outlet for gold from the Zimbabwe Plateau) and on Mozambique Island, and they pressured the sultan of Malindi into forming an alliance with them. To control the trade of the wider Indian Ocean, they captured Goa (on the west coast of India), the Strait of Malacca (the main entry point to the South China Sea), and the Strait of Hormuz (the entryway to the Persian Gulf). They also built forts in the Maluku Islands (also known as the Spice Islands). The only major setback for the Portuguese was their failure to secure a spice route through the Red Sea, which remained in Muslim hands.

The military victories of the Portuguese were not always matched by commercial success. When the Portuguese captured strategically important ports, the indigenous spice trade would simply move elsewhere, in part because Portugal produced very few trade goods that the Asian spice merchants wanted. The Portuguese responded by setting themselves up as middlemen in the ancient trade network of the Indian Ocean, trading in Indian cotton cloth, Persian horses, African ivory, and a variety of other products that were not meant for export to Europe. From their headquarters in Goa, on the west coast of India, the Portuguese governors levied customs duties on cargoes and issued letters of protection to seafaring merchants. Naming its new maritime empire the *Estado da India* (State of India), the Portuguese Crown claimed that Portugal

THE GOLD OF SOFALA Located along the Mozambique Channel south of the monsoon zone, Sofala was the main outlet for gold from the Zimbabwe Plateau. The Portuguese captured Sofala in 1505, but the trade declined as the gold-bearing veins on the Zimbabwe Plateau were exhausted and gold mining moved northward toward the Zambezi valley. This painting shows Sofala and the Portuguese fort in 1683.

was the "Lord of the Sea" in the same way that the kings and sultans on the Indian Ocean rim were the "Lords of the Land."

The Swahili Coast

The Portuguese took an immediate interest in the city-states of the Swahili Coast, which made ideal ports of call for ships traveling to and from India, and they were eager to capture the maritime trade in gold between Sofala and Kilwa, the southernmost port on the Swahili Coast, especially after Vasco da Gama reported in 1499 that Sofala was a source of "infinite gold." In 1505, a fleet of eight Portuguese warships led by Francisco de Almeida arrived in the Indian Ocean to establish Portuguese domination. Sofala was occupied with little resistance because of the quick capitulation of its aging and blind ruler. The fleet then moved north and captured Kilwa. After installing a puppet king, they built a fortress that also served as a warehouse for trade goods.

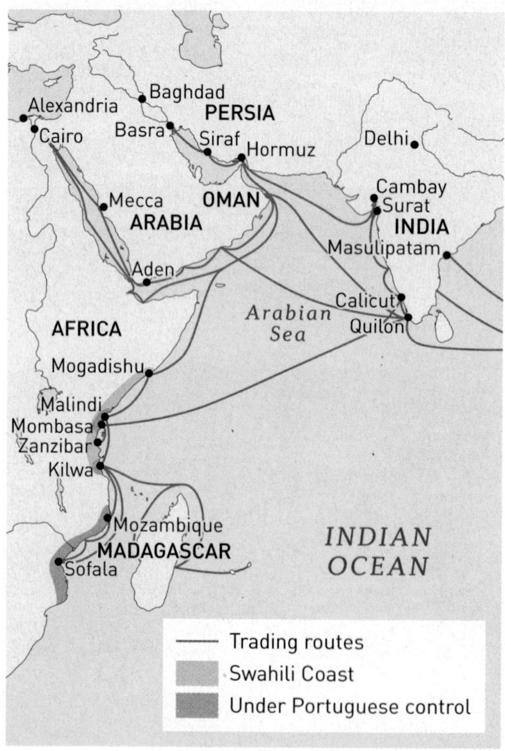

TRADE ROUTES IN THE WESTERN INDIAN OCEAN This map shows some of the major trade routes that linked the Mozambique Channel and the Swahili Coast to the Arabian Peninsula, the Persian Gulf, and India. The Portuguese captured the major African trading towns in the 1500s, but after 1648, the Portuguese and Omanis competed for influence along the Swahili coast.

Almeida then took his fleet to Mombasa, on the coast of present-day Kenya. In preparation for his attack on the city, he sent in spies at night to set it on fire, burning the wooden porches and stables that were built between the multistory stone houses. The fires raged all night, and many stone houses collapsed because the heat softened the mortar. The next morning, Almeida's troops

THE PALACE AT KILWA Built in the fourteenth century by the sultan of Kilwa, the Husuni Kubwa palace contained an octagonal pool, a grand audience court, guest rooms for visiting merchants, and the royal residence with over 100 rooms. Its grandeur mirrored the prosperity of Kilwa, which received gold from Sofala, a thousand miles to the south. For reasons that remain unclear, the palace was abandoned before it was completed.

entered Mombasa and spent 2 days plundering the town. The following year, they attacked four other island settlements. Soon the Portuguese were in control of the major trading towns of the Swahili Coast.

The Portuguese tried to impose a monopoly on trade along the east African coast, but they lacked the manpower to enforce it in the face of fierce resistance. The compliant ruler of Sofala was soon murdered by a local opposition group, as was the puppet ruler of Kilwa. Many merchants migrated out of Kilwa to engage in smuggling or to open new ports of trade in areas outside of Portuguese control. Barely a year after the Portuguese finished building their fort at Kilwa, trade had slowed to such a degree that they found it necessary to permit the local Swahili merchants to trade freely. In 1517, the Portuguese tore down their new fort because it was too expensive to maintain and served no commercial purpose, a tacit admission that they had destroyed the prosperity of Kilwa without gaining the monopoly

THE PORTUGUESE FORT AT MOMBASA Fort Jesus was built in 1593–1596 on orders from King Philip I of Portugal to serve as a military and administrative headquarters for the region. The Portuguese were later ejected from Mombasa by the Omanis in 1698.

over the gold trade that they were seeking. Half a century later, Father Monclaro, a Jesuit missionary, described Kilwa as a city that "was formerly very large and prosperous." With the gold trade gone, the merchants of Kilwa were reduced to trading in ivory, honey, and wax, which they purchased from their inland neighbors.

On the northern Swahili Coast, a revolt in Mombasa in 1528 resulted in a second Portuguese sacking of the city. By 1569, Mombasa's trade had diminished so much that its main commercial products were spears and ivory-handled daggers. In the same year, Father Monclaro described Malindi as a "city in very ruinous condition, for the sea has encroached upon almost every part of it, but what remains standing shows that it must have been very noble in ancient times." Reflecting on his voyage along the Swahili Coast in 1569, the Jesuit priest wrote,

"The principal kings here are those of Kilwa and Malindi. All are now petty rulers, poor and without power, more worthy to be called sheiks than kings. The people are generally poor and wretched in nearly all these parts, and the Portuguese are becoming so." The main result of the Portuguese conquests was to destroy the centuries-old prosperity of the Swahili Coast.

The Portuguese domination of the Swahili Coast was brought to an end by the Omani Arabs, who lived on the western shore of the Persian Gulf. After a series of rebellions in 1648 drove the Portuguese out of Oman, the sultan of Oman sought to drive them from the Swahili Coast. The Omanis captured Mombasa in 1698, then ejected the Portuguese from Zanzibar and all of their enclaves north of the Mozambique Channel, thus founding the **Omani Empire**. In short, the sultan had gained control of the regions served by the monsoon winds. But the sultan did not effectively consolidate his control, and during the eighteenth century, the Swahili trading towns operated more or less independently, or they played off the Portuguese against the Omanis. That situation allowed the maritime trade along the Swahili Coast to regain some of its former vibrancy.

The Zambezi Valley and the Zimbabwe Plateau

South of the Swahili Coast, the Portuguese sought to consolidate their position in the Mozambique Channel, where they controlled Sofala and Mozambique Island. The gold trade at Sofala was in decline because the gold-bearing veins on the Zimbabwe Plateau were becoming exhausted, and gold mining activities were moving north toward the Zambezi River valley. Consequently, the Portuguese sought to capture the gold mines for themselves. In 1570, a thousand Portuguese soldiers marched up the Zambezi valley in an effort to reach and take over the mines. Harassed by repeated attacks from local chiefs and suffering from bouts of fever, they retreated to their base on Mozambique Island to await reinforcements. When an additional 700 soldiers joined them in 1573, the combined force marched 300 miles from Sofala to the Zimbabwe Plateau, skirting the fever-ridden Zambezi valley, while a smaller unit went up the Zambezi valley to look for a rumored silver mine. Both groups failed to find any mines, either gold or silver, and the soldiers withdrew to the coast.

The only lasting impact of these invasions was the establishment of Portuguese forts and trading posts along the Zambezi River at Sena and Tete. The Portuguese soldiers and traders who were stationed in those towns often married local Tonga women. Their Luso-African descendants made the settlements relatively self-sufficient by inserting themselves as middlemen into local networks of production and trade. As generations passed, the Luso-Africans blended more and more into the larger Tonga communities, with little more than their Portuguese names to distinguish them from the local population. With their increasing self-sufficiency, the settlements became more and more independent of Portuguese control.

During the seventeenth century, the Portuguese and Luso-Africans in the Zambezi valley extended their influence by intervening militarily in disputes among the Karanga chiefdoms on the Zimbabwe Plateau. After 1629, they could trade freely on the plateau, where they opened fairs for purchasing gold and established mining camps worked by laborers whom they had commandeered from Karanga villages. After repeated failures to find fabulously rich gold mines, the Portuguese had come to understand that the gold was extracted from numerous small diggings that were easily exhausted. They also discovered that the gold supplies were not nearly as rich as they had once imagined. Vasco da Gama's 1499 claim that there was an infinite amount of gold on the plateau turned out to be a myth.

As an alternative to gold mining, the Portuguese and Luso-Africans in the Zambezi valley began to acquire large tracts of land that could be turned into estates that would attract Portuguese settlers. The African chiefdoms on the surrounding plateaus regarded the valley as unimportant, and therefore the chiefs did not oppose the Portuguese settlements. The Portuguese Crown, for its part, was eager to support the scheme in order to regain its lost authority over the Luso-African settlements. The landed estates were known as ***prazos***, and the masters of the estates were known as *prazeros*. Each prazo developed a large military force made up of armed slaves obtained through raids, purchase, and the indigenous practice of voluntary enslavement in times of famine. Large prazos commonly owned 4,000–5,000 slaves, and one was recorded to have as many as 15,000. By the mid-seventeenth century, some of the largest prazos had conquered many of the small African chiefdoms in the Zambezi valley and had even annexed parts of the surrounding plateau. Sometimes prazeros would send their armies to aid African chiefs on the plateau in exchange for land where they could establish new prazos.

One remarkable feature of the prazos was that many of the titleholders were Luso-African women. The Portuguese Crown had a practice of awarding grants of land to the widows and daughters of men who had performed extraordinary military service. The women who received these grants would often remain in Portugal while their designated male representatives settled in the Zambezi valley and married local women. Because the title deeds to the prazos required that they pass to the eldest daughter upon the death of the grantee, in practice they often passed to the Luso-African daughters of the Portuguese settlers. Luso-African women who possessed prazos were addressed by the honorific title *Dona*. Although their husbands and fathers tried to exercise control over them, many of the donas exhibited remarkable independence and amassed considerable wealth and power. Dona Ursula Ferreira, for example, married three times and accumulated two large and wealthy prazos, while Dona Ines Gracias Cardoso accumulated four. Other donas sent their slaves to exploit gold diggings or to develop new trade routes into the interior.

Despite the military might of their slave armies, the prazos in the Zambezi valley never dominated the African chiefdoms on the surrounding plateau, in part because the prazos were often at war with each other. In some cases, the wars resulted in their mutual destruction. By 1730, most of the great prazos that had been established in the seventeenth century were in decay or completely abandoned. After 1750, a new wave of Portuguese settlers arrived to establish new prazos, which were much smaller and weaker than their predecessors, rarely amassing more than a few hundred slaves. With the decline of the prazos, the African chiefdoms on the plateau conquered and annexed a number of the prazos on their borders.

Although the Portuguese settlements provoked a lot of warfare, their long-term impact on the economic and political configuration of the region was minimal because they operated more like African chiefdoms than like foreign colonizers. Institutions and practices imported from Portugal became more and more Africanized with the passage of time. Perhaps the most enduring legacy of the prazos was the descendants of the slave soldiers, who gradually coalesced into a distinct ethnic group, known as the Chikunda.

Overall, Portuguese war capitalism in the Indian Ocean was very different from the version, described in chapters 5 and 6, that predominated in the Atlantic. In the Indian Ocean, the Portuguese created a relatively self-contained system that was administered from Goa, on the west coast of India. Their objective was to insert themselves as middlemen into the ancient trading relationships that animated the commerce of the Indian Ocean world. Despite some initial success, they were ultimately disappointed. The gold from Zimbabwe was never sufficient to meet their expectations, and the settlements in the Zambezi valley kept slipping away from Portuguese control to become quasi-independent entities modeled on African chiefdoms.

The Dutch at the Cape of Good Hope

Although the Portuguese in the Indian Ocean considered themselves the Lords of the Sea throughout the sixteenth century, they found their dominance challenged by the Dutch, English, and French as the seventeenth century began. Instead of creating a commercial hub in India, the Dutch East India Company headed straight to the Maluku Islands (in modern Indonesia), which were at the center of spice production. They established their company headquarters and trading hub on the island of Java, some 1,600 miles west of the Maluku Islands, because it was more accessible to the maritime trading routes. Like the Portuguese before them, the Dutch tried to establish multi-faceted relationships for trading a variety of products within the Indian Ocean and South China Sea.

Their entry into the Indian Ocean trade forced the Dutch to develop new sea routes through the Atlantic as well. To sail from the Netherlands to Java, a ship would first head for Brazil to catch the trade winds, which carried it around the Cape of Good Hope, at the southern tip of Africa, and into the Indian Ocean. Ships following this route from Europe to Asia went nowhere near the Atlantic coast of Africa. The Atlantic trade and the Asia trade were thus entirely separate systems that relied on completely different sea routes. That is why the Dutch government established the Dutch East India Company to trade with Asia and the Dutch West India Company to trade in the Atlantic Ocean.

Mimicking the war capitalism previously practiced by the Portuguese, the Dutch East India Company ousted the Portuguese from their forts in the Maluku Islands beginning in 1605. In 1619, after they tried and failed to wrest the Strait of Malacca from the Portuguese, they seized the port of Jakarta on the island of Java (in modern Indonesia) to be their commercial hub and company headquarters. Initially focusing their trade on the Maluku and Banda Islands, they established a worldwide monopoly on cloves and nutmeg. So secure was their monopoly that the Dutch government was able to fix the price of cloves on the European market in 1677 and keep it unchanged until 1744.

The Dutch established their own sea routes between the Cape of Good Hope and Jakarta (a distance of some 6,000 miles). The Portuguese ships had normally rounded the Cape and sailed northward along Africa's eastern coast through the Mozambique Channel until they caught the monsoon winds along the Swahili Coast. The Dutch, in contrast, took a southern route by sailing due east from the Cape until they reached the region of the southeast trade winds, which took them north to Jakarta. An alternative route was to head northeast toward Jakarta and make a stopover at the island of Mauritius, some 2,500 miles from the Cape. It normally took 6 or 7 months to make the trip between the Netherlands and Jakarta in either direction. Because their sea routes bypassed most of the western Indian Ocean rim, the Dutch never tried to establish a presence along the east African coast.

The sea routes used by the Dutch East India Company involved long stretches at sea without stopping at secondary ports of call, thus creating a need for strategically placed way stations for resupplying the ships and resting the crews. Accordingly, the Dutch laid claim to the island of Mauritius in 1638 and to the Cape Peninsula (which included the Cape of Good Hope) in 1652. After replenishing its supplies at the Cape, a ship could either sail non-stop to Jakarta via the southern route or take the more direct route with a stopover in Mauritius. Of the two way stations, the one at the Cape was by far the most important because it gave the Dutch control of the transition point between the Atlantic and Indian Oceans.

The southern tip of Africa enjoyed a Mediterranean climate with winter rains and summer sun, and it was far enough away from the equator that many of the diseases that claimed the lives of Europeans in tropical Africa were unknown. The **Cape Colony** was established when the Dutch East India Company founded Cape Town and persuaded some of its employees to settle there in order to grow crops and raise sheep and cattle that they could sell to the company to resupply its ships. This original group of settlers was soon augmented by Dutch orphan girls that the company brought out to be wives for the men, and by French Protestants known as Huguenots who had sought refuge in the Netherlands during France's religious wars. By 1707, the white settler population of the Cape Colony included about 700 company employees and 2,000 Dutch and French immigrants.

CAPE TOWN IN 1683 This painting shows Cape Town just 31 years after the first Dutch East India Company settlers landed in 1652. The fort and the town are huddled near the seashore, while Table Mountain looms in the background. The harbor is filled with Dutch ships on their way to Jakarta or the Maluku Islands.

The land around the Cape Colony was relatively arid, with only 16–24 inches of rainfall per year, and no African agricultural populations had settled there. Instead, the region was inhabited by Khoikhoi cattle and sheep herders, who lived on the plains, and San hunter-gatherers, who lived mostly in the surrounding mountains. The Khoikhoi were nomadic in the sense that they periodically dismantled their settlements and moved with their cattle and sheep to new pastures according to the season. They were organized politically into chiefdoms, each containing up to 16 settlements. Prior to the establishment of the Cape Colony, they had been furnishing cattle and sheep to passing ships, and they continued to do so after the arrival of the Dutch settlers. Between 1652 and 1699, the company purchased some 20,000 cattle and 40,000 sheep from Khoikhoi herders.

The Dutch East India Company originally gave white settlers 20-acre plots on which to practice intensive agriculture, but most of them were unsuccessful at growing crops in the semiarid region and preferred to move inland from Cape Town to raise cattle and sheep on large tracts of land in imitation of the Khoikhoi. The expansion of settler groups onto Khoikhoi pastureland led to violent clashes. These conflicts culminated in a 4-year war in which the settlers captured some 1,800 head of cattle and 5,000 sheep from the Khoikhoi. As the European settlers claimed larger and larger tracts of land, the Khoikhoi and the San were squeezed out. The Khoikhoi not only lost their livestock to the settlers, but also suffered high mortality during an epidemic of smallpox, brought in by ships in 1713. Sinking into poverty, the surviving Khoikhoi sought their livelihoods as shepherds and cattle herders for the settlers. The San, in contrast, were often killed or driven into the wilderness areas on the fringes of the settled zones.

Almost from the beginning, the company brought captives to Cape Town to load and unload ships, cut wood on Table Mountain, haul water, and perform a variety of other menial tasks. Because the Dutch ships used sea routes that took them far from Africa's Atlantic coast, captives were obtained from Indian Ocean ports. During the seventeenth and eighteenth centuries, the company purchased some 4,000 captives from Madagascar and East Africa. A much larger slave trade was run privately by company officials as a way of making extra money. An average company ship coming from Asia might carry as many as 20 captives that had been privately purchased by the captain or company officials for sale in Cape Town. The captives in the private slave trade came mostly from Madagascar, India, and Indonesia, and later from Mozambique. Between 1652 and 1808 nearly 60,000 captives were privately imported. After 1711, the slaves living in the Cape Colony outnumbered the white settlers.

A typical large farm on the Cape Peninsula in the eighteenth century consisted of the Boer (the Dutch term for a settler farmer) and his family, their imported

THE INTERIOR OF THE CAPE COLONY Although the Dutch East India Company gave each white settler a 20-acre farm near Cape Town, many of them preferred to move inland to raise sheep and cattle on large tracts of land. The movement of well-armed settlers onto Khoikhoi rangeland led to wars in which the indigenous Khoikhoi herders and San hunters were gradually squeezed out.

slave laborers, and their Khoikhoi clients (who were not slaves, but were subservient to their **Boer** landlords because they had nowhere else to go). Even though the settlers had acquired extensive landholdings by conquest and theft, their population remained tiny. In 1793, there were fewer than 14,000 European settlers on the entire Cape Peninsula. Unlike European plantation owners in the New World, the Boers did not produce anything that was profitable enough to export over long distances except, perhaps, for some wool. Instead, they adopted a lifestyle based on extensive pastoralism, which they had learned from the Khoikhoi.

The Mascarene Islands: Mauritius and Réunion

A particular point of European interest in the Indian Ocean was the **Mascarene Islands** (Mauritius and Réunion), located roughly halfway between the southern tip of Africa and the southern tip of India. When Portuguese sailors first set foot on Mauritius in 1507, they found no inhabitants, but a large number of dodoes—flightless birds some 3 feet tall and weighing up to 40 pounds that were found exclusively in Mauritius. When the Dutch East India Company settled the island in 1638, they brought in pigs, cattle, and goats. To make the settlement profitable, they also brought in 300 captives from the East African island of Madagascar, who worked mostly at cutting ebony trees in the forests. The settlers engaged in farming and livestock herding, supplemented by extensive hunting and fishing, in order to feed themselves and supply food to company ships. After the company established its base at the Cape of Good Hope in 1652, however, Mauritius became less essential, because many of the company's vessels sailed from the Cape to Jakarta by the southern route, which missed Mauritius by 900 miles.

Agriculture was a continuing problem on Mauritius because cyclones and droughts destroyed crops in many years, and because even in normal years, the island's large population of rats, which had come as unintended passengers on ships, made it difficult to cultivate beans, rice, wheat, and other crops. Only sugarcane, which the Dutch introduced from Java, and sweet potatoes were immune to the rats' depredations. An additional problem was that many of the pigs turned feral. In 1666, wild pigs were reported to be "running everywhere" and killing young calves. The pigs also destroyed the nests of the dodoes, each of which contained a single egg in a heap of grass on the forest floor, and thus were most likely responsible for their extinction. The last reliable report of dodoes on Mauritius comes from 1647, although some were spotted on a small islet off the coast in 1662.

DEAD AS A DODO Dutch settlers on Mauritius hunted the dodoes for food and inadvertently created a population of wild pigs that destroyed their nests, causing the dodo's extinction by 1665–1670. This picture was painted in 1626, when dodoes were still numerous.

The colony on Mauritius failed to thrive, and the Dutch abandoned the island in 1710. In 1721, Mauritius was claimed by the French East India Company, which had already claimed Réunion, some 140 miles away. The French company wanted to use Mauritius as a stopover between France and India and as a base for naval and privateering operations. Between 1793 and 1810—a time of hostilities between Britain and France—French warships and privateers operating out of Mauritius captured more than 500 British and allied ships. To develop agriculture in the Mascarene Islands, the company imported captive Africans from Madagascar, Mozambique, and the Swahili Coast, dramatically expanding the East African slave trade. During the eighteenth century, over 120,000 captives were carried to the Mascarene Islands, where they made up as much as 85 percent of the population.

Slaves performed a variety of tasks on the island, including loading and unloading ships and growing food, but the majority of them worked in the cultivation of sugarcane. Although sugar production had failed to catch on when the Dutch first introduced it in the seventeenth century, the French governor hoped to replicate the slave-based production system that had been developed in the Caribbean. Sugar production in the Mascarene Islands never reached Caribbean levels, but by the 1790s, Mauritius was producing 5 million pounds of sugar and 20,000 pounds of cloves per year. The sugar plantations of the Mascarene Islands thus created an Indian Ocean slave trade that resembled the Atlantic slave trade, albeit on a much smaller scale.

WAR CAPITALISM IN THE MEDITERRANEAN WORLD

When the Ottoman Turks captured Constantinople in 1453, it had been the capital of the Byzantine Empire for over a thousand years. The Turks renamed the city Istanbul and made it the capital of the Ottoman caliphate, which claimed to be the successor to the prior Islamic Caliphate in Damascus, Baghdad, and Cairo. But the Turkish sultan Mehmed II (known as Mehmed the Conqueror) also bore the title "Caesar of the Romans," indicating that he was both the inheritor of the Islamic Caliphate and the inheritor of the Christian Roman Empire. In this way, he bridged two worlds. The conquest of Constantinople thus marked the emergence of the **Ottoman Empire** as a world power.

The label *Ottoman* refers to the ruling dynasty founded by Osman Gazi (who ruled 1281–1324), a nomadic Turkish horseman who led a minor Muslim warrior state located on the fringes of the Byzantine Empire. Avoiding warfare with neighboring Islamic states, the Ottomans expanded their territory at the expense of the Byzantines through a string of military victories during the fourteenth century. Because they attacked Christians, the Ottomans could claim that they were waging a jihad against infidels, but they were also launching raids to amass booty and captives.

In order to avoid the rivalries and internal schisms that had historically plagued nomadic warrior states, the Ottoman rulers developed a slave army and a cadre of slave bureaucrats. Under the *devshirme* (blood tax) system, the Ottomans sent military officers into the rural parts of southeastern Europe to

BLOOD TAX In this painting from 1558, a group of boys are selected as payment for the *devshirme*, imposed on Christian subjects by the Ottoman sultan. The boys would be trained to enter into service as soldiers or bureaucrats

scour the villages for the fittest and brightest Christian boys between the ages of 8 and 10. The boys were taken from their families and brought to Istanbul, where they were converted to Islam and trained to serve the Ottoman state. The largest number received military training and joined the elite Janissary Corps, while others became Muslim clergy, scribes, and palace administrators. The sultan thus gained an elite corps of soldiers and bureaucrats who were socially isolated from the larger population and whose loyalty was unquestioned.

Although the expansion of the Ottoman Empire after 1453 was largely accomplished by armies traveling on foot and horseback, the Ottomans also proved to be a formidable maritime power in the eastern Mediterranean and the adjoining Aegean and Black Seas. Immediately after the conquest of Istanbul, they captured Greek islands and ports in the Aegean Sea, which separates Turkey from Greece. Then they moved into the Black Sea, ousting the Genoese from the commercial center of Trebizond (which lay along the Silk Road) in 1461 and capturing the Genoese fort at Caffa in 1475.

Their main maritime opponent, however, was Venice, which had previously dominated trade in the eastern Mediterranean. The two maritime powers fought a war between 1463 and 1479, in which Venice lost part of its maritime empire and agreed to pay an annual tribute to the Ottomans. When war broke out again in 1499, the Ottomans captured several more of Venice's ports, considerably weakening its position in the eastern Mediterranean. Seeking control of production as well as trade, they captured the sugar-producing islands of Cyprus in 1571 and Crete in 1669. The days when Venice and Genoa dominated trade in the Mediterranean were clearly over. The label of war capitalism seems appropriate here because access to ports, trade routes, and resources were all determined by the outcome of warfare.

Ottoman Egypt

When the Ottomans invaded Egypt in 1517, the Egyptians had been ruled by the Mamluks for more than 250 years. The Mamluks were originally captives from the Black Sea region who were brought to Egypt as boys and trained for military service, as described in chapter 3. Even after the Mamluks seized power in Egypt in 1260, they continued to bring in new enslaved boys from the Black Sea region to refresh the military. Sons of Mamluks could not become Mamluks, although some of them were allowed to join the free cavalry, which was not considered an elite fighting force.

The career of Tumanbay II, the last Mamluk sultan of Egypt, illustrates the Mamluk system. He was born in Circassia, along the northeastern shore of the Black Sea, captured, and sold to slave traders, who took him to Egypt. After completing military school, he became a domestic slave in the sultan's household. He gradually rose through the military ranks to become a commander of a hundred Mamluk soldiers (the highest rank of military commander), and he then became prime minister. When the Mamluk sultan left Egypt in 1516 to fight the approaching Ottoman army, he left Tumanbay in charge of Egypt. After the sultan was killed fighting in Syria, Tumanbay took over the sultanate of Egypt. He had been sultan for less than a year when the Ottoman army arrived in Cairo.

The soldiers who attacked Cairo in 1517 were under the personal command of the Ottoman sultan. Although the Mamluks had a proud military tradition and a fierce reputation, their lance-wielding cavalry was no match for the muskets and cannons of the Ottomans, who killed an estimated 10,000 people during their conquest of the city. Ibn Iyas, a chronicler of the period, wrote that the carnage was sufficient to "strike terror into the hearts of man, and its horrors to unhinge their reason." When the Ottoman soldiers captured Tumanbay, they hung him from the city gate like a common criminal.

After many centuries of being ruled successively by Greeks, Romans, Arabs, and Mamluks, the Egyptian people were accustomed to being controlled by foreigners. The Mamluks, who came mostly from the Black Sea region north of Turkey, generally spoke Turkish and not Arabic, so the Ottoman Turks did not seem completely strange. Even so, the Ottoman conquest marked a major change in Egypt's status because it had been an independent state ever since the rise of the Fatimids in 969, but now it was simply a province of the Ottoman Empire. The grain produced by the peasants in the Nile valley that had in ancient times gone to Rome would henceforth go to Istanbul.

No sooner had the Ottomans conquered Egypt than they withdrew most of their soldiers to fight on the Iran-Iraq border. To maintain order in Egypt, the Ottomans allowed the Mamluk military units to reconstitute themselves. When some Mamluks sought to break away from Ottoman rule, the sultan in Istanbul sent his chief administrator to suppress the rebels and create a new administrative system that would ensure Mamluk loyalty. After that, Egypt was governed differently from the other Ottoman provinces. The Mamluk units of the Egyptian army were continually refreshed with enslaved Christian boys from the Black Sea, Bosnia, and Albania, and were counterbalanced by units of the Ottoman Janissary Corps as well as by regular army units made up of native-born Egyptians, who were often the sons of Mamluks.

The administrative system imposed by the Ottomans was based on the old Mamluk system. The governors of Egypt were Ottoman administrators sent out from Istanbul for 1-year terms. Although their terms were renewable, they were replaced frequently to make sure that they remained loyal to Istanbul and did not develop a local power base. At the lower levels of administration, many Mamluk officers were appointed as district administrators or low-level military governors, receiving the title of **bey**. They made effective administrators because they were accustomed to giving commands and had an intimate knowledge of local conditions that the administrators from Istanbul lacked. Over time, the Mamluk beys became a dominant political force within the Egyptian administration.

The bulk of the Egyptian population, however, consisted of descendants of the ancient Egyptians who made their living as farmers in the Nile valley and the Nile delta. By the sixteenth century, they spoke mostly Arabic and practiced Islam. In addition, there were nomadic Arab tribes who lived in Egypt's western desert, and settled Arab tribes who had seized large tracts of land in Upper Egypt during the final century of Mamluk rule. One of those settled tribes—the Banu Umar tribe—agreed to collect taxes on the government's behalf in Upper Egypt in return for being allowed to exercise semiautonomous authority over their own territory.

The Egyptian social hierarchy consisted of two main categories. At the top were the Ottoman and Mamluk elites—lumped together in popular discourse as "Turks"—who populated the government and the military. Below them were the indigenous Egyptians and Arabs, who were referred to as "peasants" by the ruling elites and deemed to be a servile class that was unfit for government or military service. "I will not give [military] salaries to peasants," proclaimed one Ottoman governor. "Salaries are for Turks."

In the late sixteenth century, Egypt switched from a system of direct taxation by government officials to a system of "tax farming," in which private tax collectors gathered the taxes from a locality and turned over a fixed sum to the government. If they collected more than they owed the government, they could keep the surplus. A tax farm (i.e., the authority to collect taxes in a certain locality) became a valuable entity that could be bought, sold, mortgaged, or inherited just like a piece of property. This system reduced the revenues that flowed into Egypt's central treasury because only about one-fifth of the tax collected in rural areas was turned over to the government. The rest was kept by the tax farmers, many of whom were Mamluk beys.

The conquest of Egypt gave the Ottomans privileged access to the Red Sea, which was their main gateway to the Indian Ocean spice trade. In 1538, the Ottomans assembled a fleet of more than 70 ships and 20,000 men and set out for the west coast of India. On their return, they established control over the port of Aden, which was the gateway between the Red Sea and the Indian Ocean. When a Portuguese fleet of over 80 ships from Goa tried to enter the Red Sea in 1541, it withdrew after being bombarded by Ottoman artillery. Having solidified their control over the Red Sea, the Ottomans sent four ships to the Swahili Coast in 1546 to plunder Malindi, which was allied with the Portuguese. The Ottomans were challenging Portuguese domination of Indian Ocean trade.

After an Ottoman fleet containing 30 ships and 850 soldiers was lost in the Indian Ocean in 1552, however, the Ottomans withdrew from the Indian Ocean and focused on defending their control of the Red Sea. They nevertheless maintained a degree of influence in the Indian Ocean by sending cannons and muskets to sultans in Southeast Asia to help them repel the Portuguese. In 1566, the sultan of Aceh (in modern Indonesia) proclaimed that he and the Muslims of India recognized the Ottoman sultan as their suzerain and protector. Because ports such as Aceh successfully defended themselves against the Portuguese, the indigenous pepper trade continued to thrive. A 1598 Dutch map carried an inscription about the pepper trade in Aceh, saying that "they have great store of pepper, which the ships from Surat and Cambay [ports on the west coast of India] come yearly to fetch and take to the Red Sea." A century of Portuguese domination in the western Indian Ocean had failed to kill the ancient spice trade.

The Ottoman Regencies in North Africa

Along the Mediterranean coast of North Africa, the Ottomans created three provinces known as "regencies": the Algiers Regency (in present-day Algeria), the Tunis Regency (in present-day Tunisia), and the Tripoli Regency (in present-day Libya). The stretch of the Mediterranean coast occupied by the three regencies was known to Europeans as the Barbary Coast, a reference to the Berber populations of North Africa. The only part of the Barbary Coast that remained independent was Morocco.

Unlike Egypt, which was conquered by an Ottoman land army, the three regencies were created by pirates who invaded from the sea. The person who best exemplifies this process was Khayr al-Din, who was also known by his Italian-language nickname Barbarossa (Red Beard). He was born on the island of Lesbos off the coast of Turkey, but his early life is shrouded in legend. By one account, his mother was the daughter of a Greek Orthodox priest; by other accounts, his father was a Muslim privateer or a Christian renegade. In any event, Khayr al-Din and his three brothers became **corsairs**—a term that refers to pirates who operated under the protection of a political authority.

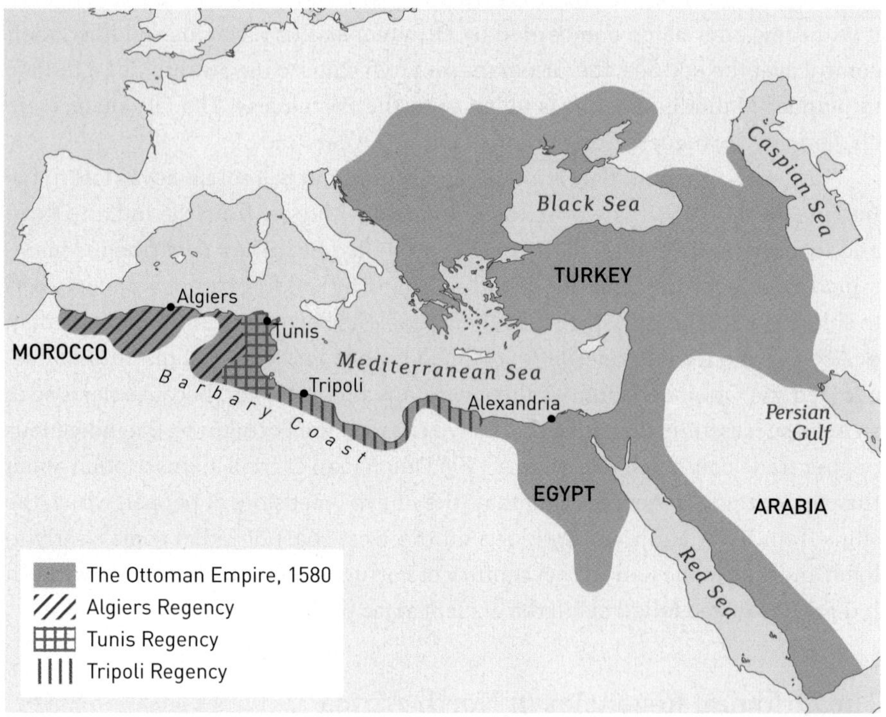

THE OTTOMAN EMPIRE IN 1580 This map shows the extent of the Ottoman Empire after its conquests in North Africa. In Egypt, Ottoman rule extended over the Nile River valley and the Arab tribes in Egypt's western desert. The regencies of Tripoli, Tunis, and Algiers, which together made up the Barbary Coast, controlled mainly the coastal strip and parts of the Atlas Mountains.

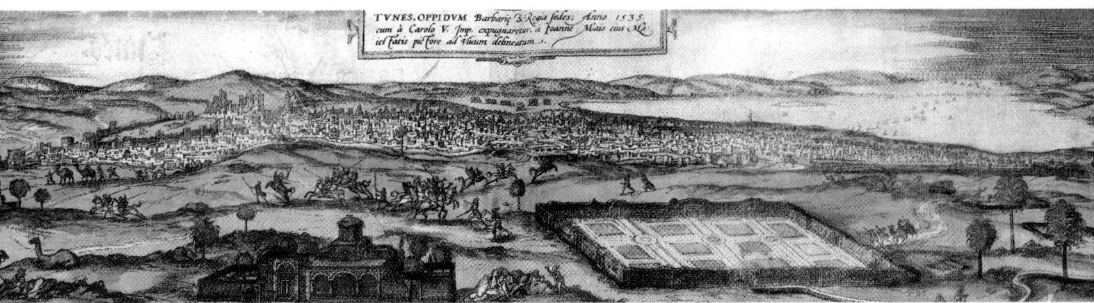

CAPTURING TUNIS In 1534, the Ottoman corsair known as Barbarossa (Red Beard) captured Tunis from Spain, but a year later the Spanish forces got it back. Their victory was celebrated in this 1535 painting by the Spanish court painter Johannes Maius. It was not until 1574 that the Ottomans recaptured Tunis and incorporated the Tunis Regency into the Ottoman Empire.

As his reputation grew, Barbarossa entered into an agreement with the local ruler of Tunis to prey on ships in the Mediterranean and share the booty. Soon he moved west along the Mediterranean coast to Algiers, where he and his brother Aruj wrested control of the city from the local tribal sheikh. When a Spanish fleet attacked Algiers, Barbarossa appealed to the Ottoman sultan for help, thus entering into an alliance with the Ottoman Empire. Although he fled the city before the reinforcements arrived, he returned in 1525 to drive out the Spanish, and the Ottoman sultan appointed him governor of Algiers. He continued to prey on Christian shipping and to attack ports on the European coast of the Mediterranean until 1533, when the sultan made him the admiral of the Turkish navy. In 1534, he captured Tunis from Spain, but lost it again a year later.

After Barbarossa's death in 1546, he was succeeded as admiral of the Ottoman navy and governor of Algiers by one of his lieutenants, named Turgut Reis, popularly known as Dragut. In 1551, Dragut attacked and captured Tripoli. As a reward, the sultan made him the bey of Tripoli, but soon he was again at sea, where he captured a Venetian ship and attacked two towns, showing that he could be an Ottoman bey and a corsair at the same time. When he was killed during a siege of Malta in 1565, a lieutenant from his fleet, named Uluj Ali, became the bey of Tripoli and was promoted to governor of Algiers in 1568. These men moved easily between the roles of corsair, admiral, and governor.

During the sixteenth century, the North African corsairs crossed the waters in oar-propelled galleys, but after 1600, English and Dutch pirates who came to North Africa to join the corsair fleets taught them how to build and sail

NORTH AFRICAN CORSAIRS ATTACK A FRENCH SHIP This painting from the early seventeenth century shows two corsair galleys attacking a French ship in the Mediterranean. The galleys, which were propelled by enslaved Christian oarsmen, were highly maneuverable, while the French ship relied on its sails, leaving it at the mercy of the winds.

square-rigged sailing ships. The corsair fleet in Algiers, for example, consisted of 36 galleys in 1581, but by 1634, it contained more than 70 sailing ships, each of which carried between 25 and 40 cannon. At about the same time, the fleet of Tunis consisted of 40 sailing ships and only 5 galleys. The adoption of sails greatly increased the range of the corsairs, and by the 1620s, they were attacking the Atlantic coasts of Portugal, Spain, France, and England. The most audacious corsair expedition went all the way to Iceland in 1627.

The corsairs captured ships and seized merchandise, but their most profitable prizes were Christian captives, whom they held for ransom, kept as galley slaves, or sold in North Africa. Although most galley slaves had a miserable existence, some of them became powerful corsairs themselves: Uluj Ali, mentioned above, was formerly a galley slave from Italy, and Murad Reis, the Muslim corsair who led the expedition to Iceland, was formerly known as Jan Janszoon from the Netherlands before he was captured by corsairs and made a galley slave in 1618. Recent scholarship estimates that over a million European Christians were enslaved by Muslim corsairs from North Africa between 1530 and 1780.

The system of government in the regencies of Algiers, Tunis, and Tripoli went through several stages of development between 1525 and 1800. The first rulers were corsair-admirals who governed with the blessing of the Ottoman sultan in Istanbul, but later the sultans sent out governors (known as pashas) who served for terms of 3 years. As outsiders who were little more than temporary visitors, they had no local power base or local support. By the seventeenth century, the Ottoman pashas had been reduced to ceremonial functions, while the real political power was held by autocratic rulers, known as **deys**, who had risen from the ranks of the Turkish military garrisons that were stationed permanently in the three regencies. Although the deys reigned as monarchs with lifetime tenure, many of them had their rule cut short by infighting within the military elite. In Algiers, for example, 11 different deys held the supreme office between 1671 and 1710, an average reign of less than 4 years. In the eighteenth century, military strongmen seized power in Algiers, Tunis, and Tripoli and established ruling dynasties that lasted into the nineteenth century.

Port cities such as Algiers, Tunis, and Tripoli displayed cosmopolitan influences that made them distinct from their rural hinterlands. Algiers was the most Turkish of the cities in North Africa; its harbor-front buildings and its long main street seemed patterned after Istanbul. In the eighteenth century, Algiers was home to native Algerians, Turks, Muslim refugees from Spain, Jews, Berbers, Arabs, white Christian slaves, and a few black slaves from sub-Saharan Africa. The famous Casbah (walled citadel) of Algiers housed several mosques, the palace, and a crowded traditional quarter with streets so narrow that two people could barely pass. Although some of the city's public buildings displayed the influence of Turkish architectural styles, the palace was a nondescript square building that was little more than functional.

The influence of the Ottoman rulers was limited mostly to the coastal cities and the narrow coastal plain; the rest of the countryside remained under the authority of tribal leaders and Muslim holy men. Each of the three regencies was divided into administrative districts run by appointed beys who operated more or less independently of Istanbul as long as they collected the taxes and delivered them to the capital. Every spring, the beys reinforced their authority by touring the countryside with troops to collect taxes, meet tribal leaders, deliver gifts, and wave the Ottoman flag. The beys knew that they could not succeed without the cooperation of the local tribal leaders, so they operated by negotiation and diplomacy rather than exercising direct authority. As a result, three centuries of Ottoman rule had minimal impact on the countryside.

Beginning in the seventeenth century, American ships came to North African ports to sell lumber, tobacco, and New England rum and buy figs, raisins, and Turkish opium. Because the American colonies were ruled by Britain at the time, its ships were protected by the British Navy. After the United States gained its independence in 1783, however, American ships became prime targets for North African corsairs. Lacking a naval presence in the Mediterranean, the American government made regular tribute payments to the North African rulers and paid ransom to recover captured American sailors. By 1800, tribute and ransom payments to the corsairs consumed 20 percent of the U.S. federal budget. A peace treaty to end the tribute payments was signed in 1815 after two wars in which the U.S. Navy launched attacks on Algiers and Tripoli. That is why the official hymn of the United States Marine Corps, written in the nineteenth century, begins with the line, "From the halls of Montezuma to the shores of Tripoli."

CONCLUSION

During the three centuries from 1500 to 1800, the war capitalism that emerged in the Indian Ocean and Mediterranean worlds was very different from the version practiced in the Atlantic world, where the states of Atlantic Europe seized land in the Americas to create plantations that were worked by captive laborers brought in from Africa. The result was an increase in violence on both sides of the Atlantic, as European settlers in the Americas pushed out indigenous peoples and predatory states arose in Africa that raided their neighbors for captives. Although the destruction engendered by the Atlantic slave trade was first felt near Africa's Atlantic coast, it spread to places as far as a thousand miles inland by the eighteenth century, bringing large sections of Africa under the influence of slavers and slave traders.

In the Indian Ocean and Mediterranean worlds, in contrast, the ravages of war capitalism were felt mostly near the coasts. In eastern Africa, the Portuguese destroyed the prosperity of the Swahili Coast, but their attempts to march inland and capture the gold mines of the Zimbabwe Plateau ended in failure. The Portuguese settlers in the Zambezi valley became more Africanized as the generations passed, and the Portuguese prazos survived by emulating the surrounding African chiefdoms. When the prazos disintegrated in the eighteenth century due to internal strife, the indigenous chiefdoms reclaimed their lost land.

In southern Africa, the Dutch and Huguenot settlers near the Cape of Good Hope destroyed the prosperity of the Khoikhoi cattle and sheep herders without developing any alternative sources of wealth. Instead, they emulated the herding techniques of the Khoikhoi and used a combination of coerced Khoikhoi workers and imported slave laborers to keep their livestock farms going. Even with coerced and enslaved labor, the settlers did little more than eke out a comfortable subsistence. They nevertheless remained integrated into the global economy because they sold their sheep and cattle to Dutch East India Company ships passing to and from Asia.

The only place in the western Indian Ocean to experience war capitalism that resembled that of the Atlantic world was the Mascarene Islands (Mauritius and Réunion), where French planters introduced Caribbean-style sugar plantations that relied on captive labor imported from Madagascar and the east coast of Africa. However, because of problems of weather and distance, the scale of sugar production in the Mascarene Islands remained small compared with the Caribbean. During the 1770s, the total value of goods arriving at Lorient, France, from the Mascarenes was less than a million French livres a year, while nearly 11 million livres worth of commodities came in from France's Caribbean colonies each year.

In the Mediterranean, the Ottoman conquests reoriented the commerce of the Mediterranean world. No longer dominated by the Italian city-states of Venice and Genoa, much of the trade in the eastern Mediterranean became oriented toward Istanbul. Grain from the Nile valley, for example, was exported to Istanbul much as it had once been sent to Rome during the days of the Caesars. In the regencies of Algiers, Tunis, and Tripoli, corsairs engaged in legalized piracy, enslaving over a million Christians and turning the Mediterranean into a war zone that extended into the Atlantic Ocean.

Except for Morocco, all of North Africa came under Ottoman rule in the sixteenth century. Yet in each of the North African provinces or regencies, local interests held more power than the Ottoman pashas sent out from Istanbul. It is ironic that those local power holders were not necessarily native born. In Egypt, the Mamluk beys and Mamluk tax farmers garnered more and more power while continuing to import new generations of enslaved soldiers from the fringes of the Ottoman Empire. In a similar way, the permanent power centers in Algiers, Tunis, and Tripoli were the army garrisons (made up of Turks, Eastern Europeans, and Christian renegades) and the corsair fleets (which were commanded by Christian renegades and Muslims from various parts of the empire). In contrast, the native-born North Africans had little influence in the government.

The situation was very different in the countryside, where the Berber and Arab tribes in the three regencies were allowed to manage their own affairs as long as they paid their taxes and refrained from outright rebellion. Because the tribal chiefs generally met with the Ottoman beys only once a year, the impact of three centuries of Ottoman rule was minimal. In Egypt, in contrast, the farmers in the Nile delta and the Nile valley were being ground into poverty by the

Mamluk tax farmers, while the settled and nomadic Arab tribes enjoyed relative autonomy.

The war capitalism that disrupted and restructured much of the world between 1500 and 1800 was based on low-level technology that relied heavily on forced human labor. The sailing ship was perhaps the most technologically advanced machine that the new global empires possessed. After 1800, however, the rise of industrial capitalism, which rested on the power of machines, would restructure relations of trade and production on a global scale and radically alter Africa's relationship with the global order.

CHAPTER REVIEW

KEY TERMS AND VOCABULARY

Omani Empire
prazo
Cape Colony
Boer
Mascarene Islands
Ottoman Empire
bey
corsair
dey

STUDY QUESTIONS

1. Why was the arrival of the Portuguese so destructive to the East African city-states?
2. Explain how the prazos in the Zambezi River valley could remain independent of the Portuguese Crown.
3. Describe the effect of Dutch settlement in the Cape Colony on the local Khoikhoi population.
4. What economic activity made the Mascarene Islands different from other European outposts in the Indian Ocean?
5. In what ways did the Ottoman conquests in North Africa reconfigure trade relations in the Mediterranean world?
6. What happened to the old Mamluk aristocracy after the Ottoman conquest of Egypt?
7. Why did the regencies of Algiers, Tunis, and Tripoli encourage legalized piracy in the Mediterranean?

PERSPECTIVES

AN AMERICAN CAPTURED BY ALGERIAN CORSAIRS

Joshua Gee was a sailor from Boston who was captured by Algerian corsairs on July 29, 1680, and spent the next 7 years as a slave working on Algerian privateering ships. In July 1687, he was ransomed by the British, as Massachusetts was a British colony at the time. After returning to Boston in October 1688, he became a shipwright and was elected to several municipal offices. His account of life with the Algerian corsairs was discovered in 1926 and published in 1942.

The first voyage I went to sea, we had a fight with two English ships, received much damage and were forced to leave them. The next day we took a ship from New Spain, a rich prize. The second voyage we fought an English ship and received much damage. She escaped, the sea being very high. The third voyage we fought a Genoese ship, which . . . escaped. After that, war was made with France, and we took many ships and did reward ourselves with clothing when we had leave to go on board the prizes which . . . favor shone on us. . . .

At our return to Algiers, news came of my first master's death on his voyage to visit his friends in the Black Sea, and then I was put to my second master, Cova Mestefa, the same that took me, being my half master at the first sale in the market. Some small time after my coming to him, one of our company being absent and he coming to the knowledge of it, caused us all to be laid down one by one, and himself with a . . . three-inch rope beat us all very severely. . . .

On another voyage we took a Portuguese flyboat soon after she came out of Portugal. She was bound for Brazil. I had leave to go on board, and I tarried all night and threw away my old clothes and put on new and as many as I could well carry. In the morning our boats came on board, and my master and others in the boat went away loaded.

After war was made with France, we chased a French ship and came not up with her till within night we boarded her and the ship blew up. I was in the hold to be ready to stop any leaks that might happen under water. The blast so lifted our ship that all our guns seemed to lift from the deck that it seemed as if the deck would fall. Considering the age and weakness of our ship, our master esteemed our deliverance miraculous and said surely God hath some particular love for someone in this ship, for whose sake we are all saved.

Of the French ship's crew, only three were saved by our boat. . . . Sometime after their being sold in Algiers, they were ransomed, and after that it was known that it was Master Marchand and the boatswain, and that they blew up their ship on purpose so that we with them might perish rather than be slaves. The captain of our ship said that had he known it before they were sold, he would have hung them at the yardarm and shot them to death.

1. *How would you describe Joshua Gee's life as a galley slave?*
2. *Why did the French crew blow up their own ship?*

Source: *Narrative of Joshua Gee of Boston, Mass. while he was captive in Algeria of the Barbary Pirates, 1680–1687* (Hartford, 1943), pp. 17–19, 21–24. Spelling modernized by Robert Harms.

THE REGENCY OF TUNIS IN 1788

When the French writer and diplomat François-René Chateaubriand visited Tunis in 1807, he was given a notebook filled with information on the state of affairs in the regency. Historians have since learned that the notebook was written in 1788 by a certain C. Nyssen. The information is presented in a question-and-answer format.

Question III. What is the population of this empire? Are the Moors [Berbers] or the Arabs more numerous? Are they taxed by tribes or individually? . . . Are there any Arabs settled in the city?

The population was calculated at four or five million souls before it was reduced by the plague, which may . . . have swept away one eighth [of the population]. The number of Arabs exceeds that of the Moors. Some taxes are paid by tribes and others by individuals. . . . There are Arabs settled in the city, but they are not the most numerous group of its inhabitants.

Question IV. Are there in the heart of the kingdom, or on the borders, many tribes who refuse to pay taxes? Are the Moors or Arabs the most intractable? Which of these two is wealthier? Do the nomadic tribes ever farm the lands of the inhabitants of the towns for purposes of cultivating them or pasturing their flocks and herds? What do these flocks and herds consist of?

There are tribes on the borders which at times refuse to pay taxes, but the troops sent to levy them soon compel payment. It is in general the Arabs that are the most intractable. There is every reason to presume that the Moors are the richest because they not only hold offices, but embark at the same time in agriculture, commerce, and manufactures. As the Arabs confine themselves to agriculture, the nomadic tribes frequently farm the lands of the inhabitants of the towns, either for tilling or for pasturing their flocks and herds, consisting of horned cattle, sheep, and camels, which serve them as beasts of burden, whose hair they spin, whose milk affords them nourishment, and whose flesh they often eat.

Fine horses are becoming very scarce because the Arabs have grown tired of breeding them and because the government and its officials took from them every adequate horse at whatever price they pleased. . . .

Question IX. Are there any caravans in the kingdom? Whither do they travel? Is the trade carried on by them considerable? What articles do they barter? . . .

Two caravans travel regularly to Tunis: the one from Constantine [Algeria] and the other from Ghadames [Libya]. The former makes eight or ten journeys a year, purchases haberdashery, jewelry, drugs, grocery, linen and woolen cloth, hardware, and hats manufactured in Tunis, paying for these articles in cattle and hard piasters. That from Ghadames rarely makes more than three journeys [a year], bringing negros and buying the same commodities as the other, and in general, whatever is necessary to supply the trade, which it carries on with the interior of Africa.

1. *How would you describe the main population groups in the Tunis Regency?*
2. *How successful was the regency government at collecting taxes?*

Source: François-René Chateaubriand, *Travels in Greece, Palestine, Egypt, and Barbary during the Years 1806 and 1807*, trans. Frederick Shoberl (New York: Van Winkle and Wiley, 1814), pp. 31, 34 of the Appendix to vol. 2.

PERSPECTIVES

THE KILWA CHRONICLE, 1520

The original Arabic manuscript of Kitāb al-sulwa fī akhbār Kulwa (Book of Consolation on the History of Kilwa)*—also known as* The Kilwa Chronicle*—was written in Kilwa between 1520 and 1530. The author does not give his name, but reveals that his maternal uncle was one of the keepers of the Kilwa treasury. It is the earliest account that gives an African Muslim's perspective on the arrival of Europeans on the Swahili Coast. His reference to the Europeans as "Franks" harkens back to the time of the Crusades. The dates are given in terms of the Islamic calendar.*

During al-Fudail's reign there came news from the land of Mozambique that men had come from the land of the Franks [the Christians]. They had three ships, and the name of their captain was al-Mirati [Dom Vasco da Gama]. After a few days there came word that the ships had passed Kilwa and had gone on to Mafia. The lord of Mafia rejoiced, for they thought they [the Franks] were good and honest men. But those who knew the truth confirmed that they were corrupt and dishonest persons who had only come to spy out the land in order to seize it. And they determined to cut the anchors of their ships so that they should drift ashore and be wrecked by the Muslims. The Franks learned of this and went on to Malindi.

When the people of Malindi saw them, they knew they were bringers of war and corruption, and were troubled with very great fear. They gave them all they asked, water, food, firewood, and everything else. And the Franks asked for a pilot to guide them to India, and after that back to their own land—God curse it! All this took place in the year which began on a Tuesday, A.H. 905 [1499 CE]. . . .

Then in the year A.H. 906 [1500 CE], which began on a Wednesday, there came al-Kabitan Bidhararis [Dom Pedro Alvarez Cabral] with a fleet of ships. He asked the people of Kilwa to send water and firewood and desired that the sultan or his son should go on board to converse with him. The amir and the people of the land decided it was best to send him an important citizen. So they sent Sayyid Luqman ibn al-Malik al-Adil. They dressed him in royal robes and sent him over.

Then they wanted water, and the Kilwa people drew it in a number of waterskins, and the porters carried it to the shore. Then they called out to the Portuguese to come ashore and take it. As they were coming, one of the principal slaves of the Amir Hajj Ibrahim, who was surnamed Hajj Kiteta, ordered the water carriers [of Kilwa] to carry the water away. So they did so. When the Christians disembarked on shore to fetch water, they saw neither much nor little water, but none at all. So they went back to their ships in anger. They set off again—God curse them!—to Malindi, and received everything they wanted in the way of water, firewood and food.

1. *How does the writer characterize the Franks (Christians)?*
2. *Why did the people of Kilwa refuse water to the Portuguese?*

Source: *The East African Coast: Select Documents from the First to the Earlier Nineteenth Century*, compiled by G. S. P. Freeman-Grenville (Oxford: Clarendon Press, 1962), pp. 47–48.

THE SWAHILI COAST IN 1569

Father Monclaro was a Portuguese Jesuit who accompanied a Portuguese military expedition that tried and failed to capture the gold mines on the Zimbabwe Plateau. In 1569, he traveled the length of the Swahili Coast that was under Portuguese control. His account reveals that the Portuguese had destroyed the former prosperity of the Swahili trading towns and left the inhabitants impoverished.

The king of Kilwa is a Moor [Muslim], as are all his subjects, and, as I was informed, was once the principal and greatest king here, because his possessions extended to Sofala before the Portuguese came to India. . . .

The city was formerly very large and prosperous, the houses were all of stone and lime with tiled roofs, but it was twice destroyed by our people because of the treachery of its inhabitants. . . . These Moors have some commerce with the islands of Comoro, and in the interior in ivory, which they buy from the Kaffirs [unbelievers] to sell to the Portuguese who are always in those parts, or to the factor of the captain of the said coast. . . .

Thence we went to Pate, which was our principal destination, with intention to destroy it because of the harm which is done there to the Portuguese. It is about twelve leagues distant from the city of Cambo, along the coast. It has a bad port, and at low tide the sea retires more than three leagues, and with the rising tide the water rushes in very furiously. Nevertheless it has a large commerce with Mecca and other parts. The city is very large, and has many fine edifices. Its Moorish priest was the chief of all on the coast.

When we arrived, we found the country deserted by all but the king and principal Moors, who begged for mercy, which was readily granted upon their paying the soldiers 12,000 *cruzados*, partly in money and partly in cloths and provisions. These Moors are very proud, and the worst enemies we have upon that coast, and so they proved themselves after we had left for Mozambique, for they took revenge by killing some peaceable Portuguese merchants who were in those parts. They also robbed and killed some Christian young men, with the excuse that a Moor was killed by the people of the captain of the coast, and they are in rebellion.

We were here nearly twenty days, until we returned to Zanzibar, and thence to Mozambique, without going to the islands of Comoro. Many of our people fell sick and died during this journey. The principal kings here were those of Kilwa and Malindi; all are now petty rulers, poor and without power, more worthy to be called sheiks than kings. The people are generally poor and wretched in nearly all these parts, and the Portuguese are becoming so already through the loss of commerce and navigation taken from them by their enemies.

1. *How would you describe the economic condition of the Swahili trading towns in 1569?*
2. *Describe the relationship between the Portuguese and the local Swahili population.*

Source: *The East African Coast: Select Documents from the First to the Earlier Nineteenth Century*, compiled by G. S. P. Freeman-Grenville (Oxford: Clarendon Press, 1962), pp. 138, 142–143.

PART 3

AFRICA IN THE AGE OF THE GREAT DIVERGENCE, 1800–1870

Sometime around 1800, Britain entered into an unprecedented period of sustained economic growth that was accompanied by advances in military, scientific, and educational development. That process later spread to Belgium, France, Germany, the Netherlands, and the northeastern United States. The historian Kenneth Pomeranz has characterized this phenomenon as the Great Divergence because it marks the historical moment when the countries of Atlantic Europe, for the first time in their history, became richer and more economically productive than any other countries in the world.

Britain's economic growth stemmed in part from the use of machines powered by waterwheels and coal-fired steam engines to manufacture articles that had previously been made by hand, and in part from a new way of organizing production. Instead of the old system of cottage industries and craft guilds that relied on highly skilled artisans, products were manufactured by unskilled wage laborers working in large factories. This new system will be referred to as industrial capitalism. The greater efficiency of industrial production substantially lowered the cost of manufactured goods: a worker with a power loom could weave cotton cloth 40 times faster than one with a hand loom, and a rolling mill produced iron plates 15 times faster than hammering by hand.

Historians have long debated why industrial capitalism first emerged in the late eighteenth century (and not in classical antiquity or some other earlier period), and why it first developed in Britain (and not in India, China, or Africa). The answer seems to be that although individual ingenuity has been found all over the globe throughout history, a system of industrial capitalism could develop only in an environment that provided an optimal combination of cheap energy, cheap labor, large markets, business-friendly institutions, and capital. To identify the key elements in Britain's Industrial Revolution, some historians have focused on factors unique to Britain, such as its improvements in agriculture, its rich coal deposits near the industrial cities, its business-friendly institutional reforms, and the work ethic of the English Puritans.

Another group of historians, however, has adopted a transnational perspective that focuses on the role of Atlantic trade and New World crops. Pomeranz has argued that imports of cheap sugar (which provided quick energy) and cheap cotton (which replaced wool) saved Britain from a crisis of depleted soils and overgrazed pastures, and thus helped to free up a portion of the population to work in factories. Imported sugar and cotton were affordable because they were produced by slave labor in the New World. Other historians with a transnational perspective have pointed out that the institutional reforms that aided the development of industrial capitalism would not have been adopted without pressure from the very merchants who had been enriched by Atlantic trade. Still others have focused on the question of where the British got the capital to finance their new industries. Although profits from its New World colonies made up only a small part of Britain's available capital, their contribution was not insignificant and may have been sufficient to put Britain over the top. In sum, many factors contributed to the rise of industrial capitalism in Britain, but the role of its overseas colonies cannot be ignored. In this sense, industrial capitalism must be viewed as a global system that could not have developed in isolation.

The rise of industrial capitalism was the most significant development in world history since the domestication of animals and plants around 11,000 BCE in the Fertile Crescent of Southwest Asia, for it changed the way people lived their lives. People in Britain who had formerly made their living as peasant farmers, sharecroppers, or landless rural laborers flocked to the cities to work up to 14 hours a day in large factories, creating an urban working class that was entirely dependent on wages. In 1835, when Alexis de Tocqueville visited the textile mills of Manchester, England, at the global epicenter of industrial capitalism, he observed that "a sort of black smoke covers the city. Under this half-daylight 300,000 human beings are ceaselessly at work." But de Tocqueville also noticed something else: "From this foul drain," he wrote, "the greatest stream of human industry flows out to fertilize the whole world." Manchester's textile mills illustrate the global nature of industrial capitalism. The cotton they spun was grown by enslaved African laborers working on plantations in the United States, and the cloth they produced was sold all over the world. The only reason why the mills were located in Manchester was that it had abundant water power and nearby coal deposits to power the machines. Unlike previous production systems in which cotton

EPICENTER OF THE INDUSTRIAL REVOLUTION A view of the industrial city of Manchester, England, in 1865. Its cotton mills placed it at the epicenter of Europe's Industrial Revolution. Alexis de Tocqueville had observed in 1835 that "a sort of black smoke covers the city. Under this half-daylight, 300,000 human beings are ceaselessly at work." The smoke came from the coal-fired steam engines that powered the machinery.

THE COAL OF NEWCASTLE The abundant coal in the region of Newcastle, England, powered the blast furnaces at the Lymington Iron Works, which produced 30,000 tons of metal per year in the 1830s. A local historian named T. Rose claimed that the usefulness of iron made it infinitely more valuable than fine gold, and he accordingly ranked the managers of the company "amongst the greatest benefactors of the human race." This picture was painted by Thomas Allom in 1835.

cloth was made in cotton-growing regions and wool cloth in sheep-herding regions, Manchester's industrial capitalism was embedded in a worldwide system of production and trade.

By lowering the cost of manufactured goods, industrial capitalism generated a worldwide scramble to find new markets and new sources of raw materials. Because Britain was more interested in obtaining raw materials for its factories than in supplying captive labor to its colonies, it led the fight to abolish the trans-Atlantic slave trade (although slavery itself was not abolished until later), and it sent out a squadron of warships to intercept slave traders along the West African coast. As the trans-Atlantic slave trade gradually wound down between 1807 and 1866, European ships increasingly visited the African coasts in search of tropical oils for European industries, spices for European cuisine, and ivory to carve into luxury items desired by Europe's growing middle class. The British referred to the new trade in commodities as "legitimate trade," a name that acknowledged the illegitimacy of its former trafficking in slaves.

Despite the major shift from a trade in human beings to a trade in commodities, the general pattern of Africa's commercial relations with Atlantic Europe did not change substantially. The European countries that had formerly trafficked in captives now sent out ships to buy commodities at the same places and often from the same African merchants. Instead of reducing their presence in Africa, some European trading nations increased it. To protect its trading privileges, the British government purchased the abandoned Dutch and Danish forts along the Gold Coast and established consulates along the major waterways of the Niger River delta, while the French retained control of their enclaves on the Senegambian coast. On the east African coast, the British, French, Germans, and Americans all established consulates on the island of Zanzibar in the 1840s to facilitate the trade in cloves, gum copal (a tree resin used in making varnish), and ivory. With the exception of French military incursions into North Africa and British conquests in southern Africa, the European trading countries seemed content to control the overseas trade in certain enclaves along the African coasts and did not attempt to explore or occupy the inland areas.

It is ironic that the era of "legitimate trade" in the nineteenth century was closely associated with an increase in slavery in Africa itself. The plantation system that the Europeans had developed in the New World began to be replicated in Africa, where enslaved laborers worked for African or Arab masters to produce tropical oils and spices for European markets. Moreover, the African and Arab caravans that traveled deep into the interior regions to obtain ivory usually brought back captives as well as elephant tusks. It has often been claimed that the internal African slave trade subsidized the ivory trade, but it was really the other way around: the profits from the ivory trade financed an expansion of the internal slave trade. In a sense, the growth of industrial capitalism in Europe triggered an expansion of war capitalism in Africa.

WHITE GOLD Ernst D. Moore (in the fedora hat), who was an ivory buyer for Arnold, Cheney, and Company of New York City, poses atop a pile of 355 elephant tusks at the company's compound in Zanzibar. Altogether, the tusks weighed 22,000 pounds. When the ivory arrived in the United States, it would be fashioned into combs, piano keys, and billiard balls. Moore later regretted his involvement in the ivory trade and wrote a book entitled *Ivory: Scourge of Africa*.

1807	**1869**	**1874**
Britain outlaws the slave trade	Suez Canal opens	Tippu Tip settles at Kasongo

8

ECONOMIC AND POLITICAL UPHEAVALS IN THE NINETEENTH CENTURY

Between 1803 and 1818, the governments of Denmark, England, the United States, France, the Netherlands, Portugal, and Spain enacted a series of laws and treaties that outlawed the transportation of African captives across the Atlantic Ocean. They did not, however, outlaw slavery in their overseas colonies. Although the effort to abolish the slave trade was partially successful, it was undermined by three problems: first, slavery itself remained legal throughout the New World, which offered a ready market for slave smuggling; second, countries such as Portugal, Spain, and France made very little effort to enforce the new anti–slave trade policy; and third, Britain's treaties with Spain and Portugal allowed slave trading to continue unabated south of the equator.

With treaties and decrees proving woefully inadequate to stop the trans-Atlantic slave trade, the British Navy established its West Africa Squadron in 1818 with an initial fleet of six ships, which grew to thirty by the mid-1840s. Forbidden by treaties from operating south of the equator, the squadron cruised along portions of the West African coast looking for slave ships and occasionally blockaded major slaving ports. Although 200,000 Africans were liberated from slave ships between 1820 and 1865, some 3.6 million captive Africans were landed in the New World

1886	**1886**	**1893**
Gold discovered on the Witwatersrand	Chokwe destroy the Lunda capital	Rabih Fadlallah conquers Bornu

FIGHTING THE SLAVE TRADE This painting shows the British Navy ship *Black Joke* attacking the Spanish slave brig *El Almirante* in the Bight of Benin on February 1, 1829. The captain's log states, "*Black Joke* captured *Almirante* Spanish Brig with 466 slaves from Lagos to Havana after an action of one hour and twenty minutes." During the years 1827–1829, the *Black Joke* captured 16 slave ships.

during that same period, with the majority of them going to Brazil. Thus the West Africa Squadron was intercepting less than 6 percent of the total traffic! What finally brought the trans-Atlantic slave trade to an end was the closing of Brazilian ports to slave ships in 1850 and the abolition of slavery in the Americas: Britain outlawed slavery in its American colonies in 1833, France in 1848, and the United States in 1865. By that time, the trans-Atlantic slave trade was effectively over.

The end of slave trading did not mean the end of commerce between Africans and Europeans. During the era of the slave trade, Europeans had always purchased hides, ivory, gold, acacia gum (used in textile dyes), and other African products along with captives, but as the trans-Atlantic slave trade came to an end, they increased their purchases of those products and sought new products to meet the demands of industrializing European economies. The industrial expansion of soap production exemplifies this process. Prior to 1790, soap was expensive in Europe and was not regularly used by ordinary people. In 1791, however, a Frenchman named Nicholas Leblanc discovered an inexpensive way to make soda ash, which could be mixed with tropical oils to make bars of soap. Soon soap making moved from homes and small shops to large factories that consumed enormous quantities of soap-making ingredients. By 1852, Britain was producing 140,000 tons of soda ash per year, and France was producing 45,000 tons, but they also needed tropical oils such as coconut oil, palm oil, and peanut oil, which could be obtained only by trade with Africa and other tropical regions of the world.

This chapter examines the changes in Africa's relationship to the world economy by focusing on three processes. The first was the rise in the production of tropical agricultural products for export to Europe. The second was the scramble for ivory in the interior regions of Africa. The third was the rise of modernizing economies in Egypt and southern Africa that were based on cotton production and mineral discoveries. In all cases, the economic changes were accompanied by major social and political changes that made life in many parts of Africa very different at the end of the nineteenth century than it had been at the beginning.

CASH CROP PRODUCTION IN COASTAL AFRICA

In the early nineteenth century, African rulers and merchants living near the Atlantic coast who had previously profited from the slave trade began to search for new ways to purchase goods that were being produced by the factories of Europe. In West Africa, growers began to produce large quantities of peanuts and palm oil for export, but those agricultural commodities could be profitably produced only within a hundred miles or so of the Atlantic coast because, beyond that limit, the cost of transportation would eat up the profits. On the island of Zanzibar, off the coast of East Africa, a unique combination of soil and climatic conditions fostered the production of cloves for export to Europe and the United States. Different regions along the African coasts made the transition from slave trading to cash crop production in different ways and with different social and political results. The discussion here will focus on four examples: Senegambia, the kingdom of Dahomey, the Niger River delta, and the island of Zanzibar.

Peasants and Peanuts in Senegambia

In the kingdoms of Kajoor and Bawol on the Senegambian coast, the nobility and their military slaves who had profited most from the slave trade lost out to small farmers who were in a better position to profit from the new trade in agricultural commodities. During the eighteenth century, the rulers of Kajoor and Bawol had come to rely on an elite corps of professional soldiers of slave origin, known as ***cheddo***. In the 1840s, Abbé David Boilat, who was born in Senegal to an African mother and a French father, described the cheddo as follows: "The *cheddo* take their orders from the kings and principal chiefs. They stop travelers on the roads, and pillage the most peaceful peasants to seize their cattle herds and their persons to sell to the Moors [Berbers] or other nations in the interior in order to buy brandy, tobacco, guns, gunpowder, bullets, swords, and knives. They are the plague of the country."

The cheddo flaunted their status as outsiders in an overwhelmingly Muslim region by rejecting Islam and openly drinking alcohol, which is forbidden to Muslims. Abbé Boilat explained that "the word *cheddo* doesn't only signify a soldier, but a scoundrel, an unbeliever, a man without faith or law." When a French Catholic missionary asked a group of cheddo soldiers what their religion was, they replied, "We are *cheddo*; our religion is to drink." By the nineteenth century, many prominent cheddo soldiers had intermarried with the noble families of Kajoor and Bawol, and so the word *cheddo* came to be applied indiscriminately to both the nobility and the military elite.

CHEDDO SOLDIER This 1840s painting by Abbé David Boilat shows a Cheddo soldier relaxing with his bottle of French brandy. The painting identifies him as a pagan because alcohol is forbidden to Muslims. Boilat explained that "the word *cheddo* doesn't only signify a soldier, but a scoundrel, an unbeliever, a man without faith or law."

The farmers in the rural villages, in contrast, were sober Muslims who viewed the cheddo soldiers and their noble patrons as a bunch of pagans. As the Atlantic slave trade in Senegambia was dying down after 1820, the cheddo soldiers were losing an important source of their income. To compensate, they increased their raids on rural villages in order to capture slaves whom they could sell into the Sahara Desert trade. Yoro Dyao, a Muslim cleric, wrote that the region was "marked by the most terrible violence, and most of the time free men were taken, rendered captive without reason, and sold so that the *cheddo* could buy themselves horses, silver, Guinea cloth, and liquor."

What saved the rural farmers of Kajoor and Bawol from oppression by the cheddo was the production of peanuts. In 1840, the French discovered that peanut oil from Senegambia could be mixed with palm oil to make soap. The farmers of Senegambia exported 5,500 tons of peanuts to France in 1854, and by 1882 they were exporting 80,000 tons a year. Peanut production put money in the hands of the Muslim farmers, who bought guns and ammunition to defend themselves from the cheddo. When a group of cheddo soldiers arrived at a rural village, the men would frequently pull out their guns and prepare for battle. Seeing themselves outnumbered and outgunned, the cheddo would retreat. After 1850, the balance of military power slowly shifted in favor of the farmers because they had a steady source of income from peanut production, while the cheddo, who would not dream of tilling fields for a living, found it more and more difficult to maintain their power and their extravagant lifestyle.

Palm Oil Plantations in Dahomey

Although the British Navy's West Africa Squadron patrolled the West African coast to intercept slave ships, there were places where the geography was conducive to smuggling. One of those places was the kingdom of Dahomey, where the rivers and lagoons in the swampy coastal plain provided opportunities for clandestine traffic. The most notorious smuggler of captives was Francisco Felix de Sousa, the king of Dahomey's commercial agent at the port city of Quidah.

Born in Brazil of mixed African and Portuguese ancestry, de Sousa came to Dahomey to work in the Portuguese fort there, but soon established himself as an independent slave trader. He used his friendship with Dahomey's King Gezo to gain an appointment as the king's commercial agent in Quidah, where he traded captives on behalf of the king and also on his own account. Controlling the commerce of the port from 1820 until his death in 1849, he gained a reputation as a master smuggler. He lavishly entertained the officers of slave ships in his private compound, which was furnished with liquor, billiard tables, roulette wheels, and other amenities that could be used to separate the sailors from their money. The West Africa Squadron captured more than 20 of the slave ships that he loaded, including several ships belonging to de Sousa himself. Nevertheless, a quarter of a million captives were carried away from Quidah and neighboring ports during the years of de Sousa's administration.

The transition from the slave trade to trade in agricultural commodities had the ironic effect of increasing the use of enslaved laborers within the kingdom of Dahomey. With the slave trade in decline, government officials and wealthy merchants in Dahomey invested their profits from that trade in the production of palm oil, which Europeans used to make soap. By the 1840s, there were many palm oil plantations owned by Dahomian officials and merchants around the port cities of Quidah and Porto Novo as well as Dahomey's capital city of Abomey. The plantations were worked by slaves, who tended the trees and engaged in the laborious processes of extracting the oil from the palm fruit and transporting it to the ports. In 1851, Abomey counted 10,000 slaves out of a total population of 30,000, and in 1855, there was a major revolt of Yoruba slaves on the Abomey plateau. The system of plantation production using slave labor was moving from the New World to the kingdom of Dahomey.

The Palm Oil Traders of the Niger Delta

In the Niger River delta, the slave trade died out even more slowly than in Dahomey, because its maze of creeks and waterways provided ideal cover for clandestine slave traders. Nearly half a million captives were taken out of Niger delta ports between 1800 and 1850. Bonny and Old Calabar, the two leading slave ports of the Niger delta, continued to export captives until 1837, when the West

Africa Squadron began concentrating its efforts there. The trading town of Nembe, hidden deep in the mangrove swamps, remained active in the clandestine slave trade until the Brazilian slave markets closed in 1850.

As the slave trade was winding down, the British began to buy palm oil that came from the oil palm trees that grew abundantly in the Igbo country just inland from the Niger River delta. The trees were owned by individual Igbo families, who harvested the fruit, extracted the oil, and sold it to African merchants, who transported it to the Niger delta. British purchases grew from 5,000 tons per year in 1827 to 30,000 tons per year in 1853. African merchants who had formerly traded in captives scrambled to monopolize the palm oil trade in certain inland regions, purchasing large numbers of enslaved laborers to load and unload the heavy casks of palm oil for transportation in dugout canoes along the delta waterways. African palm oil merchants in Old Calabar also developed palm plantations worked by slave labor. For this reason, captives continued to be brought into the Niger delta ports long after the Atlantic slave trade ended.

The decentralized nature of Niger delta societies created openings for successful slaves to become heads of trading firms and even kings, causing political and

PALM OIL SHIPS AT BONNY, NIGER DELTA This sketch published in the *Illustrated London News* in 1850 shows eight British ships in the Bonny harbor waiting to be loaded with palm oil, which the British used for making soap. The African dugout canoe in the foreground is carrying casks of palm oil to a ship. During the 1850s, British ships purchased 30,000 tons of palm oil per year from the Niger Delta ports.

social upheavals in the major delta trading ports. The canoe house system that had developed in the eighteenth century (see chapter 6) had allowed slaves who were successful traders to advance to powerful positions within the trading firms. After 1850, successful slaves began to seek political offices as well. In Old Calabar, wealthy slaves gained membership in the governing council. In Bonny, in 1854, the king was deposed and replaced by a regency council consisting of the heads of the four largest trading firms, three of whom started out as slaves. When the king regained power in 1864 and abolished the regency council, an Igbo man of slave origin named Jaja, who was the head of the largest trading firm in Bonny, moved upstream and established the independent kingdom of Opobo, cutting Bonny off from its palm oil markets. A former slave had become a king! In the later years of the nineteenth century, the kingdom of Opobo prospered while Bonny went into economic decline.

Clove Plantations in Zanzibar

Cloves, which grew exclusively in the Maluku Islands, were one of the most valuable commodities in Europe's spice trade. It was sometimes said that they were worth their weight in gold. In the 1770s, a French merchant managed to smuggle some clove trees to the Mascarene Islands in the Indian Ocean, but they did not grow well there. Then, in 1812, an Omani Arab merchant named Salih smuggled clove trees from the Mascarene Islands to Zanzibar, a small island just 22 miles off the east African coast. There, he found the soil and climate ideal for clove trees, and he established a thriving plantation. When the sultan of Oman, a kingdom in the Persian Gulf that claimed a loose hegemony over Zanzibar, visited the island in 1828, he confiscated Salih's plantation and made himself the biggest clove producer on the island. Four years later, he began to transfer the capital of the Omani Empire from the Persian Gulf to Zanzibar. By the 1840s, people all over the island were cutting down fruit trees in order to plant clove trees, and many Omani Arabs followed their sultan to Zanzibar in order to begin clove plantations of their own. The plantations were worked by slave laborers purchased from the east African mainland. By 1870, Zanzibar had between 60,000 and 100,000 slaves working on the clove plantations, and it imported 10,000 captives per year to replenish the labor force. As in parts of West Africa, the rise of international trade in agricultural commodities led to an increase in the use of slave labor in Africa itself.

THE SEARCH FOR IVORY IN THE INLAND REGIONS

In contrast to the regions near the African coasts that produced agricultural products such as peanuts, palm oil, and cloves for export, many parts of Africa produced agricultural products that did not find a ready market in Europe or were too expensive to transport to the coast. In those parts of Africa, trade with Europe and the Americas was mainly based on ivory from elephant tusks. Although ivory had long been exported to Europe, where it was used for knife handles, umbrella handles, and combs, the demand for African ivory greatly increased in the nineteenth century as pianos with ivory-topped keys and gaming tables with ivory billiard balls became staples of the middle-class lifestyle in Europe and America. British imports of ivory rose from 125 tons per year in 1820 to 800 tons per year in 1875. Along with these new uses for ivory came a shift in the sources. Whereas the hard ivory from West African elephants was suitable for knife and umbrella handles, equatorial African ivory was softer and could be carved into ornate objects and exquisite designs, and the soft East African ivory was said to be the best in the world. With the increase in demand, the price of East African ivory rose 400 percent between 1823 and 1873.

There were three main differences between the ivory trade and the trade in agricultural products. The first was that an elephant tusk was so valuable that traders could afford to transport it hundreds of miles to the coast and still make a profit. The second was that while clove trees and peanut fields produced a new crop each year, ivory could be obtained only by killing the elephants. As the elephant herds were wiped out near the African coasts, African ivory hunters and ivory merchants had to travel farther and farther inland in search of elephants. The third was that elephant tusks do not rot or spoil, so ivory caravans could leave the coast, travel far into the interior, and return several years later with loads of ivory. As a consequence of those three factors, the ivory frontier moved relentlessly inland from the Atlantic and Indian Ocean coasts during the nineteenth century. By the 1860s, some people living in the very heart of Africa were sending ivory to both the Atlantic and Indian Ocean coasts.

The ivory trade had different political effects in different parts of Africa. Along the Congo River, the Bobangi traders monopolized the river traffic, but they did not attempt to form a state or conquer territory. In Angola, the Chokwe ivory hunters destroyed the Lunda Empire and gained control of the trade routes without forming a new unified state to replace it. The opposite process was seen in eastern and northeastern Africa, where heavily armed caravans carved out states that ruled over societies that had traditionally had decentralized political systems. The states thus formed were as much commercial enterprises as political entities. To get a clearer picture of these processes, we examine the ivory trading empires of the Bobangi, the Chokwe, Msiri, Tippu Tip, Al-Zubayr, and Rabih Fadlallah, and we conclude this section with a look at a similar state-building process created by Samori Touré in West Africa, although he traded in kola nuts and not ivory.

The Bobangi in the Congo River Basin

The Bobangi canoemen along the Congo and Ubangi Rivers had been major suppliers of captives to the equatorial African coast during the eighteenth century (see chapter 6). After the slave trade went into decline, they refocused their efforts on the ivory trade, transporting elephant tusks down the Congo River in their large dugout canoes to Malebo Pool, where a 200-mile series of rapids blocked further advancement. The ivory was then transferred to caravans of Teke and Kongolese porters, who carried it to the coast for sale to Europeans. By the 1880s, ivory was coming from as far inland as Boyoma Falls, over a thousand miles from the mouth of the Congo River.

Investing the wealth they gained from their ivory sales in guns, gunpowder, cloth, and slaves, the Bobangi traders developed a society that expanded its population mainly through purchases of captives. Bobangi trading towns along the middle Congo River became populated overwhelmingly by persons of slave origin, giving rise to a system of social mobility whereby ambitious and successful slaves could become wealthy traders, or even chiefs. In this way, the Bobangi trading towns along the middle Congo were similar to the trading towns in the Niger River delta. In both cases, the towns had developed from former fishing villages and had highly decentralized political structures that encouraged entrepreneurship and economic mobility. During the 1880s, the chiefs of most of the Bobangi trading towns were people who had started their careers as slaves and had risen to wealth and power because of their success in the river trade. When a British missionary arrived at the Bobangi trading town of Lukolela in the 1880s, he reported that the chief's principal wife had great power over him "because she was free born and he was not."

The Bobangi traders did not attempt to use their wealth to establish a political or territorial empire. The dense tropical African rainforest had no long-distance overland trade routes. Instead, trade goods such as elephant tusks were taken to the nearest river to be transported by canoe, and all of the rivers in that vast watershed eventually flowed into the Congo River. To control the commerce of the middle Congo was to control the commerce of the entire Congo River basin. Under such circumstances, the Bobangi had no need to conquer territory and rule over it. They were content with monopolizing the Congo River trade and becoming wealthy.

The Chokwe in Angola

The transport of captives from Angola to Brazil increased in the early nineteenth century as the Portuguese took advantage of the treaties that allowed slave trading south of the equator, but after Brazil closed its ports to slave ships in 1850, the Angolan slave trade came to an abrupt end. The economic impact of the transition to commodity trading was especially turbulent in the Lunda Empire (see chapter 6), which had

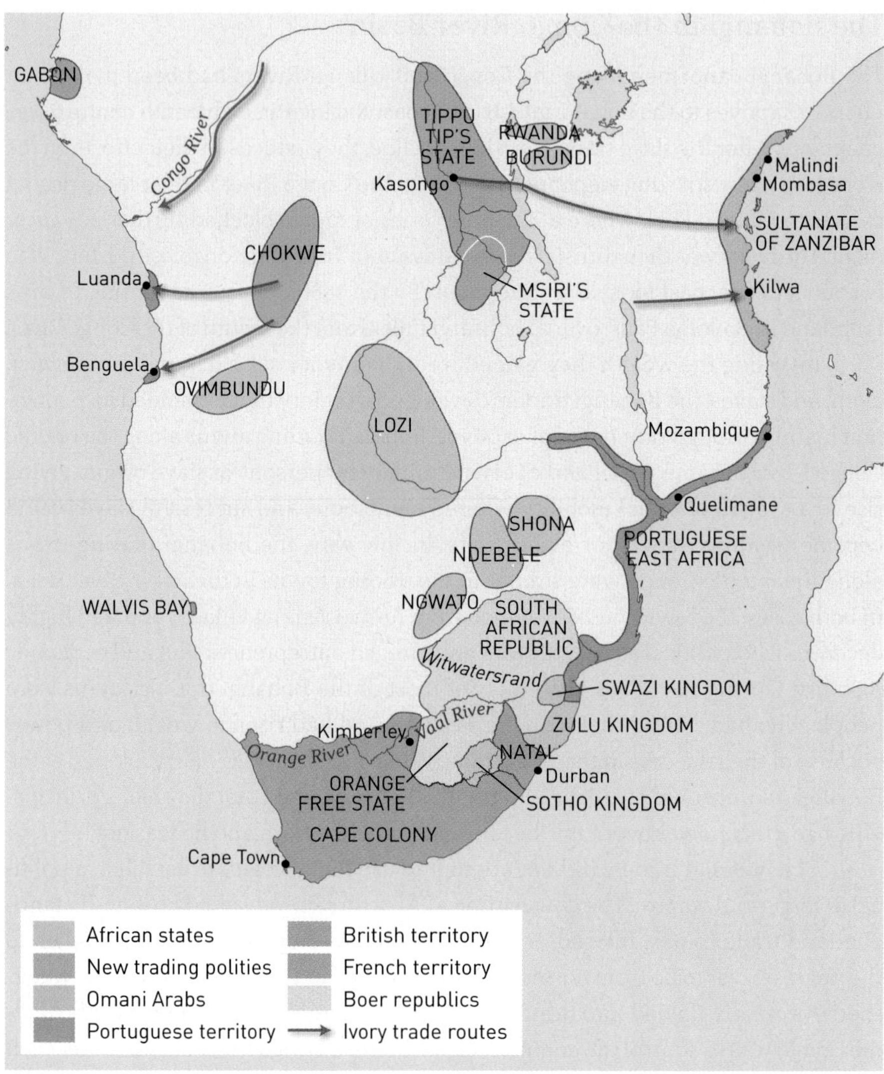

SELECTED STATES SOUTH OF THE EQUATOR IN 1880 This map shows the new ivory-trading spheres established by Msiri, Tippu Tip, and the Chokwe during the nineteenth century. In southern Africa, diamonds were discovered in the Cape Colony, and gold was discovered in the South African Republic (a.k.a. the Transvaal). The island of Zanzibar, which was the capital of the Zanzibar Sultanate, became important in the nineteenth century as a global center of clove production and the ivory trade.

been the major supplier of captives to the Portuguese. The Lunda king had developed a complex patronage system in which the luxury goods that he received via the slave trade were redistributed to lesser titleholders throughout the kingdom. The closing of the Brazilian ports to slave ships put the patronage system in jeopardy because the Lunda king had nothing else to trade for foreign luxury goods. By 1875, the trade route from the Lunda capital to the Atlantic coast had fallen into disuse, and political unrest was growing both in the Lunda capital and in the provinces of the Lunda Empire.

Living in the hinterland of Angola in between the Portuguese settlements near the coast and the Lunda Empire in the interior were highly mobile bands of **Chokwe** hunters. Although the Chokwe were considered backward and primitive by the rulers of the neighboring kingdoms, they were in a perfect position to profit from the new economic conditions. As hunters, they were experts at killing elephants, and they were also skilled at locating wild beehives containing wax, which the Portuguese used for making candles. The Chokwe began selling ivory and wax to the Portuguese in exchange for firearms, which they used to hunt elephants, and for other trade goods, which they used to purchase enslaved women. They then put those women to work processing wax into cakes for export, and they used the profits to purchase more guns and captives.

In the 1870s, the Lunda Empire was facing political unrest and fierce successional struggles. Certain contenders for power who were living in the western provinces invited Chokwe hunting bands to settle on their lands to collect ivory and wax on their behalf, and they also hired Chokwe war bands to aid them in their struggles against the ruling group in the Lunda capital. Fighting their way eastward, the Chokwe mercenaries broke faith with their employers and sacked the Lunda capital in 1886. They then initiated a reign of terror in the Lunda Empire. They raided villages, took as many captives as they could bring with them, and killed the rest of the inhabitants. Many Lunda refugees fled to the Luba kingdoms to the north and east, leaving desolation where the heart of the Lunda Empire had once been. The shift from slave trading to ivory trading had brought with it new forms of violence and conflict.

The East African Ivory Trade

Ivory had been exported from the various trading towns on the east African coast to the Red Sea and the Arabian Peninsula since the first century of the Common Era, and it was being carried to the Persian Gulf, India, and China by the ninth century, if not before. But it was only in the eighteenth century that the east African ivory trade became concentrated on the island of Zanzibar. "When the ships from India arrive in December, January, and February," wrote a French trader in 1776, "all the Moors from Kilwa, Mafia, Mombasa, etc., go to Zanzibar to buy their cargoes and distribute them subsequently in their districts in exchange for ivory tusks, provisions, and slaves." As a global center for the export of cloves and ivory, Zanzibar attracted international attention, causing the United States, Britain, France, and Germany to establish consulates there in the 1840s. The cosmopolitan nature of Zanzibar's economy is illustrated by the fact that trade was conducted there using Maria Theresa dollars (silver coins minted by the Habsburg rulers in Europe). For much of the nineteenth century, the biggest purchasers of ivory in Zanzibar were American ships from Salem, Massachusetts and Providence, Rhode Island.

Zanzibar also became east Africa's major market for captives. Although the island had never been involved in the trans-Atlantic slave trade, it became a major supplier of captives to several destinations in the Indian Ocean. Many of the captives who arrived from the east African mainland in the nineteenth century were destined for the clove plantations in Zanzibar, but others were purchased by French slave ships for the sugar plantations in the Mascarene Islands, and still others were taken to the Arabian Peninsula and the Persian Gulf, where they worked as servants, pearl divers, and laborers in date groves. The opening of the Suez Canal in 1869 greatly facilitated the shipping of dates from the Arabian Peninsula to markets in Europe and the United States, spurring a sharp rise in Arabian date production and an increased demand for slave labor in the date groves.

During the nineteenth century, Zanzibar-based trading caravans that were financed by Indian merchants living in Zanzibar went farther and farther inland in search of ivory and captives. The caravans were organized by Swahili merchants from the east African coast and Omani Arab traders who had immigrated to Zanzibar from the Persian Gulf. They generally followed trade routes that had been pioneered by Nyamwezi merchants living in what is now central Tanzania. Traveling on foot in a region where disease-carrying tsetse flies prevented the use of pack animals, these caravans often contained between five hundred and a thousand people. They traveled along well-established trade routes through regions where the local people would produce extra food to sell to the passing caravans. A caravan of a thousand people consumed a lot of food.

Hired professional porters from the Nyamwezi territory were essential elements of any caravan. The Nyamwezi became known as a "nation of porters" because nearly every young Nyamwezi man signed on to at least one or two caravan journeys in order to make some money before settling down to a life of farming, and others remained professional porters until they were too old to travel. Any Nyamwezi man who had never seen the Indian Ocean was considered an unsophisticated bumpkin. The trading town of Tabora, located roughly in the center of modern-day Tanzania, developed into the central node of the caravan routes. It was common for one gang of Nyamwezi porters to carry the loads between the coast and Tabora, and a different gang to carry the loads from Tabora to points west.

MSIRI IN KATANGA

With 24,000 tusks exported annually from Zanzibar during the 1860s, the elephant herds in the region that is now Tanzania were virtually extinct by 1872. The new destination of the ivory caravans was the region known as Katanga, located in the lightly wooded grasslands of the southern savanna roughly halfway between the Atlantic coast and the Indian Ocean coast. Possessing copper mines in addition to ivory, Katanga had once been under the control of the Lunda Empire. The main person to develop the trade between Katanga and Zanzibar was **Msiri**, a Nyamwezi trader who went to Katanga in 1850 with a heavily armed caravan to purchase ivory and copper. While there, he came to the aid of a chief who was under attack by a neighboring Lunda chief. Msiri easily won the war because his men were armed with guns while the Lunda chief had none.

Msiri returned to Katanga a year later with a larger and even more heavily armed entourage and took over the chiefdom that he had rescued a year earlier. He formed an army using local recruits and began to conquer some of the neighboring chiefdoms while forming alliances with others, thus consolidating his rule over the region and forming a kingdom known as the Yeke Kingdom. He married a woman from the village of each subordinate chief in order to bind the chiefdoms together and create an intelligence network to keep an eye on the chiefs. Finding the supply routes that brought him guns and gunpowder from the east African coast unreliable, he established relations with Portuguese traders in Angola, on the Atlantic coast. Even though he reportedly had over 500 wives, his favorite wife was Maria de Fonseca, the sister of his Luso-African trading partner in Angola.

The major obstacle to free transit between the coasts was an independent Lunda kingdom known as Kazembe. The Portuguese had earlier developed settler colonies in Angola, on the Atlantic coast (see chapter 5), and in Mozambique, on the Indian Ocean coast (see chapter 7), but had never been able to link them together. The Portuguese had sent four diplomatic missions to Kazembe between 1796 and 1831 seeking to open a trade route across Africa from Angola to the Zambezi River valley. Although the king had welcomed them with great pomp and ceremony, he had rebuffed their demands for freedom of passage through his kingdom. When Msiri established his Yeke Kingdom in the 1850s, he also found his eastern trade route partially blocked by the king of Kazembe. He responded by waging war on Kazembe. By the late 1860s, Msiri had annexed most of the territory of Kazembe, and he dominated the ivory and copper trade. His kingdom was now trading with both the Atlantic coast and the Indian Ocean coast of Africa. By uniting the east and the west trading spheres, Msiri had accomplished a goal that had long eluded the Portuguese.

Tippu Tip in Manyema

North of Msiri's Yeke Kingdom was the dense tropical rainforest, which was much less accessible to large trade caravans than the lightly wooded grasslands of the southern savanna. With ivory becoming more and more scarce, Arab and Swahili traders from the east African coast began to cross Lake Tanganyika with their Nyamwezi porters in the 1860s to search for ivory in the tropical rainforest region of Manyema (now in eastern Congo). Being over a thousand miles from the Indian Ocean coast, this region had not previously been involved in the international economy. Ivory tusks had so little value there that people used them as mortars for pounding grain or as fence posts.

The most successful of the ivory traders who penetrated this region from the East African coast was Hamid bin Muhammad el Murjebi, widely known as **Tippu Tip**, a man of mixed Omani Arab and African ancestry who was born in Zanzibar. He gained the nickname Tippu Tip because he brought guns into regions where they were previously unknown, and the local people reported that his guns made the sound "tip, tip, tip." In the 1870s, he established permanent bases in the towns of Kasongo and Nyangwe along the Lualaba (upper Congo) River. From there, his hired Nyamwezi soldiers would attack villages, seize stockpiles of ivory, and take captives, who could be ransomed with ivory or sold as slaves. When those soldiers wished to return to their homes in central Tanzania, Tippu Tip replaced them with enslaved soldiers he had captured in his wars against local chiefs.

TIPPU TIP Hamid bin Muhammad el Murjebi, known as Tippu Tip, was the most successful caravan trader in East Africa. During the 1870s, he founded a large trading state in Manyema (a region halfway between the Indian and Atlantic Oceans) that funneled ivory and captives to Zanzibar. After retiring to Zanzibar in the 1890s, he wrote his autobiography, which gave details of his career.

By the 1880s, Tippu Tip's trading and raiding state extended over 500 miles from north to south along the Lualaba

River. The trading town of Kasongo, where he had his headquarters, grew from about 1,000 people in 1874 to 20,000 by 1890. By then, Tippu Tip no longer obtained ivory by purchase, but instead received it as tribute from the chiefs he had conquered. Caravans coming to Kasongo from the east African coast now carried mostly guns and ammunition instead of trade goods. The state created by Tippu Tip operated mainly as a military and commercial enterprise that collected captives and ivory and sent them to Zanzibar.

During the 1880s, Tippu Tip's commercial agents advanced downstream along the upper Congo River to the point where they encountered traders belonging to the Bobangi-dominated networks that funneled trade down the Congo River to the Atlantic coast. The trade routes to the east had met up with the trade routes to the west. By this time, there was no part of equatorial Africa that was not in commercial contact with either the Atlantic coast or the Indian Ocean coast. Even the most remote parts of the tropical rainforest were now enmeshed in the global economy.

Ivory and Captives in the Northeastern Savanna

An east–west belt of wooded grassland runs from the Red Sea in the east to Lake Chad, in the middle of Africa. This belt, referred to here as the northeastern savanna, forms the transition zone between the Sahel, to its north, and the tropical rainforest, to its south. Lacking valuable commodities such as gold or salt, and being distant from major markets, this region had not previously been a center of commerce or slave trading. It was only with the rise in the world price of ivory that the tusks of the elephants in the northeastern savanna suddenly became valuable. With ivory ensuring the profitability of trade caravans, it was but a small step to include trading in captives as well. As in East Africa, it was the search for ivory that took the caravan traders hundreds of miles from their homes to the northeastern savanna, but they always returned with both ivory and captives. Because of its historical isolation from the wider world, the inhabitants of this region were unacquainted with guns, which made them easy targets for traders arriving in heavily armed caravans. Their situation was similar to that of the people of the tropical rainforest who had succumbed so easily to the guns of Tippu Tip.

What made the northeastern savanna unique was that its markets were not on the Atlantic or Indian Ocean coast, but on the Mediterranean coast, which was controlled by the Ottoman Empire. There were three major trade routes across the Sahel and the Sahara. The first ran up the Nile River valley to Alexandria, Egypt; the second to the Libyan port of Benghazi; and the third from near Lake Chad to the Libyan port of Tripoli. When the ivory reached the Mediterranean coast, it was purchased by British ivory traders based on the Mediterranean island of Malta. Taken together, the Mediterranean ports of Malta and Alexandria exported more

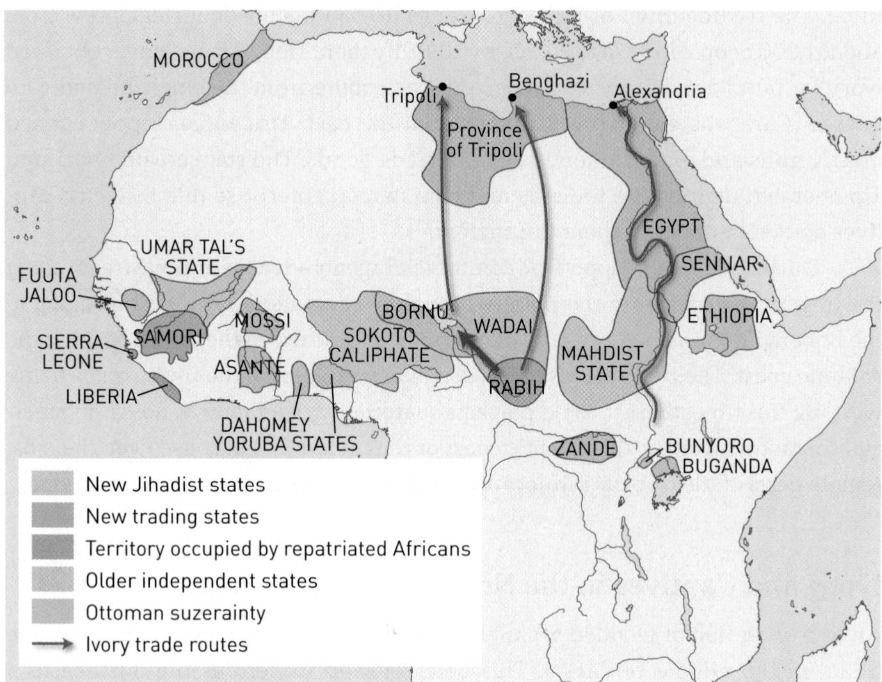

SELECTED STATES NORTH OF THE EQUATOR IN 1880 This map shows the ivory trading sphere established by Rabih in the northeastern savanna, and the cola nut trading sphere established by Samori in the northwestern savanna. Ivory collected in the northeastern savanna was taken across the Sahara to the Mediterranean ports of Alexandria, Benghazi, and Tripoli. The jihadist states will be discussed in chapter 9.

ivory per year than Zanzibar. The captives were sent on Ottoman ships to Istanbul and other destinations in the eastern Mediterranean.

Al-Zubayr in Sudan

In 1820, the Egyptian army invaded Sudan, to its south, and established the city of Khartoum, at the confluence of the Blue and the White Nile, as its administrative and commercial center. The region north of Khartoum was mostly desert or semidesert grassland inhabited by Muslims who spoke Arabic. Some of them were Arabs, but others were Sudanese, who often used fake genealogies to link themselves to Baghdad and Arabia. South of Khartoum, the semidesert gave way to the wooded grasslands of the northeastern savanna. Those terrains were populated by cattle herders and farmers who grew millet and sorghum. Because they had never embraced Islam, the Muslims in the north considered them to be pagans and savages.

Beginning in the 1840s, Sudanese merchant firms with headquarters in Khartoum mounted ivory trading and slave raiding operations to the south. As bases for their operations, they developed fortified trading settlements known as **zaribas**. By the 1860s, there was a zariba about every 20 miles along the trade routes that went south and southwest from Khartoum. The commerce of the region was divided among about a dozen merchant companies based in Khartoum.

The most successful of the Khartoum merchants was **Al-Zubayr**, who ventured into a region southwest of Khartoum, known as the Bahr el-Ghazal (Sea of the Gazelles), where no trade caravans had traveled before. He found ivory in abundance that was little valued by the local populations. Going farther into the unknown territory, he and his followers built a large fortress. When the local ruler tried to drive him away, Al-Zubayr defeated him and became the ruler of the region. He founded a capital city called Deim Al-Zubayr, where he built a strong army of enslaved soldiers. From this base, he expanded his conquests in subsequent years, establishing a network of over 30 zaribas. In 1873, he was asked by the khedive (viceroy) of Egypt to administer the lands that he had conquered on behalf of the Egyptian government. He was given the title of bey and allowed to administer his territory as he saw fit, as long as he sent £15,000 worth of ivory per year to Cairo as taxes.

By this time, Al-Zubayr ruled over a territory as large as France. His followers continued to hunt elephants and trade in ivory and other products of the region, and they also traded in captives. Many of the people enslaved in his wars were integrated into his army or put to work producing food for his soldiers, but large numbers of them were taken to Egypt, where they worked as domestic servants and agricultural laborers. Al-Zubayr's biographer and friend, H. C. Jackson, reported that Al-Zubayr himself was the biggest slave trader of all, and that his capital city of Diem Al-Zubayr was a major emporium for the slave trade with Egypt.

In 1874, Al-Zubayr invaded and conquered the kingdom of Wadai, to his northwest. This development alarmed the Egyptian government, which began to see him as a rival power. The ruler of Egypt, Khedive Ismail, summoned him to Cairo in 1875 and did not allow him to return to Sudan. Al-Zubayr's son Suleiman attempted to rule the territory in his father's absence, but he was killed by the Egyptian army in 1879.

The Rise of Rabih Fadlallah

With the collapse of Al-Zubayr's short-lived trading state, several of the armed war bands that he had created moved westward, beyond the sphere of Egyptian control, to seek their fortunes as warlords and traders. Their goal was to transplant the zariba system into the wooded grassland to the west. This region attracted them for two reasons: First, it contained elephants whose ivory could be carried north across the Sahara Desert to the Mediterranean ports of Benghazi and Tripoli, bypassing the Egyptians entirely. Second, firearms were rare in this region, so well-armed caravans could conquer and enslave the local populations almost at will.

The roving war bands established new zaribas and raided the countryside for captives, integrating the boys and young men they captured into their armies and incorporating the girls and young women as servants, concubines, or wives for the soldiers. In this way, their armies grew stronger with each victory. The rest of the captives were sold for guns and ammunition to trans-Saharan slave traders, who took them across the desert to Benghazi and Tripoli. After the Ottoman sultan issued the Decree of 1857, which forbade trade in African captives in most parts of the Ottoman Empire, slave exports from Tripoli declined, and the bulk of the slave exports shifted to Benghazi, where trade was not as closely monitored.

The most successful of the new merchant-warlords was **Rabih Fadlallah**, who had been Al-Zubayr's principal lieutenant. Rabih was born around 1840, in a village near Khartoum that was known for making bricks. As a young man, he joined the Egyptian army as a cavalryman, but left after permanently injuring his right hand during some military maneuvers. Returning to Khartoum, he reportedly met Al-Zubayr during a chess game. At the time, Al-Zubayr was looking to hire 200 mercenary soldiers for a trading expedition to the Bahr el-Ghazal, and Rabih signed on. History has not recorded who won the chess match, but Rabih had clearly impressed Al-Zubayr, and by the age of 30, had become his top lieutenant.

In 1878, after the fall of Al Zubayr's trading state, Rabih left Sudan with about 800 followers, half of whom were equipped with muskets. Moving west through the woodland savanna, he conquered the small Islamic state of Dar al-Kuti and established a base there. From that base, his soldiers roamed widely during the dry seasons to pillage, enslave, and collect ivory. After 10 years in Dar al-Kuti, his army had grown to more than 10,000 soldiers.

One of Rabih's goals was to gain unrestricted access to the trans-Saharan trade routes, which were his lifeline to the wider world. The major trade route that he was using linked Benghazi to the kingdom of Wadai, which lay in the Sahel directly north of his base in Dar al-Kuti. The sultan of Wadai, however, feared the power of Rabih's army and did not want to help him obtain arms and supplies. When the sultan refused Rabih's request to allow trading parties from the north to traverse Wadai on their way to his base, Rabih attacked Wadai's client state of Dar Runga, scattering or enslaving the population. He also launched two attacks on Wadai itself, but they ended without a clear victory. Even though the sultan of Wadai eventually allowed trans-Saharan trade caravans to proceed to Rabih's base, he maintained a strict embargo on arms and ammunition.

THE CAPITAL OF BORNU Kukawa, the capital of Bornu, was a double city, with a western town occupied by Arab merchants from North Africa and an eastern town housing the royal palace and the houses of the nobles. This 1851 drawing by the German explorer Heinrich Barth shows the central square that separated the two towns. Kukawa was destroyed in 1893 by Rabih Fadlallah, who conquered the kingdom of Bornu and built a new capital with a sumptuous palace at Dikwa.

Cut off from the sources of his military strength, Rabih decided to relocate west of Lake Chad, where he could use the trade route that ran from the kingdom of Bornu across the Sahara to Tripoli. Bornu had been an independent kingdom for over 500 years. Its capital city, Kukawa, was a double city, with a western town occupied by Arab merchants from North Africa and an eastern royal city containing the palace of the king and the residences of the important nobles. The space between the two towns was occupied by a large market, where goods from Europe and North Africa were exchanged for cattle hides, ivory, ostrich feathers, and captives, which were sent to North Africa in return.

When Rabih conquered the kingdom of Bornu in 1893, he was more than 1,200 miles west of Khartoum and roughly halfway between the Red Sea and the Atlantic coast. After capturing Kukawa, he plundered and razed it. Then he established a new capital city at Dikwa, where he built an impressive palace. In his previous conquests, he had been far more interested in commerce than in governance and had usually lived in military camps while leaving the local rulers in place to deal with day-to-day matters of state. Rabih's establishment of a new capital and a new palace in Bornu showed that he was finally ready to govern. He ruled as a king, using the same title of *Shehu* that had been used by the previous rulers of Bornu, and he kept the existing vassal chiefs in place under the watchful eyes of his lieutenants. He developed a legal code based on Muslim sharia law and instituted new systems of taxation and budgeting. Under Rabih's rule, ivory and captives continued to be sent across the Sahara Desert to North Africa.

Samori Touré in the Northwestern Savanna

In the northwestern savanna, **Samori Touré** created a commercial empire that exploited the north–south trade routes that ran between the western Sahel, to the north, and the forested regions to the south. Elephants were rare in the western savanna, and Samori, as he was known, based his commerce on kola nuts, which grew in the forested regions to the south but were consumed mainly in the Sahel. Because they were the only source of caffeine (think of Coca-Cola) in an area where coffee was not grown, kola nuts were an essential part of hospitality and ceremony in the Sahel. The trading zone where Samori operated had a centuries-old tradition of long-distance traders being the most peaceful of travelers. As they passed from village to village and from kingdom to kingdom, their personal security was guaranteed by the fact that they did not pose a threat to anyone. That situation changed because Samori used his commercial profits and contacts to introduce guns into a region where they were previously scarce. Under these circumstances, he was able to conquer a large empire in a short time.

Samori Touré, who was born around 1830, was an itinerant trader, purchasing kola nuts in the forest regions and taking them north to the Fuuta Jaloo highlands, where he traded them for cattle and salt. He also visited the gold-bearing region of Buré, where he traded kola nuts for gold. He used the gold and the cattle to buy guns and other European goods that were brought in from the Sierra Leone coast. In 1853, Samori abandoned commerce and enlisted in the army of a local ruler, gaining valuable military training and experience. A decade later, as an ex-soldier with no capital to restart his trading career, he formed a band of seven men armed with guns and invited young men in the surrounding region to join him as he set out to create an empire.

When Samori's army approached a village, he would send out a messenger who ordered the village to surrender. If they refused, he launched an attack. Many villages fought to defend themselves, protected by fortifications of thick mud walls that had only one entry and one exit. Villages that offered stiff resistance were besieged and starved until they surrendered. As oral testimony from a village in what is now southern Mali attests, "If you say that Samori captured many slaves here, it was because of famine. It was out of hunger, not because of Samori's bravery, because Samori attacked many villages without success. At that time, everyone cultivated together and kept their harvest in the field. When you were under siege, you couldn't leave the fortified village. That is why Samori laid siege to our villages. Nobody could leave. And when you were starving and without food, you finally surrendered."

SAMORI TOURÉ A kola-nut trader by profession, Samori Touré exchanged his kola for gold and cattle, which he then used to purchase guns in Sierra Leone in order to form an army and conquer territory. Seeking a unifying ideology, he proclaimed an Islamic state in 1886, but the people revolted when he ordered forced conversion to Islam. His territory was, above all, an economic space where commerce was king.

With each military victory, Samori incorporated the defeated troops into his army. Captured young men were given military training, and young women were taken as wives for the soldiers. Other war prisoners were brought to Fuuta Jaloo, a kingdom that relied almost exclusively on servile laborers for its agricultural production (see chapter 6). Samori exchanged these captives for cattle, which he sent to the Sierra Leone coast to be traded for guns. Still other captives were sent north to the Sahel or the Sahara Desert to be traded for horses. Even though horses suffered a high mortality rate in the tsetse fly–infested zone just north of the rainforest, Samori maintained a small cavalry that could unsettle his enemies by launching surprise attacks. Using his military skills and his knowledge of commerce, Samori built up a well-trained and well-equipped army that conquered a large empire in a period of about 15 years.

Samori pursued military and commercial objectives at the same time. He gained control of the city of Kankan (in modern Guinea), which was at the crossroads of north–south trade routes between the Sahel and the forest and east–west routes to the Sierra Leone coast, which provided an outlet for international trade. When the route to Freetown, Sierra Leone, was cut off, Samori opened a new trade route to Monrovia, Liberia. In the 1870s, he gained control of the goldfields at Buré and used the gold to purchase guns. Djibril Tamsir Niane, the venerable historian of West Africa, described Samori's empire as "above all, an economic space where commerce is king."

By the 1870s, Samori's empire had grown too large to be governed by simple military occupation. He established a governing council and made each council member responsible for overseeing certain government functions. In effect, the councilors functioned like cabinet ministers. But Samori also needed a unifying ideology and a basis for claiming political legitimacy. He found the answer in Islam. Although raised as a non-Muslim, he had converted to Islam under the influence of the Muslim scholars in Kankan and had learned to read the Quran. In 1884, he gave himself the title of *almamy*, which he copied from the theocratic state of Fuuta Jaloo, and in 1886, he proclaimed his conquered territory to be an Islamic state. His problems began when he ordered all of the people in his territory to convert to Islam. This announcement prompted massive revolts among the non-Muslim populations starting in 1888. In response, Samori revoked his order and set about rebuilding his ravaged empire. Although he continued to practice Islam as his personal faith, he never again tried to impose it on the people in his conquered territories.

MODERNIZING ECONOMIES IN EGYPT AND SOUTHERN AFRICA

At the northern and southern ends of the African continent, modernizing states were developing in the nineteenth century. Egypt, in the north, developed a modern army, a modern government bureaucracy, and a modern transportation and communication system with steamships, railroads, and telegraph lines, much of it paid for by cotton production. At the southern end of the continent, the white settlers in the region that is now South Africa moved from low-intensity farming to an industrial economy based on diamond and gold mining. Yet those modernizing developments did not spark similar developments among their African neighbors. Quite the contrary: economic growth in Egypt and southern Africa led to political and military instability that reverberated far beyond their borders.

Egypt

Egypt became part of the Ottoman Empire in 1517, when the Ottoman army defeated Egypt's ruling Mamluk dynasty (see chapter 7). The Ottomans incorporated Egypt's existing Mamluk military elite into the structure of their rule. Mamluk commanders were appointed to Ottoman military and civilian posts, and enslaved recruits for the Mamluk army continued to be imported from such widespread places as the Black Sea and Albania. Just as Egypt had earlier been a major supplier of grain to Rome, it became a major supplier of foodstuffs to Istanbul. Its economic importance to the Ottoman Empire diminished during the eighteenth century, however, as Ottoman authority in Egypt waned and internal turmoil undermined the country's economy.

In 1798, the French army invaded Egypt and defeated the forces of the Mamluk commanders, but a British naval blockade of the Nile delta ports persuaded the French to withdraw in 1801. In the aftermath of the French withdrawal, the Ottoman sultan appointed **Muhammad Ali**, an Albanian-born officer in the Ottoman army, as the governor of Egypt. Muhammad Ali worked to turn Egypt into a modern state with a salaried civil service and a professional army. In 1811, he organized the massacre of several hundred Mamluk officials who had previously controlled the military recruitment and tax collection systems. With the Mamluks out of the way, he reorganized the Egyptian army based on the French model and replaced the Albanian and Turkish soldiers who had been sent by the Ottoman sultan to help expel the French with Egyptian recruits and enslaved soldiers from Sudan. He also purchased large quantities of weapons from the British and French and brought in many European military and administrative advisers.

Perhaps the most lasting innovation introduced by Muhammad Ali was the production of Egyptian long-staple cotton. After a bush that produced cotton with exceptionally long fibers was discovered growing in a garden in Cairo in 1818, Muhammad Ali ordered the Egyptian peasants to plant a certain amount of cotton of this type and to cultivate cotton on state-owned lands as their annual corvée (forced-labor tax). The British cotton mills in Manchester purchased long-staple cotton at prices up to four times those they paid for ordinary Egyptian short-staple cotton because they considered it superior to all but the best American cotton. To boost production, Muhammad Ali distributed seeds, brought in experts from Syria to teach the peasants how to properly cultivate the crop and prepare it for export, sold draft animals to peasants on credit, and distributed cotton gins among the rural villages. His representatives bought the harvest at a low fixed price and sold it to British merchant houses in Alexandria for roughly twice as much. Soon cotton sales were the second-largest source of state income (after land taxes). By the 1850s, roughly 25,000 tons of cotton were being exported annually

MASSACRE OF THE MAMLUKS As a province of the Ottoman Empire, Egypt was ruled by Ottoman governors, but the old Mamluk aristocracy continued to dominate the military and the administration. After Muhammad Ali became governor of Egypt in 1805, one of his first acts was to order an ambush and massacre of several hundred Mamluks in Cairo. The suppression of the Mamluks freed him to institute his reforms and modernization projects.

to Britain, and production quadrupled during the American Civil War, when the North blockaded Southern ports to prevent American slave-produced cotton from reaching England.

Muhammad Ali's cotton initiative was part of a larger plan to improve agricultural production and increase state revenues. He eliminated tax exemptions from lands controlled by religious organizations and removed the private tax farmers (many of whom were Mamluks) in order to bring tax revenues under direct state control. He ordered updated surveys of land ownership and instituted forced labor on public works. With the new tax revenues and forced labor, he repaired the canals, reservoirs, and irrigation works that were the key to Egyptian agriculture, thereby increasing the amount of cultivated land by one-third. These improvements were carried out at enormous cost. The construction of the Mahmudiya Canal, for example, required the forced labor of 360,000 peasants, 100,000 of whom died of disease and hardship. The main beneficiaries of those improvements were the Egyptian state and the large landowners. Ordinary peasants ended up working harder and longer for less reward, and armed peasant uprisings were not uncommon between 1820 and 1840. Many of the captives brought in from Sudan after 1820 ended up working in the cotton fields of the large landowners.

European involvement with Egypt increased when the British developed a route to India via the Mediterranean and Red Seas that relied on Egypt as a transshipment point. In the 1850s, the British built railroads connecting Cairo to the port of Alexandria on the Mediterranean and to the port of Suez on the Red Sea. In this way, goods could be transferred by rail from ships in the Mediterranean to ships in the Indian Ocean, thus eliminating the need to sail around the southern tip of Africa in order to reach India or China. Not to be outdone, the French began construction of the Suez Canal, which linked the Mediterranean Sea directly to the Red Sea. After the canal opened in 1869, a ship from Europe could sail directly to India or China. Encouraged by the high prices that the British paid for Egyptian cotton during the American Civil War, when American cotton was not available, the ruler of Egypt at that time, Khedive Ismail, undertook further modernization

THE SUEZ CANAL This parade of ships celebrates the opening of the Suez Canal in 1869. By linking the Red Sea to the Mediterranean, the canal permitted European ships to sail directly to India and China without making the long trip around the southern tip of Africa. It also facilitated travel between Europe and the east African coast.

measures. He expanded and modernized his army, developed steamship service on the Nile, installed a telegraph system, and extended the railway up the Nile toward Sudan. But while modernizing his country, he was also amassing a large amount of debt.

Southern Africa

In 1795, the British seized the Dutch East India Company's colony near the Cape of Good Hope in order to gain a strategic naval base at the southern tip of Africa. After taking definitive control of the Cape Colony in 1806, they began to develop it as a place for trade and settlement similar to the British colonies of Canada and Australia. A banking industry developed in Cape Town, and British traders took their ox-wagons loaded with trade goods to visit the inland settlements of the Boers, traveling along improved wagon roads.

At the time of the British takeover, much of the land in the immediate interior was under the control of Boers, who lived on large sheep and cattle ranches that they operated with the aid of two subordinate groups: slave laborers who had been brought in from Madagascar and the Indian subcontinent, and indigenous Khoikhoi who had lost their cattle and their rangeland in wars with the settlers, and who now lived on the ranches as servants with a status little better than that of the slaves.

One year after the British took definitive control of the Cape Colony, they outlawed the importation of new slaves in accordance with the Slave Trade Abolition Act passed by the British Parliament in London. In 1828, they abolished the Hottentot Code, which had required all Khoikhoi to carry documents proving that they served a white settler master and lived on his ranch. The 1828 decree freed the Khoikhoi to leave the Boer ranches, where they had often worked for nothing more than food and shelter. Then, in 1833, the Parliament passed the Emancipation Act, by which the slaves in all British colonies were to be set free after a period of "apprenticeship" that was designed to prepare them for eventual freedom.

The Great Trek

The abolition of the Hottentot Code and the passing of the Emancipation Act foreshadowed major changes in the Boer way of life, which had been undergirded by slave and servile labor. These changes motivated many of the settlers to migrate northward, beyond the borders of the Cape Colony, in search of new lands where they could establish independent settlements free from British interference. White settlers began leaving the Cape Colony in 1834. Although they were armed with guns and mounted on horses, the African inhabitants did not at first see them as a threat because they traveled in small bands, generally consisting of a few families under the leadership of a senior male. By 1837, however, these Trekboer groups had grown much larger. A group of Trekboers led by Piet Retief, for example, set out with a hundred covered ox-wagons and thousands of sheep and cattle. By 1840, about 10 percent of the white settlers had left the Cape Colony and moved north into the interior in a movement that became known as the **Great Trek**.

The major objective of the Trekboers was to find new land for settlement, and they found it on the high plateau west of the Drakensberg Mountains. The high plateau was relatively underpopulated by Africans because the African chiefs preferred to settle with their people in areas of reliable rainfall, which were found in the mountains themselves, at elevations above 5,000 feet. For security, the chiefs built their settlements on the sides of hills and mountains rather than in the plains or river valleys. The Trekboers, in contrast, settled mostly on the plateau, where the elevation was between 3,000 and 5,000 feet and the rainfall was less reliable. The grasslands where they settled were often filled with herds of antelopes that were stalked by lions and hyenas. The Trekboers, who had no interest in growing crops as the Africans did, saw these grasslands as unclaimed land

THE GREAT TREK This 1836 painting shows a Trekboer wagon crossing a mountain stream. The Boer settlers began leaving the Cape Colony in 1834. By 1840, about 10 percent of the white settlers had left the Cape Colony and moved north into the interior, where they seized land belonging to African chiefdoms.

to be had for the taking. They did not understand that although the African chiefs lived in clustered settlements on the mountain slopes, they projected power and made claims over a much larger landscape.

When the Trekboers arrived in a new area, they initially sought good relations with the local chiefs. In some cases, the chiefs welcomed them, just as they welcomed any strangers fleeing from a rival chiefdom. In other cases, the chiefs tried to enlist them as allies in their wars with rival chiefs. But relations often broke down, and warfare erupted between Trekboers and chiefdoms. When threatened with attack, the Trekboers would arrange their wagons in a circle surrounded with piled-up thornbushes. From this circle, they could inflict withering gunfire on their spear-wielding attackers. With their horses and guns, the Trekboers could launch lightning raids on their African adversaries in return. Because the Trekboers and the Africans both valued cattle, warfare between the two groups often turned into cattle raids. In one encounter in 1837, a trekker commando of 135 armed horsemen captured 7,000 cattle in a period of 9 days.

In the early 1850s, the British officially recognized the independence of the Trekboer groups living in the territories north of the Cape Colony, opening the way for the establishment of two independent states, which became known as the **Boer republics**. The major rivers in southern Africa, which ran either west toward the Atlantic Ocean or east toward the Indian Ocean, made useful markers for defining the borders of the new states. The Trekboers who had headed north from the Cape Colony and settled in the area between the Orange River and the Vaal River called their region the Orange Free State because its southern boundary was defined by the Orange River. Other Trekboers who had continued farther north across the Vaal River referred to their region as the Transvaal (trans-Vaal), although the official name for their state was the South African Republic (not to be confused with the later Republic of South Africa).

Despite their adoption of a republican form of government with constitutions, elected presidents, and legislative bodies that represented the interests of the white settlers, both the Orange Free State and the Transvaal were little more than collections of scattered settlements. They had weak central institutions and suffered from endemic conflict that was punctuated by occasional rebellions and even civil wars. Their central governments controlled only a portion of the vast territory that they claimed. Nevertheless, their formal recognition as independent states by Britain allowed the Trekboers to obtain legally recognized titles to the land they had seized from African chiefs.

In the Transvaal, each adult male Trekboer was given two 6,000-acre ranches, covering a total area of 19 square miles, and his male children were each entitled to receive two ranches upon reaching 16 years of age. Through speculation and land deals, many individuals acquired seven or eight ranches, and one man amassed over a hundred. In the ensuing land rush, land companies and investors from the Cape Colony secured titles to uninhabited land in hopes of selling it later for a profit. In an economy dominated by subsistence ranchers, the government had very little money, and it often paid government officials with grants of land, which cost the government nothing.

The white settlers developed laws and administrative structures to ensure their domination of the African inhabitants of the plateau. The 1860 constitution of the South African Republic stated that "the people are not prepared to allow any equality of the non-white with the white inhabitants, either in Church or State." In areas with relatively high concentrations of white settlers, the local African communities were allocated land where they could live under their own chiefs, but they could be forced to relocate if their land was desired by new white settlers or expanding white ranches. Instead of paying taxes, the chiefs were required to supply laborers to the white ranches on demand. In order to ensure the security of the white settlements, the chiefs were not allowed to own horses or guns, nor were they permitted to make alliances with other chiefs. Settlers in frontier areas, in contrast, often allowed the local Africans to live on their vast landholdings in return for free labor, and absentee landlords encouraged Africans to live on their land in return for rent in grain or livestock.

By 1870, the white population of the Boer republics had grown to about 50,000. The majority of the white settlers lived as subsistence ranchers in areas of unreliable rainfall where they could prosper only with the aid of vast tracts of land and coerced African labor. Largely cut off from the outside world, they got their supplies of sugar, flour, coffee, tools, and firearms from itinerant traders who came up from the Cape Colony in covered ox-wagons. They paid for those items by selling livestock and wool from their ranches, as well as ivory and ostrich feathers they obtained by hunting.

The Discovery of Diamonds

Up until 1870, the interactions of the white settlers in southern Africa with the global economy were largely limited to exporting wool, ivory, and ostrich feathers and supplying the ships that rounded the Cape of Good Hope. That situation changed abruptly when diamonds were discovered in a frontier region beyond the Cape Colony. After the discovery of an 83-carat diamond in 1869, a horde of prospectors and speculators converged on an 80-mile stretch along the Vaal River, where they dug into the sand and gravel riverbed with picks and shovels in hopes of finding diamonds that had washed down from underground beds in the distant mountains. They lived in rough mining camps with names such as Last Hope and Fools Rush, where liquor, gambling, and prostitution provided the main amusements. Moving along the riverbed from shallow dig to shallow dig, few of them found any diamonds.

Twenty miles to the south and well away from any river or stream, diamonds were discovered in "dry diggings" on three Boer ranches that together covered 58 square miles. Underneath those ranches were diamond "pipes" (necks of long-extinct volcanoes) that contained the richest diamond deposits in the world. Poor-quality diamonds were found in the black soil near the surface, but the prospectors soon discovered that underneath a layer of limestone was a deep layer of yellow clay that contained richer diamond deposits. As miners rushed to the dry diggings, the owners of the three ranches sold claims that gave a prospector the right to dig in a space roughly 30 feet by 30 feet for £100 each. Before the end of 1871, these claims were selling for as much as £4,000. Sensing an opportunity for a new source of revenue, the British annexed the area and attached it to the Cape Colony. By 1872, 20,000 whites and 30,000 blacks (most of whom worked for white prospectors, but some of whom were independent miners) had converged on the area and were living in mining camps. One of those mining camps—named New Rush—grew into the town of Kimberley, which became known as the "city of diamonds."

At first, a single white prospector with a few African laborers could work a claim, but as the miners dug deeper, the earthen walls between claims often crumbled and water seeped into the pits, requiring pumps and other equipment that most miners lacked. Furthermore, with so many diamonds pouring onto the world market in such a short time, the price of uncut diamonds in London collapsed in January 1872. Many diamond buyers left southern Africa, followed by miners with diamonds that nobody wanted in their pockets. As a further discouragement, the miners had reached the limit of the diamond-bearing yellow soil and had struck a hard blue soil that they believed contained no diamonds. Believing that the diamond rush was over, the De Beer brothers, who owned what had been the richest diamond-bearing ranch, sold it to a syndicate of merchants for £6,000.

The southern African diamond-mining industry was resurrected by two developments. The first was the discovery that the hard blue soil was not impenetrable, and that it contained an even greater density of diamonds than the yellow soil above it. Working the blue soil more than 80 feet below the ground, however, required equipment and investment that were beyond the capacity of the small claim holders. The second development was the arrival of a new kind of entrepreneur who sought to expand the scale of the mining operations. Chief among these entrepreneurs were **Cecil Rhodes**, the son of an English country parson, and Barney Barnato, who grew up in London's overcrowded and poverty-stricken East End.

Arriving at the diamond fields with little or no money, both Rhodes and Barnato managed to acquire some capital, and soon they each owned enough

FIELD OF DIAMONDS The discovery of diamonds at Kimberley in 1869 sparked a diamond rush that brought 20,000 white prospectors and speculators to the diamond fields, where they lived in rough mining camps. This engraving from an 1871 photograph captures the rough and chaotic nature of life in the diamond fields.

claims to dream of creating a giant monopoly that could regulate the world diamond market. Rhodes formed a partnership with Alfred Beit, a German diamond merchant in Kimberley, who put Rhodes in contact with Nathan Rothschild, a member of the wealthy European banking family and the head of the NM Rothschild & Sons bank, England's leading supplier of international venture capital. Backed by the substantial resources of the Rothschilds, Rhodes forced Barney Barnato to merge with him in 1888 to form De Beers Consolidated Mines. Named after the former landowners who had sold their diamond-bearing ranch for £6,000, De Beers Consolidated Mines soon monopolized southern African diamond production, and by the end of the century it had a virtual monopoly on worldwide diamond sales.

As the diamond-mining companies became profitable, they needed a large number of African laborers to dig the pits and haul up the soil. In order to attract workers, the mining companies initially offered attractive wages, which could be used to buy useful items such as plows, wagons, and rifles. In response, Africans from all over southern Africa flocked to Kimberley at a rate of two or three thousand a month. Distant African rulers sent parties of workers to earn money and bring back guns. African farmers living in the immediate vicinity, in contrast, sought plows and wagons to expand their farming operations in order to supply Kimberley with grain. One merchant in 1876 was selling one plow per day to African farmers. The majority of the black laborers worked until they had earned enough to buy the goods they needed and then returned home, causing a constant turnover of the labor force.

Because of fear that the workers would steal diamonds or swallow them and excrete them later, the companies introduced a system of closed compounds, where the workers slept in dormitories and ate in dining halls. The compounds were surrounded by high fences made of corrugated iron and topped by wire netting to keep diamonds from being thrown over to waiting conspirators on the other side. Workers often spent months at a time in the compounds and had to endure a period of quarantine before they were allowed to leave.

The Gold Rush

While the diamond companies were being consolidated in Kimberley, an even more significant mineral discovery was made some 270 miles to the northeast, in the Transvaal. In 1886, outcrops of gold-bearing rock were discovered in a range of rocky hills known as the Witwatersrand (from the Dutch term meaning "ridge of white waters"), near the modern city of Johannesburg. Unlike California, where the gold lay near the surface and could be easily recovered by freelance gold diggers, the Transvaal contained gold-bearing reefs that were stacked like thin dinner plates, sloping downward beneath the surface at angles of 25 degrees or more to depths of over 3 miles. Most of the gold was therefore deep underground; the visible outcrops were nothing more than the outer edges of the reefs. Although the total amount of gold in the Witwatersrand was enormous, no single reef was particularly rich, which meant that a lot of labor had to be invested for each ounce of gold recovered.

Following the discovery of gold, miners and prospectors flocked to the region, and the town of Johannesburg (named after the two surveyors who laid out the streets, Johannes Meyer and Johannes Russik) sprang up almost overnight. By 1888, some 450 mining companies had been formed. Half the white male population from the diamond-mining city of Kimberley showed up there, as did some of the biggest businessmen from Cape Town. Alfred Beit, Cecil Rhodes, and Barney Barnato, the diamond magnates from Kimberley, all started gold-mining companies and bought up claims. "If there is anyone in Johannesburg who does

GOING FOR GOLD The Eersteling gold mine, which opened in 1871, was the first gold mine in the Transvaal. Prospectors who rushed to Eersteling later spread out in all directions in hope of finding more gold, thus leading to the discovery of the rich Witwatersrand gold deposits in 1886.

not own some scrip in a gold mine," wrote one observer in 1888, "he is considered not quite right in the head."

At first, the prospectors worked the surface outcrops, but soon they were digging directly beneath those outcrops, believing that the gold veins ran straight down. At depths beyond 100 feet, however, the character of the rock changed, making it much more difficult and expensive to extract the meager amounts of gold it contained. When word of this got out in 1889, Cecil Rhodes sold all his gold claims, and a third of the white population of Johannesburg packed up and left, causing a 60 percent drop in the value of gold shares. Three banks in Cape Town failed because they had invested heavily in the gold mines, and many leading citizens of Cape Town faced financial ruin.

The gold-mining industry in the Transvaal was saved by Joseph Curtis, an American mining engineer working for the Kimberley diamond merchant Alfred Beit. Following the theory that the gold-bearing reefs descended diagonally instead of vertically, Curtis drilled a borehole at a spot 1,000 feet south of the main outcrop and struck the main gold-bearing reef at a depth of 635 feet. With financial backing from Beit (who was himself financed by the Rothschilds), he quietly bought up ranches south of the main outcrop. By 1893, drillers were striking the main reef at depths of half a mile. The success of deep-level gold mining renewed Cecil Rhodes's interest in the Witwatersrand goldfields, where he bought up controlling interest in a number of small mining companies and established Consolidated Gold Fields of South Africa, which became one of the most powerful gold-mining groups. Because deep-level mining required heavy equipment and substantial capital investments, a variety of other investors from Britain, Europe, and the United States poured money into gold-mining companies in the Transvaal.

The global market for gold operated very differently from the international diamond market. Diamonds are expensive—in part because they are attractive, but also because they are rare. If competing diamond companies flooded the world market with stones, they would quickly lose their value. That is why Cecil Rhodes and Alfred Beit fought so hard to create a worldwide monopoly on diamonds. Gold, on the other hand, was the basis of the national currencies of most European and American countries, a circumstance that made the demand for gold virtually unlimited. Moreover, the price of gold was fixed by law in countries using the gold currency standard, and therefore the quantity of gold on the market did not affect the price one way or the other. For these reasons, a variety of different mining companies could coexist on the Witwatersrand without harming the gold-mining industry as a whole. In order to work together on matters of common interest, the leading mining companies formed the Chamber of Mines in 1889.

In addition to capital, the mining companies also needed heavy inputs of labor. Nearly a hundred thousand Africans were working in Witwatersrand gold mines by the end of the nineteenth century, and the Chamber of Mines coordinated efforts to keep their wages as low as possible. When the wages were reduced by 20 percent in 1896, there were widespread protests from the black miners, but a combination of drought and a rinderpest epidemic that killed off 80–90 percent of the cattle in southern Africa forced many Africans to seek work in the mines to earn money for food. Few of the Africans who lived near Johannesburg worked in the mines, however, because they were employed on white settler farms or worked as independent farmers producing food for the miners and for the city of Johannesburg.

Instead, the vast majority of the mine workers came from farther away and worked for a season before returning home. At first, many of them were Zulus, who were imported in large gangs from their homeland near the Indian Ocean coast. By the end of the century, however, about two-thirds of the mine workers were coming from what is now southern Mozambique. They were preferred by the mining companies because they would often stay at the mines for 2 or 3 years at a time, whereas workers from nearby regions usually went home to work in their fields during the agricultural season.

The discovery of gold and diamonds transformed the economy of southern Africa in three major ways. First, a region that had been largely isolated from the global economy became a magnet for international investment as European and American miners, engineers, businessmen, and merchants flocked to southern Africa. Second, the need to bring equipment, supplies, and personnel to the mines set off a boom in railroad building. By 1885, a railroad linked the Kimberley diamond mines to Cape Town, and by 1895, the Witwatersrand goldfields had rail links to all of the major port cities in southern Africa, from Cape Town to Delagoa Bay. Like mining, railroad building required large infusions of capital and massive amounts of African labor. Third, large numbers of Africans who had previously made their living as independent farmers and cattle herders were now becoming wage laborers. Because the African workers were given unskilled, low-wage jobs (skilled, high-wage jobs were reserved for whites), most of them did not become permanent mine workers, but engaged in migratory labor, traveling to the mines and working for a certain period of time before returning home to work on their own farms. In the three decades between 1870 and the end of the century, the economy of southern Africa had been transformed from a subsistence economy based on low-intensity ranching to a modern capitalist economy that brought fortunes to some and low-wage labor to others.

CONCLUSION

The gradual end of the trans-Atlantic slave trade prompted Europeans and Africans alike to reset the economic relationships between Africa and the global economy. In areas near the Atlantic and Indian Ocean coasts, Africans stepped up the production of agricultural products such as peanuts, palm oil, and cloves, which they exported to Europe. In the inland regions, African trade caravans probed farther and farther into the interior in search of ivory. In the process, they brought previously isolated regions of Africa into contact with the global economy. By the 1860s, trade routes from the Atlantic coast were meeting up with trade routes from the Indian Ocean and the Mediterranean Sea. At the northern and southern extremities of Africa, states with modern bureaucracies, infrastructures, and armies emerged.

The economic upheavals had varying social and political ramifications. Near the coasts, Senegambia and the Niger delta saw major social upheavals as the old slave trading elites were supplanted by peasant producers and former slaves, while the Omani Empire moved its capital to the fertile island of Zanzibar, to which Arab immigrants from the Persian Gulf flocked in order to start clove plantations. In areas far from the coasts that were rich in ivory, African trade caravans armed with muskets easily dominated local populations who fought them with traditional weapons. The results of these conflicts were varied. In Angola, the Chokwe ivory hunters destroyed the once formidable Lunda Empire without creating a successor state to replace it. In East Africa, caravan traders such as Msiri and Tippu Tip built powerful empires that were as much commercial enterprises as political entities. A similar pattern prevailed in the northeastern savanna, where ivory traders such as Al-Zubayr and Rabih built large, but short-lived, empires, while Samori's empire in the northwestern savanna foundered for lack of political legitimacy. The Bobangi canoemen along the middle Congo River were an exception because their control of strategic points along the river gave them a near monopoly on the trade of the entire Congo basin. Growing wealthy from the ivory trade, they saw no need to conquer territory or establish a land empire.

The modernizing economies of Egypt and southern Africa developed in places that were gateways to the Indian Ocean. Egypt controlled the passage from the Mediterranean Sea to the Red Sea, a route that was serviceable only with the aid of railroads and a modern canal, while British control of the Cape of Good Hope regulated the passage of ships between the Atlantic and Indian Oceans by the sea route. In both cases, modernization was paid for using local resources: cotton production in Egypt, and diamonds and gold in southern Africa. Egypt and southern Africa became enclaves with trappings of modernity that did not spill over into neighboring regions. On the contrary, they provoked warfare and chaos just beyond their borders.

CHAPTER REVIEW

KEY TERMS AND VOCABULARY

cheddo

Chokwe

Msiri

Tippu Tip

zariba

Al-Zubayr

Rabih Fadlallah

Samori Touré

Muhammad Ali

Great Trek

Boer republics

Cecil Rhodes

STUDY QUESTIONS

1. Compare the decline of the trans-Atlantic slave trade in Africa north of the equator with that in Africa south of the equator.
2. In what ways did the production of agricultural commodities for export create social and political upheavals in coastal areas of Africa?
3. What was the connection between rising world market prices for ivory and the creation of new states in the interior regions of Africa?
4. Why did Msiri's Nyamwezi form a successful state in the southern savanna while the Chokwe did not?
5. Explain how the zariba system facilitated the spread of merchant-warlords in the northeastern savanna.
6. Why do some historians refer to Muhammad Ali as the father of modern Egypt?
7. In what ways did the discovery of diamonds and gold in southern Africa transform life for Europeans and for Africans?

PERSPECTIVES

A PRINCESS IN ZANZIBAR

Princess Salme was born in Zanzibar around 1840. Her father was Said bin Sultan, the sultan of Zanzibar and Oman, and her mother was a slave concubine who had been born in Circassia, near the Black Sea. As one of the only women in Zanzibar who could both read and write, Princess Salme wrote a personal memoir that provided a rare glimpse into life in the sultan's harem. When her father died in 1856, all of his potential successors were sons born of slave mothers.

My mother was a Circassian by birth, who in early youth had been torn away from her home. Her father had been a farmer, and she had always lived peacefully with her parents and her little brother and sister. War broke out suddenly, and the country was overrun by marauding bands; on their approach the family fled into an underground place, as my mother called it—she probably meant a cellar, which is not known in Zanzibar. Their place of refuge was, however, invaded by a merciless horde, the parents were slain, and the children carried off by three mounted Arnauts [Ottoman mercenaries]. . . .

She came into my father's possession when quite a child, probably at the tender age of seven or eight years, as she cast her first tooth in our house. She was at once adopted as [a] playmate by two of my sisters, her own age, with whom she was educated and brought up. Together with them she learnt to read, which raised her a good deal above her equals. . . . Her greatest pleasure consisted in assisting other people, in looking after and nursing any sick person in the house; . . . I well remember her going about with her books from one patient to another, reading prayers to them.

She was in great favour with my father, who never refused her anything, though she interceded mostly for others, and, when she came to see him, he always rose to meet her half-way—a distinction he conferred but very rarely. . . .

My father had only one . . . legitimate wife, at my time, as far as I recollect; his other wives, or Sarari, . . . numbering seventy-five at his death, had all been purchased by him gradually, and the former, his first wife, Azze bint Sêf, a princess of Oman by birth, reigned as absolute mistress over the household. In spite of her very small size, and of her plain exterior, she possessed an immense power over my father, who willingly submitted to all her arrangements. She treated all the other wives and their children in a very imperious, haughty, and pretentious manner; happily for us she had no children of her own, who could not have failed to be as disagreeable in their way! All my father's children, thirty-six in number, when he died, were by his Sarari, and there was consequently no difference between us.

1. *How do you reconcile the apparent contradiction that Princess Salme's mother was a slave, yet she lived in a palace?*
2. *Describe the relationship between the sultan's freeborn wife and his many slave concubines.*

Source: Emily Ruete, *Memoirs of an Arabian Princess: An Autobiography by Emily Ruete, née Princess of Oman and Zanzibar* (New York: Appleton, 1888), pp. 4–5.

TIPPU TIP CREATES A STATE

Hamid bin Muhammad el Murjebi, known as Tippu Tip, was the most successful African explorer, caravan trader, and state builder in nineteenth-century East Africa. Of mixed East African and Omani Arab ancestry, he grew up in Zanzibar, where he attended Quranic school. He wrote his autobiography in Swahili using Arabic characters. In this excerpt, he tells how he established his authority over the trading towns of Nyangwe and Kasongo, on the Lualaba (upper Congo) River, which became the core of his empire in the Manyema region. These events took place in 1874–1875.

Going on we reached Nyangwe. My kinsmen from the coast said to me, "Stay here, let us be together!" I told them "I'm going to Kasongo, to my kinsman Muhammed bin Said el Murjebi [a.k.a.] Bwana Sige." They pressed me but I demurred and went off. I passed Kihandai, Kibogo and Kabanga, and all the locals came to me; and the chiefs of each area wanted me to stay and be their chief. However, I demurred and the people of Nyangwe told me that in Kasongo people were in difficulties, there was famine. Further, the people were in difficulties over their slaves who had run off and were now unobtainable. I told them, "Never mind, on my arrival everything will be in the hands of Almighty God!" On the morning of the third day I arrived in Kasongo. My kinsmen were overjoyed at my arrival and invested me with full authority for the area. What the people had told me in Nyangwe I could see for myself, especially hunger. And the people themselves were in a rebellious frame of mind, especially the Wazua, who were both numerous and rebellious, and also, among others, the people of Ugera. . . . I stayed there for two months, in the third month they made away with a group of some 200 of my slaves. We looked for them but couldn't find them. I held a meeting with those Arabs who were in Kasongo. . . . They had with them only a relatively small number of guns. . . . When I saw the state of affairs I said to them "Well, what is to be done? The locals seem to have rebelled." They told me, "We leave both large and small matters to you; all authority is yours and no one will argue with you."

I decided on war and we fought the locals for three months until they all announced their submission and willingness to live in peace. All authority over them was in our hands, and in the matter of ivory they had no right to sell even the smallest tusk, and any work that we needed doing, they brought men to do it. Food was plentiful, both rice and every other kind. People from Nyangwe came and bought rice in Kasongo, calling the country Bungala because of the quantity of rice. They bought it for ivory. There was peace. And those people who asked me to be their chief when I left Nyangwe to come to Kasongo appeared, killing people as they travelled on the roads. I dealt with all those areas through which the roads passed. There was peace again, and even women travelled; there was no one about who would not either pay them respect or give them food.

1. *Why did the coastal ivory traders at Kasongo and Nyangwe want Tippu Tip to be their chief?*
2. *How did the ordinary residents respond to Tippu Tip's rule?*

Source: Tippu Tip, *Maisha ya Hamed bin Muhammed el Murjebi, yaani Tippu Tip, Kwa Maneno Yake Mwenyewe [The Story of Hamed bin Muhammed el Murjebi, known as Tippu Tip, in His Own Words]*, trans. W. H. Whitely (Nairobi: East African Literature Bureau, 1966), pp. 77, 79.

PERSPECTIVES

IVORY TRADERS TRAVEL SOUTH FROM KHARTOUM

Al-Zubayr Rahma Mansur was born on the island of Wawissi in the Nile River north of Khartoum. He attended Quranic school in Khartoum before beginning his career as a caravan merchant in 1856. Along with other merchants from Khartoum, he journeyed south in search of ivory. He later ruled a territory the size of France and was appointed bey (district administrator) of the Bahr el Ghazal by the khedive of Egypt. In 1900, he recounted his life story to his friend H. C. Jackson, who wrote it down. In this excerpt, he recounts his first trading trip to the south.

We did not cease to journey for a length of time on the White Nile, until we arrived at the Port of the Bahr el Ghazal. This Port is called Meshra el Rek and beyond it vessels cannot proceed to the south. We disembarked with our bales and our merchandise on the second of Safar [the second Islamic month] of the same year. Then we passed through the country of the Gangiya, until we arrived on the seventh of the month at the land of the Jur, where Ali Amuri had a station called Ashur, named after the Sheikh of the District.

Now at this time there were in the Bahr el Ghazal many merchants, besides Ali Amuri, scattered throughout the country, each one with a zariba to which he could fly for shelter and into which he could put his goods. Those most in demand were beads of all sorts and colors, cowries, and tin. These are the ornaments for the men and women, and these the inhabitants preferred to silver and gold, exchanging them for ivory, rhinoceros horns, ostrich feathers, rubber, iron, copper, and other products of the country.

I continued to live with my friend Ali Amuri assisting him in his commerce. But there had passed but a few months when the natives rose against the merchants, envying them, their possessions. At length, in the year 1857, they collected from all directions and stormed the zaribas, killing some of the merchants and carrying off their goods as trophies. They also attacked the zariba of Ali Amuri, but I led his men and opened fire on the savages, routing them and killing large numbers: Praise be to God, the High, the Mighty. When the merchants heard of my success they flocked round, and I became in high estimation with them, so that the natives of the country were afraid and did not dare to renew their attack. My friend Ali Amuri, seeing that I was the cause of his escape, loved me exceedingly and gave me a share in his profits, to wit one tenth of all his ivory. When the country was tranquil again, he left me in his camp and went to Khartoum, where he was absent for six months, returning with more merchandise. On his arrival he found that I had amassed such abundance of goods from the products of the country, as he would not have been able to accumulate in many years. This increased his respect for me and he offered me a partnership in his traffic. But my soul inclined to travel and I determined to commence trading by myself.

1. *What was the significance of the zaribas?*
2. *How did the inhabitants of the Bahr el Ghazal react to the traders from Khartoum?*

Source: H. C. Jackson, *Black Ivory and White, or the Story of El Zubeir Pasha, Slaver and Sultan as Told by Himself* (Oxford: B. H. Blackwell, 1913).

MANIFESTO FOR THE GREAT TREK

Piet Retief was a Boer farmer living in the Cape Colony who led a large group of Trekboers out of the colony and into the interior of southern Africa to escape British rule. As a spokesman for the disgruntled farmers, he published this manifesto in the Grahamstown Journal *on February 2, 1837, outlining his grievances against the British. The "vagrants" he mentions in article 1 are most likely former Khoikhoi laborers who were allowed to leave the white farms after the British abolished the Hottentot Code in 1828.*

1. We despair of saving the colony from those evils which threaten it by the turbulent and dishonest conduct of vagrants, who are allowed to infest the country in every part; nor do we see any prospect of peace or happiness for our children in any country thus distracted by internal commotions.
2. We complain of the severe losses which we have been forced to sustain by the emancipation of our slaves, and the vexatious laws which have been enacted respecting them.
3. We complain of the continual system of plunder which we have ever endured from the Caffres [Africans] and other coloured classes, and particularly by the last invasion of the colony, which has desolated the frontier districts and ruined most of the inhabitants.
4. We complain of the unjustifiable odium which has been cast upon us by interested and dishonest persons, under the cloak of religion, whose testimony is believed in England, to the exclusion of all evidence in our favour; and we can foresee, as the result of this prejudice, nothing but the total ruin of the country.
5. We are resolved, wherever we go, that we will uphold the just principles of liberty; but, whilst we will take care that no one shall be held in a state of slavery, it is our determination to maintain such regulations as may suppress crime, and preserve proper relations between master and servant.
6. We solemnly declare that we quit this colony with a desire to lead a more quiet life than we have heretofore done. We will not molest any people, nor deprive them of the smallest property; but, if attacked, we shall consider ourselves fully justified in defending our persons and effects, to the utmost of our ability, against every enemy. . . .
9. We quit this colony under the full assurance that the English Government has nothing more to require of us, and will allow us to govern ourselves without its interference in future.
10. We are now quitting the fruitful land of our birth, in which we have suffered enormous losses and continual vexation, and are entering a wild and dangerous territory; but we go with a firm reliance on an all-seeing, just, and merciful Being, whom it will be our endeavor to fear and humbly to obey.

By authority of the farmers who have quitted the Colony,
(Signed) P. Retief

1. *What were the main grievances of the Boers?*
2. *What kind of state did the Boers hope to create in the new territory?*

Source: Originally published in the *Grahamstown Journal*, February 2, 1837. Reprinted in *Select Constitutional Documents Illustrating South African History, 1795–1910*, selected and edited by G. W. Eybers (London: Routledge & Sons, 1918), pp. 144–145.

NGUNI VILLAGE Speakers of Nguni languages in southern Africa lived in circular villages consisting of round huts surrounded by a fence. Such villages were referred to as *kraals*. This painting by George French Angus in the 1840s shows a kraal near the Umlazi River in South Africa. The artist noted that "this kraal is without the enclosure for cattle in the center, as is usual for most of the kraals." The skin hanging from the flagpole indicates that the village headman is at home.

1808
Crown Colony of Sierra Leone proclaimed

1812
Sokoto caliphate established

1828
Death of Zulu King Shaka

9

RELIGIOUS MOVEMENTS AND STATE-BUILDING STRATEGIES IN THE NINETEENTH CENTURY

At the same time that global industrial capitalism was impinging on Africa in new ways (as described in chapter 8), powerful currents of change related to universal religions, new state-building strategies, and innovative military tactics were sweeping the continent from the West African Sahel to southeastern Africa. On the West African coast, former American slaves and Africans liberated from slave ships created settlements from which they spread the teachings of Protestant Christianity, while intellectuals such as Samuel Ajayi Crowther and Edward Wilmot Blyden sought to define a message that was both fully Christian and fully African. In the Sahel, variants of Sufi Islam emphasized the role of charismatic leaders who rejected the established Islamic institutions and claimed spiritual authority based on personal visions from God. The spread of Sufi brotherhoods in the nineteenth century provided an organizational base for Muslim religious innovators to launch jihads and create new theocratic states. By the end of the nineteenth century, the religious and political landscape of the Sahel had been completely transformed.

A very different kind of change developed near the Indian Ocean coast of southern Africa, where local chiefs used new strategies of state building and military organization to transform small independent chiefdoms into large kingdoms

1836	1852	1885
Fall of Oyo Empire	Umar Tal declares jihad	The Mahdi captures Khartoum

with formidable, self-sustaining armies. Unlike rulers of the past, these state builders were less interested in controlling territory, towns, or trade routes than in amassing and redistributing large quantities of cattle. Cattle were a movable form of wealth, and the circulation of cattle via gifts and exchanges was the glue that held extended families, chiefdoms, and kingdoms together. The result was the formation of a series of movable kingdoms that drifted northward from near the southern tip of Africa almost to the equator. In contrast to the Atlantic coast in the era of the slave trade, where movable wealth had often taken the form of human captives, the cattle kingdoms of southern Africa integrated their war captives into their military system and used them to help raid for more cattle.

The new religious ideas and state-building innovations that emerged in the nineteenth century transformed the political landscape of Africa both north and south of the equator, but took place mainly in areas that were not well integrated into the global economy. The Islamic jihads, for example, first erupted in what is now northern Nigeria, a region that is distant from both the Atlantic Ocean and the Mediterranean Sea. The state-building innovations in southern Africa began near the coast of the Indian Ocean, which was mostly "sail by" country for ships heading for the Mozambique Channel and the Swahili Coast. While one set of economic and political transformations was taking place in the overseas trading zones (described in chapter 8), different dynamics were at work in areas that were not significantly involved in international trade. The rapidity of change was astonishing. Kingdoms and empires throughout Africa that had once seemed formidable collapsed and gave way to entirely new states. The political map of African kingdoms and empires in 1885, on the eve of colonization by the Europeans, bore little resemblance to the map that had existed at the beginning of the century.

CHRISTIAN INFLUENCE IN WEST AFRICA

Christianity has a long history in Africa. Egypt was a major center for early Christian thought, and Egypt and Ethiopia later became bastions of the monophysite teachings about the unitary nature of Jesus Christ that had divided the Christian world in the fifth century (see chapter 3). In the sixteenth century, the Kongo Kingdom was recognized by the pope in Rome as one of the world's Christian kingdoms (see chapter 5), and pockets of Christianity developed around areas of Portuguese settlement in Angola. On the West African coast, in contrast, despite centuries of interaction between Africans and Christian Europeans, the spread of Christianity had been negligible during the era of the slave trade, in part because the Europeans who came there were primarily slave traders who limited their interactions with Africans to the commercial sphere.

The British Colony of Sierra Leone

The situation in West Africa changed in 1792, when a thousand former American slaves, most of whom were Protestant Christians, settled on the Sierra Leone coast. During the American Revolutionary War, they had been persuaded to join the British army in return for the promise of freedom, but after the British lost the war, they were taken to a desolate area of Nova Scotia, Canada, where they struggled with poor soils and a harsh climate. To alleviate these problems, a group of British anti-slavery activists formed the Sierra Leone Company and resettled them at a spot they called Freetown, on land purchased from a local chief. There, the skilled and enterprising ex-slaves built the town in the North American style.

By 1798, Freetown had about 400 American-style houses built along streets laid out in a grid pattern. The settlers were joined in 1799 by a group of 500 escaped slaves from Jamaica who had been rounded up and deported by the British. In 1808, the British proclaimed Freetown and the nearby settlements to be the crown colony of Sierra Leone and placed it under the rule of a British governor. Freetown became the home port of the British Navy's anti–slave trade West Africa Squadron, and over the subsequent decades more than 100,000 Africans liberated from slave ships were settled in and around the colony. The liberated

FREETOWN IN 1874 Freetown was founded by British anti-slavery activists as a haven for ex-slaves from Canada and Jamaica. After becoming part of the British crown colony of Sierra Leone in 1808, Freetown became the home port for the British Navy's West Africa Squadron. During the nineteenth century, over 100,000 Africans liberated from slave ships were resettled there.

Africans, who came from many regions of Atlantic Africa, spoke a total of 128 African languages, but the largest groups were Igbo and Yoruba ex-captives from what is now southern Nigeria.

The settlers did not mix well with the local African populations. The Nova Scotians and Jamaicans were thoroughly westernized and saw themselves as more British than African. Likewise, the settlers who had been liberated from slave ships, who found themselves cut off from the cultures of their homelands, also tended to adopt Western culture and Christianity. These tendencies were reinforced by the Anglican Church Missionary Society, which set up schools and churches for the settlers. By the 1850s, the different groups of settlers had amalgamated into a single cultural group, known as Creoles, and had developed their own language, called Krio, which was a mixture of English and the African languages of the liberated captives.

Education was important to the Creoles of Sierra Leone. In 1827, the Church Missionary Society founded a secondary school in Freetown, called Fourah Bay College (British private secondary schools were called "colleges"), to train the Creole settlers to be teachers and clergymen. Graduates of the school gradually replaced British missionary teachers in the elementary schools, and by 1861, Creole Anglicans had replaced the British in the clergy. In the 1860s, a greater percentage of children in Freetown attended school than did in England, and some of the Creole students went on to study law and medicine in Britain. In 1876, Fourah Bay College upgraded its curriculum to become a university and established an affiliation with Durham University in England, a move that allowed graduates to gain internationally recognized degrees. The revised curriculum included Latin, Greek, Hebrew, Arabic,

FOURAH BAY COLLEGE, SIERRA LEONE Founded in 1827 by the Church Missionary Society to spread Christianity and train teachers, Fourah Bay College was originally a private secondary school, but it became a degree-granting university in 1876 after establishing an affiliation with Durham University in England. This building was completed in 1848.

French, German, history, and natural science, enhancing Freetown's reputation as "the Athens of West Africa."

The American Colony of Liberia

Two hundred miles down the Atlantic coast from Freetown, a private organization known as the American Colonization Society was creating a separate settlement colony for free blacks and ex-slaves from the United States. The project was supported by many American slave owners and pro-slavery advocates, who feared that the growing numbers of free blacks in the United States would incite enslaved blacks to revolt or run away. Many African American leaders opposed the settlement scheme because they felt that slaves had helped build the United States and would now be deprived of the fruits of their labor.

In 1821, the first group of African American settlers arrived to found the settlement of Monrovia, named after U.S. President James Monroe. The group included free blacks from the United States, ex-slaves who had been promised liberty on the condition that they would move to Monrovia, and African captives liberated from slave ships by the U.S. Navy. In subsequent years, various state branches of the American Colonization Society sponsored their own colonizing ventures, establishing the colonies of Maryland, Port Cresson, Mississippi, and others along the coastal strip that came to be known as Liberia. One of Liberia's leading intellectuals, Edward Wilmot Blyden, characterized Liberia as "a little bit of South Carolina, of Georgia, of Virginia—that is to say, of the ostracized, suppressed, depressed elements of those states tacked on to West Africa—a most incongruous combination with no reasonable prospect of success."

In 1839, the various settlements united under the name of the Commonwealth of Liberia and began operating as an independent nation, even though they were not recognized as such by any other countries. In 1847, following a dispute over Liberia's demand that British ships pay customs duties, the U.S. government absolved itself of any responsibility for Liberia by recognizing it as an independent republic. In contrast to Sierra Leone, which received some material support from the British government, Liberia was now entirely on its own. Despite the scarcity of funds, the independent Liberian government sought to promote education, and in 1863, it opened Liberia College, an American-style undergraduate institution sponsored mainly by the New York Colonization Society.

The **Republic of Liberia** consisted of scattered settlements near the coast. It had a constitution that was almost identical to that of the United States, but it applied only to the settlers. Relations with the local Africans had gotten off to a rocky start in 1821, when members of the American Colonization Society demanded a grant of land from the African King Peter at gunpoint. Africans resented the settlers' presence on their land, and on more than one occasion, they took up arms against the newcomers. The settlers, for their part, were mostly African American Christians who viewed African culture with condescension bordering on contempt. A continuing point of conflict in both Liberia and Sierra Leone was that the settlers were vehemently opposed to the slave trade, whereas many of the local African chiefs were still profiting from it. During the first half of the nineteenth century, more than 170,000 captives were taken out of the region by the illegal slave trade, mostly on Spanish and Portuguese ships.

Religious and Intellectual Leaders

Although tiny, the settler colonies of Sierra Leone and Liberia produced several religious and intellectual leaders whose influence extended far beyond the boundaries of their settlements. The most famous of these leaders were Samuel Ajayi Crowther and Edward Wilmot Blyden. **Samuel Ajayi Crowther** was born in 1809 in the Yoruba country of what is now southwestern Nigeria. He was captured in the wars that accompanied the breakup of the Oyo Empire (described later in this chapter) and was bought and sold several times before being sold to Portuguese slave traders on the Atlantic coast. After the Portuguese slave ship on which he was traveling was intercepted by the West African Squadron in 1822, he was taken to Freetown, Sierra Leone. Three years later, he joined the Anglican Church in Freetown and took the name Samuel Crowther, after an eminent British clergyman. He

BISHOP SAMUEL AJAYI CROWTHER After being rescued from a slave ship and settled in Freetown, Crowther studied theology in England and became an Anglican minister. Sent as a missionary to Nigeria, he translated the Bible into Yoruba. In 1864, he was named bishop of West Africa and given an honorary Doctor of Divinity degree from Oxford University.

used his Yoruba name—Ajayi—as his middle name. Displaying a talent for language learning, he was sent by the Anglican Church Missionary Society to study in England, and he continued his studies at Fourah Bay College in Sierra Leone. He later returned to England to study theology, where he was ordained as a Christian minister by the Anglican bishop of London.

In 1843, Crowther was sent to what is now Nigeria to found a Christian mission among the Yoruba people and to translate the Bible into the Yoruba language, for which he established a writing system. Even though Yoruba was his mother tongue, he conducted extensive research to find just the right words to translate Christian concepts such as "God," "sin," and "salvation." In his travels through the Yoruba country, he frequently sat down with the elders to discuss theology and other serious matters, writing down all the "suitable and significant words" and watching their mouths to get the exact pronunciation for his phonetic transcriptions. In tracing out the words and their various uses, he delved deeply into the traditions and customs of the Yoruba, even going so far as to study the esoteric vocabulary of the Egungun secret society and the Ifa divination cult. His Yoruba Bible set the standard for all later translations of Christian scriptures in Africa. In addition to translating the Bible and the Anglican *Book of Common Prayer*, he wrote a grammar and dictionary of Yoruba, a primer for the Igbo language, and a grammar and dictionary of the Nupe language. In 1864, he was awarded an honorary doctorate of divinity by Oxford University and was ordained as the Anglican Church's first bishop of West Africa.

Because he had married a Muslim woman from his Portuguese slave ship, Crowther had a lifelong interest in Christian-Muslim relations. In his mission work, he enjoyed courteous and friendly relations with Muslim rulers and clerics, with whom he participated in long discussions searching for common ground between the Bible and the Quran. One of the most vexing issues was the Christian doctrine of the Trinity (which holds that God exists in three persons: God the father, Jesus the son, and the Holy Spirit). The Muslims rejected that doctrine because they held that there is only one God, not three. With his deep knowledge of several African languages and Christian doctrine, Crowther worked to define a form of religious faith that was both Christian and African.

Another West African intellectual of notable influence was **Edward Wilmot Blyden**, a free black man from the Caribbean island of St. Thomas. As a boy, he was mentored by an American Protestant pastor, John Knox, who was impressed by Blyden's studiousness and intelligence. Encouraged by Knox, Blyden went to the United States to study for the ministry at Rutgers Theological College, but when he arrived, he was refused admission due to his race. After two other American theological colleges turned him down for similar reasons, Blyden traveled to Liberia to seek his fortune. He arrived in 1850, just 3 years after it had become an independent

EDWARD WILMOT BLYDEN Born on the Caribbean island of St. Thomas in 1832, Blyden migrated to Liberia after being denied admission to American theological schools because of his race. He had a varied career as a journalist, diplomat, professor, and president of Liberia College. He wrote several books in which he expressed appreciation for African culture and gave a stinging critique of racism and capitalism.

republic. Blyden became a newspaper editor and high school principal. After Liberia College opened in 1863, he served as professor of classics, professor of Islamic studies, and later president of the college. He also held a variety of diplomatic posts in England, the United States, and France, and he served as secretary of state for the Liberian government. In addition, he worked in neighboring Sierra Leone as a representative of the government to the African populations in the interior. In this capacity, he came into contact with the Muslim educational centers in the hinterland of the Sierra Leone coast and visited the Islamic kingdom of Fuuta Jaloo (see chapter 6).

Regardless of the positions he held, Blyden was constantly thinking about how the black race fit into the larger panorama of Western cultures, African cultures, Christianity, and Islam. He rejected white racist ideology and sought to free African Americans and Africans from any notion of cultural inferiority. He urged them to be proud of black achievements and contributions to world civilizations. Pointing to the role of black slave labor in developing commercial agriculture in the United States, and to the Caribbean slave colonies whose work financed England's Industrial Revolution, Blyden defined and analyzed a capitalist world system that relied on the exploitation of African labor. In his book *African Life and Customs*, Blyden celebrated African cultures for their music, poetry, and art, and he praised the African ethos of community solidarity, by which neighbors helped one another while also welcoming strangers and guests. At the same time, he urged Africans to educate themselves in modern science and learn new technologies to fully develop the resources of Africa.

Blyden also took an interest in the relationship of Christianity to Islam. In his 1887 book *Christianity, Islam, and the Negro Race*, he argued that Islam was more authentically African, especially because the Christianity practiced in West Africa had been introduced by European colonizers. Although he remained a Protestant, he advocated a synthesis of Africa's "triple heritage"—indigenous, Muslim, and Christian. The colonies of Sierra Leone and Liberia were melting pots containing a variety of cultural elements from both sides of the Atlantic. In this culturally rich environment, intellectuals such as Crowther and Blyden sought to point the way toward a harmonious synthesis of African and Western traditions.

ISLAMIC REVOLUTIONS IN THE WEST AFRICAN SAHEL

In contrast to North Africa, where Islam was initially spread by conquest and accompanied by cultural Arabization, the spread of Islam south of the Sahara before 1800 was a largely peaceful process carried out by indigenous evangelists anchored in peaceful clerical communities that sprouted up near major towns and trade routes. Rather than trying to conquer or co-opt the existing states, the clerics normally made a pact with the local rulers: the political leaders would be allowed to enter the clerical towns only for religious purposes, and the clerics, for their part, would stay out of politics. These clerical communities had deep local roots and were firmly embedded in the cultural traditions of West Africa. They represented what the historian Lamin Sanneh has called "the pacifist tradition in West African Islam." Only on rare occasions (see chapters 5–6) did Muslim clerics abandon that tradition and call for jihad.

That predominantly peaceful tradition was ruptured in the nineteenth century when a series of jihads broke out across the West African Sahel. They were not wars against unbelievers for the purpose of spreading Islam; instead, they were reform movements carried out in places where the population was largely or partially Muslim. The West African jihads are often described as Islamic revolutions rather than holy wars because they were usually carried out by civilians against established Islamic states. Their goal was to create a pure and just Islamic state to replace a lax and corrupt one.

These jihads were associated with variants of Sufism, a mystical form of Islam. A Muslim saint who had mystical visions would attract disciples and found a fraternal order commonly known as a brotherhood. Future generations of followers would link themselves to the founder through spiritual genealogies that listed the Sufi teachers and saints who had preceded them. In the late eighteenth and early nineteenth centuries, new currents of Sufi thought and practice were spreading southward across the Sahara Desert, operating within the larger tradition of Sunni Islam, which had predominated in North Africa since the fall of the Fatimids in the twelfth century.

Two Sufi orders became enormously influential in West Africa during the nineteenth century. The first was the Qadiriyya, which was founded in Baghdad in the twelfth century. It gained a following among the scholars and clerics at the Al-Azhar Mosque and University in Cairo in the late eighteenth century and spread south across the Sahara Desert via trade routes. The other influential Sufi order was the Tijaniyya, founded in Algeria by Ahmad al-Tijani in the 1780s. Al-Tijani, who had spent time in Cairo before settling in Algeria, preached that the Prophet Muhammad had appeared to him in a vision and commanded him to start a new Sufi order. Whereas the Qadiriyya, with its emphasis on religious learning, had a somewhat elitist tinge, the Tijaniyya had more populist appeal because it emphasized adherence to a strict moral code and zeal in spreading the Islamic faith. During the nineteenth century, these two Sufi brotherhoods spread so widely in the West African Sahel that affiliation with either the Qadiriyya or the Tijaniyya became the equivalent of being a Muslim.

Although it may seem anomalous, there are several reasons why jihads could emerge from a mystical and inward-looking form of Islam. One is that many of the mystical clerics insisted that they received visions calling them to take religious action. The best example is Usuman dan Fodio (discussed below), who was the architect of the jihad movement in the West African Sahel. He believed that the twelfth-century founder of the Qadiriyya, Abdul Qadir Jilani, had appeared to him in a vision and handed him the "Sword of Truth," which he was to use against the enemies of God. He also claimed that Jilani had subsequently appeared in visions to offer him advice at key moments of crisis. Without these mystical underpinnings, Usuman would not have launched a jihad. A second reason is that the mysticism of the Sufi orders inclined them to emphasize prophetic beliefs about the *Mahdi*—the Islamic deliverer who would appear at the end of time—and the *Majaddid*—the renewer who appeared once in each century to prepare the way for the Mahdi. Although Usuman dan Fodio denied being the Mahdi, he did claim to be a Majaddid, and he believed that his jihad was preparing the way for the divine event that would signal the end of time. A third reason is that the Sufi brotherhoods provided an organizational framework that Islamic reformers could use to mobilize the common people against what they saw as decadent ruling elites. The older Islamic traditions of secluded clerical villages and Muslim scholars at royal courts had been less amenable to the mass mobilization of the common people.

This section examines the three major jihads that erupted in the West African Sahel in the nineteenth century: the jihad of Usuman dan Fodio, the jihad of Sheikh Ahmad, and the jihad of Umar Tal. In analyzing these jihads, it is important to distinguish between the motivations of the leaders and those of their followers. Although the leaders appear to have been motivated primarily by religious zeal, their followers joined for a variety of religious, economic, political, and personal reasons. The leaders railed against corruption and exploitation under the existing regimes and explained how the common people would be better off under a reformed Islamic state. But they also knew that some people joined their cause out of personal ambition. After his successful jihad, Usuman dan Fodio noted that he himself had not profited in any way, but he expressed regret that some of his followers had used the jihad as an opportunity to indulge their greed and lust for power.

The Sokoto Caliphate and Usuman dan Fodio

The Islamic revolutions that reshaped the political map of the West African Sahel in the nineteenth century began in Hausaland, a region far from the Atlantic Ocean that had not been affected by the Atlantic slave trade in any significant way. Located in what is now northern Nigeria, Hausaland was occupied by people who lived in walled cities and spoke the Hausa language. In the sixteenth century, seven independent Hausa kingdoms dominated the landscape. Small Muslim communities began to develop in the Hausa kingdoms after 1500, and some Muslim scholars settled in the larger Hausa cities under the patronage of the royal courts. By the eighteenth century, certain Islamic practices, such as the use of Muslim names, had become widespread throughout Hausaland, but they existed side by side with traditional religious customs and rites. Some Hausa rulers practiced Islam, but others ignored it. Sometimes one ruler would be a strict Muslim, but his successor would emphasize traditional religious practices. Thus did Islam wax and wane in the royal courts of Hausaland.

In the eighteenth century, the religious tensions in Hausaland were exacerbated by ethnic tensions. Although most of the land was occupied by Hausa-speaking farmers, it was also home to clans of nomadic Fulani cattle herders, who were granted permission by the Hausa kings to pasture their herds, and in return were required to pay a special cattle tax, an imposition the herders deeply resented. Although some of the Fulani clans ignored or rejected Islam, others embraced it, and at least one Fulani clan—the Toronkawa clan—developed a tradition of Islamic learning and scholarship. It was from this clan that a young scholar named **Usuman dan Fodio** emerged. Born in 1754, he studied with a number of Islamic scholars in Hausaland and became a member of the Qadiriyya brotherhood.

In 1774, Usuman dan Fodio became a tutor to the royal family in the Hausa kingdom of Gobir. Although he succeeded in exerting some religious influence over the king, his teaching was ignored by the king's successor, King Nafata, who rejected Islam and resurrected traditional religious practices. Usuman left the royal court and began to preach among the common people. He condemned the cattle tax and other taxes that he deemed oppressive, and he advocated the adoption of Islamic law, which he thought was more just and fair. Alarmed by Usuman's preaching, the king decreed that no person could become a Muslim unless their father was a Muslim. He banned turbans for men and face coverings for women, thus depriving Muslims of their most visible marks of religious identity. When King Nafata died after a short reign, his successor invited Usuman to the royal palace for a conversation. Instead of talking, however, he pulled out a musket and tried to shoot the Muslim cleric. The gun misfired, and Usuman was able to escape. His growing band of followers believed that his escape was a sign from God that Usuman should rule the kingdom. As Usuman's following grew, the king threatened to send an army against him and his followers. In response, Usuman's followers began to arm themselves, and in 1804, Usuman dan Fodio declared a jihad against the King of Gobir.

Usuman's army consisted mainly of Fulani archers, Hausa farmers armed with swords, and a small cavalry made up mostly of Fulani scholars who proved to be surprisingly tough and skilled fighters. Victory in the early battles allowed them to capture cavalry horses to use in future battles. With each victory, Usuman's following and his army grew. After conquering the kingdom of Gobir, his forces moved on to conquer the other Hausa kingdoms. By 1812, the rebels had gained control over most of Hausaland and established a theocratic Islamic state that they referred to as a caliphate. Usuman dan Fodio held the title of caliph. The new state was referred to as the **Sokoto caliphate** because its capital was the city of Sokoto. The caliphate was divided into a series of emirates, each ruled by an emir, that were under the loose control of the caliph. Usuman was, in effect, replicating in miniature the structure of the former Islamic Caliphate that had ruled the Muslim world from Baghdad until 1258. The establishment of the Sokoto caliphate in 1812 marked the end of the first phase of the jihad, but the caliphate continued to expand for much of the century, eventually becoming one of the largest states in West Africa.

Jihad along the Middle Niger

Usuman dan Fodio's jihad became a source of inspiration for other Muslim clerics throughout the western and central portions of the Sahel. A direct offshoot of Usuman's jihad developed in Masina, which occupied the fertile Middle Niger floodplain, located where the Niger River flows through the Sahel between Segu and Timbuktu. The leader of that jihad was Ahmad bin Muhammad (known as Sheikh Ahmad), a Fulbe man from Masina who had earlier traveled to Hausaland to become a student and disciple of Usuman dan Fodio. Like his teacher, he became a member of the Qadiriyya brotherhood. He was reported to have fought in Usuman's army during the jihad in Hausaland. Before beginning his own jihad in Masina, he sought and received a battle flag from Usuman, an act that showed his continuing subordination to his spiritual master.

After gaining control of Masina sometime after 1810, Sheikh Ahmad fought against the army of Segu in 1818. Prior to the jihad, the nomadic Fulbe cattle herders of Masina, who were largely Muslim, had paid tribute to the kingdom of Segu, which was ruled by a pagan military elite supported by a slave army (see chapter 6). The enslaved soldiers of Segu rejected Islam and maintained a hedonistic lifestyle that was offensive to many Muslims. The highly motivated jihadists led by Sheikh Ahmad freed themselves from Segu's rule and moved east to capture the trading cities of Jenne and Timbuktu. Patterning his Islamic state on the Sokoto caliphate, Sheikh Ahmad took the title of caliph and organized his state along theocratic lines, with an emir (governor) and a *qadi* (judge) appointed to rule each province. He also established an alliance with the Kunta, the Arab tribe that controlled the Sahara Desert trade north of Timbuktu. Together, the caliphate of Masina, the Kunta Arabs, and the Sokoto caliphate in Hausaland formed a kind of economic common market that dominated the north–south commerce of the Middle Niger region and the Niger bend.

The Jihad of Umar Tal

In contrast to Usuman dan Fodio in Hausaland and Sheikh Ahmad in Masina, who were both members of the Qadiriyya brotherhood, **Umar Tal** was a member of the rival Tijaniyya brotherhood, which placed greater emphasis on the role of the holy man and allowed for personal interpretations of the Islamic scriptures, even if they differed from the scholarly commentaries. As a Sufi cleric, he emphasized the prophecies about the coming of the Mahdi. He rejected the claims of his followers that he was the Mahdi, but he did believe that he was a Majaddid (renewer), and he even claimed to be the Mahdi's right-hand man.

Umar Tal grew up in the western province of the kingdom of Fuuta Toro, which occupied the middle Senegal River valley along the southern edge of the

Sahara Desert. Although Fuuta Toro was an Islamic state with an elected ruler, the people of the western province felt disaffected with their leadership because they paid a disproportionately large share of taxes, but did not get a share of the customs duties paid by the French merchants who traded along the middle Senegal River. As a young Muslim scholar, Umar left Fuuta Toro in 1826 for an extended trip to Cairo, Mecca, and possibly Damascus and Jerusalem. During his journey, he engaged in discussions and debates with some of the finest scholars in the Muslim world. Umar emerged from his travels firmly attached to the teachings of the Tijaniyya brotherhood. In 1831, he arrived in Hausaland and settled in Sokoto. By this time, Usuman dan Fodio had died, and the Sokoto caliphate was ruled by his son, Muhammad Bello, who had been Usuman's military commander during the jihad. Umar Tal married Muhammad Bello's daughter and undoubtedly learned a great deal about the organization and history of the jihad in Hausaland.

In 1840, Umar Tal arrived in the theocratic kingdom of Fuuta Jaloo (see chapter 6), where he devoted himself to teaching, to writing, and to forming a small community of disciples. As an adherent of the Tijaniyya brotherhood, he emphasized the essential role of holy men such as himself in guiding the believers to a true knowledge of God. In accordance with Tijaniyya teachings, he believed that a true understanding of Islam came through the mystical connection between the holy man and God, not through the legal reasoning and intellectual understanding of the Muslim scholars. He also claimed to have received a mystical formula from God that granted him divine guidance in times of trouble.

When the theocratic rulers of Fuuta Jaloo began to see his growing popularity and influence as a threat in 1849, Umar and his disciples moved to the small pagan kingdom of Tamba, where he continued to attract followers. Getting involved in long-distance commerce, he developed trading relations with Fuuta Jaloo and with Freetown, Sierra Leone, where he purchased guns and ammunition from the British. He soon transformed the village where he had settled into a fortified town with thick walls, a citadel, and several thousand inhabitants. He organized his followers into fighting units and even created a unit of blacksmiths to repair guns. Those activities posed a clear threat to the King of Tamba, who dispatched an army in 1852 to destroy Umar's town. As the army approached, Umar announced that he had received divine authorization to wage a jihad. Umar's forces won the battle with withering firepower, and the jihad had begun. In 1853, Umar took the capital of the Tamba kingdom and went on to capture the nearby Buré goldfields. This victory gave his forces plenty of money to purchase more guns and ammunition from the British in Freetown. With a strong and well-equipped army, Umar moved northeast toward the Middle Niger region and turned his attention to the kingdom

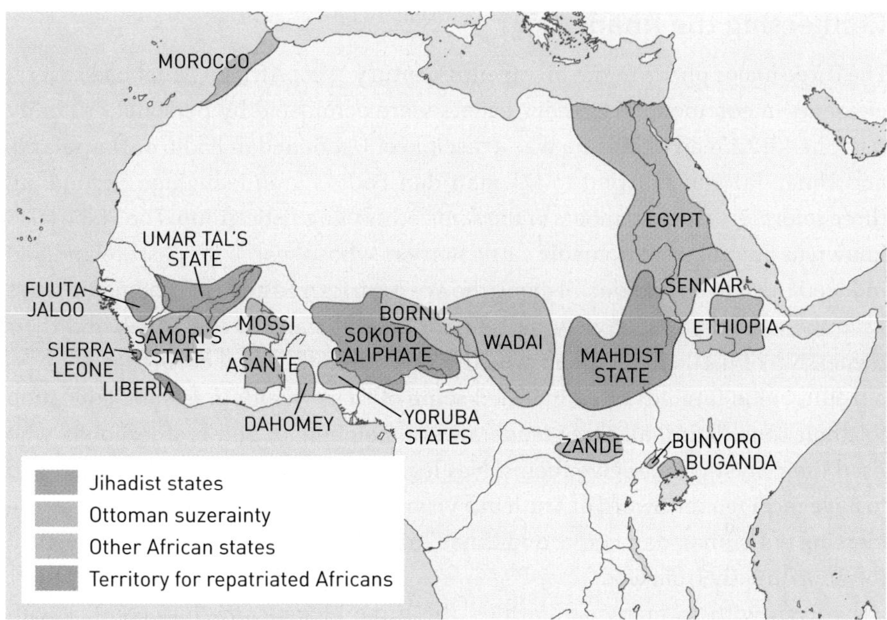

JIHADIST STATES OF THE SAHEL, 1880 This map highlights the states of the Sahel in existence in 1880 that were created by a jihad. Fuuta Jaloo, the westernmost state on this map, was created in the eighteenth century, while Umar Tal's Tukolor Empire, the Sokoto caliphate, and the Mahdist state were nineteenth century creations. Bornu was the site of a failed jihad.

of Kaarta, which was ruled by a pagan aristocracy supported by a slave army (see chapter 6).

Needing more troops, Umar visited his home kingdom of Fuuta Toro, along the middle Senegal River, to recruit soldiers and followers for the jihad he was waging along the Middle Niger. Citing the presence of the French trading forts along the middle Senegal, he told the people, "This country has ceased to be yours. It has become the country of the Europeans. Join me and emigrate to the East!" His recruiting efforts were so successful that about 20 percent of the inhabitants of Fuuta Toro left their homes and fields to follow the reformer. Strengthened by his new recruits, Umar's forces captured Segu in 1860, then moved up the Niger, where they conquered the caliphate of Masina (which had itself been formed by a jihad a half century earlier), and advanced all the way to Timbuktu. Umar Tal was killed in 1864 while suppressing a rebellion in Masina. His son Amadu took his place, inheriting an empire (known as the Tukolor Empire) that stretched more than 900 miles from the middle Senegal River valley to the Niger bend.

Connecting the Jihads

The three major jihads in the nineteenth-century West African Sahel had several elements in common. First, their leaders were connected by personal or family ties: Sheikh Ahmad of Masina was a disciple of Usuman dan Fodio of Hausaland, and Umar Tal was married to Usuman dan Fodio's granddaughter. Second, all three reformers were members of the same ethno-linguistic group. The Fulbe (also known as Fulani) were nomadic cattle herders whose search for pastureland had induced them to spread out all along the West African Sahel. Their nomadic ways gave them an expansive view of the peoples and states of the Sahel, and their ownership of cattle made them wealthy relative to the neighboring farmers. As a result, Fulbe families often invested some of their wealth in Islamic education for their sons. Third, all three leaders were members of Sufi brotherhoods who used their mysticism to give themselves legitimacy: Usuman dan Fodio claimed to have received the Sword of Truth in a vision; Sheikh Ahmad was fortified by the blessing of Usuman dan Fodio; and Umar Tal claimed to have received a mystical formula directly from God.

Even with so many similarities, the three jihads came into conflict with one another, in part because their leaders represented rival Sufi brotherhoods: Usuman dan Fodio and Sheikh Ahmad had joined the Qadiriyya, whereas Umar Tal had joined the Tijaniyya. Because of doctrinal differences, Umar Tal found that his preaching was not welcome in Fuuta Jaloo, a state that had itself been formed in a jihad a century earlier, and Umar Tal's army later conquered the caliphate of Masina, which had been created by the jihad of Sheikh Ahmad. It is perhaps ironic that Umar Tal was killed while putting down a rebellion in Masina. Taken together, the three jihads sparked an upsurge in warfare, caused the displacement of populations, and reconfigured the political and religious landscape of the West African Sahel.

THE YORUBA WARS

The **Yoruba Wars**, which engulfed much of what is now southwestern Nigeria between 1813 and 1893, were not jihads, but they were set off by the jihadist movements in the Sahel. An offshoot of the jihad that had created the Sokoto caliphate in 1812 later destroyed the capital of the Oyo Empire (a non-Islamic state), causing the Oyo nobility to flee southward and the empire to implode. The subsequent relocation of the Oyo capital far to the south provoked a series of wars among Yoruba states that sought to be the successor to the defunct empire. Historians know those wars as the Yoruba Wars because they were fought mainly by people in the Yoruba ethno-linguistic group. Lasting for 80 years, they caused massive population displacement, facilitated the rise of warlord states, and sent nearly 400,000 captives to the Americas via the illegal slave trade. One of those captives was Samuel Ajayi Crowther, who was later rescued from a Portuguese slave ship. Even though these wars in the south had no religious associations, they would not have occurred without the breakup of the Oyo Empire, which was the direct result of a jihad. Therefore, it seems appropriate to discuss the jihad and the Yoruba Wars as successive phases of a single process in order to illustrate the unforeseen consequences of jihad in areas beyond the frontiers of West African Islam.

The Yoruba constitute the third-largest ethno-linguistic group in Africa. They occupy a territory as large as England, located in the southwestern part of what is now Nigeria. For many centuries, they have lived in densely populated towns and would travel as far as 20 miles to work on their farms. At the center of each town was the palace of the local king, who was known as the *oba*. Often described as a sacred or divine ruler, the oba had great religious authority. Living in seclusion and rarely appearing in public, the oba ruled with the help of a council of chiefs. Prior to 1500, a number of small Yoruba kingdoms developed, each governed by a "great oba" who lived in the capital city and had authority over the lesser obas in the surrounding towns.

The Oyo Empire

During the sixteenth and seventeenth centuries, the Yoruba kingdom of Oyo began to extend its authority over the other Yoruba kingdoms to create the Oyo Empire. When a kingdom was conquered and incorporated into the Oyo Empire, it did not lose its identity or its individual political organization. It simply acknowledged the authority of the king of Oyo and paid tribute. The Oyo Empire reached its maximum extent around 1750. At the center, it contained a core group of six kingdoms that were under the direct control of the king of Oyo. Beyond this core were other Yoruba kingdoms that had more autonomy, but nevertheless recognized the authority of Oyo. On the periphery were non-Yoruba kingdoms that paid tribute, but were not otherwise under Oyo control. A relative peace prevailed among the Yoruba kingdoms during the eighteenth century because the king of Oyo used his prestige and religious authority to settle disputes and prevent wars. But there was always the possibility that warfare might break out among the component kingdoms if the Oyo Empire, which held them together, were to disintegrate.

The Oyo Empire was located in the grasslands north of the coastal forest zone. This geographical situation had two consequences. First, the capital city of Oyo Ile, located in the far northern part of the empire, became a major commercial center for the exchange of forest products from the south for products from the Sahel. Trade caravans from Oyo Ile visited markets in all the Yoruba kingdoms.

They were also in touch with the commercial centers of the Sahel as far away as Jenne and Timbuktu. From the north they imported salt, glassware, leather goods, and horses. Prisoners of war were often taken north to be traded for horses, but those captured in the southern regions were taken south to the Bight of Benin, where they were traded for sea salt or sold to Europeans for cloth and other goods that could be taken north to the Sahel and traded for horses. Second, the empire's grassland location allowed it to use horses for military purposes. It had two cavalries, a heavy one that rode large horses imported from the Sahara and fought with heavy lances and spears, and a light one that rode smaller ponies from the Sahel and fought with throwing spears and bows and arrows. The army of Oyo did not adopt guns until the nineteenth century.

The Destruction of Oyo

The warfare that engulfed the Yoruba kingdoms was triggered by an Islamic jihad that destroyed Oyo Ile, the capital of the Oyo Empire. The capital was located in the far north of the Yoruba country, not far from Hausaland, where Usuman dan Fodio had led a successful jihad and established the Sokoto caliphate. The commander-in-chief of the Oyo army, General Afonja, was disgruntled because he had been passed over by the council of chiefs when a new king was chosen, so he formed an alliance with a Muslim preacher from Hausaland in order to launch a jihad against the new king. Seeking support among the Muslim Hausa slaves and Fulbe cattle herders living in Oyo, he announced that slaves could earn their freedom if they ran away from their masters and joined his jihad. General Afonja was not a Muslim himself, but he capitalized on the energy and fervor of his Muslim followers to launch a rebellion that he hoped would bring him to power.

If General Afonja was using his Muslim allies for his own political purposes, they were also using him for the purpose of extending Usuman dan Fodio's jihad beyond Hausaland. In 1823, they killed General Afonja and launched a war to claim the northern part of the Oyo Empire as a province of the Sokoto caliphate. After seizing control of most of the northern towns of the empire, the jihadist army marched on Oyo Ile in 1836. Fearing the coming attack, the king and his people abandoned the city and fled over a hundred miles south, where they founded a new capital city, known simply as Oyo. Although the rulers still enjoyed religious and symbolic authority in their new capital, they no longer held military or economic power. They had been reduced to ceremonial figureheads who were respected and honored, but not feared.

The destruction of the Oyo Empire gave way to violent conflict between Yoruba kingdoms as they battled for supremacy. Swelling with refugees, the towns of Ibadan and Ijayi emerged as thriving cities and soon grew into the capitals of rival states, each of which sought to replace the defunct Oyo Empire. Both Ibadan and Ijayi expanded through conquest—Ijayi to the west and Ibadan to the east. Ibadan attacked Ijayi in 1844 and again in 1860, finally defeating it in 1862 to become the most powerful state in the region. After 1877, a series of revolts against Ibadan plunged the region into a new round of warfare that lasted until 1893.

The Yoruba Wars not only reconfigured the political map of Yoruba country, but also brought about many changes in the structure and power relations of Yoruba society. In the first place, there was massive population displacement and a proliferation of war refugees. People fled their towns as individuals or in small groups, and sometimes entire towns would move from the grassland into the coastal forest region in order to find safety from cavalry charges. A second consequence was the rise of local warlords who took advantage of the chaos to establish military and political power. Displaced men would join the warlords' armies in return for protection, giving rise to a class of professional soldiers, especially after guns became common in the 1840s. The old military system of the Oyo Empire, in which a mass of conscripted soldiers were supported by elite cavalry troops, gave way to well-trained infantries equipped with firearms. Successful warlords lived in large compounds with hundreds of followers, relatives, and slaves. Although their lack of religious sanctification meant that they could never become obas, their compounds were often larger than the palaces of the obas. As a result of the wars, this new group of warlords supported by professional armies became the dominant military and political force in Yoruba country. The jihad in the north had set off a chain reaction that continued to reverberate over the people living in the south.

THE MAHDIST JIHAD IN SUDAN

The Mahdist jihad in Sudan is here considered separately from the jihads in the West African Sahel because it came from different religious roots, spread in response to a very different political landscape, and had no known connections with the jihads discussed above. In the nineteenth century, the region directly south of Egypt that is now the modern country of Sudan was known by the Arabic term *Bilad al-Sudan*, the land of the blacks. In 1820, Muhammad Ali, the governor of Egypt (see chapter 8), sent an army up the Nile River valley to conquer and annex the territory. Because Egypt was a province of the Ottoman Empire, the army was made up mostly of Turks from various regions of Anatolia and Albanians from southern Europe (Muhammad Ali was himself an Albanian). The people of Sudan, however, described the invaders simply as "Turks."

In 1824, the invaders built a fort and a garrison at the confluence of the Blue Nile and the White Nile, which would quickly grow into the city of Khartoum and become the political and economic hub of Sudan. The urban population grew so rapidly that the mosque built in 1829–1830 was demolished in 1837 and a larger one was built in its place. As the army of conquest gave way to an army of occupation, its ranks were augmented by enslaved soldiers from Sudan itself. In 1835, every locality under Egyptian control was ordered to supply enslaved recruits to the army. Despite the infusion of captive Sudanese soldiers, the occupiers continued to be known as "the Turks."

We noted earlier that Islam in the West African Sahel was dominated by two Sufi orders, the Qadiriyya and the Tijaniyya. In the eastern part of the Sahel—where Khartoum was located—a third Sufi order had gained a foothold. The Khalwatiyya Sufi order had originated in the fourteenth century in what is now Afghanistan. Its name refers to a method of withdrawing from the world for mystical purposes. The order was known for its strict ritual training and its dervishes—disciples who lived austere lives of extreme poverty. During the eighteenth century, a Khalwatiyya cleric named al-Sammani established a new suborder that became known as the Sammaniyya, and it was this suborder that was brought to the valley of the Nile around 1800. A member of this suborder, by the name of Muhammad Ahmad, would eventually lead the jihad that conquered Sudan.

Muhammad Ahmad, the Mahdi

Muhammad Ahmad was born in 1844 to a family directly descended from the Prophet Muhammad. Deeply religious since childhood, he joined the Sammaniyya order as a young man and settled on the island of Abba in the White Nile, south of Khartoum. There, he built a mosque and gained a reputation for holiness and supernatural powers, attracting a small group of followers. In 1881, when he was 37 years old, he sent letters to the important leaders in Sudan announcing that he was **the Mahdi**, the divine leader chosen by God to bring justice and equity to the earth at the end of time. Both Sunni and Shia Islam held beliefs about the eventual coming of the Mahdi, and Sufi Islam had generated quite a bit of Mahdist speculation over the centuries, though few people had actually declared themselves to be the Mahdi. In addition to claiming the religious title of the Mahdi, Muhammad Ahmad declared himself "Imam," the leader of the faithful, and "Successor of the Apostle of God," which identified him as the successor of the Prophet Muhammad. "He who doubts that I am the Mahdi," he proclaimed, "is a renegade; he who opposes me is an infidel; and he who wages war against me will neither succeed in this world nor in the world to come."

THE MAHDI Muhammad Ahmad of Sudan declared himself to be the Mahdi (the Islamic deliverer who appears at the end of time) and launched a jihad to drive the Egyptians and Turks out of Sudan in order to set up an Islamic state. Although militarily successful, he died before fully establishing his ideal state. This woodcut is based on a drawing of the Mahdi in 1884.

The Egyptian government, which had controlled Sudan since the 1820s, saw this announcement as a threat, especially after Muhammad Ahmad urged the Sudanese to cease paying taxes to the "infidel Turks." The Egyptian government dispatched steamboats carrying soldiers up the Nile to arrest Muhammad Ahmad at his island retreat, but his followers, armed with only spears, swords, and clubs, ambushed the soldiers and drove them away. Hailed as a miracle, the victory enhanced Muhammad Ahmad's reputation as the true Mahdi. Once the Egyptian soldiers and their steamboats had retreated, Muhammad Ahmad and his followers made a long march to the hill country that marked the boundary between Arab settlements to the north and black African territory to the south. Because of Muhammad Ahmad's reputation, a variety of people flocked to the hills to join him. Some of them were pious Muslims who truly believed that he was the Mahdi who would apply Islamic law and practice in its full rigor. Others were simply Arabs from farther north who had come to the southern fringe of the Arab Sudan to work as boatmen, traders, and soldiers of fortune while Al-Zubayr and other merchants from Khartoum were pioneering the slave and ivory trade in the south (see chapter 8). They joined Muhammad Ahmad's movement out of economic and political interest. Still others were black cattle-herding nomads who resented any control by the Egyptian government. Together, these three groups made up a formidable fighting force.

The Mahdi's prestige mounted in 1881 and 1882 as more attempts by the Egyptian army to crush the growing Mahdist movement failed just like the first.

The newly confident Mahdi now took the offensive and proclaimed a jihad against Kordofan, a province of Sudan ruled by an Egyptian governor. Kordofan had a mixed population that included seminomadic Arab tribes and several groups of black African cattle-herding nomads. The Mahdi encouraged all of these ethnic groups to rise up against the Egyptian governor, and those rebellions paved the way for the arrival of the Mahdist army in full force. By now the army had been strengthened by the addition of enslaved black soldiers who had formerly fought for Egypt, but had been captured in battle and integrated into the Mahdist army. By early 1883, the last two Egyptian army garrisons in Kordofan had surrendered. In response, the Egyptian government sent out an expeditionary force of 8,000 men led by a former British officer in the Indian army. As the Egyptian army advanced into Kordofan, the Mahdi sent messages to the Egyptian soldiers proclaiming that it was hopeless to fight against the soldiers of God. The army of the Mahdi, now numbering some forty thousand troops, easily defeated the Egyptians, eliminating their last serious opposition.

From their base in Kordofan, the armies of the Mahdi moved west to conquer the Sultanate of Dar Fur and south to conquer the Bahr el-Ghazal region that had formerly been ruled by Al-Zubayr. In April 1884, the Mahdist army captured Al-Zubayr's former capital of Deim Al-Zubayr. A locally raised army of holy warriors who pledged their allegiance to the Mahdi occupied the Suakin Province, bordering the Red Sea. The remaining prize was Khartoum—the commercial and administrative capital of Sudan. With the capture of Khartoum in January 1885, the Mahdist forces controlled most of Sudan, excluding the southern equatorial regions and parts of the far north. For the most part, the Egyptians and the Turks had been driven out.

The Mahdist State

Establishing a new capital at Omdurman, across the White Nile from Khartoum, the Mahdists formed a government that embodied Muhammad Ahmad's vision of a true Islamic state. They believed that the Mahdi derived his power and legitimacy directly from God, and that lesser officials had only the authority bestowed on them by the Mahdi. The new regime modified Islamic law by rejecting the authority of the four main schools of Islamic jurisprudence and giving equal weight to the precepts of the Mahdi. To the Muslim profession of faith ("There is no god but God, and Muhammad is God's messenger"), they added a phrase stating that Muhammad Ahmad was "the spiritual successor of the Prophet Muhammad." They also modified the Five Pillars of Islam, replacing the duty to make a pilgrimage to Mecca with the duty to fight in holy wars. Such modifications of long-standing Islamic belief and practice would have been rejected as heretical had not Muhammad Ahmad been regarded as spiritually connected to the Prophet Muhammad and, through him, to God. In 1884, Muhammad Ahmad severed his ties to the Sammaniyya Sufi order that had birthed his movement. He wanted to be seen as the leader of all Muslims, not merely the head of a minor Sufi order. His successor would ban Sufi orders altogether.

Muhammad Ahmad saw his conquest of Sudan as the first stage in a larger project to conquer and expand the Muslim world, but that dream was cut short in June 1885, just 6 months after the fall of Khartoum, when he died from a sudden illness. After the death of the Mahdi, leadership of his movement was taken over by Abdallahi ibn Muhammad, the main commander of the Mahdist army, who took the title "Successor of the Mahdi." After suppressing a series of revolts challenging his leadership, Abdallahi sent his army to expand his territory eastward into the Christian kingdom of Ethiopia and northward into Egypt. Transforming Sudan from a theocratic state into a despotic state with himself as the absolute ruler, he developed an elite bodyguard of 9,000 men—half of them enslaved soldiers and half free Sudanese—commanded by his son, Uthman, whom he was grooming to be his successor. Abdallahi ibn Muhammad also created an elaborate and centralized bureaucracy composed of civil servants inherited from the very Turco-Egyptian regime that the Mahdi had tried to destroy. He instituted a set of taxes and fees that resembled the former Turco-Egyptian tax system. One of his major administrative innovations was to develop separate treasuries for different branches of the government, which allowed him to siphon off a substantial portion of the government's revenue into his own private treasury. By the 1890s, the religious movement that had originally propelled the Mahdist regime to power was dying out, replaced by a secular absolutist monarchy.

Among the jihads discussed in this chapter, the Mahdist jihad in Sudan was in many ways unique: it was the only jihad in which the leader declared himself to be the Mahdi and the successor to the Prophet Muhammad; the only one with aspirations to conquer the entire Muslim world; and the only one in which the Ottoman Empire (which claimed to be the legitimate successor to the early Islamic Caliphate) was seen as the enemy. Despite these features, it nevertheless had certain elements in common with the jihads in the West African Sahel. First, it emerged from the mystical vision of an adherent of a Sufi brotherhood. Although Muhammad Ahmad eventually broke with that group, it gave him his start and provided the initial energy for his movement. Second, his attacks were initially directed at the Muslim army of Egypt, which showed that he was not waging a war against unbelievers. Ironically, he sought military support from black Sudanese cattle herders and former slave soldiers, who were mostly non-Muslim. Later on, he conquered certain non-Muslim areas of Sudan in order to enlarge his territory, but his was primarily an Islamic reform movement aimed at creating a pure and just Islamic state. Although he was spectacularly successful in warfare, he died before he could create his ideal Islamic state. After his death, his successors reverted to the kind of despotism and corruption that his movement had fought against for many years.

POLITICAL AND MILITARY REVOLUTIONS IN SOUTHERN AFRICA

Northeast of the European settlements at the Cape of Good Hope (see chapters 7 and 8), African populations occupied the territory between the Indian Ocean coast and the Drakensberg mountain range, which runs parallel to the coast about a hundred miles inland. The area was kept fertile by rain clouds coming in from the Indian Ocean, which typically brought more than 30 inches of rain per year. The people spoke closely related Bantu languages belonging to the Nguni linguistic subfamily. Many of the Nguni languages were mutually intelligible—in fact, they were so closely related that some linguists suggest that we should think of the Nguni subfamily as a continuum of dialects rather than a cluster of separate languages. The linguistic homogeneity of the region reflects its cultural homogeneity and suggests that the different ethno-linguistic groups that lived there were all descended from a common ancestral population.

Living in a relatively lush environment, the Nguni speakers made their living by a combination of farming and cattle herding. Unlike the drier environments in southern Africa, where people such as the Khoikhoi (see chapter 7) engaged in nomadic cattle herding, the fertile lands of the Nguni speakers allowed them to live in fixed villages. They cultivated fields of maize (corn) and sorghum, while the young men moved the cattle from pasture to pasture according to the season. A family's wealth was determined by the number of cattle it owned, and it could not obtain wives for its sons without paying a bride-price in cattle to the families of their brides. A family with large herds could therefore have both wealth in cattle and wealth in people. Because cattle were so important, warfare often took the form of cattle raids.

In 1800, the Nguni speakers were organized politically into a variety of small and medium-sized chiefdoms. Chiefs performed a variety of functions, such as regulating access to land, offering protection to people and their livestock, and settling major disputes. They were also spiritual leaders, responsible for performing rituals that were thought to bring prosperity to the community and maintain harmony with the spirits of their ancestors. Chiefs were often referred to as "rainmakers," but the term was understood broadly to mean that the chiefs' duty was to protect the prosperity and well-being of the community.

Each chiefdom was dominated by an extended chiefly family from which the successors to the reigning chief were chosen. The chiefly family and its allied families constituted the aristocracy of the chiefdom. A second social tier was made up of common people who were not related to the aristocratic families. Commoner families who were unhappy with the conditions in the chiefdom could leave and seek the protection of another chief. The third social tier was composed of poor people without cattle, who survived by becoming clients or servants of wealthy families. Often their condition was little better than slavery. Prosperous chiefdoms grew by attracting immigrants, while less prosperous chiefdoms were at risk of shrinking as people moved away. A southern African proverb summed up the situation by stating that a chief without people was no chief at all.

A key function of the chiefs was to organize the initiation rites that granted young men the status of full adults. The initiation process included circumcision rituals, but the young men were also trained to hunt and spent a period rendering services to their chief. A group of young men who went through initiation together formed an age set. In the late eighteenth century, certain chiefs began extending the length of time during which young men served as initiates, and eventually they abandoned the circumcision ceremonies altogether, which prolonged the period of adolescence and kept the young men under the control of the chief. The age sets were increasingly used as military regiments and police units for the chiefs, and the members regularly performed tasks such as building the chief's house, cultivating his fields, and guarding his cattle. This system strengthened the power of the chiefs and allowed them to take full advantage of the labor and fighting capacity of the young men.

By the early nineteenth century, two of the chiefdoms had successfully absorbed smaller neighboring chiefdoms to expand into fully-fledged kingdoms, dominating the region politically and militarily. The first was the Ndwandwe Kingdom, ruled by Zwide, and the second was the Mthethwa Kingdom, ruled by Dingiswayo. As in other parts of Africa, the small chiefdoms they conquered did not disappear, but were incorporated as vassal states. The Ndwandwe and Mthethwa Kingdoms were inherently unstable because many of the chiefs they had conquered were looking for any opportunity to break away and regain their independence.

Historians have puzzled over why this process of state building and political expansion took off in the second half of the eighteenth century. Some have looked at the Portuguese slave and ivory traders who came to Delagoa Bay (now Maputo, Mozambique), but this trade was minimal prior to the 1820s, when Brazilian slave ships began seeking captives from southeastern Africa after Britain outlawed the Atlantic slave trade. Others have pointed to encroachments by the European settlers in the Cape Colony, but those events took place far to the south of Zwide's and Dingiswayo's kingdoms. The most probable explanation is that the enlarged states were simply an expansion and refinement of certain social institutions and military tactics that had long been known in southern Africa. When one chiefdom expanded and became a dominant military power, then other chiefdoms felt compelled to adopt similar practices for self-preservation.

Shaka and the Zulu Kingdom

One of King Dingiswayo's smaller vassal states was the Zulu chiefdom. When its chief died in 1816, a struggle for succession among his sons ensued, from which the deceased chief's eldest (but not favorite) son **Shaka** emerged as the new Zulu chief, with the aid and support of King Dingiswayo. The chiefdom that Shaka ruled was tiny—covering only 6 square miles—and had an army of fewer than 500 men. Dingiswayo encouraged Shaka to develop his age regiments and expand his military forces in order to help defend the western flank of the Mthethwa Kingdom.

In building up his army, Shaka took an innovative military approach. In contrast to previous armies of the region, which had fought using a combination of long throwing spears and short stabbing spears, Shaka's regiments relied heavily on short, broad-bladed stabbing spears, which were used in conjunction with 4- to 6-foot-tall shields made of cattlehide. Using a battlefield formation known as "the horns of the ox," Shaka sent out a relatively small force (known as "the chest"), marching in close formation, to engage the enemy, while more mobile

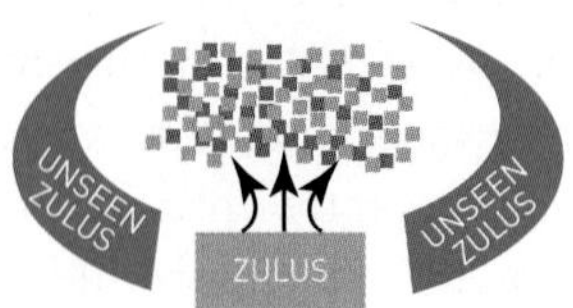

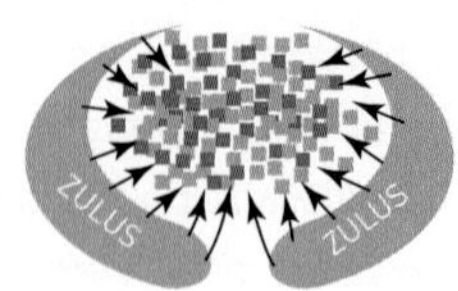

HORNS OF THE OX Shaka deployed a battle formation known as the "horns of the ox," which he compared to the head of a Cape buffalo. Soldiers in the "chest" section engaged the enemy, while the two "horns" encircled them, ready to close in at the appropriate moment.

units (known as "the horns") on both sides moved at greater speed to surround and engulf them.

In 1818, the rivalry between the Ndwandwe and Mthethwa Kingdoms escalated into warfare. When the fighting became intense, Dingiswayo summoned his vassal Shaka and his regiments, but was killed in battle before Shaka could arrive. The death of Dingiswayo created an opportunity for his vassal chiefs to break away, causing his kingdom to splinter into its component parts, a process that was accelerated when Shaka assassinated Dingiswayo's rightful heir. Shaka quickly emerged as the strongest chief among the ruins of Dingiswayo's kingdom.

After repelling an attack from Zwide's regiments, Shaka began to conquer neighboring chiefdoms and absorb their regiments into his own army. The following year, Zwide's army invaded Shaka's territory. Shaka repelled the invasion and launched successful counter-raids into Zwide's territory, capturing large numbers of cattle. Zwide's defeats by Shaka's regiments provoked the disintegration of his kingdom as several of his generals broke away and moved north with their followers to establish independent kingdoms of their own. By 1819, Shaka was the dominant political and military leader in the region between the Mkhuze and Thukela Rivers, a distance of about 125 miles. By amalgamating a variety of small chiefdoms through conquest and negotiation, he had created a powerful state, known as the **Zulu Kingdom**.

SHAKA THE ZULU Using innovative military formations and organizational arrangements, Shaka transformed his small Zulu chiefdom into a powerful kingdom and forced rival chiefs to flee the territory. This sketch by James Saunders King was made in 1824, just 4 years before Shaka was killed by two of his brothers.

The kingdom that Shaka had cobbled together consisted of three regions. The core region was made up of chiefdoms that had kinship or traditional ties to the old Zulu chiefdom. They were surrounded by a second tier of chiefdoms that lacked such ties, but were nevertheless considered an integral part of the Zulu Kingdom. Those chiefdoms provided the majority of the recruits for the Zulu regiments. The third region, on the periphery of the Zulu Kingdom, contained chiefdoms that operated independently, but acknowledged the hegemony of the Zulu king and provided the kingdom with a buffer zone against attacks. Beyond these buffer states were regions outside of the kingdom, where Shaka sent his regiments to raid for cattle.

The key to holding the Zulu Kingdom together was Shaka's control over the young, unmarried men in the age regiments. To complement the male age regiments, he created noncombatant age regiments of single young women, which provided labor for the state. Young people could not marry until they had provided several years of satisfactory service. When they had completed their duties, Shaka released them from military service and gave permission for the men in a certain regiment to choose wives from a certain women's regiment. At that

ZULU WAR GAMES Zulu King Mpande looks on as two Zulu regiments—one with black shields and one with white shields—engage in military exercises. The kraal (enclosed village) in the background is one of the 14 military capitals maintained by the Zulu king. The larger houses in the center were for the king's women. This picture was painted in the 1840s by George French Angus, who claimed that he was the only Englishman ever allowed to enter the women's houses.

point, those two regiments disbanded and were replaced by new recruits. This practice marked a major change in the Zulu social system because marriage had traditionally been an arrangement between two families and marriage partners had generally been chosen by the parents. Now, Shaka told the young men and women when to marry and where to look for mates. Shaka also received young, unmarried women who were sent to him as tribute and kept them secluded in a royal enclosure. He called them the "sisters and daughters of the king," and he gave them in marriage to rich and powerful men in order to link them to the royal family through artificial kinship ties. By inserting the Zulu state into the system of marriage and family formation, Shaka created an effective tool for integrating a collection of previously independent chiefdoms into a powerful and stable centralized state.

Yet another mechanism for integrating the conquered chiefdoms into the kingdom was the giving of gifts of cattle to subordinate chiefs and influential men, as well as to soldiers when they were finally released from military service and allowed to marry. Such a system required continuous infusions of cattle. Whenever Shaka's armies returned victorious from a battle, they brought with them as many cattle as they could seize. One historian has referred to Shaka's military system as a "perpetual cattle raiding machine."

Shaka's Zulu Kingdom reached its greatest extension in 1826, after his regiments successfully invaded the remnants of Zwide's former kingdom and seized large herds of their cattle. But just 2 years later, Shaka was stabbed to death by two of his brothers. One of the assassins, Dingane, claimed the throne and suppressed all opposition by executing chiefs who had been loyal to Shaka and assassinating all but two of his remaining brothers. He won the support of the senior regiments by relaxing the marriage laws and giving the soldiers generous gifts of cattle so that they could set up their own homesteads. Although Dingane did not try to expand the borders of the kingdom beyond those established by Shaka, he frequently sent his regiments out to raid for cattle far from their homeland. Having steady infusions of cattle to redistribute to vassal chiefs was essential for maintaining their loyalty. By this time, the component chiefdoms had become so well integrated into the Zulu Kingdom that even a major shock such as Shaka's assassination did not cause it to break up.

The Ngoni and the Wars of Displacement

The disintegration of Zwide's Ndwandwe Kingdom following its defeats by Shaka in 1818 and 1819 unleashed a period of instability that would reverberate throughout southeastern Africa. Several of Zwide's generals broke away and moved northward with their regiments into what is now southern Mozambique in order to create new kingdoms for themselves. The most successful of them were Zwangendaba, Soshangane, and Nxaba. Over time, these breakaway groups became collectively known as the **Ngoni**.

There were three keys to the Ngoni's success. First, they had battle-hardened standing armies based on the age-regiment system. These well-trained armies could easily overwhelm the more peaceful chiefdoms, which had traditionally relied on poorly trained farmers who were hastily mobilized in times of war. Second, the age-regiment system was useful for integrating young boys from conquered populations into the Ngoni armies and creating loyal subjects. Third, because their wealth was measured in cattle instead of land, they were highly mobile and were able to relocate frequently, settling in any place that had adequate pasture for their livestock. The continuous desire to increase their herds and armies propelled the Ngoni to move farther and farther north in search of new conquests. By the 1860s, some of them were living and fighting 2,000 miles north of their birthplace.

The Ngoni group that had the greatest impact on southeastern Africa was led by **Zwangendaba**, described by one historian as "one of the most remarkable leaders in African history." When Zwide's kingdom began to disintegrate, Zwangendaba and his followers fought their way north into what is now southern Mozambique, incorporating captured people into their regiments and growing stronger with each victory. The people of southern Mozambique, who did not use a regimental system, were no match for Zwangendaba's forces. The only real threat came from two other offshoots of Zwide's kingdom: the regiments led by Soshangane and Nxaba. The three militarized groups coexisted for a time in southern Mozambique and sold some of their war captives to Portuguese slave traders at Delagoa Bay, but they eventually came into conflict with one another. In the early 1830s, Soshangane defeated the other two Ngoni chiefs and forced them to migrate north and west.

Having driven out his only serious rivals, Soshangane established the Gaza Kingdom, incorporating conquered chiefdoms as vassal states and integrating their young men into his military regiments. At its height, his kingdom stretched along the Indian Ocean coast from the Limpopo River to the Zambezi River, a distance of some 800 miles, and extended about 600 miles inland from the coast. The assimilation of conquered peoples into the regimental system was most effective in the core regions of the kingdom, while many of the peripheral chiefdoms paid tribute to Soshangane, but otherwise operated more or less independently. Soshangane also demanded tribute from the Portuguese traders and settlers at Delagoa Bay and elsewhere, whom he incorporated into his kingdom as vassals and protected in exchange for oversea commodities. He also controlled the prazo lands in the Zambezi valley that had earlier been settled by Portuguese

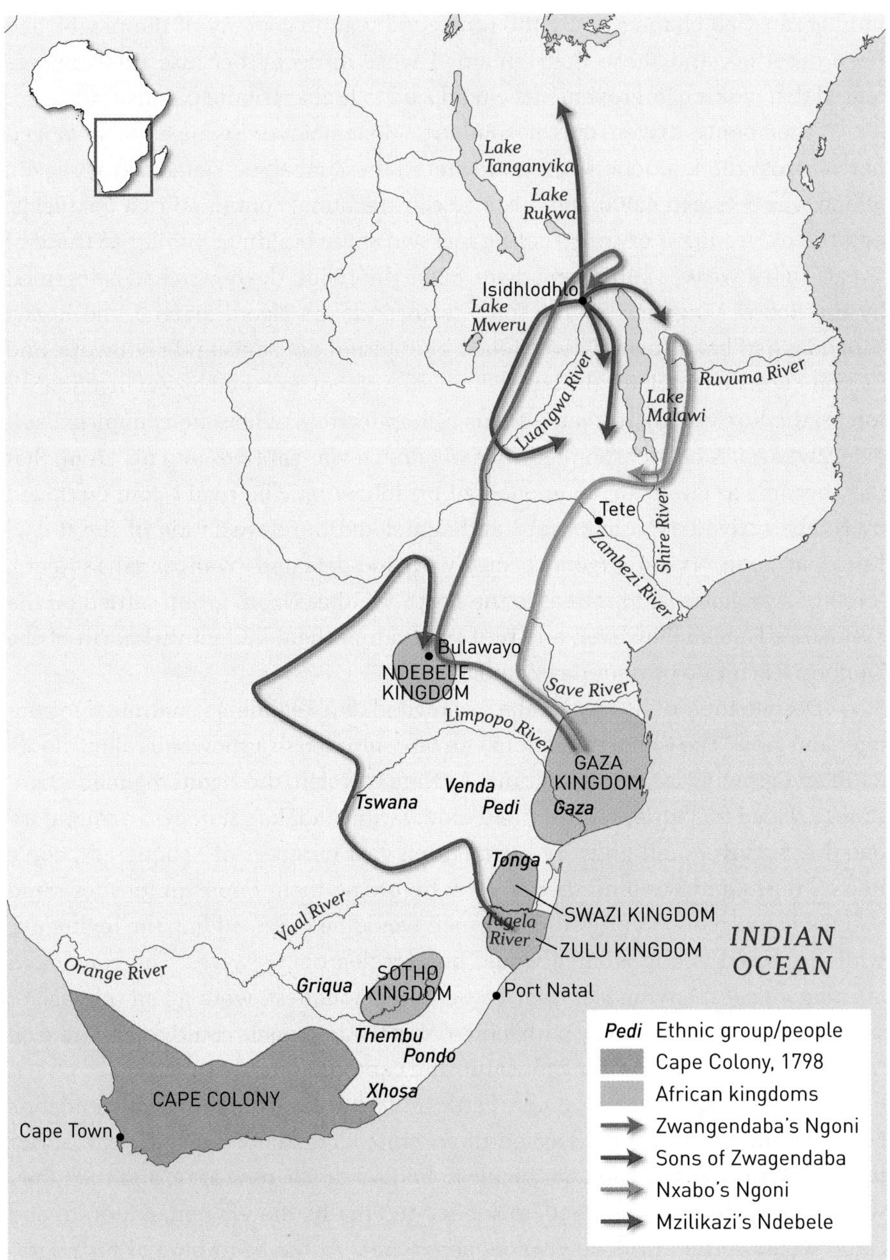

WARS OF DISPLACEMENT IN SOUTHERN AFRICA, 1798–1848 The arrows show the movements of armed Ngoni and Ndebele regiments. Zwagendaba's Ngoni and Nxabo's Ngoni both left Soshangani's Gaza Kingdom and migrated northward along the high plateau that runs parallel to the Indian Ocean coast. After Zwagendaba died in 1848, his five sons split up and founded independent chiefdoms. Mzilikazi's Ndebele took a more circuitous route to found the Ndebele Kingdom on the Zimbabwe Plateau.

immigrants (see chapter 7). By the nineteenth century, many of the prazos had been deserted, and those that remained were in decay because their owners feared that making improvements would lead to higher tribute payments.

After being driven out of southern Mozambique, Zwangendaba moved north across the Limpopo River and entered the Zimbabwe Plateau. This region, which was between 4,000 and 5,000 feet in elevation, contained rich goldfields, and the old tradition of constructing massive stone buildings similar to those of Great Zimbabwe was still strong there. Since the 1680s, the region had been ruled by the Rozwi Kingdom. By the time Zwangendaba's Ngoni arrived, the Rozwi Kingdom had been severely weakened by internal divisions and civil wars, and its army was no match for the battle-hardened Ngoni. Pursued by Zwangendaba's forces, the Rozwi king retreated to his hilltop fortress, where he committed suicide. Zwangendaba incorporated so many Rozwi war captives into his group that they became a significant component of his following. The rival Ngoni group led by Nxaba arrived soon afterward and completed the devastation of the Rozwi Kingdom. Soon, Nxaba's Ngoni clashed with and defeated Zwangendaba's Ngoni, forcing Zwangendaba to retreat to the north. Neither Ngoni group settled on the Zimbabwe Plateau, however, and by 1835, both of them had moved north of the Zambezi River into present-day Zambia.

Despite their defeat by Nxaba, Zwangendaba's regiments continued to conquer and grow. The Ngoni migrations can be compared to a snowball rolling down a hill and growing larger all the time. As they traveled, the Ngoni regiments constantly raided for cattle, captives, and food. Zwangendaba's state was a migratory one that survived and grew by assimilating vast numbers of conquered people into its ranks and winning their loyalty by giving them opportunities for rapid social advancement. Captured young men would be inducted into the regiments, while captured young women would be parceled out as wives. The conquered farming villages, having lost their cattle in the conquest, were given the task of supplying the Ngoni military with food so that the regiments could concentrate on their primary activity: raiding for cattle and captives.

The continuous need for more cattle and more captives kept Zwangendaba's Ngoni on the move. They relocated their entire state about every 4 years. Prior to moving, they would send out scouts to find a suitable new area, and then they would dispatch their regiments to subdue it. Finally, the women, children, and cattle would settle in the newly conquered area. At the beginning of his migrations, Zwangendaba's state had consisted of a single royal village and its attached regiments, but later it contained seven territorial units, each dominated by a large military town that housed the regiments and members of the royal family. Each time the Ngoni moved, they re-created this administrative structure and settlement pattern in their new location.

Zwangendaba died near the southern tip of Lake Tanganyika in 1848. He had led his people on a migration of more than 2,000 miles, leaving famine and devastation in his wake. His group had grown from a few hundred to more than a hundred thousand people, from a variety of ethnic groups, who had been assimilated and had become Ngoni. In a dispute over succession among Zwangendaba's sons, his coalition fragmented into five major groups, which split off and went their separate ways. The migration routes of the Ngoni had never been haphazard, but had been dictated by the environment. They avoided the tsetse fly–infested lowlands, where their cattle were in danger of being infected with sleeping sickness, as well as the dry plains, where cattle would have to be constantly on the move in search of grass and water. Instead, they sought highland areas with adequate rainfall for lush pastureland. By the 1870s, however, the offshoot Ngoni groups had run out of suitable land for further migration, and they settled permanently in present-day Tanzania, Malawi, and Zambia. The wars of displacement were over.

Mzilikazi's Ndebele Kingdom

A final offshoot of the Ndwandwe Kingdom was Mzilikazi's Ndebele Kingdom. Mzilikazi was born in a small chiefdom controlled by the Ndwandwe Kingdom. After the death of his father, the chief, he was installed as the new chief by King Zwide. In the aftermath of Zwide's defeats by Shaka in 1818 and 1819, Mzilikazi and his regiment abandoned Zwide and fought briefly for Shaka's Zulu Kingdom before striking out with perhaps two or three hundred followers to create a new kingdom on the high plateau west of the Drakensberg Mountains. Over time, Mzilikazi's followers came to be known as Ndebele.

Unlike the kingdoms built by Dingiswayo, Zwide, and Shaka, which incorporated entire conquered chiefdoms as vassal states, Mzilikazi incorporated conquered people into his kingdom as individuals, not as groups. After capturing a village, Mzilikazi would resettle the older men and women at some distance from their old homes. Captured young women would become the wives of senior soldiers. Captured children were taken to be raised by Ndebele families. Young boys were trained to be spear carriers for the soldiers. If they proved brave and reliable, they were allowed to become soldiers and join the regiment. Those who assimilated quickly found a path to rapid promotion. One captive, for example, rose to become the ruler of two villages.

Mzilikazi's kingdom was organized around the age-regiment system. Young men lived permanently in three large military towns and were not allowed to marry until they had devoted a number of years to military service and distinguished themselves in battle. Men who had been released from their military duties and permitted to marry constituted a reserve military force. They lived in

MZILIKAZI'S ROYAL KRAAL After separating from Shaka, Mzilikazi moved with his regiment to the high plateau west of the Drakensberg Mountains, which he dominated during the 1820s and 1830s. This picture of his kraal on the plateau was painted by Cornwallis Harris in the 1820s. Note the large enclosure for cattle in the middle of the village.

small villages near the military towns so that they could be quickly mobilized in times of war. Because the kingdom had been constructed by conquering alien peoples in a hostile territory, there was no hierarchy of traditional chiefs. Instead, the main administrative authorities were the commanders of the regiments. The regiments headquartered in the military towns raided for cattle and captives, ranging as far as present-day Botswana and Zimbabwe.

In 1836, Boer families from the Cape Colony arrived on the plateau during the Great Trek (see chapter 8). At first Mzilikazi paid them no heed, but when larger groups of trekkers appeared later that year, he saw them as a threat and launched an attack. Circling their wagons and loading their guns, the Boers repelled the first attack, as well as a second one a few days later. The Boer counterattack on Mzilikazi's capital in January 1837 forced Mzilikazi and his regiments to flee to the north. In November, further raids on his remaining military settlements were conducted by a Boer commando force of 300 men equipped with guns and horses. Mzilikazi's spear-wielding regiments were no match for the mounted riflemen. With his military settlements in flames and his people in flight, the king fled with his soldiers, cattle, and followers on a long march north in search of good pasture for his cattle and a new home for his people. After traveling through parts of what is now Botswana, they settled on the Zimbabwe Plateau in 1838, after a journey of nearly 1,500 miles. The Ngoni regiments of Zwangendaba and Nxaba had destroyed the Rozwi Kingdom when they had passed through several years earlier, so Mzilikazi's regiments had little trouble conquering the land and incorporating the populations into his new state.

It was on the Zimbabwe Plateau that Mzilikazi established his final state, which became known as the Ndebele Kingdom. Large military settlements were built in key districts, and smaller posts were constructed to guard the frontiers. Because men remained attached to their regiments after marriage, both young and old were subjected to the military authority of the regimental commanders. Each military settlement became the capital of a province. Because the provincial commanders were commoners who had risen through the military ranks, there was little danger that the provinces would try to break away, as was the case in kingdoms in which the provinces were governed by hereditary chiefs.

A three-tiered class structure developed in the Ndebele Kingdom that reflected the complex history of Mzilikazi and his followers. The aristocracy was composed of descendants of Mzilikazi's original followers. Next came the descendants of the people who were incorporated into the kingdom before it was displaced by the Boers. Lowest in prestige were people from the Zimbabwe Plateau who were incorporated after Mzilikazi had settled there. Like the Ngoni kingdoms of Zwangendaba, Soshangane, and Nxaba, the Ndebele Kingdom was put together by assimilating people from a variety of linguistic and ethnic groups.

CONCLUSION

The political landscape of Africa in 1880 was very different from what it had been in 1800. On the West African coast, in the colonies of Sierra Leone and Liberia—established with the support of Christian abolitionists in England and slaveholders in the United States, respectively—Western-educated intellectuals of African descent struggled to bridge the gaps between Christianity, Islam, and indigenous African religions. Samuel Ajayi Crowther, who was educated in Sierra Leone and England, went to spread Christianity in the southern portions of the former Oyo Empire. Thus an empire whose political institutions had long been based on uniquely Yoruba religious concepts was now becoming Muslim in the north and Christian in the south as universal religions encroached on local ones.

The Islamic jihads that erupted across the Sahel created a number of new states while destroying older ones. The jihadist armies were less interested in conquering non-Muslim areas than in conquering states with significant Muslim populations that were ruled by lax or corrupt Muslim rulers. The primary goal of the jihads was less to expand Islam than to reform and purify it in areas where it was already established. An example of the complexity of this process can be seen in Masina, in the Middle Niger region, where a jihad organized by members of the Qadiriyya brotherhood was driven out 50 years later by a jihad waged by Umar Tal and his Tijaniyya brotherhood. On the southern fringes of the Sokoto caliphate, the once-mighty Oyo Empire disintegrated. The northern part (which had a significant Muslim minority) was absorbed into the Sokoto caliphate, while new, independent successor states emerged in the non-Muslim southern part.

Southern Africa, in contrast, was rocked by the emergence of militarily powerful kingdoms in a political landscape that had previously been dominated by small chiefdoms. These developments were made possible by the expansion of the age-regiment system and its use to integrate conquered people into the society of their conquerors. As the Ngoni and Ndebele groups moved north, they absorbed so many new people of a variety of ethnic and linguistic origins that the descendants of the original groups became distinct minorities. The system's success was evident in the fact that the conquered people came to be thoroughly assimilated and to identify as Ndebele or Ngoni. In a similar way, the people in Shaka's kingdom came to see themselves as Zulu, even though the term had previously denoted only a tiny chiefdom. Despite the momentous changes in Africa's economic relations with the wider world in the nineteenth century, the Zulu, Ngoni, and Ndebele remained true to their own political systems and their own internal dynamics. Although they interacted with English, Boers, and Portuguese, they did not allow their economic and political systems to be subordinated to the demands of global economic forces. In the process of their 2000-mile migration north over less than three decades, the Ngoni devastated large regions and reshaped the political map of the kingdoms and chiefdoms of southeastern Africa.

If we add together the new states discussed in this chapter and those created by the new adaptations to the capitalist global economy (see chapter 8), it becomes evident that very few parts of sub-Saharan Africa escaped the economic, religious, and political transformations of the nineteenth century. Although some of the newly created states, such as the Zulu Kingdom in southern Africa and the Sokoto caliphate in the West African Sahel, have survived in one form or another up to the present day, many of the older states, such as Oyo, Bornu, Lunda, and Rozwi, were destroyed and replaced by unstable regimes dominated by warlords, religious zealots, armed traders, or nomadic cattle herders. It was in this destabilized political landscape that Africans would face the greatest challenge to their sovereignty in their entire history: the colonial partition of the African continent.

CHAPTER REVIEW

KEY TERMS AND VOCABULARY

Republic of Liberia
Samuel Ajayi Crowther
Edward Wilmot Blyden
Usuman dan Fodio
Sokoto caliphate
Umar Tal
Yoruba Wars
the Mahdi
Shaka
Zulu Kingdom
Ngoni
Zwangendaba

STUDY QUESTIONS

1. How did the Westernized settlers of African descent in Sierra Leone and Liberia relate to the local African cultures?
2. Why did African Christian thinkers such as Crowther and Blyden try to find common ground between Christianity and Islam?
3. How do you explain the upsurge in Islamic jihads in West Africa in the nineteenth century?
4. Outline the main connections between the jihads of Usuman dan Fodio, Ahmad bin Muhammad, and Umar Tal.
5. What made the Mahdi's religious movement in Sudan different from similar movements in the West African Sahel?
6. Why did Shaka's military innovations lead to a stable Zulu kingdom, whereas commanders such as Zwangendaba who used similar military tactics spent their lifetimes on the move?
7. How did the Ngoni military system reconfigure the political and ethnic maps of southern Africa?

THE LIBERIA PROJECT

Edward Wilmot Blyden was born in St. Thomas, then part of the Dutch West Indies, and moved to Liberia in 1850. Starting out as a journalist, he became the editor of the Liberia Herald, *held government positions as secretary of state, minister of the interior, and ambassador to Britain and France, and served as president of Liberia College. In a lecture that he delivered at Lower Buchanan, Grand Bassa County, Liberia, in 1908, he reflected on the accomplishments and challenges of the Liberia settlement project.*

This year we celebrate the eighty-sixth anniversary of the founding of the city of Monrovia by the Negro settlers from America. The colony is nearly ninety years old. The Republic has just celebrated its Diamond Jubilee. Still Liberia is called by foreigners an experiment. Nothing of the kind has ever happened before in the world's history. A group of returned exiles—refugees from the house of bondage—settled along a few hundred miles of the coast of their Fatherland, attempting to rule millions of people, their own kith and kin, on a foreign system in which they themselves have been imperfectly trained, while knowing very little of the facts of the history of the people they assume to rule, either social, economic or religious, and taking for granted that the religious and social theories they have brought from across the sea must be adapted to all the needs of their unexpatriated brethren.

Liberia is a little bit of South Carolina, of Georgia, of Virginia—that is to say—of the ostracized, suppressed, depressed elements of these States—tacked on to West Africa—a most incongruous combination, with no reasonable prospect of success; and further complicated by additions from other sources. We take a little bit from England, a little bit from France, a little bit from Germany, and try to compromise with all. We have no definite plan, no dominating race conception, with really nothing to help us from behind—the scene whence we came—and nothing to guide us from before the goal to which we are tending or should tend. . . . We are severed from the parent stock—the aborigines—who are the root, branch, and flower of Africa and of any Negro State in Africa. . . .

Our progress will come by connection with the parent stock. The question, therefore, which we should try to study and answer is, What are the underlying principles of . . . *African* life? Every nation and every tribe has a right to demand freedom of life and abundance of life, because it has a contribution to make peculiar to itself towards the ultimate welfare of the world. But no nation can have this freedom of life, and make this contribution, which no other nation can make, without connection with its past, of which it must carefully preserve the traditions, if it is to understand the present and have an intelligent and inspiring hope of the future.

---

1. *Do you agree with Blyden's statement that "nothing of the kind has ever happened before in the world's history"?*
2. *Why did Blyden emphasize the importance of understanding the "underlying principles of African life"?*

Source: Edward Wilmot Blyden, *The Three Needs of Liberia: A Lecture Delivered at Lower Buchanan, Grand Bassa County, Liberia, February 26, 1908*, 2nd ed. (London: C. M. Phillips, printer, 1908), pp. 1–3.

LAUNCHING A JIHAD

Usuman dan Fodio was a member of the Fulani minority living in the Hausa kingdom of Gobir, in what is now northern Nigeria. He launched a successful holy war against the governments of the Hausa kingdoms and founded the Sokoto caliphate. In his Book of the Difference between the Governments of the Muslims and the Governments of the Unbelievers, *Usuman dan Fodio rejects the legitimacy of rulers who are unbelievers and lays out the principles for a proper Islamic government.*

The intention of the unbelievers in their governments is only the fulfilling of their lusts, for they are like the beasts. God Most High has said: "they are but as the cattle; nay, they are farther astray from the way!; they eat as cattle eat, and the fire shall be their lodging." . . .

The purpose of the Muslims in their governments is to strip evil things from religious and temporal affairs, and introduce reforms into religious and temporal affairs, and an example of stripping evil things from religious and temporal affairs is that every governor of a province should strive to fortify strongholds and wage holy war against the unbelievers, and the war-makers and the oppressors, and set up a military station on every frontier, and combat every cause of corruption which occurs in his country, and forbid every disapproved thing. An example of introducing reforms into religious and temporal affairs is that the governor of every country shall strive to repair the mosques, and establish the five prayers in them, and order the people to strive to read the Quran, and make [others] read it, and learn knowledge, and teach it; and that he should strive to reform the markets and set to rights the affairs of the poor and the needy, and order the doing of every approved thing. These qualities which have been mentioned in this section are the qualities of the way of the Muslims in their governments, and he who follows them in his emirship, has followed the way of Paradise, which is the straight way. God Most High has said: "and that this is My path, straight; so do you follow it, and follow not divers paths lest they scatter you from His path." And he who follows the path of the Muslims in their governments, he has obeyed God and His Messenger and God Most High has said: "whosoever obeys God and the Messenger, they are with those whom God has blessed, Prophets, just men, martyrs, the righteous; good companions they."

. . . The foundations of government are five things: the first is that authority shall not be given to one who seeks it. The second is the necessity for consultation. The third is the abandoning of harshness. The fourth is justice. The fifth is good works.

1. *What was Usuman dan Fodio's view of the purpose of Muslim governments?*
2. *What specific reforms did he intend to introduce?*

Source: M. Hiskett, "Kitab al-farq: A Work on the Habe Kingdoms Attributed to Uthman dan Fodio," *Bulletin of the School of Oriental and African Studies*, vol. 23, part 3, 1960, pp. 567, 569–570.

SHAKA GOES TO WAR

Shaka, the founder of the Zulu Kingdom, has been variously depicted as a nationalist hero and a bloodthirsty tyrant. This account was written in the Zulu language by Magema M. Fuze, a mission-educated Christian, in the early twentieth century and was published privately in 1922 under the title Abantu Abamnyama *[The Black People]. In this excerpt, Fuze recounts Shaka's war against King Zwide, who had killed Shaka's adoptive father, King Dingiswayo. The account emphasizes Shaka's brilliance as a military strategist.*

Shaka, being angered by the murder of his "father" Dingiswayo, marshalled the Zulu and the Mthethwa and the Hlubi people to arms. . . . The army sallied forth and made for the Ndwandwe country. But Zwide was very strong, and more fearsome than the other chiefs; therefore Shaka, whilst making an advance movement, wanted to draw the Ndwandwe army downwards [southwards], and as he was doing all these movements, he was devising a plan to draw Zwide into the Zulu country. And what did he intend by this? Shaka knew very well that the Ndwandwe army did not depend on cattle on the hoof for food when it fought, but on rations of millet which it carried with it, and his intention was to harass it until it became short of food and suffered from hunger. It was for this reason that he first advanced and then retreated. . . .

As for Shaka, he wanted to draw it towards the Mhlathuze river, so that it should fight at Nkandla and Nsuze, where the country is extremely broken. He had proclaimed to all the homesteads in the Zulu country that the foodstuffs should be removed, and that the homesteads should be abandoned and destroyed by fire.

And so the son of Langa [i.e., Zwide] brought his army forward until the whole of the Mahlabatini area of the Zulu country was occupied. And when the son of Senzangakhona [i.e., Shaka] saw the enemy, he arranged his own forces in inaccessible places. When he was about to launch the attack, he ascended a small hill known as Khomo near Sibhudeni. He mounted the Khomo hill and from there launched it and observed it.

There the two armies attacked one another, and there was the smell of war, and the dust rose up high. Well! Seeing that the Ndwandwe were so strong, what was the outcome? The Zulus were so enraged that their anger could only be quenched with water [a Zulu saying], and they were fighting a fight of death. For in fact, before the clash, Shaka had given the order that the bundles of spears were to be abandoned, and that each man was to carry a short stabbing spear together with only one spear for throwing as the army was about to engage. No-one carried three or more spears as was formerly the custom. . . .

The army fought with great intensity until darkness fell, and it was dreadful. For several days it fought with terrible fury. The horror continued until Shaka realized that he had mauled Zwide's forces considerably, and that they were hungry through not being able to get food anywhere, their own supplies which they carried with them being quite exhausted.

---

1. *What does the author see as Shaka's motivation for this war?*
2. *Explain the role of terrain and food supplies in Shaka's battle plans.*

Source: Magema M. Fuze, *The Black People and Whence They Came: A Zulu View*, translated by H. C. Lugg, edited by A. T. Cope (Pietermaritzburg, South Africa: University of Natal Press, and Durban, South Africa: Killie Campbell Africana Library, 1979), pp. 47–48.

FLEEING THE NGONI

Narwimba was born in East Central Africa in the highland region between Lake Malawi and Lake Tanganyika at the time when Ngoni war regiments were expanding into the region. She was uprooted several times by the Ngoni depredations, traveled long distances, and eventually joined a Christian community led by Moravian missionaries. When she was an old woman known as Grandmother Narwimba, she told her life story to a missionary, who wrote it down.

I was born in a village on the Songwe in the land of Urambya. While I was still a little child, terror came upon our land, for the Ngoni attacked our village and we fled before this terrible enemy to Karonga in the Konde country. Chief Chungu, who was then a very powerful chief, allowed my parents to settle in his land. We lived there in peace for a number of years.

When I was grown, a man came to woo me. He had to work for my parents. He tilled a large field of millet for some years during the rainy season; he brought many presents and he built them a new hut. When my father was satisfied, the man was allowed to take me to his hut and I became his wife. My husband's name was Sambi Simuchimba. Six children were born to us in the Konde country. Five of them died in infancy and we were left with one daughter named Chifuwa.

After some years, the Ngoni, those robbers and murderers, came to the Konde country and made war upon us. In the battle with them, my husband fell. Nor could our great Chief Chungu defend himself against the enemy.

Now I was a widow, and I had to see which of my husband's relations would take me to wife. In the Nyika country, some days' journey from where I now live, dwelt my husband's only sister. She had one son, named Mirambo. When he had obtained her [his mother's] consent, he took me and my child to Chitete and I became his wife. I bore Mirambo six children—three boys and three girls; of these four died. Do you know what it is like? I have mourned so many times. When they laid my children in the ground, I have lamented and wept myself hoarse until I could weep no more.

Alas! there was no peace in our country. The Ngoni, who live on Lake Nyasa, went far and wide through the land plundering and murdering. They burned the harvests in the field or mowed down what was too green to burn. All who fell into their hands were slaughtered or taken into slavery. Sometimes the enemy stayed a year, sometimes two. When they had laid waste to the land, they went back to their own country. My husband and I fled before them. We sought shelter with different chiefs and had to beg or we should have starved. Not until the enemy left the country could we return to Chitete, build up the ruined huts, and, when the rains came, till the fields.

---

1. *What was Narwimba's view of the Ngoni?*
2. *What survival strategies did Narwimba employ?*

Source: Marcia Wright, *Strategies of Slaves and Women: Life Stories from East/Central Africa* (New York: Lilian Barber Press, 1993), pp. 47–49.

PART 4

AFRICA IN THE AGE OF THE NEW IMPERIALISM, 1870–1940

Despite the rise of industrial capitalism in Atlantic Europe, the older pattern of European war capitalism continued to reign in the rest of the world well into the nineteenth century. At the southern tip of Africa, Britain captured the Cape Colony from the Dutch in 1806 and established the settler colony of Natal in 1843. It seized Hong Kong in 1841, imposed unequal treaties on China in 1842, 1858, and 1860, and took over India from the British East India Company in 1858. The French, in a similar vein, seized Algeria in 1830 and parts of Southeast Asia in the 1860s. Then came a pause as that phase in the expansion of European domination seemed to have run its course.

By 1880, however, Britain's demand for industrial raw materials and its need for new markets for its manufactured goods had reached a point at which the British government was ready to launch an aggressive expansion into distant territories that were not yet colonized. The French government was on a similar path, and other nations in Atlantic Europe quickly followed suit. This new round of imperial expansion in the late nineteenth century is known to historians as the "New Imperialism" because it was driven by the needs of European industrial economies and facilitated by the use of industrial technology.

Although examples of the New Imperialism could be seen in various parts of the world, its major thrust was toward the one continent that had hitherto largely escaped direct European control—Africa. During the 1880s, England, France, Germany, Portugal, and Belgium carved up the continent into a series of colonies as each of those countries staked its claim on certain regions of Africa to bolster its economic growth at home or enhance its status as a Great Power. That process is known as "the scramble for Africa."

The colonialism that the nations of Atlantic Europe imposed on Africa in the late nineteenth century differed significantly from the earlier colonization of the New World, where European diseases such as smallpox wiped out a large part of the Native American population. Unlike the Native Americans, Africans did not die in large numbers from exposure to European diseases because Africa had never been isolated from the Eurasian landmass, and therefore most diseases known in Europe were also known in Africa. Rather, it was the European visitors to Africa who experienced high death rates from tropical diseases unknown in the colder parts of Europe, causing the coast of West Africa to be known as the "white man's grave." During the four centuries prior to 1850, when Europeans were turning large parts of the world into settler colonies, they came to Africa primarily to trade and return home.

Five major changes altered the relationship between Africa and Europe after 1850 and created the conditions for the European scramble for Africa. The first was a change in the nature of the trade between the two regions. European commerce with Africa prior to 1850 was dominated by the slave trade, which was supplied with captives from wars among independent African chiefdoms and kingdoms. Under those circumstances, Europeans had little economic interest in imposing a colonial order that would end the wars and reduce the supply of captives. The decline of the Atlantic slave trade during the nineteenth century and the rise of commerce in minerals, animal products, tropical oils, and spices altered that situation. Warfare in the African interior, which had once fed the slave trade, came to be seen as disruptive to what the British called "legitimate trade."

A second major change was the increasing use of steam-powered trains and ships. Africa's trade with Europe had remained limited prior to 1870 because of the difficulty of transporting products of legitimate trade over long distances to coastal ports. In tropical Africa, tsetse flies carried the disease trypanosomiasis that was fatal to horses, donkeys, and oxen, and therefore trade goods had to be transported by human porters. The high cost, slow pace, and limited carrying capacity of these porters meant that only high-value goods such as gold, salt, and ivory could be profitably transported over long distances.

The 1840s were a period of railroad-building fever in Britain, inspiring a general belief that railroads were the key to Africa's economic future. The British built railways for the government of Egypt beginning in the 1850s, and they built railways in southern Africa in the 1870s and 1880s after the discovery of diamonds and gold there. Those activities prompted British dreams of a "Cape to Cairo" rail line that would run the length of the African continent. The importance of railroads in opening up commerce in the Congo River basin was made clear by the explorer Henry Morton Stanley, who claimed in 1882 that "the Congo basin is not worth a two-shilling piece in its present state. To reduce it into profitable order, a railroad must be made between the lower Congo and the upper Congo, when with its accessibility will appear its value."

Similarly, the success of steamboats in the United States after 1807 and in England after 1812 prompted Europeans to envision regular steamboat traffic on the major African rivers. The French used steamboats on the Senegal River as early as 1819, and by the 1860s, stern-wheel steamboats with shallow drafts made it possible for private British trading companies to navigate through the Niger delta and open up the Niger River to overseas commerce. Stanley was so keen to use steamboats on the Congo River that in 1879 he had two river steamboats dismantled and carried around the rapids by porters so that they could be reassembled on the upper river.

The third area of change was military technology. During the era of the slave trade, huge quantities of muskets and ammunition had poured into the coastal regions of Africa, and after 1800, ivory traders carried muskets into the far interior. With so many muskets in Africa, a similarly armed European military troop would have been at a disadvantage against African forces. However, major innovations in firearms following the American Civil War altered this equation. Repeating rifles, first used in the

Civil War, came into general use after the introduction of the Winchester repeating rifle in 1867. The Civil War also inspired the Gatling gun, a clumsy device with 6–10 barrels rotating around a central shaft. The first true machine gun was the Maxim gun, introduced in 1884 by the American Hiram Maxim, who manufactured it in England. It could shoot 11 bullets per second from a single barrel. The military advantage of the Maxim gun was summed up by the British poet Hilaire Belloc in his poem "The Modern Traveller" (1898): "Whatever happens, we have got / The Maxim Gun, and they have not."

HIRAM MAXIM'S MACHINE GUN The Maxim gun, the world's first machine gun, made its appearance in 1884, just when European armies were moving into Africa. It could fire 600 rounds per minute. In many cases, Maxim guns tipped the battles in favor of the European forces. This photo shows Hiram Maxim, the inventor and manufacturer, demonstrating his weapon.

African rulers, for their part, tried to modernize their military arsenals as best they could. Breech-loading rifles first reached West Africa in the 1870s. Samori Touré reportedly imported 6,000 French breech-loading military rifles through the port of Freetown in 1890, and his blacksmiths quickly learned how to repair and even replicate them. King Behanzin of Dahomey obtained four Krupp cannons with steel barrels and three machine guns from German merchants living in Ouidah, and he claimed to have a factory that produced gunpowder and firearms. In equatorial Africa in 1884, Tippu Tip obtained over a thousand rapid-fire rifles from the sultan of Zanzibar. Most African armies, however, were unable to match the Europeans' firepower. When a British force armed with rapid-firing Snyder-Enfield rifles marched on the capital of the Asante Empire in 1874, the British commander remarked that the British would have been annihilated if the Asante army had been armed with rapid-firing rifles instead of outdated muskets.

The fourth area of change was in medicinal discoveries that allowed Europeans to survive in the tropical African disease environment. The main killers of Europeans were mosquito-borne diseases, such as malaria and yellow fever, and waterborne diseases, such as cholera, typhoid fever, and amoebic dysentery. Outside of the Mediterranean climate zones at the northern and southern extremities of the African continent, the probability of death for a European was 50 percent in the first year of residence and 25 percent each year thereafter. Europeans had earlier encountered tropical diseases in the New World, but the African disease environment had proved to be twice as lethal as that of the Caribbean. During the 1850s, however, it was discovered that daily doses of quinine could prevent the *falciparum* malaria that was responsible for the majority of European deaths in Africa. As the use of quinine spread, the first-year death rate for Europeans fell from 50 percent to 5–10 percent. This innovation helps explain why the great expansion of European exploration and missionary activity in Africa did not take place until after 1850.

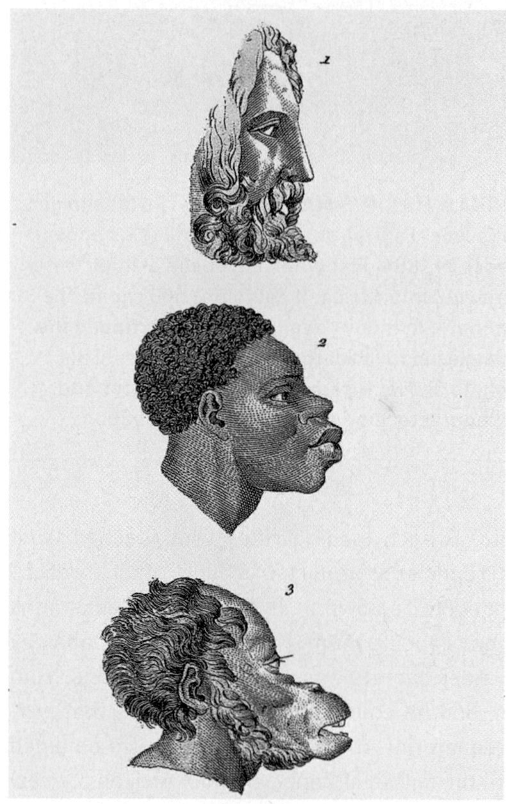

RACIST IDEAS ON DISPLAY The French naturalist Julien-Joseph Virey used the Great Chain of Being theory in 1824 to rank Africans between apes and Europeans, thus making Africans seem less than human. Drawings such as this one were used to popularize racist ideas. Note how the features of the African's head are distorted and exaggerated to make it seem more ape-like.

The fifth change was the rise of so-called scientific racism, by which Europeans sought to justify whatever prejudices they held against people of color by appealing to the biological ideas of their time. Drawing on the medieval notion of the Great Chain of Being—a linear hierarchy of all living organisms with Europeans at the top—scholars of natural history began to study human skulls in order to classify the different races, focusing on the facial angle as the primary indicator of their place in the hierarchy. Some of these natural scientists claimed that Africans possessed a facial form somewhere in between those of Europeans and apes. The development of Darwin's theory of evolution did little to overturn that basic scheme. In his 1871 book *The Descent of Man*,

Darwin put Europeans at the top of the evolutionary ladder, while ranking Africans and Australian aborigines just above the gorilla.

Racist ideas were popularized by exhibitions such as "human zoos," in which Africans, Native Americans, and other non-Western people were put on display. That trend reached its most extreme expression when the Bronx Zoo in New York City displayed an Mbuti pygmy from the Congo rainforest named Ota Benga, who was exhibited in the Monkey House along with an orangutan. The exhibit ran for only a few days before it was shut down because of protests from black ministers, but it attracted nearly 40,000 visitors in a single day, putting it on par with Coney Island as a major attraction. Many of the visitors believed that they were seeing the "missing link" between humans and apes, an idea that fused racist thought with evolutionary theory.

These changes and others gave the nations of Atlantic Europe the tools and concepts that they would use to colonize the African continent. The conquest of the African continent would have seemed unthinkable to them in 1800, or even 1850, but by the 1880s, the scramble for Africa was under way.

A HUMAN ZOO Human zoo exhibitions in which non-Western people were put on display like animals were popular in Europe and America during the late nineteenth and early twentieth centuries. This photo shows Ota Benga, an Mbuti pygmy from the Congo rainforest who was displayed in the Monkey House of the Bronx Zoo. Although the exhibition was shut down after a few days in response to protests by black clergymen in New York City, Ota Benga later grew depressed and committed suicide.

THE SENEGALESE RIFLEMEN RAISE THE FRENCH FLAG OVER TIMBUKTU Originally recruited from Senegal, this elite corps of African troops was instrumental in the French conquest of West Africa. Although the French had made incursions into the Timbuktu area since 1880, they formally occupied the city in December 1893 in order to stop the Tuareg from disrupting the trans-Saharan trade routes. This drawing was published in *Le Petit Journal* in Paris in February 1894.

1882	1884-1885	1896
British invasion of Egypt	Berlin Conference for the partition of Africa	Ethiopians win the Battle of Adwa

10

THE COLONIAL PARTITION OF AFRICA, 1870–1918

By 1870, Europeans had been trading along the Atlantic, Mediterranean, and Indian Ocean coasts of Africa for four centuries, but they had made only feeble attempts to build settlements or conquer territory. The major exceptions were at the northern and southern extremities of the continent—the only two regions with a Mediterranean climate that was hospitable to European settlers. In the north, the French conquered Algeria in 1830 and made it an official part of France in 1848. In southern Africa, the British seized the Cape Colony from the Dutch in 1806 in order to gain military and commercial control of the gateway between the Atlantic and Indian Oceans, and they established the settler colony of Natal in the fertile coastal strip between the Indian Ocean and the Drakensberg Mountains in 1843. The European conquests of Algeria and Natal were the last gasp of the settler colonialism that had dominated the world ever since Columbus discovered America. In the vast territories between the northern and southern extremities of Africa, however, tropical climates and tropical diseases had discouraged European settlement. Europeans possessed a few toeholds along the coasts and major rivers, but little more. Even counting the British and French colonies in northern and southern Africa, Europeans controlled less than 10 percent of the African continent in 1870.

The Africa that European colonizers encountered in the 1870s and 1880s was a very different place from the Africa of a hundred years earlier. Many of the kingdoms and empires that had flourished in the eighteenth century had subsequently

1899–1902	1904–1907	1905–1907
Anglo-Boer War	Herero genocide	Maji Maji Rebellion

fractured or disappeared. In the West African Sahel, the kingdoms of Segu and Kaarta had been wiped out by the jihadist forces of Umar Tal. Farther south, the powerful Asante Empire was shrinking as its northern provinces rebelled and its southern provinces sought alliances with the British, and after 1836 the Oyo Empire disintegrated into a series of warring mini-states. South of the tropical rainforest, the Kongo Kingdom remained decentralized in the wake of its destructive civil war, and its kings remained too weak to command large armies. In the southern savanna, the Lunda Empire dissolved into its component parts following its defeat by the Chokwe. In southern Africa, the Rozwi Kingdom on the Zimbabwe Plateau had succumbed to attacks by the mobile regiments of Zwangendaba's Ngoni. In the place of those former kingdoms were the new African conquerors, such as Tippu Tip, Samori Touré, Umar Tal, Muhammad Ahmad (the Mahdi), and Zwangendaba, whose innovative military tactics or access to firearms made them militarily strong, but often left them politically weak for lack of popular support in the conquered territories.

EUROPEAN EXPANSION INTO THE AFRICAN INTERIOR

Technological and medical advances in Europe during the nineteenth century had made it possible for European nations to conquer and colonize Africa, but deciding whether or not they should actually do so was a different proposition altogether. Conquest and colonization would be costly in money and lives, and the payoff was far from certain. That is why the governments of the European nations were initially reluctant to move into the interior of Africa, preferring instead to establish trading monopolies along certain stretches of the African coast while avoiding the interior regions. In 1868, for instance, the British captured the fortress of Magdala in the Ethiopian highlands in order to free several dozen British and European detainees held by Emperor Tewodros II. After looting the fortress and freeing the prisoners, the British marched back to the coast, dismantled the railroad they had built for hauling military supplies, and departed. The British acted in a similar way in 1874, after they had gained a trading monopoly over the Gold Coast by buying out the Dutch and Danish forts and proclaiming the coastal Fante Confederation to be a British crown colony. When the inland Asante Empire challenged Britain's monopoly, a British army sailed to the Gold Coast, marched inland, and sacked the Asante capital. After signing a treaty with the Asante king and receiving an indemnity of 50,000 ounces of gold, the British quickly withdrew in order to avoid the expenses and complications of a formal occupation.

Although European governments were reluctant to involve themselves with the interior regions of Africa, explorers sponsored by private geographical societies and missionaries sponsored by church mission societies moved aggressively into the very areas their governments avoided. European ships had explored the Atlantic and Indian Ocean coasts of Africa since the 1450s, but nearly 400 years later, most of the interior was still unknown territory to Europeans. They had huddled in their coastal enclaves and had largely refrained from traveling inland for fear of disease or attack. The "New Map of Africa," published in Dublin in 1805 and based on "the latest authorities," showed numerous coastal towns but left most of the interior blank, labeling it simply as "unknown parts." A map published in 1839 by the London-based Society for the Diffusion of Useful

A MOSTLY BLANK MAP The "New Map of Africa," which claimed to be based on "the latest authorities," shows the state of European knowledge about Africa in 1805. Note that the interior of the continent is largely blank, reflecting European ignorance of Africa's geography. That knowledge increased only marginally during the first half of the nineteenth century, but expanded during the second half, when explorers crisscrossed the continent.

Knowledge had only slightly less blank space than the Dublin map. Prior to the mid-nineteenth century, the Europeans had clearly lacked either the desire or the capacity to travel into the interior regions of Africa.

Geographical Societies

This situation changed with the rise of geographical societies in the major European nations during the nineteenth century. There were 12 geographical societies in Europe by 1870, and 29 by 1890. They raised money to sponsor exploration and disseminated the findings of the explorers through publications, conferences, and public lectures. The International Geographical Congress held in Paris in 1875 attracted 1,500 participants from 34 countries and included well-attended discussions about how to fill the gaps in the knowledge about the interior of Africa. That same year, the German explorer Georg Schweinfurth told the Egyptian Geographical Society that "no question has acquired more general significance for science today than the exploration of Africa." The Brussels Geographical Conference, held a year later, focused exclusively on strategies and initiatives for exploring Africa. Over the next 2 years, 11 European countries plus the United States established special committees for exploration in Africa.

In contrast to earlier European travelers in Africa, who had written travelogues about their adventures, the new breed of explorers were regarded as scientists who were gathering important data. Verney Lovett Cameron set the standard in his trek across Africa in 1873–1876, when he made nearly 4,000 measurements of altitude, 1,000 measurements of latitude and longitude, and 600 lunar observations, which were then used to help cartographers render more accurate maps. Explorers were also expected to write detailed descriptions of the flora and fauna they observed, as well as the languages and the customs of the people they encountered. In short, they were collecting information that would be useful to future colonizers. European newspapers regularly reported on the progress of the explorers, portraying their exploits in heroic terms. Some of their books became runaway best sellers, and they developed an intense rivalry over who was the greatest explorer. Two of the most famous explorers—David Livingstone and Pierre Savorgnan de Brazza—were given lavish state funerals in which they were praised as national heroes.

Missionaries

The nineteenth century also saw a surge in Christian missionary activity in Africa. The earliest European missionaries had been the Portuguese Catholics who traveled to the Kongo Kingdom, Angola, and Ethiopia in the sixteenth century. They focused on converting African kings and nobles in the hope of creating Christian kingdoms. In Ethiopia, which was already a Christian kingdom affiliated with the Egyptian Coptic Church, the missionaries briefly convinced the emperor to switch allegiance to the Roman Catholic Church in exchange for military aid from Portugal. Popular discontent, however, soon forced him to abdicate the throne in favor of his son, who reestablished the traditional ties to the Egyptian church. The early missionaries in Kongo and Angola introduced some European cultural elements in clothing styles, naming patterns, musical instruments, and burial customs along with Christian religious beliefs, but they did not seek to bring about a radical transformation of African societies. Catholic missionary societies fell on hard times after the Jesuit order was disbanded by the Pope in 1773 and religious orders in France were suppressed in the wake of the French Revolution. When Napoleon conquered Rome in 1809, he sent the Pope into exile and dissolved the *Propaganda Fide*, the organization responsible for Catholic missions. By 1820, Catholic missionary activity in Africa had reached its lowest point since the sixteenth century.

A new zeal for missionary endeavors, led initially by Protestant churches, arose in Europe and America during the nineteenth century. Several Protestant denominations founded missionary societies between 1792 and 1860, beginning with British Baptists, Anglicans, and Wesleyan Methodists as well as Scottish Presbyterians; the movement then spread to France, Switzerland, the Netherlands, Germany, and the United States. The Protestant awakening, as it was called, was followed by the formation of new Catholic missionary organizations such as the Holy Ghost Fathers, the Society of African Missions, and the White Fathers. All those mission societies remained relatively independent of their national governments and even of the Vatican.

The first concentrated missionary activities in Africa by the new mission societies involved work with the liberated Africans who settled in Sierra Leone and with the African American settlers in Liberia. The missionaries were not only preaching their Christian faith, but also helping to create a new social order composed of Africans who were Christian, educated, and practiced in European and American ways. That model was extended to other parts of Africa after 1850, when advances in the prevention and treatment of tropical diseases allowed greater numbers of European missionaries to survive in the tropical climate. The early missionaries often founded Christian villages, located some distance from existing settlements so that the new converts could develop a new kind of spiritual life apart from the traditional influences of their society. In contrast to the earlier missionaries who had sought to convert African kings and spread Christianity from the top down, the missionaries of the nineteenth century were trying to spread Christianity from the bottom up. Missionary zeal could sometimes lead to competition among rival religious organizations. Such conflicts were often resolved by dividing up the territory among the different mission societies, granting each one a monopoly over a certain region.

Nowhere was religious rivalry fiercer than in the East African kingdom of Buganda. Anglican Protestants, Catholic White Fathers, and Muslim clerics from Zanzibar all gained converts in Buganda in the 1880s. King Mwanga, who was suspicious of all foreign religious influences, ordered twenty-six of his Catholic and Protestant page boys burned alive on a great funeral pyre for resisting his sexual advances, and he initiated a wave of anti-Christian persecution. When the persecution died down, Mwanga sought to placate the new religious factions and neutralize their influence by forming religion-based military units, which were given large landed estates to provide them with income and subsistence. The plan backfired, however, and by 1886, the new military units had become the power bases for the different religious factions. Over the next decade, the politico-religious landscape shifted frequently as the rival factions jockeyed for power and influence.

As beneficiaries of the Industrial Revolution, missionaries brought to Africa not only Christian beliefs, but also technology and science. Missionaries carried medicines that were previously unknown in many parts of Africa, and they introduced ox-drawn plows to areas of southern Africa where they had not been used before. They put steamboats on the Congo River, Lake Malawi, and Lake Tanganyika before those regions were under formal European control, and they advocated modern forms of communication such as telegraph lines. The most important innovations brought by missionaries were related to literacy and printing. Mission societies developed ways to write various African languages using the standard 26-letter Roman alphabet. The Protestant missionaries translated all or parts of the Bible into those languages and set up printing presses to produce vernacular-language Bibles. Catholic missionaries preferred their Latin Bible, as they did in Europe, but they translated and printed catechisms, devotional books, selections from the Bible, and books on the lives of saints. All of this activity required educated African Christians to read the mission publications, and so the missionaries produced textbooks in local African languages for their schools. The creation and maintenance of schools became an indispensable aspect of missionary activity.

THE SCRAMBLE FOR AFRICA

The term **scramble for Africa** refers to the period from the late 1870s to the late 1890s—a time when the European powers made claims on African territory, signed treaties with one another to fix the borders of their new colonies, and mobilized armies to conquer the territories they had claimed. As the term implies, the scramble was not a coordinated or well-planned effort among the European powers to gain control of Africa. Rather, it was the result of fierce competition and rivalry. When one European power claimed exclusive rights to a certain part of Africa, its rivals scrambled to claim the other parts for fear of being left out. The process was as chaotic as it was brutal.

The spark that may have set off the scramble for Africa was the decision by the French colonizers in Senegal in 1879 to build an 800-mile railroad running east from the port city of Dakar to the Middle Niger region, which would pass through territory that the French did not control. Over the next 3 years, the French moved inland, establishing forts and surveying for the rail line. African misgivings about this activity were revealed by the ruler of Segu, who detained the leader of the French survey team for 10 months. In building a railroad between the Atlantic Ocean and the Middle Niger River, the French had, in effect, committed to annexing the vast territory in between.

While the French were making far-reaching decisions in Senegal, a crisis was brewing in Egypt. Under the rule of Khedive Ismail, Egypt had undertaken a major program of modernization, building over a thousand miles of railroads, continuing to modernize the army, and transforming Alexandria into a great Mediterranean port. Much of this modernization had been financed by foreign loans incurred during the American Civil War, when American cotton was kept off the market and the demand for Egyptian cotton soared. When the war was over and American cotton reentered the world market, the price dropped, and Egypt found itself unable to repay its loans. Facing bankruptcy, Khedive Ismail agreed in 1878 to grant British and French officials joint control of Egypt's finances.

Although the Anglo-French collaboration made some progress toward paying off the debts, it put new strains on Egypt's domestic budget. With military pay falling into arrears, the army mutinied in 1879 and 1881, and in June 1882, 50 Europeans were killed in a riot in Alexandria. Fearing that Egypt was descending into chaos and that British investments in the Suez Canal were in danger, a British army invaded Egypt in September and defeated the Egyptian army in a series of battles. The British had initially planned to secure the Suez Canal, restore order, and then withdraw (as they had earlier done in Ethiopia and Asante), but when they discovered that the Egyptian government had collapsed, they decided to stay on and rule Egypt themselves. British Prime Minister William Ewart Gladstone remarked, "We have done our Egyptian business, and we are an Egyptian government." Egypt was now a British colony, and the Anglo-French Dual Control agreement was in tatters.

Events moved at lightning speed over the next 2 years. In November 1882, the French parliament ratified a treaty that the explorer Brazza had signed with the Teke King Makoko, which gave France sovereignty over a vast territory north and west of the Congo River. In a debate that lasted less than an hour, nobody thought to ask if King Makoko understood that by affixing his X to a treaty written in French, he was signing away his country. In February 1884, the British government signed a treaty with Portugal recognizing Portugal's claims over the mouth of the Congo River (although the treaty was never ratified by the British parliament), and later that year, Germany proclaimed protectorates over Namibia, Cameroon, and Togo.

The Berlin Conference of 1884–1885

By late 1884, it had become clear that a scramble for Africa was under way, and some Europeans worried that it could lead to war among European nations that made rival claims to African territory. To prevent that from happening, 12 European countries, plus the United States and Turkey, met in Berlin between November 1884 and February 1885 to set some ground rules for the partition of Africa. The first issue discussed at the **Berlin Conference** was the Congo River basin, a vast area that had been largely unknown to Europeans until Henry Morton Stanley traced the course of the river in 1876–1877. Instead of awarding control to a major European nation, however, the conference decided to give most of it to King Leopold II of Belgium, who promised to make it a free-trade zone, where companies from all nations could conduct business. Because the territory was awarded to King Leopold personally (and not to Belgium), the colony was called the Congo Free State.

The second issue discussed at the conference was the lower Niger River. After Britain fought off a proposal to make it an international free-trade zone similar to the Congo, the conference recognized Britain's predominant position on the lower and middle Niger. The final issue was how to handle any new European claims to African territory. The conference participants decided that claims would be recognized by the other European powers only if the claimant exercised "effective occupation of the territory." The Berlin Conference thus marked the end of the period when European governments could claim territory that they did not actually control and the beginning of their efforts to conquer and occupy the claimed territories.

Partition on the Ground

The European conquest and partition of Africa would take many years. It was not accomplished in a single war, but rather in a long series of wars fought in far-flung places with a shifting cast of soldiers, foes, and allies. One key to the

Europeans' success was their use of African soldiers. Beginning in 1857, the French in Senegal had created professional African military units known as the Senegalese Riflemen, made up largely of former slaves. In addition, they incorporated prisoners of war and escaped slaves into their army as they moved across the West African Sahel. The result of this strategy could be seen in the French force that attacked Segu in 1890: it consisted of 103 French officers, engineers, and artillery specialists; 634 regular African soldiers; and 1,466 irregular African soldiers who were unpaid but allowed to plunder and collect booty.

Other colonial invaders also relied on African troops. The Italian military column that fought (and lost) the decisive Battle of Adwa in Ethiopia in 1896 consisted of a hundred Italians and over 4,000 African soldiers, a group that included escaped slaves, fugitives from a criminal past, and other marginalized persons seeking a fresh start and a steady paycheck. Hausa soldiers from what is now northern Nigeria formed the core of the British expeditionary force in southern Nigeria in 1893, and Hausa soldiers were recruited to fight in the Congo for the Belgian King Leopold II. Soldiers from Zanzibar, who were conditioned by years of working in trading caravans, were much in demand by European armies in East Africa and the Congo.

The other key to European success was enlisting African allies. This approach is sometimes referred to as the "divide and conquer" strategy. African rulers had no way of knowing that large parts of Africa had already been partitioned at the Berlin Conference, or that the European nations were under diplomatic pressure to establish "effective occupation" of territories. Operating on the assumption that the Europeans had come to plunder, enslave, and then depart, some chiefs allied themselves with the European armies in order to gain an advantage over rival chiefs. They soon discovered, to their chagrin, that this time the invaders had come to stay.

During the colonial invasion of Tippu Tip's Manyema Empire, for example, Ngongo Luteta, who was one of Tippu Tip's top generals, decided to switch sides after being on the losing end of several skirmishes. He delivered his soldiers and 2,000 guns to fight for King Leopold's Congo Free State. At about the same time, a Luba chief named Lumpungu, who had chafed under the domination of Tippu Tip's empire, entered into a military alliance with the colonial forces, contributing his soldiers and 3,000 guns. The two defections tipped the odds in favor of the colonial forces. When the final phase of the war began, the colonial forces consisted of a handful of Belgian officers, three or four hundred regular African troops (mostly Hausa mercenaries and some locally recruited Africans), and twenty thousand allied African troops.

THE FIRST WAVE OF AFRICAN RESISTANCE

Despite the technological and strategic advantages enjoyed by the European invaders, African resistance was often vigorous and prolonged. The advance of the invading armies was normally accompanied by heavy fighting and destruction. Instead of a single conquest of Africa, there were hundreds of conquests of individual villages, chiefdoms, and kingdoms, each with its own story. This section will give four examples of European conquest and African resistance, including one in which the European invaders were defeated and driven out.

Samori Touré in West Africa

The major obstacle to the French conquest of West Africa was Samori Touré, the cola nut trader and conqueror who had created a powerful empire in the 1870s (see chapter 8). After his attempt to establish Islam as the ideological foundation of his political system incited a popular rebellion against his rule in 1887, he had rebuilt his state on the basis of personal loyalty to himself. Although he had initially negotiated peacefully with the French, he feared that a conflict with them was inevitable. He began to purchase large quantities of modern firearms from British traders in Freetown, Sierra Leone, and his blacksmith shops copied them to produce similar models. He also hired African soldiers who had previously fought for the British and French colonial armies to teach his soldiers European military tactics.

In 1891, when the French drove Samori out of his capital at Kankan after heavy fighting, he retreated to the southeast, evacuating people and food supplies along the route and burning the houses in his wake to force the French army to travel through scorched-earth territory. When the French sent caravans with food and supplies, Samori's forces attacked them. Samori soon established a new empire beyond the reach of the French by conquering parts of existing states such as Abron and Kong. After his forces beat back French advances in 1895, 1897, and in July 1898, he retreated to the Dan Mountains, where lack of food and constant harassment by the local population led many of his soldiers to desert to the French side. A French reconnaissance force caught him by surprise in September 1898 and arrested him. He was sent into exile in Gabon, where he died 2 years later of bronchial pneumonia.

Mahdist Resistance in Sudan

Like the French, the British faced determined resistance and occasional defeat. Some of the bloodiest fighting was in Sudan, which had been progressively taken over by Egypt during the nineteenth century. Britain gained authority over Sudan

THE SQUARE THAT BROKE The Battle at Abu Klea, where the Mahdist forces in Sudan inflicted heavy damage on the British Camel Corps, was remembered for its fierce hand-to-hand fighting. Despite their losses, the Camel Corps reached Khartoum in January 1885 only to find that the city had fallen 2 days earlier.

in 1882 as a consequence of establishing a protectorate over Egypt. With the jihad led by Muhammad Ahmad, who called himself the Mahdi, conquering large areas of Sudan (see chapter 9), the British sent General Charles Gordon to evacuate the Egyptian garrison in Khartoum, which was located at the junction of the Blue Nile and the White Nile. Instead of evacuating the Sudanese capital, however, Gordon fortified it and called for reinforcements to make a stand against the Mahdi's army. When the Mahdi's forces surrounded the city in April 1884, the British sent a relief expedition to Khartoum. Traveling up the Nile on a flotilla of over 200 small boats that could navigate the rapids, the relief expedition split up. The largest group continued by boat, and the Camel Corps formed a flying column of some 1,400 men to travel by land and meet up with General Gordon's steamboats just north of Khartoum.

When the Camel Corps approached the wells at Abu Klea on January 16, 1884, after traveling 43 miles over desert sands without any water, they found the wells in the hands of Mahdist forces. In the battle the next day, the British soldiers formed a square with all their guns pointing outward in order to fight off an attack

MAXIM GUNS AT OMDURMAN Maxim guns are arrayed against the Mahdist forces of Sudan at Omdurman (across the Nile from Khartoum) in 1898. The British had 20 Maxims on wheels (as shown here) and 24 more mounted on riverboats on the Nile. After the fighting stopped, a British officer remarked that it was "not a battle, but an execution."

from any direction, but the Mahdist forces broke through the square and fought the British hand to hand. Although the Camel Corps used camels to travel from place to place, they fought their battles on foot like infantry soldiers. What saved the British forces from annihilation was the dense mass of camels in the middle of the square, which prevented the Mahdist forces from effectively occupying the center. Despite their losses at Abu Klea and again at Abu Kru 2 days later, the Camel Corps finally rejoined the Nile and arrived at Khartoum on two riverboats on January 28, 1885, only to discover that the Mahdist forces had taken the city 2 days earlier, and that General Gordon and the Egyptian garrison were all dead. The boats turned around and headed back to Egypt.

Sudan remained under Mahdist control until 1898, when the British returned with **Maxim guns** (the earliest machine guns) and heavy artillery to rout the Mahdist forces at Omdurman, just across the White Nile from Khartoum. Armed with 20 Maxim guns, and backed up by 11 steam-powered gunships on the Nile fitted with another 24 Maxim guns, the British killed 11,000 Mahdist soldiers and severely wounded another 16,000, while their forces suffered only 47 killed and some 400 wounded. One eyewitness described dead bodies "spread evenly over acres and acres," and concluded that what he had seen "was not a battle, but an execution."

Decentralized Resistance in Southeastern Nigeria

Resistance to the British invaders took a very different form in the forests of southeastern Nigeria, where the Igbo people had a decentralized political system in which each village was independent and there were no chiefs. Instead, each village was governed by a council of elders representing the major lineages. Not wishing to invade the numerous Igbo villages one by one, the British decided that all of the Igbo people were under the occult control of the Arochukwu oracle (see chapter 6) and that every anti-British act throughout Igbo country was inspired or ordered by him. As a result, the British devised a plan to invade the town of Arochukwu and capture the oracle. The invading army consisted of 74 British officers and 3,464 African soldiers supported by several Maxim guns.

In early December 1901, four military columns converged on Arochukwu and captured the town in a single day. They failed to capture the oracle, but they blew up the sacred grove where he made his pronouncements. Then the four columns marched through southern Igboland, where they destroyed villages, looted barns filled with yams, and seized more than 25,000 rifles and percussion cap muskets. Fifteen thousand refugees fled to two Catholic missions that were located north of the fighting area. Outnumbered and outgunned, many of the Igbo villages capitulated, but others built stockades across the roads and dug trenches along the sides of the roads to ambush the advancing columns. In one village, the British forces reported that after they had occupied the marketplace and formed a defensive square, the Igbo villagers "made a determined attack on all sides of the square, advancing with great bravery, but were repulsed with heavy loss, suffering principally from the effect of the Maxim and M/m gun fires." Once again, it was the Maxim gun that tipped the balance in favor of the British.

The British conquest of Igboland has been referred to by Nigerian historians as a "conquest in detail" because it was carried out village by village. Many villages that initially surrendered to the British resumed their independent ways as soon as the troops moved on. In the years following the Arochukwu campaign, the majority of British military expeditions were in areas that had previously been conquered, but had refused to stay conquered. By 1904, the area of British authority extended only about 50 miles inland from the coast and a few miles on either side of the Niger and Cross Rivers, and by 1910, a missionary wrote that "almost continual expeditions, which the newspapers never mention, take place in the interior of the country." It was not until the end of World War I that the British could finally claim control of Igbo country.

Ethiopians Drive Out the Italians

The most successful resistance against the invading Europeans was mounted by the kingdom of Ethiopia. In 1885, the Italians seized the Red Sea port of Massawa and moved inland to occupy the Eritrean Plateau, just north of Ethiopia. They then moved into northern Ethiopia, and from there they proclaimed a protectorate over the entire kingdom. In response, Ethiopian Emperor Menelik II began importing large quantities of firearms. By 1893, he was in possession of a large number of repeating breech-loading rifles (including American-made Remingtons and Winchesters) and 42 French-made Hotchkiss mountain artillery pieces that he had purchased from an arms dealer in Paris. Weighing only 362 pounds, including the wheeled carriage, the Hotchkiss mountain guns could be dismantled and carried over rough terrain by mules.

THE BATTLE OF ADWA This popular Ethiopian painting of the 1896 Battle of Adwa was produced in the 1940s by an unknown artist. Emperor Menelik II is at the far top left, and Empress Taitu is on a horse at the bottom left. The Ethiopian general is on a horse in the center, wearing a lion's-mane headdress. Saint George, the patron saint of Ethiopia, hovers above the battle throwing a spear at the Italians. Ethiopian soldiers are shown full face (which symbolizes good people), while the Italians are shown in profile (which symbolizes bad people). After the Ethiopian victory, the Italians withdrew from the country.

The Ethiopian and Italian armies met in the rugged mountains near Adwa on March 1, 1896. Menelik positioned his forces in a natural saddle between two large hills that protected their flanks and provided a platform for the Hotchkiss guns. Spotting an opening between the two advancing Italian brigades, he directed 15,000 soldiers into the gap and split the Italian forces. By 9:30 in the morning, the **Battle of Adwa** was effectively over, although the fighting continued well into the afternoon. The Ethiopians completely routed the Italian forces, capturing 11,000 rifles and all of their artillery.

One key to the Ethiopian victory was their Hotchkiss guns, which were able to take out the Italian artillery batteries because they had a longer range. With its rifled barrel, the Hotchkiss gun had a range of 2 miles with a high degree of accuracy. It was a rare moment when African forces had the advantage of superior weapons. After the battle, the Italians withdrew and signed a treaty recognizing the independence of Ethiopia. As a result, Ethiopia remained an independent kingdom throughout Africa's colonial period. Today, Ethiopians celebrate March 2 as a national holiday that commemorates the victory at Adwa.

EUROPEAN EXPANSION IN SOUTHERN AFRICA

The pattern of European conquest was somewhat different in southern Africa. The British already had control over the Cape Colony and Natal, and white Boer emigrants from the Cape Colony had already moved north and established the Orange Free State and the South African Republic. North of those colonies, the Portuguese were slowly expanding their territory inland from the Indian Ocean coast in Mozambique and from the Atlantic coast in Angola. In the 1880s, however, the middle zone between Mozambique and Angola, which the British called "Central Africa," was still unconquered. The Portuguese had long dreamed of extending their two colonies inland until they controlled all of Central Africa, thus creating a band of Portuguese rule that extended across Africa from east to west. The British, however, also hoped to control the region, which was essential to their dream of a Cape to Cairo railroad. Yet another incentive for colonization in Central Africa was the gold mines of the Zimbabwe Plateau, which had supplied gold to the Indian Ocean trading networks for centuries. Some Europeans believed that they were the legendary mines of the biblical King Solomon.

We saw in chapter 9 how the Ngoni regiments of Zwangendaba and Nxaba had migrated northward to the Zimbabwe Plateau in the 1820s, destroyed the Rozwi Kingdom, and then moved on to the north in search of new pastures for their cattle. In 1838, the Rozwi territory was conquered again, this time by the migrating regiments of Chief Mzilikazi, who had been driven out of the South

African plateau by Boer settlers (who had themselves left the Cape Colony during the Great Trek). After a migration of some 1,500 miles, Mzilikazi and his followers settled on the Zimbabwe Plateau, where he founded a state that became known as the Ndebele Kingdom. He subsequently tried to conquer the Shona chiefdoms to the east, but they defended themselves and maintained their independence.

Mzilikazi nevertheless claimed sovereignty over many of the Shona chiefdoms, and he exacted tribute from them in return for leaving them alone. Chiefs who refused to pay were subject to periodic raiding. When Mzilikazi died in 1868, he was succeeded by his son, Lobengula. By the 1880s, King **Lobengula** was besieged by a variety of English, German, Portuguese, and Boer seekers of gold-mining concessions. He refused them all, in part because he suspected that the Portuguese and Boers wanted his land as well as his gold. But then he encountered a concession seeker who was much harder to refuse: Cecil Rhodes.

King Lobengula versus Cecil Rhodes

Cecil Rhodes (whom we met in chapter 8) had made a fortune by investing in diamond and gold mines in what is now South Africa. He was convinced that the legendary goldfields on the Zimbabwe Plateau would yield as much gold as his mines on the Witwatersrand, and he referred to the Zimbabwe Plateau as the "second Rand." Knowing that King Lobengula had been denying mining concessions, Rhodes approached him with cunning and duplicity. First, he sent John Moffat, a trusted missionary, to persuade Lobengula to sign a treaty of friendship with Britain. The treaty stipulated that Lobengula would not enter into treaties with any other foreign powers, nor cede any part of his country without the consent of the British high commissioner.

Rhodes then sent his agents to King Lobengula to negotiate an agreement by which Rhodes would gain mining rights in return for providing the king with modern weapons. The king agreed, under the erroneous belief that the British were interested only in his minerals and not in his land, and also because he hoped that granting a monopoly to Rhodes would rid him of the other concession seekers. Rhodes's agents assured Lobengula that no more than 10 white men would mine in his territory, but that promise was left out of the English-language version of the agreement, which Lobengula signed with an X. Moreover, the agreement contained vague language that allowed the miners to do "all things that they may deem necessary" to procure gold and make a profit. When Lobengula later discovered that he had been tricked into signing away his country, he dispatched two ambassadors to London to renounce the agreement, but the British government ignored his request.

Rhodes then created a new company called the British South Africa Company (BSAC). He used his agreement with King Lobengula to obtain a charter from the British government that allowed the company to "make treaties, promulgate laws, preserve peace, and maintain a police force, and acquire new concessions" in the region from the Molopo River (which forms the border between present-day South Africa and Botswana), to the Great Lakes of Central Africa, some 1,500 miles to the north. The charter, in effect, gave the BSAC the authority to act like the government of a sovereign state. It also gave Rhodes official authorization to do just about anything he wanted in the vast territory of Central Africa.

Rhodes and the Pioneer Column

Within a year of receiving his charter, Rhodes sent a group of 200 white men recruited from the Cape Colony to settle permanently on the Zimbabwe Plateau and engage in farming and mining. Each had been promised 15 gold claims (amounting to about 23 acres apiece) and roughly 5 square miles of land. They were accompanied by 200 soldiers from the company's private army, who were equipped with breech-loading rifles, 7-pound field guns, and Maxim guns. The "pioneer column," as it was called, did not seek to enter Lobengula's Ndebele Kingdom, but instead skirted its eastern borders and settled among the weaker independent Shona chiefdoms, seizing land and mining locations.

Lobengula, who claimed hegemony over the Shona chiefdoms, considered sending soldiers to expel the white intruders, but he feared that such an action would provoke a war with the British. Instead, his soldiers launched several raids into independent Shona chiefdoms to assert his claims to sovereignty over the entire region. The BSAC responded by declaring war against the Ndebele Kingdom, using the raids as a pretext. It launched an attack led by BSAC horsemen, who had each been promised 20 gold claims and 10 square miles of land. When their rapidly moving flying column entered Lobengula's capital city of Bulawayo on November 3, 1893, they found it abandoned and burned. Lobengula had destroyed his city and fled northward across the Zambezi River with his troops to seek refuge among the Ngoni, but he died of smallpox a few months later.

The white settlers soon discovered, to their chagrin, that most of the gold mines had been worked out long ago, and that the Zimbabwe Plateau would never be a "second Rand." They had, however, seized good farmland and pastureland, so the BSAC decided to create a colony of white settlers who would own large farms worked by African laborers. Accordingly, it claimed all the land in the central part of the former Ndebele Kingdom and forced the Ndebele chiefs into outlying areas with poor land and water resources. Those who chose to remain on their land were

SPIRIT MEDIUMS IN CAPTIVITY This rare photo shows Charwe, who channeled the fertility spirit Nehanda (left), and Gumboreshumba, who channeled the hunting spirit Kaguvi, in prison after their capture in 1897. The two spirit mediums were executed for encouraging the Shona people to rebel against the white settlers brought in by Cecil Rhodes and his British South Africa Company. Nehanda-Charwe's heroism later became a source of inspiration for Zimbabwe's liberation struggle in the 1970s.

forced to labor on white farms. The BSAC also conducted cattle raids, seizing about 160,000 head of cattle and moving them to the white farms. To support its occupation, the BSAC began building a railway to Bulawayo. In 1895, the territory was named Rhodesia, in honor of Cecil Rhodes.

The Ndebele Resistance

The following year, however, the people of the former Ndebele Kingdom rose in rebellion against the white settlers. The British South Africa Company rushed in reinforcements and put down the rebellion after 6 months of heavy fighting. The Ndebele rebellion inspired the people in the Shona chiefdoms to the east to rebel as well. They did so partly in response to white settlers raiding Shona villages to forcibly recruit laborers and company tax collectors launching raids to seize cattle.

Women as well as men took part in the rebellion; while the men attacked white settlements, the women would make off with their cattle. The Shona rebels received inspiration and blessings from local spirit mediums, the most prominent of whom was a woman named Charwe, who was a medium of the fertility spirit Nehanda. The British reported that **Nehanda-Charwe** was "by far the most important wizard in Mashonaland," as shown by the gifts and tribute she received from Shona chiefs for bringing rain and fertility to the land. The rebellion lasted until December 1897, after Nehanda-Charwe had been captured. She was later executed by the British and buried in a secret grave because they feared that her burial place might become a shrine or pilgrimage site that would strengthen anti-British resistance. Despite the British efforts to erase her from popular memory, she remained a revered historical figure and a symbol of courage and resistance.

The Anglo-Boer War

The final war in the European partition of Africa was fought not against African chiefs or kings, but against the white Boers who had established two independent republics—the Orange Free State and the South African Republic—to the north of the British-controlled Cape Colony. In these "republics," Africans, who made up the overwhelming majority of the population, were not allowed to vote.

The underlying issue was control of the rich gold mines on the Witwatersrand, which was located in the Boer-dominated South African Republic. Roughly one-third of the world's gold production came from those mines. Investors, businessmen, engineers, and prospectors flocked to the region from a variety of European countries and the United States, although the vast majority of them were British. Wary of the influx of foreigners, the Boer government imposed taxes on the mining industry and instituted tariffs, licensing, and other administrative controls. It also alarmed the British by building a railroad to the Portuguese-controlled port on Delagoa Bay, thus bypassing the British-controlled ports in the Cape Colony and Natal. The mining magnates, including Cecil Rhodes, wanted the Boer government to institute policies more favorable to their interests, but white foreigners did not have the right to vote in the South African Republic. To further diminish foreign influence, the Boer government increased the residency requirement for voting from 5 years to 14 years.

When Cecil Rhodes became the prime minister of the British-run Cape Colony in 1890, he used his influence to pass a series of laws favorable to the diamond mine owners and industrialists, including one, known as the Glen Gray Act, that pushed Africans off their land to make them available as laborers in white-owned industries. He was frustrated, however, because he had no way to impose similar policies in the goldfields of the Witwatersrand, which were located in the Boer-dominated South African Republic. The solution, as he saw it, was to take over the goldfields.

With the complicity of the British colonial secretary, Joseph Chamberlain, and some of the mining magnates, Rhodes sent out a raiding party of 500 men commanded by Leander Starr Jameson that was supposed to take the mining city of Johannesburg by surprise and hand the country over to the British. On January 2, 1896, the raiders were captured 25 miles short of Johannesburg. The failure of the Jameson raid persuaded Chamberlain that direct British action was needed. Britain issued an ultimatum to the Boers and sent troops to South Africa. Believing that war was inevitable and not wishing to wait until more British troops arrived, the two Boer republics declared war on the British on October 11, 1899.

The **Anglo-Boer War** lasted 3 years. At its peak, the British had 200,000 soldiers on the ground. In all, about 450,000 men in uniform, drawn from Britain and other British Commonwealth countries, served on the British side. The British captured the South African Republic's capital, Pretoria, during the first year, forcing President Paul Kruger to flee to Europe, but Boer commandos waged fierce guerilla warfare in the rural areas, harassing British forces, disrupting transportation lines, and raiding supply depots.

The British responded with a scorched-earth strategy. They burned 30,000 Boer farmsteads, destroyed crops, poisoned wells, and seized livestock. To protect their supply lines, they used armored trains and built 8,000 fortified blockhouses (many of them linked together by telephone lines and nearly 4,000 miles of barbed-wire fences) to protect key points. They rounded up white women, children, and the elderly, as well as Africans who were suspected of helping the Boers—100,000 people in total—and put them in detention camps, where disease was rampant due to abysmal sanitary conditions and shortages of food. An estimated 28,000 whites and 14,000 Africans died of disease while interned. By the end of the war, roughly one-half of the white population of the Boer republics was either a prisoner of war or held in a detention camp. All of those measures wore down the Afrikaners, who signed a treaty recognizing British sovereignty in 1902.

AN AFRICAN SCOUT DIRECTS BRITISH TROOPS This drawing from the *Illustrated London News* in 1899 shows British troops guided by an African scout on their way to Mafeking. During the Anglo-Boer war, many Africans aided the British against the Boers by serving as scouts, wagon drivers, messengers, cattle drivers, and guards.

The Anglo-Boer War has often been portrayed as a "white man's war," but Africans played key roles on both sides. African farm laborers who remained loyal to their Boer landlords provided essential support services, such as driving supply wagons and taking care of Boer farms when their landlords were away fighting. Other Africans favored the British over the Boers. More than 50,000 Africans were employed as wagon drivers, cattle drivers, scouts, messengers, and guards for the British army. The fortified blockhouses that were the key to the British strategy were each manned by seven British soldiers and four African night guards. In many cases, African scouts directed the British troops.

The most significant actions of the African population, however, came in taking advantage of the chaos and dislocation of the war to reclaim their land. In both of the Boer republics, the great majority of the land had been seized by the government and given to white settlers, reducing the Africans to tenant laborers. In one area, the Africans removed all Boer property markers to show that the white settlers no longer owned the land. Many Boer soldiers returned from the battlefield to find armed Africans blocking them from their former farms. When General Louis Botha, the commander in chief of the Boer army, went home to visit his farm, the local Africans told him that he was not welcome and should move on. Boer leaders cited the attacks by armed Africans as one of their primary reasons for surrendering. During the peace negotiations, the British betrayed their African allies by promising that all Boer soldiers who laid down their arms would get their land back.

THE CHANGING MAP OF AFRICA

On May 5, 1898, the *Independent*, a New York weekly magazine, published a set of maps of Africa to show the changes that had taken place over the previous half century. The smaller inset map was labeled "Africa 1848." It showed the territory of French domination along the Mediterranean coast of Algeria, Ottoman Turkish hegemony over much of northeastern Africa, Portuguese domination along the coasts of Angola and Mozambique, and British domination at the southern tip of the continent. Inland from the coasts, however, the interior was largely blank, with vast areas labeled "Unexplored Areas" or "Great Desert."

The main map, which showed Africa in 1898, was mostly filled in with colors representing the British, French, German, Portuguese, Italian, and Spanish colonies. Ethiopia and Liberia (which had been recognized as an independent republic by the United States in 1847) were shown as independent countries, as was Morocco, which would be divided between France and Spain in 1904, and Libya, which would be colonized by the Italians following the Italo-Turkish war in 1911–1912. The area of Sudan controlled by the Mahdi was shown as disputed territory, but that situation would soon change when the British defeated the

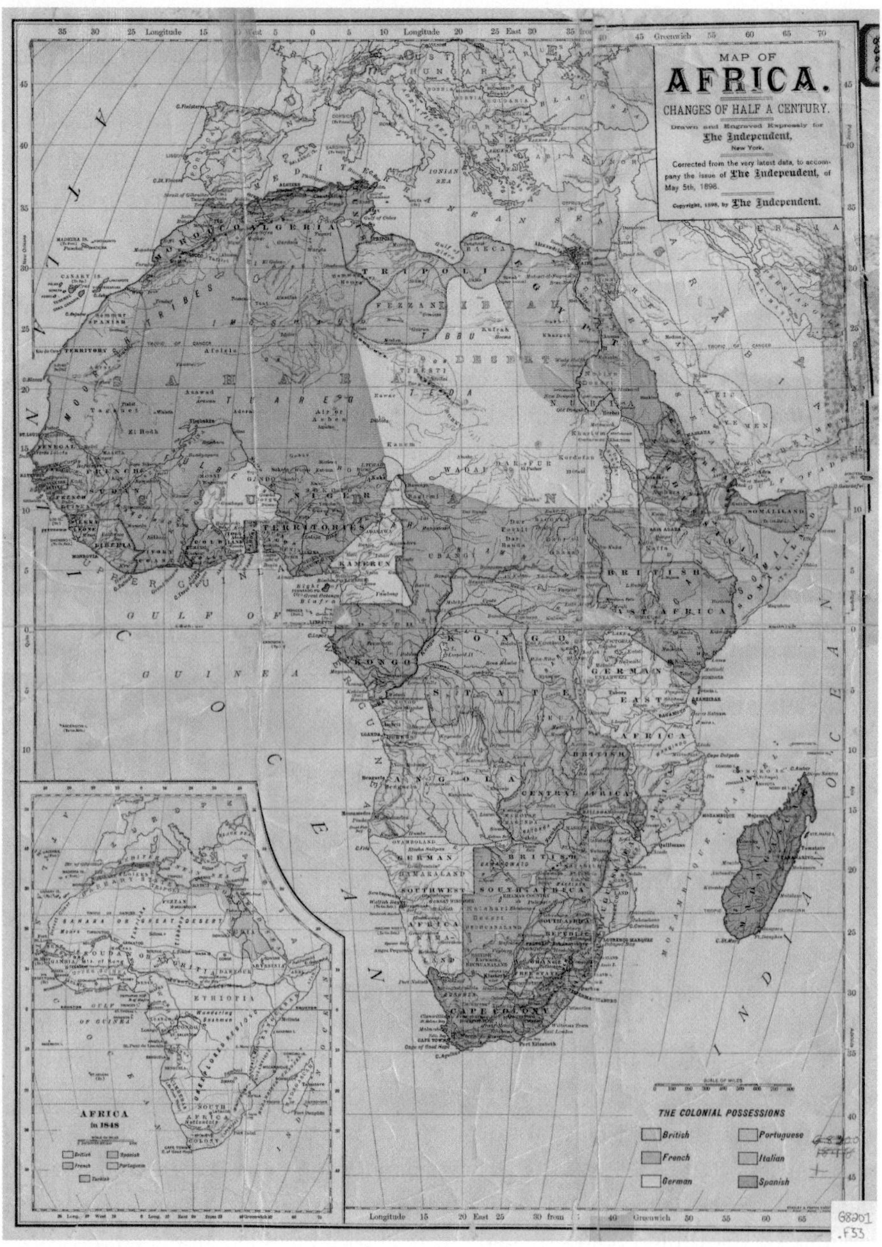

THE CHANGING MAP OF AFRICA The map of Africa was changed radically between 1848 and 1898 by the colonial partition of the continent. Notice that the 1848 map in the lower left corner is mostly blank, whereas the larger 1898 map is filled in with colors representing the European colonial powers.

Mahdi's forces at Omdurman 4 months later. When viewed together, the two maps of Africa capture the rapidity of its change from a continent filled with independent empires, kingdoms, chiefdoms, and village democracies to a continent filled in with the colors of colonial rule.

EARLY COLONIALISM

Once the Europeans had established "effective occupation" of their African colonies, they had to figure out how to govern the territories that they had seized. The partition of Africa had not been carefully thought out or planned; indeed many of the European commanders on the ground had advanced without waiting for orders from their superiors, and in some cases they went into battle despite specific orders to halt and wait for instructions. They were making it up as they went along. For Africans, the colonial occupation was unlike anything they had ever known. Warfare in precolonial Africa had often taken the form of cattle or slave raids, in which the attackers took what they wanted and then left. In other cases, vanquished chiefs and kings had been forced to pay tribute, but they had been otherwise left to manage local affairs as they saw fit. The total domination exercised by the colonial conquerors was something new entirely.

The first order of business for the Europeans was to establish their authority. Knowing that they were distrusted and hated, colonial officials often resorted to brutality to instill fear in the African populations. Gabriel Louis Angoulvant, the French governor-general of Côte d'Ivoire, made this point very clearly in 1908 when he wrote, "What has to be established above all is the indisputable principle of our authority. On the part of the natives, the acceptance of this principle must be expressed in a deferential welcome and absolute respect for our representatives." He added that "signs of impatience or disrespect toward our authority are to be repressed without delay." Angoulvant also articulated the outlines of the colonial project, which required that Africans demonstrate their acquiescence to the colonial authority "in the full payment of taxes, in serious cooperation in the construction of [railroad] tracks and roads, in the acceptance of paid porterage, and in following our advice in regard to labor." In other words, he planned to use the taxes and labor power of the African population to advance the colonial project.

During the early years of colonial rule, the boundaries between colonies were frequently adjusted by bilateral treaties, and the names of the colonies were sometimes changed as colonial administrative systems were organized and reorganized. The region referred to in this chapter as the French Congo, for example, was at first a part of the colony of Gabon and was sometimes called Gabon-Congo.

It was renamed Middle Congo in 1903, separated from Gabon in 1906, and took the name French Congo in 1910, when it became a part of a larger entity called French Equatorial Africa. To minimize the confusion, this book will use the names of the modern African countries whenever possible, except for cases in which the colonial names had a specific historical meaning during the periods under discussion.

Building Railroads

One priority in many of the colonies was to build railroads, a task that required massive amounts of conscripted African labor. Workers were usually recruited by force, and they could not walk off the job if they were dissatisfied with their meager pay. The British dream of a Cape to Cairo railroad was never realized, but many shorter rail lines were built to carry African commodities from the interior to the coast for transshipment to Europe.

Two of the most ambitious railway projects were along the lower Congo River, where some 200 miles of rapids and waterfalls separated the mouth of the river from the middle Congo, which was navigable by steamboat for a thousand miles. The task was to build a railroad through the rugged Cristal Mountains and around the rapids. It was further complicated by the fact that the Belgian King Leopold II controlled the south bank of the river, while parts of the north bank were controlled by the French. Because of tensions between the Belgians and the French, both colonial powers would build railroads that ran roughly parallel to each other and, in some places, were only a few miles apart.

The first attempt at a railway through the Cristal Mountains was made by King Leopold's Congo Free State. Although the line was only 241 miles long, the project took 8 years to complete, employing up to 60,000 workers at a time. To maintain discipline, many workers were brought to the work site in chains, like members of a prison chain gang, and the 200-man railway police force administered frequent floggings to recalcitrant workers. Many workers died as a result of accidents (such as the explosion of a train car full of dynamite), poor nutrition, lack of shelter, and disease. Although Congo Free State officials would admit to only 1,800 African deaths, local legend held that each railroad tie represented the loss of one African life.

The French, who controlled parts of the north bank of the Congo River, complained that the Belgians charged them too much to transport their merchandise by railroad and that bottlenecks caused delays of up to 6 months. Moreover, the Belgians were reluctant to allow French troops and supplies on their railroad. As a result, the French decided to build their own 312-mile-long railroad through the

Cristal Mountains, running roughly parallel to the north bank of the Congo River. For a labor force, they conscripted nearly 16,000 workers from the surrounding region, but many men fled into the bush, and entire villages migrated elsewhere to escape the recruiters. With very few men left in the immediate area, French colonial officials began to conscript workers from other French colonies. As the recruiters approached villages, people fled, hid in the dense forests, or rebelled. Faced with massive resistance, the recruiters simply rounded people up at gunpoint and led them away with ropes around their necks. During the 12 years of construction, nearly 130,000 conscripted workers labored on the railway. Abysmal conditions and lack of food in the workers' camps led to a high mortality rate. Between 16,000 and 23,000 workers died, either in the camps or while fleeing through the bush.

These two rail lines running roughly parallel to each other illustrate some of the contradictions and ironies of early colonialism. On the one hand, the rail lines helped to integrate the Congo River basin into the modern global economy and brought an end to the long caravans of conscripted human porters that had previously transported products to the coast. To inaugurate their railroad, Belgian colonial officials erected a monument that depicted three African porters and bore the inscription, "The railway freed them from porterage." Yet the two railroads had been built with massive amounts of forced African labor, at a high cost in human lives. Even more ironic is the fact that the two railways essentially covered the same ground. Rivalries between the Congo Free State and the French Congo prevented the two colonies from cooperating to develop a single rail line.

Red Rubber in the Congos

Another major project of early colonialism was to find products that could be exported to pay the costs of the colonial conquest and colonial administration. In the 1890s, the product of choice was wild rubber. The development of pneumatic bicycle tires in Europe in the 1890s, along with increasing industrial uses of rubber for hoses, springs, tubing, washers, and diaphragms, created a rising demand for rubber. In 1897, French officials in Mali noted that rubber was the only product worth exporting from that colony. It was the leading export product in Guinea, Angola, and Tanzania, and by 1900, Guinea, Angola, Ghana, and the Congo Free State were among the five leading rubber producers in the world (the other was Brazil). The boom in African wild rubber came to an end after 1910 when increasing quantities of high-quality rubber from plantations in Southeast Asia became available in Europe, but only after its two-decade run had brought unprecedented suffering and destruction to the inhabitants of the two Congos.

Congo Free State Concession Companies

In most parts of Africa that exported rubber during the boom years, itinerant African merchants would purchase wild rubber collected by villagers and transport it to the coast. This type of free commerce in rubber never developed in the Congo Free State, however, because King Leopold II parceled out huge tracts of land to chartered concession companies, which were given monopolies over all resources in those concessions. In 1892, the king decreed that Africans who collected ivory and wild rubber in the tropical rainforest had to deliver it to state agents or concession companies. The largest of the concessions, which covered an area ten times the size of Belgium, was reserved for King Leopold himself.

HORRORS OF THE RUBBER SYSTEM Many Congo villagers who failed to meet their fortnightly rubber quotas were manacled and put to work on chain gangs, as seen in this rare 1904 photo. Sometimes women would be taken hostage and held until their husbands produced the required rubber. Such brutal mistreatment produced widespread rebellions against the rubber companies.

The concession companies moved into their assigned territories with private armies, made up largely of locally recruited former slaves. The company soldiers and agents established rubber posts throughout their concessions and made lists of all the adult males in each village. Each man was given a quota of 8 pounds of rubber, which he had to deliver to the post every 2 weeks. If he fell short, he could be flogged with a rhinoceros-hide whip called a *chicotte* or imprisoned. Alternatively, his wife or children could be held hostage until the rubber was delivered. If a village fell short of its quota, the chief was imprisoned. The records of one post show that 44 chiefs were in prison in July 1902 alone. At another post, 55 women hostages were hanged when their husbands failed to bring in rubber on time. Violence and fighting were endemic to this process of rubber collecting, and one rubber post imported 17,600 rifle cartridges and 22,755 loads for muzzle loaders in a single year. "The only way to obtain rubber is to fight," claimed one state official. Because of the violence and bloodshed associated with rubber collection, the Congo rubber concession system was often referred to as **Red Rubber**.

By using such violent methods, the rubber companies made record profits. When the Anglo-Belgian India Rubber and Exploration Company (ABIR) reported a net profit in 1898 that was 12 times the amount of its initial investment, two Belgian economists wrote that "such a result is perhaps without precedent in the annals of our industrial companies." They failed to note that the neighboring concession run by the Société Anversoise was running profits 60 percent larger than ABIR's. The largest and most profitable rubber concession in the Congo Free State was the Crown Domain, which was exploited by agents working directly for King Leopold II. The king kept its operations a secret and left no record of his profits, but because the Crown Domain was 10 times larger than Belgium itself, they must have been enormous.

Despite the initial high profits, the rubber concession system was not sustainable. With such high quotas, the wild rubber resources of the rainforest were rapidly depleted. As rubber became harder and harder to find, people migrated out of the concession areas or sought refuge in the dense rainforest. A missionary who traveled through King Leopold's private concession reported "numerous sites where only recently thousands of people had been living. Here and there a few blackened sticks showed where the huts had been. But never a man or woman or child. All was as still as the grave." Other Africans rebelled against the rubber companies. One company reported that 142 of its soldiers were killed during the first 6 months of 1905. With rubber production and profits in freefall, the rubber companies packed up and left the Congo Free State. As a result of the abuses and atrocities of the rubber companies, the Belgian parliament voted in 1908 to take the Congo Free State away from King Leopold and make it a colony run by the Belgian government. It was thereafter known as the Belgian Congo.

French Congo Concession Companies

The neighboring French Congo established a similar concession system in 1899. The concession companies received a monopoly on the products of the soil (mainly rubber and ivory) for a period of 30 years. In return, the companies were to create private military and police forces and pay rents and customs to the state. The result was a veritable land rush as different groups of investors competed to gain concessions in the French Congo. By the end of 1899, 40 concession companies had been granted monopolies covering 70 percent of the territory of the French Congo.

Although the French colonial government made some feeble attempts to limit the abuses of the concession companies, many of them operated just like those in King Leopold's Congo Free State. One company's methods included taking hostages, flogging people with the *chicotte*, and the outright killing of men, their wives, and even their children. An official investigation of that company reported the proven murders of 750 people and the probable murders of 1,500 more. When Pierre Savorgnan de Brazza, the former governor-general of the French Congo, made an inspection tour of the colony in 1905, he reported that "the kidnapping of women in native villages is a common practice." He also noted that many regions were depopulated because the people had fled, and that other regions were in full rebellion against the concession companies. The abuses and atrocities inherent in the rubber concession system in King Leopold's Congo Free State had found their way into the French Congo as well.

THE SECOND WAVE OF AFRICAN RESISTANCE

As the machinery of colonial rule took shape, it became clear to Africans that the level of domination by the colonial administrations was different from anything they had experienced before. Instead of extracting tribute from chiefs, the colonial administrations began to collect annual taxes from the head of every household. Whereas precolonial African rulers had summoned laborers for special projects such as building the king's palace, the colonial rulers conscripted massive amounts of labor to build roads and railroads. And the constant demand for porters was a burden on the populations. People resisted those demands in a variety of individual ways, but also collectively, and the African continent was rocked by armed rebellions. The list of rebellions in Africa during the time between the initial colonial conquest and the end of World War I is a long one, but a few examples will illustrate the wide variation in the causes and methods of the rebellions and in European responses.

The Hut Tax War in Sierra Leone

The British had established the crown colony of Sierra Leone in 1808 for the purpose of resettling victims of the Atlantic slave trade (see chapter 9), but that colony occupied only the coastal regions of Sierra Leone. In 1896, the British extended their authority by proclaiming a protectorate over the inland areas, which were inhabited mainly by the Mende and Temne people. Their rebellion was a response to the imposition of British rule, forced labor for road building, and above all, the imposition of an annual hut tax of 10 shillings on all houses with at least four rooms and 5 shillings on smaller houses. The chiefs opposed the tax not only because it was financially burdensome, but also because they saw it as a threat to their sovereignty.

The rebellion broke out in Temne country, organized by a charismatic war chief named Bai Bureh. After Bai Bureh's forces had successfully resisted the British colonial army for 2 months, the Mende people rose in a rebellion organized by members of the Poro secret initiation society. Soon a rebel army was reported to be marching toward the capital city of Freetown to expel not only the British, but also the English-speaking Creoles who had settled there earlier in the century. In response, the British brought in soldiers from Nigeria to put down the rebellion. The British commander later observed that the **Hut Tax War** had involved "some of the most stubborn fighting that has been seen in West Africa." The British governor of Sierra Leone attributed the rebellion to "the growing political consciousness of the African." He was saying, in effect, that once the Africans had figured out what the British were up to, they didn't like it.

The Baule Rebellion in Côte d'Ivoire

The Baule people of Côte d'Ivoire were farmers, gold miners, and cloth weavers who had a decentralized political system with numerous village chiefs. In 1898, the French began to set up administrative posts in the region. Needing labor for their posts, they created "liberty villages" where runaway slaves could work for the French in exchange for liberty from their Baule masters. Baule chiefs saw this action as a threat to their control over their labor force. When Baule chiefs began to ambush French supply caravans, the French moved more troops into the area, which exacerbated the problem because the Baule people were forced to provide food and porters for the additional troops. After the French imposed taxes in commodities and labor on each household in 1900, resistance to the French became widespread, and by 1902, Africans had revolted throughout Baule country.

The French commander was frustrated in his efforts to quell the revolt in a politically decentralized society. He complained that the French could not win simply by vanquishing a king or capturing a capital city, because the Baule had neither. Instead, he proposed a strategy of total war: "We must methodically destroy their goods, capture their flocks, liberate their slaves, and track down the hideaways of the families of the fighters to make them prisoners." At the same time, the French tried to win over the chiefs by rebating 25 percent of the taxes they collected and offering them political gifts, commercial favors, and educational opportunities for their children.

By 1904, many of the rebellious chiefs had submitted to the French, and the fighting died down. The French governor met with a group of Baule chiefs and explained that their tax money would be used to build good things for them such as roads, a telegraph line, and a railway. One of the chiefs responded that it was the local people who built the roads with their labor and then paid for them with their taxes;

that the telegraph line would mainly serve the colonial administrators; and that there was no guarantee that the railroad would ever be built. "In reality," he said, "you take our money because you are the master, and the master has a right to extract anything he wants from his slave." The colonial governor and the Baule chief had diametrically opposite understandings of the meaning and purpose of colonial taxation.

Tensions were rekindled in 1908, when a new French governor increased the tax on each head of a household and imposed communal labor obligations in order to compel the Baule to produce crops such as cocoa or cotton for the European market. At the same time, he instituted a tax on guns and decreed that people who paid the tax would receive a permit to purchase 250 grams of gunpowder. In 1908 alone, nearly 700,000 musket-charges of ammunition flowed into the Baule country. The new governor was, in effect, giving people both the incentive and the means to revolt. In the following year, the Baule did exactly that, and in response, the French brought in four companies of Senegalese soldiers and created two new brigades of locally recruited troops.

Over the next 2 years, the colonial forces launched six major offensives in the Baule territory. They won every battle, but the Baule would simply melt away into the bush to fight another day. In response, the French tried to destroy the agricultural base of the Baule economy by confiscating food stores and uprooting crops through two successive growing seasons. When famine set in in 1910, the Baule began to surrender. Between 1900 and 1911, the combination of warfare, famine, epidemics, and large-scale migration reduced the Baule population by hundreds of thousands.

The Maji Maji Rebellion in Tanzania

In the German colony of Tanzania, the governor sought to boost revenue by growing cotton to supply the textile mills in Germany. Fearing that individual farmers could not grow cotton successfully, he ordered each village headman to establish a communal cotton field, which would be worked by the men of the village. Each man was supposed to work 28 days per year in the cotton field, but in practice men usually worked much more. Men who failed to do the required work were beaten or imprisoned. The work was burdensome enough, but more problematic was that the cotton-growing season coincided with the season for growing food crops, so food production suffered. While the men were working in the cotton fields, wild pigs sometimes destroyed their subsistence crops. It was no accident that the **Maji Maji Rebellion** began at the start of the 1905 cotton-picking season, and that one of the first rebel actions in many areas was to burn the cotton fields.

As the rebellion spread, it transcended ethnic divisions and loyalties to particular chiefs. What initially unified the rebels was a religious ideology developed by a prophet named Kinjikitile. Believing that he had become possessed by a subordinate spirit of the local deity Bokero, he built a large spirit-hut where people could come to communicate with their ancestors, and he distributed a special kind of holy water (*maji* is the Swahili word for water) that would protect people against German bullets. Crowds thronged to his spirit-hut to obtain the magic water. Kinjikitile was hanged by the Germans a month after the rebellion broke out, but by then, his assistants had fanned out to neighboring regions with the magic water and were encouraging people to join the rebellion. Local chiefs who opposed the movement were swept aside by popular fervor; in one case, an emissary of the movement took over as the new chief. Three months after the rebellion started, it had spread throughout the southeastern quarter of Tanzania.

At first, the rebels had great success because there were only a handful of African colonial soldiers in the area. But the Germans quickly rushed in forces from the coast and mounted three military expeditions to attack the rebels. When the German colonial soldiers began to kill rebel fighters, people lost faith in the magic water. By then, however, the rebellion had gained a great deal of momentum, and the rebels had no intention of surrendering.

After German forces encircled and scattered the main rebel army in 1906, the rebels returned to older established patterns of ethnic organization and guerilla warfare. The Germans responded with a scorched-earth strategy against the guerilla fighters, seizing the food supplies for their troops and preventing the cultivation of crops. "The fellows can just starve," declared Captain Richter of the German army. By the time the rebellion was over in July 1907, 2 years after it began, famine had covered the land, and perhaps one-third of the region's population was dead.

The Herero Genocide in Namibia

The Herero were cattle herders living in Namibia. Located at the southern tip of Africa, it was the only German colony in Africa with a climate suitable for large-scale European settlement. In 1894, the colonial government encouraged German settlers to establish farms on lands it had confiscated from the Herero, seizing their cattle and forcing the men to become laborers on the farms. When the Herero learned in 1903 that the Germans planned to divide their territory with a rail line and force them into crowded reservations, they made plans to drive the Germans out. In January 1904, they began attacking German farms, and they briefly occupied the settler town of Okahandja. Within 4 months, they destroyed nearly every German farm in the territory and made off with most of the cattle.

The colonial governor desperately sent telegrams to Berlin to ask for reinforcements, and ships loaded with German troops set off from Hamburg in

May—the first of an expeditionary force that would grow to 20,000 men. The German commander, Lothar von Trotha, outlined his plan in a letter: "It was and is my policy to use force with terrorism and even brutality. I shall annihilate the revolting tribes with streams of blood and streams of gold. Only after a complete uprooting will something emerge." Von Trotha's forces defeated the main body of Herero rebels at the town of Waterberg in August 1904 and pushed the retreating Herero into the Omaheke Desert. Fleeing women, children, and unarmed cattle herders were slaughtered. The commander then sealed off the desert to keep the Herero from returning and placed troops to guard the water holes, leaving thousands of refugees to die from thirst and starvation. Starving Herero who surrendered were chained, put in concentration camps, and used as forced laborers. Many of them died in the camps.

The **Herero genocide** has not been forgotten. A United Nations report in 1985 estimated that the Herero population of 80,000 was reduced to 15,000

SURVIVORS OF THE HERERO GENOCIDE This photo shows starving survivors of the Herero revolt against the German colonizers. The Germans drove them into the Omaheke Desert and placed soldiers at the water holes to keep them away. The United Nations has characterized the German actions as genocide because more than three-quarters of the Herero population was starved to death or shot.

starving refugees between 1904 and 1907. It characterized the episode as one of the earliest examples of genocide in the twentieth century.

The Mad Mullah in Somalia

During the scramble for Africa, the coastal lowlands in the Somali Peninsula were divided among the British and the Italians, with France gaining a small foothold around the port of Djibouti. Muhammad Abdullah Hassan grew up in these semiarid lowlands among nomadic pastoralists who herded camels and horses. A poet and a devout Muslim, he came under the influence of the Sudanese mystic Muhammad Salih. After receiving spiritual training under Salih in the early 1890s, he returned home to spread the teachings of the Salihiya religious order. He preached that the British were infidels who were destroying their religion and that the Christian Ethiopians, who lived in the highlands to the west, were in league with the British. He also called for Somali unity and independence, thus attracting people who did not necessarily agree with his extreme religious views. Because of his fanatical zeal and sometimes erratic actions, the British referred to him as the **Mad Mullah**.

After obtaining weapons from the Ottoman Empire, Sudan, and other Arab nations, Hassan attacked an Ethiopian garrison in 1900 and then launched raids into the British-protected area. In response, the Ethiopian emperor, Menelik II, proposed joint Ethiopian-British military action against him. During the next 5 years, the Dervish army, as the rebel forces were called, inflicted heavy losses on Ethiopian, British, and Italian forces. By 1913, Hassan had established an independent state, known as the Dervish state, and built a series of forts that dominated the hinterland of the Somali peninsula. The Dervish state retained its independence until 1920, when the British attacked its capital aided by the latest military technology—12 airplanes carrying 20-pound bombs. This episode exemplifies the complex patterns of resistance and collaboration in early colonial Africa. Menelik II had routed the Italians from Ethiopia in the Battle of Adwa in 1896, but 4 years later, in the face of a threat from Islamic jihadists, he proposed an alliance with the British.

CONCLUSION

Although some Europeans offered benevolent-sounding justifications for the conquest of Africa, such as ending the internal slave trade or spreading Western civilization, its fundamental reasons were economic. It was industrial capitalism that allowed for the European conquest and partition of Africa in the first place. Innovations in the manufacturing and design of weapons after 1850 gave the Europeans military advantages over African armies that would have been unimaginable a few decades earlier, and new medical discoveries greatly increased the chances of European survival in tropical environments. In addition, Europeans were no longer seeking outlets for their surplus populations or monopolies over exotic spices and stimulants, as they had done in earlier stages of European expansion. Rather, they sought raw materials for their factories and expanded markets for their manufactured products.

Writing in the aftermath of the scramble for Africa, the British economic historian Allan McPhee explained it as follows:

> The Scramble for Africa was nothing more than a visible token of the demand which had been gradually arising in Europe for the products of Africa. The products were no longer slaves, nor merely palm oil products; they now consisted of cotton and rubber, coffee and groundnuts, hides and minerals. Henceforth, penetration of the interior was imperative so as to safeguard and encourage supplies of the new commodities.

Frederick Lugard, who commanded the British West African Frontier Force, put it more succinctly: "The partition of Africa was, as we all recognize, due primarily to the economic necessity of increasing the supplies of raw materials and food to meet the needs of the industrialized nations of Europe."

One advantage that the Europeans had during their conquest of the African continent was that they, as outsiders who had traveled hundreds or thousands of miles to reach various parts of Africa, had a vision of the continent as a whole. African chiefs, kings, and villagers, on the other hand, were often enmeshed in local and regional politics and had no way of knowing what was going on in other parts of Africa. They also had no way of discerning the long-range intentions of the invaders. Africans had known raids, wars, and conquests throughout their history, but the total domination exercised by the European invaders was something entirely new. That is why there were two waves of armed African resistance to colonialism: the first when the armies of the Europeans invaded their territory, and the second after the full extent of the colonial project had been revealed.

By the end of World War I, armed rebellions had largely ceased in Africa. All of them had failed, in part because the Europeans could always bring in reinforcements from other colonies or from Europe. The repression of the rebellions had often been savage, and large numbers of Africans had lost their lives. Africans would continue to engage in strikes, protests, and occasional riots to oppose specific colonial policies, but the hope that the colonizers could be driven out by armed force was mostly gone. In the aftermath of the wars of partition and the rebellions of the early colonial period, the colonizers began to seek political accommodation with their African subjects, and Africans began to look for ways to endure, or even prosper, under colonial conditions. A kind of stalemate settled over the continent.

CHAPTER REVIEW

KEY TERMS AND VOCABULARY

scramble for Africa
Berlin Conference
Maxim gun
Battle of Adwa
Lobengula
Nehanda-Charwe
Anglo-Boer War
Red Rubber
Hut Tax War
Maji Maji Rebellion
Herero genocide
Mad Mullah

STUDY QUESTIONS

1. Why did the nations of Atlantic Europe largely refrain from seeking colonies in Africa until the 1880s, even though they established colonies in the Americas and Asia?
2. Of the various factors that led Europeans to seek colonies in Africa in the 1880s, which do you think are the most important?
3. Assess the strengths and weaknesses of the invading European armies.
4. Assess the strengths and weaknesses of the African armies that were defending their territory.
5. How do you explain why some African chiefs collaborated with the incoming colonial armies?
6. What do the early colonial administrative actions of the Germans, Belgians, and French tell us about the original motives for colonialism?
7. Why did many Africans rise in rebellion after the initial establishment of colonial rule?

SELLING CLOTH IN THE CONGO

One of the incentives for European colonization in Africa was to gain exclusive access to new markets for the products of European factories. The explorer Henry Morton Stanley gave this address in 1884 to the Chamber of Commerce in Manchester, England, a city whose cotton cloth industry was at the epicenter of the Industrial Revolution. Note how he tempts the Manchester captains of industry with the promise of new markets for their cloth and then pivots to ask for a gunboat on the Congo River.

I was interested the other day in making a curious calculation, which was, supposing that all the inhabitants of the Congo basin were simply to have one Sunday dress each, how many yards of Manchester cloth would be required; and the amazing number was 320,000,000 yards, just for one Sunday dress! (Cheers.) Proceeding still further with these figures I found that two Sunday dresses and four every-day dresses would in one year amount to 3,840,000,000 yards, which at 2d. per yard would be of the value of £16,000,000 [the equivalent of nearly $2 billion today]. The more I pondered upon these things I discovered that I could not limit these stores of cotton cloth to day dresses. I would have to provide for night dresses also—(laughter)—and these would consume 160,000,000 yards. (Cheers.) Then the grave cloths came into mind. . . . I estimate that, if my figures of population are approximately correct, 2,000,000 die every year, and to bury these decently, and according to the custom of those who possess cloth, 16,000,000 yards will be required, while the 40,000 chiefs will require an average of 100 yards each, or 4,000,000 yards. . . . I discovered that I had neglected to provide for the family wardrobe or currency chest, for you must know that in the Lower Congo there is scarcely a family that has not a cloth fund of about a dozen pieces of about 24 yards each. . . . Now, 8,000,000 families at 300 yards each will require 2,400,000,000. (Cheers.) You all know how perishable such currency must be; but if you sum up these several millions of yards, and value all of them at the average price of 2d. per yard, you will find that it will be possible for Manchester to create a trade—in the course of time—in cottons in the Congo basin amounting in value to about £26,000,000 annually [the equivalent of over $3 billion today]. (Loud cheers.) . . .

Now, if your sympathy for yourselves and the fate of Manchester has been excited sufficiently, your next natural question would be as follows: . . . we beg to ask you what Manchester is to do in order that we may begin realising this sale of untold millions of yards of cotton cloth? I answer that the first thing to do is for you to ask the British Government to send a cruiser to the mouth of the Congo to keep watch and ward over that river until the European nations have agreed among themselves as to what shall be done with the river, lest one of these days you will hear that it is too late. (Hear, hear.)

1. *Why would textile manufacturers in Manchester, England, be interested in the Congo River basin?*
2. *Why did Stanley recommend placing a gunboat at the mouth of the Congo River?*

Source: H. M. Stanley, *Address of Mr. H. M. Stanley on England and the Congo and Manchester Trade to the Manchester Chamber of Commerce, 21 October, 1884* (Manchester: A. Ireland & Co., 1884), pp. 12–13.

THE MAJI MAJI REBELLION

The Maji Maji Rebellion in Tanzania was the largest African uprising against colonial rule, engulfing the southern half of the colony. The following account of the beginning of the rebellion was compiled from the oral testimonies of local elders gathered by G. C. K. Gwassa in 1966–1967. Two of the main characters in this story are the prophet Kinjikitile and his assistant, Mpokosi who ran a military training camp.

The song of Mpokosi during likinda [the training camp] was in the Ngindo language. He used to take his fly-whisk and his calabash container for medicine, and he went around sprinkling them [the recruits] with medicine. It was like military drilling with muzzle-loaders, and under very strict discipline. . . .

During that time they were dressed in their military attire called *Ngumbalyo*. . . . The song was entirely in riddles. Thus the question "what are you carrying?" meant "what do you want to do?" The answer "we are carrying peas" meant "we are carrying bullets," and they used peas in their guns during drilling. "Creeping peas" are those that creep, and it meant that they were marching to the battlefield. "Creeping, creeping"—that was walking, that is military marching. "Destroy the red earth."—that meant tear the European apart or destroy him.

And as they returned . . . to their camp they sang many times, "Let us fight him today." They sang the same song as they marched to the battlefield.

[Kinjikitile] told them, "The Germans will leave. War will start from up-country towards the coast and from the coast into the hinterland. There will definitely be war. But for the time being go and work for him. If he orders you to cultivate cotton or to dig his road or to carry his load, do as he requires. Go and remain quiet. When I am ready I will declare the war." Those elders returned home and kept quiet. They waited for a long time. Then the elders wondered, "This *mganga* [prophet, i.e., Kinjikitile] said he would declare war against the Germans. Why then is he delaying? When will the Europeans go? After all, we have already received the medicine and we are brave men. Why should we wait?" Then the Africans asked themselves, "How do we start the war? How do we make the Germans angry? Let us go and uproot their cotton so that war may rise."

Only a few shoots of cotton were affected, not the whole field. . . . Ngulumbalyo Mandai and Lindimyo Machela uprooted the first two shoots. Then Jumbo [Chief] Mtemangani sent a letter to Kibata through his wife. . . . She was to report to the *akida* [Arab overseer working for the Germans]. . . .

There at Kibata they began to fight. They fought for a whole week. Then the Arab ran out of ammunition. His village was surrounded by warriors. Then those jumbes [chiefs] who had gone to rescue him arranged for his escape to Miteja and thence to Kilwa. Then they plundered the shops and all property. But Kinjikitile had told them not to plunder. That was their mistake.

1. *What was the purpose of uprooting the cotton plants?*
2. *How much authority did the prophet Kinjikitile have over his followers?*

Source: *Records of the Maji Maji Rising*, part 1, edited by G. C. K. Gwassa and John Iliffe, Historical Association of Tanzania Paper No. 4 (Nairobi: East African Publishing House, 1968), pp. 11–13.

PERSPECTIVES

RED RUBBER

This account of the period of forced rubber gathering in the Congo (1892–1910) was written in 1954 by Leon Bangeli, a retired schoolteacher from Lifumba, a riverside village in the heart of the rubber region. Recalling events he had witnessed or heard about in his childhood, his narrative shows how relations between the local people and the white intruders evolved from trade to forced rubber gathering to forced provision of foodstuffs. He shows that the people of the region remember the rubber period as marked by horrendous violence. Note that the narrator refers to white colonial officials by their African nicknames, and that Chief Ioma refers to the white people as "ghosts" because of their white skin.

Mangala [an African soldier who worked for the whites] and the whites landed their boat and went to see Ioma, the great patriarch who had sold the whites some ivory tusks. But in the transaction, Ioma had cheated them. Because even during the sale he had regretted it in his heart and said, "There go my ivory tusks with those ghosts." When the whites and Mangala arrived at Ioma's house, the patriarch said to his people, "Here come the ghosts. We had thought they were gone for good, but now they have come back!" There was a great battle; a massacre.

When Ioma saw that his people were being killed, he fled with those who remained. The whites returned to Bonjongo, their headquarters.

The whites sent Mangala to Chief Ioma to tell him, "Ioma and his people must come here." The people launched their dugout canoes and arrived at Bonjongo. The whites said to them, "It is very good to live in peace, but bring us recruits to serve as soldiers." Ioma acquiesced and said to the whites, "I will inform my kinsmen."

He recounted the story to his kinsmen and they gave men to serve as soldiers from each village—20 men in all. They conducted the recruits to the white man, who said, "That is good, but now go and produce rubber." They replied, "How should we do it?" The whites explained, "After you have cut into the rubber vines, rub the latex on your stomach until it congeals into a ball." They produced the first rubber and brought it to him. But the whites said, "Go and produce more rubber; one basketful for each village." And they produced it.

After that, he placed a sentry in each village; that is, a soldier who lived there and collected the rubber. If a village did not bring enough rubber, the hands of the inhabitants would be cut off. This was a time of extermination. The rubber époque lasted for a long time.

Then Ikoka [Charles Lemaire, a colonial official] came to replace Ntange [Léon Fiévez, a colonial official] at a time when the people were still producing rubber. And Ikoka said, "The rubber work is finished. Now, bring me chickens, cassava bread, fish, and meat. Go hunting and bring me the kill. If a village doesn't bring enough, we will fight you." Each time that we went to deliver the goods and one village didn't bring enough, the soldiers would go and kill some people there or seize them and destroy their village. That time of war was named "the taking of the hands."

1. *Why did Chief Ioma supply soldiers to aid the whites?*
2. *How did the forced rubber collection come to an end?*

Source: E. Boelaert, H. Vinck, and Ch. Lonkama, "Arrivée des Blancs sur les Bords des Rivières Equatoriales," *Annales Aequatoria*, vol. 16 (1995), pp. 42–43. Translated into English by Robert Harms.

THE HERERO MASSACRE AS GENOCIDE

The following report was prepared by a sub-commission of the United Nations Economic and Social Commission on Human Rights regarding the question of the prevention and punishment of the crime of genocide. When the report was released on July 2, 1985, it was the first official U.N. report to classify the 1904 massacre of the Herero by German colonial troops as genocide. Here are the relevant excerpts from what has become known as the Whitaker Report.

Genocide, particularly of indigenous peoples, has also often occurred as a consequence of colonialism, with racism and ethnic prejudice commonly being predisposing factors. In some cases occupying forces maintained their authority by the terror of a perpetual threat of massacre. Examples could occur either at home or overseas: the English for example massacred native populations in Ireland, Scotland and Wales in order to deter resistance and to "clear" land for seizure, and the British also almost wholly exterminated the indigenous people when colonizing Tasmania as late as the start of the nineteenth century. Africa, Australasia and the Americas witnessed numerous other examples. . . .

Toynbee stated that the distinguishing characteristics of the twentieth century in evolving the development of genocide "are that it is committed in cold blood by the deliberate *fiat* of holders of despotic political power, and that the perpetrators of genocide employ all the resources of present-day technology and organization to make their planned massacres systematic and complete." The Nazi aberration has unfortunately not been the only case of genocide in the twentieth century. Among other examples which can be cited as qualifying are the German massacre of Hereros in 1904,* the Ottoman massacre of Armenians in 1915–1916, the Ukrainian pogrom of Jews in 1919, the Tutsi massacre of Hutu in Burundi in 1965 and 1972, the Paraguayan massacre of Aché Indians prior to 1974, the Khmer Rouge massacre in Kampuchea between 1975 and 1978, and the contemporary Iranian killings of Baha'is. A number of other cases may be suggested. It could seem pedantic to argue that some terrible mass-killings are legalistically not genocide, but on the other hand it could be counter-productive to devalue genocide through over-diluting its definition.

1. *What is the connection between colonialism and genocide?*
2. *What was the role of General von Trotha in the Herero genocide?*

*General von Trotha issued an extermination order; water-holes were poisoned and the African peace emissaries were shot. In all, three quarters of the Herero Africans were killed by the Germans then colonizing present-day Namibia, and the Hereros were reduced from 80,000 to some 15,000 starving refugees.

Source: United Nations Economic and Social Council, Commission on Human Rights, Sub-commission on Prevention of Discrimination and Protection of Minorities, Thirty-Eighth session, Item 4 on the provisional agenda, Review of Further Developments in Fields with Which the Sub-commission Has Been Concerned: Revised and Updated Report on the Question of the Prevention and Punishment of the Crime of Genocide, prepared by Mr. B. Whitaker, E/CN.4/Sub.2/1985/6 (July 2, 1985), pp. 7–10.

HARVESTING COCOA IN GHANA Farmworkers processing cocoa pods on a farm in Ghana, 1925–1935. They split open the pods by hand and scoop out the beans, which are covered with a white pulp. The pile of wet cocoa beans will be covered with banana leaves and left to ferment for 5–6 days, while the pulp turns into a liquid and drains away. By 1911, Ghana was the world's no. 1 producer of cocoa.

1919
German colonies redistributed

1922
Egypt gains nominal independence

1925
Gezira irrigation scheme opens in Sudan

11

MAKING COLONIAL STATES, 1914–1940

The brutal regimes that characterized early colonial rule in Africa were not sustainable in the long run. After suppressing numerous rebellions across the continent, the colonial powers began the process of transforming their occupied territories into colonial states with regular administrations, policies, and laws. This transition was already under way in the early twentieth century, but it was interrupted by the outbreak of World War I. From July 1914 until November 1918, the major European colonial powers were totally consumed by the war. Having exhausted their national treasuries, Britain and France were forced to rely on loans from the United States to sustain their military efforts. It was only after the Treaty of Versailles formally ended the war on June 28, 1919, that the colonial powers could develop new, more sustainable systems of colonial rule.

This chapter first looks at the impact of World War I in Africa, then explores the patterns and practices of colonial rule that the European powers adopted in the aftermath of the war. This period will be referred to as "high colonialism" to distinguish it from the "early colonialism" that reigned prior to World War I and the "late colonialism" that developed after World War II. High colonialism took very different forms in different colonies, depending on the colonizer and the number of white settlers who lived in the colony.

1926	1929	1931
Firestone establishes rubber plantation in Liberia	Women's War in Nigeria	Revolt of Leverville palm oil workers

A comment about the names of the colonies is in order here. Many of the colonies were given names that differed from those later adopted by the independent countries that succeeded them. The Gold Coast, for example, became Ghana; French Sudan became Mali, Southern Rhodesia became Zimbabwe, Nyasaland became Malawi, and so on. In order to reduce the confusion resulting from shifting names, this chapter, like the previous one, normally uses the modern names of the countries, even though the colonial names may have been different. A major exception is made in the case of the two colonies named Congo, which are referred to as the Belgian Congo and the French Congo, respectively.

WORLD WAR I

The Great War, as World War I was called at the time, was one of the deadliest military conflagrations in world history. The aggressors (known as the Central Powers) were Germany, Austria-Hungary, and the Ottoman Empire, and the defenders (known as the Allies) included Britain, France, Russia, Italy, and the United States. European countries that had colonies in Africa could be found on both sides of the conflict. After the initial clashes in 1914, the fighting in Europe settled down to a stalemate during 1915 and 1916, which was broken when the United States entered the war on the side of the Allies in April 1917, paving the way for their victory. By 1919, the Allies had prevailed on all fronts.

The war was a watershed in the geopolitical history of the twentieth century. In addition to redefining national borders in Europe, it led to the fall of ruling dynasties in Germany, Russia, Austria-Hungary, and Turkey, and it created the conditions for the Russian Revolution and the Armenian genocide. The use of new military technology such as airplanes and submarines caused unprecedented slaughter and destruction. Altogether, some 8,500,000 soldiers died from wounds or disease, and an estimated 13 million civilians died from disease, displacement, starvation, and massacres.

World War I spilled over into Africa in three ways. First, colonial powers drafted African soldiers to fight on their behalf on European battlefields. Some 180,000 soldiers from France's African colonies, for example, were called up to fight in Europe. Second, Germany's African colonies found themselves at war with neighboring colonies under Allied rule. The war was especially devastating in eastern and central Africa, where Tanzania—a German colony at the time—bordered on British, Portuguese, and Belgian colonies. With African soldiers fighting on both sides, the war was accompanied by shortages of food, weakened populations, and epidemic diseases that caused large-scale civilian deaths. In all, over a hundred thousand African soldiers died in the war, and over 300,000 civilians died from war-related famine and disease. Third, Egypt was the staging

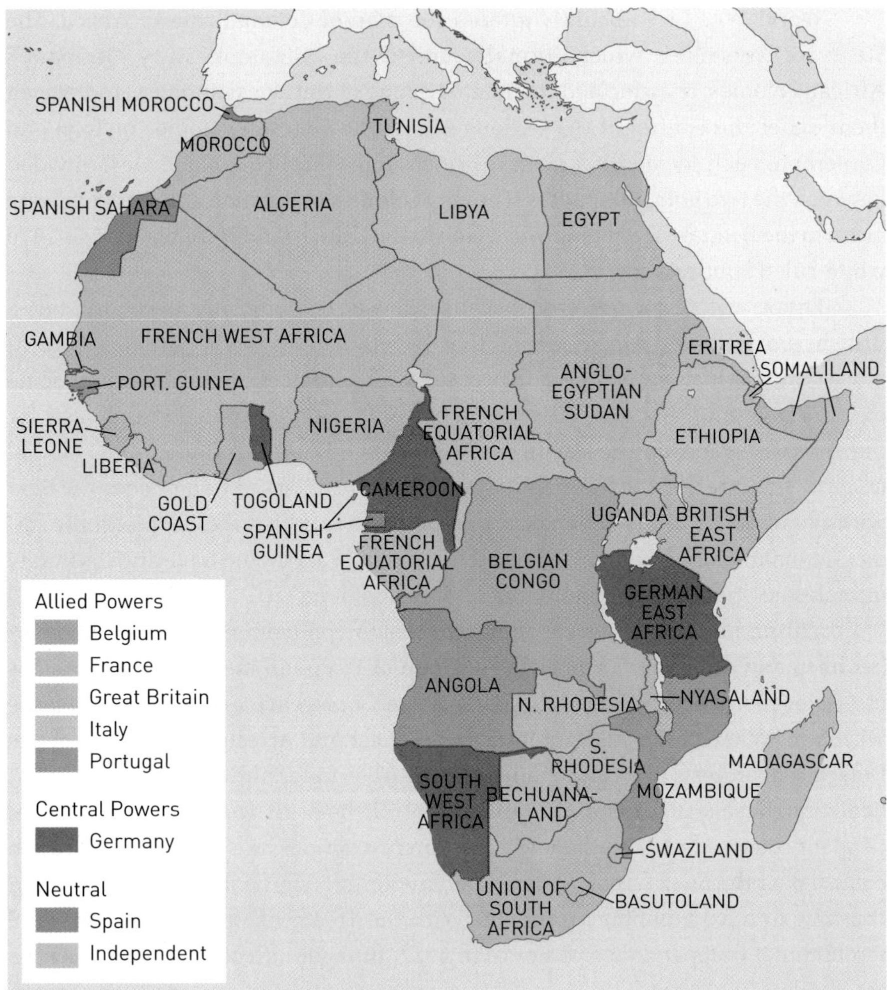

COLONIAL AFRICA AT THE OUTBREAK OF WORLD WAR I The Central Powers were represented by Germany, which controlled Togoland, Cameroon, South West Africa, and German East Africa (which included Tanganyika, Rwanda, and Burundi). The Allies were represented by France, Britain, Italy, and Portugal. Although Belgium was occupied by the Germans during the war, the Belgian Congo's colonial army, consisting mainly of African troops, fought against the Germans in Cameroon and German East Africa.

area in the British effort to drive the Ottoman Turks out of Palestine and Syria. In 1916, the British had three armies with a total of 400,000 soldiers based in Egypt. Although there was no fighting in Egypt itself, many Egyptian peasants and their camels were drafted to provide support to the British armies, and the camel corps suffered considerable losses while fighting on the front lines.

World War I significantly altered the map of colonial rule in Africa. The Treaty of Versailles, which formally ended the war, took away Germany's African colonies, transformed them into League of Nations mandates, and placed them under the control of the various Allies. The German colonies of Togo and Cameroon, each located between a British and a French colony, were divided between the two colonial powers. The tiny colonies of Rwanda and Burundi were given to the Belgians, Tanzania was given to the British, and Namibia was given to white-ruled South Africa.

Egypt was a special case because it was not officially a colony, but a British protectorate, which meant that it retained its own national government under British supervision. Egyptian intellectuals were intrigued by some of U.S. President Woodrow Wilson's Fourteen Points that provided the basis for the Treaty of Versailles negotiations. Point 5 stated that in adjudicating colonial claims, "the interests of the populations concerned" should have equal weight with the interests of the colonizers, and point 12 said that the people in the former Ottoman Empire (which collapsed during the war) should have an "absolutely unmolested opportunity of autonomous development."

Wilson had not meant for those phrases to apply to Egypt (which had earlier been an Ottoman province), but a group of Egyptian intellectuals known as the Delegation asked to go to the Paris Peace Conference and discuss the issue with him. When the British refused this request and arrested the leader of the Delegation, protests and riots against the British erupted throughout the country. Realizing that Egypt was spinning out of control, the British proclaimed it an independent country in 1922, albeit with certain restrictions: the British would retain control over the Suez Canal, Sudan, and Egyptian foreign policy, and they would continue to have a military presence. With the Treaty of Versailles in 1919 and the nominal independence of Egypt in 1922, the map of colonial rule in Africa assumed its final form.

FROM OCCUPIED TERRITORIES TO COLONIAL STATES

As Europe began to recover from the ravages of World War I, the colonial powers resumed the task of transforming their African colonies from occupied territories into self-sustaining colonial states with institutions such as administrative bureaucracies, taxation systems, armies, and courts of law. In light of Wilson's emphasis on "the interests of the populations concerned," they felt the need to justify their continued domination of African peoples. The British sought to portray colonialism as a win-win situation. Frederick Lugard, who served as the governor-general of Nigeria from 1914 to 1919, argued in his 1922 book, *The Dual*

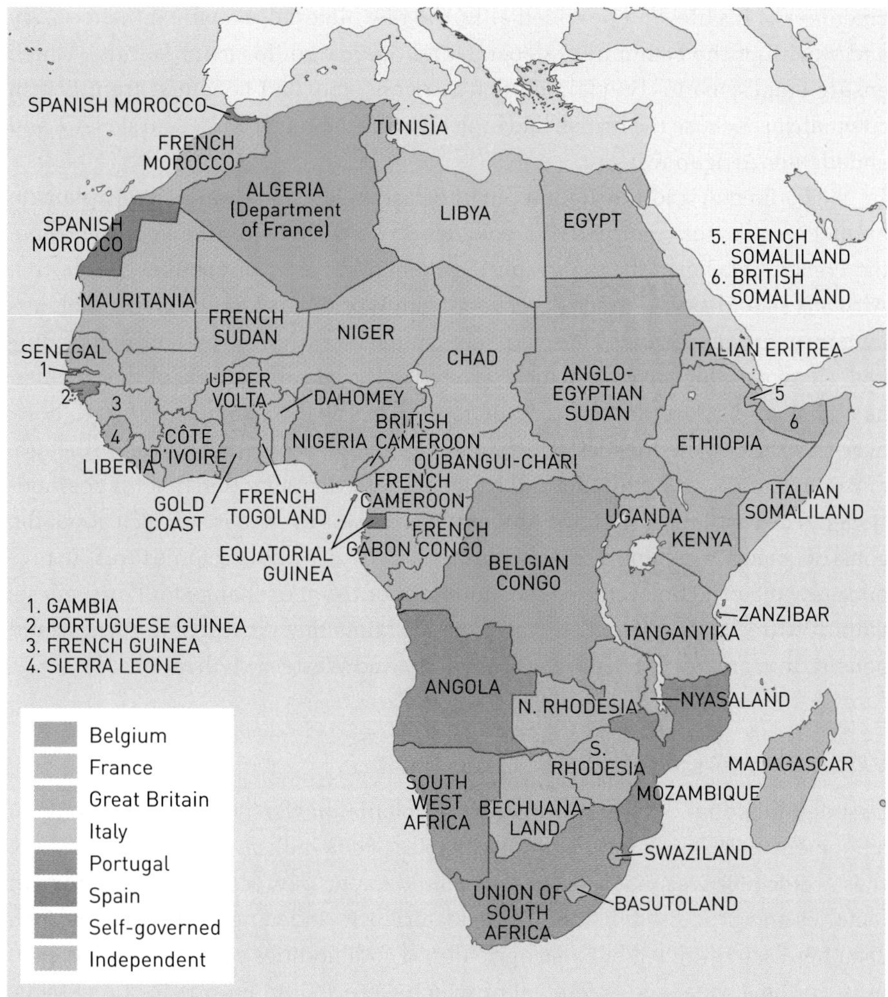

AFRICA AFTER WORLD WAR I After the war, the former German colonies were divided up among Britain, France, Belgium, and South Africa. South West Africa is shown here as self-governed because it was under the authority of self-governed South Africa. After Egypt became an independent kingdom in 1922, it was no longer a nominal province of the Ottoman Empire, nor a protectorate of Britain.

Mandate in British Tropical Africa, that "Europe is in Africa for the mutual benefit of her own industrial classes and of the native races." Sensitive to class conflicts in Britain, he added that the beneficiaries of colonialism included not just British industrialists, but also British commoners. "The products of the tropics," he wrote, "have raised the standard of comfort of the [British] working man, added to the amenities of his life, and provided alike the raw materials on which the industry and wealth of the community depend, and the market for manufactures which ensure employment." He claimed that Africans, too, had benefited from British colonialism because the British had built railroads, abolished internal slavery, and ended inter-African warfare.

The French and Portuguese, in contrast, made no secret of their plans to extract wealth from their African colonies. In his 1923 book, *The Improvement of the French Colonies*, Albert Sarraut, the French minister of colonies, wrote that Africans should assist France's recovery from World War I by supplying "soldiers for its army, money to pay off its war debts, and material and products for its industry." There was much wealth to be exploited in the soil and subsoil of the colonies, he claimed, but it needed to be made more accessible. Sarraut recognized, however, that the colonies needed substantial improvements in transportation, health, and education in order to achieve the higher levels of production that France envisioned. The Portuguese dictator Antonio Salazar was even more explicit about the goals of Portuguese colonialism. He wrote that the role of the colonies was "to produce raw material and sell it to the Mother Country in exchange for [Portuguese] manufactured goods." He also made vague claims that Africans, in turn, would benefit from greater exposure to Christianity and Western civilization.

Principles of Colonial Rule in Africa

Despite individual differences among the colonial powers, they seemed to be in agreement on certain fundamental principles of colonialism in Africa. The first of these principles was that the colonies should export raw materials for European factories and processing plants. Those materials included natural resources such as minerals and timber, but also agricultural commodities such as palm oil, peanuts, cotton, cocoa, and coffee, all of which were sent to Europe for processing. In order to encourage or coerce Africans to produce products needed in Europe, colonial governments required Africans to pay their taxes in cash, thereby forcing rural villagers to produce export crops to earn money for taxes. When the tax system failed to produce enough crops, the colonial governments simply ordered people to grow more or else face punishments.

The second principle was that colonial rule should create conditions whereby European companies and settlers could go to Africa for business ventures in order to make profits that would be repatriated to Europe. British colonial secretary Joseph Chamberlain told the Birmingham Chamber of Commerce in 1896 that "the Foreign Office and the Colonial Office are chiefly engaged in finding new markets and in defending old ones. The War Office and Admiralty are mostly occupied in the defense of those markets, and for the protection of our commerce." Within that broad framework, it was up to private companies and settlers to exploit the resources of the colonies. Louis Franck, the Belgian minister of colonies, elaborated on that theme when he wrote, "The merchant, the industrialist, and the planter are the driving powers of a colony. Without them, no country in the world would be able to bear the considerable expense of colonization. The State cannot itself attempt the economic development of our territories." In the age of industrial capitalism, the British, French, Portuguese, and Belgian governments were in Africa to expand their national economies by enriching their nations' private companies.

The third principle was that the colonies should be financially self-sufficient. Each colony was expected to raise enough tax and customs revenue to cover the expenses of colonial administration. One historian has referred to this principle as "hegemony on a shoestring," but it could also be called "colonialism on the cheap." During the worldwide Great Depression, for example, the Belgian Congo colonial government was running annual deficits while Belgian companies were draining nearly 8 trillion Belgian francs of profit from the colony. After much negotiation, the Belgian government reluctantly agreed to provide a small subsidy to the colonial administration, but only on a temporary basis.

Colonial administrations sought to save money by keeping the number of European administrative and military personnel to a minimum and relying as much as possible on African chiefs, soldiers, police, and clerks to attend to the day-to-day work of governing. At the same time, the colonial governments sought to increase their revenue by extending tax collection to every household and increasing exports so that they could collect more customs duties. Whatever money the Africans had left over after paying their taxes could be used for buying products imported from Europe, on which the colonial government also collected customs duties. Whenever goods entered or exited the colony, the colonial government gained revenue.

The fourth principle was that colonial projects for economic development were to be limited in scope. The colonizers were not planning to build factories or to replicate the European Industrial Revolution in Africa. Rather, they envisioned a globally integrated economic system in which the colonies provided a steady supply of agricultural commodities and raw materials to be processed in European factories by European workers. In order to meet European demand, Africa needed further improvements in its transportation networks; elementary schools to produce literate workers for the colonial administrations and European companies; court systems to guarantee property rights and punish criminals; and basic medical care to fight epidemics and keep workers healthy. Beyond meeting those basic needs, however, no further economic development was envisioned.

The fifth principle was that the costs of economic development projects should be borne as much as possible by the Africans themselves. Expensive projects such as railroads were financed by loans that the railroads would repay from their hauling charges. The labor required for building roads, bridges, telegraph lines, and colonial administrative buildings would be forced labor recruited from rural villages. In the French colonies, for example, each able-bodied man was required to do 15 days of forced labor each year, and some people were sent outside their districts to work on major public projects for up to a year under a legal loophole known as the "second portion." The Portuguese colonies, too, relied heavily on forced labor for building roads and other public works. Recruitment and supervision of forced laborers was increasingly farmed out to African chiefs and soldiers. The colonizers failed to acknowledge that successful economic development would require major investments in transportation, health, and education that they were unable or unwilling to make. Taken together, these five principles underlay the wide variety of specific policies implemented by the different colonial powers.

Racist Underpinnings of Colonial Rule

Colonial laws and policies were based on the racist assumption that Africans and colonial Europeans lived in completely different cultural universes that should remain separate and unequal. Colonial rulers accordingly established a racial hierarchy composed of white "Europeans" (administrators, soldiers, businesspeople, and settlers) on the top and black "natives" on the bottom, with different laws and regulations for each group. Frederick Lugard, the architect of British colonial administration, acknowledged that black Africans were human beings, but he believed that they were far nearer to the animal world than to Europeans. He claimed that Africans were lacking in self-control, discipline, and foresight and lacked the power of organization and management. "The virtues and defects of this race-type," he wrote, "are those of attractive children."

Different colonial powers implemented the racial hierarchy in different ways. In British colonies, racial distinctions were reflected in policies such as residential segregation in the cities, and in special "native courts" that applied "customary law" to Africans, whereas whites were subject to British law. Similar distinctions could be found in the French colonies, but the most visible manifestation of the unequal treatment of Africans was the ***indigénat***, a law that allowed French colonial administrators to inflict swift and immediate punishments on Africans for any real or perceived challenge to their authority. Half of the punishments meted out under the *indigénat* in the 1930s were for failure to pay taxes or complete forced-labor assignments, but Africans were also jailed or fined for offenses such as not planting enough peanuts, selling pepper to African traders, and emptying their reserve granaries. In one instance, a colonial administrator used his authority under the *indigénat* to force people to spend their nights in the marshes of the Middle Niger floodplain, slapping the water to quiet the frogs that disturbed his sleep.

Whereas the British maintained a strict binary division between "natives" and "Europeans," the French, Portuguese, and Belgians created an intermediate category for Africans who were educated in colonial or mission schools and had adopted a European lifestyle. In French colonies, such persons were known as *assimilés* (assimilated ones) or ***évolués*** (evolved ones) and were exempt from the summary discipline of the *indigénat*. In the Portuguese colonies, the *assimilados* (assimilated ones) were usually mission-educated Christians who obtained employment in the colonial administration and received exemptions from forced-labor requirements. In the Belgian Congo, a person with an *évolué* certificate was exempt from corporal punishment, had access to European courts, and was allowed to walk through a white neighborhood after 6 p.m. without being arrested. The very existence of such in-between categories revealed the stark contrast between the rights of "Europeans" and those of "natives."

Indirect Rule

All colonial regimes relied on local chiefs and headmen to collect taxes and enforce colonial laws, but they differed on how they related to preexisting African chiefdoms and kingdoms. When the British conquered large African states, they generally sought to keep the existing African administrative systems more or less intact so that they could be redirected to serve British policy interests. The British referred to this approach as **indirect rule.** The French, in contrast, broke up large African states and appointed chiefs who were loyal to the French, even if they lacked local legitimacy, but they later switched to a modified form of indirect rule. The Portuguese took a different approach and drew their district administrators from the white settler community that was already in place, using local chiefs only for the lowest levels of colonial administration.

Systems of indirect rule relied on a colonial stereotype holding that Africa was neatly divided into a series of homogeneous "tribes" that occupied clearly delineated territories. "Tribes" were said to be governed by "paramount chiefs," who in turn supervised lesser chiefs and village headmen. As previous chapters have shown, the historical reality was much more complex. The political boundaries of precolonial African states rarely coincided with ethnic or linguistic boundaries, a situation that often frustrated colonial officials. A British colonial official in Zimbabwe noted that in 1924, "the tribes were in a very disorganized state," but by 1929, he could boast that he had artificially created a more streamlined "tribal" organization. In a similar way, a French official who was trying to consolidate several tiny chiefdoms to form a "tribe" in the French Congo in 1937 wrote, "Even if there were enough interest in abolishing the numerous land chiefs to create tribes, it would be impossible to find among the land chiefs individuals influential enough to be appointed as chief of the tribe." In both cases, the administrators were trying to alter African political systems to make them conform to the colonial model of a "tribe."

Although indirect rule weakened the chiefs by reducing their customary authority, it also strengthened them by freeing them from accountability to their own constituents. Backed up by the power and might of the colonial government, the chiefs could use their position to their personal advantage by levying fines, banishing rivals, conscripting labor, or seizing land. Colonial governments were generally willing to tolerate such abuses as long as the chiefs collected taxes, mobilized labor, arrested lawbreakers, and kept the peace. One scholar has gone so far as to characterize indirect rule as a system of "decentralized despotism." A closer look at colonial governance in the British, French, and Portuguese colonies will illustrate how the principles of indirect rule were implemented in practice.

British Indirect Rule

The principles and practices of British indirect rule were elaborated by Frederick Lugard in *The Dual Mandate in British Tropical Africa*, in which he sketched out a model of an administrative system whereby African "paramount chiefs" supervised "district headmen," who in turn supervised "village headmen." Lugard explained that there should not be two sets of rulers—one British and one African—but a single government in which the African chiefs had well-defined duties. "The chief himself," Lugard wrote, "must understand that he has no right to place and power unless he renders his proper services to the [colonial] state." The British retained for themselves the exclusive right to raise and command armies, impose taxes, make laws, appropriate land, and choose successors to deceased chiefs. In essence, the chiefs could keep their traditional titles and ceremonial trappings, but would otherwise be agents of British policy.

The most difficult problems in implementing a system of indirect rule came in areas where the people had decentralized political systems with no identifiable chiefs. The Igbo people of southern Nigeria (see chapters 6 and 10) are the most notable case in point. In precolonial times, their village-oriented political system did not recognize any authority higher than the council of village elders. After the British gained military control of Igbo country, they sought local leaders to appoint as chiefs. Because the village elders were religious leaders as well as civil authorities, they were reluctant to ally themselves with the British, and they put forward undesirables, or men of little status, in order to insulate themselves from the colonial administration. The British then appointed those "nobodies" as chiefs by giving them a written warrant and an official British cap. They thus became known as **warrant chiefs.**

The warrant chiefs were unpopular because they frequently abused their newfound authority, and they became even more unpopular in 1928, when they were ordered to collect taxes from all the male heads of household. The following year, after a rumor spread that the warrant chiefs would begin collecting taxes from women as well, crowds of women up to 10,000 strong staged protests, throwing sand at the warrant chiefs, beating them with sticks, and seizing their British caps. The protests spread over two provinces and did not end until colonial soldiers began firing into the crowds at point-blank range, killing and wounding dozens of unarmed women. Because women had organized and carried out the protests, the events became known as the Women's War. In the aftermath of the protests, the British created local governing councils that were more in keeping with Igbo customs.

French Direct and Indirect Rule

The French system of administration developed out of France's experience in conquering the West African Sahel, where the older established African states had already been destroyed in the nineteenth century by the jihad of Umar Tal (see chapter 9) and the conquests of Samori Touré (see chapter 8). With no "traditional" authorities to rely on, the French conquerors simply appointed chiefs based on their loyalty to France. Many of the appointed chiefs were of different ethnicities and spoke different languages than the people they governed. In cases in which the French conquered intact kingdoms, they at first kept them whole as "protectorates," but later stripped the kings of any real authority or removed them from power entirely. Dividing the kingdoms into administrative units of more or less equal size, they frequently appointed chiefs from families that had not traditionally exercised authority.

French policy became more like that of the British after World War I, when the governor-general of French West Africa ordered French administrators to identify the traditional lineage heads and accord them special consideration when selecting chiefs. Where chiefs no longer existed, they looked for the person most acceptable to the local population. In rehabilitating the status of the traditional chiefs, the governor-general had no intention of restoring their previous authority. Echoing his British counterpart Frederick Lugard, he wrote, "There are not two authorities in the district, French authority and native authority; there is only one. Only the [French] *commandant* of the district commands. The native chief is only an instrument, an auxiliary."

Portuguese Settlers as Administrators

Circumstances in the Portuguese colonies of Angola, Guinea-Bissau, and Mozambique differed from those in the French and British colonies because Portuguese settler populations were already in place at the time of the scramble for Africa. The Portuguese could thus staff their colonial administrations with locally hired Portuguese settlers who were accustomed to living in Africa and had some knowledge of African languages. The smallest colonial administrative unit in Portuguese colonies was the "post," which was staffed by a Portuguese official who commanded an African security force to help him collect taxes, recruit forced labor, arrest lawbreakers, and suppress dissent. Local chiefs, who were arbitrarily appointed by the Portuguese, had even less autonomy than their counterparts in French colonies.

AGRARIAN ECONOMIES IN AFRICAN PRODUCER COLONIES

As we consider the period of high colonial rule, it is useful to make a distinction between two types of colonies. The vast majority of the colonies had very few white settlers, and their colonial administrations concerned themselves mainly with governing and taxing African producers. Colonies of this type will be referred to as producer colonies. The other type consisted of settler colonies such as Algeria, South Africa, and Zimbabwe, in which large numbers of white settlers had control of significant amounts of productive farmland. In these colonies, colonial policies were aimed at supporting the white producers and turning Africans into migratory wage laborers for white farms and enterprises. Colonies that were primarily producer colonies, but contained pockets of settler or plantation agriculture, were in an intermediate situation. In those cases, Africans were often caught between demands for their labor and their desire to produce cash crops for themselves.

The main purpose of the African producer colonies was to generate profits for European companies and revenue for the colonial governments. In order to accomplish those goals, the colonies needed to produce agricultural commodities that were in demand on the world market. Peanuts and palm oil were already being exported from Africa in the nineteenth century, and their production expanded significantly in the century that followed. Cocoa and coffee were introduced beginning in the 1890s. As we've seen, colonial governments required farmers to pay their taxes in cash (as opposed to paying in kind) in order to force them to produce goods that had cash value on the world market. The rise of cash crop production affected gender relations, as women remained responsible for growing the food crops to feed the family, while men often claimed a monopoly on the money generated by cash crop production.

Cocoa, Coffee, and Peanuts

Cocoa and coffee are tree crops that grow well in the West African forest belt. In Ghana, African residents of the coastal strip obtained cocoa seedlings from the colonial botanical garden and moved into the sparsely populated forest belt to find land to grow their crop. They formed companies that bought up large blocks of land from local chiefs and subdivided it for individual use. By 1911, Ghana was the world's number one producer of cocoa. Not waiting for the colonial government to build an infrastructure, the Ghanaian cocoa farmers pooled their money to build roads and bridges to help transport their products to the coast. In the late 1930s, when the price of cocoa dropped because of the worldwide Great Depression, Ghanaian cocoa farmers and chiefs banded together to withhold their cocoa from the market, forcing British cocoa buyers to raise the price.

In neighboring Nigeria, African Christian clergymen traveled inland from the coast to carry seedlings and spread the word about cocoa growing. Once cocoa caught on, local Nigerian merchants began to invest their profits in forest land for cocoa farms. Expanding deep into the forest away from the towns, the cocoa farmers built small hamlets so they could stay near their farms. By the 1930s, African farmers from the savanna region north of the forest were also moving into the forest to grow cocoa. In Côte d'Ivoire, the first coffee and cocoa plantations were established by French plantation owners, who took advantage of the colonial government's forced-labor system, but by the 1920s, more and more Africans were establishing cocoa and coffee farms in the forests. By the late 1930s, Côte d'Ivoire was exporting 50,000 tons of cocoa per year, Nigeria was exporting 100,000 tons, and Ghana was exporting 250,000 tons.

The bulk of the West African population, however, lived in the savanna, where the crops they could grow had little or no value in the world market. If they failed to pay their taxes, they risked punishments such as being beaten in front of their children, forced to sit in the hot sun for hours balancing a heavy rock on their head, or held under water in a colonial form of waterboarding. Some desperate people borrowed money from their chief, leaving a daughter behind as a pawn; others fled to neighboring colonies in hopes of finding lower tax rates; while still others undertook seasonal migrations to earn money working in regions that produced peanuts or cocoa.

In French West Africa, many young men traveled to the peanut-growing regions in western Senegal in order to earn money to pay their families' taxes. Workers would travel as far as 600 miles and spend up to a month on the road. Arriving in a famished condition, they made an oral contract with an African landlord in which they received land to cultivate their own peanuts in return for working 3 or 4 days a week in the landlord's fields. Other young men would travel south into the forest belt to find work logging exotic hardwoods or laboring on African-owned cocoa or coffee farms. The head of the household would often send different family members to different places so that if one failed to earn enough money, another might succeed. French officials reported that up to half of the villagers in the savanna regions in any given year were away seeking money to pay their taxes.

Cotton Colonialism

Cotton was the commodity that drove the Industrial Revolution. By the beginning of the American Civil War in 1861, mechanized textile mills had sprung up in Britain, continental Europe, and the northeastern United States. Cotton cloth production embodied the globalization of the industrial age because the cotton itself was grown hundreds or even thousands of miles away from the textile factories. The climate in Europe and the northern United States was too cold and too lacking in sunlight to grow cotton, so the textile mills looked southward for their supplies. With global cotton consumption quadrupling between the end of the American Civil War and 1920, Europeans looked to their African colonies for new supplies of "white gold," as cotton was sometimes called.

Africa was no stranger to cotton. Even before the Old Kingdom in Egypt was formed, two varieties of cotton that are indigenous to Africa were domesticated in the Nile valley. Although ancient Egyptians wore mostly linen cloth made from flax, cotton was grown and spun in Meroe by the sixth century BCE. By 1100 CE, the spinning and weaving of cotton were widespread in the Nile valley and the northern savanna. With the spread of Islam in West Africa, the use of cotton cloth expanded further because Muslim standards of modesty required people to cover up most of their bodies. As early as 1068, the Sanhaja Berbers of the western Sahara Desert (see chapter 3) were described as people who covered their faces with veils so that only their eyes were visible. In the northern savanna, many families grew small amounts of cotton for their own needs, often intercropping it with food crops.

Market-Driven Cotton Production

African cotton gained international importance in the nineteenth century, when Egyptian long-staple cotton, which many believed to be the best in the world, became Egypt's number one cash crop. Egypt's latitude was similar to that of

Georgia, Mississippi, and Alabama, the major cotton-producing regions in the United States. Although cotton could grow in Africa's more tropical latitudes, it did not do as well there, and the quality was not as good. Cotton requires a lot of sunlight during the growing season, and the amount of daylight near the equator seldom exceeds 12 hours throughout the year. That factor helps to explain why cotton yields in Egypt were seven times greater than those in Nigeria, Uganda, or Mozambique.

Following the example of Egypt, the British hoped to develop irrigated cotton production in Sudan in the Gezira triangle, formed by the confluence of the Blue Nile and the White Nile. From their experiments, they concluded that Gezira was the "finest cotton growing country in the whole of the British Empire." Equally important, it produced the exact variety of cotton required by the textile mills in Lancashire County, England. Their scheme called for building a dam on the Blue Nile and irrigation canals to distribute the water to individual fields. Twenty thousand workers were mobilized to build the 2-mile-long Sennar Dam, which was completed in 1925.

The people who lived in the Gezira triangle were forced to sell their land to the British for a nominal sum and become tenants on land they had previously owned. They acquiesced largely because they had been conquered in war. As a familiar Arabic saying went, "The master of the sword is the master of the land." Acting much like ancient Egyptian pharaohs, the British claimed ownership of the land and the irrigation system. Tenant families were each allocated 30 acres of land, of which 10 had to be used for cotton, 10 left fallow each year for crop rotation, and 10 used for food and fodder crops. The tenants received 40 percent of the profit from cotton sales, with the rest going to the colonial government and the cotton company. By the late 1930s, the irrigation scheme covered more than a million acres and was worked by 25,000 farm families.

The British tried to use the free-market approach to encourage cotton growing in northern Nigeria. They built a 700-mile railroad line to haul bales of cotton to the coast, and they sent out government officials to encourage people to grow cotton in order to earn money to pay their taxes. The *Times* of London predicted that all of northern Nigeria would soon be "filled with cotton plantations." The local farmers quickly discovered, however, that they could make twice as much money by growing peanuts instead. When the railroad first reached Kano in 1912, over 3,000 tons of peanuts piled up in the streets awaiting transportation during the first month. Moreover, much of the cotton being produced was sold to the local weavers, who matched or exceeded the prices offered by the British. Cotton exports picked up in the 1920s, when imported cloth began to drive local weavers out of business, but they never exceeded 25,000 bales a year, a tiny fraction of what the British had originally anticipated.

FIELDS OF COTTON Tenant farmers at the Gezira irrigation scheme in Sudan work at thinning the cotton plants to improve the yield. A typical cotton field had at least 30,000 plants per acre. Each tenant family was required to plant a minimum of 10 acres of cotton each year.

The British were more successful at expanding cotton production in highland Uganda, where exceptionally fertile soils and two rainy seasons a year provided favorable conditions for cotton growing. The first cotton growers were women, but the British were determined to establish cotton as a man's crop. In 1923, the British agricultural director stated that "cotton growing could not be left to the women and old people." At the beginning, the British used coercion to get men to grow cotton by ordering them to plant it on communal plots under the control of the chief. Even though cotton cultivation was initially coerced, it did not generate the steady resistance found in most other African colonies. That was because the main food crop in Uganda was the plantain banana, which was harvested little by little year round and therefore did not interfere with the cotton harvest. By 1938, Uganda was exporting 16 times more cotton than Nigeria.

Forced Cotton Production

In most of the tropical regions of Africa, however, cotton was a controversial crop. Low prices and poor yields led farmers to prefer food crops that could be eaten or sold in the local market. In 1935, a chief in French West Africa told a colonial official that "if the merchants offered a higher price, then everyone would grow cotton." Cotton had other disadvantages as well: it rapidly depleted the phosphorus and nitrogen in the soil, and its growing season coincided with those of major food crops, forcing families with limited available labor to choose between food and cash crops.

In French West Africa, the colonial administration initially tried to promote voluntary cotton production, but when that failed, it quickly turned to coercion. Each village was ordered to have a village cotton field, laid out and measured by a colonial agricultural monitor, to be worked collectively by the villagers. Villagers later recalled that "they never paid us for the cotton. We farmed for free." In 1935, the colonial government mounted a vigorous publicity campaign to promote voluntary cotton growing, but to no avail. Instead, there were reports of farmers fleeing their villages to avoid forced labor in the communal cotton fields.

The failure of forced cotton production prompted the French colonial government to embark on a scheme to build dams and canals to irrigate the semidesert land near the Niger bend in order to grow cotton. Using Egypt as their model, the French predicted that irrigation would produce cotton yields 10 times greater than rain-fed agriculture. Aggressively recruiting African settlers for the scheme with misleading promises and administrative pressure, the French administrators ordered chiefs to provide them with quotas of settlers. Officials reported that the roads were filled with people fleeing their villages to avoid the recruiters. In all, the **Niger scheme** never put more than 250 square miles of land under cultivation (out of a projected 6,000), and it never supported more than 30,000 African settlers (out of a projected 360,000). In contrast to the French fantasy of turning the Niger bend into a "second Egypt," the irrigated fields yielded only 20–50 percent as much cotton per acre as the British Gezira triangle scheme in Sudan. That was because the French never found a variety of cotton that was ideally suited to the soil and climate of the Niger bend.

The Belgian Congo moved into large-scale cotton production beginning in 1920, when it divided the colony into concession areas, granted European companies monopolies over the cotton produced there, and required African farmers to grow a certain amount of cotton. Cotton company agents and government cotton monitors visited the villages and ordered each household to prepare a field of a specified size, giving them a rigid calendar for planting, weeding, and harvesting. Each planter kept a booklet in which the cotton monitor noted how much seed the person had received from the cotton company and how much cotton the household produced each year. Up until the 1930s, the cotton companies kept the prices low, and most of the money the farmers earned from the harvest went to pay taxes.

In the Belgian Congo, as in many other parts of Africa, women did the bulk of the work in cotton production. A colonial agricultural report noted that "the greatest part of agricultural work, if not the totality, is performed by women." Yet the cotton companies made payments for the cotton to the male heads of household, whom they considered to be the owners of the cotton fields. A man with several wives could thus collect payments for the cotton production of each wife. As cotton prices increased in the 1940s, men used the cotton money to buy prestige items such as bicycles, while the women who produced the cotton got some cloth from their husbands, or perhaps nothing at all.

Congo law imposed a penalty of 7 days of hard labor plus a substantial fine for failure to produce sufficient cotton, but in practice, many people who failed to keep up with the schedule were whipped on the spot with a *chicotte*. Many of the African cotton monitors who enforced the work schedule were ex-soldiers who knew very little about agriculture, but a great deal about intimidation. The colonial government forced people to grow more cotton by raising the tax rates nearly eightfold between 1922 and 1930. One colonial administrator concluded in 1937 that "it has become increasingly evident that the basis for the major part of our economic success in the Belgian Congo is forced labor in the strictest sense of the word."

Portugal was the last colonial power to embrace forced cotton production. Modeling its cotton policy on that of the Belgian Congo, Portugal gave cotton companies exclusive concessions to purchase cotton at fixed prices from local farmers in Mozambique, who would be pressured to grow it. The project did not get off to a good start. When the people of one district brought in their first harvest in 1932, they were told that their cotton was third-class, and they were paid only 20 *centavos* per kilogram. The following year, they refused to grow cotton. By 1937, only 80,000 African farmers were growing cotton. To increase Mozambique's cotton production, the colonial government issued a decree that established required agricultural production and mapped out large areas of the colony where farmers would be forced to grow cotton. By 1940, half a million farmers in Mozambique were growing cotton under threat of punishment.

AGRARIAN ECONOMIES IN WHITE SETTLER COLONIES

African colonies with a significant number of white European settlers operated in a very different manner from producer colonies. These colonies were most often found in the Mediterranean climate zones of North Africa and South Africa or on high plateaus with cooler weather and less exposure to malaria-carrying mosquitoes. In all cases, the general plan was for white farms and businesses to produce cash crops and minerals for export, with Africans supplying the labor. Africans worked for white farms and businesses to earn money to pay their taxes.

Algeria

In Algeria, at the northern edge of Africa, 10,000 square miles of the best agricultural land near the Mediterranean coast had been allocated to European settlers by 1921. The country was 90 percent desert, so arable land was rare. The seized land was given to over 200,000 European settlers, half of whom came from southern France and the rest from Italy and Spain. The settlers became known as the *pieds noirs*, "black feet" in French, although the origins of the term remain obscure. Some say it refers to their black leather shoes, while others say that the soles of their feet were blackened because they were too poor to wear shoes.

At first, the Europeans grew mostly hard and soft wheat, but they soon turned to vineyards and wine making. The Algerian wine country, at a latitude similar to that of central California, had a long growing season, moderate-to-warm temperatures, and little seasonal variation in temperatures between winter and summer. By 1914, nearly half of the settlers' land was taken up by vineyards, which demanded labor-intensive cultivation. Cheap labor was easy to obtain because over half a million Algerians had lost their land during the expropriations following the colonial conquest, and they depended on income from wage labor on settler farms. By the mid-1930s, Algeria was the third-largest wine producer in the world (after France and Italy). In contrast to grape production, which continued to be labor-intensive, wheat production began to be mechanized in the 1930s by the increasing use of tractors and combine harvesters. A single combine harvester could replace a hundred workers.

Faced with inadequate land for smallholder agriculture and diminishing employment opportunities on the settlers' farms, many young Algerian men began to cross the Mediterranean to seek work in France. By 1925, over 100,000 Algerians were working in France, where they took the most undesirable jobs and often lived in appalling conditions to earn enough money to send back home to support their families.

South Africa

The most extreme application of the settler colony system was at the opposite end of the continent, in South Africa. Following its victory in the Anglo-Boer War of 1899–1902 (see chapter 10), Britain entered into a series of negotiations with the British and Boer settlers, resulting in the formation of the Union of South Africa in 1910. The agreement united the Cape Colony and Natal, which had been under British control, with the Orange Free State and the South African Republic, which had been controlled by the Boers. In the newly formed Union of South Africa, laws were passed by a parliament made up of exclusively white representatives.

The Union of South Africa was officially a British colony with a British governor-general, but it had the status of a self-governing dominion within the British Empire, which made it similar to Canada, Australia, and New Zealand. In an effort to satisfy both the British and the Boer settlers, English and Afrikaans (a variant of Dutch) were both recognized as official languages. Government functions were divided geographically: the administrative capital was Pretoria (in the former South African Republic), but the parliament met in Cape Town (in the former Cape Colony), and the Supreme Court met at Bloemfontein (in the former Orange Free State). While the system of government bent over backward to placate the different factions of the white settler minority, the African majority was virtually ignored.

With the white settlers firmly in charge, the parliament passed the **Natives Land Act** on June 19, 1913, which prohibited Africans from owning land outside of the "native reserves" that were being established. The **native reserves** were somewhat like the Indian reservations in the United States. The main difference was that in South Africa, the Africans made up more than two-thirds of the population, yet they were initially allocated only 7 percent of the land. Describing the African reaction to the Natives Land Act, the African journalist Sol Plaatje wrote, "Awakening on Friday morning, June 20, 1913, the South African Native found himself, not actually a slave, but a pariah in the land of his birth." The native reserves were made up of small and medium-sized blocks of land scattered throughout the eastern half of the country. The only substantial block was in the territory of the former Zulu Kingdom, but even there, whites had acquired legal title to much of the best land.

At the time the Natives Land Act was passed, a great many Africans were living outside the areas that had been designated as native reserves. Most of them lived on land that was owned by white farmers, where they worked as tenants or sharecroppers. Many white farmers were absentee landlords who did not work on their land at all, but simply leased it out to African tenants and showed up at harvest time to collect their rent. Under such conditions, African tenants could live as semi-independent farmers even if they lacked a legal title to the land. The Natives Land Act changed all that. It prohibited Africans from paying rent or sharing the harvest with the landlord, essentially turning African farmworkers into migratory wage laborers who lacked any rights to the land, not even as tenants or sharecroppers.

Spearheading the African opposition to the Natives Land Act was a newly formed organization called the South African Native National Congress, which would later shorten its name to the African National Congress, or ANC. The general secretary of the organization was the young African journalist Sol Plaatje,

PROTESTING THE NATIVES LAND ACT This photo shows the delegation of black South Africans that traveled to London in June 1914 to protest the 1913 Natives Land Act. Seated in the center is John Dube, the founder and president of the South African Native National Congress (SANNC), which was the forerunner of the African National Congress (ANC). Sol Plaatje, the general secretary of the SANNC, is seated on the right.

who had worked tirelessly to document the effects of the law on Africans. He participated in the ANC delegation to the South African parliament in Cape Town and even traveled to London to demand repeal of the law, but to no avail. The ANC's protests against the Natives Land Act made it the leading organization in South Africa that worked to defend the rights of Africans, a fact that would not be forgotten when black South Africans were finally allowed to vote in free elections in 1994.

In his book *Native Life in South Africa*, Plaatje described the eviction of African tenants from the land they had lived on and worked on for years. He described "countrymen and country women driven from home, their homes broken up, with no hopes of redress, on the mandate of a government to which they had loyally paid taxation without representation." Those who were expelled sought refuge in the native reserves, which became so overpopulated with people and cattle that the original vegetation disappeared, wells dried up, and soil erosion became an increasing problem. Under such conditions, smallholder farming in the reserves collapsed as families eked out a living on tiny plots, while able-bodied males sought wage labor on white farms and businesses. New legislation in 1936 increased the land allocated to Africans from 7 percent to 13 percent of the country, but did little to alleviate the problems.

By 1936, over half a million African men were living outside the reserves as wage laborers for white employers. Those who sought work in the towns and cities were harassed by the Native Urban Areas Act, which proclaimed that the urban areas were the preserve of white people and tolerated Africans only as units of labor. Africans who lost their jobs or completed their contracts could be expelled from urban areas and sent back to the native reserves. Back in the reserves, women struggled to produce enough food to maintain their families and to support the young, the old, and the infirm while so many of the able-bodied men were away.

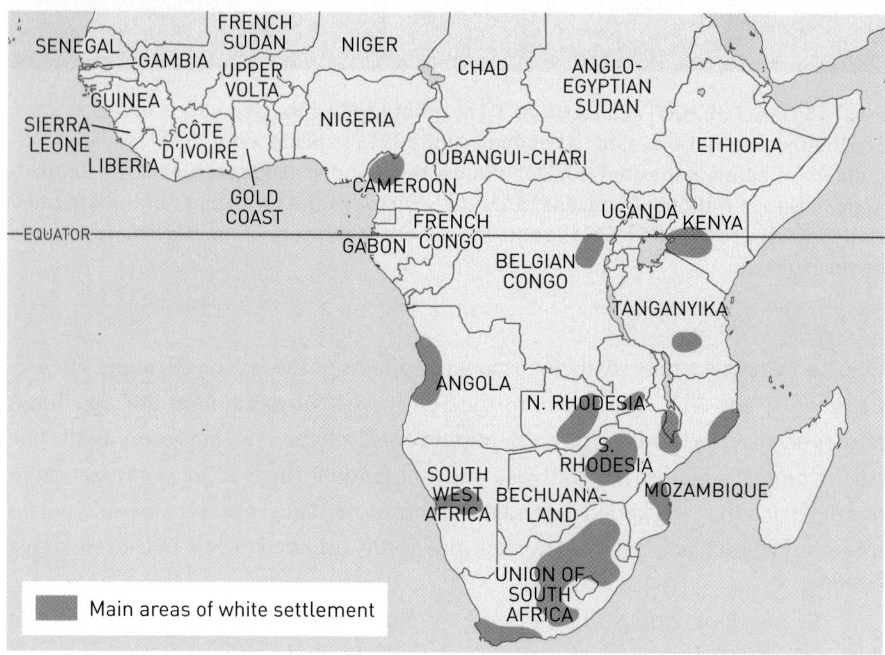

WHITE SETTLER AREAS IN SUB-SAHARAN AFRICA, 1920–1940 The major areas of white settlement were in South Africa and Southern Rhodesia (present-day Zimbabwe), but other colonies had pockets of white settlement as well. They were usually located in areas of high elevation that had a cool climate and were free of mosquito-borne diseases.

Zimbabwe

A similar set of developments took place on the Zimbabwe Plateau to the north of South Africa. This was the area to which Cecil Rhodes's British South Africa Company, which had obtained a charter from the British government, brought his "pioneer column" of armed settlers from South Africa in 1893 to mine for gold (see chapter 10). Even though the gold deposits turned out to be not nearly as rich as Rhodes had imagined, gold nevertheless produced important profits for the company and made up 50–60 percent of the colony's exports through the 1930s. When the imposition of a hut tax, which forced Africans to earn cash to pay their taxes, failed to produce enough mine workers, the company instituted a policy of forced labor, known as *chibaro*. Under this system, people were simply rounded up and marched to the mines, where they were forced to sign on for a year's labor. Those who refused were whipped or had their granaries burned down. The company's labor recruiters cast a wide net, and some workers had to walk up to 750 miles to reach the mines. Because of the poor working conditions and low pay, the mine workers usually referred to their condition as "slavery." During the 1920s, about 40,000 African men per year worked in the gold mines of Zimbabwe under ***chibaro*** **contracts**.

When the gold mines turned out to be less profitable than the company had expected, it tried to attract white settlers to start farms. The company had been seizing land from Africans ever since Rhodes's pioneer column first arrived, so fertile land was readily available. After the Africans revolted against the company in 1896–1897, Rhodes had punished them by seizing even more land and dividing the territory between African reserves and regions set aside for white settlers. By 1907, the BSAC directors decided that the time had come to put an end to the myth that Zimbabwe was a "second Rand." An estates department was set up in 1908 to promote European settlement, and a land bank was set up in 1912 to make loans to "persons of European descent." By 1914, over 5 million acres had been sold to white farmers. A typical white farm covered 5 square miles. As more settlers arrived, they often picked out land that was already being cultivated by Africans. As one colonial officer noted, "In selecting their land, they have naturally been guided by the number of natives located thereon, whose knowledge of the productive powers of the soil must necessarily be the best guide."

When the British South Africa Company's charter ran out in 1923, Southern Rhodesia, as it was then called, became a self-governing British colony with a parliament made up of white settlers. The 1930 Land Apportionment Act, passed by the white parliament, increased the amount of land for white settlers to approximately half the country. There were about 50,000 white settlers at the time, while over a million Africans had to share the other half. During the 10 years following the Land Apportionment Act, over 50,000 Africans were forcibly moved into reserves. As land confiscation and forced resettlement made the Africans' fields smaller, it became harder and harder for African farmers to make an independent living through smallholder agriculture. With no other option, they were forced to work for whites, either in the mines or on the white farms.

Initially, the white farms produced corn for the local mine workers, but by 1914 they were also exporting over 20,000 tons of corn a year to Britain. Tobacco was added to the repertory of settler crops when it was discovered that Virginia tobacco thrived in the sandy soils of Mashonaland (the region where the Shona people lived). By 1928, nearly a thousand white-owned tobacco plantations were producing 24 million pounds of tobacco a year on former Shona land. Tobacco cultivation was a labor-intensive activity that required about one African worker per acre. Because the tobacco-growing region was crossed by two major labor-migration routes to the South African mines, the farms found a steady supply of workers who had already been forced into migratory labor by taxes or labor recruiters.

SETTLERS AND PLANTATIONS IN AFRICAN PRODUCER COLONIES

Although Algeria, South Africa, and Zimbabwe are the most prominent examples of a colonial system whereby white settlers seized African land and turned independent African producers into migratory wage laborers, there are smaller examples of this phenomenon elsewhere, in colonies where African producers predominated. Such areas were usually located in highlands that had a climate hospitable to European settlers. They drew African laborers mostly from the surrounding regions. In the tropical regions, international corporations such as Lever Brothers and Firestone carved out vast plantations in the midst of African producer colonies.

Pockets of White Settler Farming

One prominent pocket of white settler farming was in the mountains of the Belgian Congo, where over 30 square miles of land were granted to 72 settlers in 1928 to establish coffee plantations. Coffee was a labor-intensive crop that employed large numbers of women and children at harvest time. Because the wages were not adequate to attract workers, the plantations would simply requisition workers from the chiefs, who would compel people to work on the plantations. Another such area was the highlands of central Mozambique, where settler-owned tea plantations employed about 25,000 African workers by 1940. A third pocket of white settlement was the Shire Highlands in Malawi, where Europeans established tea and coffee plantations.

The best-known example of a white settler enclave in a colony otherwise dominated by African smallholders is the **White Highlands** in Kenya. In precolonial times, the region had been occupied by Maasai cattle herders and Kikuyu farmers, but epidemics of rinderpest (a deadly cattle disease) and smallpox had swept through East Africa during the 1890s, decimating the cattle herds, wiping out well over half the population, and leaving the appearance of a nearly empty land. Soon after a railroad line was completed in 1902, the British colonial administration mounted a campaign to attract European settlers to help make the railroad profitable. Newspaper ads touted Kenya as "Britain's youngest and most attractive colony." They proclaimed that there was "no richer soil in the British Empire" and extolled "the advantage of native labor to supplement your own effort."

A SETTLER ESTATE IN THE HAPPY VALLEY This imposing settlers' house was located in the Wanjohi Valley—often called the Happy Valley—in the White Highlands of Kenya. The settlers here were mostly British and Anglo-Irish aristocrats who enjoyed famously hedonistic lifestyles while their African tenants did all the farm work.

Many of those who answered the ads were wealthy British aristocrats who dreamed of becoming gentlemen farmers who didn't actually do any work. Sixty-nine of the settlers were listed in *Burke's Peerage*, the definitive guide to the British aristocracy. Some of the land grants were enormous: Lord Delamere received nearly 300 square miles of land, and even settlers of modest means could obtain a thousand acres. By 1920, nearly 9,000 square miles of prime land had been confiscated by the British, and the number was later increased to 12,000 square miles. In a country where much of the land was semidesert, and only 10 percent of the total land area was suitable for cultivation, white settler farms covered half of the arable land. To provide labor for the white farms, the British not only instituted a hut tax on the African population, but also prohibited Africans from growing coffee or corn for income. The profitable crops were the legal monopoly of the white settlers.

The main form of African labor in the White Highlands was the "squatter" or "labor tenant" system, in which Africans were allocated land for growing crops or grazing by a white landlord in return for a certain amount of labor per year. The system changed over time as the settler community became better entrenched and more politically powerful. In 1918, a squatter could work for the settler 3–4 months a year in return for the right to cultivate a 6-acre plot of land and graze up to 30 sheep and goats. The wages were so low as to be almost insignificant, but the squatters stayed on in order to maintain access to land for cultivation and stock grazing. In 1931, over 100,000 Africans lived as squatters in the White Highlands, a number that would double by 1945. Conditions became even more difficult for squatters in 1937, when a new law extended the number of required working days to 240 and gave settlers the legal authority to limit the size of squatters' fields and reduce or eliminate their livestock.

Company Plantations

In addition to farms run by white settlers, a variety of plantations were established in African agricultural areas by European companies. One of the earliest examples was in Tanzania, where in 1898, the German East Africa Company began a plantation to produce sisal, a fibrous plant that is used for making ropes and twine. By 1938, Tanzania was supplying over one-third of the world's sisal. As the industry grew, the plantation's labor force came from increasingly remote regions of Tanzania. That was because many of the Africans in the more accessible regions had taken to growing cash crops such as coffee and cotton and therefore saw no need to engage in migratory labor. The labor force was augmented by migrants from as far away as Mozambique, Burundi, and Zambia. By 1948, over 120,000 Africans were working on the sisal plantations.

A second example of the effects of company plantations comes from the Belgian Congo, a heavily forested colony that was well suited to producing palm oil. A British soap manufacturer, Lever Brothers, calculated that it was spending too much money paying market price for palm oil produced by African farmers in southern Nigeria, and it sought a more favorable arrangement for procuring its supplies. In 1911, Lever Brothers signed an agreement with the Belgian Congo's colonial government, which granted the company exclusive rights to the palm oil produced in a territory of nearly 4,500 square miles. Instead of creating traditional palm plantations with long rows of trees, the company sought to create "natural plantations" by choosing areas with wild groves of oil palm trees. Using the same colonial law that King Leopold had once used to give rubber companies ownership of all the wild rubber in the forests (see chapter 10), the company claimed ownership of the palm groves, to the exclusion of the local residents. Its plan was to hire workers from the region to harvest bunches of palm fruit and carry them to processing plants.

The first post set up by the company was called **Leverville,** in honor of the Lever brothers. The colonial government assigned the company a European military officer and 15 African soldiers who would accompany the labor recruiters in order to intimidate potential recruits and protect the recruiters from the hostility of villagers. In many cases, the villagers fled in advance of the recruiters. By 1922, the company employed nearly 7,000 workers in the Leverville region. Workers lived in camps composed of straw-hut shelters in which 10–20 men slept, one against the other. They were fed a portion of rice and a piece of dried fish once a day, and nothing on Sunday. The cost of the food was deducted from their pay.

In 1931, a drive to forcibly recruit workers set off a major revolt in the region of Leverville. Finding that the men had fled from a certain village in advance of their arrival, the company recruiters locked up the women in a warehouse as hostages. When the recruiters arrived at another village 3 days later, they were met with volleys of arrows. Soon the whole region was in full revolt. Local spiritual leaders urged people to stop wearing European cloth and to throw away their colonial money in hopes that the spirits of their ancestors would intervene to help them drive out the whites. The colonial government called in soldiers, who spent 5 months putting down the revolt. At least 500 Africans were killed in the clashes, but only one person died on the government side.

The final example is the plantation system established in Liberia by the **Firestone Tire and Rubber Company** of Akron, Ohio. Although Liberia was an independent country, ruled by descendants of the American ex-slaves who had settled there in the nineteenth century (see chapter 9), the relationship between the settler government in the capital city and the African chiefs in the interior was similar to those in the European colonies. In 1926, the Firestone Tire and Rubber Company signed an agreement with the Liberian government that gave the company the right to lease up to a million acres of land (1,500 square miles) for rubber plantations. Because the Liberian government was deeply in debt to British banks and the U.S. government, Firestone gave it a $5 million loan to retire its debts and finance needed public works. Firestone was now the Liberian government's chief creditor. When Liberia fell behind on its payments in 1933, Firestone asked the U.S. government to dispatch a warship to Liberia, but the issue was resolved by diplomatic means.

The rubber plantation agreement gave Firestone enormous influence over the Liberian government. The Liberians had to accept a financial adviser designated by the president of the United States, five American customs and revenue officials designated by the U.S. State Department, and four American army officers recommended by the president of the United States to lead the Liberian Frontier Force. The Liberian government, on the other hand, was responsible for providing an adequate labor supply to the plantations. For its part, Firestone established two plantations that covered 100,000 acres and contained about 10 million rubber trees.

From the beginning, Firestone had a hard time finding enough workers willing to work for 2 cents an hour, and its agreement with the Liberian government prevented it from bringing in laborers from outside the country. The rubber company urged the Liberian government to conscript whatever men it could find and

TAPPING RUBBER TREES Workers on a Firestone Tire and Rubber Company plantation in Liberia tap a rubber (*Hevea*) tree by cutting channels to allow the latex to drip into a little cup. The League of Nations reported in 1930 that the workers were often forced or coerced into plantation labor by their chiefs, who were on the payroll of the company.

to extend the hut tax to even the most remote towns and villages. Firestone also paid chiefs 1 cent per day for each worker they supplied. In 1929, the International Labor Conference reported that Firestone was using forced labor, but a League of Nations report the following year absolved the company and pinned the blame on Liberian government agents. The report noted, however, that the chiefs had been reduced to "mere go-betweens, paid by the government to coerce and rob the people." The examples of Lever Brothers and Firestone illustrate how plantation economies often resulted in forced labor.

MINING ECONOMIES AND MIGRATORY LABOR

Mines made up a special category in the colonial economy, for they often drew their labor force from a large area that included neighboring colonies. Their impact was therefore regional in scope. Moreover, mines operated year round, whereas agricultural labor on white farms and plantations was often seasonal. A third distinctive characteristic of mining was that miners were mostly male, whereas women as well as men often worked on white farms and plantations.

The South African Gold Mines

The largest mining operation in Africa continued to be the South African gold mines, which employed about 200,000 workers in 1920 and double that number by 1938. Because the few well-paying jobs were monopolized by white employees, the only jobs available to Africans were unskilled positions with dangerous conditions, low pay, and no possibility of advancement. As a result of this system, the mines were constantly scouring the southern third of Africa for workers. After 1932, when recruitment in southern Africa became insufficient, the mines began to recruit in Central Africa instead. The flow of labor from any given area fluctuated from year to year, but the mines cast such a wide net that there was seldom a shortage of labor. The workers were motivated by three factors. First and foremost was the need for money to pay taxes. Second was the desire to buy nice clothes or other modern consumer goods. Third was the desire among young men for money to pay the bride-price so that they could get married. Although a mining income could help meet the needs mentioned above, it was not adequate for supporting a family. Men were able to leave home in search of work only because the women in their home communities produced and marketed the crops, cared for the livestock, and raised the children, ensuring that the men would have a family and community to return to. Thus the entire system of migratory mine labor rested on the agricultural production of women.

In 1932, the mines received permission to recruit "tropical" workers from Zimbabwe, Zambia, Botswana, and Malawi. In order to bring workers to the mines, the recruiting agency built over 700 miles of roads in northern Botswana, and it also built roads and recruitment camps in Zambia and Malawi. Trucks transported workers along the roads. The agency even established motor-barge transport on the Zambezi and Okavango Rivers and provided rudimentary medical exams at the recruitment camps to weed out applicants with health problems. By 1939, the "tropical areas" were contributing about 25,000 recruits a year.

Once the workers arrived at the mines, they were housed in compounds that typically had a dining hall, washrooms, and large dormitory rooms filled with bunk beds. A room 16 feet by 25 feet would house 40 men, and a room 40 feet by 32 feet would house 80, but the workers complained that the rooms sometimes held twice that many. Each compound was fenced in to prevent easy communication between the miners and the local population, and many compounds had only a single gate. Although the gates were generally unlocked, they had turnstiles that forced miners to go through one at a time. The chief authority was the white compound manager, who was assisted by a force of black compound police, who had the authority to send any black miner to the lockup at any time and for any reason. Alcohol was forbidden in the compounds, except for once or twice a week, when the mines served modest amounts of locally brewed low-alcohol beer that the mine owners called "Kaffir beer" and the miners called "compound beer."

Unattached women migrated to the mining areas to provide leisure-time services to the large concentrations of men who were away from their families. The most prominent were the ***shebeen* queens,** who opened unlicensed drinking establishments known as *shebeens*. In southern African societies, brewing sorghum beer was traditionally viewed as women's work, and these women used their skills and knowledge to brew beer for sale to the mine workers. Because it was illegal for Africans to brew beer and sell it in the mining areas, the women developed varieties of beer with shorter brewing times to minimize the dangers of police raids, and they developed stronger brews to distinguish their beer from the weaker compound beer served by the mines. A police report in 1919 noted that the women "are constantly being arrested and convicted, but as soon as one liquor den is closed others are opened."

By the 1930s, the *shebeen* business in the Witwatersrand was dominated by women from nearby Lesotho, who had left their homes to earn money and also to escape from the strictures of custom and patriarchal authority. Sotho male elders referred to those women derisively as *matekatse* (those who wander) or *matlolaterata* (those who jump the fence), yet ordinary Sotho regarded them with a mixture of resentment, anxiety, and awe because they were shrewd businesswomen who managed to run profitable establishments while avoiding the police who sought to shut them down.

The Copperbelt

The **Copperbelt** region, located in the southern Belgian Congo and northern Zambia, had produced copper bracelets and copper crosses (which served as currency) for centuries. The northern part of the Copperbelt, in the Belgian Congo, was known as Katanga. The Belgian mining company Union Minière opened its first copper mine there in 1911, and by 1931 it had become the world's largest producer of copper. The mines relied on labor-intensive production techniques that required large numbers of manual laborers. Workers lived and worked in unhealthy conditions, and medical facilities were rudimentary or nonexistent. In 1913–1914, more than one in five mine workers died of pneumonia, dysentery, or other diseases.

The job of finding men to work in the mines initially fell to various private labor-recruiting companies, but in 1910, the Belgians set up a single private company, called the Katanga Labor Exchange, which worked closely with the colonial government to recruit laborers from all parts of the Belgian Congo. By 1925, labor shortages at the mines were becoming acute. The director of the exchange wrote, "Genuinely voluntary labor hiring has become increasingly rare. Unless the stubborn natives can be subjected to direct constraint, recruitment drives will bring in fewer and fewer laborers. This is what makes the labor problem truly crucial." In response, the

COPPER MINING IN KATANGA Mine workers at the Kisanga copper mine in Katanga, Belgian Congo, in the late 1920s. The men pictured here were recruited from the mountains of Rwanda, nearly a thousand miles away.

exchange began to recruit workers from the Manyema district of the Congo (Tippu Tip's former territory) and from the colonies of Rwanda and Burundi, which the Belgians had taken over from Germany after World War I. Recruits from the mountains of Rwanda and Burundi suffered a death rate of nearly 10 percent from respiratory diseases, due partly to difficulties in adapting to the lowland climate.

The labor crisis finally prompted the mining company to undertake long-overdue reforms. First, it brought in more machines to substitute for manual labor. Between 1923 and 1929, the proportion of ore extracted by machine rose from 10 percent to 84 percent. Second, it sought to increase the efficiency of the labor force by providing more comfortable and hygienic housing and better food. Third, it began a process of labor stabilization by developing a group of skilled, permanent African workers who settled in the area with their families.

The southern part of the Copperbelt lay in Zambia, which was under the control of Cecil Rhodes's British South Africa Company until 1924, when it became a British colony. It was not until the British government took over that copper mining, undergirded by South African and U.S. capital, took off. Unlike the open-pit mines in Katanga, the Zambian mines were underground. They were richer in copper, but harder to work. Because the Zambian Copperbelt region had a population density of less than two persons per square mile, it was initially necessary to bring in laborers from farther south. Recruits traveled up to 2 months on foot to reach the mines.

In contrast to Cecil Rhodes, who had envisioned Zambia as nothing more than a labor reservoir, the British colonial governor was an advocate of white settler agriculture. He accordingly reserved the better agricultural land near the rail lines for white settlers willing to produce corn and other foodstuffs for the mines or for export, and he pushed the Africans into native reserves. A 1937 government report noted that in one district, "the total number of adult males liable for tax is estimated at 60,000 and 70,000. There are no economic crops, no native industries of any importance, nor, owing to the presence of endemic pleuro-pneumonia, has there been any market for cattle during the last 22 years." Reduced to subsistence farming on poor and sometimes overcrowded land, many Africans found it necessary to seek cash by working on white farms or in the copper mines.

After 1931, the mining companies no longer needed labor recruiters because more men were looking for work than they could hire. The key to attracting workers was that the Zambian mines allowed men to bring their wives. The housing provided in the mining compounds was woefully inadequate (sometimes several couples shared a room), but the mining companies gave the women 5-acre garden plots on company land where they could grow food for family consumption or for sale. By the 1930s, some 2,000 plots were producing peanuts, corn, beans, and green vegetables. In 1934, the women sold 600,000 pounds of vegetables to the Roan Antelope Mine alone. The women also grew corn and millet, which they used in brewing beer; a woman who brewed beer every week could earn substantially more than her husband. By the mid-1930s, about half the male mine workers were living in the compounds with their wives, and many couples were raising children who might grow up to be mine workers. The presence of women was advantageous for the mines as well, because it helped them cut costs and stabilize the labor force.

The Kilo-Moto Gold Mines

The final example to be considered here is the Kilo-Moto gold-mining complex in the Belgian Congo, which consisted of two separate mines located approximately 100 miles apart. The region where the mines were located, slightly north of the equator in the mountains bordering the western rift of the East African Rift System, receives abundant rain and has fertile volcanic soils that can produce a variety of food crops, and was therefore one of the most densely populated regions of the Belgian Congo, so there was no need to recruit mine workers from far away. That situation, however, put a lot of pressure on the local populations.

Mining operations began at Kilo in 1905 and at Moto in 1911. Up until 1926, the mines belonged to the colonial government, which recruited the labor force. A government official reported in 1914 that "nothing is done according to the law. People are forced to supply food; women are forced to work without contracts; workers are recruited by force; and their chiefs send them to work with threats of prison sentences." He later described the recruitment process: "In preparation for Mr. Stocker's labor recruitment trips, various chiefs were warned to have

KILO-MOTO GOLD MINING These workers are digging for gold in open pits at the Kilo-Moto gold mines in the Belgian Congo. The mines employed 40,000 workers in 1940, most of whom were local, so that a third of the men in the region were absent from their villages at any given time.

supplies of workers ready. On reaching a village, Mr. Stocker would find chained natives lined up for him. He had the chains struck off and took the men away." Confirmation of these practices can be found in the register of the Catholic mission at Kilo: "Increasing numbers of men are being snatched from their villages for mine work," wrote a priest on September 6, 1914. Two years later, the villages in the Kilo region were forced to relocate along newly built roads to facilitate labor recruitment and the provision of food to the mines.

In 1926, the colonial government sold the Kilo-Moto mines to a private company, which created the Kilo-Moto Recruiting Agency to recruit full-time workers. While continuing to receive aid from the local colonial administration, the recruiting agency instituted a program of paying chiefs 12 francs for each full-time worker they supplied. In 1930, for example, one chief received 9,456 francs, an amount equal to the annual wages of 22 mine workers. The Catholic missionaries reported in 1931 that "everyone agrees that if the chiefs did not force them to do so, no natives would leave their villages to go to work at the mines."

When the company took over in 1926, the Kilo-Moto mines employed 22,000 workers. That number grew steadily, reaching 41,000 workers in 1940. Most of the workers came from within the Kilo-Moto region. Although the Congo Commission on Labor had decreed in 1925 that no more than 25 percent of the adult men in any given district could be taken away for migratory labor, a 1930 government commission report revealed that 35 percent of the adult males in the Kilo-Moto region had been taken to work in the mines. That situation placed a huge burden on the women, who not only grew the food for their families, but could often be seen on the roads carrying 60-pound loads of foodstuffs toward the mines. The commission discovered that the governor of the province where the mines were located had raised the recruitment limit to 35 percent under pressure from the mining company. Because of the economic importance of the gold mines, the governor-general of the Belgian Congo decided to keep the limit at 35 percent of the adult male population. That policy remained in effect until 1944.

CONCLUSION

During the high colonial period, each African family became more integrated into the global economy, either by producing cash crops or by working for a mine or plantation that produced goods for the international market. A drop in the world market price of cocoa or palm oil had serious repercussions in rural villages, and a rise in demand for gold or copper could send recruiters farther and farther afield in search of labor. Yet the world market was always mediated through the colonial governments. If the market did not provide enough incentive for African farmers to grow certain crops, then the colonial governments resorted to compulsion. The needs of European factories usually trumped the incentives of the market.

As the colonial system matured, the colonial powers came to rely more and more on African chiefs, soldiers, and police to keep the peace, collect taxes, enforce crop production quotas, round up workers to build roads and railroads, and recruit laborers for the mines and plantations. Initially, the British and the French followed very different governing strategies, with the British trying to preserve large African kingdoms while the French were trying to break them up. After World War I, however, the French system became more like the British one, with so-called traditional chiefs forming the base of the colonial administrative pyramid. The chiefs had to navigate their contradictory position in which they were simultaneously the leaders of their people and colonial civil servants who could be dismissed if they failed to carry out administrative orders.

The goals of the colonial administrations varied according to colony type. In colonies with environments favorable to European settlers—such as Algeria, South Africa, Zimbabwe, and the White Highlands of Kenya—the primary goal was to ensure the economic success of the settlers by creating favorable market conditions and supplying them with cheap African labor. The colonial administrations achieved this by imposing taxes on the Africans to force them to earn cash and by giving the white settlers a monopoly on the most profitable crops.

In colonies with few European settlers, in contrast, the goal was to use taxes and production quotas to induce Africans to produce the raw materials and agricultural products needed by European factories and consumers. Africans were enthusiastic producers of edible cash crops such as peanuts, and of tree crops such as coffee and cocoa that did not interfere with food production, but they were more resistant to cotton production, which took time and land away from their primary goal of producing food. This situation created an ongoing conflict because the very commodity that the European colonizers wanted the most was the one that Africans were least interested in producing. However, cotton production was embraced in Egypt and Sudan, where the yields were high, and in Uganda, which had extraordinarily fertile soils and two rainy seasons a year.

In parts of Africa where people produced staple crops, such as millet, sorghum, cassava, and yams, that were not marketed internationally, earning enough money to pay taxes was a major problem. The most common solution was to send the younger men away to work as migrant laborers, often for years at a time. In West Africa, the migrant laborers usually worked for African employers in the production of peanuts, coffee, and cocoa, but in the southern half of the continent they were more likely to work in the mines, on corporate plantations, or on white settler farms. The men spent as long as 2 months traveling to the work region on foot, although over time, the construction of roads and the growth of truck transportation eased the journey. At the workplace, they lived in crowded compounds or rough camps with poor sanitary conditions and lousy food, and they often did not see their wages until after they returned home. The exodus of men from the rural villages placed a huge burden on women to keep up the family farms while also meeting government-imposed production quotas. In the Belgian Congo, the colonial administration was worried enough about the exodus of men from the rural villages that they set a limit of 25 percent of the adult male population (35 percent in the Kilo-Moto Economic Zone). It is doubtful that those limits were seriously enforced. In parts of French West Africa, the male absentee rate exceeded 50 percent.

Although many men engaged in migratory labor because they were forcibly recruited or because they had no other way to pay their taxes, others saw it as an opportunity. Many young men saw migratory labor as a way of earning money to pay the bride-price required to marry and start a family. In precolonial times, young men generally had little money, so they depended on the family elders to furnish the bride-price, thus giving the elders a major say in the choice of the bride. By earning their own bride-price, the young men began to break free of the elders' control, thus creating a growing shift in generational power.

A major consequence of migratory labor was that the migrant laborers developed a wider vision of Africa. Prior to engaging in labor migration, most rural Africans saw Africa through the lens of their own village and the surrounding neighborhood. Their identification with groups larger than their own family focused on their village and their chiefdom. Once they arrived at the mines and the plantations, however, they met people who spoke different languages and lived by different social and cultural codes. The gold mines of South Africa employed workers not only from all parts of South Africa, but also from Mozambique, Botswana, Zimbabwe, Malawi, Zambia, Namibia, and Angola. Suddenly, Africa looked bigger and more diverse than the individual migrant had previously imagined.

At the same time, the migrant laborers became more conscious of the unique qualities of their own language and culture. In the South African gold mines, speakers of the Zulu language from both inside and outside the boundaries of the Zulu Kingdom discovered their common heritage, just as Luba speakers from Kasai and those from Katanga discovered their common culture in the Copperbelt. It has been said that when American college students tour Europe, they develop both a wider sense of cultural diversity and a deeper sense of what it means to be an American. The migrant laborers in Africa had a similar experience. The migrants began to think about the world beyond their village and chiefdom in different ways and to see themselves as simultaneously members of a particular ethno-linguistic group, subjects of a particular colonial state, and, more broadly, as Africans.

CHAPTER REVIEW

KEY TERMS AND VOCABULARY

indigénat

évolué

indirect rule

warrant chief

Niger scheme

Natives Land Act

native reserve

chibaro contract

White Highlands

Leverville

Firestone Tire and Rubber Company

shebeen queen

Copperbelt

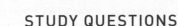

STUDY QUESTIONS

1. Assess the impact of World War I on Africans.
2. Why did the colonial powers prefer indirect rule over direct colonial administration?
3. How did the colonial governments pressure African farmers to produce cash crops?
4. Why did African farmers embrace cash crops such as peanuts and cocoa, but reject forced cotton production?
5. How did white settlers in South Africa and Zimbabwe force African farmers to become wage laborers?
6. Name the ways women participated in the mining economy.
7. What were the social consequences of labor migration to mines and plantations?

PERSPECTIVES

THE DUAL MANDATE

Frederick Lugard was the architect of the British system of indirect colonial rule. In his 1922 book, The Dual Mandate in British Tropical Africa, *he outlined his views on how colonial rule should ideally be organized. In the following excerpt, he uses the emirates of Northern Nigeria as his model for how to organize a system of indirect rule.*

The object . . . is to make each "Emir" or paramount chief, assisted by his judicial Council, an effective ruler over his own people. He presides over a "Native Administration" organized throughout as a unit of local government. The area over which he exercises jurisdiction is divided into districts under the control of "Headmen," who collect the taxes in the name of the ruler, and pay them into the "Native Treasury," conducted by a native treasurer and staff under the supervision of the chief at his capital. Here, too, is the prison for native court prisoners, and probably the school. . . . Large cities are divided into wards for purposes of control and taxation.

The district headman, usually a territorial magnate with local connections, is the chief executive officer in the area under his charge. He controls the village headmen, and is responsible for the assessment of the tax, which he collects through their agency. He must reside in his district and not at the capital. He is not allowed to pose as a chief with a retinue of his own and duplicate officials, and is summoned from time to time to report to his chief. . . .

A province under a [British] Resident may contain several separate "Native Administrations," whether they be Muslim Emirates or pagan communities. A "division" under a British District Officer may include one or more headmen's districts, or more than one small Emirate or independent pagan tribe, but as a rule no Emirate is partly in one division and partly in another. The Resident acts as sympathetic adviser and counselor to the native chief, being careful not to interfere so as to lower his prestige, or cause him to lose interest in his work. . . .

The tax—which supersedes all former "tribute," irregular imposts, and forced labor—is, in a sense, the basis of the whole system, since it supplies the means to pay the Emir and all his officials. The district and village heads are effectively supervised and assisted in the assessment by the British staff. The native treasury retains the proportion assigned to it (in advanced communities a half), and pays the remainder into Colonial Revenue.

1. *Outline the chain of command proposed by Lugard.*
2. *What was the significance of colonial taxes?*

Source: Frederick Lugard, *The Dual Mandate in British Tropical Africa* (Edinburgh: Blackwood, 1922), pp. 200–201.

THE WOMEN'S WAR

The Women's War of 1929 in southern Nigeria is unique in the annals of anti-colonial mass protest because it was organized as a series of peaceful protests. The initial success of the protests ended only after soldiers began firing on unarmed women. Afterward, the British colonial government held hearings to determine what had happened. On April 17, 1930, a woman named Nwanyima recounted how a crowd of women gathered in the town of Oloko to confront Warrant Chief Okugo.

The Testimony of Nwanyima

294TH WITNESS, NWANYIMA (F.A.) was called and sworn.
THE CHAIRMAN: What is your name?
WITNESS: Nwanyima.
THE CHAIRMAN: Where do you live?
WITNESS: Obikabia.
THE CHAIRMAN: You remember when all the women collected together last December?
WITNESS: Yes, Sir.
THE CHAIRMAN: Would you tell us how they came to collect?
WITNESS: I will tell you, so far as I know. The trouble started from Oloko. We were at home and we heard that the Oloko people had said that we should come to them because what they had heard was not pleasant. We went there and asked them why they cried out, raised alarm. They replied that Okugo had said that women should pay tax. We joined the Oloko women to shout out.

There and then we asked Okugo about it. Our spokeswomen asked Okugo about it. We sat back and listened. Okugo was unable to deny the statement. Oloko women gave evidence and Okugo was imprisoned [by a crowd of women who surrounded his house] and those of us who came from distant towns returned to our respective homes.

When we returned home we said that we would go and tell our clerk to bring the matter to the notice of the District Officer because we could not pay tax and that we were suffering already from the tax paid by our husbands and sons. We said that, as regards taxation, we women did not wish to pay tax and we did not wish to pay the tax of men also. We were overburdened.

We were also annoyed about market, trade was not satisfactory, not good. Oil, no value for it. Kernels, no profit. We asked the white men "How is it that you now dislike our produce and yet you have asked us to bring oil and kernels to the factories?" When we take oil to them instead of taking it in the ordinary way, they ask us to boil it and then pour it into a measure in order to strain the sediments. This process entails much waste of oil. The same thing applies to kernels. You have to wait there for a long time to prepare the kernels. They examine the kernels and if they find shells amongst them they make us pick them out.

We asked that we should go into the matter with the white men as to produce prices and also as to why women should pay tax because women are under men and there is no reason why women should pay tax. We were arrested—women were arrested—and imprisoned. Some of the women are still in prison. We want those who have been imprisoned to be released. We did nothing.

1. *What was the motivation behind the women's protests?*
2. *Why did Nwanyima think it unfair for women to pay tax?*

Source: Proceedings of the Commission of Inquiry into the Disturbances in the Calabar and Owerri Provinces, 1930 (CE/K5A), pp. 658–660; reprinted in Toyin Falola and Adam Paddock, *The Women's War of 1929: A History of Anti-Colonial Resistance in Eastern Nigeria* (Durham, NC: Carolina Academic Press, 2011), p. 597.

PERSPECTIVES

THE GOLD COAST FARMERS' HYMN

When the price of cocoa dropped in the 1930s because of the worldwide Great Depression, African cocoa farmers and chiefs in Ghana (formerly called the Gold Coast) banded together to withhold their cocoa from the market in order to force British buyers to pay higher prices. To encourage the farmers, Joseph Ben Gaisil wrote "The Gold Coast Farmers' Hymn." It was printed in the February 25, 1938, issue of the African Morning Post, *a newspaper serving Accra, Ghana. The song suggests that Ghanaian cocoa farmers had developed a distinct identity and a sense of pride in their profession.*

Oft in slav'ry, oft in woe
Onward Brethren farmers go
Pull the tug, protect with might
God your strength, your course being right

Let not courage from thee flee
Soon shall victory speed to thee
Let not fears your course impede
Chiefs, your cause of justice plead

Let your strong hearts still be glad
March in hopeful armor clad
Fan the fire all into flame
Play with them the trickish game

Onward then in battle move
If your crops are yours, then prove
Show your freedom to the foe
Onward Gold Coast farmers go

Father, Gov'ment unto thee
With our complaints do we flee
Peace and justice is our cry
Towards us turn thy justice eye

—Joseph Ben Gaisil

---

1. *Why did the author compare the farmers to slaves?*
2. *What was the role of the colonial government in the conflict?*

Source: *African Morning Post* (Accra), February 25, 1938, p. 2.

COTTON PROTEST SONGS

These songs were usually sung by women during a protest, or while walking to the cotton fields in the morning, or while carrying sacks of cotton to the trading stations. The first five songs were sung in Mozambique, while the sixth was sung in the Belgian Congo. Regardless of their origin, all of the songs express similar sentiments.

Song no. 1 (from southern Mozambique)

Tell the administrator that we haven't paid our taxes.
Tell him that no matter how many sacks of cotton we sell,
we still won't have enough to pay even one hut tax. . . . Tell him that we don't have time to grow food,
and that we're hungry.

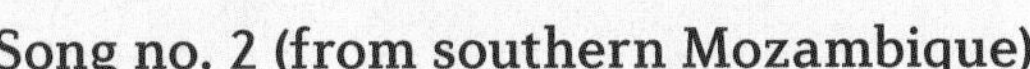

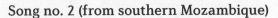

Song no. 2 (from southern Mozambique)

You have to flee, men, because the *capataz* [overseer] is coming.
Flee men, flee women, the man of cotton is coming.

Song no. 3 (from southern Mozambique)

We worked and were paid nothing
We were forced to work in the fields
We carried cotton on our head
We were seized and we cried
We were beaten in this land
Lopes beat us.

Song no. 4 (from southern Mozambique)

We are fed up from suffering under the Portuguese
We are being tortured by cotton
We are fed up from suffering under the Portuguese.

Song no. 5 (from central Mozambique)

I cultivate my cotton,
    I suffer, my heart is weeping,
    . . .
I've taken it to the Boma [trading station] there,
    I suffer, my heart is weeping,
They've given me five escudos,
    I suffer, my heart is weeping,
When I reflect on all this,
    Oyi – ya – e – e
I suffer, I do,
    I suffer, my heart is weeping.

Song no. 6 (from the Belgian Congo)

Ah! There was a lot of cotton!
White man has just bought it,
How come I have only a little money left!
What happened?

---

1. *What were the main complaints of the women?*

2. *What was the relationship between growing cotton and paying taxes?*

Source: Song no. 1: Raúl Honwana, *The Life History of Raúl Honwana: An Inside View of Mozambique from Colonialism to Independence, 1905–1975* (Boulder, CO: Lynne Rienner Publishers, 1988), p. 88; songs nos. 2–4: Allen Isaacman, *Cotton Is the Mother of Poverty: Peasants, Work, and Rural Struggle in Colonial Mozambique, 1938–1961* (Portsmouth, NH: Heinemann, 1996), pp. 223–224; song no. 5: Leroy Vail and Landeg White, *Capitalism and Colonialism in Mozambique: A Study of Quelimane District* (Minneapolis: University of Minnesota Press, 1980), p. 352; song no. 6: Osumaka Likaka, *Rural Society and Cotton in Colonial Zaire* (Madison: University of Wisconsin Press, 1997), p. 119.

WASHING HIS FOLLOWERS' FEET Isaiah Shembe, the founder of the Nazarite Baptist Church in South Africa, conducts a foot-washing ceremony, in which the pastor becomes the servant of his followers. Starting out as an itinerant evangelist and faith healer, Shembe founded dozens of congregations among the Zulu people. His group was part of the larger religious movement known as the Zionist churches.

1914	1921	1925
Bubonic plague erupts in Senegal	Simon Kimbangu arrested in Belgian Congo	Amadu Hamallah arrested in Mali

12

ENCOUNTERS WITH MODERNITY, 1914–1940

The years following World War I were times of great social and cultural upheavals in Africa. These changes were promoted in part by colonial governments and Western missionaries and initiated in part by Africans themselves as they came into greater contact with the global economy, modern biomedicine, and universal religions. Young men who traveled hundreds of miles on foot to work in the mines of southern Africa or the peanut fields of West Africa returned home with a wider perspective on Africa and the world. In a similar way, children who received some rudimentary Western education in colonial-era primary schools, and adults who sought modern biomedical health care at colonial-era hospitals or clinics, were keenly aware that the world was changing.

In the wake of the Industrial Revolution, social and cultural change had been accelerating all over the world. Europe had not only undergone an unprecedented transformation in technology and manufacturing, but had also experienced a major social transformation. Instead of aristocratic landlords who controlled masses of landless peasants, European states were now dominated by wealthy industrialists and financiers who had often risen from modest means by their own talents and entrepreneurial visions. They dominated a growing class of free landless laborers who had left the rural areas and were now utterly dependent on the industrialists for jobs. To support the growing industrial economy, universal primary-school education was introduced in France, Britain, and Belgium after

1927	**1927**	**1930**
Amadu Bamba dies in Senegal	Achimota College opens in Ghana	Joseph Babalola begins preaching in Nigeria

1880, and aspects of modern biomedicine based on germ theory were developed in parts of Europe at about the same time. European religious groups—especially the Protestants—embraced modern technology and stressed the industrial-age virtues of discipline, hard work, and thrift over older Christian values such as piety, purity, and ascetic mysticism. Given the colonial relationship between Europe and Africa, it is no surprise that echoes of those industrial-age changes would be felt in African nations, too.

When the European powers began to rethink their colonial policies after World War I, they concluded that they needed to do more than simply exploit Africa's natural resources: they needed to develop its human capital as well. Louis Franck, the Belgian minister of colonies, advocated "progressive development" among the African population because, in his words, "without the natives you can accomplish nothing in the colonies." In a similar vein, the French minister of colonies, Albert Sarraut, wrote that economic growth and "human development" must go hand in hand. French colonial policy, he emphasized, should not only establish commercial centers, but also build schools and hospitals. The problem with such progressive sentiments lay in the harsh realities of tight colonial budgets and the fundamental colonial principle that government initiatives should be funded by the Africans themselves through their taxes and labor. In the late 1920s, for example, the Belgian Congo colonial administration spent less than 20 percent of its meager budget on social and humanitarian programs such as health care and education, while the rest went mostly to administration, public works, and the military.

The challenges of living under colonialism prompted many Africans to reevaluate the religious paradigms by which they understood the world. Both Christianity and Islam spread during the colonial period, in part because they spoke to universal fears and aspirations, and in part because they created connections with the larger world beyond the village and the farm. That is why migrant laborers were often among the first converts to universal religions. Nevertheless, personal issues and local conditions could not be ignored in the pursuit of universal truths, and those circumstances gave rise to locally based Christian and Muslim movements led by charismatic preachers and teachers. To many Africans, the goal was to create a new religious synthesis that bridged the personal, the local, and the global. Africans were selectively embracing modernity, and they were doing so on their own terms.

THE END OF SLAVERY

It is hard to say just how many enslaved people there were in Africa at the beginning of the twentieth century, but it was estimated that 30–50 percent of the people in the Sahel were slaves, and that the total number of slaves in Africa ran into the millions. Although Britain and France had allowed slavery in their American colonies until 1833 and 1848, respectively, by the time of the scramble for Africa in the late nineteenth century, the major European powers were firmly set against slavery. Just 4 years after the Berlin Conference of 1884–1885 had inaugurated the partition of Africa (see chapter 10), the signatories to the Berlin agreement reconvened in Brussels to discuss the suppression of slavery and the internal slave trade in Africa. The Brussels Anti-Slavery Conference of 1889–1890 was partly a publicity stunt to generate support for the colonial conquest of Africa and partly a ploy by King Leopold II of Belgium to consolidate his control over the Congo River basin, but it nevertheless illustrates how closely the issues of slavery and colonialism were intertwined.

Colonial officials in Africa found themselves caught between two opposing forces. On the one hand, humanitarian and religious organizations in Europe were pushing for the elimination of slavery in Africa for moral reasons, and the metropolitan governments believed that abolishing slavery would create a class of landless laborers who could work for European enterprises. On the other hand, the very African chiefs who were the linchpin of indirect rule were often the biggest slaveholders. Frederick Lugard, the high commisioner for Northern Nigeria, worried that if slavery were to be abolished, "the upper classes would be reduced to misery and starvation, and, as a consequence, to hostility against the Europeans who had brought this chaos about." As for the slaves themselves, Lugard worried that liberation would "produce a mass of unemployed vagrants and increase the criminal classes," and he feared that it would lead to increased prostitution among the women. The solution to that dilemma in both British and French colonies was to "delegalize" slavery instead of abolishing it outright. Under **delegalization**, slavery was not a recognized legal status, so slave owners could no longer go to a colonial court to reclaim runaway slaves as their legal property. The corollary, however, was that the colonial administration would refrain from taking any positive steps to free existing slaves.

Two examples will illustrate how delegalization worked in practice. In French West Africa, the colonial administration delegalized slavery in 1903 and outlawed new enslavement and slave trading in 1905. During the next decade, as many as a million slaves left their masters. One reason for the massive slave exodus was that many of the slaves were first-generation captives who had been enslaved in the nineteenth-century wars of Samori Touré (see chapter 8) or the jihad of Umar Tal (see chapter 9). Some of them had been slaves for as few as 15 years, and they still had an attachment to their home regions and native languages. Upon returning home, they could find land to farm and perhaps reconnect with relatives.

About two-thirds of the slaves, however, stayed with their masters, in part because slavery in Africa was a social institution as well as a labor relationship.

Women slaves were more likely to stay than men because many of them had married, borne children, and been integrated into local households. Second- or third-generation slaves were also more likely to stay because they no longer spoke the language of their ancestral homelands and usually had no place to go. Those who stayed used the threat of flight as leverage to renegotiate the conditions of their servitude. Some sought an in-between solution: they founded new villages and cleared new fields, but continued to render services to their former masters in order to maintain their relationship with a powerful patron.

In contrast, the British in Northern Nigeria approached the issue of slavery with great caution. They delegalized slavery in 1901, outlawed new enslavement, and declared that all children of slaves born after 1901 were free, but they did nothing for the people who were already enslaved. The continuing importance of slave labor could be seen during the peanut boom of 1912–1914 (see chapter 11), when the emir of Kano and other large landholders used slave labor to grow peanuts for export. Unlike French West Africa, where colonial officials often helped ex-slaves find land and construct villages, the British used vagrancy laws to detain runaway slaves and invoked land tenure laws to deny them farmland. To ensure that the masters were compensated for the loss of their slaves, the British required slaves to purchase their own freedom. A British official explained that this was done to "prevent vagabondage and occupation of the land by hordes of masterless runaway slaves." Instead of leaving, many ex-slaves entered into sharecropping arrangements with their former masters. Even so, over 200,000 slaves in Northern Nigeria—roughly 10 percent of the slave population—abandoned their masters and returned to their home regions. Slavery continued in some regions of Nigeria until it was definitively abolished in 1936.

In the 1930s, slavery as a socioeconomic institution gradually disappeared from Africa, mainly because the colonial economy provided ex-slaves with alternative ways to make a living. The growth of cash crop production allowed ex-slaves to find work in peanut fields and on cocoa farms. In Senegal, for example, some former slaves cultivated peanuts on newly accessible land along the railway line, while others gained access to land by joining the Muride Muslim brotherhood (described later in this chapter). Other ex-slaves joined Christian mission stations, enlisted in colonial armies, engaged in migratory labor, or drifted into the urban centers, where they worked as porters, canoemen, cooks, construction workers, dockworkers, guards, and domestic servants. The existence of alternatives to slavery made it easier for those who stayed in place to gradually free themselves from reliance on their former masters.

The abolition of slavery in Africa produced neither the bonanza of cheap wage laborers that some Europeans had envisioned nor the hordes of vagrants, criminals, and prostitutes feared by Lugard. In the wake of colonial laws delegalizing (but not abolishing) slavery, the slaves, using a variety of options, mostly freed themselves. Despite its slow progress and uneven application, the colonial abolition of slavery had unleashed a major restructuring of both the social and economic order.

MEDICINE AND PUBLIC HEALTH

Every African community had people who were skilled at setting broken bones, assisting in childbirth, and providing herbal remedies for various ailments. The Azande people in Sudan, for example, had a pharmacopoeia of more than 400 therapeutic materials for treating over a hundred different diseases. Among the Akan people of southern Ghana, researchers have catalogued 217 medical preparations using 103 different ingredients in various combinations. To diagnose a patient, the healer would listen to the patient, smell or touch the stomach, look at the color of the eyes, feel the joints, or strike the soles of the feet to observe a change in color. Medicines could be eaten, drunk, rubbed on the body, inhaled, absorbed in a bath, or administered as an enema.

When an illness proved too strong for herbal remedies, people often attributed it to witchcraft or to the displeasure of ancestors or local spirits. Diviners and priests were called on to block the witchcraft or appease the spirits to allow the patient to heal. A diviner was a diagnostician who tried to understand the spiritual and psychological dimensions of the disease. Diviners could be either men or women. Women diviners among the Igbo often combined divination with herbal healing. In some cases, the diviner would trace the disease to a breakdown in social relations within the family or the community and try to bring about social reconciliation so that physical healing could take place. In other cases, diviners would go into a trance to discover the diagnosis. Priest or priestess healers could perform exorcisms or identify the evil person who was casting a spell on the patient. It was common for people who were sick to shop around to find just the right herbalist, priest, or diviner to treat their specific illness. In their most general forms, the strategies of healing in Africa were not that much different from those of early modern Europe, where witch-finders pitted white magic against black magic and priests performed exorcisms to cast out demons.

The idea that disease is caused by germs that can be counteracted by drugs is very recent in Western culture. Prior to the development of **germ theory**, people in Europe believed that an individual illness was the result of sinful behavior and that epidemics were caused by invisible noxious vapors. The major scientific discoveries of germ theory were made by the French chemist Louis Pasteur in the 1860s and the German physician Robert Koch in the 1870s and 1880s. Once the theory was accepted by the scientific community, modern biomedicine slowly gained popular acceptance in Europe and America, despite its rejection by certain religious groups, such as the Christian Scientists.

Germ theory and the biomedical treatment of disease had just begun to gain currency in Europe at the time of the scramble for Africa. European missionaries who arrived in Africa in the late nineteenth century still died at high rates: fully half the Baptist missionaries who arrived in the Belgian Congo between 1878 and 1888, for example, died of tropical diseases. But survival rates slowly improved after the biological causes of certain tropical diseases were identified. In 1893, the Church Missionary Society in England founded Livingstone College in an effort to train missionaries in the elements of practical medicine so that they could make medical care part of their missionary work. Similarly, the Catholic White Fathers received medical training during their novitiate.

Hospitals and Medical Training Programs

By 1936, Catholic missionary orders operated over 200 hospitals in Africa, and various Protestant missions had established hospitals as well. In Malawi, for example, the Scottish Presbyterian Mission operated 26 hospitals, while Protestant missions operated 29 hospitals in Nigeria. In rural areas, these hospitals were often rudimentary. In 1944, a district medical officer in northern Ghana described two of his hospitals as "mud sheds, each with 15 beds." The conditions at one of them were so poor that he refused to operate on patients there, and he described the operating theater at the other as "open to the four winds." Emergency nighttime operations were done by the light of a lantern held by an aide.

The colonial governments saw modern biomedicine as necessary to preserve the human capital essential to their colonial projects. The French minister of colonies, for example, wrote in 1923 that improvements in medical care were crucial because the colonizers had a "duty to preserve the populations that they governed," and also because "labor is the keystone of the economic edifice that we must build." By the mid-1930s, the basic colonial medical system was firmly in place. In the French colonies, each capital city had its own hospital, and each administrative district in the countryside had one or more medical centers, each staffed by a European doctor assisted by African auxiliaries. Below them in the medical hierarchy were infirmaries run by African auxiliaries and dispensaries run by African nurses. Health care in British colonies varied widely from place to place. By 1936, Uganda had 4 hospitals for Europeans and 23 hospitals for Africans, in addition to 93 rural dispensaries that were financed by local taxes. Nigeria had 12 hospitals for Europeans, 57 hospitals for Africans, and 300 rural dispensaries financed by the local communities. The Belgian Congo had 25 government

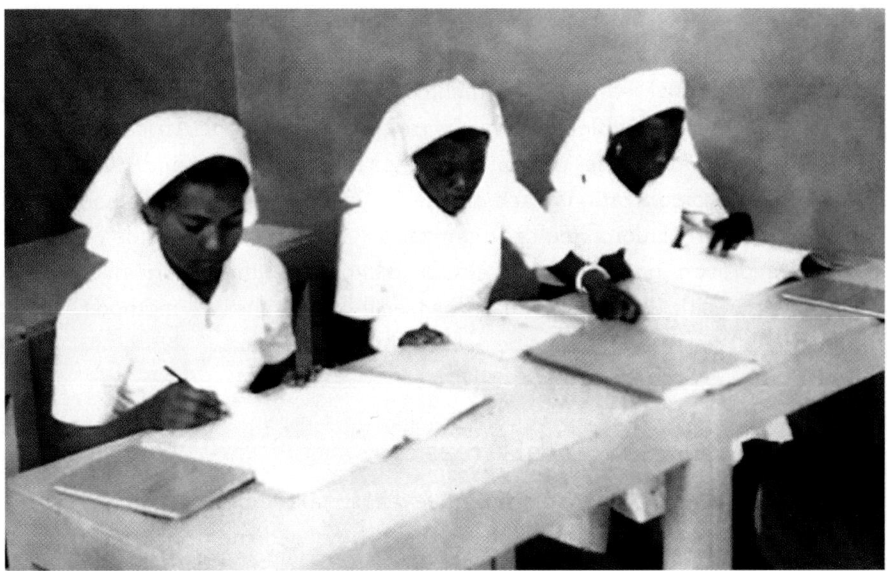

NURSES IN TRAINING These nursing students, photographed in the 1930s, are studying at the government hospital in Lubumbashi, Belgian Congo. In 1936, the Congo had 2,000 African nurses and medical assistants.

hospitals for Europeans as well as 70 government hospitals for Africans, which treated 85,000 African inpatients and over 800,000 outpatients in 1936.

The expansion of colonial medical services by missions and colonial governments would not have been possible without African medical workers. The Belgian Congo in 1936, for example, had 174 European doctors and 243 European nurses, aided by 2,000 African medical assistants and nurses. Similarly, French West Africa had about 250 European doctors and nurses and about 2,000 African medical assistants and nurses. No colonial governments trained Africans to be fully qualified medical doctors, but they did provide intermediate-level training for African medical assistants. By the 1930s, the British had instituted training programs for medical assistants in South Africa, Uganda, and Nigeria, while the French had a similar program in Senegal, and the Belgians another in the Congo. Both male and female nurses were normally trained at government or mission hospitals.

How effective were the treatments and biomedicines administered in the colonial hospitals and clinics? The record is mixed. The scientific breakthroughs of the nineteenth and early twentieth centuries had mostly focused on European diseases, so many of the diseases of the tropical regions of Africa were poorly understood by European doctors. One useful medical breakthrough was the drug neosalvarsan, discovered in 1912, which could treat syphilis and tropical yaws. Despite some risky side effects, it was in great demand among Africans. Serious research on tropical diseases got going in Africa itself only in the mid-1920s, aided by grants from organizations such as the British Colonial Development Fund and the League of Nations Health Organization. The bulk of the funds went into research on preventing sleeping sickness (also known as human African trypanosomiasis, a parasitic disease spread by the tsetse fly), but the best methods of controlling that disease continued to be debated into the 1930s.

Healing Practices in Rural Areas

Africans in rural areas, where there were few hospitals or medical centers, gradually became aware of modern biomedicines. They used the drugs that worked (when they could obtain them), but they did not abandon their traditional healers. Instead, many Africans practiced a kind of medical pluralism that acknowledged the coexistence of different healing therapies that were based on very different theories of causality. In the lower Congo (the former Kongo Kingdom), for example, an illness could be treated by a diviner, by kin-group therapy, by purification therapy, or by Western biomedicine. All four systems coexisted. Colonial governments banned what they called "witchcraft" and "fetish belief," but they did not make systematic efforts to suppress traditional healing practices. In British East Africa, for example, the colonial administration allowed traditional practitioners to offer their own systems of therapy as long as they restricted them to their own communities. In 1930, the colonial governor of Uganda pointed out the futility of banning traditional healing practices by noting that such laws would lack popular support and would be impossible to enforce.

Nevertheless, the colonial medical officers and the traditional healers shared some common ground. Uganda's medical director noted that many practitioners of traditional medicine "are much respected, and it is indeed possible that a study of the herbs used by some of them might add to the list of remedies such as quinine, which the pharmacopoeia owes to primitive medicinal practices." At the same time, African healers watched the practitioners of modern biomedicine to see if there were some useful techniques that they could adopt. Nowhere did the two systems overlap more than in the practice of midwifery. In Sudan, where the British sponsored a school for the training of midwives, the women educated there would revert to traditional Sudanese birthing methods if they ran out of medicine or if their modern equipment broke.

Fighting Epidemics

The one area in which the colonial medical services could successfully impose European medical techniques on a mass scale was campaigns against epidemics. Since medieval times, Europeans had fought epidemics by quarantining sick individuals and establishing a protective barrier—known as a ***cordon sanitaire***—to isolate infected areas. Campaigns against epidemics were very different from ordinary health care in a clinic or hospital: they were fighting a specific disease instead of treating illnesses on a case-by-case basis, and they were protecting territory more than they were protecting individuals. To get a sense of the methods and results of colonial campaigns against epidemic diseases, let's look at two examples: bubonic plague in Senegal, and sleeping sickness in the Belgian Congo.

The Plague in Senegal

The bubonic plague broke out in Senegal in 1914 and continued its periodic ravages over the next 30 years. French officials tried to isolate infected areas by imposing travel restrictions and even encircling villages with soldiers. They burned the houses of plague victims and sometimes burned down entire villages. The mass burials of plague victims in lime pits offended the local populations because they violated Islamic burial standards. Such unpopular measures would have been vindicated if they had worked, but their effectiveness was questionable. Dr. André Lafont, the director of the Bacteriological Laboratory in Dakar, Senegal, argued that the *cordons sanitaire* in Dakar were futile, and the head of the colony's health services noted that in some cases the *cordons sanitaire* made the situation worse by trapping people in infected areas. As both the plague and the campaign against it continued over decades, Africans reacted in a variety of ways. Rural villagers often found the plague-control measures oppressive; Muslim leaders declared that the plague had been sent by God; and members of the educated elite generally approved of the control efforts because they saw Western biomedicine as an expression of modernity.

Sleeping Sickness in the Belgian Congo

In the Belgian Congo, the campaign against sleeping sickness was a similarly massive public health effort, also lasting over 30 years. The parasite that causes sleeping sickness, which lives in the blood of infected persons, was spread by the large biting tsetse flies that haunted the riverbanks and lake shores. The flies would bite people indiscriminately, picking up the parasite from the blood of the infected and depositing it into the blood of the healthy. Colonial officials tried to slow the spread of the disease by making maps identifying infected and noninfected zones; establishing quarantine camps to isolate infected individuals; and creating *cordons sanitaire* by relocating whole villages and regulating travel. They also introduced a system of medical passports, requiring people in certain areas to prove that they were not infected before they were allowed to travel along the roads and rivers. In an effort to cure the sick, the colonial administration sent out inspection teams that toured the countryside and conducted mandatory physical examinations to identify infected persons. At first, they tried to cure them with injections of the drug atoxyl, which was not only ineffective, but was 40 percent arsenic and caused a third of the patients to go blind. By 1930, however, the Belgians had newer drugs that were less toxic, and they established a series of injection centers in the afflicted regions.

It is difficult to assess the anti–sleeping sickness campaign in the Belgian Congo. In the first place, the Belgians were trying to solve a problem that was partially of their own making. The massive population displacements unleashed by the colonial conquest and by forced rubber collection (see chapter 10) had contributed to the initial spread of the disease. Second, most of the people infected prior to 1925 died, although the quarantine measures and *cordons sanitaire* probably kept the disease from spreading even farther than it did. The cure rate improved

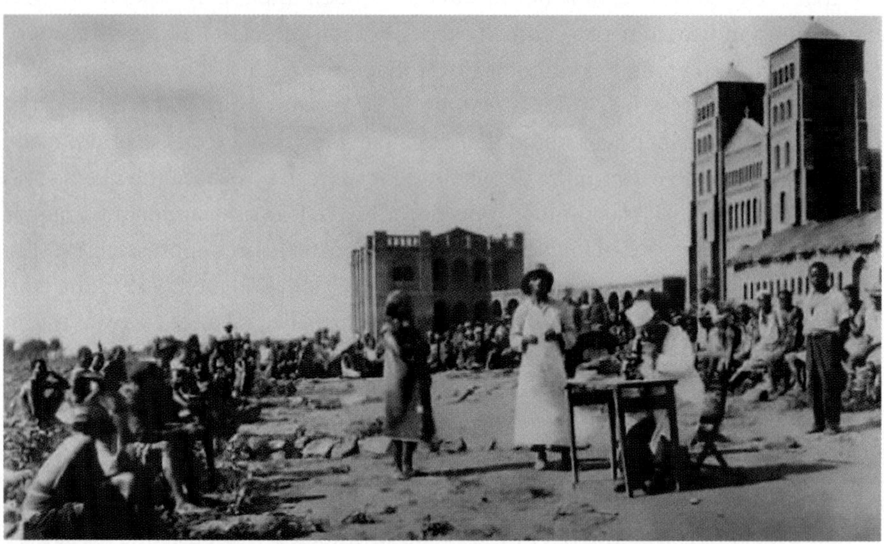

ANTI–SLEEPING SICKNESS CAMPAIGN These medical examinations in Ankoro, Belgian Congo, were part of the anti–sleeping sickness campaign in the 1930s. The African medical assistant examines blood samples with his microscope, while the African nurse (wearing a pith helmet) supervises the operation.

in the 1930s with the development of new drugs, injection centers, and more effective screening, and by 1930, the inspection teams screened nearly 3 million people each year. One inescapable conclusion, however, is that the anti–sleeping sickness campaign became the main mechanism by which the colonial government imposed its authority and control over the subject populations.

Belgian officials saw the anti–sleeping sickness campaign as a vindication of their colonial rule, but many Africans viewed it as just another colonial intrusion into their lives. Because the epidemic coincided with the imposition of colonial rule, many Africans saw sleeping sickness as a white man's disease, and some saw it as a form of biological warfare that the Europeans had unleashed on Africa. In the early years of the campaign, entire villages fled when the medical inspection teams approached, in part because they feared the painful lumbar punctures, and in part because they feared being quarantined even if they were still asymptomatic. People also tried to evade the travel restrictions, especially young men who wanted to seek work in the mines. By the 1930s, however, people gradually came to accept the anti–sleeping sickness campaign as a normal part of life under colonial rule.

SCHOOLS AND SCHOOLING

Colonial administrations and private European enterprises needed a core group of Africans with formal education along Western lines to serve as interpreters, scribes, accountants, and clerks. Although most of the Africans who were qualified for those positions had studied at mission schools, the colonial administrations also took an interest in their education. As early as 1856, the French had established a school in Senegal to train interpreters and educate the sons of chiefs; in 1906, the British established a school for the sons of chiefs in Sierra Leone; also in 1906, King Leopold II established a school for clerks and technical schools for railway and steamboat mechanics in the Congo.

Literacy and writing were not alien concepts in Africa. In the parts of Africa where Islam predominated, basic literacy in Arabic was common, and many people pursued higher education in Islamic law and sciences in cities such as Cairo, Marrakesh, Jenne, Timbuktu, and Labé (in Fuuta Jaloo). Ethiopia had Christian priests and monks who were literate in the ancient liturgical language Geez as well as in the modern Ethiopian language Amharic, which was written with the same alphabet. Literacy in European languages was first brought to Africa by Christian missionaries beginning in the late fifteenth century. The Kongo Kingdom and Angola had educated Christian elites who were literate in Portuguese and Kikongo, the native language of the Kongo Kingdom. The founding of Fourah Bay

College in Sierra Leone in 1827 made Freetown a major center for Western education, especially in 1876, after it established a formal affiliation with Durham University in England. In South Africa, the Scottish Presbyterian Mission established a post-primary school at Lovedale in 1841 to train Christian teachers and pastors. Despite those efforts, literacy outside of the Muslim areas remained limited to a tiny minority of the population.

Primary Education

After World War I, the colonial administrations sought to expand their networks of schools to reach greater numbers of Africans. The idea of primary education for the masses was a relatively recent one that grew out of the Industrial Revolution in Europe. France had first established universal free education in 1881. In addition to literacy and arithmetic, the French schools taught notions of order, cleanliness, and efficiency that were designed to soften "the savagery and harshness natural to peasants." Britain established universal free primary education in 1891. In addition to reading, writing, and arithmetic, pupils in Britain learned habits of regular attendance, punctuality, orderly behavior, and submission to the teacher's authority. Primary education was designed to produce workers for Britain's industrializing economy, not to prepare students for higher education. Even by the 1930s, fewer than 15 percent of British schoolchildren went on to high school. In Belgium, universal primary education was not established until the eve of World War I.

Schools in British Colonies

It was in the shadow of Europe's experiment with mass education that Frederick Lugard, the architect of Britain's system of indirect rule, proclaimed in 1925 that the moral, social, and economic progress of Africa depended on expanded access to Western-style primary education. As a member of the British Advisory Committee on Education in Tropical Africa, he argued that primary education for the masses was more important than higher education for the few. The goal of primary education, he emphasized, was to instill "higher standards of duty and efficiency" in African young people. One important difference between schooling in Europe and in Africa, however, was that education in Europe was culturally conservative. In Europe, education transmitted the accumulated knowledge and values of Western culture. Primary schooling in Africa, in contrast, was designed to be an instrument of cultural change.

The British sought to expand primary education at minimal expense by relying on mission schools that were staffed by local African teachers. Hence it was Africans—and not foreign teachers—who brought Western education to the masses. The village schools offered up to 3 years of primary education with

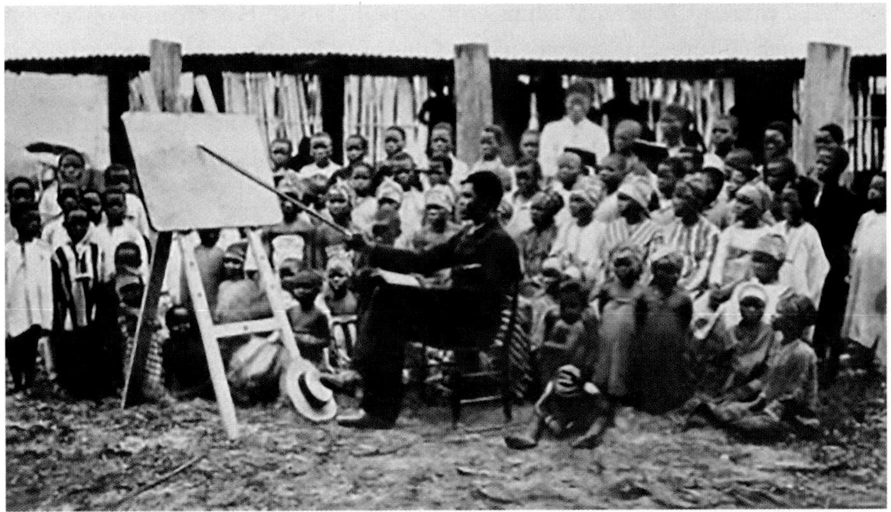

PRIMARY EDUCATION An African teacher and pupils pose in front of a mission school in the Niger Delta region of Nigeria, ca. 1900. The primary education system in the British colonies relied on the missions and mission-trained African teachers.

classes conducted in the local African languages. The curriculum emphasized Christianity and industrial-age moral virtues such as punctuality, regular attendance, and following instructions. To provide teachers for the village schools, the missions established teacher-training institutions, but the demand for qualified teachers frequently outstripped the supply, and most teachers in the village schools had only 3 or 4 years of schooling themselves. Because African teachers were poorly paid, they often left for better-paying jobs with the colonial administration or European businesses, adding to the chronic teacher shortage.

Schools in French Colonies

Education in the French colonies was very different from the British model in two ways: first, the French did not rely on mission schools, and second, all of the classes were conducted in French. In contrast to the British idea of mass education articulated by Frederick Lugard, the French sought to create a small educated elite. The French education policy was originally formulated in French West Africa, a region one-third larger than the United States that was divided into eight separate colonies. Its population was heavily Muslim, and the French did not want to antagonize the Muslims by bringing Christian missionaries into Muslim areas. Although many Muslims in French West Africa were literate in Arabic, and some had received advanced Islamic education, the French colonial administration needed a cadre of African Muslims who were literate in French and conversant with French culture. One attempt to meet this need was the establishment of four schools that combined traditional Islamic education with instruction in French in order to produce interpreters, teachers for Quranic schools, and judges for the Islamic courts who would be sympathetic to French colonial rule.

The vast majority of schools in French West Africa, however, were secular institutions run by the colonial government that emphasized French language and culture. At the base of the education system were 2-year "initiation schools" in the rural villages, where classes were taught in French by African teachers. The best students from the initiation schools could continue for 2 more years at regional schools located in urban areas and rural administrative centers. In addition to the French language, they studied European history, geography, science, arithmetic, and hygiene. For the students who advanced to the next level, the capital city of each of the eight colonies had a 4-year higher primary school, which offered admission by competitive exams. The higher primary schools employed European-educated teachers with university degrees, and their equipment was equal to that of schools in France. The education system in the French colonies was aptly summed up by the governor-general of French West Africa as "Instruct the masses; separate out the elite."

Schools in Belgian and Portuguese Colonies

In the Belgian Congo, the colonial government sought to expand existing mission school networks by giving each mission station up to 500 acres of land, where it was expected to build a school and start a farm to be worked by the students. Proceeds from the farm would help cover the school's expenses. That policy cost the state nothing because it simply confiscated land from Africans and gave it to the missions. Classes were conducted in African languages, and religious and moral education was considered more important than technical or literary instruction. The vast majority of students attended primary schools that offered only 2 years of instruction in the local language and were taught by a teacher with scarcely more education than the students.

The Portuguese colonies had a more limited primary education program. They relied almost exclusively on Portuguese Catholic missions to provide a 3-year course of what they called "rudimentary education." Instruction had to be in Portuguese, which made it difficult to find enough qualified African teachers. Because the missions depended heavily on government subsidies, their educational activities were limited by the states' meager budgets. Under these conditions, many of the schools taught little more than the Catholic catechism. Schools in rural areas were often linked to large Portuguese-owned farms, where children learned farming along with reading. The main purpose of those schools was to produce trained farmworkers.

Effects of Primary Education

The various colonial projects to expand primary education had mixed results. The French government schools maintained high standards, but reached only about 4 percent of the total population in French West Africa, and even less in French Equatorial Africa, which had only a single higher primary school, located in Brazzaville. The British were reaching 10–13 percent of the total population in their West African colonies by relying on mission schools, but those schools were of uneven quality, and they taught in local languages. The Portuguese education system reached only about 3 percent of the population, and the schools were of poor quality and often aimed more at training farmworkers than providing education. The most successful expansion of schooling—at least in terms of numbers—came in the Belgian Congo, where over a million school-aged children received schooling in local languages by 1938, even though most of them would not have a chance to advance beyond the second grade. In sum, the primary schools were inadequate to create the kind of skilled and disciplined labor force envisioned by the colonial education departments. Their major effect, beyond providing some basic literacy in local languages, was in spreading Christianity and making pupils aware of the much wider world that lay beyond their village.

Advanced Schooling

In all the colonies, there was a demand for Africans who were proficient in European languages to fill clerical, accounting, and technical positions in the colonial administrations. The French met this need with the **William Ponty School**, near Dakar, Senegal, a high school attended by the best graduates of the higher primary schools. It was mostly for the training of teachers, with a curriculum that emphasized proficiency in French. Students who wanted more technical training could switch to the medical school, the veterinary school, or the school of marine mechanics, all in Dakar. The major shortcoming of the William Ponty School was that it was very small, admitting only about 80 incoming students each year. In 1938, the French opened a secondary school for girls in Rufisque (near Dakar). Admitting only about 30 students per year, it had a curriculum similar to that of the William Ponty School, with the addition of classes in sewing, cooking, and child care.

The British opened several post-primary schools to give students training in English. In Muslim areas, they established Gordon College (British colonial high schools were referred to as colleges) in Sudan and **Katsina College** in Northern

PROTOZOOLOGY CLASS Students in a protozoology class at Yaba Higher College, which was founded in 1934 near Lagos, Nigeria.

Nigeria. The schools took in boys who had come up through the Muslim education system, taught them the skills needed by the British administration, and socialized them to an elite culture of government service. For students in non-Muslim areas, the British opened **Achimota College** in Ghana and Makerere Government College in Uganda. To provide university-level education, the British established Yaba Higher College in Nigeria, which offered "training of a university or professional character" in a few selected subjects and gave out diplomas that were not recognized outside of Nigeria. In South Africa, the South African Native College at Fort Hare began to offer post-secondary education after 1923.

Frederick Lugard, the former governor-general of Nigeria, had opposed giving Africans a purely academic education because he believed that it would lead to "an emancipation of thought" that would undermine respect for British authority. Well-educated Africans, he warned, would be "out of touch with the people, imbued with theories of self-determination, and acutely sensitive to any fancied racial discrimination." Lugard was correct in his assessment that well-educated Africans would not be content to live under colonial rule. Among the graduates of Katsina College in Nigeria were Ahmadu Bello, who became the premier of Northern Nigeria, and Abubakar Tafewa Balewa, who became the first prime minister of independent Nigeria. Five graduates of Achimota College in Ghana went on to become presidents of Ghana, one graduate became president of The Gambia, and one became the president of Zimbabwe. Former students of the South African Native College at Fort Hare include Nelson Mandela, the first black president of South Africa, as well as the first presidents of Tanzania, Zambia, and Zimbabwe.

RELIGIOUS CHANGE

At the time of the scramble for Africa, Christian communities could be found in Egypt and Ethiopia, Sierra Leone and Liberia, Angola and Mozambique, and at the southern tip of Africa, while Islam was dominant in North Africa, the Sahara Desert, the Sahel, and the Swahili Coast. In the southern two-thirds of Africa, however, most people followed more localized religious traditions that did not make universal claims. Most precolonial African religions were characterized by a complex of local shrines, sacred places, deities, and spirits that could be invoked to help navigate the challenges of daily life. Both Christianity and Islam spread in Africa during the colonial period, usually at the expense of these local religions. Although the colonial administrations represented Christian countries that had state-sponsored churches, they worked to keep Christian missionaries out of the Muslim regions for fear of provoking unrest or rebellions. Followers of local religions, on the other hand, often found themselves challenged by the universal claims of both Christianity and Islam.

The Spread of Mission Christianity

By the beginning of World War I, some 10,000 Christian missionaries (4,000 Protestant and 6,000 Catholic) were living and working in Africa. Schools, churches, and mission communities became centers for disseminating Christian beliefs along with the trappings of modern Western culture. Trousers and skirts were considered proper Christian clothing, along with shoes for those who could afford them. Carrying a Bible to church on Sunday was a powerful symbol, even for those who were unable to read it. The traditional African 4-, 5-, or 6-day week, which was usually defined in reference to market days, was replaced by the 7-day Christian week in which Sunday was set aside as the day of worship. While the churches banned certain forms of traditional dancing, they often promoted alternative activities for young people, such as soccer games, spreading the sport all over Africa. Africans began to take Christian names, which they often appended to their given names to conform to the system of first and last names common

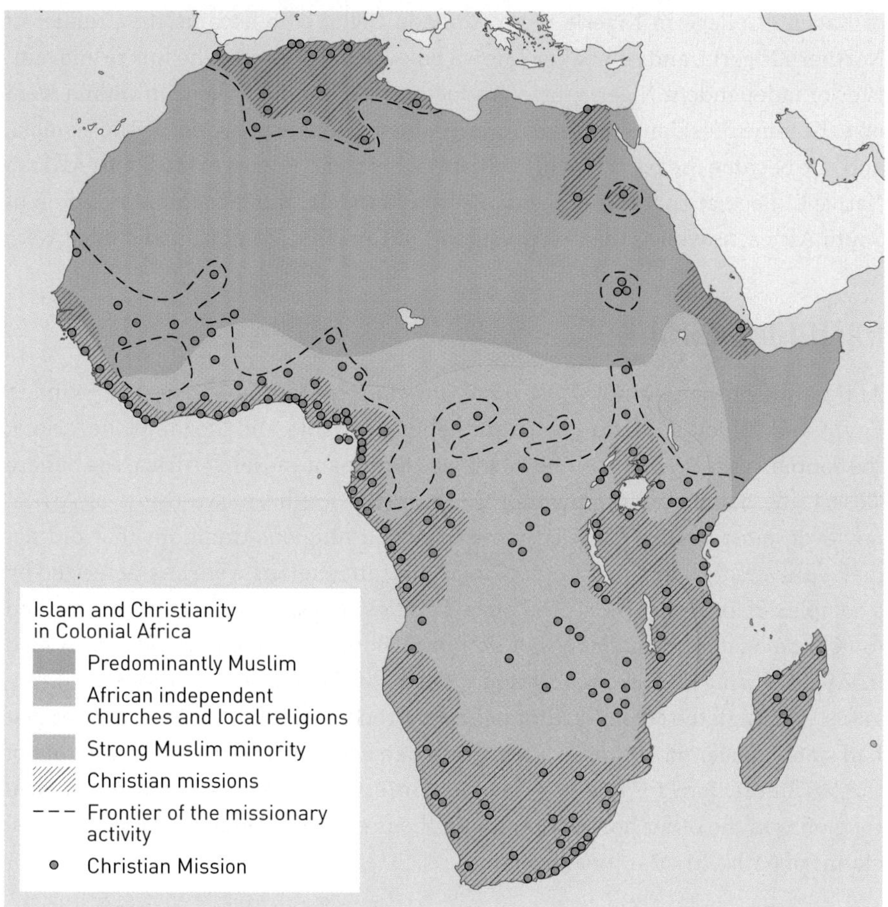

ISLAM AND CHRISTIANITY IN COLONIAL AFRICA This map traces a rough outline of Muslim and Christian areas in Africa during the high colonial period. Importantly, local religions did not necessarily disappear in the regions dominated by Islam or Christianity.

in Europe. Churches also promoted new economic activities. African pastors in southern Nigeria encouraged the planting of cocoa trees, and missionaries in South Africa promoted the use of plows.

During World War I, certain African Christians who were not affiliated with any mission society emerged as important evangelists. The most prominent example is **William Wade Harris**, a Liberian who was once imprisoned for his opposition to the African American rulers of that country. While in prison, he had a vision of the archangel Gabriel, who proclaimed him a prophet. Moving across

A SOCCER TEAM African soccer players pose with French colonial officials in French West Africa in the 1930s. Missionaries and colonial officials often promoted soccer as a game for young people, thus spreading the sport all over Africa. Soccer has since become the national sport in all the African countries.

the border into neighboring Côte d'Ivoire and Ghana, he traveled from village to village and preached about the imminent return of Jesus Christ. To prepare for this climactic event, he told people to be baptized, accept the authority of the Bible, obey the Ten Commandments, and attend Sunday worship. Tens of thousands of people were baptized under Harris's preaching, and huge bonfires could be seen as they burned the ritual objects of the traditional religions. It was the largest campaign of mass conversion to Christianity that Africa had ever seen.

Harris did not try to start his own church. Rather, he encouraged people to join the existing Methodist churches in Ghana or the Catholic churches in Côte d'Ivoire, although some of his followers in the more remote areas formed their own Harrist churches. He had been preaching for only a year when the French colonial authorities in Côte d'Ivoire declared him a disruptive element and decided to expel him from the colony. Harris and three women companions were arrested, stripped, beaten, and imprisoned in the port town of Bassam until Harris could be sent back to Liberia by ship.

In the decade following the Harris revival, similar independent evangelistic movements gained momentum in Ghana and Nigeria. In the Niger Delta, where an Igbo preacher named Garrick Braide was holding revival meetings, the Methodist mission once received a letter reporting that some 8,000 souls had been converted to Christianity and were looking for a church to join.

The Growth of African Independent Churches

By the end of World War I, some African Christians were feeling dissatisfied with the missionary churches they belonged to. At the root of their dissatisfaction was the fact that the missionaries who came to Africa had been heavily influenced by the European scientific and technological revolutions of the nineteenth century. Although the Bible is filled with stories of miraculous happenings and divine interventions, the missionaries seemed more interested in the miracles of modern technology. They prayed for the sick, but generally relied on modern biomedicine for a cure. Regarding personal and national wealth, the missionaries believed in gradual progress through hard work and righteous living rather than through divine intervention.

African traditional religions, in contrast, had always had an instrumental component. They provided charms, sacrifices, diviners, and oracles that would help a person cure an illness, grow crops successfully, or succeed in business. People were in the habit of shopping around for spiritual help: if one charm didn't work, perhaps another would do the job; if one diviner failed, perhaps another would succeed. The mission churches, in contrast, did not emphasize direct divine intervention to solve personal problems. They focused instead on universal themes such as heaven and hell, sin and salvation, and the benefits of living righteously. Many Africans, therefore, felt that the churches did not provide a sufficient arsenal of spiritual weapons to navigate the challenges of daily life.

A similar problem arose in relation to witchcraft. In popular discourse, talking about witchcraft was a concrete way of talking about the problem of evil in the world. Many Africans believed that evil deeds and misfortune were not random, but were often the result of witchcraft, which was itself a consequence of breakdowns in social relationships and community solidarity. Traditional African religions provided a variety of methods for combating witches with the aid of ritual objects, diviners, and anti-witchcraft cults. Although the missionaries believed in evil, sin, and the devil, they granted no credence to witchcraft. Many Africans felt that the mission churches, by denying the existence of witchcraft, were leaving them defenseless against the powers of evil.

Because mission theology was often ambiguous in relation to the practical problems of everyday life, many people hedged their bets by relying on the churches to answer the big questions about the meaning and purpose of life, while at the same time relying on charms and local diviners to solve everyday problems and protect them from witchcraft. Others, however, sought out churches that would satisfy a broader spectrum of spiritual needs. That desire was at the root of the independent faith-healing churches that sprang up in sub-Saharan

Africa. To gain insights into this phenomenon, let's look at three examples: the Zionist churches in southern Africa, the Aladura churches in Nigeria, and the Kimbanguist churches in the Belgian Congo.

The Zionist Churches in Southern Africa

The **Zionist churches** in southern Africa (not to be confused with the Jewish Zionist movement that led to the creation of the state of Israel) had their origins in the town of Zion, Illinois, in the United States. Situated on the shore of Lake Michigan about 40 miles north of Chicago, the town was founded in 1900 by a Scottish evangelist named John Dowie, who was known for staging elaborate "divine healing" events in front of large audiences. Zion, Illinois, was governed by Dowie as a theocracy, in which smoking, drinking, eating pork, and using modern medicine were banned. Illness was to be healed by prayer alone. Residents were required to deposit all their money in Dowie's Zion Bank, which was not legally incorporated or regulated.

One of Dowie's followers was a small-time real estate speculator named John G. Lake, who moved to Zion to learn more about faith healing. Soon after Lake's arrival, John Dowie was removed from office for fraud and financial mismanagement, so Lake switched his allegiance and became a follower of Charles Parham, a Pentecostal evangelist who was holding revival meetings nearby in a large tent. Lake learned to "speak in tongues" (seen as a gift from the Holy Spirit), and he soon became co-leader of a group that conducted exorcisms. After Parham was arrested for pedophilia and the townspeople threatened to run Lake out of town because of botched exorcisms that left at least two people dead, Lake spent $25.00 for a third-class steamship ticket to South Africa.

Arriving in South Africa in 1908, Lake started the Apostolic Faith Mission (AFM) and barnstormed across the country. He gained fame by claiming that he had brought a young girl back to life through prayer after she had been dead a full 35 minutes. He also claimed the ability to heal the sick, speak in tongues, and cast out demons, all talents that were not in the spiritual repertory of the regular missionary churches. A historian who reviewed the evidence on Lake's 5-year ministry in South Africa concluded that he was "the foremost religious con man ever to reside in South Africa," but some Africans nevertheless found that his approach to Christianity contained some ideas that they could use to make their faith more meaningful.

Even before Lake left South Africa in 1913, Africans began to break away from his Apostolic Faith Mission and start their own churches. One of the first to do so was Daniel Nkonyane, a co-director of the AFM who taught that one of the keys to healing was maintaining a proper relationship with one's ancestors, an aspect the mission churches were neglecting. He founded a church among the Zulu people that came to be called the Christian Catholic Apostolic Holy Spirit Church in Zion. By 1927, Nkonyane's church counted 10 congregations in South Africa and had begun to expand into Swaziland.

Another offshoot of Lake's ministry was led by Isaiah Shembe, a Zulu man with a preacher's certificate from the African Native Baptist Church. While traveling with John G. Lake in 1910–1911, he absorbed Lake's tent-revival style of preaching and studied his methods of healing. After parting from Lake, Shembe undertook extended evangelistic tours throughout Zululand, where he became known for casting out demons. He baptized his converts by immersing them in a river instead of dabbing water on their foreheads (as most mission churches did), forbade the wearing of shoes in church, and allowed people to wear traditional Zulu garments instead of Western clothes. Zulu chiefs were initially hostile to his message, but 15 of them eventually joined his Nazarite Baptist Church, and the Zulu king took Shembe's daughter to be one of his wives. By then, Shembe had completed his transformation from a faith healer's apprentice to a prophetic church leader, well connected to Zulu royalty.

A third breakaway group was formed by an African man from Lesotho named Edward Lion, who had worked closely with John G. Lake on his faith-healing tours. Lake turned Edward Lion into a faith-healing superstar and used his story to raise money in the United States. "Lion received the power of God," Lake wrote with his characteristic hyperbole, "and he manifests a greater measure of the healing gift than I believe any man ever has in modern times." Before returning to the United States, Lake appointed Edward Lion to be the leader of the AFM, but in 1917, Lion formed his own church and founded a town named Zion City, where he ruled like a spiritual king and likened his followers to New Testament apostles. Zion City's reputation was tarnished, however, when a local chief fined Lion for impregnating a young woman during confession, and when South African authorities intervened to stop him from taking all the money that male members earned working in the gold mines as migratory laborers.

Edward Lion's ministry was soon superseded by that of Engenas Lekganyane, who had become a well-known faith healer under Lion's tutelage and dreamed of building a Zion City of his own. In 1920, Lion sent Lekganyane to preach in the Transvaal, where the young man soon founded congregations that surpassed Lion's in size. In 1924, Lekganyane split with Lion and formed the Zion Christian Church (ZCC), which went on to become the largest Christian denomination in South Africa. In 1942, he purchased a farm in Lesotho and founded a settlement called Zion City Morija, which grew to be much larger than the Zion City of his mentor. Ironically, Zion City Morija was being built in Lesotho just 5 years after John Dowie's original Zion Tabernacle in Zion, Illinois, burned to the ground.

The churches founded by Nkonyane, Shembe, Lion, Lekganyane, and similar prophetic leaders are referred to as Zionist churches because they traced their roots to Zion, Illinois, and usually included the word "Zion" in their names. Zionist churches were characterized by prophetic leaders who claimed direct revelations from God through dreams and visions. Because of their fiercely independent nature, the Zionist churches underwent frequent schisms as their prophets undertook itinerant wanderings and the afflicted went from one leader to another in search of healing. In contrast to the missionary churches, the Zionists emphasized divine healing, casting out demons, and witch-finding. Sunday worship services featured participatory public prayer, sacred dances, speaking in tongues, and purification rites that included the public confession of sins. Congregants often wore white robes as symbols of purity, although green robes were sometimes worn to symbolize the Holy Spirit. Zionist churches baptized their converts by immersion in a river to symbolize the baptism of Jesus in the River Jordan. They generally accepted polygyny, but banned the eating of pork. Women were often in the majority in Zionist congregations, in which they served as local leaders and played key roles in healing ceremonies and worship services. Some women went on to found new Zionist churches based on their personal prophetic visions.

Despite their many religious innovations, the Zionist churches did not stray too far from their missionary roots. They sang from the old missionary hymnbooks (with the exception of Shembe's churches, which composed their own hymns), and they did not reject Western forms of worship. "We do just as in Zion, Illinois," one prominent Zionist leader told a Lutheran missionary. Despite their emphasis on prophetic visions and direct revelations, Zionists acknowledged the Bible as the ultimate authority on religious matters. The son of Isaiah Shembe told his congregation, "There is nothing that Shembe did which cannot be found in the Book; and the things he did and taught, he took out of the Bible." Although some scholars have interpreted Zionism as a fusion of Christianity and traditional African religions, one prominent historian has more accurately characterized it as "a particular form of missionary Christianity which may have seemed attractive because of apparent parallels with traditional religious culture." The main issue that drove the Zionist project was not the desire to fuse Christianity and traditional African religions, but to find a form of Christianity that could better satisfy traditional concerns.

The Aladura Churches in Nigeria

The **Aladura churches** developed among the Yoruba-speaking peoples of southern Nigeria. Their roots go back to the World War I era, when the Spanish flu pandemic was raging across the region. A young schoolmistress named Sophie Odunlani, who taught in an Anglican school, believed she had a vision from God and began to preach that people could be healed through Christ alone. She joined up with a man named J. B. Sadare, a member of the local Anglican Diocesan Board, who was holding prayer meetings in his home, and soon a small group of about 60 people left their Anglican mission churches and formed a small independent church of their own. The group rejected modern medicines out of faith in the healing powers of God. Its members became known as "Aladura" (people of prayer) because they prayed more often and more publicly than other Christians.

The congregation gained an international dimension when one of the members came upon an article called "The Seven Principles of Prevailing Prayer," written by a certain Pastor Clark, who led the Faith Tabernacle in Philadelphia, Pennsylvania. Soon, Faith Tabernacle publications were circulating widely among literate Yoruba. Several Aladura members maintained a lively correspondence with Pastor Clark, seeking his advice on a variety of issues, and went on to found small Faith Tabernacle congregations in various Yoruba towns. The relationship with Philadelphia came to an end in 1928, when Pastor Clark was expelled from his own church for adultery. At the same time, another group of African Christians who emphasized the power of prayer was forming. It was led by a woman known as Captain Abiodun, who had seen a vision of an angel while in a trance at the age of 15 and had founded a prayer group called Seraphim, which staged annual processions of people wearing white robes. Because of its emphasis on prayer and rejection of both European and African medicines, Seraphim was also considered an Aladura church.

The big breakthrough for the Aladura churches came in 1930, when a Yoruba steamroller driver named Joseph Babalola had a vision in which God told him to quit his job in the public works department and preach the Christian message. After being baptized in the lagoon behind the Faith Tabernacle Church in Lagos, he traveled to the Yoruba town of Oke-Oye to begin his ministry. Preaching several times a day in an open field, he commanded people to burn all their traditional ritual objects and to rely on God alone for protection and success. As his reputation spread, the crowds grew. It was said that within a span of 3 weeks he healed 100 lepers, cured 60 blind people and 50 lame people, and brought a dead child back to life. Stories spread that barren women became pregnant, mute people spoke, witches confessed, and demons were exorcised. The Methodist missionaries, on the other hand, dismissed those stories as "grotesquely inaccurate."

As Joseph Babalola traveled across Yoruba country preaching to crowds numbering in the thousands, bonfires roared as people burned their ritual objects, traditional shrines were destroyed, and Methodist and Anglican churches were emptied. Babalola's evangelistic journey was interrupted in March 1932, when he

PREACHING THE WORD This photo shows Joseph Babalola preaching in the 1930s. The Christ Apostolic Church (CAC), which he founded, became the largest of the Aladura (people of prayer) denominations and the one closest in theology to traditional Protestant churches.

was sentenced to 6 months in prison for taking part in a witch-finding ordeal, an event that confirms that his willingness to fight witches was part of his popular appeal. Emerging from prison, he continued to travel to various parts of Nigeria, and in 1936, he even traveled as far as Ghana. Some of his followers went out to preach on their own, and a number of independent prophets also arose in the religiously charged atmosphere of the time. Aladura churches such as the Faith Tabernacle were becoming a major religious group in Nigeria.

Despite the success of their own evangelists, the Faith Tabernacle congregations in Nigeria were not trying to separate themselves from the wider world of Christianity. They affiliated for a time with a British faith-healing church that sent them some missionaries, but the groups parted ways after it was discovered that the missionaries were secretly taking quinine tablets to protect themselves from malaria, thus exposing their lack of faith in God. In 1940, Joseph Babalola teamed up with a prosperous Yoruba cocoa farmer named Isaac Akinyele to unite and organize the loose coalition of Faith Tabernacle churches. The result was the Christ Apostolic Church (CAC), which became the largest of the Aladura denominations and the one closest to traditional Protestant churches in opposing polygyny, dancing, drumming, and drinking. It placed a high value on education and built up its own network of schools. The complex relationship between Aladura and missionary churches can be illustrated by looking at the family of Isaac Akinyele, who went on to lead the CAC for many years. Isaac was later chosen to be the olubadan (traditional ruler) of Ibadan, one of the largest cities in sub-Saharan Africa, while his twin brother Alexander became the Anglican bishop of Ibadan. Both of them were revered figures in Nigeria.

Because the religious revivals of the 1930s had produced a multiplicity of prophets, faith healers, and small independent congregations, the Aladura churches exhibited tremendous variation in their views on issues such as polygyny, witchcraft, and the validity of certain prophetic visions. While the CAC churches were the closest to traditional Protestantism, the Seraphim churches founded by Captain Abiodun were the closest to traditional Yoruba culture, and they welcomed charismatic women as prophets and leaders. Across the spectrum of Aladura churches, women were more numerous than men, and most congregations had special men's societies and women's organizations. The women's organizations were generally more powerful because they were larger and often counted wealthy female traders among their members. Despite their wide variation in belief and practice, the Aladura churches were united by their emphasis on prayer and their independence from European missionaries.

The Kimbanguists in the Belgian Congo

The largest independent Christian church movement in Africa developed in the Belgian Congo, where it flourished despite vigorous efforts by the colonial government to stamp it out. It was led by **Simon Kimbangu**, who was brought up at a mission station run by the British Baptist Missionary Society and joined the Baptist Church as a young man. He taught at the Baptist mission school for a time, and was then sent to be an evangelist in the village of Nkamba, 12 miles away. Beginning in 1918, he believed that he heard voices calling him to be a prophet, but he tried to ignore them. It is said that on April 6, 1921, he laid his hands on a critically ill woman and healed her, and soon thereafter he brought a dead child back to life. People began to flock to Nkamba to be healed or to receive his blessing. In his preaching, he condemned polygyny and sensual dancing, and he outlined a doctrine of nonviolence that included obedience to authority and love of one's enemies. Two Baptist missionaries who traveled to Nkamba to investigate the rumors about Kimbangu were unable to observe a single miracle during their brief visit, but a fellow missionary wrote, "It seems to me that this is the most remarkable movement which the country has ever seen. I am every day receiving letters from our Congolese members and adherents telling of the wonderful cures they themselves have witnessed."

Simon Kimbangu was not trying to form a breakaway church, and the Baptist Missionary Society was the initial beneficiary of his preaching. A missionary noted that in the wake of Kimbangu's preaching and healing, the Baptist chapels in the villages were full while the Catholic chapels were empty. Village leaders besieged the mission with requests for schoolteachers and materials; in 3 months, the mission sold more than 500 hymnbooks. Kimbangu's assistants began to spread his message, and a number of would-be prophets emerged who emulated Kimbangu's style. All of this was rather disconcerting to the Belgian colonial authorities, who worried that Kimbangu would use his newfound popularity to organize an anti-colonial rebellion.

On June 6, 1921, just 2 months after the beginning of Kimbangu's ministry, the Belgian colonial authorities sent soldiers to arrest him. After being tried by a military court that did not allow defense counsel or defense witnesses, he was convicted of sedition and hostility toward whites, and sentenced to 120 lashes followed by execution. One piece of evidence used against Kimbangu was a song sung by his followers, which the Belgians interpreted as inciting a rebellion, but which was actually a Kikongo translation of the well-known Protestant hymn "Onward Christian Soldiers," which compared the spread of Christianity across the globe to an advancing army led by Jesus Christ carrying a Christian cross. "The Belgians know nothing of Protestant worship and its treasury of hymns," complained a Baptist missionary. Eventually, the trial came to the attention of King Albert of Belgium, who commuted Kimbangu's sentence to life in

SIMON KIMBANGU IN PRISON This rare photo shows Simon Kimbangu (right) in prison in Lubumbashi, Belgian Congo. After a career as a Baptist preacher and faith healer that lasted only 2 months, he was sent to prison for the rest of his life. The photo had to be taken surreptitiously because the Belgian colonial authorities sought to erase any public acknowledgment of Kimbangu.

prison. He was sent to Lubumbashi, some 850 miles away from Nkamba, so that his followers could not visit him. Fearing that he might try to send messages to his followers, the authorities kept him in solitary confinement for most of the next 30 years.

Even though Simon Kimbangu was tucked away in a distant prison, the colonial government was still worried about his followers. In the wake of his trial, many of Kimbangu's followers withdrew from the mission churches and began meeting on their own. Many believed that he would miraculously return to Nkamba. In response, the colonial authorities razed the village of Nkamba and placed guards at the spring across the valley from the village where people came to collect healing water. Simon Kimbangu's wife, Mary Mwilu, built a small house near the spring. Kept under constant surveillance by soldiers and periodically threatened, she became the spiritual mother of Kimbangu's followers. In 1922, the colonial government banned the followers of Kimbangu from holding meetings, and people identified as Kimbanguists were rounded up and deported.

In 1924, the solicitor general of the Belgian Congo declared that the followers of Kimbangu constituted "a grave danger" to European colonial rule because they showed "unity and solidarity." He wrote that "we must continue the struggle against Kimbanguism as one of our civilizing tasks." The government accordingly closed all Kimbanguist churches and schools, sent soldiers to patrol the roads, and ordered another round of deportations. Those who escaped deportation slowly returned to the mission churches, but some Kimbanguist groups continued to meet in secret. In all, some 100,000 people were deported to more than 30 different regions of the Belgian Congo, where they initially lived in concentration camps under harsh conditions. As an unintended consequence of these deportations, Kimbanguist teachings spread to all parts of the Belgian Congo. By the 1960s, the Church of Jesus Christ on Earth by the Prophet Simon Kimbangu, as it was called, was the largest independent church in Africa, with over half a million members.

Understanding African Independent Churches

The Zionist churches in southern Africa, the Aladura churches in Nigeria, and the Kimbanguist churches in the Belgian Congo are just three examples of the independent Christian movements that were springing up all over Africa in the colonial period. They, and the other Christian movements across the continent, attracted followers for three reasons. First, they offered direct divine assistance in practical matters such as curing illness or achieving prosperity. Second, they confronted witchcraft instead of denying its existence. And third, they added a local dimension to the universal claims of Christianity: they believed in one universal God, but they also followed a local prophet or preacher. Although the majority of

African Christians still attended missionary churches, the trend toward independent churches would grow over time. By the 1960s, there were some 5,000 independent church denominations operating in 34 African countries.

Islam and Colonial Rule

Islam had long been the dominant religion in the North African Maghreb (Morocco, Algeria, and Tunisia), which was colonized by France, and in the Nile Valley (Egypt and Sudan), which was colonized by Britain. In the region just south of the Sahara Desert, however, the religious situation was more ambiguous. French West Africa contained some powerful Islamic states, and it had significant Muslim populations in the towns along the trade routes. As a universal religion, Islam had been embraced for centuries by traders, who often traveled together with Muslim clerics and scholars. Commercial centers such as Timbuktu and Jenne had become renowned centers of Islamic higher learning that attracted scholars and students from long distances (see chapter 4). Despite the long-standing presence of Muslims in the region, however, many people in rural agricultural villages of French West Africa maintained their traditional beliefs and practices throughout the precolonial era. That situation changed during the colonial period, when the number of Muslims increased rapidly. Between 1924 and 1936, for example, the number of Muslims increased more than 60 percent. It is perhaps ironic that French West Africa was ruled by a Catholic country at the time when Islam expanded more rapidly than it had in the previous thousand years.

By the time of the scramble for Africa, the French already had considerable experience in governing Muslim populations, having briefly controlled Egypt from 1798 to 1801 and having taken over Algeria in 1830. In colonizing North Africa, the French acquired a population that was overwhelmingly Muslim. In French West Africa, in contrast, the proportion of Muslims was much smaller, but Muslims nevertheless controlled the largest kingdoms, the trade networks, and the schools. The key to governing French West Africa, therefore, was reaching an accommodation with the Muslim elites.

From their experience in Algeria, the French knew that the Muslim population was not monolithic, but rather was divided in its loyalty among different Muslim brotherhoods. The French accordingly made a distinction between "good" and "bad" brotherhoods in French West Africa. The worst, in their eyes, was the Tijaniyya, which had established its own jihadist state in the nineteenth century under the leadership of Umar Tal (see chapter 9). The French had fought a series of battles against Tijaniyya armies during their conquest of the middle Niger valley in the 1890s, and they remained deeply suspicious of the Tijaniyya in the aftermath. To them, the Tijaniyya was an implacable enemy.

After 1910, however, the French reached an accommodation with a major Tijaniyya leader named Malik Sy after he preached a sermon explaining that jihad was not an appropriate response to French colonial rule. He later circulated a text in which he wrote that "God has given special victory, grace, and favor to the French." During World War I, Malik Sy urged his followers to enlist in the French army, and he lost his eldest son in the fighting. Following Malik Sy's death in 1922, his son-in-law Seydou Tal (who happened to be the grandson of the nineteenth-century jihadist leader Umar Tal) became an important diplomatic figure in French West Africa who sought to bridge the gap between Islamic and French culture. "It is moving to think," wrote the French governor of Mauritania, "that the grandson of our greatest enemy is our greatest friend."

Islamic Reform Movements in French West Africa

The Tijaniyya leaders not only accommodated themselves to French rule, but looked to the French for support when they were challenged by a local Islamic reform movement. The leader of the movement, **Amadu Hamallah**, was himself a member of the Tijaniyya, but his followers relied on their own interpretations of Tijaniyya texts, rather than respecting the traditional chain of transmission from teacher to student, and they claimed that Hamallah had received revelations directly from the Prophet Muhammad. They also used an altered form of an obligatory daily prayer, repeating it eleven times instead of the traditional twelve and using a special eleven-bead rosary to keep count. Feeling disrespected, the local Tijaniyya leaders sought French aid to crush the reformers.

There is no evidence that Amadu Hamallah ever made anti-French statements or tried to rally his followers against the French. In fact, he seemed mostly oblivious to them. French officials, however, claimed that all Islamic reform movements were inherently dangerous because they tended to attract the young and the most troublesome elements of society. The presence of ex-slaves and members of despised occupational castes among Hamallah's followers appeared to prove their point. Moreover, French officials began to interpret Hamallah's altered prayer, with its accompanying eleven-bead rosary, as a kind of secret code to rally his followers.

Under pressure from the local Tijaniyya leaders, many of whom were direct descendants of Umar Tal, the French declared Amadu Hamallah to be a dangerous enemy. In 1925, he was arrested and sentenced to 10 years of exile in neighboring Mauritania. When violent altercations between members of the Tijaniyya and followers of Hamallah's disciples broke out in Mauritania, Hamallah was shipped off to Côte d'Ivoire, even though he had been living a week's journey away from the town where the clashes took place. After he returned to his home in 1936, the French remained suspicious of him. During his exile, he had begun abridging his prayers. Noting that Muslim soldiers on their way to battle followed a similar practice, French officials interpreted Hamallah's abbreviated prayers as a secret call to battle. When a personal dispute between Hamallah's son and some local nomads turned violent, the French blamed Hamallah. They sent about a hundred of Hamallah's followers into exile in scattered parts of French West Africa and deported him to France, where he died of pneumonia in 1943. Although the French had formerly considered the Tijaniyya to be their implacable enemy, they now saw it as a "good brotherhood," and the cleric who tried to reform it had become the new enemy.

An even more complicated situation developed in relation to the Muridiyya, a Muslim brotherhood founded in the 1880s by a cleric named **Amadu Bamba**, who established a village called Touba, or "conversion," in Senegal. Bamba had been associated at one time or another with both the Qadiriyya and Tijaniyya, but he was not satisfied with either one. He spent most of his time studying the Quran and writing devotional poetry, but nevertheless attracted a community of followers. Some of his followers aspired to become scholars and clerics, but many were former Cheddo soldiers (see chapter 8) who were told that they could gain a place in paradise by working in the cleric's peanut fields.

Because of Amadu Bamba's brief association with the Tijaniyya, and because of the presence of former Cheddo warriors among his following, the French feared that he would lead a rebellion. As a result, they exiled him to Gabon for 7 years. When he returned, he found that his followers had become even more popular during his absence, in part because they had little connection to the colonial administration. Fearing Bamba's growing popularity, the French again sent him into exile. It was during his second exile that he had a revelation and declared that his group was now a new Sufi brotherhood that was separate from the Tijaniyya. He called it the Muridiyya, a term that referred to the disciples of a spiritual leader. His followers were called Murides.

After his return from his second exile in 1907, Amadu Bamba became an enthusiastic supporter of the French. "Thanks to French occupation," he declared, "the inhabitants who, far from being Muslims, were pillagers living at the expense of travelers and the weak, have changed to become calm and peaceful. Now, the sheep and the jackals march together." In making reference to "pillagers" and "jackals," he was clearly referring to the former Cheddo warriors working in his peanut fields. His Muride brotherhood continued to attract followers, especially ex-slaves, who could work on the brotherhood's farms for 8 years and would then be given land and allowed to marry. By 1912, the growing brotherhood had 68,000 disciples working under the authority of 162 sheikhs (teachers/supervisors).

AMADU BAMBA The only known photograph of Amadu Bamba, the founder of the Muslim Muride brotherhood, was taken in 1913 in Diourbel, Senegal. By this time, the French colonial government had decided that his doctrine of hard work held economic benefits for the colony.

Following Amadu Bamba's death in 1927, his followers continued to expand peanut cultivation, and they even built their own rail line to carry their crops to the coast.

Islamization from Below

An even larger expansion of Islam took place in rural villages, where young men who engaged in migratory labor learned the basics of Islam while working in the cities or in African cash crop regions and carried the knowledge back to their homes. In such situations, Islamization often occurred through the gradual adoption of Islamic practices and attitudes, in contrast to the dramatic conversions that characterized the Christian revivals in Côte d'Ivoire and southern Nigeria. One historian has characterized this process of Islamization as "gradual religious drift." Two examples of this phenomenon, among the Diola of Senegal and in the Buguni region of Mali, will illustrate how it worked.

The Diola people lived in Senegal, where they made their living as rice farmers. Their traditional religion was organized around a series of shrines that had different religious and practical functions, and each person would seek membership in one or more shrines. New shrines arose as new Diola prophets had visions, and old ones could die out if they lost their followings. Even though the Wolof kingdoms immediately to the north had been

Muslim for centuries, Islam had not spread among the Diola before the twentieth century.

When Islam did attract a following among the Diola, it was not because of pressures from their neighbors, but because of economic interests. During the 1920s and 1930s, there was a push toward Islam led by wealthy young men who were either successful peanut growers or had earned their money in cities. The French authorities in Senegal had made efforts in the years immediately following World War I to encourage production of peanuts as a cash crop. They imposed and rigorously enforced a high head tax, distributed free seed peanuts, and constructed roads to carry the crop to market. Diola farmers were able to adopt the new crop without diminishing their rice production because peanuts and rice were planted and harvested at different times of the year. Because peanuts did not grow well in the low-lying inundated zones used for rice cultivation, they did not take land away from rice farming. As a result, peanut farming grew rapidly during the 1920s, and new opportunities for wealth grew with it.

Young men who had achieved financial independence from their elders through peanut farming had two practical reasons for embracing Islam. First, they wanted to be free to marry whom they pleased and did not want to wait until they had gone through the village initiation ceremonies, which were held only once every 20 years. Because patriarchal authority and the initiation rituals were undergirded by the traditional shrines and priests, conversion to Islam was a way for young men to free themselves from the social control of the elders. Second, Muslim clerics who visited the area had long been accepted as ritual specialists who had spiritual powers analogous to the traditional shrine priests. When a devastating drought struck during the early 1930s, and prayers at the traditional shrines failed to produce the needed rain, some communities sought the aid of Muslim holy men. When the rains returned shortly after Muslim clerics had blessed the barren fields, the popularity of Islam soared.

The expansion of Islam during the 1930s was astonishingly rapid. In one village, the resident Muslim cleric left to pursue advanced studies in 1928, when the Diola people were only beginning their conversion to Islam. When he returned in 1941, he found that most of the population was Muslim. The major holdouts were the elders, who feared losing their traditional authority. The young men, on the other hand, embraced Islam and sought an alternative path to authority and respect through Islamic education. By 1934, there were 85 Quranic schools operating in the Diola region. By the late 1930s, conversion to Islam was aided by a "snowball effect" that created peer-group pressure on young men to convert. "Whoever you were, you saw your friends converting," one man explained.

Similar processes of Islamization were taking place 600 miles away from the Diola (900 miles by the winding road), in the Buguni region in southern Mali. Buguni was a poor region that produced few cash crops beyond a little obligatory cotton, so most families did not earn enough money to pay their taxes. Their solution was to send out one or more sons for migratory labor each year. The peanut basin of Senegal was a popular destination. By working 5 or 6 months through the peanut season, a migrant could earn 200–400 francs, enough to pay the 9-franc head tax and have money left over for marriage expenses or investments in cattle. A more convenient, if less lucrative, destination was Côte d'Ivoire, where the typical working contract was only 3 months long. Migrants who arrived there initially worked as lumberjacks and wood haulers, earning 35 francs a month, and they later worked as laborers on African-owned cocoa farms. Other migrants went to Guinea, where they dug deep pits to look for gold. In all of these cases, the young men worked for African employers, and those employers were usually Muslims.

When young men went off to seek work in distant regions, the best way to find food, lodging, and jobs was by tapping Muslim networks and connecting to Muslim communities. Upon arriving in a town, the migrants would go to the mosque to pray and make contacts. It was advantageous to adopt a Muslim name, learn some Arabic greetings, and know the protocols of Muslim prayer. As one migrant explained, "When you went on migration, you were forced to enter into the host's customs, such as religion. If at that time you did not pray and you found yourself among people who prayed, you were forced to change and start praying. Otherwise they would not even consider you for work." The migrant workers saw Islam as a tool for succeeding in the wider world beyond their village. As one village elder explained the connection, "When people started to migrate, everyone began to pray, one after another."

Whatever their original motives for learning the basics of Islamic practice, many migrants found that participation in the prayers gave them a sense of religious belonging and a feeling of solidarity with fellow migrants. At the work sites, Muslim migrants sought out others from their home region to pray together at a mosque or form informal prayer groups. Many migrants abandoned Islam once they returned home, but those who engaged in repeated migratory cycles often developed an Islamic cultural style that grew into a religious orientation. Whereas the first migrants usually hid their Muslim practices after returning home, later migrants practiced Islam more openly.

In 1928, French officials reported that mosques were being built and Quranic schools were being established in Buguni, and we know from oral testimony that many unauthorized neighborhood Quranic schools were springing up at about the same time. During the 1930s, the French appointed several Muslim chiefs to replace unpopular traditionalist chiefs, which made it easier for young Muslims to practice their faith overtly despite the opposition of the traditionalist power associations. As young people began to practice Islam more openly, returning migrants began to criticize certain traditional practices and urged their fellow villagers to embrace Islam. A split developed between the young migrant laborers, who were increasingly Muslim, and the traditionalist elders, who were increasingly marginalized. After World War II, when enough young people had converted to make conversion a matter of peer pressure, the growth of Islam in Buguni reached a tipping point. Soon Islam became the dominant religion in Buguni, all without any dramatic interventions by traveling Islamic clerics.

CONCLUSION

The Industrial Revolution initiated a series of social and cultural changes, which first erupted in Europe and soon reverberated around the world. Colonial policies aimed at improving "human capital" in Africa, through schooling and biomedical health care, were limited by lack of funds and shortages of personnel. Even though many colonial-era changes were initiated by missionaries and colonial officials, the new policies could not have been implemented without substantial African input. Slavery was delegalized by colonial officials, but over the subsequent decades African slaves mostly freed themselves. Most of the children in primary schools were taught by African teachers, and the hospitals and rural health clinics were staffed by African nurses and medical assistants. In a similar way, much of the expansion of Christianity was carried out by African catechists and evangelists, who often spread the Christian message in advance of the missionaries.

Africans found ways to participate in those changes on their own terms. When slavery was delegalized, not all slaves left their masters. Instead, the spectrum of responses ranged from immediate flight to long-term accommodation. Africans responded to modern biomedicine by adopting a kind of medical pluralism that could accommodate the coexistence of different healing therapies based on different theories of medical causality. The African role in shaping the impact of new ideas can best be seen in the plethora of independent Christian churches that sprang up all across Africa. Although the majority of African Christians during this period belonged to traditional missionary churches, a significant minority joined independent churches, which promised direct divine intervention to heal the afflicted, promote prosperity, and fight witchcraft. In Muslim areas, new Islamic brotherhoods emerged, existing ones were challenged by reformers, and young migrant laborers brought Islam to non-Muslim villages. Africans everywhere were picking and choosing among the new ideas and belief systems that infiltrated their continent. Africans had long held to a pluralistic framework by which they could absorb new ideas without necessarily rejecting the old ones, and as new options arose, they continued to select the ones that seemed the most useful and adapt them to meet their needs. Despite tremendous changes and cultural influences from abroad, African cultures were still vibrant and still recognizably African.

CHAPTER REVIEW

KEY TERMS AND VOCABULARY

delegalization
germ theory
cordon sanitaire
William Ponty School
Katsina College
Achimota College
William Wade Harris
Zionist churches
Aladura churches
Simon Kimbangu
Amadu Hamallah
Amadu Bamba

STUDY QUESTIONS

1. Why did many former slaves choose to stay with their former masters after slavery was delegalized?
2. What did the colonial powers gain from encouraging rudimentary education and modern biomedicine?
3. What were the key differences between the school systems in British, French, and Belgian colonies?
4. Why were the colonial authorities so slow to offer higher education opportunities?
5. How did colonial public health campaigns against epidemics impinge on the daily lives of Africans?
6. Explain why so many independent African Christian churches developed during the colonial period.
7. How did Islam spread in French West Africa during the colonial period despite the French colonial government's opposition to popular Muslim leaders?

KWAME NKRUMAH AT ACHIMOTA COLLEGE

Kwame Nkrumah entered Achimota College in Ghana when it first opened its doors in 1927. He went on to be the leader of Ghana's independence movement and the country's first prime minister and president. In this excerpt from his autobiography, he reveals his affection for the school and discusses its role in arousing his feelings of nationalism.

About this time [1927] the Prince of Wales' College at Achimota was officially opened by the Governor, Sir Gordon Guggisberg, before a large and colorful gathering of chiefs and government officials. Among the chiefs was the Kumasihene, a notorious ruler of Ashanti who had earlier been deported to the Seychelles by the Governor because of alleged participation in human sacrifices.

But the figure to whom all Africans looked that day was Dr. Kwegyir Aggrey, assistant vice-principal and the first African member of the staff. To me he seemed the most remarkable man that I had ever met and I had the deepest affection for him. He possessed intense vitality and enthusiasm and a most infectious laugh that seemed to bubble up from his heart, and he was a very great orator. It was through him that my nationalism was first aroused.

He was extremely proud of his color but was strongly opposed to racial segregation in any form and, although he could understand Marcus Garvey's principle of "Africa for the Africans," he never hesitated to attack this principle. He believed conditions should be such that the black and white races should work together. Co-operation between the black and white peoples was the key note of his message and the essence of his mission, and he used to expound this by saying: "You can play a tune of sorts on the white keys, and you can play a tune of sorts on the black keys, but for harmony you must use both the black and the white."

I could not, even at that time, accept this idea of Aggrey's as being practicable, for I maintained that such harmony can only exist when the black race is treated as equal to the white race; that only a free and independent people—a people with a government of their own—can claim equality, racial or otherwise, with another people. . . .

Looking back on Achimota days, I realize that they were among my happiest, probably because they were the last days of leisure I have ever enjoyed—days when I could read, without fear of being disturbed, the book that interested me most; have long discussions with my friends on an endless variety of topics or wander through the woods surrounding the college, alone with my thoughts. I graduated in 1930 and the time came for me to leave Achimota. With the lines of our farewell hymn, "Forty Days and Forty Nights," still on my lips, I sadly left the college walls.

1. *What was Kwame Nkrumah's disagreement with Dr. Kwegyir Aggrey?*
2. *Why did Nkrumah look back fondly on his days at Achimota College?*

Source: Kwame Nkrumah, *Ghana: The Autobiography of Kwame Nkrumah* (New York: Thomas Nelson & Sons, 1957), pp. 14, 20.

NOKUTELA DUBE: AN AFRICAN WOMAN MISSIONARY

Nokutela Dube was born into a Zulu family in Natal (South Africa). She spent 8 years studying at the Inanda Seminary, a school for girls sponsored by the American Board of Missions. In 1894, she married John L. Dube, who would later become the founding president of the South African Native National Congress (SANNC), which was the forerunner of the African National Congress (ANC). She shares here how she and John began their missionary work among the Zulu.

About six months after our marriage, God called us to a new field. It was not until this time that I felt that God had called me out to his work. He was calling us to a people most of whom had not heard of Christ. We did not have very much money for the expense of moving, for we were not drawing any salary at this time, but we said if the Lord has called us he will provide the means; and he did. My brother offered to take us with his wagon. . . .

How glad we were when we stood on the top of a mountain and saw the Incwadi. This place is on the Umkomas Valley, near the mountains which divide Transvaal and Natal. It is about a hundred miles from our former home on the coast. Our hearts went up in prayer to God as we looked, and saw nothing but *kraals* with no sign of Christian civilization. We had a little mud hut given us, and after we had put in all our things we had just enough room to sleep. . . .

The first Sunday we were there, two hundred people came to hear the story we had to tell them—the story which was told to the shepherds: though old, yet it is ever new. Our people believe in a Great Great (*Unkulunkulu*), who has withdrawn himself into the heavens on account of man's sinfulness, and has no communication with them. So they worship the spirits of their ancestors. Mr. Dube in his first sermon told them that he had found the way to reach this Great Great, and they showed a great interest.

We at once started a class meeting to instruct them in Christian living, and it soon numbered fifty. A day school was started with scholars from the ages of four to forty, or more. . . . In connection with my practical work among women I saw more clearly their needs. In our country the women do most of the field work, and their husbands stay home and tan skins, with which they make short skirts for their wives. Every girl is worth ten cattle; when she is to be married the husband pays these to the father of the girl.

God has enabled us to build two church buildings, in one of which a church was organized before we left with thirty members and a large class under instruction. Since we left twenty-seven have been received into church membership. There are two day schools connected with these churches.

1. *What was Nokutela Dube's opinion of the people of the Incwadi?*
2. *How did the Dubes get the people interested in the Christian message?*

Source: Nokutela Dube, "Africa: The Story of My Life," *Life and Light for Woman*, vol. 28 (1898), pp. 110–113.

PERSPECTIVES

CONGOLESE CONCEPTS OF WITCHCRAFT

Witchcraft was understood very differently in Africa and in the West. In Africa, talking about witchcraft was a popular way of talking about evil in the world. Those suspected of witchcraft were usually men who looked and acted normally. The following excerpts from 1910 and 1965 explain how witchcraft functioned in the lower Congo. They indicate that half a century of Western colonialism increased anxieties about witchcraft instead of diminishing them.

How Witchcraft Works

Witchcraft is recognized when a person who is having an argument with another predicts misfortune for him as a curse; if the utterance takes effect, then the one who said it is not innocent, but is suspected of being a witch. . . . Acts of witchcraft are best recognized in human malevolence. . . .

Although witches recognize one another, no witch can ever admit to himself that he is one. Non-witches just use their eyes. If they see a woman who always seems to have money, they know she controls a money *kundu* [evil spirit]. If they see a hunter who always hits his quarry, they know he controls a gluttony *kundu*. That's how people figure out witchcraft.

From Konda Jean, *Mavanga ma Kindoki*, Cahier No. 120, Laman Collection, Lidingö, Sweden, ca. 1910.

Bewitching People

The witch is someone who has hidden knowledge by virtue of which he obtains secret techniques, usually employed secretly. Witchcraft usually appears where there is jealousy, envy and the like. A person who has this hidden knowledge can do someone else harm without letting him know whence the hurt comes. He learns the techniques of sorcery; with them the witch can send a curse to someone else who is at a distance. A witch sends curses with two intents: (1) to distress the victim for a time, (2) to seize his life. These things are done by someone whose entire soul is gripped by jealousy.

Witchcraft also manifests itself very strongly in connection with malice and theft. In this regard there is a kind of witchcraft everybody knows about, called *kinkondi* or *kimpungu*. If a man has lost something or had something unexpected happen to him, he may go to an *nkondi*-operator or to one who possesses *mpungu* to control the source of the difficulty. Then the magician, acting on behalf of the enquirer, sends a curse; everything that is done is counted in the name of the client, not of the diviner himself. The client may have two intentions: (1) to know the origin of the event that has befallen him, (2) to counteract the origin of the event. In the latter case he may intend to cause the offender to suffer, or seek his life.

We are saying that the witch and possessor of *kundu* [evil spirit] are the same sort of person: those who cause harm to the souls and bodies of others. In this sense of causing harm, there is no doubt that witchcraft is real. In general, those we call witches are malicious, greedy, and jealous people who are, in effect, murderers because they all have the same motive: killing others or preventing them from enjoying human happiness.

From Yakobi Munzele, *Bakulu beto ye Diela diau*. 1965. Mimeographed essay.

1. *According to Konda Jean, how does a person recognize the presence of witchcraft?*
2. *How does Yakobi Munzele define witchcraft?*

Source: John M. Janzen and Wyatt MacGaffey, *An Anthology of Kongo Religion*, University of Kansas Publications in Anthropology, no. 5 (Lawrence, KS, 1974), pp. 45–46.

EXILING AMADU BAMBA

The Muslim marabout (itinerant preacher) Amadu Bamba became so popular in Senegal that the French colonial administrators saw him as a threat to their authority. They exiled him in Gabon for 7 years, but when he returned in 1902, he was more popular than ever. Below, French administrators correspond about sending him into exile a second time. Note that they sometimes refer to Amadu Bamba using the honorific title Serigne, whereas Bamba always refers to himself in the third person.

Amadu Bamba's reply when he was summoned to present himself before the French commandant within 8 days: "It is the servant of God who sends this reply, a servant of God who has no other Master. He informs the Commandant that peace comes to those who walk the straight path. In addition, he acknowledges that he has received the summons, and he replies that he is a servant of God and does not recognize any other master but God and gives homage to God alone; [not to the] very high, the venerated, the rich, and the great. Peace comes to those who walk the straight path."—from the Journal of the French Administrative Post at Diourbel, May 1903.

Telegram from the French administrator at Thiès to the governor-general of French West Africa, May 7, 1903: "Urgent! The marabout Amadu Bamba has let it be known that he does not recognize any master but God, and he refuses to come when we summon him. I consider the situation particularly serious because passions can get overheated. Given the religious influence of this rebellious marabout, we fear that the French administrator is powerless to assure order as long as the marabout stays in Baol."

Report from the French administrator at Diourbel to the governor-general of French West Africa, May 22, 1903: "People from Kontor, Kaël, and Goréte came to see me, and they confirmed that Serigne Bamba has decided not to leave his village no matter what efforts we make [to summon him]. Those who want to see him or speak to him have to go to Mbaké; but as for him, he can't be bothered. They estimate that about 7,000 people are currently in Mbaké. Even allowing for exaggeration on the part of the natives, it would not be surprising if there were 2,000 or 3,000 individuals.

The number of new converts grows each day, and it swells the throng of his fanatic disciples or Murides who crisscross the country spreading extraordinary rumors about the power and glory of Bamba. All of the facts, actions, and words relating to that marabout are scrambled and turned in his favor. People are saying that Bamba no longer fears the Europeans; that guns will not fire and gunpowder will not go off against him; his exile in Congo becomes a triumphant voyage to France, etc. etc., and a thousand other fabrications of that sort. In short, he has become the unique person who gets all of the public attention.

As for me, I tend to believe that he seeks to create an independent religious power center, which will inevitably be hostile to us and will be a counterbalance to our authority."

1. *Why did Amadu Bamba refuse the summons of the French administrator?*
2. *Why did the French fear Amadu Bamba?*

Source: Oumar Ba, compiler and editor, *Ahmadou Bamba Face aux Autorités Coloniales, 1889–1927* [Documents Recueillis], (Abbeville, France: F. Paillart, 1982), pp. 97, 100. Translated by Robert Harms.

PART 5

AFRICA IN THE AGE OF GLOBAL WAR, 1935–1990

By the mid-1930s, the British, French, Portuguese, and Belgian colonial governments had developed systems of indirect rule by which decisions made in metropolitan or colonial capitals would be carried out in the most remote regions of Africa. To colonizers and Africans alike, it looked as if colonial rule had stabilized into a system that would remain in place for decades, if not centuries.

The major calls for African independence during the interwar period came not from Africa, but from the Pan-African movement led by the African American author, intellectual, and civil rights activist W. E. B. Du Bois. Between 1919 and 1927, he organized four Pan-African Congresses to bring together people of African descent living in the Americas, the Caribbean, Europe, and Africa in order to discuss their common grievances arising from worldwide white racism. The second Pan-African Congress, held in London in 1921, issued a strong condemnation of colonialism in Africa, noting that Britain had "declined to . . . grant to colored colonies those rights of self-government which it freely gives to white men." After the fourth Pan-African Congress, held in New York City in 1927, the movement lost steam and became inactive for the next eighteen years. Both in Africa and in the wider world of the African diaspora, it seemed as if colonialism was securely entrenched in Africa for the foreseeable future.

That sense of a colonial equilibrium would be ruptured by two global wars. One of them—World War II—was a "hot war" that lasted a decade, from 1935 to 1945; the other was a "cold war" that divided much of the world into two competing camps for nearly half a century. Taken together, World War II and the Cold War created the global context in which Africans regained their independence and formed African-ruled states.

World War II was the most destructive conflagration in global history, leaving between 50 million and 80 million people dead (including those who died from war-related disease and famine). It was called a "world war," but it was actually a series of interrelated wars fought in scattered locations across the globe. The aggressors were the Axis powers (Germany, Italy, and Japan), who were opposed by the Allies (mainly the British Commonwealth, the United States, and the Soviet Union). Both alliances included countries with African colonies, although it was the Allies who had the larger stake in Africa because Germany had lost its African colonies following World War I. (Portugal, which also had African colonies, maintained neutrality during the war.) Africa was involved with the conflict in several ways. First, Ethiopia, East Africa, and North Africa saw heavy fighting. Second, areas of Africa outside the theater of war became sources of recruits and raw materials for the colonial powers as Africans were mobilized to aid the European war effort. The experience of the war changed attitudes toward colonial rule in both Europe and Africa.

World War II reconfigured economic and political power around the globe. When the war came to an end on September 2, 1945, the nations of Atlantic Europe that had once ruled the world were devastated. World War II was the first war in history in which aerial bombing of cities was a regular military strategy: Germany's bombing raids on

London killed 20,000 civilians and damaged or destroyed a million homes, while the Allied bombing of Berlin killed at least 20,000 civilians and reduced the central city to rubble. To help Europe recover from the war, the United States provided $12 billion (the equivalent of $120 billion in 2016) in aid through the Marshall Plan between 1948 and 1952 to rebuild the European economies. The war left the United States, which had developed the atomic bomb during the war, as the strongest military power in the world, followed by the Soviet Union, which tested its first atomic bomb in 1949 and became an imperialist power by establishing hegemony over much of Eastern Europe in the final phase of the war. The colonial powers of Atlantic Europe—Britain, France, Belgium, and Portugal—were forced to adjust to their diminished role in the world order.

Both the British and the French realized that it was important to maintain peaceful relations with their African colonies in the postwar era, but they went about it in opposite ways. Britain was the first colonial power to conclude that maintaining a worldwide empire in the face of increasing nationalist opposition in the colonies was not feasible. Accordingly, it granted independence to India and Pakistan in 1947 and to Sri Lanka, Burma, and Palestine the following year. Whereas the British began to plan for the eventual independence of their African colonies, the French sought to win the support of Africans by integrating the colonies more closely into a worldwide French Community. They were determined to reestablish control over their colonies after the war, and they resorted to aggression when they deemed it necessary. In 1945, they violently suppressed anti-French demonstrations in Algeria, leaving 6,000 dead, and in the following year, they fought anti-French unrest in Indochina by bombarding the port city of Haiphong with a warship. In 1947, the French repressed an uprising on the African island of Madagascar, leaving as many as 89,000 people dead.

No sooner had World War II ended than the world was again split into two rival camps at the outbreak of the Cold War. On one side was the United States and its Western European allies, who formed a military alliance called the North Atlantic Treaty Organization (NATO). They favored democratic government and substantially free market economies in which governments nevertheless provided limited economic regulation and a social safety net. On the other side was the Soviet Union and the Eastern European countries it had liberated from the Germans during World War II. The Soviet Union operated under communism, a Marxist-socialist ideology that favored a strong central government that controlled all aspects of the economy and society. In Asia, China was also emerging as a new communist power, which was sometimes an ally of the Soviet Union and sometimes a rival.

The Cold War dominated global international relations for nearly a half century, from 1945 to 1991. It was called the Cold War because it consisted mostly of threats, espionage, proxy wars, and strategic maneuvering that stopped short of a military conflagration between the protagonists themselves. The core areas of the globe occupied by authoritarian communist governments or capitalist democracies were more or less fixed by 1950, and therefore the Cold War was played out mainly in what was then called the Third World: the formerly colonized countries that the protagonists believed could be persuaded to align themselves with one camp or the other.

When the former colonial regions of Africa became independent beginning in 1957, they became a new battleground in the Cold War. Cold War ideologies influenced African movements for independence, wars of liberation, and post-colonial development policies. On the communist side, both the Soviet Union and China were strong advocates for African independence and socialist governments. On the side of the capitalist democracies, which referred to themselves as the Free World, the United States had emerged as the undisputed leader. Its policies toward African independence were ambiguous and often contradictory because it did not want to antagonize the major colonial powers such as Britain, France, Belgium, and Portugal, who were its key allies in the fight against communism. Even after the initial wave of African independence, Cold War tensions and rivalries had a major impact on African countries until the collapse of the Soviet Union in 1991.

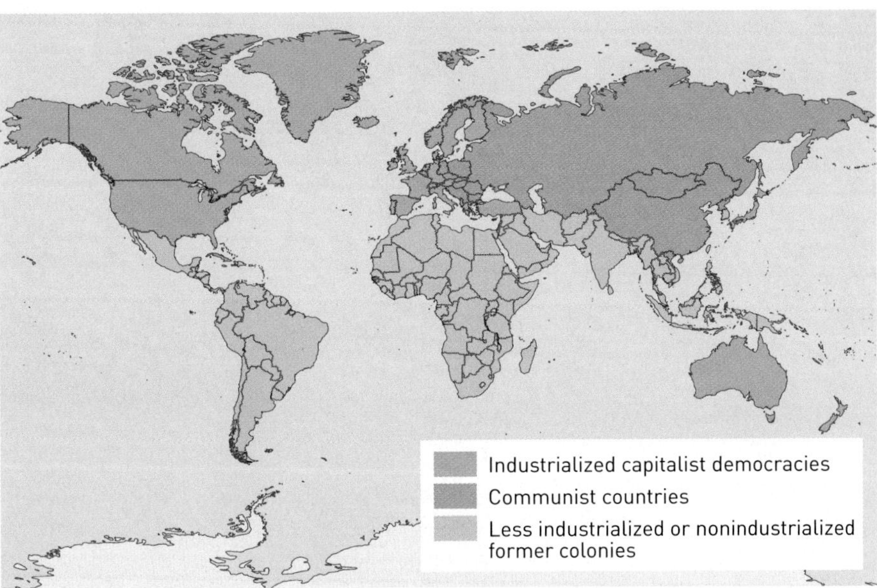

THE THREE-WORLD ORDER, 1947–1991 This map shows the three-part division of the world throughout the years of the Cold War: the industrialized capitalist democracies in Western Europe and North America, which referred to themselves as the Free World; the communist countries, mainly China and the Soviet Union; and the less industrialized or nonindustrialized former colonies, collectively known at the time as the Third World.

HAILE SELASSIE WITH HIS TROOPS Ethiopian Emperor Haile Selassie (center) reviewing his troops in 1935. At the time, Ethiopia was the only country in Africa that had not succumbed to foreign colonization. In a speech at the palace in Addis Ababa on August 12, he warned of the possibility of war. Less than 2 months later, the Italians invaded from Eritrea. As the Italian army approached the capital on May 2, 1936, Haile Selassie fled the country for England, but he returned to the liberated capital 5 years later.

1935	**1943**	**1945**
Italy invades Ethiopia	Axis forces with-draw from Africa	Terracing campaigns begin in East Africa

13

LATE COLONIALISM: DEVELOPMENT AND CHANGE, 1935–1965

Even though most parts of Africa were spared from the fighting during World War II, in part because the most intense African battles were fought in the sparsely populated Sahara Desert, the war years were a time of intensified colonial oppression as the colonial governments scoured the African countryside for military recruits; extracted forest products such as rubber and timber; mobilized farmers to increase their production of cotton, peanuts, and palm oil; and intensified the mining of copper, cobalt, uranium, gold, and industrial diamonds. In the aftermath of the war, the European colonial powers continued to seek resources from Africa for rebuilding their war-devastated economies. Realizing that the intensive mobilization of people and resources that characterized the war years was not sustainable, they began to devise plans to improve infrastructure, education, health care, and agriculture in Africa in order to increase the economic output of their colonies. They also developed plans to cope with the explosive growth of Africa's cities.

After discussing the impact of the war itself, this chapter describes the new postwar development policies and assesses their results. It makes five main points: First, postwar development plans continued to focus on increasing mineral and cash-crop exports to Europe, rather than signaling a significant change in colonial policy.

1946	1947	1950
Radio Brazzaville begins broadcasting	French West African railway workers strike	10-year plan in Belgian Congo

Second, the development projects were financed in large part by revenue raised in the colonies themselves, or by loans that would be repaid from the colonies' future revenue. Third, even with significant African contributions, the costs to the colonial powers were heavy enough to make them realize that continuing colonial rule would be expensive in the long run. Fourth, many of the development projects entailed unprecedented intrusions by colonial authorities into the lives of ordinary Africans and thus provoked strong resistance, which in turn cast doubt on the viability of state-directed development. Fifth, expanding African economies required urban laborers for transportation hubs, warehousing, processing of agricultural products, and a variety of other jobs. Because it was no longer feasible to depend on temporary migrant workers from the countryside, a large and permanent urban workforce was developing that was not afraid to demand better wages and working conditions.

WORLD WAR II

Conventional accounts of World War II state that it began on September 1, 1939, when Germany invaded Poland. If one takes a more global view, however, then it could also be said that the war began 4 years earlier, on October 3, 1935, in Africa. That was the day Italy invaded Ethiopia, the only country in Africa that had never succumbed to colonial rule. The Italians had invaded before, in 1896, but the Ethiopian army had successfully repelled them at the Battle of Adwa (see chapter 10). The Italians had withdrawn to the north and occupied the tiny colony of Eritrea on Ethiopia's northern border, but nearly 40 years later, they came back for a second try. On October 6, 1935, the Italians captured Adwa, and 7 months later they entered the Ethiopian capital of Addis Ababa. By then, the Ethiopian emperor, **Haile Selassie**, had fled to England. Flush with victory, Italian dictator Benito Mussolini proclaimed the creation of his new Italian East African Empire, consisting of Eritrea and Ethiopia.

After the war broke out in Europe in 1939, the British and French sought African soldiers to augment their military strength. The British obtained troops from their African colonies by a combination of aggressive recruitment and outright conscription. The French, for their part, desperately sought military assistance from their African colonies as they braced for the coming German invasion. One resource was the Army of Africa, based in French North Africa, which contributed 42 regiments of Algerian, Tunisian, and Moroccan soldiers. Another was the Senegalese Riflemen, a military force made up of African soldiers from all over French West Africa. Between September 1939 and June 1940, some 100,000 men from French West Africa were drafted into the French military.

The Italian Campaigns

In 1940, with World War II raging in Europe, Italy launched two separate military campaigns against British colonies in Africa. The first was known as the East African Campaign. From their base in Ethiopia, Italian forces moved east into Somalia to expel the British, west into Sudan to capture two British garrisons, and south into Kenya, where they captured two towns in the sparsely populated northern region of the country. The British quickly mobilized to defend their colonies and drive the Italians out of Ethiopia. They brought in two infantry divisions from India, 27,000 soldiers from South Africa, and several brigades of African soldiers from Ghana and Nigeria, and they expanded the East African army, known as the King's African Rifles, to 20,000 strong.

The key to liberating Ethiopia, however, lay with the irregular Ethiopian resistance forces known as the **patriots.** Emperor Haile Selassie, who had been in exile in England, entered Ethiopia from Sudan and joined up with an elite British Special Forces unit known as the Gideon Force. Traveling through the countryside, they used powerful loudspeakers to rally the patriots. Women as well as men joined the patriot army. In the region near Addis Ababa, a separate patriot army commanded by Abebe Aregai, the former chief of police in Addis Ababa, was consolidating its control over the countryside, but it was not powerful enough to attack the city. The Italians were finally pushed out of the capital on April 6, 1941, by a British army made up of East African, South African, Ghanaian, and Nigerian troops. Accompanied by thousands of Ethiopian patriot soldiers, Haile Selassie entered the capital on May 5, 1941, 5 years to the day after he had fled the city. In the aftermath of the war, the former Italian colony of Eritrea was placed under Ethiopian control, and the British reaffirmed Ethiopia's sovereignty.

Italy's other military foray into Africa was the North African Campaign, which began in 1940. From their colony in Libya, the Italians invaded Egypt in hopes of capturing the Nile valley and linking up with the Italian forces in Ethiopia. After a British counteroffensive nearly destroyed the Italian army, the Germans came to Italy's aid. They sent in the Afrika Korps, commanded by the German field marshal, Erwin Rommel, who was known as "the Desert Fox" because he would launch surprise attacks and then disappear into the desert sands. By late 1942, the British had driven the Axis forces from Egypt and Libya, and finally defeated them in May 1943 in Tunisia with the help of their American allies, who were moving in from the west. Over 230,000 German and Italian troops were captured, including most of the Afrika Korps. This victory left the Allies well positioned to invade Italy from Libya (the straight-line distance across the Mediterranean from Tripoli to Rome was only 214 miles).

THE DESERT FOX IN LIBYA German field marshal Erwin Rommel (left) rides through the desert between Tobruk and Sidi Omar in Libya during the siege of Tobruk in 1941. Rommel led the Afrika Korps' 15th Panzer Division to victories throughout 1940 and 1941, earning the nickname "the Desert Fox" for the stealth of his attacks. Note the camouflage paint on his vehicle.

The Divided French Colonies

After France surrendered to Germany in June 1940, the Germans installed a collaborationist government (known as the Vichy government because its capital was the French city of Vichy) led by Marshal Philippe Pétain, which was allowed to maintain control of France's colonies as long as they remained officially neutral in the war. Initially, the governors of France's African colonies, with one exception, pledged loyalty to the Vichy government. The exception was the governor of Chad, a landlocked colony in French Equatorial Africa, who sought to maintain trading relations with the British colony of Nigeria. Chad instead sided with the **Free French Forces**, a group in exile, led by General Charles de Gaulle, that opposed the Vichy government. Once Chad had joined the Free French Forces, the governors of the other colonies in French Equatorial Africa (but not those in French West Africa) followed suit. The French colonies then settled into a stalemate: the governors in French North Africa and French West Africa remained loyal to the Vichy government, while those in French Equatorial Africa pledged their loyalty to the Free French Forces.

That stalemate was ruptured in 1942 when the Americans landed in French North Africa. Under the command of General Dwight D. Eisenhower, the American invasion (known as Operation Torch) was part of a coordinated Allied effort to trap the Germans in a pincer movement by having the British invade Libya from Egypt while the Americans invaded French North Africa and moved east. After the Americans captured Algiers, the capital of French North Africa, on November 8, 1942, they merged the French colonial Army of Africa with de Gaulle's Free French Forces and replaced the pro-Vichy administrators with ones who were loyal to de Gaulle. With French North Africa under the control of the Free French Forces, de Gaulle moved his headquarters to Algiers in May 1943.

In response to those events, the collaborationist governor-general of French West Africa resigned and was replaced by a new governor-general who supported the Free French Forces. From then on, all of France's African colonies were under the control of the Free French Forces, with Algiers as their provisional capital. The Free French governors used their African colonies to recruit soldiers and supply raw materials for the Allies, imposing forced labor and mandatory production of cash crops as part of the "war effort." The most onerous of these impositions was forced rubber gathering, a relic of the early colonial period that was resurrected during the war. Africa was a vital part of the Allied war strategy, but the burden was borne by ordinary Africans who had nothing to do with the war. Many chiefs in West Africa became very unpopular because they were obligated to conscript soldiers and mobilize forced labor.

World War II ended with Japan's surrender on August 15, 1945, shortly after the Americans dropped atomic bombs on Hiroshima and Nagasaki. The uranium in those bombs came from the Shinkolobwe mines in the Belgian Congo. Throughout the war, African soldiers had been involved in the fighting. When Germany invaded France in June 1940, nearly 10 percent of the soldiers defending France were Africans. Some of them bore the full brunt of Germany's mechanized Panzer divisions and suffered heavy casualties. About 15,000 of these African soldiers were captured and spent the war in German prison camps. During the liberation of France in 1944, as many as 100,000 French African soldiers fought for the Allies. African soldiers from the British colonies, for their part, fought first in the Ethiopian and East African campaigns, then in North Africa, and many of them went on to participate in the invasion of Italy in 1943–1944. The British also sent 120,000 troops from Africa to help drive the Japanese out of Burma. In all, half a million African soldiers from the British colonies served in World War II. Some 15,000 of them were killed, and thousands more became prisoners of war. Africa was thus involved in World War II from the initial invasion of Ethiopia in 1935 to the final mushroom cloud 10 years later.

ECONOMIC AND HUMAN DEVELOPMENT IN POSTWAR AFRICA

As the war was coming to an end, the British, French, and Belgians began to rethink their approach to colonial rule. The old colonial policies of military conscription, forced labor, and maximum extraction of natural resources were no longer sustainable. The governor-general of the Belgian Congo, for example, acknowledged that the rural populations of the Congo were worn out, having been pushed to the limit by the colonial government during the war. The new idea underlying postwar colonial policies was that economic development should benefit the Africans as well as the colonial rulers, so that the Africans would become willing (though not equal) partners in colonial ventures. The colonial powers used this renewed emphasis on development as a justification for holding on to their colonies in the postwar world. Article 73 of the United Nations charter, signed by Britain, France, and Belgium in 1945, approved of this kind of intervention, stating that U.N. members should promote the "political, economic, social, and educational advancement" of non-self-governing territories (i.e., colonies). The colonial powers preferred to emphasize economic, social, and educational advancement because they were less threatening than political advancement. Our analysis begins by looking at the postwar development policies of Britain, France, and Belgium. Then we examine the effects of the development-oriented colonial state on different areas of African life.

Postwar Development Policies

In his 1942 report to the British Colonial Office, entitled *Native Administration and Political Development in British Tropical Africa*, Lord Hailey, Britain's foremost expert on African affairs, wrote that the colonial administration could no longer be merely an agency for keeping order, but instead must be committed to "the improvement of the economic and social life of the colonial population." Such a statement marked a departure from earlier British justifications for colonialism, which had emphasized military security and anti-slavery campaigns. Immediately after the war, Britain's colonial secretary announced that the new British policy was "to develop the colonies and all their resources so as to enable their people speedily and substantially to improve their economic and social conditions."

To finance the new development efforts, the British government allocated £120 million over a 10-year period to the Colonial Development and Welfare (CDW) Fund and encouraged individual African colonies to draw up a **10-year plan** for development. Ghana and Nigeria, for example, developed 10-year plans for improvements in water supplies, town planning, communications, education, hospitals, and agriculture. Although helpful, the CDW funds were rather modest: CDW grants accounted for only one-sixth of the colonies' expenditures on development, with the rest of the funds coming from each colony's own revenue or from external loans (which would be repaid from the colony's future revenue).

The Marketing Board funds in Ghana and Nigeria illustrate how African farmers became a major source of development loans. In an attempt to minimize yearly price fluctuations for major export commodities such as cocoa and coffee, each colony's **Marketing Board** purchased the commodities from the farmers at prices well below world market value and deposited the difference in a special fund. If world market prices dropped too low, then money from the fund could be used to subsidize the amount paid to farmers, thus keeping prices stable. However, world commodity prices in the postwar years were generally above average, so the Marketing Board accumulated large surpluses that could be loaned out for development projects. In reality, the Marketing Board's holdings consisted of money that had been confiscated from African farmers. It was the cocoa and coffee farmers who were unwittingly financing substantial portions of the development plan.

The French also adopted a development-oriented approach to colonial rule. In 1944, as the war was nearing an end, the leader of the Free French Forces, Charles de Gaulle, convened a conference in Brazzaville, French Congo, to discuss the role of France's African colonies in the postwar order. The final declaration of the Brazzaville Conference repeated France's well-worn call for the "development of the productive potential of the colonies," but it also recognized the need to raise African purchasing power and improve African standards of living. Breaking from the older idea that the colonies existed solely to supply raw materials for European industries, the conference recommended that French colonial governments undertake pilot programs to encourage industrialization in the colonies themselves. Worried about the low productivity of traditional African agriculture, the conference recommended sending an envoy to the Soviet Union to study its collective farms.

To implement their development plans after the war, the French set up the Investment Fund for Social and Economic Development, thereby departing from their previous policy that the colonies should pay for themselves. Sixty-four percent of the fund went to improving transportation infrastructure, 18 percent went to social expenditures such as education and health care, and 18 percent was used for improving agriculture. All grants from the fund had to be matched by revenues raised in the colonies themselves. Although a few of the projects promoted industrial diversification, most of them simply promoted increased exports of the major cash crops. The results failed to live up to the lofty rhetoric of the Brazzaville Conference.

In the Belgian Congo, Governor-General Pierre Ryckmans also believed that a fundamental change in colonial policy was needed. He acknowledged that the

Congo had been built on a "skimming economy," which had skimmed off the most easily accessible natural resources and exported them to Europe. Future growth, however, would have to come from increases in domestic production and internal trade among the African population. To meet that challenge, the Belgian colonial government developed a 10-year plan for the Congo, which would be financed by foreign loans (mainly from banks in the United States) that would be repaid through increased exports—in other words, African farmers and workers would repay the loans. The plan was heavily focused on improving transportation infrastructure, but it also envisioned improvements in education, health care, agriculture, and city planning.

The colonial development funds and the 10-year plans signaled a reorientation and restructuring of the colonial regimes. Colonial states became "development states" by beefing up their departments of transportation, education, public health, urban planning, and agriculture. Whereas the early colonial state could be characterized as a conquest state that focused on military occupation, and the high colonial state of the interwar years had focused on experiments with indirect rule, the late colonial development state, with its emphasis on economic and human development, was acquiring some of the attributes of a modern bureaucratic state, although the key policy decisions were still made in London, Paris, and Brussels.

One of the great ironies of late colonialism was that the new projects for improving the situation of ordinary Africans required unprecedented government intrusion into their lives. The conquest state and the high colonial state had imposed new burdens on top of the traditional rhythms of everyday African life, but the development state of the postwar years sought to transform selected aspects of everyday life itself. It was the attempt to remake African agricultural practices that most intruded into the lives of ordinary people. In some parts of Africa, so many colonial agricultural agents were swarming over the rural villages that it looked to some like a second colonial occupation. To better understand the impact of the development state in postwar Africa, the remainder of this chapter looks at changes in transportation, education, health care, agriculture, and urban life during the late colonial period.

Transportation

Ever since the beginning of colonial rule in Africa, transportation was the highest development priority of colonial administrations: King Leopold II of Belgium had once remarked that "colonization is transportation," and Frederick Lugard, the architect of British indirect rule, noted in 1923 that "the material development of Africa may be summed up in one word—transport." In most of tropical

Africa, tsetse flies carrying sleeping sickness had historically prevented the use of pack animals, and porters still trudged along winding paths carrying loads of goods on their heads well into the colonial period. During World War I, for example, the French used 125,000 porters to carry 4,200 tons of foodstuffs. In 1926, the British calculated that head porterage cost 2 shillings and 6 pence per ton-mile, while truck transportation cost only 1 shilling, and railway transportation cost 2 pence.

The initial phase of creating a transportation network had focused on railroads. By the eve of World War II, almost every colony had at least one major railroad line that ran from the interior to a port city in order to export the products of the country. A look at the railroad map of Africa in 1938 shows a curious pattern whereby rail lines in neighboring colonies ran parallel to one another, but did not meet up, because of rivalries among the colonial powers. The most striking example of this phenomenon was along the lower Congo River, where French and Belgian rail lines ran roughly parallel to each other on the north and south banks (see chapter 10). The only region where the rail lines intersected to any degree was southern Africa, which had significant white settler populations.

Roads and Automobiles

During the interwar period, trucks began to challenge the supremacy of railroads. The 3-ton **Albion A10 truck**, with its 32-horsepower engine and chain drives to the rear wheels, became the standard vehicle on the roads of British colonies until the 1950s. It had been the workhorse truck of the British army during World War I, and it was well suited to the challenges of African dirt roads. Albion trucks began to get some competition when a Nigerian car dealer named William Akinola Dawodu imported Model T Fords and Firestone tires from the United States.

THE WORKHORSE OF COLONIAL AFRICA
Because they were considered rugged and reliable, Albion trucks were widely used in both British and French colonies during the interwar years. Built in Scotland, the Albion A10, shown here, was powered by an in-line 4-cylinder, 32-horsepower engine. It used a chain drive to propel the back wheels and boasted a carrying capacity of 3 tons.

The importance of roads went well beyond the limited vehicular traffic they carried. Even by 1952, Nigeria and Ghana had only about 20,000 vehicles each. For colonial administrations, roads facilitated the assertion of colonial power and extended effective administrative control. In 1926, the governor-general of French Equatorial Africa complained that his subdistrict officers were separated from their superiors by weeks of travel along forest paths, and he argued that motor-vehicle roads would permit more effective administration by cutting down communication and travel time. For ordinary Africans, the roads became major pathways for people traveling on foot to the markets, towns, and mines. Women carrying agricultural produce to markets were a common sight along the roadways. Moreover, trucks carrying merchandise could always add a few passengers on top of the load and thus serve as an informal bus service. Roads also restructured human geography as villages relocated closer to the roads for better access to goods and transportation. In some cases, people were forced by the colonial government to move their villages nearer to the roads, but in other cases people moved on their own.

Most of the motor-vehicle roads were simple dirt roads built and maintained with forced labor. Continuous maintenance was required in tropical Africa because the torrential rains washed out roadbeds and carved deep gullies in the ground. By 1938, Nigeria had one of the best road systems in tropical Africa, with 168 miles of asphalt roads and 23,000 miles of dirt and gravel roads; French West Africa, which was one-third larger than the United States, had 30,000 miles of dirt roads and tracks; and the Belgian Congo, which was the size of the United States east of the Mississippi, had 27,000 miles of dirt roads. As a point of comparison, the United States in 1939 had nearly 300,000 miles of paved intercity highways, half a million miles of hard-surfaced county and town roads, and over 2 million miles of dirt roads.

After World War II, a new phase of road building, financed in part by the colonial development funds, was launched. By the 1950s, asphalt roads were cheaper to build than railroads, causing railroad building to fall into disfavor. The 3-ton Albion trucks seen in the British colonies in the interwar years were replaced by trucks as large as 15 tons, and four-wheel-drive Marmon-Harrington trucks from the United States could pull a trailer to haul a total of 25 tons. By 1955, Nigeria had 28,000 miles of roads, of which 1,000 miles were asphalt and another 2,000 miles were gravel; French West Africa as a whole had nearly 50,000 miles of roads, of which 72 miles were asphalt and 400 miles were gravel; and the Belgian Congo had 66,000 miles of primary and secondary dirt roads. The most serious deficiency was in French Equatorial Africa, a territory the size of India, which by 1950 had only 11,000 miles of dirt roads. In contrast, India had 350,000 miles of roads, of which 85,000 miles were hard surfaced. A British report in 1956 recommended that neighboring colonies begin to integrate their transportation networks. Too many roads simply ended at the border.

Air Transport

Air transportation first came to Africa during the interwar years. Although the Cape to Cairo railroad that Cecil Rhodes had dreamed of in the late nineteenth century (see chapter 10) never became a reality, air service from Cairo, Egypt, to Cape Town, South Africa, began in 1932. With frequent stops at intermediate airports, the trip took 11 days. The French began regularly scheduled flights across the Sahara Desert to Dakar, Senegal (the capital of French West Africa), and on to Brazzaville, French Congo (the capital of French Equatorial Africa), and from there to Lubumbashi, in the Belgian Congo's copper mining region, to the Portuguese colony of Mozambique, and finally to the French-ruled island of Madagascar. With all the intermediate stops, the trip from France to Madagascar took 8 days. In the Belgian Congo, most of the important mining and administrative centers had some form of air service by 1938.

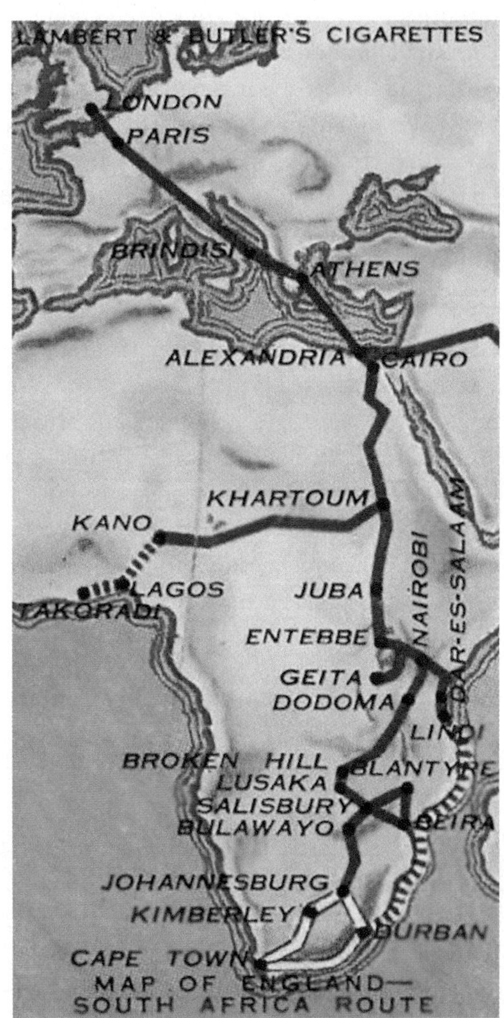

LONDON TO JOHANNESBURG This cigarette-card image shows the air route from England to South Africa, along with the branch route from Khartoum, Sudan, to Lagos, Nigeria. In 1936, Imperial Airways provided twice-weekly flights to South Africa and weekly flights from Khartoum to Nigeria.

During World War II, new airports were built in sub-Saharan Africa to supply the armies fighting in North Africa. Entebbe Airport in Uganda became a key hub because it was at the intersection of the north–south air routes between Cairo and Cape Town and the east–west routes between British colonies in East Africa and West Africa. After the war, Pan American World Airways established regular service from New York to West Africa and South Africa, and in 1952, the British Overseas Airways Corporation established the first jet service from London to Johannesburg, South Africa. Airports continued to be improved all over Africa: the airport at Dar es Salaam, Tanzania, was renovated in 1954 to meet international standards; a new airport capable of accommodating the largest airplanes was built at Nairobi, Kenya; and the airport at Brazzaville, French Congo, was also upgraded to international standards, bringing Brazzaville within 22 hours of Paris. The list goes on and on.

Education

The expanded economic activity that the colonial rulers envisioned in their postwar development plans required more workers who could read and write in African or European languages, could do basic arithmetic, and were familiar with certain Western scientific notions such as germ theory. They also wanted employees who were dependable, punctual, and accustomed to following instructions. All of those skills and behaviors were being taught in colonial schools. The British, French, and Belgian colonial regimes accordingly expanded their education systems following World War II, while Portugal languished behind.

Education in British Colonies

There were three types of schools in the British colonies. Mission schools were the core of the education system, and the colonial governments facilitated their efforts by giving them subsidies and including generous amounts of religious education in the official curriculum that all schools had to follow. Government-run schools paid their teachers salaries that were comparable to equivalent grades in the civil service. **Native Authority schools**, run by local chiefs and councils, were popular in areas with large Muslim populations, where Christian mission schools were not welcome. In all three types of schools, classes were conducted in the local language during the 4 years of primary school, but for those students who had the opportunity to attend middle school, English was gradually introduced into the curriculum. By the fourth and final year of middle school, all instruction was in English. The British spent nearly £9 million from the CDW Fund on education between 1946 and 1954, but given the budgetary limits, they believed that the best hope for future expansion of education was through Native Authority schools financed by the host communities themselves.

Opportunities for post-primary education in British colonies were still scarce. Only 10 percent of the children who completed 4 years of primary school had an opportunity to go on to middle school, and even fewer went to secondary school. Nigeria, for example, had over a million students in primary schools in 1953, but only 2 percent of that number were in secondary school. Six university-level institutions were operating in the British colonies by the mid-1950s, but the number of students was small: University College at Ibadan, Nigeria, had 527 students, University College of Gold Coast had 349, and Makerere College in Uganda had 448.

Despite the limited access to post-primary education, English literacy spread in the postwar era. One example comes from southern Nigeria, where a growing number of taxi drivers, mechanics, clerks, teachers, small businessmen, market women, and traders could read and write English. In response to the demand for reading material, African printing shops produced inexpensive booklets containing stories, plays, and advice on a variety of subjects. Sample titles included *Life Turns Man Up and Down, The Quack Doctor, The Disappointed Lover, How to Avoid Mistakes and Live the Good Life*, and *The Way to Make Friends with Girls*. The writing style, laced with riddles and jokes, showed the influence of oral traditions, thus connecting the new medium of writing to traditional forms of oral expression. The center for these publications was the southern Nigerian city of Onitsha, where the Tabansi Bookshop began publishing booklets by local authors in 1947. Soon other printing shops were producing booklets and selling them in the Onitsha main market, where as many as 200 titles were available on any given day. Because the booklets were sold primarily in the Onitsha market, they became generically known as **Onitsha market literature**. The Nigerian

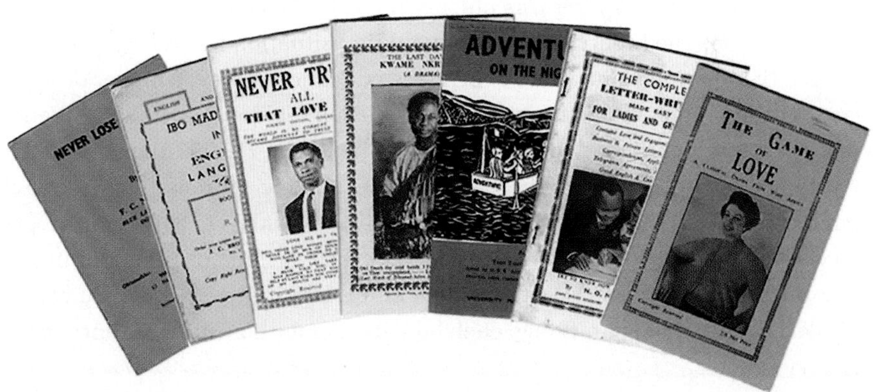

ONITSHA MARKET LITERATURE The term refers to the popular booklets that were sold at the large market in Onitsha, Nigeria, in the middle decades of the twentieth century. Written by and intended for "common" people, this literature covered a range of genres, including fiction, current events, plays, social advice, and language study. Over 200 English-language titles by local authors were on sale at the market in the postwar years.

novelist Chinua Achebe later urged that Onitsha market literature be taken seriously by scholars because it describes "the social problems of a somewhat mixed-up but dynamic, even brash, modernizing community."

Education in French Colonies

The education system in the French colonies relied heavily on the colonial state rather than on the missions. In 1953, 75 percent of the students in French West Africa (which had a large Muslim population) were in government schools and 25 percent were in mission schools. In French Equatorial Africa, which had a predominantly non-Muslim population, more than half of the students were in government schools and the rest were in mission schools. In order to be certified, mission schools had to follow the government curriculum and employ teachers whose training was on par with that of government-school teachers. All instruction was given in French, and the curriculum and examination standards sought to mimic those of metropolitan France. By the 1950s, French West Africa had 33 secondary schools. To provide higher education, the French established the University of Dakar in Senegal in 1953, and they provided some scholarships for African students to study in French universities.

Although the French system provided a good education for those who made it through primary and secondary school, it was less useful for the vast majority of students, who received only 2 years of primary education. Because all classes were conducted in French, many pupils gained only a superficial knowledge of French, which was quickly forgotten once they returned to normal village life. The French tried to remedy that situation by adding "complete schools" that offered 4 or 6 years of primary education. An even bigger problem was that the French education system reached so few people. In 1953, French West Africa (which included eight colonies) had only 217,000 pupils enrolled in primary schools and another 9,000 in secondary schools, while French Equatorial Africa (which included five colonies) had only 127,500 pupils in primary schools and 2,500 in secondary schools. The vast majority of children in the French colonies never went to school at all! In contrast, the British colony of Nigeria and the Belgian Congo each had about a million students enrolled in primary schools.

Education in the Belgian Congo

The colonial education system in the Belgian Congo relied almost entirely on mission schools, which could receive government subsidies if they met certification requirements. Prior to World War II, only mission societies with headquarters in Belgium could receive subsidies for their schools (a rule that effectively excluded

Protestants), but after the war, the colonial authorities expanded the subsidies to all mission societies regardless of nationality. In 1949, some 415,000 children studied in certified schools, whereas 515,000 pupils still studied in non-certified schools that were not up to the standards. Overall, about 50 percent of all school-aged children in the Belgian Congo attended a 2-year primary school that taught classes in African languages.

By 1950, about 4,000 students were enrolled in secondary schools, but many of them were offered only a year or two of vocational training suitable for clerks and teachers, instead of a full 4-year academic curriculum. Only one-tenth of 1 percent of the students who entered primary school in 1950 would have an opportunity to graduate from high school. Provisions for university education advanced even more slowly. Lovanium University opened in Kinshasa in 1954 with subsidies from the Belgian government as a project of the Catholic Church. By 1957, it had 86 Congolese enrolled in regular university courses and another 74 in remedial pre-university courses. Opportunities for studying in Belgian universities were even more limited. By 1957, there were only 12 Congolese studying at Belgian universities. By the time the Congo gained independence in 1960, only about 30 Congolese held university degrees.

Education Results Compared

The varying results of the French, British, and Belgian approaches to education in Africa can be partially explained by their policies toward Christian missions. In French West Africa, where missionaries were kept out of large territories to avoid offending the Muslim population, only 1 percent of the total population was enrolled in school in 1953, whereas 2 percent was enrolled in French Equatorial Africa, which had very few Muslims and was more welcoming to missionaries. In contrast, 3 percent of the population of British Nigeria was enrolled in a combination of mission schools, government schools, and Native Authority schools. The Belgian Congo, which relied almost exclusively on mission schools, enrolled an astonishing 8 percent of the total population, even though most primary schools offered only 2 years of education.

One of the major differences between the British, French, and Belgian colonial education systems was in their approach to the use of African languages. Because the French conducted all classes in the French language, the reach of the primary school system was limited by the number of African teachers with a sufficient knowledge of French. The British and Belgian education systems, in contrast, could reach many more people because the primary schools used local or regional African languages, making it easier to find teachers. Students in African-language primary schools learned to read the Bible or the Catholic catechism in their own language. They could write notes and letters to family and friends, and they could read local signs and notices, but they could not access the wider world of books, newspapers, and magazines written in English or French.

Health Care

Two developments that came out of World War II had the potential to revolutionize health care in Africa. One was penicillin, one of the first antibiotics used to treat a spectrum of bacterial infections. Penicillin was discovered in London in 1928, but it was not until 1943 that pharmaceutical companies were able to produce it in sufficient quantities to supply the Allied troops. By sharply reducing deaths from infected wounds, penicillin became the wonder drug of World War II. It was first made available to the American public in 1945. The major uses of penicillin in Africa were in treating venereal diseases, yaws, and tropical ulcers. In using penicillin to treat venereal diseases, colonial officials were treating a problem that was largely of their own making. The migratory labor system had created ideal conditions for men to contract venereal diseases during their sojourns in the cities, mining towns, and plantation centers and to carry the diseases back to their home villages.

The other development was the discovery of DDT, a powerful insecticide that could be used to kill the mosquitoes that carried malaria, typhus, and dengue fever. It was used to protect the troops in the later stages of World War II, especially during the fighting in southern Europe and the South Pacific. In 1955, the World Health Organization began its Global Malaria Eradication Program by spraying DDT on the walls of houses to kill mosquitoes before they could carry the malaria parasite from one person to another. The program largely eliminated malaria in the Caribbean, the Balkans, India, large swaths of the South Pacific, and parts of North Africa.

Tropical Africa, the most malaria-infected area on earth, presented the program with special logistical problems. The distances were vast, the roads were few, tropical African mosquitoes were active year round, and the mud walls of rural houses absorbed the DDT and thus diluted its strength. There never was a massive malaria eradication campaign in Africa similar to the one in India, where 150,000 people were hired to spray DDT on interior walls. Instead, the efforts focused on towns, and on rural regions where mosquito activity was seasonal. The city of Sokoto in Northern Nigeria made an ideal test site. There, 80,000 homes were sprayed in 1954, causing a marked reduction in the mosquito population. The government of Zimbabwe, a colony dominated by white settlers, also undertook a massive spraying campaign in 1955 to create a malaria-free belt around two-thirds of the colony. The campaign effectively eradicated malaria in the Copperbelt region of Zambia, an outcome described as one of the outstanding achievements of modern medicine. Despite such efforts, malaria continued to be a major cause of illness and death in tropical Africa.

The British, French, and Belgians had different approaches to the distribution of health care in their colonies. The British invested in hospitals that maintained high standards, whereas the French had fewer and smaller hospitals, relying instead on inexpensive medical centers with affiliated dispensaries. Patients at the medical centers depended on their families and friends to bring them food and keep them company, whereas many of the British hospitals kept their patients in near isolation. Both the French and the Belgians made extensive use of mobile teams to fight epidemics.

Improvements in public health and health care may help to explain Africa's rapid population growth after World War II. According to United Nations statistics, the African population increased from 136 million in 1920, to 175 million by 1940, to 200 million by 1950, and to 250 million by 1960. During the 1920s, 1930s, and 1940s, the growth rate remained steady at about 1.2 percent per year, but during the 1950s, the growth rate nearly doubled to 2.1 percent per year. At that pace, the population of Africa would double every 32 years.

AGRICULTURE AND THE SECOND COLONIAL OCCUPATION

The influx of colonial agricultural agents who arrived in Africa after World War II to try to remake African farming practices is referred to as the **second colonial occupation**. In contrast to popular innovations such as trains, schooling, and modern biomedicine, which people could take or leave, change in farming practices involved fundamental issues of livelihood and survival. Because planting and harvesting took place only once a year, the consequences of using new techniques that did not work could be catastrophic. That is why farmers were reluctant to adopt new farming methods proposed by outsiders, especially ones with little or no knowledge of local conditions. Even when the new agricultural techniques were useful and appropriate, they were often taught to the wrong people. As a French colonial official wrote, "Although women play such an important role in agricultural production, the extension services never approach her, but always her husband or brother." Despite the predominant role of women in African agriculture, the colonial agricultural services neglected women and promoted male farming.

British planners were attracted to large, dramatic projects. Perhaps the most famous was the million-acre Groundnut Scheme in Tanzania, where the British planned to produce peanuts using mechanized agriculture. They hoped to produce 600,000 tons of peanuts per year on fields that covered an area the size of Connecticut. The British claimed that the Groundnut Scheme would give the African people "an ocular demonstration" of the superiority of Western methods and technology. They found available land in a part of Tanzania that was sparsely populated, but they never asked why African farmers had never settled there. Once the clay-like soil had been opened up by large plows, torrential rains beat it down, and the hot tropical sun baked it into a ceramic-like crust. Not easily discouraged, the British brought in army tanks left over from the war to pull armor-plated plows that could break through the crust. When the British finally abandoned the project in 1951, they had not produced enough peanuts to replace the original seed.

BUSH BLASTING More than 100,000 acres of African bushland were strip-cleared, using chains dragged between bulldozers, to make way for the 170-mile-long lake that would form behind the Kariba Dam. The local farmers were expelled from the fertile Zambezi valley and resettled on marginal lands, which later came to resemble the edge of the Sahara Desert.

A second large-scale British development project was the **Kariba Dam** on the Zambezi River, which forms the border between Zambia and Zimbabwe. The inspiration for the project came from the Hoover Dam in the United States, and the financing came in the form of a loan from the newly created World Bank—the largest loan given out by the bank in its first decade of existence. The purpose of the dam was to supply electric power to the Zambian copper mines and to the growing industrial belt around the white settler city of Harare, Zimbabwe. When the dam was finished in 1959, the bottled-up waters flooded the Zambezi valley and formed Lake Kariba, which stretched upstream for 175 miles and

KARIBA DAM WORKERS ON STRIKE The British recruited thousands of workers from all over British Central Africa to build the Kariba Dam on the Zambezi River in the 1950s. More than a million cubic yards of concrete went into the dam, which rose 420 feet above the valley floor, making the work extremely dangerous. These armed workers are on strike for better wages and working conditions.

spilled over the banks for 10 miles on each side of the river. In terms of volume, it was (and still is) the largest artificial lake in the world.

The lake created a major problem for the 50,000 Africans who had farmed the Zambezi valley's rich alluvial soils before being forcibly moved out and resettled by the colonial authorities. The worst resettlement area was Lusitu, where 6,000 people were settled on a tract of land that could not support more than 2,000. Soil erosion and a decline in fertility quickly followed. An American anthropologist who spent considerable time in the area wrote that the "wind-swept barren land expanded as the years went by" so that "Lusitu resembled areas in the West African Sahel." Although the displaced people were largely forgotten, a great deal of international attention was focused on the plight of wild animals trapped on islands by the rising waters. Over a 4-year period, some 6,000 animals were rescued through an international project known as Operation Noah.

The Terracing Campaigns

Another major front in Britain's second colonial occupation was in the mountains of East Africa. The problem, as the British saw it, was rapid population growth during the interwar period. Prior to World War I, the populations of East Africa had suffered an ecological and demographic collapse resulting from famines, epidemics, colonial conquest, and anti-colonial rebellions. It was during that period of declining African population that white settlers had grabbed so much land in the Kenyan highlands that the region became known as the White Highlands. After 1920, however, the East African population began to grow rapidly, leading to land scarcity on the fertile mountain slopes, which became acute after World War II. Among the Kikuyu people of central Kenya, for example, the cost of an acre of land rose from 100 goats in 1939 to over a thousand in 1952.

When land became scarce, fields were kept in continuous cultivation instead of being left fallow to allow soil nutrients to regenerate, which led to declines in fertility and increased erosion. The Africans wanted the British to make more land available to them or to allow them to produce high-value cash crops such as coffee, but the British agricultural officers insisted that the solution lay in culling livestock, removing steep slopes from cultivation, and building terraces to block the downhill flow of rainwater. The arduous task of building and maintaining the terraces fell mostly to women, in part because of the new colonial gender division of labor, which funneled men into migratory labor and left women with most of the farm work. Although fields had traditionally been worked by individual households, the British terracing schemes often required communal labor because a single terrace would cross the fields of several households. The communal terracing campaigns marked a new level of colonial intrusion into farmers' lives and aroused widespread opposition, spearheaded by women. Three examples will show how these schemes worked in practice.

In the Muranga district in central Kenya, British agricultural engineers decided that terraces should be built running parallel to the ridges, and the chiefs were ordered to mobilize the people into labor gangs. Because so many men were absent doing migratory labor, the vast majority of the work was done by women. The largely female labor gangs constructed over 10,000 miles of terraces in 1945 and 1946, which was not only exhausting work, but also reduced the available cropland: 4–6 feet were lost to terraces for every 3-foot drop in the slope. In July 1947, 10,000 people gathered for a political meeting and passed a resolution that women should not be forced to join the terrace construction gangs. After that meeting, the project was temporarily suspended. When one chief attempted to restart forced terracing in 1948, more than 2,000 women demonstrated outside the district commissioner's office. In the following month, the women refused to participate in a communal grass-planting campaign, and the chief ordered them arrested, causing large crowds of women to protest the arrests. By the end of 1948, the protests had subsided and terracing resumed, but discontent continued to simmer just below the surface.

The second example comes from the Morogoro district in Tanzania, where the British agricultural officers decided that the slopes of the Uluguru Mountains needed to be covered with bench terraces—wide terraces built in a step fashion. The problem was that the topsoil layer was very thin, so that making bench terraces often displaced the topsoil and left the land sterile. When the terracing project was first announced in 1949, the local farmers ignored it, rightly believing that it was best to disturb the topsoil as little as possible. In 1954, however, the colonial agricultural officers ordered all taxpayers to work 3 days a week constructing terraces. That time was later remembered by the local farmers as a period of hunger.

When protests broke out the following year, the colonial government decided to hold public meetings to try to convince people of the value of terraces. Aware of the possibility of violence, the British brought extra police along with them. At one of the meetings, the crowd of some 4,000 people shouted, "We don't want terraces; give us back our old ways." The local chief began to scold the people, saying, "Even if you object, you will still be digging terraces until the time of your grandchildren." The meeting soon turned into a full-scale riot, in which the people threw stones at the British and the police retaliated by throwing smoke bombs and firing into the crowd, killing one protester. Soon after that, the terracing scheme was abandoned.

A third example comes from the Usambara Mountains in Tanzania. The population of the region had expanded from 80,000 in 1920 to over 200,000 in 1946, and land shortages were becoming a problem, especially after the colonial government created a forest reserve where cultivation was forbidden and allocated the best land on the plains to European sisal plantations. The British colonial government's solution to land shortages was a communal terracing scheme that used ridges to turn the mountainsides into grids of raised squares. As was often the case, the job fell heavily on the women because many of the men were away working on sisal plantations. The scheme generated opposition because it undermined the social principle that every member of the community had a right to enough land for subsistence. In keeping with that principle, marginal lands had traditionally been left fallow for the poor to use, but now that the fields were being terraced, the owners were reluctant to lend them to poor people.

Resistance to terracing was led by the women, who showed up for gang labor carrying tiny weeding hoes that were useless for building terraces and invaded the meetings held by sub-chiefs. The British described them as "well-rehearsed female storm troopers, who chanted in unison their dislike of ridge cultivation." In the end, continued opposition forced the British to abandon the scheme. The entire staff of British agricultural officers left the region in 1958, and the 57 policemen who had worked as enforcers of the scheme were fired.

Collective Farming in the Belgian Congo

In the Belgian Congo, increased production of cash crops was the only viable alternative to the skimming economy, so agriculture was a major component of the Congo's economic development. In devising their 10-year plan, which was implemented in 1950, the planners acknowledged that the previous colonial policy of forcibly relocating populations closer to roads for administrative convenience had hurt agricultural production, as it had caused some of the most fertile areas to be abandoned. They admitted, too, that their attempts to introduce European-style plowing had often brought about a decrease in the fertility of the soils. Nevertheless, they hoped that future agricultural research would bring better results.

The colonial government's main program for agricultural improvement called for the creation of collective agricultural villages, known in French as *paysannats* (peasantries). Instead of each farmer selecting individual field sites in the surrounding forest and bush, as was the traditional practice, the colonial authorities that established the peasantries created one enormous collective field for the whole village. The field was divided into strips, one for each family. Family members would start by cultivating a patch at one end of their strip. Over a period of 20 years, they would work their way toward the far end, abandoning each patch as the soil became exhausted. After 20 years, they would start again at the beginning, where the soil's nutrients would have naturally regenerated after so many years of lying fallow. The advantage of the system was that it created very large collective fields that could be worked with tractors and other farm implements. The major disadvantage was that soil quality often varied randomly across the large collective field, depending on what vegetation had previously covered it. As a result, some families got strips that were fertile, while others got less fertile ground. The system also ran afoul of local customs and laws regarding land rights.

The 10-year plan called for settling half a million rural families in peasantries, which would have represented a quarter of the Belgian Congo's entire population. Such a massive reordering of the countryside was reminiscent of the rural collectivization campaigns in the Soviet Union. In implementing the scheme—often against local resistance—the colonial government bypassed the African chiefs in favor of direct intervention by colonial officials. The Congo's governor-general explained the approach as follows: "From a praiseworthy concern to do things quicker and better, we wanted to take everything in hand and direct the Congolese masses, willy-nilly, to a happiness that conforms to our ideas." A Soviet central planner could not have expressed it better.

Consequences of Rural Development

Rural development projects—however well intentioned—signaled an unprecedented intrusion by colonial officials into the lives of ordinary Africans. One consequence of the second colonial occupation was to undermine the system of indirect rule through local chiefs. In contrast to the relatively passive role that colonial authorities played before the war, when they were content to let the chiefs collect taxes and recruit labor, they now expected the chiefs to act as their partners, assisting the colonial authorities in their effort to impose revolutionary changes in the work rhythms of ordinary people. In central Kenya, chiefs who failed to construct enough terraces were quickly replaced, which led to a rapid turnover of local leadership. The authority of chiefs was also weakened in the Belgian Congo, where the governor-general noted that "our old conception of indirect rule—timid and attenuated as it has been from the beginning—has not ceased to grow weaker." Chiefs were put in an impossible position: those who did not implement colonial projects aggressively enough were replaced or bypassed, but those who did so became unpopular among their communities and sometimes faced protests or outright rebellion.

A second consequence of the second colonial occupation was that women began mobilizing for political action. African women had always played a major role in agriculture, but their responsibilities intensified during the colonial period. As men left their villages for months or years at a time for migratory labor, the burden of farming was left more and more to the women to handle on their own. When the colonial governments began to intervene directly in African farming techniques, as in the terracing campaigns, the bulk of the extra labor fell to the women. When the government introduced improved seeds or techniques, the labor-saving innovations were typically reserved for male farmers, while the women reaped little benefit. It is not surprising that women were often at the forefront of protests.

CITIES AND URBAN LIFE

Africa has always had cities. In ancient times, North African cities such as Memphis, Alexandria, and Carthage were among the largest and most important cities in the world. In West Africa, trading cities such as Timbuktu and Jenne grew large and prosperous, as did East African port cities such as Mombasa, Kilwa, and Mogadishu. Precolonial kingdoms had capital cities, such as Timbo in Fuuta Jaloo, Kano in the Sokoto caliphate, Kumasi in the Asante Empire, and São Salvador in the Kongo Kingdom. Some precolonial city-states, such as Accra, Ghana, grew into colonial capital cities.

The Growth of Colonial Cities

In twentieth-century tropical Africa, the great majority of the larger cities were what one geographer has termed **colonial cities** because they developed during the colonial period as seaports, commercial centers, or colonial administrative capitals. The colonial cities were inhabited mostly by Africans who came from the rural regions. In southern Africa, where white settlers were numerous, there were cities that a geographer has called "European cities" because they were built to attract white settlers. Some of them were even designed to replicate cities in Europe. Africans eventually outnumbered the white settlers in these European cities, but they were restricted to living in suburban "locations" or in crowded neighborhoods far away from the city center.

Migrants to the colonial cities initially came to work for colonial administrations and European enterprises. As the African neighborhoods grew, other Africans arrived to open shops and provide essential urban services, such as supplying firewood or charcoal for cooking. Although colonial officials sometimes worried that Africans would lose their African culture in the cities, the reality was that migrants usually moved into ethnic neighborhoods where most people spoke their language and followed familiar customs. During this period, most of the larger African cities attracted the bulk of their immigrants from the nearby hinterlands. Thus Lagos, Nigeria, was a predominantly Yoruba city; Nairobi, Kenya, was a predominantly Kikuyu city; Kinshasa, Belgian Congo, was a predominantly Kongolese city; and so on.

On the eve of World War II, most colonial cities in the tropical regions of Africa were still relatively small, with populations ranging from 10,000 for Libreville, Gabon, to 65,000 for Accra, Ghana. During and after the war, the cities grew rapidly as rural people flocked to the urban areas for better jobs, educational opportunities, and biomedical health care. Some migrants came because of jobs in domestic industries, such as food processing and beer brewing, in the new industrial districts; other migrants created their own urban economy by providing goods and services to one another. By 1960, several cities in tropical Africa had populations of 400,000 or more. The rapid growth created an urgent need for upgrading the basic urban infrastructure by adding new streets, water pipes, drainage ditches, and refuse removal systems. That is why all the postwar development plans allocated money to urban planning. The graph on the next page shows the growth of selected cities.

Colonial cities generally had areas dominated by a permanent urban population of Africans with relatively good jobs as clerks, teachers, taxi drivers, or mechanics, while other areas of the city were home to newcomers who hoped

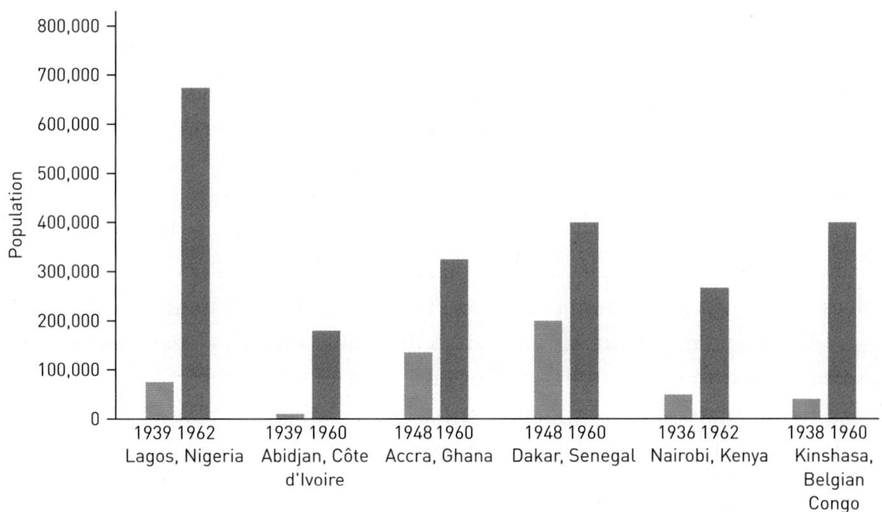

THE EXPLOSIVE GROWTH OF CITIES This bar graph shows the growth of Lagos (Nigeria), Abidjan (Côte d'Ivoire), Nairobi (Kenya), and Kinshasa (Belgian Congo) between the 1930s and 1960s. The bars for Accra (Ghana) and Dakar (Senegal) show less spectacular growth because they cover a shorter time period—from 1948 to 1960.

to become permanent residents, or to floating populations of young people who planned to earn money for a few years and then return to their rural villages. Some people moved back and forth between city and countryside in a process known as straddling. While recent migrants continued to embrace the ethnicity of their rural region, families who had lived in a city for several generations sometimes developed special urban ethnic identities, such as "Lari" in Brazzaville or "Kinois" in Kinshasa, that had no counterparts in the countryside.

Cities and Work

The cities and larger towns were magnets for African men seeking work as salaried employees such as civil servants, teachers, and clerks; as skilled laborers such as railroad and steamboat mechanics, carpenters, and bricklayers; as domestic servants; and as casual laborers who worked for daily wages at a variety of manual jobs. Dockworkers and railway workers were prime prospects for a casual labor system because ships arrived irregularly at the ports and freight trains arrived only every few days. But dockworkers and railway workers also had a certain amount of leverage with their employers and the colonial governments because the ports and railroad terminals were the key bottlenecks in the export-based economy. Without their labor, the economy would have ground to a halt.

It was this leverage that gave many urban workers the confidence to fight for better wages and working conditions. Whereas migratory and forced laborers who fulfilled short-term contracts in mines and plantations were often willing to put up with low pay, poor lodging, bad food, and onerous working conditions because they knew that they would soon be going home, workers who saw themselves as part of a permanent urban working class were often more assertive.

African women were also drawn to the cities, not only to earn money, but also to escape the patriarchal authoritarianism of the rural villages. Women found it difficult to find wage labor in urban areas, especially since the European residents usually hired men as their domestic servants (whom they referred to as "houseboys" or simply "boys"). As a result, large numbers of young and unattached women made their living in the urban areas as self-employed entrepreneurs. In Accra, Ghana, for example, 75 percent of the women worked as traders, selling fish, meats, fruits, vegetables, beads, pottery, copper basins, and cloth. Although some Accra women became wholesale merchants who had credit with overseas firms, the great majority were petty traders who eked out a modest living. Women dominated the local markets all over West Africa, as well as in the Belgian Congo, Zimbabwe, Zambia, and Malawi.

In Nairobi, Kenya, where a large proportion of the shopkeepers were Indian men, a substantial number of unattached women worked in the sex and hospitality trades. There were many unmarried men in Nairobi, as well as married men who had left their families behind in the rural regions. They often lived in small rented rooms that they shared with two or three other men. Given those circumstances, many women found that they could make a living by providing men with the comforts of home. Although some women walked the streets in search of clients, others lived in clean, well-furnished rooms, where they would offer tea, conversation, sex, and perhaps a meal to the men who knocked on their doors. By this means, some women earned enough money to build houses of their own or send money back to their families in the countryside.

Urban Labor Strife before World War II

Men who worked as wage laborers lived under a constant fear that their wages would not keep up with the cost of urban living. In contrast to rural villages, where people could meet their subsistence needs through a combination of farming, hunting, fishing, gathering, and gardening, city folk depended on their wages to cover all their needs. As prices rose, wages often remained stagnant. Labor unrest first surfaced in the mid-1930s during the worldwide Great Depression, when there was an outbreak of strikes in a variety of places, including the port and railhead cities of Dakar, Senegal, and Mombasa, Kenya. Dockworkers in Dakar, who were concerned that their wages were falling behind the rising cost of living, staged a general strike in 1936, at the beginning of peanut export season. After a 1-day strike, they received raises of between 34 percent and 50 percent. Their success inspired a wave of strikes by commercial workers, seamen, tugboat crews, gardeners, domestic servants, and others. The strikes soon spread to other port cities in Senegal, such as Rufisque and St. Louis.

In 1939, a similar series of strikes broke out in Mombasa, Kenya, where Public Works Department employees held a strike for increased housing allowances. The strike spread to other groups of workers, including the casual dockworkers, who staged a 3-day strike to win a 1-hour reduction in the standard workday, which ensured that more casual laborers would be hired. In 1942, as wartime inflation continued to erode the value of wages, another series of strikes rolled through Mombasa, beginning with 2,000 railway workers and extending to most of the government departments and other large employers. The strikes won additional cost-of-living adjustments for many of the workers.

Urban Labor Strife after World War II

After the war, the nature of labor protests changed in two ways. First, the issues were no longer solely wages and work hours. Now, they also addressed the structure of the labor force and the overall allocation of wages and salaries among different categories of workers. Second, the strikes were increasingly organized by labor unions. In the French colonies, unions had been outlawed during the war, but they were permitted to form again after the war was over. In the British colonies, a few unions for African workers had been formed in the 1930s, but the formation of trade unions accelerated in the 1940s after the British Colonial Office promulgated the Trade Unions Ordinance, which provided for the legal registration of trade unions and set ground rules for the resolution of labor disputes. A look at strikes in 1947 in Ghana, French West Africa, and Tanzania illustrates these developments.

Ghana had known trade unions such as the Gold Coast Railway African Workers Union since the 1930s, but unions became much more active in the postwar era. The Gold Coast Mine Employees Union was formed in 1944, and in the following year, the Gold Coast Trades Union Congress was founded to bring together all the separate unions into a single organization. In 1947, Ghana experienced a series of strikes involving a variety of industries and over 46,000 workers. It began with the railway workers, who staged a 15-day strike just as the cocoa harvest needed to be transported to the coast. Because world cocoa prices were high, the workers felt that there was money available to raise their wages. As the strike spread to other industries, over 30,000 gold miners went on strike for over a month. In the end, the gold miners received not only a wage hike, but also added indemnities such as paid annual leave, sick leave, and overtime pay. As for the railway workers, their strike ended in a compromise.

The railway workers' unions in French West Africa, led by the Federation of Native Railroad Workers, went on strike in 1947–1948. This strike was exceptional for two reasons. The first was the geographical scale of the labor dispute, which spread throughout French West Africa along the different rail lines—the longest being the Dakar-Bamako line, which was over 800 miles long. Second, the strike was less about specific salary hikes than it was a demand for a single pay scale, based solely on merit, that would apply to black and white workers equally, with no regard to race or nationality. A similar issue of concern was the structure of the African workforce itself. The railway company employed over 15,000 "auxiliaries" who were classified as "temporary workers," despite the fact that many of them worked full-time and had years of experience. The unions wanted them to be reclassified as full-time workers and paid according to the single pay scale.

In the ensuing negotiations, the railway company and the workers agreed to a single pay scale in return for a reduction in the total workforce. But the workers and the unions disagreed with the company on the details of the arrangement, and when the French labor commission's report was accepted by the unions but rejected by the company, the workers went on strike. The strike, which lasted 5 months, took a toll on the railway workers and their families, who struggled to survive with no income. It finally ended in 1948, when a new governor-general arrived with a new set of proposals. According to the final agreement, over 30 percent of the railway workers were to be considered full-time, as opposed to 12 percent before the strike. Most important, a single pay scale for wages and salaries was implemented, and all workers received a 20 percent increase. After a long struggle, the principle of equal pay for equal work, regardless of race, had been established.

The 1947 strike in Dar es Salaam, Tanzania, showed certain similarities to the strikes in Ghana and French West Africa. Dar es Salaam was a port city and a railhead on the Indian Ocean coast. The strike originated with casual dock-workers, who were seeking higher wages to keep up with inflation, but a week later it spread to railway workers, and from there it spread along the rail line to towns in the country's interior, then to the sisal plantations in the southern highlands, and even to the Groundnut Scheme, where the field workers struck for 13 days. A month after it began, it reached the Uruwira lead mines near Lake Tanganyika.

As the strike spread, the workers' demands shifted from specific salary levels to the general principle of equal pay for equal work. The Tanzanian workforce had a complex racial hierarchy, which included whites, Indians, Arabs, and Africans, and equally complex pay scales. "We are now tired of these zigzag regulations," stated a manifesto written by African workers. "Equal pay for equal work is not recognized, and this can easily be seen from our present salaries, which have entirely been based on racial prejudice." Another manifesto proclaimed, "The time has now come when equal pay for equal work is claimed." Although African workers failed to achieve equal pay scales, they gained wage increases of 40–50 percent. The 1947 strike had been organized by the workers without the aid of trade unions, but in its aftermath, the dockworkers founded the Dar es Salaam Dock Workers and Stevedores Union and began to build a two-story union clubhouse. However, the union was banned in 1950 after a failed dock strike led to a riot, and the clubhouse was never finished.

The strikes in Ghana, French West Africa, and Tanzania show how labor protests expanded and changed during the course of a strike. A strike that began in a specific industry could easily incite strikes in other sectors of the economy, as when the strike by Tanzanian dockworkers spread to railway workers, then to sisal plantations, and even to the Groundnut Scheme. The goals of the strikes were also subject to change, as when specific grievances about pay that did not keep up with inflation were generalized to include the structure of the urban labor force and the principle of equal pay for equal work. The strikes' wide applicability and adaptability was a result of having a common enemy: they gave voice to a shared repertory of postwar grievances that did not so much target a particular company or government agency as the colonial government itself.

Cities and Leisure

People came to the cities to work, but they also enjoyed leisure. The rhythms of the urban workweek left a certain amount of downtime that needed to be filled with activities such as organized sports, music and dancing in bars, and movies. After the war, sports stadiums, bars, and movie theaters were opening all over Africa. By 1956, for example, there were 40 movie theaters in Nigeria, 26 in Ghana, and 90 in French West Africa. A brief look at three colonial cities in tropical Africa—the Belgian colonial city of Kinshasa, the French colonial city of Brazzaville, and the British colonial city of Dar es Salaam—will illustrate the growth and development of modern leisure activities.

Kinshasa

Kinshasa is located on the Congo River, just upstream from the impassable rapids. It was in Kinshasa that the rail system leading to the coast converged with the riverboat system leading to the interior of the country, so the city was the key transportation hub of the Belgian Congo. A major activity for young and old alike in the postwar era was playing or watching soccer. Belgian Catholic missionaries had taught the game to schoolchildren in the 1920s (see chapter 12), and by the beginning of World War II, Kinshasa had 53 teams playing in six divisions. The wealthier teams wore soccer cleats, while the poorer ones played barefooted. A Belgian missionary known as Father Raphael was the driving force behind the expansion of sports facilities in postwar Kinshasa. He helped to develop three soccer stadiums, the largest of which was the King Baudouin Stadium (named after the reigning Belgian king), which opened in 1952 and could hold 30,000 spectators.

For adult evening activities, there were a variety of open-air beer gardens with names such as Congo Bar, Oscar Kashama Bar, and Congo Fifi. A typical bar consisted of a walled-in space with a slightly raised dance floor in the middle. Chairs and tables were set up around the dance floor, and the beer was sold under a canopy at one end. A typical musical group consisted of a singer accompanying himself on a guitar, mandolin, or accordion, backed up by a rhythm section of one or two musicians playing on drums or empty beer bottles. The music that emerged after the war—known as *maringa* music—had roots in the Congo, West Africa, and Latin America. The West African component came from the considerable West African community living in Kinshasa, while the Latin American influence came via 78 rpm records made in Cuba. The African tunes and rhythms that had traveled across the ocean during the slave trade era were now returning home.

What made Kinshasa a magnet for musical groups was the rise of radio stations and recording studios. Radio Congolia, founded by a Belgian during World War II, broadcast for only 60–90 minutes a day, but it regularly played dance music from Kinshasa bars, usually broadcast live from the studio. After the radio station folded in 1948, it was replaced by a colonial government station that broadcast programs for Africans that included modern Congolese music. The first recording studio in Kinshasa was opened in 1948 by a Greek refugee from the war, and four others, also operated by Greeks, opened during the 1950s. These studios, which were rudimentary affairs, made tape recordings that were sent to Europe to be pressed into 78 rpm or 45 rpm records.

Musical groups would try out their songs in the bars before recording them in a professional studio, but the bulk of their profits still came from live performances.

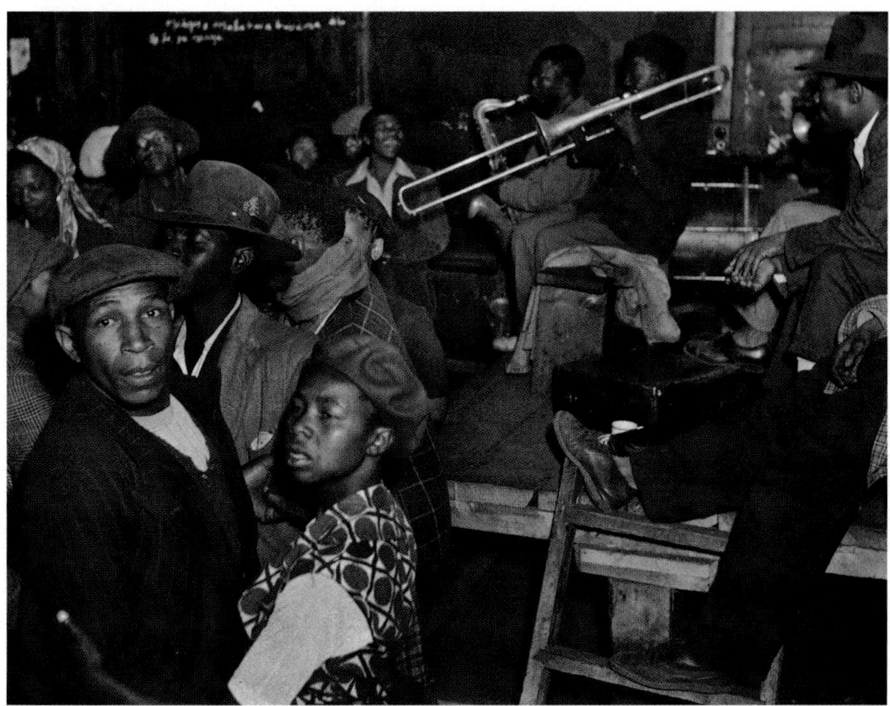

NIGHTLIFE Music and dancing at a night spot in Johannesburg, South Africa, in 1955. During the 1940s and early 1950s, the Johannesburg suburb of Sophiatown was a legendary hub of black culture known for its jazz and blues clubs. Under apartheid (see chapter 14), the black residents of Sophiatown were forcibly evicted on February 9, 1955, and the town was flattened. After that, music and dancing for black South Africans continued to thrive in the black townships located farther out from Johannesburg.

A group such as OK Jazz retained a reference to its professional roots, as the "OK" referred to the Oscar Kashama Bar, where it often played. So few people in Kinshasa had record players or electricity that the musicians didn't sell many of their records, and most people who wanted to hear recorded music would go to bars in the evenings. Under such conditions, even popular musicians found it hard to support themselves with their music. One of the legendary musicians of the 1950s, Jamais Kalonga, made his living by working for the colonial government transportation company. By making music in their spare time, Kalonga and others made Kinshasa into the recording capital of Africa. One of the studios, Ngoma, listed nearly a thousand titles in its 1955 catalog.

Brazzaville

In Brazzaville, located across the Congo River from Kinshasa, children played soccer on the streets, kicking around lemons from local trees with their bare feet. When a lemon got too squishy, they replaced it with another; it could take a whole pile of lemons to get through a game. In 1948, there were 30 top-tier soccer teams in Brazzaville with a total of 750 players, all of whom wore proper soccer cleats. These teams were sponsored by organizations such as the Catholic Church, government departments, schools, and companies. In addition, there were 26 junior teams that played barefooted because they could not afford shoes. A city league was founded in 1953 for the top-tier teams, which played their matches in Brazzaville's two large stadiums, each of which held thousands of fans. Young people learned the game by playing for primary-school teams or for neighborhood teams, which organized championships for each area of the city. All soccer games were strictly amateur, and the players received no compensation, although a few were recruited by teams in Paris and Marseilles.

Another form of leisure activity was going to the movies. After World War II, five movie theaters that screened American and French films opened in the African sections of Brazzaville. Because few in the audience understood English, and many of them had poor French as well, listening to the dialogue was not as important as watching the action. American Westerns were particularly popular because it was easy to tell the good guys from the bad guys. If a film lacked sufficient action, the crowd would jeer, demand their money back, or, occasionally, riot. The leaders of the Catholic Church worried that gangster films were contributing to juvenile delinquency and that movies showing white people engaged in fighting, immorality, and frivolity would cause Africans to lose respect for Europeans. "Isn't it better to show decent whites at work?" wondered the monseigneur. But the governor-general responded that such movies would fail to draw an audience.

Open-air bars with dance floors and live bands multiplied in the postwar era. As often happens in large metropolitan cities, different bars catered to different ethnic clienteles: Gaiété Brazza, for example, attracted mostly people from West Africa, whereas Chez Faignond was popular with Congolese as well as with Belgians who came over from Kinshasa (which still had legal segregation). Well-dressed women sporting the latest fashions, hairstyles, and headscarves came in groups and sometimes performed songs and dances. The music in the bars was similar to that in Kinshasa, and people in both Kinshasa and Brazzaville would sometimes take the ferry across the Congo River to hear a certain band on the other side.

In 1946, the French opened Radio Brazzaville, which had the most powerful transmitter in Africa and brought the music of Brazzaville and Kinshasa to an international audience with short-wave broadcasts reaching as far as the United

States. Programs on Radio Brazzaville were aimed at Europeans, but a separate channel tailored for African audiences (called Radio AEF) began broadcasting in 1950. Battery-powered radios were not yet available, but homes without electricity (which was the vast majority in Brazzaville) could pay a monthly fee to be connected to radio "distribution points" scattered throughout the city. The most popular Brazzaville musicians crossed the Congo River to record their songs in the studios of Kinshasa. Even as their audiences and popularity grew, two of the best—Paul Kamba and Bernard Massamba—never got rich from their recordings, and they continued to make a living from their day jobs as low-level civil servants.

Dar es Salaam

Like Kinshasa and Brazzaville, Dar es Salaam, Tanzania, grew from a small town into a colonial capital. Located on the Indian Ocean coast, it had substantial European, Arab, and Indian communities in addition to its African population. Its population grew rapidly during and after World War II, reaching nearly 70,000 by 1948 and 130,000 by 1957. Like other rapidly growing cities, Dar es Salaam suffered from inadequate housing and urban infrastructure, as well as from shortages of food and fuel. The cultural amenities of urban life provided a respite from the harsh material conditions and served as a basis for the organization of social life. Soccer teams and musical groups were part of larger social clubs that connected people across ethnic and class lines.

Schools and government agencies had sponsored soccer teams since the 1920s, but the 1940s saw the emergence of street teams in African neighborhoods, which developed into soccer clubs that welcomed both players and fans as members. The clubs were places where friends gathered to drink coffee (it was a predominantly Muslim city) and play table games, and where members would assist one another in finding jobs, housing, and even marriage partners. By 1955, there were 38 registered soccer clubs in Dar es Salaam, with championship matches played in the Ilala Stadium, which had been built in 1947 with government funds. Two of the soccer clubs—Yanga and Sunderland—fielded Dar es Salaam's most prominent soccer teams in the 1950s, and they developed an intense rivalry: the Yanga players, who came from the Swahili Coast, were derisively referred to as "fish mongers," while the Sunderland team, which included Arab and Indian players, was dismissed as a bunch of "foreigners."

Because of Dar es Salaam's location on the Indian Ocean, it received musical influences from both the Arab and the Western worlds. *Taarab* music was originally sung in Arabic to the accompaniment of Southwest Asian instruments at the court of the Sultan of Zanzibar, but in the 1920s, ***taarab* bands** began to perform songs in Swahili for popular audiences. Over time, the orchestras grew larger, adding

European instruments such as violins, mandolins, and double basses. *Taarab* bands in Dar es Salaam in the 1950s played mostly at weddings and other festive occasions. Because the *taarab* musicians were Muslims who did not drink alcohol, they did not perform in bars. *Dansi* bands, in contrast, performed dance music with Latin rhythms and Swahili lyrics. The names of the bands often revealed the ethnic or regional origin of the musicians, as in the Western Jazz Band (from western Tanzania) or the Nyamwezi Jazz Band (from the Nyamwezi ethnic group). Both *taarab* and *dansi* bands created social clubs that included musicians and nonmusicians as members. Any money that the band earned by playing at weddings, concerts, or bars went into a fund that could be used to buy musical instruments or help members in need.

Leisure activities were a major way in which people defined the differences between urban and rural life. We can get a glimpse of how folk in Dar es Salaam felt about their city from the words of a *dansi* song recorded in 1950, which offered advice to migrants: "When you go out to a dance, a soccer game, or the market / The women are really hot, and the bandits are really hot / All they want is one thing: that is your money / Be careful my child, there in Dar es Salaam." On the other hand, city dwellers sometimes exhibited an annoying sense of urban superiority when they returned home to their rural villages. A resident of Dar es Salaam described a typical homecoming in 1956: "What? You live in a village without electricity? No movie theatre? No dance hall? No bands? What a dump!" Despite the cultural divide between city and village, most people learned to navigate both worlds and move seamlessly between them.

CONCLUSION

World War II disrupted the equilibrium of high colonial rule in Africa. Although the fighting took place mostly in Libya, Ethiopia, and Tunisia, it also spilled over into Egypt, Somalia, Kenya, and Sudan. The British, French, and Belgian colonies in Africa became recruiting grounds for soldiers and sources of raw materials, including the uranium in the two atomic bombs that the Allies dropped on Japan to end the war. As a result, much of the harshness that had characterized early colonial rule returned as colonial governors struggled to meet their quotas for the war effort. The end of the war did not bring about the end of colonial demands, however, because Britain and France had been devastated by the war and were deeply in debt.

After the war, Britain, France, and Belgium began to realize that if their colonial rule was to be sustainable, then Africans needed a larger stake in the system. They accordingly drew up development plans to make improvements in transportation, public health, education, urban planning, and agriculture. Although the funding for those projects was hopelessly inadequate in relation to the need, and although much of it came from the Africans themselves, it was nevertheless a considerable investment for the colonial powers given that they were still rebuilding from the devastation of World War II. It was clear from the process of drafting development plans that bringing the colonial economies up to speed would be expensive and time-consuming.

While some of the development efforts, such as new schools and hospitals, were enthusiastically received by the African populations, others were resisted. Development planners did not hesitate to intrude on African life if they thought they were making changes for the better. Major illustrations of this phenomenon are the peasantries of the Belgian Congo and the forced terracing campaigns in Kenya and Tanzania. Such campaigns to transform agriculture generated resistance against the colonizers rather than support.

The postwar era saw rapid growth in the cities as rural Africans migrated there in search of jobs, education, biomedical health care, and the trappings of modernity. Strikes became frequent in the colonial cities as workers struggled to keep up with postwar inflation and fought for equal pay for equal work. The cities were not only the site of work, however, but also the site of play, as the growth of soccer matches, movie theaters, new forms of music, and new types of nightlife contributed to the diversity of African urban culture. It was in this changing environment that voices began calling for African independence.

CHAPTER REVIEW

KEY TERMS AND VOCABULARY

Haile Selassie

patriots

Free French Forces

10-year plan

Marketing Board

Albion A10 truck

Native Authority school

Onitsha market literature

second colonial occupation

Kariba Dam

colonial city

taarab band

STUDY QUESTIONS

1. Name the different ways in which Africans were involved in World War II.
2. Why did the colonial powers place a new emphasis on economic and human development after World War II?
3. Who ended up paying for the postwar development initiatives?
4. What was the second colonial occupation, and why did many Africans resist it?
5. Why were women the major instigators of rural protests?
6. Why did strikes break out in certain sectors of the economy and not in others?
7. What were the advantages and disadvantages of moving to cities during the postwar era?

AN AFRICAN SOLDIER SPEAKS

African soldiers who served in colonial armies during World War II frequently returned home with changed outlooks, tastes, and expectations. Robert Kakembo, who was born in Uganda, East Africa, joined the King's African Rifles in 1939 and fought in the campaign to drive the Italians from Ethiopia. In his memoir An African Soldier Speaks, *he wrote only briefly about the war itself and focused instead on his hopes for the future.*

The war has shown the white man that the African hungers for knowledge, for literacy, for Christian moral standards, is sincere and earnest. The African has surpassed all European expectation in his intellectual ability. "The sons of yesterday's savages," writes one European, "are demanding to become fighter-pilots. They are all yearning for progress." . . .

Now the African soldier has learned to read and write; he is used to reading newspapers, to listening to wireless broadcasts, to seeing films, to playing games, both outdoor and indoor ones. The question is, will this man, this widely traveled and educated soldier, go back and be satisfied to go back home to his village and live in the same old dull conditions that he lived in before the war? You know as well as I do that we have men demobilized from the forces who have been highly trained in all branches of warfare of a mechanized army, which is producing an outlook and an intensification of mentality that will never submit to the neglect that the uneducated masses, back home in the villages, undergo. . . .

I hear a lot of dissatisfaction with conditions back in villages and reserves from men who return from leave. They have begun to feel the dullness and backwardness of their homes, and they want a drastic change in the whole system of African life.

It regrets me to say that with the exception of a few things done or being done here and there, the general attitude of our trustees is still just to quietly amble along with no sign of hurry. Native governments where Indirect Rule is practiced have not awoken to this drastic change that is taking place in the life of their people. From West Africa, African representatives were sent to England to give their views and suggestions on post-war reconstruction—in Uganda the African has never heard of such a thing as post-war reconstruction. To them things are all right as they are, and the British Government just looks on.

The African soldier is used to wearing boots, to smoking cigarettes, meat is a daily item in his food, tea and coffee have become his essential breakfast; and he must continue to have these things and it will need money to get them. The African soldier's pay is between 28s. and 32s. a month. And that does not include his clothing and ration. The question is, will the Government raise the pay of the ordinary African laborer, which is from 6s. to 20s. a month? Will the Government provide work for everybody?

1. *Name some of the ways that Robert Kakembo was changed by his experience in World War II.*

2. *What is his opinion of the "native governments" (i.e., the chiefs)?*

Source: R. H. Kakembo, *An African Soldier Speaks* (London: Livingstone Press, 1947), pp. 22–23.

A WORKER'S LAMENT

Many African soldiers returned home from World War II to find bleak prospects for jobs and housing. In anticipation of that outcome, a soldier from Ghana on active duty wrote this psalm. Basing it on the Biblical Psalm 23, the writer reproduced the archaic language of the King James Bible. The psalm was printed in the African Morning Post, *Accra, Ghana, on September 2, 1944. His mention of the "pool" is a reference to the foreign cartels that fixed the price of cocoa.*

A PSALM 23

by an African laborer

The European Merchant is my shepherd,
And I am in want,
He maketh me to lie down in cocoa farms;
He leadeth me beside the waters of great need;
He restoreth my doubt in the pool parts.
Yea, though I walk in the valleys of starvation,
I do not fear evil:
For thou art against me.
The general managers and profiteers frighten me.

Thou preparest a reduction in my salary
In the presence of my creditors.
Thou anointest my income with taxes;
My expense runs over my income.
Surely unemployment and poverty will follow me
All the days of my poor existence,
And I will dwell in a rented house forever!

1. *Who does the soldier identify as his main enemy?*

2. *What is his outlook on his future?*

Source: *The African Morning Post*, Accra, Ghana, September 2, 1944. Reprinted in J. Ayo Langley, *Ideologies of Liberation in Black Africa, 1856–1970: Documents on Modern African Political Thought from Colonial Times to the Present* (London: Rex Collings, 1979), pp. 415–416.

A CALL TO ACTION

African wage laborers had a precarious existence that was always threatened by a rise in prices or taxes. When the British colonial government in Zambia (then called Northern Rhodesia) raised taxes in 1935, the workers at the Nkana copper mine decided to go on strike. This call to action was originally written and circulated in the Bemba language by G. Lovewey. It was translated into English by an African clerk so that it could be included in the government's report on the strike.

Listen to this, all you who live in the country. Think well how they treat us and to ask for a land. Do we live in good treatment? No! Therefore let us ask one another and remember this treatment. Because we wish on the day of 29th April, every person not to go to work. He who will go to work, and if we see him it will be a serious case. Know how they cause us to suffer: they cheat us for money; they arrest us for loafing; they persecute us and put us in jail for tax. What reason have we done?

Secondly do you not wish to hear these words? Well listen, this year of 1935. If they will not increase us more money, stop paying tax. Do you think they can kill you? No. Let us encourage; surely you will see that God will be with us. See how we suffer with the work and how we are continually reviled and beaten underground. Many brothers of us die for 22s. 6d. Is this money that we should lose our lives for? He who cannot read should tell his companion that on the 29th April not to go to work. These words do not come from here; they come from the wisers who are far away and enable to encourage us.

That all. Hear well. If it is right, let us do so.

We are all of the Nkana
Africans—Men and Women.
I am glad,
G. LOVEWEY.
Translated by N. Mafuleka, Native Clerk.
5th April, 1935.
NKANA MINE.

1. *Why was the author unhappy with the mining company?*
2. *What was his plan to remedy the situation?*

Source: Report of the Commission Appointed to Enquire into the Disturbances in the Copperbelt, Northern Rhodesia (Lusaka: Government Printer, 1935), p. 59, reprinted in Nancy J. Jacobs, *African History through Sources*, vol. 1 (Cambridge: Cambridge University Press, 2014), p. 279.

THE FOOTBALL SHOE CONTROVERSY

Following an injury to a player during a soccer (football) match in Brazzaville, French Congo, in 1936, the white president of the Native Sports Federation banned the wearing of soccer shoes, forcing the players to go barefooted. This outraged the players, who saw it as an assault on their hard-won status as educated Africans who wore shoes. Below is a petition from the captains of the four leading soccer teams in Brazzaville, followed by a statement from the white secretary of the federation expressing his reservations about the ban.

Petition from the Captains of the Four Leading Soccer Teams in Brazzaville to the Governor-General of French Equatorial Africa

For the first time, a player had the misfortune to break a leg during a match. This incident resulted in the death of our sadly missed comrade after about two months in hospital. Because of this, . . . the President has asked that all players play bare footed, and, beyond this, has excluded teams that wear shoes. Since he has not achieved the hoped-for results, the President has disqualified and excluded for life all players using shoes.

We ask ourselves, Mr. Governor-General, why Mr. Benilan has not proposed that these players show up at the office or workshops in bare feet? We do not wear shoes out of vanity or ostentation, but quite simply, as we wear trousers or shirts. So, why are these articles imported into our country? And, since whites first began to play football, has there never been a single occasion when they had an accidental injury?

The Native Sports Federation has only once spent money on football shoes. It was in 1934 when twenty-two pairs of shoes were distributed to two teams, and that is all. Yes, we do not pay our dues, but we have arranged, ourselves, to buy shoes. So what are the President and Secretary complaining about?

We love association football, Mr. Governor-General, and that has always been why we have played. Since Mr. Benilan no longer wants us in that federation which, nevertheless, belongs to us, allow us, Mr. Governor-General, to request permission to establish an autonomous native association for association football. In that way, we will be able to continue playing as we have done for a long time, and will no longer be dependent on the Sports Federation of Mr. Benilan.

Reservations about the Ban Expressed by the White Secretary of the Native Sports Federation

Many Federation players are accustomed to playing in shoes, and, in everyday life, they are being worn more and more frequently. It will be difficult to apply this decision and, without doubt, some will leave the Federation. This will compromise the results of our next tournament, which will be reduced to school teams and youth teams only.

1. *What does this incident reveal about racism in colonial sports?*
2. *Why was wearing soccer shoes so important to the African players?*

Source: Phyllis M. Martin, *Leisure and Society in Colonial Brazzaville* (Cambridge: Cambridge University Press, 1995), pp. 109–110.

FIRST PRIME MINISTER OF GHANA Kwame Nkrumah, who became the first prime minister of independent Ghana in 1957, greets a crowd as he rides through a town in an open car. A graduate of Ghana's Achimota College, he studied theology, education, and philosophy in the United States, and then studied law and philosophy in London. He founded Ghana's first mass political party, the Convention People's Party, in 1949. In his autobiography, he described himself as a "non-denominational Christian and a Marxist Socialist."

1950–1954	1952–1956	1956–1957
Apartheid laws in South Africa	Mau Mau rebellion in Kenya	Battle of Algiers

14

STRUGGLES FOR POLITICAL INDEPENDENCE, 1940–1968

During the darkest days of World War II, the Allies began to plan for the postwar international order. In 1941, American president Franklin D. Roosevelt and British prime minister Winston Churchill held a secret meeting off the coast of Newfoundland and signed a document known as the **Atlantic Charter**. The other Allies, including the Free French Forces and the Belgian government-in-exile, signed on in London 6 weeks later. The Atlantic Charter proclaimed, among other things, "the right of all peoples to choose the form of government under which they will live," and it called for the restoration of the "rights of self-government." The catch was that such high-minded phrases applied only to the signatory powers; they were not meant for their colonies.

Nevertheless, both the British and the French realized that the colonial system of indirect rule, by which policies crafted in London or Paris were handed down to colonial governors and implemented by local African chiefs, required substantial reforms. In his 1942 report to the British Colonial Office, Lord Hailey advocated that the colonies "be given a full opportunity to achieve self-government." He did not suggest a timetable, but he assumed that African self-government would not come anytime soon. Power, he emphasized, would remain in the hands of the colonial governments until the British decided that a given colony was "ready" for independence, by which he meant having a modern government with British-style parliamentary institutions that would look out for British

1957	1958	1960
Ghanaian independence from Britain	Guinean independence from France	Congolese independence from Belgium

THE RIGHT OF ALL PEOPLES American president Franklin Delano Roosevelt (seated, left) and British prime minister Winston Churchill (seated, right) signed the Atlantic Charter in August of 1941 to define Allied goals for the postwar world. Clause no. 3 of the Charter proclaimed "the right of all peoples to choose the form of government under which they will live," but the Allies did not apply that principle to the colonized peoples in Africa.

interests. The timetable for eventual independence was somewhat clarified by a 1947 Colonial Office report, which estimated that some of Britain's colonies might achieve "full responsibility for local affairs" (but not for national or international affairs) within a generation. Although the British were in no hurry to end colonial rule, they nevertheless differed from the French, Belgians, and Portuguese in that they could at least envision a day when their African colonies would be independent countries.

The French, in contrast, had a more rigid vision of colonial rule. At the Brazzaville Conference, held in the French Congo in 1944, Charles de Gaulle's opening remarks acknowledged the African contribution to France's war effort by noting that "up to the present, it has largely been an African war." To squash any talk of self-government for the colonies, however, the final declaration of the

CHARLES DE GAULLE IN BRAZZAVILLE The leader of the Free French Forces during World War II, Charles de Gaulle, speaks at the opening of the Brazzaville Conference to discuss the future of France's African colonies in January 1944. He acknowledged the critical support that Africans provided during the war, but ruled out the possibility of future independence for the African colonies.

conference clearly stated that "the eventual establishment of self-government in the colonies—at however remote a date—must be ruled out." The declaration nevertheless called for the creation of representative assemblies in each colony, and for African representation in the drafting of a new French constitution after the war. These calls were an admission that the French system of indirect rule through local chiefs was no longer sufficient.

Despite British and French reluctance to even consider granting independence to their African colonies in the near future, the British colony of Ghana became an independent state in 1957, the French colony of Guinea gained its independence a year later, and the Belgian Congo became independent in 1960. By 1963, all of the colonies in the northern two-thirds of Africa (with the exception of Guinea-Bissau, Equatorial Guinea, and Djibouti) were independent states. A more mixed pattern could be observed in the southern third of Africa, where Britain granted independence to Zambia, Malawi, Botswana, Lesotho, and Swaziland between 1964 and 1968, but Portugal clung to its colonies of Angola and

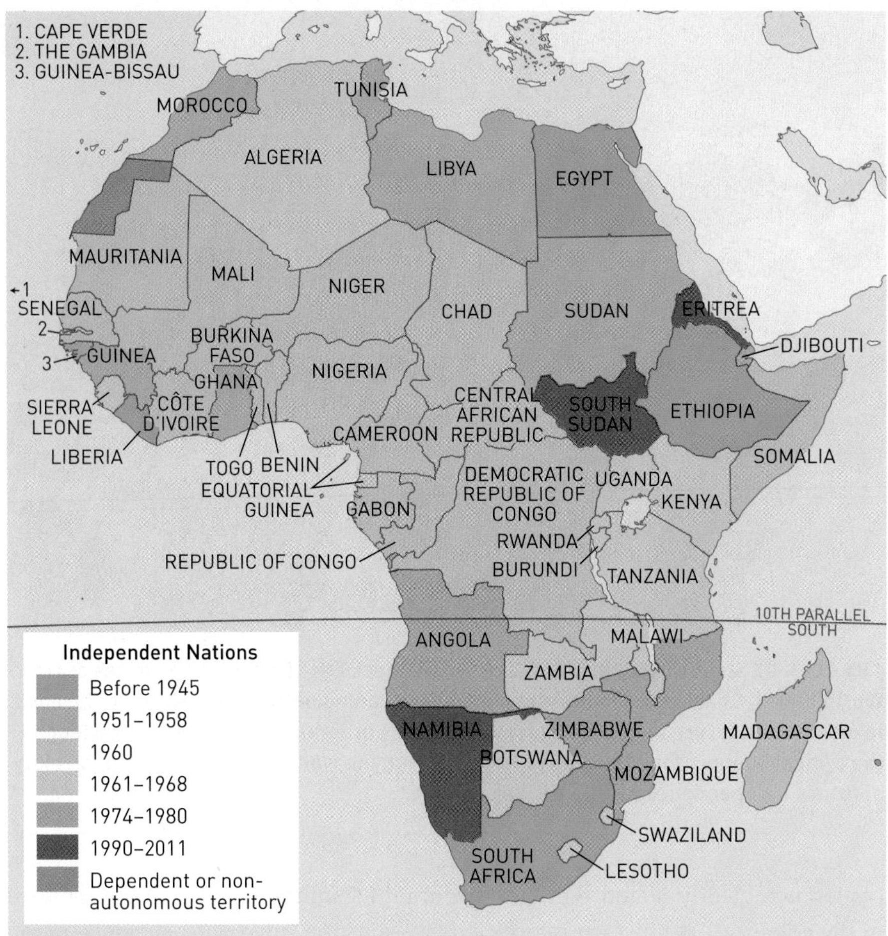

INDEPENDENCE IN AFRICA The year 1960 saw the greatest number of African countries gain independence at one time. South Africa received its independence from Britain in 1931 under white minority rule. Eritrea broke away from Ethiopia in 1993, and South Sudan achieved its independence from Sudan in 2011.

Mozambique, while the white settler governments in South Africa and Zimbabwe passed draconian laws to increase their domination over the indigenous black populations.

This chapter examines the political struggles and policy discussions that led up to independence for the great majority of the African colonies, and it also explores the reasons why Africans living in certain colonies experienced increasing repression instead. Like the previous chapter, this one concentrates on the years following World War II, but whereas chapter 13 focused on economic and lifestyle changes in Africa, this chapter looks at political mobilization and the drive toward independence. In most British and French colonies, Africans mobilized peacefully for protests and political rallies, but in others, such as Kenya, Algeria, and South Africa, where white settler–dominated governments blocked African aspirations, the liberation movements took a violent turn.

POSTWAR POLITICAL REFORMS

In the aftermath of World War II, many Africans in British and French colonies were demanding a voice in how they were governed. This group included African soldiers who had fought for Britain and France during the war, young people graduating from mission and government schools, employees of the colonial administrations, workers in the mines and transportation hubs, and farmers who had been displaced by white settlers or alienated by colonial development schemes. Just as the British and French governments had very different visions regarding the eventual independence of their African colonies, they also had different approaches to political reform. The French created a uniform system that was applied to all their African colonies, while the British devised plans tailored to the unique conditions in each colony.

Representative Assemblies in French Colonies

The French instituted a series of political reforms in the immediate postwar years: trade unions and political parties were allowed to operate legally; forced labor and arbitrary punishments were abolished; and Africans gained new legal rights and access to courts. Most important, Africans were permitted to elect representatives at three different levels of the government. At the lowest level, they elected representatives to the Territorial Assemblies that were established in each of the twelve French colonies in Africa (the French referred to the individual colonies as "territories"). At the next level, each of the Territorial Assemblies sent five members to the Great Council of French West Africa or French Equatorial Africa. Finally, elected African representatives were added to the French National Assembly in Paris, where their presence symbolized the integration of the colonies with metropolitan France.

These new forms of political participation were largely a sham: only certain categories of Africans (such as veterans, civil servants, registered property owners, and people literate in French or Arabic) were allowed to vote; white French citizens living in the colonies were vastly overrepresented because of separate voter rolls; the Territorial Assemblies and Great Councils were relatively powerless advisory bodies; and the African representatives in Paris were too few to have much impact. Yet every 18 months or so, there was an election in one French colony or another; African political parties formed and competed; and elected representatives gained political experience. All of those activities created hope that they might someday lead to greater self-government.

Constitutional Reforms in British Colonies

Meanwhile, the British system of indirect rule through African chiefs was coming under increasing attack from educated Africans and colonial officials alike. In Malawi, for example, the African nationalist leader Hastings Banda wrote in 1946 that "the chiefs do not express the feelings, desires, and aspirations of the Africans any more than dukes, earls, and barons express the feelings, desires, and aspirations of the British people." That same year, a British colonial official wrote that the traditional chiefs were not equipped to implement the new economic development plans and recommended that more educated Africans be brought into local government. He dismissed the system of indirect rule as "a mere expedient to provide the Central Government with cheap local agents to carry out the details of its day to day administration." By 1947, the British Colonial Office was ready to abandon the concept of indirect rule in favor of local and regional councils that included educated Africans.

The transition from a system of indirect rule through chiefs to a system of rule through elected representatives can be illustrated by the development of the new constitutions in Ghana and Nigeria. As a first step on the long road to eventual self-government, the British introduced a new constitution in Ghana in 1946 that provided increased African representation in the national Legislative Council. This advisory body, made up of colonial officials, European businessmen, African chiefs, and educated Africans, normally met for about 1 week each year. Under the 1946 constitution, 18 of the 30 members would be selected by councils of chiefs, thus giving Africans a majority. The British hoped that the enlarged Legislative Council would "satisfy the legitimate aspirations of the political class" for several decades and would thus allow "a period for the healthy growth of local government." The British were still thinking in terms of decades, not years.

In reality, the new constitution would last for only 4 years. In 1950, the new colonial governor found it to be inadequate and ordered the drafting of a new Ghanaian constitution. In contrast to the 1946 constitution, which was drawn up by the British governor, this one was written by an all-African committee that included only 9 chiefs among its 36 members. The resulting Coussey Constitution, named after the African judge who chaired the committee, scrapped the Legislative Council and created a National Assembly with 38 members elected by universal suffrage, 37 members selected by councils of chiefs, and 9 appointed Europeans. Not only did the Africans have an overwhelming majority, but the elected members outnumbered the chiefs. The first general election under the new constitution was held in 1951.

A similar process unfolded in Nigeria, which adopted a new constitution in 1947. The Richards Constitution, as it was called, created a pyramid structure in which chiefs selected delegates to the regional councils, which in turn selected delegates to the national Legislative Council. Sensing that public opinion had moved ahead of British plans, a new colonial governor, John Macpherson, began drafting another new constitution in 1949 after consulting with village and regional councils. This new constitution (known as the Macpherson Constitution) scrapped the national Legislative Council in favor of an elected National Assembly and gave legislative powers to elected regional assemblies. It also paved the way for Nigeria's first general election in 1952. Africans in both Ghana and Nigeria were clearly rejecting indirect rule through chiefs in favor of elections with universal suffrage.

THE WHITE SETTLER PROBLEM

While Africans in colonies with very few white settlers, such as Ghana and Nigeria, were gaining a greater voice in national affairs, the path to independence was more difficult in colonies with significant white settler populations. The settlers in those colonies had seized the best farmland and exploited cheap African labor, and they wanted to be sure that any political changes did not undermine their dominant position. As a result, Britain and France sometimes found themselves drawn into conflicts that were triggered by African resentment of the white settlers, such as the rebellions that erupted in Kenya and Algeria.

The Mau Mau Rebellion in Kenya

The **Mau Mau rebellion** was one of the most significant threats to colonial rule in East Africa since the Maji Maji Rebellion in Tanzania in 1905–1907 (see chapter 10). The rebellion began in 1952 among the Kikuyu people in the Kenya Highlands, a region where aristocratic white settlers controlled enormous expanses of land, while the Kikuyu people lived as squatters on settler farms or in the increasingly overcrowded Kikuyu reserve. Although the insurgents are generally referred to by the name Mau Mau, they themselves did not use that term. Instead, they called themselves the Land and Freedom Army, a name that expressed their grievances as well as their goals.

The Origins of the Mau Mau Rebellion

Although most of the land in colonial Kenya was owned and worked by Africans, the white settlers' estates in the White Highlands were a glaring exception. There, the land was worked by African laborers who were not paid regular wages, but were instead allowed to raise livestock and farm for themselves on small plots in exchange for their labor. They were known as labor tenants or squatters (see chapter 11). Fearing that the Africans might try to acquire "squatters' rights" to land, the white settlers made plans after World War II to reduce them to simple wage laborers with no land rights. Toward that end, the settlers began to limit squatter livestock and expel as many squatters as possible.

Many of the Kikuyu squatter families who were forced out had lived on settler farms for over 30 years, and they returned to the Kikuyu reserve only to discover that their ancestral farmland had been taken over by senior members of their subclans or by wealthy Kikuyu farmers and chiefs. Lacking land in the reserve, some ex-squatters returned to the White Highlands and accepted whatever conditions the white settlers imposed on them; some became wage laborers for prosperous Kikuyu farmers in the reserve; and others flocked to the city of Nairobi, where they struggled to survive by doing odd jobs, hawking merchandise, brewing beer, and engaging in prostitution or crime. In 1947, more than half of Nairobi's population was made up of the Kikuyu poor.

There were thus a large number of Kikuyu who had grievances against the colonial state, the white settlers, and the wealthy Kikuyu farmers and chiefs. Although people understood very well that British colonial policies were behind their plight, it was sometimes easier for them to direct their anger at the chiefs and rich Kikuyu landowners who were profiting from the very policies that caused their suffering. It is not surprising, therefore, that the first person killed by the insurgents when the fighting broke out in 1952 was a wealthy Kikuyu chief named Waruhiru, who was shot while driving home from Nairobi in his Hudson sedan.

The military phase of the rebellion was organized by the Kikuyu War Council in Nairobi, which obtained weapons and sent them to military camps in the thick bamboo and cedar forests that bordered the Kikuyu reserve. Thousands of young men and hundreds of young women left their homes for the forests, where they received basic military training from Mau Mau commanders, most of whom were veterans of World War II. By 1953, as many as 30,000 young men and women were living in military camps scattered throughout the forest. Many were armed with nothing more than machetes and spears, but British army rifles, submachine guns, and light machine guns were nevertheless reaching the forest camps. Young women from Nairobi and the Kikuyu reserve carried food, money, and information to the forest fighters. Because rivalry among the different forest commanders prevented a coordinated military strategy, the attacks were often isolated hit-and-run operations that did little to change the outcome of the rebellion. A common Mau Mau tactic was to attack a guard post and then retreat before the regular colonial soldiers arrived to reclaim it.

A State of Emergency

Alarmed by the growing unrest, the British declared a state of emergency on October 20, 1952. That same day, 12 military transport planes arrived with the first contingent of British army soldiers, and 3 days later, a British warship anchored in the harbor at Mombasa. The British also brought in units of the King's African Rifles (a colonial army made up of African soldiers) from Uganda and Tanzania. To patrol the Kikuyu reserve, they sent in large numbers of African police and created a Kikuyu Home Guard made up of Kikuyu loyalists. By mid-1953, 10,000 British and African regular troops, 21,000 police, and 20,000 Kikuyu Home Guard troops (only 3,000 of whom were armed with rifles) were involved in the fighting. The British also had a small air force that dropped 50,000 tons of bombs on suspected Mau Mau camps in the forest.

Even with such a formidable force, the British were making little progress against the rebels, so they began to intervene directly with the Kikuyu population. To prevent squatters in the White Highlands from aiding or joining the rebellion, the British loaded thousands of them onto trucks at gunpoint and hauled them back to the Kikuyu reserve. Knowing that the fighters in the forest were getting arms and supplies from Nairobi, they launched Operation Anvil to rid the city of rebel influences. Sweeping through the Kikuyu neighborhoods, the security forces sent 24,000 people to detention camps and deported 9,000 women and children back to the overcrowded reserve. Africans who remained in Nairobi had to carry a photo-ID passbook, available only to people whose loyalty was vouched for by a government official, a prominent loyalist, or a white employer.

Occupying the Kikuyu Reserve

The most drastic measures, however, were aimed at the Kikuyu reserve itself. To isolate the forest fighters from their sources of food and supplies in the reserve, the British used forced labor to construct a 50-mile-long ditch that was 10 feet deep, 16 feet wide, and filled with barbed wire, booby traps, and sharpened bamboo stakes. Police stationed at posts every half mile patrolled the ditch 24 hours a day. In an even more drastic action, the British ordered the Kikuyu to abandon their scattered homesteads and build compact Emergency Villages that were surrounded by barbed-wire fences and overlooked by watchtowers. Women who worked in their fields during the day had to be accompanied by armed guards.

By the end of 1954, over a million people had been forcibly relocated into roughly 800 Emergency Villages. Most of the villages were designed to keep suspected Mau Mau sympathizers under constant surveillance, although some were built to protect Kikuyu loyalists from possible Mau Mau reprisals. The British also built over a hundred detention camps, where, on any given day, some 80,000 suspected Mau Mau supporters were held in harsh and brutal conditions until they confessed to having taken the Mau Mau oath, renounced it, and gave up the names of their comrades. Those who refused to confess faced various forms of torture, such as beatings, floggings, electric shock, and waterboarding. Overall, between 160,000 and 320,000 Kikuyu spent time in the detention camps.

To gain support among the Kikuyu living in the reserve, the British introduced a program for consolidating fragmented land holdings and giving the owners full legal title. Because loyalist elders were in control of the consolidation committees, loyalist families gained land while Mau Mau supporters lost out. As the tide of war began to turn in favor of the British, more Kikuyu in the reserve sided with the loyalists. In the end, nearly as many Kikuyu men joined the loyalist Home Guard as joined the Mau Mau fighters in the forest, and loyalist Kikuyu women often fought

DETENTION CAMP A detention camp in rural Kenya for people suspected of aiding the Mau Mau fighters. Suspected Mau Mau supporters were often tortured until they confessed to having taken the Mau Mau oath and gave up the names of their comrades. The wooden tower at the back of the camp is a gallows. Over 1,000 insurgents were hanged during the Emergency.

to defend their crops and livestock against Mau Mau raiders who came in search of food supplies. Although the British press depicted the Mau Mau rebellion as a war against the white settlers, the rebels killed only 32 white civilians during more than 4 years of fighting, while over 1,800 civilian Kikuyu loyalists died in Mau Mau attacks. An estimated 20,000 Mau Mau insurgents were killed by British and loyalist forces.

With the Kikuyu reserve in a state of lockdown, the regular British and African troops were freed up to launch operations in the forest. The Mau Mau military commander known as General China (because he was an admirer of Mao Zedong) was captured in 1954, and Stanley Mathenge, another top commander, mysteriously disappeared the following year. When Dedan Kimathi, the symbolic figurehead of the Mau Mau fighters, was captured in October 1956, the fighting was effectively over. A month later, the last British army troops left Kenya, more than 4 years after the declaration of the state of emergency. The British had preserved their colonial rule, but at great cost. The Mau Mau rebellion reminded the British of how important it was to reach an accommodation with the African elites in their colonies.

The Algerian War of Independence

The French colony of Algeria had been legally incorporated as a part of France (see chapter 10), which meant that the European settler minority in Algeria had full rights as French citizens. The Muslim Berbers and Arabs who made up the majority of the population, however, were largely excluded. Muslim discontent could be seen in the Manifesto of the Algerian People, a document drawn up in 1943 that called for equal rights, agricultural reform, and the eventual creation of an independent Algerian state. The high hopes of the Algerian nationalists were dashed after World War II, when the French National Assembly passed the Algerian Statute, a law that provided only for a relatively powerless Algerian Assembly, which was divided into two groups of representatives with 60 votes each. One group was elected by 460,000 European settler voters, and the other by 1.3 million Algerian Muslim voters, rendering the vote of one white settler equal to three Muslim votes. On top of this intrinsic imbalance, when the first election for the Algerian Assembly was held in 1948, the French rigged the ballot, arrested pro-independence election officials, and withheld voter registration cards to make sure that those Muslim candidates who favored independence would be in the minority. Disillusioned with the electoral fraud, angry Muslims responded with cries of "Give us arms." In 1954, a group of Algerian militants formed the National Liberation Front (NLF) and began to plan a war for national independence.

Rebels in the Countryside

On All Saints' Day, November 1, 1954, the NLF launched 70 simultaneous attacks in scattered locations in the mountains of eastern Algeria. To build support for their movement, the rebels passed out leaflets urging people to join the armed conflict. The number of attacks mounted each month: the NLF launched a total of 178 attacks in November and 201 more in December; then, after a break for winter, they launched 455 attacks in May and 501 in June. Rebel groups would infiltrate a rural village and kill pro-French Algerians as well as Muslim policemen and administrators who worked for the French. Once they had secured the area, the rebels moved into the village and relied on local women to provide them with food, water, clothing, and information. In remote areas with European settler farms, they cut grapevines, killed cattle, and attacked settlers. Because they operated in small groups, the fighters were usually able to evade the columns of jeeps, armored personnel carriers, and tanks that the French sent into the mountains.

The NLF leaders had hoped to shock the French into negotiations for independence, but their plan backfired. The French arrested scores of known militants and rushed in reinforcements to support the 50,000 or so troops who were already there. By 1955, there were some 120,000 French troops in Algeria. In order to cut the rebels off from the general population, they displaced whole villages and emptied out rural areas. The French declared a state of emergency in areas of fighting, which allowed them to conduct collective reprisals against villages, carry out summary executions, and generally follow a policy of shooting first and asking questions later. Their instructions were explicit: "Every rebel using weapons or seen carrying a weapon must be immediately shot; every suspect who tries to escape must be fired upon." In order to intimidate the rural population, French soldiers destroyed villages deemed sympathetic to the rebels, executed prisoners, and dumped bodies in the streets for all to see. The harsh actions of the French army galvanized Algerian support for the rebels.

The Battle of Algiers

In the fall of 1956, the focal point of the fighting shifted to the capital city, Algiers. Bordering the Mediterranean Sea, Algiers was a predominantly European city, with some 300,000 European residents. It was also home to about 80,000 Algerian Muslims, who lived mostly in the old quarter known as the Casbah, an overcrowded and decaying maze of narrow streets and twisting alleys that ran between the three-story mud-brick and stucco houses. The **Battle of Algiers**—as it is now known—was not really a battle in the classic sense, but an ongoing street fight between rebel terrorist bombers and French security forces that lasted from late 1956 to late 1957. The purpose of the bombings was to move the war from the rural mountains to the locus of French power.

The bombing campaign was the work of Saadi Yacef, a baker who had grown up in the Casbah. On orders from the NLF leadership, he created an elaborate network of secret passages, safe houses, and hidden bomb factories. He recruited three expert bomb-makers as well as a small group of women whose French appearance enabled them to carry bombs through checkpoints unimpeded. He also amassed a group of 1,500 fighters and organized them into semiautonomous cells, so that if one cell was captured, its members could not disclose confidential information on the others. The bombing campaign began on September 30, 1956, when a pair of NLF women detonated two bombs at crowded cafés in the center of the city. A third bomb at the Air France terminal failed to detonate due to a faulty timer. That was the opening of a larger campaign of bombings and shootings in the European part of the city.

Knowing that the Algiers police force was no match for the well-organized rebels, the French army brought in the Tenth Parachute Division, 8,000 men strong, and gave it complete authority over the city. Dividing the city into squares, the troops cordoned off each section, set up checkpoints, and conducted house-to-house searches to locate weapons or known NLF rebels. Men were strip-searched and women were searched with metal detectors. The French developed a network of informers and set up an index-card system that identified the suspicious people living on each street. Some 30–40 percent of the men in the Casbah were arrested and interrogated over the course of the battle. Interrogation often included various methods of torture, such as electric shock, waterboarding, and sexual assault. If rebel leaders were caught, they were interrogated and then executed by a firing squad in the public square.

The bombings stopped briefly in February 1957, after soldiers intercepted one of Saadi Yacef's bomb carriers and tortured him until he divulged the location of his bomb factory. Raiding the factory, the soldiers seized 87 bombs and 150 pounds of explosives. By June, however, Yacef had built a new factory and was again planting bombs in the center of Algiers. On September 24, soldiers acting on a tip raided Yacef's hideout and captured him, along with his favorite female bomb carrier, Zohra Drif. His capture marked the end of the Battle of Algiers, but the war in the countryside continued. No longer seeking victory on the battlefield, the NLF broke up its battalions into small units and reverted to guerilla tactics in hopes of gaining a political victory by waging a war of attrition.

The End of the Fighting

The war did not come to an end until the collapse of the French Fourth Republic and the establishment of the Fifth Republic under the leadership of President Charles de Gaulle. Because Algeria was officially a part of France, it could gain independence only with the consent of the French voters. In a referendum held in January 1961, voters in France and Algeria approved a proposal by de Gaulle that called for the "self-determination of the Algerian people," and de Gaulle subsequently entered into negotiations with the NLF. The European settlers in Algeria responded by forming their own army, which used terror tactics copied from the NLF to fight against de Gaulle and Algerian independence. In the month of January 1962, they set off 48 bombs in Paris. Following a second referendum in France and Algeria, de Gaulle officially recognized Algerian independence on July 3, 1962. Shortly thereafter, some 800,000 European settlers left Algeria and returned to France.

Like the Mau Mau rebellion in Kenya, the Algerian war of independence sent a message to the major colonial powers that colonial rule could be sustained only at great cost. It is one of the ironies of the postwar era that elections were being planned in some British and French colonies at the same time troops were being sent to others. It was the presence or absence of European settlers that made all the difference because the settlers feared losing their privileged access to land and cheap labor if Africans were to gain self-government.

MOVEMENTS TOWARD INDEPENDENCE

In 1950, only four countries in Africa could be considered independent. The first was Ethiopia, which had historically been independent except for the brief Italian occupation of 1935–1941. The second was Liberia, which the United States had recognized as independent since 1847, but was governed by an African American settler minority. The third was South Africa, which was a self-governing dominion within the British Commonwealth, but was ruled by a white settler minority. And the fourth was Egypt, which the British had granted incomplete independence in 1922. By 1968 the number of independent African countries had risen to over forty.

Decolonization came in three waves. The first wave swept across North Africa, bringing independence to all of the countries north of the Sahara Desert by 1956, except for Algeria, where the European settlers kept pressure on the French to resist independence until 1962. The second wave extended across tropical Africa, beginning with Ghana's independence from Britain in 1957 and Guinea's independence from France in 1958. The third wave, which spread through the southern third of Africa between 1975 and 1994, will be discussed in the next chapter.

The First Wave: North Africa

Egypt, the only independent country in North Africa, had officially become a constitutional monarchy in 1922, but the British had retained a large military presence, along with control of the Suez Canal, control of Egypt's foreign policy, and joint Anglo-Egyptian control of Sudan. That situation changed in 1952, when a group of young Egyptian military officers, led by **Gamal Abdel Nasser**, staged a military coup. They sent King Farouk into exile and set up a Revolutionary

REVOLUTIONARY COMMAND COUNCIL Lieutenant Gamal Abdel Nasser (seated, second from left) poses with members of Egypt's Revolutionary Command Council on June 20, 1953. Nasser served as Egypt's prime minister from 1954 to 1956 and as president from 1956 to 1970. Seated at the far right is Anwar Sadat, who succeeded Nasser as president in 1970.

Command Council to run the country. Two years later, they reached an accord with the British that required all uniformed British troops to depart, and they wrote a new constitution that declared Egypt "a sovereign independent state."

Egypt and Britain nevertheless remained entangled in two major issues. The first was the Suez Canal, which the accord left under British control. In a surprise move in 1956, the Egyptians seized the canal and expelled the British. In response, Britain, France, and Israel invaded the canal zone, but American president Dwight D. Eisenhower demanded the withdrawal of all foreign troops, leaving the canal in Egyptian hands. The other sticky issue was Sudan, Egypt's neighbor to the south, which had been jointly governed by Britain and Egypt since the nineteenth century. Both countries agreed to withdraw in 1956 and allow Sudanese independence. By the end of 1956, therefore, Egypt had disentangled itself from Britain, and it was finally the sovereign independent state that its new constitution proclaimed.

Libya, Egypt's western neighbor, had formerly been an Italian colony, but the Italians were forced to relinquish their claims in the same treaty that renewed Egypt's independence at the end of World War II. When the Allies withdrew in 1951, Libya gained its independence as the United Kingdom of Libya.

Farther to the west was French North Africa, which consisted of Algeria (which was officially a part of France), flanked on either side by Tunisia and Morocco. The latter two were not colonies, strictly speaking, but rather "protectorates," because the French had taken them over as intact states, leaving their own kings and administrative systems in place. The French government had encouraged French, Italians, and other Europeans to settle in Tunisia and Morocco, but the number of settlers never approached anything like the million or so who had settled in Algeria. Dissatisfaction with French colonial rule surfaced in Tunisia in 1952, when protests erupted in the cities and rebels in the countryside launched attacks against European settlers. Strikes and violent demonstrations broke out in Morocco at about the same time. When the French became bogged down in the Algerian war of independence, they found it expedient to grant independence to Tunisia and Morocco in 1956 rather than face the possibility of fighting in all three colonial possessions. By 1962, when the war in Algeria finally came to a close, a string of five newly independent countries occupied the Mediterranean seaboard from Morocco to Egypt.

The Second Wave: Tropical Africa

The second wave of decolonization swept across tropical Africa between 1957 and 1968, during which time over 30 separate colonies in tropical Africa became independent countries. Each one has its own story of political movements, grassroots mobilization, protests, and negotiations that resulted in its independence. To get a sense of how this process played out in different settings, we look at the drive toward independence in three tropical African colonies: Ghana (a British colony), Guinea (a French colony), and the Belgian Congo.

Ghana

After World War II, popular discontent with British colonial rule surfaced in several segments of the Ghanaian population. In the rural areas, the African cocoa farmers were on the verge of revolt. The problem originated when swollen-shoot disease, which is spread by mealybugs, infected the cocoa trees. In 1946, the Department of Agriculture began to dispatch crews to the African cocoa farms to identify and remove infected trees, but they often cut down healthy trees as well as diseased ones. As one farmer explained, "The agricultural people entered my farm with a gang of laborers and cut down the trees—trees in full bearing. When I protested, they said they would take me to court." By the end of 1947, some

2.5 million cocoa trees had been cut down, and another 4 million had been marked for removal. Some farmers were convinced that the Department of Agriculture was trying to wipe out the Ghanaian cocoa industry.

Discontent was also brewing in the cities and towns as a result of high prices for imported goods. The Africans blamed the United Africa Company, which exported cocoa and imported general merchandise, and the Lebanese merchants who dominated the retail trade. At a time when world cocoa prices were unusually high, it was rumored that the merchants were charging high prices for their merchandise in order to recoup the money they were paying for cocoa. A boycott organized by a local chief forced the merchants to cut their profit margins, but distrust remained high.

Yet another group growing progressively angrier was the Gold Coast Ex-Servicemen's Union, an organization of World War II veterans. After risking their lives for Britain in the war, many of them had returned home to poverty, unable to find work in spite of their military service.

Those and other sources of discontent came together in the Accra riots of 1948. The spark that ignited the riots was a protest march by the World War II veterans, who wanted to hand a petition to the colonial governor. When police blocked their route, some veterans threw stones at the police, who retaliated by firing on the crowd, killing two veterans and wounding others. Soon, rioting broke out in central Accra: crowds set fire to the offices and shops of the United Africa Company and attacked European-owned stores suspected of price gouging. When similar riots broke out in cities and towns across the country, the British declared a state of emergency. In the aftermath of the riots, the British proposed the constitutional reforms described earlier in this chapter, which replaced the Legislative Council with an elected National Assembly and called a general election for 1951.

THE CONVENTION PEOPLE'S PARTY. The run-up to the 1951 election saw the emergence of a new political party called the Convention People's Party (CPP), led by **Kwame Nkrumah**. A graduate of the elite Achimota high school in Accra (see chapter 12), Nkrumah had spent 10 years in the United States, earning degrees in theology, education, and philosophy, and he subsequently studied law and philosophy in London. During his time in England, he broadened his political perspective by helping to organize the Fifth Pan-African Congress in Manchester and by attending meetings of the British Communist Party. He later summed up his personal philosophy by writing, "I am a non-denominational Christian and a Marxist Socialist. I have not found any contradiction between the two."

After returning to Ghana in 1947, Nkrumah founded the CPP, which advocated "immediate self-government." The CPP initially found support among youth groups and women, two traditionally disenfranchised groups that Nkrumah brought into the political process. He also picked up support among the cocoa farmers and the trade unions, thus forming a coalition that spanned both the rural and urban areas. When the constitutional reforms in the wake of the Accra riots fell short of immediate self-government, Nkrumah called for a campaign of civil disobedience, boycotts, and strikes in order to force the colonial government to convene a Constituent Assembly to draw up a new constitution. The government sentenced him to 3 years in prison for promoting an illegal strike, attempting to coerce the government, and sedition.

Nkrumah was in prison when the 1951 election was held, but he nevertheless won his district in Accra with over 95 percent of the vote. The election was also a victory for the CPP, which won 34 of the 38 elected seats in the newly created National Assembly. As the leader of the majority party, Nkrumah was released from prison and became the prime minister of Ghana, with substantial authority over the colony's internal affairs. In the 1954 and 1956 elections, the CPP maintained its political dominance by winning roughly 70 percent of the seats. Historians have not yet pinpointed the moment when the British accepted that Ghana was on a path to full independence, but it happened sometime between 1954 and 1956. In a special ceremony on March 6, 1957, Kwame Nkrumah declared Ghana to be an independent country.

THE DOMINO EFFECT. Two weeks before Ghana officially became independent, British prime minister Harold Macmillan asked the Colonial Policy Committee to prepare a secret report on the prospects for independence in the other British colonies. The report, issued in September 1957, predicted that Nigeria would gain full independence in 1960 or 1961 and Uganda in 1967. Six other British colonies were slated to gain internal self-government within the next 10 years, with full independence to follow sometime after that. But events were moving faster than British policy anticipated. Independence in Ghana had started a kind of domino effect that could not be stopped or slowed down. All of those British colonies were fully independent by 1965.

Why did Britain let go of its African colonies so easily? One answer is that Britain had been shedding its colonies around the globe since the end of World War II. It had granted independence to India in 1947 and Malaya in 1957, and the Colonial Policy Committee's secret report anticipated independence in such far-flung places as Cyprus, Singapore, and Guyana as well as Africa. In other words, decolonization in Africa was just one more step in a larger process of dismantling Britain's global empire. A second answer is that the British had discovered that development projects such as large dams, terracing schemes, and wholesale removal of cocoa trees provoked political opposition. In Kenya, for example, the chiefdoms that bore the brunt of the forced terracing campaigns were the same ones that later produced the Mau Mau fighters, and Kwame Nkrumah in Ghana had gained the support of the cocoa farmers by opposing the colonial campaign against swollen-shoot disease. Independent African governments, the British reasoned, might be more successful at implementing modern development schemes than foreign colonizers. A third answer points to labor unrest in the most advanced sectors of the colonial economy. A wave of strikes in colonies such as Ghana, Nigeria, Kenya, and Tanzania had shown that Africans no longer accepted their assigned role as cheap labor and were demanding equal pay for equal work. Colonialism was about to get more expensive.

At a more fundamental level, however, the British had come to believe that they could use treaties and trade agreements to maintain the economic and strategic advantages that came with colonialism while shifting the costs of economic and human development to independent African governments. Once "colonialism on the cheap" had ceased to be a viable policy option, British enthusiasm for colonial ventures waned. The Colonial Policy Committee's secret report in 1957 made it clear that independent African countries would no longer be eligible for Colonial Development and Welfare funds. In short, decolonization would save Britain money without reducing the flow of agricultural commodities and raw materials from Africa. For Britain, the potential advantages of decolonization were beginning to outweigh the risks.

Guinea

When the French convened their Constituent Assembly in Paris in November 1945 to draw up a new constitution in the aftermath of World War II, 6 of the 586 delegates were black Africans from French West Africa and 2 more were from French Equatorial Africa, giving Africans hope that their desires for greater equality would be fulfilled. But the constitution of the French Fourth Republic that resulted from the assembly seemed to the African delegates to be no less detrimental to African aspirations than the previous one. Several of the disappointed delegates proposed a conference to organize for African political rights. The conference, held in Bamako, Mali, in October 1946, was attended by some 800 to 1,500 people representing all the French African colonies. Its main outcome was a political party known as the African Democratic Rally (ADR), which was initially allied with the French Communist Party. Like the French party, the ADR was not a revolutionary party, but instead advocated for greater local autonomy and greater equality with French citizens. The ADR established branches in most of the French African colonies, becoming the largest political party in French Africa.

Guinea was one of the eight territories (i.e., colonies) that made up French West Africa, and the ADR established itself there in 1947, soon boasting of

5,000 members. By the end of the year, there were ADR committees in most of the districts and urban centers in Guinea. One of the founding members of the ADR in Guinea was **Ahmed Sékou Touré**, a great-grandson of the nineteenth-century warlord and state builder Samori Touré (see chapter 9). Sékou Touré had considerable experience as a labor organizer, having been expelled from technical school in 1937 for organizing a strike. After becoming a post-office clerk, he cofounded the Postal, Telegraph, and Telephone Workers Union in 1945. The following year, he became the secretary-general of the Confederated Trade Unions of Guinea, an umbrella organization that brought all the separate unions together. In that position, he organized such divergent groups as domestic servants, dockworkers, and laundrymen. By 1952, the Confederated Trade Unions of Guinea counted 20 affiliated unions with a total of 3,000 members. He went on to become the secretary-general of the ADR's Guinean branch in 1952.

THE LEGAL FRAMEWORK. In 1956, the French were worried that their colonial empire was slipping away. Having lost Vietnam in 1954, they were fighting a war in Algeria and negotiating independence with Tunisia and Morocco. In an effort to shore up support in the remaining territories, the French National Assembly in Paris passed a law known as the Legal Framework, which provided for increased popular participation in government. Representatives to the Territorial Assemblies were to be elected by universal suffrage, and the separate voter rolls that had formerly privileged French nationals were eliminated. The Territorial Assemblies would no longer be mere advisory bodies, but would have legislative powers over most government departments, including agriculture, health, and education. Each Territorial Assembly would elect members to the Territorial Executive Committee that made administrative decisions. Despite these new arrangements, however, the appointed French governor and the appointed French district officers remained in place, awkwardly coexisting with the elected bodies. Elections for the Territorial Assemblies were scheduled for 1957.

In the run-up to the 1957 election in Guinea, the ADR could count on support from a variety of groups. First was the urban working class, especially members of trade unions. Second were World War II veterans, many of whom had returned from the war only to find poverty and unemployment. Third were the rural populations who had engaged in popular resistance against the traditional chiefs. The chiefs became extremely unpopular during the war because they had forcibly recruited labor and military conscripts, imposed mandatory cash-crop production, and forced women to provide them with unpaid labor. Fourth were the ex-slaves in the former Fuuta Jaloo, many of whom were descended from victims of Samori Touré's slave raids in the nineteenth century. In a reference to Ahmed Sékou Touré's great-grandfather, the ADR created the slogan, "If Samori

Touré could make you slaves, Sékou Touré can make you free." The fifth group was women. The ADR organized a conference in 1954 for urban women to articulate their demands, such as more schools for their children, more public water taps, and more maternity wards. Women also composed and sang a variety of songs praising ADR leaders and ridiculing their opponents, which became a key way of spreading the ADR's message. Other women became shock troops in the urban street brawls that broke out between rival political parties. Politics, the Guineans were discovering, could get rough!

When the election was held in March 1957 under the new Legal Framework, the ADR won 75 percent of the vote and was awarded 56 out of 60 seats in the Territorial Assembly. Sékou Touré, the secretary-general of the ADR party in Guinea, was elected vice president of the Territorial Executive Committee (the French governor served as president). One of the first acts of the new ADR government was to abolish the position of chief throughout Guinea and rely instead on elected local councils. In Guinea, the old colonial system of indirect rule through chiefs was officially dead.

REFERENDUM ON THE FRENCH CONSTITUTION. Because of a new crisis in metropolitan France, the reforms brought about by the Legal Framework of 1956 would be short-lived. When the French government suggested in 1958 that it might end the war in Algeria by negotiating with the rebels, a segment of the French military rebelled and threatened to invade Paris unless Charles de Gaulle was named the leader of France. De Gaulle agreed to assume power, provided that he could write a new constitution for what would become the French Fifth Republic. The new constitution was mainly concerned with metropolitan France, but some of its articles dealt with the status of the colonies, which were seen as part of the larger French Community. For that reason, people in the colonies were allowed to vote on whether to approve the new French Constitution. In France's African territories, suffrage had been expanded gradually since the end of World War II until universal suffrage was implemented in 1956. In Guinea, for example, the electorate increased from 131,000 in 1946, to 1 million in 1956, and to 1.4 million in 1957.

A draft of the new constitution was unveiled for public comment on July 29, 1958. It created a worldwide French Community consisting of France and its overseas territories. Each territory could attain internal self-government, depending on its individual circumstances, but France would retain control of a long list of functions, including foreign policy, defense, courts, currency, economic and financial affairs, strategic resources, and higher education. The territories could no longer send representatives to the French National Assembly, only to the newly created Senate of the French Community, which met for only 2 months each year and had no political powers. The preamble to the constitution stated that the new political institutions were being offered "to those overseas territories which have expressed the will to adhere to them" by voting in favor of the constitution.

The consequences of a Yes or a No vote were a major topic of discussion when de Gaulle toured Africa in August 1958 to rally support for his new constitution. Upon learning that some African territories might hesitate to ratify the constitution for fear of being bound forever to France, he agreed to modify it in order to give territories the right to opt for independence at a later date, but he insisted that any territory that chose independence would immediately cease to be a member of the French Community. When he arrived in Guinea on August 25, Sékou Touré asked him to modify the draft further to include the right to full independence *within* the French Community, but de Gaulle refused, saying that a No vote would mean the end of all French administrative, technical, and educational assistance. "Guinea," he later told his French colleagues, "is not indispensable to France. Let her assume her responsibilities."

As the referendum approached, the Guinea branch of the ADR met in Conakry to decide on its position. The trade unions, student organizations, women's organizations, and teachers' union all favored a No vote, which would mean immediate independence for Guinea and the withdrawal of French assistance. When Sékou Touré entered the meeting hall, shouts of "NO, NO, NO" erupted from the 680 delegates. Rather than give his prepared speech, he simply asked the group for their verdict on the new constitution. When cries of "NO, NO, NO" again filled the room, he announced that the matter was decided—the party would vote against the new French constitution. That evening, the ADR unanimously adopted a resolution calling for a "No" vote, and 2 days later, the other major political party in Guinea followed suit.

THE AFTERSHOCKS. When the referendum was held on September 28, 1958, some 94 percent of the voters in Guinea voted No. The French administration in Guinea threw what can best be described as a massive temper tantrum. In vacating their offices, they destroyed archives, ripped telephones off the walls, and unscrewed lightbulbs from their sockets in their attempt to leave the Guineans with as little as possible. On October 2, just 5 days after the referendum, Guinea proclaimed itself a sovereign and independent republic, with Ahmed Sékou Touré as president.

Guinea proved to be the exception in the 1958 referendum: all the other French territories in Africa approved the new constitution by large margins and thus stayed in the French Community. Two years later, however, Senegal and Mali began to negotiate with the French government for independence. Realizing that self-government for the African colonies was inevitable, de Gaulle began negotiating terms that would allow them to maintain some of the advantages of the colonial relationship. Accordingly, the French amended their new constitution on June 4, 1960, to state that a territory could become independent without having to leave the French Community—the middle ground that Sékou Touré had vainly sought in Guinea. By the end of 1960, all territories in French West Africa and French Equatorial Africa had become independent countries. French colonialism was like a house of cards: remove one card, and the others soon fall.

INDEPENDENCE FOR GUINEA Ahmed Sékou Touré (center), the first president of independent Guinea, addresses Guinea's parliament on October 4, 1958, just 2 days after he had proclaimed Guinea to be an independent country.

Why did the French give up their African colonies so quickly during 1958–1960? For one thing, they were becoming resigned to the fact that their worldwide colonial empire was disintegrating despite their best efforts to hold on to it. They had been militarily defeated in Vietnam in 1954; they were bogged down militarily in Algeria; and they had already granted independence to Tunisia and Morocco in 1956. After the rancorous split with Guinea, they feared that their "take it or leave it" approach would result in the loss of their other African territories. By granting territories full independence *within* the French Community, they could retain many of the colonial institutions that bound the territories to France. Some of those institutions simply modified their names, as when the Bank of West Africa became the Bank of West African States and the Investment Fund for Economic and Social Development became the Aid and Cooperation Fund. But some technical agencies, such as ORSTOM (the Office for Overseas Scientific and Technical Research) and CTFT (the Technical Center for Tropical Forestry), carried on into the post-colonial era without even a change of names.

The Belgian Congo

In the decade after World War II, the Belgian colonial administration was focused on making improvements to transportation, agriculture, public health, and education, as outlined in its 10-year plan (see chapter 13), but, in contrast to Britain and France, it was not even discussing political reforms. The only alteration to the ongoing system of indirect rule through chiefs was that the Belgian colonial officials frequently bypassed the chiefs in the name of greater efficiency. When a professor at a Belgian university published a plan in 1955 to move the Congo gradually toward self-government over a period of 30 years, Belgian colonial officials dismissed it as a pipe dream. It was only in 1957 that the colonial administration agreed on a plan for elected councils in the African sections of selected cities, and another for elected councils in rural chiefdoms that would be slowly implemented over a period of years. Beyond such local-level reforms, no further political changes were anticipated.

There were nevertheless Congolese political activists who were keenly aware that political change was afoot in Africa. On August 21, 1958, Africans in Kinshasa huddled around their radios as French president Charles de Gaulle told an audience in Brazzaville (just across the Congo River from Kinshasa) that independence from France was theirs for the taking. Four months later, a Congolese political activist named **Patrice Lumumba** attended an All-African Peoples' Conference in Accra, Ghana, hosted by Kwame Nkrumah, the president of newly independent Ghana. Organized by the eight African states that were already independent, the conference was attended by more than 300 delegates from 28 African countries and colonies. Some delegates held up signs with slogans such as "Africa Must Be Free" and "Down with Imperialism and Colonialism."

THE BIRTH OF POLITICS. One impediment to political activity in the Congo was the lack of political parties. The most important secular organizations that transcended the boundaries of the chiefdoms were the ethnic associations in cities. Originally founded as social and cultural organizations, they gained a political dimension with the approach of municipal council elections and talk of future self-governance. The final months of 1958 saw the formation of ethnic and regional political parties with names, such as "The Confederation of Ethnic Associations of Katanga," that displayed their ethnic and regional orientation. The only truly national political party was the Congolese National Movement (CNM), founded by Patrice Lumumba. With a diverse group of supporters from different ethnic groups and different regions of the Congo, the CNM viewed the Congo as a single political unit and rejected regional separatism. Its party platform called for independence through peaceful negotiations within "a reasonable period of time," but did not suggest a specific date.

Tensions that were building up around the issue of independence came to a head in Kinshasa on January 4, 1959, when the police disbanded a meeting of the Kongo Association, an ethnic association that had recently become a political party. As the disappointed activists started to leave, a fistfight with a white bus driver quickly turned into a general melee that was joined by some of the 20,000 fans who were leaving a soccer match at King Baudouin Stadium. Soon, the entire African section of Kinshasa was engulfed in a riot. It took 4 days for the army to quell the unrest, leaving 47 Congolese dead and hundreds more wounded. Meanwhile, the unrest spread to other parts of the country. On January 13, just 9 days after the start of the Kinshasa riot, King Baudouin of Belgium gave a radio address announcing his decision to "lead the people of Congo toward independence." It was a perfect illustration of the old saying, "If you are being run out of town, get in front of the crowd and make it look like a parade."

LUMUMBA CAMPAIGNS IN THE BELGIAN CONGO Patrice Lumumba steps out of his car at a campaign stop during the run-up to the May 1960 parliamentary elections. More than a hundred political parties put up candidates, but Lumumba's political party, the National Congolese Movement, emerged from the elections as the largest political party in the Belgian Congo. He became the Congo's first prime minister when it gained its independence on June 30.

THE BRUSSELS ROUND TABLE CONFERENCE. Instead of making concrete plans for Congolese independence, the Belgian colonial authorities busied themselves with plans for the 1959 election of municipal councils, an exercise that was becoming increasingly irrelevant because the major political parties, such as Lumumba's CNM and the Kongo Association, had decided to boycott it. In order to start a serious conversation about independence, the Belgian Socialist Party (which was the major opposition party in the Belgian parliament) called for an extended discussion about independence between high-ranking members of the Belgian government and the major Congolese party leaders and chiefs. The **Brussels Round Table Conference**, as that discussion was called, convened on January 20, 1960. Because the conference had no official standing, its organizers hoped for little more than to hear everybody out and perhaps kick around some ideas. The Belgian delegates came to the conference with no real plan of their own and were surprised to find that the Congolese delegates had met ahead of time to form a common front and speak with one voice. It would take a psychologist, or perhaps a professional poker player, to fully understand the dynamics of the meetings, but as the discussions continued, the stakes escalated, and momentum toward full independence increased. By the time the conference finished its work on February 20, the Belgians had agreed that the Congo would be granted its independence as of June 30, 1960, which was little more than 4 months away.

It is almost breathtaking to ponder how quickly the Belgian Congo went from a "colony forever" to an independent state. The uniqueness of its situation can be seen in comparison with Ghana and Guinea. In Ghana, Kwame Nkrumah had served as prime minister, with a majority of the seats in the National Assembly, for 6 years prior to Ghana's independence. In Guinea, Ahmed Sékou Touré had served as vice president, with a majority of the seats in the Territorial Assembly, for over a year prior to independence. The Belgian Congo, however, had 4 months to write a constitution, create government institutions and ministries, and organize its first-ever national parliamentary elections. Historians have made much of the fact that on the day of its independence, the Congo had only 16 university graduates, but it is perhaps more pertinent to note that none of the delegates to the Round Table Conference had any experience with democratic political institutions or with running a modern bureaucratic state.

While the leaders of the major Congolese political parties were busy creating a representative government and campaigning for the May elections, the Belgians called for a second Round Table Conference in Brussels—this one to discuss economic issues. The Congolese delegates to this conference were mostly young, inexperienced people who knew very little about economics or finance, whereas the Belgian delegates were, in the words of one delegate, "the great white sharks of Belgian finance." This time, the Belgians knew exactly what they wanted. First, Belgian companies operating in the Congo that had been incorporated under the lax Congo laws received the right to reincorporate under Belgian law so that a future Congolese government could not regulate or nationalize them. Second, the stocks owned by the Congo colonial government would not be transferred to the independent government, but rather to a joint Belgian-Congolese development company. Third, the Special Katanga Committee, a government agency that had oversight over the copper mining industry, was disbanded. One Congolese delegate reported feeling like "one of those cowboys in a Western who lets himself be bamboozled time and time again by professional con men." The Congolese had won the political round table, but had lost the economic one.

TOWARD INDEPENDENCE. When the first national parliamentary election was held in late May, more than a hundred political parties put up candidates. Most of the seats were won by candidates from ethnic or regional parties, leading to a highly splintered parliament. Lumumba's Congolese National Movement was its largest single party, with 33 seats out of 137 (no other party had more than 12). In the complex negotiations to form a government in the Congo's newly created parliamentary system, Patrice Lumumba became the prime minister, and Joseph Kasavubu, the leader of the Kongo Association (which represented the inhabitants of the former Kongo Kingdom), became the president. It is an interesting historical footnote that Kasavubu was now the president of a state that was more than 30 times larger than the old Kongo Kingdom.

Why did the Belgians give up the Congo so quickly after dragging their feet for so long? For one thing, independence in Ghana and Guinea had created expectations among the educated and urban Congolese that their turn was coming. Second, the riots in Kinshasa and other Congo cities had convinced the Belgian government that suppressing popular aspirations could be a bloody, expensive, and ultimately futile effort. The ongoing war in Algeria gave it a glimpse of what its colonial future might look like. Third, Belgian public opinion was largely indifferent to the Congo. The Congo had originally been the personal colony of King Leopold II, and the Belgian government had taken it over in 1908 only after being assured that it would not cost the Belgian treasury any money. The colonial project had never been popular with the Belgian people. Fourth, the Belgian government believed that it could protect the profits of the Belgian companies operating in the Congo even after independence, and that Belgium would benefit financially from having the companies incorporate under Belgian law.

COUNTERCURRENTS IN THE SOUTHERN THIRD OF AFRICA

1960 was a banner year for independence in Africa, as 17 former British, French, and Belgian colonies became sovereign and independent nations. Ralph Bunche, the African American diplomat who was the undersecretary of the United Nations, proclaimed 1960 "the year of Africa." More decolonization followed during the 1960s, and by 1968, 43 African colonies had emerged as independent countries. But not all of Africa was moving toward independence. Very different processes were under way in the southern third of Africa. In the Portuguese colonies of Angola and Mozambique, there was a renewed push to attract European settlers. In South Africa and Zimbabwe, the white-dominated governments proclaimed their independence from their colonial overlords, but they did so in a way that suppressed the rights of the black majority instead of enhancing them. For most Africans living in the southern third of Africa, the prospects of eventual self-government seemed to be growing dimmer with each passing year.

Portuguese Resistance to African Independence

In the aftermath of World War II, Portugal amended its constitution to reclassify its colonies as "overseas provinces" in order to keep the United Nations from interfering with them and to forestall any talk of eventual independence. The Portuguese dictator Antonio Salazar adopted the concept of **Luso-tropicalism**, which had been developed by the Brazilian sociologist Gilberto Freyre. The basic idea of Luso-tropicalism was that Portugal had been a multicultural and multicontinental nation since the fifteenth century, and that the loss of its overseas territories would therefore represent a dismemberment of the Portuguese nation itself. Freyre was invited to visit President Salazar in Portugal in 1951, and his theories were taught in the School of Colonial Administration in Lisbon.

Portugal's postwar development plans for its African colonies differed from those of the other major colonial powers in that they were primarily aimed at attracting more Portuguese settlers. In Angola, the Portuguese upgraded the roads, bridges, airfields, railways, and harbors in order to attract white settlers from Portugal's poverty-stricken rural hinterlands and urban slums. As a result, the settler population of Angola expanded from 80,000 to nearly 200,000 during the 1950s. Some of those settlers started coffee plantations on land confiscated from Africans, who were reduced to landless plantation workers, making Angola one of the four largest coffee producers in the world. In Mozambique, the Portuguese focused on building large dams on the Limpopo and Zambezi Rivers to generate electricity (much of which was sold to Zimbabwe and South Africa) and to provide water for irrigated agricultural settlements. Portuguese settlers were given free passage to Mozambique, where they received extensive grants and loans to get established. As a result, the white settler population of Mozambique doubled during the 1950s from 50,000 to 100,000. It was clear that the Portuguese were not planning to grant self-government to their African colonies in the foreseeable future.

Apartheid in South Africa

South Africa was a self-governing dominion within the British Commonwealth, governed by and for the white minority. In the years following World War II, Africans flocked to the urban centers in search of work, causing the urban population to rise from 1.7 million in 1946 to more than 2 million in 1951. With housing in short supply, shantytowns with makeshift dwellings of corrugated iron and cardboard sprang up on the fringes of cities. More than 100,000 people, for example, were living on the fringes of Johannesburg, where clean water, sanitation, and health facilities were scarce.

With the 1948 elections approaching, the campaign of the National Party, which represented white supremacists and Boer nationalists, used a crudely racist message to spread fear of "the black menace" among the all-white electorate. It promised to implement a program called **apartheid**, the Boer word for "apartness" or "separateness." The term is somewhat misleading because the goal was never to keep the races completely apart: white-owned businesses, mines, and farms could not function without black labor, and most white households could not function without black servants. Under apartheid, black and white South Africans would continue to interact on a daily basis, but always in situations in which the whites dominated.

The Apartheid Laws

The apartheid system, instituted when the National Party came to power after the 1948 elections, was based on the unequal division of land between Africans and white settlers. Ever since the 1913 Natives Land Act (see chapter 11), Africans had been allowed to own land only in specially designated native reserves, which made up only 13 percent of South Africa's land, even though Africans made up 80 percent of its population. The new apartheid laws built on this fundamental inequality. The Bantu Authorities Act of 1951 authorized the government to appoint chiefs and headmen in the native reserves to allocate land and enforce laws, thus creating a colonial-style system of indirect rule over the portion of the African population that was living in the reserves. The Pass Law Act of 1952 required every black South African to carry a passbook at all times while in a designated white area. Every change of employment or residence had to be approved by the authorities and recorded in the passbook. People who failed to keep their passbook up to date could be fined or imprisoned. Convictions for pass law violations rose from 232,000 in 1951 to 414,000 in 1959.

Other laws also enforced inequality. The Population Registration Act of 1950 required everyone in South Africa to register as either White, Native, or Colored (mixed-race), and those in the Native category had to designate a government-approved "tribe." The Group Areas Act of 1950 divided urban areas into racially exclusive zones. Any Africans living in areas zoned for whites were forcibly removed. One of the biggest removal campaigns was in Sophiatown, a suburb of Johannesburg, from which over 50,000 Africans were forcibly relocated in 1955. The Bantu Education Act of 1953 shut down the mission schools for Africans and replaced them with government-run schools that prepared young people for menial or low-level jobs. The minister of native affairs, Hendrik Verwoerd (who later became prime minister) explained that "the natives will be taught from childhood to realize that equality with Europeans is not for them." These and other apartheid laws were designed to make sure that even though black and white South Africans lived in the same country, they inhabited different worlds.

Black Opposition to Apartheid

In response to the apartheid laws, the **African National Congress (ANC)**, the major African rights organization in South Africa, organized its Defiance Campaign in 1952. The campaign marked a militant turn for the ANC, which had previously relied on petitions and delegations. The campaign was based on the principles of nonviolent civil disobedience developed by Mohandas K. Gandhi during his 21 years in South Africa. (Although Gandhi is best known as the father of India's independence, his tactics were developed earlier in South Africa.) Volunteers in khaki uniforms with black, green, and gold lapel ribbons (a symbol of African nationalism) defied the apartheid laws by entering areas reserved for whites, sitting in whites-only cafés, and burning their passbooks in public. When they were arrested, they refused to pay a fine to get out of jail. Using the slogan, "No bail, no defense, no fine," the resisters sought to overload the prisons and courts in order to strain the apartheid machinery to the breaking point. The leader of the resisters was a young Johannesburg lawyer named **Nelson Mandela**, who was president of the ANC Youth League. As the "volunteer-in-chief" of the Defiance Campaign, Mandela acquired a driver's license in March 1952 so that he could become a "one-man taxi service" for the ANC resisters.

The Defiance Campaign began on April 6, 1952, the 300th anniversary of the arrival of the first white settlers in South Africa. In the peak month of September, some 2,500 resisters were arrested in 24 cities and towns. Although the uniformed resisters were well disciplined, their activities inspired mass demonstrations in the cities of Port Elizabeth and East London that were harder to control. When police fired on the demonstrators, the protests turned violent, and rioters began burning municipal buildings and attacking white people. Seeing that the demonstrations had gotten out of hand, the ANC leadership called off the Defiance Campaign at the end of the year. By then, over 8,000 resisters had been arrested, and paid membership in the ANC had risen from 7,000 to over 100,000.

The failure of the Defiance Campaign to achieve any meaningful reform, and the subsequent arrest of 20 ANC leaders, left the organization without a clear plan for the future. To clarify its goals, the ANC joined with several other anti-apartheid organizations (including white and Asian groups) in 1955 to approve a document known as the **Freedom Charter**. It opened with the statement, "South Africa belongs to all who live in it, black and white." The most striking feature of the Freedom Charter was its multiracial character: it proclaimed equal status for all national groups and races, and it guaranteed human rights for all. It also called for a strong national government to redistribute land among all those who worked on it and to nationalize the mines, banks, and heavy industry. Some black activists rejected the multiracial approach of the Freedom Charter and formed a rival organization called the Pan-Africanist Congress (PAC), which celebrated African identity. In his inaugural address in 1959, PAC founder Robert Sobukwe made reference to the nationalist movements springing up across Africa and said, "We aim, politically, at government of the Africans, by the Africans, for the Africans, with everybody who owes his loyalty to Africa and who is prepared to accept the democratic rule of the majority being regarded as an African." Whereas the ANC sought equal status for all races, the PAC preferred a clear subordination of whites and Asians to the black majority.

MANDELA & TAMBO, ATTORNEYS Nelson Mandela as a young lawyer in his law office in Johannesburg, South Africa, where he provided affordable or free legal representation to black South Africans who ran afoul of the apartheid laws. Nelson Mandela and his law partner, Oliver Tambo, had been founding members of the ANC Youth League in 1943.

A rivalry soon developed between the ANC and the PAC. When the ANC announced plans to hold a series of nationwide demonstrations on March 31, 1960, while simultaneously sending delegations to meet with government leaders and local authorities, the leaders of the PAC called their own massive protests for March 21, 10 days earlier. PAC supporters assembled at police stations across

THE SHARPEVILLE MASSACRE South African demonstrators protesting passbook laws at Sharpeville on March 21, 1960, flee from police who opened fire on the crowd. Most of the dead and wounded were shot in the back as they fled. The Sharpeville massacre marked the beginning of a government offensive against black activist groups.

the country without their passbooks so that the police would have to arrest them. Most of the demonstrations were peaceful, but at Sharpeville, where 300 police faced a crowd of 5,000 protesters, a scuffle broke out between police and demonstrators. When several of the demonstrators began to throw rocks at the police, some of the police began firing into the crowd. By the time the gunfire stopped, 69 Africans were dead and 180 were wounded, most of them shot in the back as they tried to flee. Later that day, a similar incident took place near Cape Town, some 750 miles to the south, where police fired into a crowd of 6,000, killing 2 and setting off a riot. A week later, the white government introduced legislation to declare the ANC and PAC illegal organizations and rounded up over 18,000 ANC and PAC activists nationwide. Most were released after several months, but both the ANC and the PAC had been crippled.

Homelands and Separate Development

At the same time that the African colonies in the northern two-thirds of Africa were gaining their independence, the all-white electorate in South Africa voted in 1961 to cease being a self-governing dominion within the British Commonwealth and to instead become an independent republic with no formal ties to the Commonwealth. Instead of bringing new rights to the African population, South Africa's independence gave the white government more leeway to implement its new program of "separate development," which was, in effect, phase two of the apartheid system. The former native reserves were renamed "tribal homelands" and were slated to become semiautonomous, self-governing entities that would eventually be given full independence. Although the South African government was mimicking the discourse of independence going on elsewhere in Africa, its real purpose was to create a miniature South African colonial empire within its borders, because none of the homelands was large enough to be viable as an independent country. The largest homeland consisted of a series of disconnected territories that occupied a total of 17,000 square miles, while the smallest occupied only 3,000 square miles.

To implement the new separate development policy, the white government launched a massive campaign of ethnic cleansing that eventually forced as many as 3.5 million black South Africans from their land. People who worked for white employers were relocated to designated black residential areas, while many others were sent to the overcrowded homelands, even if they had never lived there before. The relocation campaign was followed by the Black Homelands Citizenship Act, which cancelled the South African citizenship of all black South Africans and made them officially citizens of one of the homelands, regardless of where they lived. Many people had never set foot in the homeland to which they were assigned. All black South Africans living in the white-controlled areas of South Africa thus become foreigners with no political rights.

The separate development program was launched at a time when the ANC was still reeling from the arrests and detentions in the wake of the Sharpeville massacre. Its efforts to bring about change by nonviolent means had failed. Rather than turn the ANC into a violent organization, it established a separate organization called Spear of the Nation, which would conduct campaigns of sabotage against South Africa's economic and administrative infrastructure. It was headed by Nelson Mandela. To prepare for the sabotage campaign, some fighters went to China to train in guerilla warfare, and Mandela himself spent time at a guerilla warfare training camp in Algeria. Spear of the Nation opened its campaign of sabotage in December 1961 with bombings in three cities. Over the next 18 months, the group carried out some 200 acts of sabotage. The main targets were electric pylons, post offices, jails, railway signals, and Bantu Administration offices.

The white government fought back against the sabotage campaign by detaining people without charge for long periods, using torture to extract information, and sending spies to infiltrate the organization. Nelson Mandela was arrested in August 1962, and the other Spear of the Nation leaders were captured a year later on a farm near Johannesburg. They were sentenced to life in prison for sabotage and taken to Robben Island, a tiny prison island 4 miles off the coast from Cape Town. Mandela would remain on Robben Island for 18 years before being transferred to another prison. At the time of Mandela's sentencing in 1964, the ANC leadership was decimated, and the apartheid state seemed stronger than ever. Independence for South Africa had brought heightened repression to the African population.

Zimbabwe's Unilateral Declaration of Independence

Zimbabwe, South Africa's northern neighbor, was a British colony led by white settlers under an arrangement that the British called "responsible government." Although Zimbabwe had a population of only 220,000 whites and 3.8 million Africans, the white settlers occupied more than 50 percent of the land. Zimbabwe was governed by an all-white Legislative Council. Africans were not excluded from voting, but income and property qualifications meant that only 380 Africans were eligible to vote in 1953. A new constitution, adopted in 1961, called for a Legislative Assembly of 65 members, 15 of whom were Africans, but strict income, property, and education requirements still regulated which Africans were allowed to vote. Armed with its new constitution, Zimbabwe's white settler government requested independence from Britain in 1964.

The British denied the settlers' request for independence, demanding immediate improvement in the political status of the African population, progress toward ending racial discrimination, and evidence that the plans for independence were acceptable to the population as a whole. In response, Zimbabwe's prime minister, Ian Smith, secured the support of the traditional chiefs and called an election, in which his Rhodesian Front party won all 50 of the white seats in the Legislative Assembly. When the British found those actions inadequate, Smith threatened to declare independence from Britain unilaterally. The British responded that such a declaration would be "an open act of defiance and rebellion" that no British Commonwealth nation would recognize. After further inconclusive negotiations, Ian Smith issued a **Unilateral Declaration of Independence (UDI)** on November 11, 1965. The British refused to recognize Zimbabwe's independence, but did nothing to stop it.

As in South Africa, national independence in Zimbabwe brought new repression to the African population. Even before Ian Smith announced his Unilateral Declaration of Independence, the white government had arrested the leaders of the two major African political parties for speaking out against it, and some of the

Africans who opposed the UDI were already traveling to other countries for training in guerilla warfare. Smith boasted that African majority rule would not come in a thousand years, but events would prove otherwise.

CONCLUSION

The dozen or so years between 1956 and 1968 saw an astonishing reversal in the political status of the Africans living under colonial rule, as 43 colonies emerged as independent countries. Historians are still struggling to understand how such a massive transition happened so quickly. To find an answer, we need to consider both the circumstances of the colonial powers and the circumstances in Africa. Once Britain, France, and Belgium had embraced postwar policies of development instead of the simple extraction of resources—the "skimming economy," as the Belgians called it—they began to realize that bringing their colonies up to speed in terms of transportation, education, public health, urban infrastructure, and agricultural production would be costly. Yet having started down that path, they could not reverse their course without paying a heavy political price, both in the colonies and in international opinion. One could argue that, at a certain point, it was advantageous for them to walk away and leave the challenges to African leaders, even though the Africans had far fewer resources at their disposal. After all, a variety of British, French, and Belgian companies were firmly implanted in the African colonies, and they would continue to send African raw materials and agricultural products to Europe, just as before.

Meanwhile, in Africa, there were growing signs of discontent. The prolonged rebellions in Algeria and Kenya against the abuses propagated by white settlers demonstrated that maintaining the colonial status quo would be costly in lives and treasure. The postwar upswing in labor unrest in the cities, where workers demanded equal pay for equal work, and in unrest in the countryside, where the agricultural practices of the second colonial occupation were facing increased resistance, convinced the colonial powers that rebellions, strikes, and rural unrest would become increasingly costly to contain. Another important factor was a new group of African political leaders, such as Kwame Nkrumah in Ghana and Ahmed Sékou Touré in Guinea, who showed themselves to be adept at organizing political parties and mobilizing popular opinion in favor of self-government. These leaders thus presented a viable alternative to the increasingly obsolete system of colonial rule by faceless colonial bureaucrats and traditional chiefs. The major exception was the Congo, where the Belgians at first resisted decolonization and then decided to leave the colony on only 4 months' notice, with no idea who would replace them. In all cases, however, the timing and form of independence arose from the complex interplay between African assertiveness and colonial repositioning.

Independence came in two waves during the 1950s and 1960s. The first wave swept across North Africa, where Libya became independent in 1951 as a result of the Italian defeat in World War II, Britain withdrew its military forces from Egypt in 1954, Sudan, Tunisia, and Morocco gained independence in 1956, and Algeria's war of liberation was finally resolved by its independence in 1962. The second wave was in tropical Africa, where Ghana gained independence from Britain in 1957, Guinea gained independence from France in 1958, and the Congo gained independence from Belgium in 1960. These events seemed to open the floodgates to Independence Day ceremonies in colonies all over tropical Africa.

In the southern third of Africa, however, the trend toward independence ran into several obstacles. The first was Portugal's dictator, Antonio Salazar, who saw the Portuguese colonies as essential to Portugal's prestige as a world power. To foreclose any possibility that Portugal's African colonies would ever become independent, he amended the Portuguese constitution to change the status of the colonies to "overseas provinces" and made a push to attract more white settlers. The second obstacle was the white settlers in South Africa and Zimbabwe, who dominated those colonies' export economies and sought to protect their privileged access to land and cheap labor. Instead of moving toward greater rights for the black majorities, the white settler minorities in South Africa and Zimbabwe declared themselves independent from Britain in order to continue and even enhance their domination over those majorities. It was this situation that created the conditions for the coming third wave of independence in Africa.

CHAPTER REVIEW

KEY TERMS AND VOCABULARY

Atlantic Charter
Mau Mau rebellion
Battle of Algiers
Gamal Abdel Nasser
Kwame Nkrumah
Ahmed Sékou Touré
Patrice Lumumba
Brussels Round Table Conference
Luso-tropicalism
apartheid
African National Congress (ANC)
Nelson Mandela
Freedom Charter
Unilateral Declaration of Independence (UDI)

STUDY QUESTIONS

1. What were the key differences between British and French policies regarding independence for their African colonies?
2. Why did the Mau Mau rebellion in Kenya find support in both the Kikuyu reserve and the city of Nairobi?
3. How do you explain the complete victory of the Congolese nationalists at the first Brussels Round Table Conference in 1960?
4. Why did the Portuguese resist independence for their African colonies?
5. What were the major elements of the apartheid system in South Africa?
6. Why did the ANC in South Africa turn to armed violence?
7. In what ways did the presence of white settlers in certain colonies make the path to African independence more difficult?

MAU MAU'S DAUGHTER

Wambui Waiyaki Otieno was the daughter of the first African to be the chief inspector of police in colonial Kenya. She was educated at mission schools and had planned to pursue her education in England before the British declaration of a state of emergency in 1952 changed her life. At the age of 18, she ran away from home to join the Mau Mau supporters in Nairobi. She became a spy and a scout for the insurgents and helped them plan their operations. In her memoir, she sketched out the crucial role of women in Kenya's anti-colonial struggle.

I furnished the relevant information to the Mau Mau, and the subsequent battle became the biggest the Mau Mau had ever launched against a colonial installation. It came to be known as "The Great Battle of Naivasha" and is still remembered by many. The whites and their collaborators died in large numbers, for we had taken them completely unawares. Many died at the hands of Muiru, who had strategically positioned himself at a vantage point. He felled the enemy one by one as they unsuspectingly ran into his trap. He was later captured and detained. The fight spilled from the station precincts into the surrounding areas. As a result, many squatters in the Rift Valley farms suspected of aiding the movement by scouting and spying were later deported to remote areas.

Scouting or gathering intelligence was not a simple task, and the War Council knew that without scouts no war would be waged or won. As I mentioned before, scouts had to be women for various reasons. Women normally look innocent and are able to change with every setting. Scouting in war is really espionage or the transportation of vital information or valuable items from one location to another; scouts also had to see to the maintenance of our weapons.

A spy had to go to an area that the fighters intended to attack and find out all the essential details. Such a place could be near a police station or a Home Guard post. One would first have to make friends, find out the comings and goings thereabouts, and then assess the situation: Did the officers drink exceptionally heavily? Or were they fascinated by women? Who posed no threat after what specific hours? How many officers would remain aware of their surroundings after specific hours?

All these sundry details would have to be unearthed before a scout could report to the War Council. These reports had to be precise, as a small mistake could cause the fighters to incur heavy losses. The scouts were the ones who arranged the whole attack, including details such as the number of attackers required and the weapons to be used, from which direction to attack, and in which direction to run in case of trouble. Even the place of retreat for regrouping was decided upon by the scout. It had to be a hideout that could not be discovered. If the program failed, the results were disastrous and it would be blamed on the particular scout who had planned it.

The reader might infer from my narratives that scouting was an easy job. To the contrary, it was an occupation full of unpredictable pitfalls with danger lurking in every corner. Scouts lived from day to day, as one wrong move could mean death.

1. *In what specific ways did Wambui Waiyaki Otieno aid the Mau Mau rebellion?*
2. *Why does she say that women made the best scouts?*

Source: Wambui Waiyaki Otieno, *Mau Mau's Daughter: A Life History*, edited by Cora Ann Presley (Boulder, CO: Lynne Rienner, 1998), pp. 42–43.

FUTURE CONSTITUTIONAL DEVELOPMENT IN THE COLONIES

On January 28, 1957, British prime minister Harold Macmillan asked the Colonial Policy Committee to submit an estimate of "the probable course of constitutional development in the colonies over the years ahead." Eight months later, the committee submitted its report; at the top was the word "SECRET." Ghana is not mentioned because it was already independent.

1. The Prime Minister asked that an estimate should be made of the probable course of constitutional development in the Colonies in the years ahead, and that this study should set out the economic, political and strategic considerations for and against the grant of independence.

4. (a) Independence
The following territories are likely to obtain independence within, and become candidates for membership of, the Commonwealth within the next ten years: Federation of Malaya, in August 1957; Nigeria, perhaps in 1960 or 1961 (or quite soon thereafter); West Indies Federation, perhaps in 1963; Central African Federation (after 1960); Singapore, if it joins the Federation of Malaya.

(b) Internal Self-Government
The following territories, listed geographically, appear the most likely to show significant developments in internal self-government during the next ten years: Singapore, Cyprus, Gibraltar, Kenya, Uganda, Tanganyika, Zanzibar, Sierra Leone, The Gambia, Aden Colony, Somaliland Protectorate, Mauritius, British Guiana, and British Honduras. Malta has had internal self-government for ten years, and the integration scheme would maintain this arrangement. . . .

6. (a) Budgetary implications for the United Kingdom. Ministers have decided against any regular pattern of Government-to-Government aid for independent Commonwealth countries, and by corollary against embarking on new schemes in such countries.

(b) Effect on flow of investment funds from the United Kingdom. Grants made available under the Colonial Development & Welfare Acts in the current period (1955–60) to all Colonial Governments account for only one-sixth of their expenditure on development. The remaining five-sixths are being found from their own resources and external loans.

(e) Effect on United Kingdom trade. The Colonies are of considerable trade importance to the United Kingdom. In 1956 United Kingdom exports to the Colonies were valued at £422 million or 13 percent of total United Kingdom exports. In 1956 the United Kingdom imported from the Colonies goods to the value of £376 million or 10 percent of the United Kingdom's total imports.

Any premature transfer of power which resulted in serious political troubles and a lasting deterioration in a territory's economic circumstances would of course seriously affect United Kingdom trading and financial interest in that territory. On the other hand, assuming an orderly transfer of power and no appreciable falling off in a territory's economic activity, the grant of independence need not adversely affect the United Kingdom's trading position in the territory concerned.

1. *What is the report's recommendation for giving development grants to colonies after they gain their independence?*
2. *What are the predicted economic effects of the colonies' independence on the British economy?*

Source: "Future Constitutional Development in the Colonies: Memorandum for Cabinet Colonial Policy Committee by Sir N. Brook, 6 September, 1957." In *The Conservative Government and the End of Empire, 1957–1964*, edited by Ronald Hyam and Roger Louis, series A, vol. 4 of *British Documents on the End of Empire*, edited by S. R. Ashton and A. N. Porter (London: The Stationery Office), pp. 29–34.

PERSPECTIVES

REJECTING THE FRENCH COMMUNITY

The party conference of the Guinea branch of the African Democratic Rally, held in Conakry on September 14, 1958, shook the French Community when it decided to reject the new French constitution and seek immediate independence. Bocar Biro Barry was a young activist in the teachers' union who attended the conference. In 1991, he recounted the scene to historian Elizabeth Schmidt. He begins by referencing the visit of a delegation sent by Félix Houphouët-Boigny, the party leader from Côte d'Ivoire, which flew in to persuade Sékou Touré to vote in favor of France.

It was there that things were played out. That was the day fixed for the territorial congress to decide if one must vote "Yes" or "No." It was there that Houphouët sent a delegation—to plead with Sékou to vote "Yes." He wanted all the territories of the RDA [African Democratic Rally]—Conakry, Bamako, Niamey, Abidjan, Cotonou—to vote "Yes" to please General de Gaulle. Afterwards, one would see about independence.

So, this delegation arrived here at the airport at 10 o'clock in the morning. They went to the Territorial Assembly building. The congress of Boulbinet was at the port of Boulbinet—there where the people fish. There was an old hangar there—a place where they smoked the fish. That is where they held the congress. . . .

He [Sékou] arrived at the territorial congress after the delegation's departure. We—the young people, the teachers' union—we were in the room, impatient. We said to ourselves, "The delegation of Houphouët is there. It is to corrupt Sékou. If he ever accepts to vote 'Yes,' we will liquidate him." That was whispered amongst ourselves in the conference room. All the secretaries-general were there—it was a territorial congress for which all the political leaders had been called to Conakry. All the subsections were led by teachers. There was an overwhelming majority of teachers, of young people. The youth of Guinea and the FEANF [Federation of Black African Students in France] were there. We were there, side by side with the trade unions and the youth movements. All of us, we were for the "No."

He arrived toward one o'clock. It was hot. Everyone was irritable. He arrived in the room. As soon as he entered, everyone cried, "No!" I still remember as if it were today. Everyone cried, "NO, NO, NO, NO, NO!" We were all sure that he had been led astray by Houphouët's delegation. He arrived. He sat down, calmly at first. The people continued to cry, "NO, NO, NO, NO, NO, NO!" He rose. He began to speak.

The conference lasted five minutes. Because he was a great maneuverer, a great opportunist, he saw which way the wind was blowing, and he said to himself, "If I say the other thing, they are going to liquidate me." So, he said, "The 28th of September, we must vote. What will be the vote of the *Parti Démocratique de Guinée*?" The people cried, "NO, NO, NO, NO, NO, NO!" There we were. He saw that the atmosphere was for the "No." It was at this moment that he changed sides. . . . The teachers' union, the youth movement, and the students could have cast Sékou Touré aside for Koumandian Kéïta. That was what frightened Sékou.

1. *List the different groups that attended the meeting in Boulbinet.*
2. *How did the activists persuade Sékou Touré that the ADR should vote No in the constitutional referendum?*

Source: Bocar Biro Barry, oral testimony, January 21, 1991, quoted in Elizabeth Schmidt, *Cold War and Decolonization in Guinea, 1946–1958* (Athens: Ohio University Press, 2007), pp. 160–161.

NELSON MANDELA'S SPEECH FROM THE DOCK

Nelson Mandela had been in prison for 2 years for inciting workers to strike when he was put on trial, along with 19 other ANC leaders, in 1964. As the first of the group to be tried, he opened his defense by saying, "I am the first of the accused." He then followed up with a speech that was nearly 3 hours long. Many historians believe that the "Rivonia Trial Speech," as it is called, was the most important speech he ever gave. In this excerpt, he outlines the destructive impact of the apartheid system on black South Africans.

The lack of human dignity experienced by Africans is the direct result of the policy of white supremacy. White supremacy implies black inferiority. Legislation designed to preserve white supremacy entrenches this notion. Menial tasks in South Africa are invariably performed by Africans. When anything has to be carried or cleaned the white man will look around for an African to do it for him, whether the African is employed by him or not.

Because of this sort of attitude, whites tend to regard Africans as a separate breed. They do not look upon them as people with families of their own; they do not realize that they have emotions—that they fall in love like white people do; that they want to be with their wives and children like white people want to be with theirs; that they want to earn enough money to support their families properly, to feed and clothe them and send them to school. And what "house-boy" or "garden-boy" or laborer can ever hope to do this?

Pass laws, which to the Africans are among the most hated bits of legislation in South Africa, render any African liable to police surveillance at any time. I doubt whether there is a single African male in South Africa who has not at some stage had a brush with the police over his pass. Hundreds and thousands of Africans are thrown into jail each year under pass laws. Even worse than this is the fact that pass laws keep husband and wife apart and lead to the breakdown of family life. . . .

Africans want to be paid a living wage. Africans want to perform work which they are capable of doing, and not work which the Government declares them to be capable of. Africans want to be allowed to live where they obtain work, and not be endorsed out of an area because they were not born there. Africans want to be allowed to own land in places where they work, and not to be obliged to live in rented houses which they can never call their own. Africans want to be part of the general population, and not confined to living in their own ghettoes. African men want to have their wives and children to live with them where they work, and not be forced into an unnatural existence in men's hostels. African women want to be with their menfolk and not be left permanently widowed in the Reserves.

Africans want to be allowed out after eleven o'clock at night and not to be confined to their rooms like little children. Africans want to be allowed to travel in their own country and to seek work where they want to and not where the Labor Bureau tells them to. Africans want a just share in the whole of South Africa; they want security and a stake in society. Above all, we want equal political rights, because without them our disabilities will be permanent. I know this sounds revolutionary to the whites in this country, because the majority of voters will be Africans. This makes the white man fear democracy.

1. *What did Nelson Mandela list as the most destructive aspects of the apartheid system?*
2. *According to Mandela's speech, what did the Africans want?*

Source: "Nelson Mandela's Statement from the Dock at the Opening of the Defense Case in the Rivonia Trial, April 20, 1964," Nelson Mandela Foundation, accessed January 12, 2017, http://db.nelsonmandela.org/speeches/pub_view.asp?pg=item&ItemID=NMS010; reprinted as "Read the Most Important Speech Nelson Mandela Ever Gave," *Washington Post*, December 5, 2013.

SOCIALIST SOLIDARITY A rally celebrating the solidarity of Angola and Cuba in 1977, just 2 years after the Marxist-oriented MPLA took over the government of independent Angola. The large portrait on the left shows Agostinho Neto, the first president of Angola, and the one on the right shows Cuban president Fidel Castro. By the end of 1975, 25,000 Cuban troops were in Angola to assist the Neto regime in its civil war against UNITA, which was backed by the United States and white-ruled South Africa. The civil war in Angola thus reflected the global politics of the Cold War.

1961
Murder of Patrice Lumumba

1966
Ouster of Kwame Nkrumah in Ghana

1967
Tanzania adopts African socialism

15

AFRICA IN A BIPOLAR WORLD, 1960–1990

African countries were gaining their independence at a time when the Cold War was in full flower across the globe. The Communist Party under Mao Zedong had taken over China in 1949; a communist movement led by Ho Chi Minh had driven the French out of Vietnam in 1954; and in 1959, Fidel Castro led a successful communist revolution in Cuba, some 90 miles from the United States. Communism and capitalist democracy were not just competing ideologies, but two heavily armed camps that could support or topple governments and also assist or defeat anti-colonial rebellions. The United States, the Soviet Union, and China all saw Africa as a Cold War battleground in which the emerging African nations were either potential allies or potential enemies.

The political environment of the Cold War provided opportunities for African governments and liberation movements in two major ways. First, in countries that had recently gained their independence, the governments could choose between following a capitalist path that favored free markets and sought investments from large international companies or following a socialist path by which the government formulated development plans and oversaw their implementation. The former European colonial powers and the Americans pressured African governments to follow the capitalist path, whereas the Soviet Union and China gave support to governments that followed the socialist path. Second, the Cold War offered African liberation movements and newly independent governments

1974	1975	1980
The Derg takes over in Ethiopia	Portuguese colonies gain independence	Independence for Zimbabwe

opportunities for military support. This effect was seen mostly in southern Africa, where Russia and China were major supporters of armed liberation movements, whereas the United States and South Africa supported groups that favored a capitalist orientation. Given the intense global competition between capitalism and communism, almost any government policy could be interpreted as favoring one side or another.

COLD WAR COMPETITION IN CONGO-KINSHASA

An early manifestation of Cold War rivalry in Africa could be seen in the events that followed the Belgian Congo's independence from Belgium. The new nation (known today as the Democratic Republic of the Congo, or Congo-Kinshasa for short) became independent on June 30, 1960. Its constitution, which was based loosely on the Belgian parliamentary system, called for a prime minister, who was the head of the government, and a president, who held the largely ceremonial position of head of state. The position of Congolese prime minister went to Patrice Lumumba, whose political party had won the most seats in the pre-independence election. Six days after independence, the Congolese army revolted against their Belgian officers, plunging the country into chaos and prompting the Belgian soldiers who had not yet left the Congo to begin a re-occupation of their former colony. Six days after that came the **Katanga secession**, in which the copper-rich province of Katanga, which provided much of the Congolese government's revenue, declared itself an independent country and asked for Belgian protection. The chief of staff of the Belgian army arrived in Katanga 2 days later to organize its military forces with the help of Belgian paratroopers. At this point, the secessionist state of Katanga was being run cooperatively by Katangese politicians, the Belgian mining company Union Minière, and the Belgian army.

In response to the spiraling disintegration of the Congo, the United Nations Security Council passed a resolution that called on Belgium to withdraw its troops, but said nothing about ending Katanga's secession. In desperation, Prime Minister Lumumba sent a telegram to the Soviet Union asking it to intervene against the Belgians and end the secession of Katanga. The Soviet leader, Nikita Khrushchev, replied that the Soviet Union "would not hesitate to take resolute measures" if the "imperialist aggression" of the Belgians continued. When Lumumba's telegram was intercepted by the U.S. Central Intelligence Agency, the Congo suddenly became a new front in the Cold War.

In Washington, CIA director Allen Dulles was convinced that Lumumba was a communist, even though Lumumba himself denied it. The CIA had been deceived the previous year when it had accepted assurances from Cuban revolutionary leader Fidel Castro that he was not a communist, only to find out later that he had been lying all along. The agency did not want to get burned again. The CIA station chief in Kinshasa, Larry Devlin, feared that the Congo under Lumumba would follow the "Cuban path" and might pull all of equatorial Africa into the Soviet orbit. A more balanced judgment, however, came from other CIA analysts, who concluded that Lumumba was less of an ideologue than an opportunist. They suspected that he could be bought, but could not be counted on to stay bought.

By August, the Americans had decided that Lumumba had to go. At a meeting of the U.S. National Security Council in Washington on August 18, President Eisenhower gave the green light for his assassination. Even after Lumumba was ousted in a military coup by Colonel Joseph Mobutu, the army chief of staff, the CIA's assassination plot continued. "Lumumba in opposition is almost as dangerous as in office," wrote Larry Devlin. To assist Devlin in his plans, the CIA sent him an expert on untraceable poisons and two shadowy third-country nationals, code-named Rogue and Win, who could not be linked to the United States. Devlin came up with at least eight different schemes for assassinating Lumumba, but he found it difficult to get past the blue-helmeted U.N. soldiers who were guarding Lumumba's residence. After Lumumba was placed under house arrest by Colonel Mobutu, the CIA found it impossible to get to him without giving itself away.

During an unusually heavy tropical rainstorm on November 27, 1960, Lumumba escaped from his heavily guarded compound in the back of a car and headed for Kisangani, some 1,600 miles away, via a dirt road that ran through the tropical rainforest. His convoy was intercepted 4 days into the journey, while it waited for a ferry to cross the Sankuru River. Lumumba was returned to Kinshasa and held prisoner at a military camp for several weeks while the CIA, the Belgians, and Colonel Mobutu discussed what to do with him. They finally decided to send him to the breakaway state of Katanga, where he was considered an enemy because of his efforts to quell its secession. On January 17, 1961, he was flown to an airport in Katanga. When darkness fell, he was driven to a secluded spot in the wooded savanna and executed by a firing squad. In the end, it was the Katanga authorities and their Belgian allies who killed Patrice Lumumba, although it was done with American encouragement and approval.

Following the assassination, the United Nations took the lead in bringing Katanga back into the Congo. The Belgian paratroopers left, but Katanga used its substantial copper revenues to hire a motley assortment of mercenaries (including former members of the French Foreign Legion), who were trained by Belgian officers. United Nations troops invaded Katanga in August 1961, but their advance was stalled for over a year, until U.S. president John F. Kennedy pushed for a renewed offensive that ultimately proved successful. The reunited Congo became

LUMUMBA IN CAPTIVITY Hands tied behind his back, ousted Congolese prime minister Patrice Lumumba is roughly handled by Congolese soldiers in Kinshasa. He was later sent to the breakaway province of Katanga, where he was executed.

a U.S. client state, and it would remain so through the end of the Cold War. The elaborate plot to kill Lumumba showed just how much Cold War politics had intruded into African affairs.

THE FATE OF DEMOCRACY

The story of the Congo-Kinshasa crisis, replete with its military coup, political assassination, and foreign interference, foreshadowed the fates of many of the African countries that gained their independence in the 1950s and 1960s. By the end of the 1970s, only Botswana and Gambia had remained functioning multiparty democracies. In some cases, the dominant political party had declared the country to be a one-party state; in others, the president had assumed authoritarian powers and taken the title of "president for life"; and in still others, the original elected government had been overthrown by a military coup.

What happened to the hopeful affirmations of freedom and democracy that were proclaimed with such enthusiasm during the Independence Day ceremonies? Each country has its own story, but all of them share some common elements. First, the citizens of Africa's newly independent countries had no previous experience with multiparty democracy. Colonial rule had been highly autocratic, and even African chiefs had been reduced to transmitting and enforcing orders from the colonial administration. Although constitutions based loosely on the British, French, or Belgian parliamentary system were hastily drawn up prior to independence with the aid of a few nationalist leaders and chiefs, they were not grounded in a consensus of the citizenry. The movements for independence had been aimed more at getting rid of the colonial rulers than at installing a particular form of government to replace them.

Second, the postwar colonial states in Africa had been "development states" that were focused on issues of infrastructure and the economy. In that context, the nationalists saw independence first and foremost as a means to accelerate economic growth and achieve a fairer distribution of its benefits. For many citizens and government officials, better roads, schools, and health clinics were a higher priority than a functioning parliamentary democracy on the British or French model. Governments in newly independent countries could make the argument that multiparty elections created conflict at a time when the country needed to unite under a strong leader to work together for economic development and rising standards of living.

Third, the colonial system of indirect rule had precluded any spirit of national unity. Under indirect rule, each officially recognized ethnic group was governed by its own chiefs and judged according to its customary laws. As a result, there was little sense of loyalty or affection for the nation as a whole. People seeking political office could best mobilize support by working with their own ethnic group and speaking in their mother tongue, which led to the formation of political parties along ethnic and regional lines. Even political parties that courted a nationwide following often had an ethnic or regional base.

Under such fragmented conditions, economically favored regions of a country were tempted to secede in order to keep their wealth for themselves: the rich cocoa-producing region of Ghana sought a separate independence in 1956; the copper-rich Katanga province seceded from Congo-Kinshasa in 1960, as we've seen; and the oil-rich southeastern region of Nigeria seceded in 1967, forming the short-lived state of Biafra. All those attempts at secession failed, but they highlighted the artificial nature of the colonial boundaries and the fragile unity of the newly independent states. When African heads of state formed the Organization of African Unity in 1963, its charter called for respecting "the territorial integrity of each state." A resolution adopted a year later was more explicit, calling on the member states to "respect the frontiers existing on their achievement of national independence."

The fourth element was the Cold War. Authoritarian rulers could remain in power even after losing popular support if they had military and financial backing from outside countries. Staunchly anti-communist leaders could be assured of the backing of the United States or their former colonial overlords, whereas leaders who followed a socialist path could expect support from the Soviet Union or China. The newly independent countries of Africa provided the American, Soviet, and Chinese governments with an opportunity to demonstrate that their models of governance and development were superior to those of their adversaries. The Cold War rivals wanted their African allies to succeed and their African opponents to fail, even if it meant supporting repressive regimes or organizing military coups.

Authoritarianism in Ghana

The examples of Ghana and Senegal illustrate two different trajectories of democratic rule in the aftermath of independence. In the 1956 election leading up to Ghana's independence, the Convention People's Party (CPP), which favored a modern centralized government, faced strong opposition in the region occupied by the former Asante Empire. During the colonial period, the rulers of Asante had enjoyed a special status in the British system of indirect rule. They saw their hierarchy of traditional chiefs as the embodiment of Asante culture and tradition, and they sought to retain their privileges under the new government. When the CPP won the nationwide election with a total of 400,000 votes, compared with 300,000 votes for the Asante nationalists, the Asante leaders went to London in a futile effort to appeal for a separate independence. The struggle between the CPP and the Asante nationalists underlined the ethnic and regional divisions in the new country and revealed the particular challenges posed by a parliamentary democracy. Ghana's prime minister, Kwame Nkrumah, sought to overcome the disunity by increasing his own authority. Three years after Ghana became independent, he introduced a new constitution that declared Ghana a republic rather than a parliamentary democracy. That constitution replaced the position of prime minister, who governed through the parliament, with a president, who could rule by decree, appoint or dismiss government officials, and accept or reject legislation that the parliament passed. Nkrumah also implemented the Preventive Detention Act, which allowed the government to imprison people for up to 5 years on mere suspicion. Nkrumah had become, in effect, a constitutional dictator. The following year, he made an extended visit to China, the Soviet Union, and the communist

PRESIDENT OF GHANA Kwame Nkrumah is inaugurated as president of Ghana in 1960, after voters approved a new constitution making Ghana a republic with an executive presidency. He stands on a carved stool, which is reminiscent of the Golden Stool of the Asante kings and suggestive of his increasing authoritarianism. In 1964, he amended the new constitution to make himself "president for life."

nations of Eastern Europe to gather their support and get their advice for developing his country on a socialist model. In 1964, he organized a plebiscite, which many people believed was rigged, in order to declare Ghana a one-party state led by the CPP.

Nkrumah's assumption of authoritarian power was motivated in large part by his desire to advance his ambitious program for national development, which included restructuring the economy along socialist lines and greatly expanding schools, health facilities, and the country's infrastructure. The best way to reach those goals, he believed, was with a modern centralized government that was not encumbered by the "feudal backwardness" of traditional chiefs or by squabbles among political parties. His approach might have been tolerated by the Ghanaian people if his ambitious development programs had succeeded, but by 1964, the government was bankrupt and was financing its projects with high-interest loans from European banks.

Nkrumah also alienated the army by building his elite Presidential Guard into a well-equipped regiment commanded by Soviet officers, while common soldiers often struggled to acquire basic necessities such as boots and gas. In 1966, while Nkrumah was on a visit to North Vietnam and China, a group of police and army officers staged a military coup and took over the government. There is considerable circumstantial evidence that the American CIA assisted with the coup, although its exact role has never been confirmed. Kwame Nkrumah never returned to Ghana. He died of cancer in 1972 while undergoing treatment in Romania. The experience of Ghana reflected the clash between regional and national loyalties, the tension between development and democracy, and the influence of Cold War politics.

Political Rivalry in Senegal

Things turned out differently in Senegal. In the 1959 elections leading up to Senegal's independence, the Senegalese Progressive Union, headed by **Leopold Senghor**, won all the legislative seats, shutting out the regional parties. Based on the French political system, the government of Senegal had a bicephalous executive structure with both a president and a prime minister. Senghor became the president, and his political ally, Mamadou Dia, became the prime minister, but the arrangement fostered political rivalry and power struggles within the executive branch. During a dispute over agricultural policy toward peanut farmers in 1962, the National Assembly introduced a motion of censure against Dia, who responded by ordering the arrest of the four representatives who had led the campaign against him. The army then surrounded the National Assembly and arrested Dia, who was sentenced to life in prison for an attempted coup.

In the wake of that incident, certain political parties were banned, and a new constitution was adopted that eliminated the office of prime minister and strengthened the presidency, creating a winner-take-all electoral system that effectively turned Senegal into a one-party state. As president of Senegal and head of the party, Leopold Senghor was extremely powerful, and the National Assembly became a rubber stamp for all laws he proposed. Even with a compliant assembly, he frequently governed by direct decree.

Following urban demonstrations and anti-government strikes in 1968 and 1969, however, it was President Senghor who led the way in relaxing his authoritarian policies and who reestablished the office of prime minister in 1970. Five years later, the National Assembly established a limited multiparty system, authorizing four political parties that represented the four officially recognized political ideologies (Marxist, Socialist, Liberal, and Conservative) rather than regions or ethnicities. In the 1978 elections, Senghor's Socialist Party won 82 of the 100 seats

SENGHOR SPEAKS President Leopold Senghor speaks at Senegal's Independence Day ceremony on June 20, 1960. Although he went on to oust his prime minister and govern Senegal as a one-party state for several years, he later restored limited multiparty democracy.

in the National Assembly. Three years later, President Senghor resigned and left the country to live in France, demonstrating that he had no interest in being president for life.

Military Coups

Once an African state had adopted one-party rule, the only way to reform the government or its policies was by force. As a result, **military coups** became a common means of regime change during the 1960s and 1970s. The military officers who staged coups did so for a variety of personal and ideological reasons, and the military regimes they instituted varied widely in their approach to governance. The historian Paul Nugent has classified these military regimes into four types: caretaker regimes, which step in to prevent a descent into chaos and then restore civilian rule; reforming regimes, which try to reform and restructure the government before returning to civilian rule; usurper regimes, which take over the office of the president and the dominant political party with no intention of restoring civilian rule; and military Marxist regimes, whose leaders use their regime to impose a socialist ideology.

In some cases, however, a single military ruler may go from caretaker or reformer to usurper. In 1965, Colonel Joseph Mobutu, the army chief of staff of

Congo-Kinshasa, staged a military coup and declared that for the next 5 years he would personally rule as a reforming regime. Two years later, however, he formed a political party called the Popular Revolutionary Movement, which became the country's supreme political institution. As time went on, the lines separating the government, the party, and President Mobutu became increasingly blurred as the reformer became a full-fledged usurper. He remained in office until 1997, when he was forced into exile by a rebellion after 32 years of personal rule.

Idi Amin in Uganda

The most deadly usurper regime was that of **Idi Amin**, who came from the small Kakwa ethnic group in northwestern Uganda. When Amin became commander of Uganda's armed forces in 1970, he altered the ethnic composition of the military by recruiting Kakwa soldiers from his home area and Nubians from across the border in southern Sudan. This move alarmed Ugandan president Milton Obote, who demoted Amin and increased recruitment from his own Lango ethnic group. When Amin heard a rumor that he might be arrested for misappropriating army funds, he responded by staging a military coup on January 25, 1971.

Speaking on Radio Uganda, Idi Amin announced that he would form a caretaker regime that would relinquish control as soon as new elections could be held. A week later, however, he became a usurper. Declaring himself the president of Uganda, Amin suspended certain provisions of the Ugandan constitution, put soldiers in charge of most government agencies, and decreed that the military could arrest any person on suspicion of any crime. Amin rapidly expanded the army, which grew from 1,000 at the time of Uganda's independence to 25,000 by the late 1970s. Junior officers from Amin's home region were rapidly promoted, so that by 1977, 60 percent of the top army officers were from the Kakwa-Nubian group.

As "president for life" of Uganda, Amin dismantled the political structure and established a highly personalized dictatorship in which he governed with the aid of a murky inner core of loyal Kakwa and Nubian army officers. Human rights groups estimate the number of people murdered and massacred by Idi Amin's soldiers at 250,000 to 500,000. Idi Amin's military dictatorship came to an end in 1978, when he sent his army to invade neighboring Tanzania. The Tanzanian army, aided by various Ugandan resistance groups, drove out the Ugandan army and marched on the Ugandan capital of Kampala. When Uganda's capital fell on April 10, 1979, Idi Amin fled to Libya and later went into exile in Saudi Arabia.

Other Military Coups

During nearly three decades between 1956 and 1984, 56 successful military coups took place in 26 countries of sub-Saharan Africa. Fourteen countries experienced

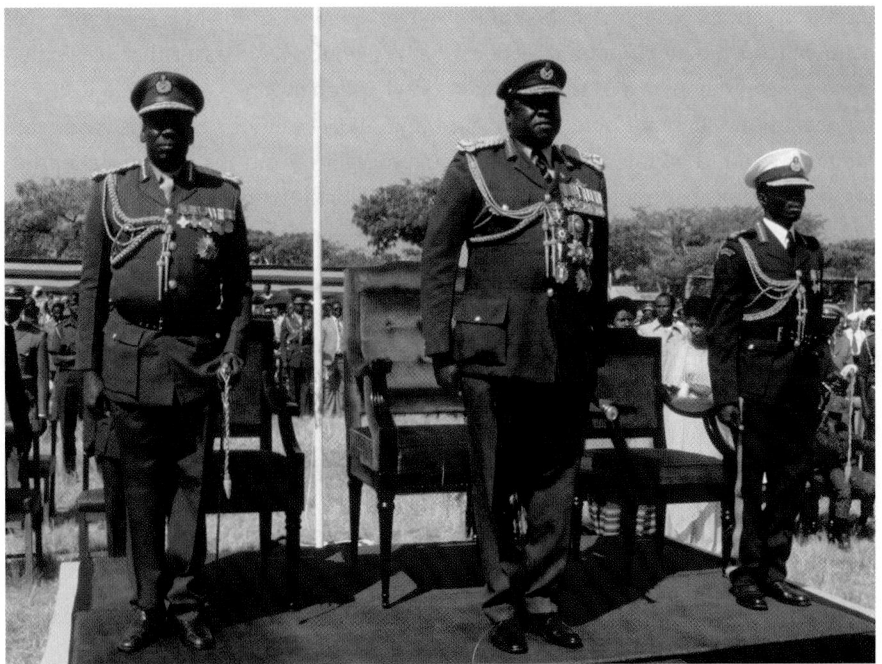

DICTATOR OF UGANDA General Idi Amin (center), Uganda's "president for life," watches a military parade in 1979, shortly before he was ousted by an invading army from neighboring Tanzania. A domineering figure, Amin seized power in a military coup in 1971 and ruled Uganda as a dictator with the help of a small group of Kakwa and southern Sudanese army officers.

more than one military coup as they alternated between military and civilian rule: Ghana had five coups, and Benin had six. By the 1980s, military rule had become the standard in sub-Saharan Africa, with 65 percent of its inhabitants and over half of its states governed by military regimes. Despite their claims of being revolutionary, military regimes often operated much like the civilian governments that preceded them and pursued similar development strategies, usually with similar results.

A slightly different pattern could be seen in North Africa, where three of the five states had gained independence as constitutional monarchies. In Egypt, which had been independent since 1922, King Farouk was overthrown by a group of military officers in 1952 (see chapter 14). One of those officers, Gamal Abdel Nasser, ruled as president until 1970, and when he died he was replaced by his vice president, Anwar Sadat, who had also participated in the 1952 coup. Libya, a former Italian colony, gained its independence in 1952 as a constitutional monarchy under King Idris. The king was overthrown in 1969 by a small group of army officers led by Muammar Gaddafi, who ruled for 42 years until he was killed during a rebellion in 2011. Morocco gained independence as a constitutional monarchy in 1956 and held its first parliamentary elections in 1963. Two years later, however, the king declared a state of emergency and suspended the parliament to rule as an autocratic monarch. The two North African states that were not monarchies—Algeria and Tunisia—were governed as autocratic one-party states after their independence.

SOCIALISM VERSUS CAPITALISM

Post-colonial African states were first and foremost development states. They would be judged by their citizens on how well they provided for development by fostering economic growth and facilitating improvements in transportation, education, and health care. Although the newly independent African states had no choice but to embrace the various manifestations of development, independence gave their leaders new choices about how development was to be achieved. The two major options were defined by the ideologies of the Cold War: a capitalist model, with economies dominated by large foreign companies, or a socialist model, in which the government took a leading role in planning.

Ghana versus Côte d'Ivoire

The choice faced by African leaders can be illustrated by the wager that Ghana's president Kwame Nkrumah made with his neighbor, Félix Houphouët-Boigny, the leader of Côte d'Ivoire. At a meeting with Nkrumah in 1957, Houphouët-Boigny said, "Let us each undertake his experiment, in absolute respect of the experiment of his neighbor, and in ten years we shall compare the results." Thus began a decade of competition between the capitalist-oriented policies of Houphouët-Boigny and the socialist-oriented policies of Nkrumah.

Nkrumah referred to his policies as socialism, but he differed from the leaders of communist countries such as China and the Soviet Union in that he did not try to remake the rural economy. Instead, he favored a mixed economy that included a dam on the Volta River to produce cheap electricity, state-run manufacturing industries, and mechanized state farms that coexisted with small family farms. Instead of mobilizing the masses, he was bypassing them. His main goal was to modernize the economy as quickly as possible; he said that Ghana must mobilize its brainpower and manpower resources "to accomplish in a single generation what European countries took 300 years to achieve."

In order to pay for these development projects, he reduced the prices that the Marketing Board paid to cocoa farmers, levied a special tax on cocoa farmers, and required all wage laborers to contribute to a compulsory savings scheme that would finance development. Nkrumah had originally come to power with the support of the cocoa farmers and the labor unions (see chapter 14), but now he was squeezing them to finance his development projects! Despite those maneuvers, it was not long before Ghana was sinking into debt. The government ministries were overspending their budgets, the world price of cocoa was falling, and the new state industries were operating well below their expected capacity.

Côte d'Ivoire, on the other hand, was much less ambitious. During the 1960s, it invested a third as much as Ghana did in development projects. Its 10-year plan called for spending half of the available development money to strengthen the sectors of the economy that were already the most productive, such as cocoa farms, coffee farms, and private agro-processing industries. As a result, Côte d'Ivoire ran budget surpluses throughout the 1960s.

In terms of the wager with Ghana, Côte d'Ivoire had two advantages. The first was its trade agreement with France, which gave preferential tariffs to Ivoirian agricultural products. The French, in effect, were subsidizing Côte d'Ivoire's exports. Its second advantage was that it had a great deal of unused forest land, which the government made available for purchase by cocoa and coffee farmers. Between 1960 and 1975, cocoa production increased sixfold and coffee production doubled as the formerly unused land was put into service. The commodity boom came to an end in the late 1970s, however, when the world market price for cocoa crashed, in part because of overproduction. The Ivoirian economy, which had been growing at a robust pace of nearly 7 percent per year, slowed to about 1 percent a year for the duration of the 1980s.

Who won the wager? If the bet had been called in 1970, Kwame Nkrumah would have lost. Western economists were characterizing Ghana's economic performance as appalling and catastrophic, while hailing Côte d'Ivoire's as the "Ivoirian miracle." However, if the bet had been called in 1980, 10 years later, then it would have been clear that neither Nkrumah nor Houphouët-Boigny had winning strategies, as neither economy was growing at a desirable rate. The final results had less to do with socialism or capitalism than with the basic fact that both Ghana and Côte d'Ivoire depended on the export of cash crops in a fickle world market. Perhaps the most significant takeaway from the West African wager is that both sides agreed that the state had an obligation to promote economic development; they just disagreed on the means.

Regardless of their official ideologies, most African governments presided over mixed economies with whatever foreign investment they could attract and whatever government investment they could afford. The vast majority of economic activity was generated by family farms, cottage industries, small businesses, and local traders. Despite decolonization, the post-colonial economies were not appreciably different from those of the late colonial era.

Socialist Rural Transformations

Despite the growth of cities during the colonial period, the vast majority of Africans still made their living by farming the land. And while the cities prospered and embraced the trappings of modern life, the rural areas often seemed poor and backward in comparison. The slow pace of rural development in much of Africa prompted some African leaders to embrace ambitious plans for massive and rapid agrarian change on a socialist model. To explore this phenomenon, let's examine three such projects, in Tanzania, Guinea, and Ethiopia.

Ujamaa in Tanzania

Six years after Tanzania became independent, President Julius Nyerere announced his new policy of African socialism. He referred to it as ***ujamaa***, using the Swahili word for "familyhood." The idea was that the people of Tanzania were like one big family, whose members could be called upon to work collectively on certain projects and share the results of their labor. Nyerere nationalized the key financial, manufacturing, and trading institutions in Tanzania, but the heart of his plan was rural development through the creation of communal *ujamaa* villages. With 96 percent of the Tanzanian population living in rural areas and making their living by farming, he noted that "Tanzanian socialism must be firmly based on the land and its workers."

Most rural people in Tanzania did not live in villages, but on individual family farms scattered across the countryside. Although their settlement patterns might have seemed haphazard when seen from the air or plotted on a map, the farm sites were, in fact, carefully chosen. Factors such as soil fertility, elevation, rainfall, water sources, and pasture for livestock were all taken into consideration. Given the microecological diversity of Tanzania, the scattered settlement pattern made a lot of sense. President Nyerere, however, reasoned that grouping people into villages would enhance productivity and economic efficiency. An editorial in the Dar es Salaam *Daily News* stated that "proximity is a necessity of development. For when people abandon their isolation and come together into well-planned and laid-out villages, they can be reached by social services, and they can effectively operate in cooperation. Only then can they begin to develop."

When it was first initiated in 1967, the villagization program got off to a slow start because Nyerere initially believed that participation in *ujamaa* villages should be voluntary. The big push for *ujamaa* villages came in 1973, when Nyerere announced his new policy of compulsory and universal villagization. Two potential obstacles to forced villagization had earlier been removed when the government had replaced local chiefs with elected local councils in 1963 and had nationalized all the land in 1967.

Young men who were members of the Tanzanian Youth League were responsible for implementing the villagization program, called Operation Planned Villages. They issued orders for people to move, supervised the layout of the new villages, and oversaw the construction of the houses. Despite women's historically predominant role in farming, and even though the official ideology called on men and women to work side by side to build the nation, Operation Planned Villages gave the authority to young men, many of whom had little agricultural knowledge. Women were encouraged to adopt more domestic duties and attend to their families and children.

Operation Planned Villages was conducted with almost military precision. Planning teams were allowed as little as a day to select a site and prepare a plan for a single village before moving on to the next. Villages were often placed near roads for administrative convenience, regardless of soil quality. It was later discovered that roughly 60 percent of the *ujamaa* villages were located on land unsuitable for permanent cultivation. Once a site was selected, military trucks were sent out to round people up and bring them to the new location, where they would have to build their own houses. In some cases, their vacated houses were bulldozed and their crops were burned to discourage anyone from returning. Many people were removed from fertile valleys or productive uplands and resettled on arid hills near a road. By 1976, some 5 million rural Tanzanians had been forcibly moved into villages.

The massive displacement caused by Operation Planned Villages coincided with a sizable drop in Tanzania's food production. The government of Tanzania spent so much money on food imports in 1974–1975 that, according to President Nyerere, it could have bought a cow for every family in Tanzania. Defenders of the program pointed out that 1974–1975 were years of unusually low rainfall, if not outright drought. But a World Bank report concluded that it was the disruption of agriculture by the villagization program that was largely to blame.

In 1975, all *ujamaa* villages were ordered to establish communal fields, in which villagers were obligated to work a certain number of days per year. The government agricultural officers insisted that economies of scale could be achieved if a large number of people with hoes worked together to farm a communal tract of land, and the Tanzanian mass media spread the message by showing pictures of large groups of people wielding their hoes together. In the few villages that were

***UJAMAA* VILLAGE** Women in the *ujamaa* village of Vijiji Vya work collectively to till a field in 1974. Prior to the villagization program, most rural people in Tanzania lived in individual homesteads instead of villages.

fortunate enough to receive tractors, new problems emerged because the tractors could plow much more land than the villagers could plant, weed, and harvest.

The key to successful farming in this area of uncertain rainfall was proper timing. Fields had to be planted and harvested at certain times in relation to the onset or termination of the seasonal rains. At crucial moments during the agricultural season, however, people disappeared to work on their own fields, then returned to work the communal fields when conditions were no longer optimal. Because the communal fields were underproducing, many villages abandoned communal labor entirely and divided up the communal fields, making each household responsible for a certain plot. By 1978, communal production had decreased to the point where the government announced that villages in Tanzania should no longer be called *ujamaa* villages because they had not adopted a socialist way of life. By then, Operation Planned Villages was effectively over. The program not only had failed to transform agriculture, but had frequently caused decreases in agricultural production. Nevertheless, many *ujamaa* villages had benefited from health care facilities and schools. By 1978, the number of rural health centers had tripled, dispensaries for medicines had been set up in some 8,000 villages, and over 90 percent of Tanzanian children attended primary school.

State Farms in Guinea

Plans to create a socialist revolutionary state were also launched in Guinea by President Ahmed Sékou Touré after the country gained independence from France in 1958. One year after Guinea became independent, the state declared all land public domain, which granted the state unbridled authority to seize land for communal production. The government set up communal fields to be worked by mandatory labor, the revenue from which was to contribute to community services. The project provoked resistance, as many people associated the mandatory labor on the communal fields with the forced labor on the chief's plot during the colonial period. When the government discovered that the communal plots generally produced smaller yields than private smallholder farms, it abandoned the program.

Rather than forcing small farmers into arrangements that they did not want, the government tried to bypass them by setting up 360 large state-owned farms called *Fermes Agro-Pastorale d'Arrondissement* (FAPAs) beginning in 1979. In addition to producing crops, the state farms were supposed to modernize farming in Guinea by serving as agricultural experiment stations and testing grounds for mechanized farming techniques. They were equipped with large tractors, plows, and other farm implements purchased from the communist countries of Eastern Europe. The FAPAs were run by civil servants with degrees from the government agricultural school, although most of the actual farm work was done as mandatory labor by the neighboring smallholders. The FAPAs were set up on land that had been seized from former colonial plantations or simply appropriated by the government. Because of the expensive personnel and equipment they required, over a quarter of the government's agricultural budget went to the FAPAs.

The FAPAs were largely failures. Their rice yields were about half those of ordinary smallholder farmers, and in some cases the FAPAs were harvesting only 70 kg of rice per hectare, in contrast to neighboring smallholders, who averaged about 300 kg. Three years after the FAPAs were launched, only a quarter of the 500 original tractors were still running. The staff may have had diplomas in agriculture, but their training was largely theoretical. The local farmers, whom the FAPAs were supposed to teach, scoffed at the young civil servants with their fancy diplomas who could not tend their own crops properly. Because the FAPAs were such a drain on the national budget, they were abolished and transformed into independent cooperatives in 1984. After President Sékou Touré died of heart disease later that year, the cooperatives were quietly abandoned, leaving broken farm machinery rusting beside the roads.

Land Reform in Ethiopia

In Ethiopia, Emperor Haile Selassie was toppled in September 1974 by a military coup conducted by a group of junior officers collectively known as the **Derg**. Six months after taking power, the Derg nationalized all rural land and outlawed private land ownership. The large commercial farms became state farms, and the vast estates of the traditional landed aristocracy were divided up and distributed to landless families. Each rural household was given use rights to a plot of land not to exceed 24 acres (most were much smaller), but was not given direct ownership.

To implement the land reform, the government closed the university and the high schools and sent 60,000 students (mostly from the cities) out into the countryside for 2 years to organize peasant associations, which were to serve as the base for future rural development. By 1980, some 25,000 peasant associations had been formed, although many of them existed in name only. The government planned to transform the peasant associations into producer cooperatives that engaged in communal farming. Despite all of its planning and organizational activity, per capita food production actually fell each year by half a percent throughout the 1970s.

When the peasant associations failed to increase agricultural production, the Derg decided to take more direct measures. In 1985, they introduced a compulsory villagization program that was designed to move some 33 million small farmers from their scattered individual homesteads into concentrated villages. The leader of the Derg, Mengistu Haile Mariam, justified the scheme by saying, "The scattered and haphazard habitation and livelihood of the peasants cannot build socialism." He believed that traditional small-scale farming was the chief obstacle to modern agriculture. As in Tanzania, the government promised that it would eventually provide schools, health care, clean water, roads, and perhaps tractors to the planned villages.

The movement of farmers into the planned villages began in 1985, when the country was still reeling from the severe drought of 1984–1985. Taking advantage of the chaos induced by the drought, the Derg managed to move over 8 million people into 15,000 planned villages over the next 3 years, using food aid from Western countries as an inducement. Although many people moved peaceably because they needed food or did not want to oppose government authority, others moved only under extreme coercion by armed party officials, who tore down their houses, burned their thatched roofs, and forced them to destroy the planted cactus fences that served as livestock corrals to discourage them from moving back. In the area near the Somali border, many people fled daily into Somalia to escape forced villagization.

Although the inhabitants of the new villages received their own family plots to cultivate, government officials made it clear that their long-term goal was to transition to communal farming. The best land was often reserved for communal fields, while the family plots were located on less fertile ground. In most cases, the promised amenities of village life never materialized, because the government was broke. As the 1980s wore on, the pressure for collectivization diminished, in part because of continued resistance by the farmers and in part because of the government's inability to provide the promised agricultural aid. By the time the Derg was toppled from power in 1991, the villagization scheme was effectively over. For all the massive movements of people into villages, less than 2 percent of Ethiopia's arable land was being farmed communally.

Socialist Experiments Evaluated

The experiences of Tanzania, Guinea, and Ethiopia show how hard it was to significantly increase agricultural production in areas dominated by smallholders. The colonial powers had tried and failed, and the independent socialist governments had failed as well. Perhaps the farmers were already squeezing maximum production from the soil, and any further improvement would have required massive investments in fertilizers and specialized equipment that poor farmers or poor governments were in no position to make. The socialist experiments in agricultural transformation can be criticized for their naïve faith that grouping people together would automatically yield economic benefits, their arrogance in ignoring the extensive knowledge of the farmers, their broken promises, their poor planning, and their inadequate execution. But at least they made a serious effort. Many other African governments were content to let things continue the way they had been in the late colonial period. Those governments did not fail, because they did not even try. But neither did they succeed.

THE THIRD WAVE OF INDEPENDENCE

During the 1960s, when most of the African countries located north of the equator were moving toward independence, much of southern Africa was still under some form of colonial rule. The list included the Portuguese colonies of Angola and Mozambique, as well as the former British settler colonies of South Africa and Zimbabwe, which were nominally independent but ruled by the white settler minority. There was also Namibia, the former German colony that had become a colony of South Africa in the aftermath of World War I. A major reason why colonialism remained entrenched in those areas was their relatively large numbers of white settlers, who had no place to go if they were driven out. A few of the settler families in South Africa had been there since the seventeenth century, and many of the settlers in the Portuguese colonies had come there to escape dire poverty in Portugal. Over time, the settlers had become so accustomed to dominating and exploiting Africans that the idea of living together in a situation of racial equality seemed unthinkable to them. In such situations, Africans had no way of gaining independence other than fighting wars of liberation.

In looking for a strategy to defeat the powerful colonial armies, African liberation movements had to look no further than the Communist Party in China. Mao Zedong, the leader of the Chinese Communist Party, had developed the concept of a **people's war**, which was a type of long-term revolutionary struggle. In contrast to the Russian Revolution, which had broken out among the urban working classes, Mao Zedong's strategy in China was to gain the support of the rural population. "The mobilization of the common people throughout the country will create conditions that will make up for our inferiority in arms," wrote Mao.

Mao's strategy was to consolidate control over the rural regions with a mixture of guerrilla warfare and politically popular programs such as land reform. Rebellions that began in remote rural areas would gradually expand to encircle the cities, and guerrilla fighting units would gradually be replaced by mobile army units, and finally by a conventional army. This strategy proved successful in China, where Mao's followers fought the Japanese invaders during World War II and the Chinese Nationalist government after that. On October 1, 1949, Chairman Mao, as he was called, stood at the Gate of Heavenly Peace in Beijing and declared the birth of the People's Republic of China. Mao's theories of a people's war heavily influenced the wars of liberation in Africa.

Wars of Liberation in Portuguese Africa

The Portuguese colonies became the sites of the major liberation struggles of the 1960s. Portugal had been the first major European colonial power in Africa, and now it was also the last. During the 1950s, the white settler populations of Angola and Mozambique had doubled (see chapter 14) as a result of Portuguese recruitment efforts and investments in infrastructure. The small West African colony of Guinea-Bissau, on the other hand, was treated differently because the climate there was considered unhealthy for Portuguese settlers. Accordingly, the colony's export economy depended on peanuts produced by African farmers, and Portuguese investment remained minimal. By the early 1960s, Guinea-Bissau had only 36 miles of paved roads.

Angola

Africa's wars of liberation from Portugal began in 1961 in northern Angola, in the region formerly occupied by the Kongo Kingdom (see chapter 5). The Kongolese people living there were resentful of the Portuguese for confiscating their land and forcing them to labor on the coffee plantations. Living near the border of the former Belgian Congo, they were well aware that the Belgians had left in 1960, and they wanted the Portuguese to leave as well. Some hoped that once the Portuguese were gone, the old Kongo Kingdom could be restored. Militants planned a series of violent uprisings for March 15, 1961, preparing to burn bridges, crops, and plantation buildings, but not intending to attack anyone.

As often happens in such volatile situations, events got ahead of the plans. On the day before the planned uprisings, a group of conscripted laborers on the Primavera Plantation gathered at the home of the plantation manager to demand the 6 months of overdue pay they were owed. The discussion grew heated, and the plantation manager allegedly pulled out his gun and shot several of the protesters, inciting the group to attack and kill him with their machetes. When word of the incident got out, bands of rebels armed with machetes or stolen guns began a campaign of violence and destruction throughout the coffee-growing region.

Within 2 months, the rebellion had spread across most of northern Angola. As many as 750 Portuguese were killed in the first 3 months, along with several thousand African contract workers from southern Angola who were loyal to the Portuguese. In response, well-armed settler militias began attacking African villages, and the Portuguese army moved in with trucks provided by NATO. Portuguese aircraft strafed and firebombed African villages. In the first 6 months of fighting, an estimated 20,000 Africans were killed, and another 150,000 fled across the border to Congo-Kinshasa as refugees. Thus began the largest anti-colonial rebellion in Africa's history.

The war against Portuguese colonialism in Angola, which would continue for 13 years, was waged by three major liberation groups. In the northern region, where the war began, the rebellion was organized by the National Front for the Liberation of Angola (FNLA), whose leaders lived in exile in Kinshasa. The FNLA found strong support among the Kongolese ethnic group, but because of its ethnic base, its reach never extended beyond northern Angola. The second group was the National Union for the Total Liberation of Angola (UNITA), formed in 1966, which had an ethnic base among the Ovimbundu people of southern Angola. The third group was the **People's Union for the Liberation of Angola (MPLA)**, which was founded by educated and mixed-race Africans living in the Angolan capital city of Luanda. One of its early leaders was Deolinda Rodrigues de Almeida, who is remembered as the "mother of the revolution" for organizing the women's division of the MPLA and for her role in attacking a prison where MPLA members were held. When the MPLA was driven out of Luanda by the Portuguese, its leaders relocated to Brazzaville, where the powerful transmitters of Radio Brazzaville (see chapter 13) allowed them to spread their message to a broader audience. The MPLA leaders were modernizers, and they were strongly influenced by Marxist ideology. Because they saw the war in national terms, they eschewed ethnic appeals and espoused gender equality: women served as combatants and also worked to educate peasants in liberated areas.

FIGHTING THE PORTUGUESE Soldiers of the MPLA (Popular Movement for the Liberation of Angola) fight a battle against Portuguese colonial forces in 1968. One of three rival anti-colonial armies, the Marxist-oriented MPLA took over Angola from Portugal in 1975 and entered into a protracted civil war with its rival, UNITA.

The military tactics used by the three rebel groups were further evidence of the influence of the Cold War on African wars of liberation. The FNLA uprisings of 1961 were disorganized and uncoordinated affairs that did not reflect a larger strategic vision. Drawing on popular anger, the FNLA hoped to shock the Portuguese into leaving Angola, much as the Kinshasa riots in 1959 had provoked the quick exodus of the Belgians (see chapter 14). The MPLA, in contrast, followed Mao Zedong's concept of a protracted people's war, which required social control through political indoctrination, organization of the masses, and bases in safe rural areas, while the fighting itself was carried out by a combination of guerrilla units, people's militias, and a revolutionary army. They even created 35-mm training films to explain the concept. The founder of UNITA, who was wary of communism, nevertheless went to China in 1966 with some of his top military commanders for extensive training in guerrilla warfare.

The war in Angola went through three phases. The first was the uprising of 1961, which was put down in a particularly brutal fashion. The second phase, from 1962 to 1966, was referred to by one historian as the "limited revolutionary struggle" because there was sporadic conflict, but the rebel activity did not pose a serious threat to Portugal's control of the colony. The final phase began in 1967, when UNITA established itself in the southern part of Angola and the MPLA established a military presence in eastern Angola, where few Portuguese settlers lived and Portuguese administrative control was weak. The liberation fighters never won a decisive military victory over the Portuguese, but they grew stronger with each passing year.

Mozambique

In Mozambique, on the Indian Ocean coast, three different independence movements emerged during 1960–1961, but they united in 1962 to form a single organization called **Front for the Liberation of Mozambique (FRELIMO)**, with headquarters in Dar es Salaam, Tanzania. FRELIMO was headed by Eduardo Mondlane, a Mozambican who held a Ph.D. from Northwestern University and had worked for the United Nations Trusteeship Council in New York City. At the time of FRELIMO's founding, he was a professor of sociology and anthropology at Syracuse University, but he returned to Africa in 1963. He not only wanted to gain independence for Mozambique, but also hoped to transform it into a socialist

FROM PROFESSOR TO REBEL Eduardo Mondlane (left) left his job as a sociology professor at Syracuse University to head the FRELIMO liberation movement in Mozambique in 1963. He was assassinated by a package bomb in 1969. To his right is Samora Machel, who led FRELIMO after Mondlane's death and became the president of Mozambique after the Portuguese withdrawal in 1975.

society. His socialist goals became official in 1968 when they were approved by FRELIMO's Second Party Congress.

The war for Mozambican independence began in late 1964, when FRELIMO sent 250 fighters to attack a Portuguese base in northern Mozambique. In response, the Mozambican colonial government arrested some 1,500 FRELIMO militants and destroyed its operations in the south. FRELIMO had more success in the Makonde country of northern Mozambique, where it sought to drive out the Portuguese as well as initiate a socialist revolution. It created communal villages, organized producer cooperatives, and mounted education and health campaigns in the territories it held. Some FRELIMO policies were opposed by certain Makonde chiefs, who wanted to get rid of the Portuguese but had no interest in socialist revolution. The leaders of FRELIMO, in turn, concluded that Mozambican peasants were being exploited by two different groups of people—the Portuguese and the local chiefs—and that the authority of the chiefs would therefore have to be destroyed before a new social order could be constructed.

From early in the war, FRELIMO commanders recruited young women to assist the fighters, a policy that was in line with FRELIMO's ideology, which favored overturning traditional age and gender hierarchies. By 1966, male elders in the liberated zones were complaining that the sight of young women with rifles slung over their shoulders violated traditional gender norms. In 1967, FRELIMO formed a Female Detachment composed of young women who had received political and military training in Tanzania. Although members of the Female Detachment occasionally participated in armed combat, they were particularly effective in gathering intelligence and mobilizing support in areas not yet under FRELIMO control because the Portuguese did not recognize them as fighters. In the liberated zones, they organized and managed schools, health posts, and collective agricultural projects.

By 1969, FRELIMO expansion had stalled, and the Portuguese were so confident in their control that they began construction of the Cahora Bassa dam on the Zambezi River. It would be the fifth-largest dam in the world and would provide electricity and irrigated farmland to attract even more Portuguese settlers. FRELIMO's attempts to stop the construction failed, but its attacks kept 20,000 Portuguese soldiers bottled up defending the dam. In 1970, with the dam construction under way, the Portuguese launched Operation Gordian Knot to drive FRELIMO out of its strongholds in the Makonde country. This time they had a new weapon: helicopters. The Americans had learned to use helicopters for tropical warfare during the Vietnam War, and Portuguese officers went to the United States for training in helicopter-based warfare. In addition to helicopters, the Portuguese mobilized some 35,000 soldiers for the operation.

Rather than fight the concentrated Portuguese forces in the north, FRELIMO forces retreated across the western border to Malawi and began to launch attacks in central Mozambique. Operation Gordian Knot was suspended at the onset of the rainy season in November 1970 because the heavy cloud cover rendered the helicopters ineffective. After that, the Portuguese army launched no further large-scale operations and instead relied on search-and-destroy missions by smaller units, another tactic borrowed from the U.S. experience in Vietnam. The FRELIMO rebels returned from their safe havens across the border and resumed their operations.

A SINKING SHIP This propaganda poster from Mozambique in the early 1970s makes the claim that the future belongs to FRELIMO. At the top is a well-armed and confident-looking group of FRELIMO soldiers. At the bottom is a drawing of a sinking ship named "Salazarismo," or Salazarism, a reference to the policies of the late Portuguese dictator Antonio Salazar. Piloting the ship is Marcello Caetano, who took over in Portugal after Salazar's death and continued his policies.

By 1972, the military situation had shifted in favor of FRELIMO. The rebels had expanded their liberated zones in northern and central Mozambique and were beginning to operate in the south. They had also begun to raid settler-owned sugar, cotton, and sisal plantations and to impede traffic on roads and railroads. With FRELIMO's fighting force swelling to 10,000 fighters and armed with increasingly sophisticated weapons from the Soviet Union and China, the Portuguese found themselves operating more and more out of isolated strongholds in rebel-dominated territory. By then, FRELIMO controlled about a quarter of Mozambique and exercised authority over a million people. Although

FRELIMO had not defeated the colonial army, the Portuguese realized that neither could they defeat FRELIMO.

Guinea-Bissau

The third Portuguese colony in Africa was Guinea-Bissau, which was located on the West African coast, sandwiched between the French colonies of Guinea (known as Guinea-Conakry) and Senegal. Because of its location, the people of Guinea-Bissau were well aware of it when French Guinea received independence in 1958 under the leadership of Sékou Touré (see chapter 14). The people of Guinea-Bissau had a variety of grievances against Portuguese colonial rule. Peanuts were the colony's main export, and the Portuguese had pushed the African peanut farmers hard to increase their production, which resulted in overuse of the land and declining soil fertility. In addition, the Portuguese paid the farmers far less for their peanuts than a peanut farmer could earn on the other side of the border, in Senegal. In 1953, over a tenth of the peanut crop was smuggled north into Senegal, and entire families were abandoning their farms and migrating there to take advantage of the higher prices.

One person who understood the plight of the peanut farmers was Amilcar Cabral, an agricultural engineer from Guinea-Bissau who had earned a degree from the Higher Institute of Agronomy in Lisbon. In 1952, he was put in charge of an agricultural experiment station near the colony's capital city of Bissau. The following year, he was asked by the Portuguese governor to carry out an agricultural survey of the colony. Over the next 5 months, he and his team of 30 researchers interviewed chiefs and farmers in 356 villages scattered across 41 administrative districts. In the aftermath of the survey, nobody knew rural Guinea-Bissau better than he.

Cabral's main passion, however, was gaining independence from Portugal. In 1956, he founded the African Party for the Independence of Guinea and Cape Verde (PAIGC), a political organization that agitated for independence. When the Portuguese began to arrest nationalist activists in 1959, he moved the party headquarters to Conakry, in the former French colony of Guinea. The PAIGC began limited guerrilla warfare 2 years later, sending small raiding parties to attack military posts and ambush Portuguese soldiers. Because Cabral had a Marxist orientation, he persuaded China to offer training in guerrilla warfare and the Soviet Union to supply arms.

By 1964, the PAIGC had a military command structure and a mobile army, known as the People's Revolutionary Armed Forces, and was running a full-scale guerrilla war. At the village level, it formed people's militias, which took orders from the PAIGC military commanders but had some latitude in how they carried out their missions. In areas under its control, the PAIGC offered health and education services and tried to improve agriculture by introducing new strains of high-yielding rice and new crops such as potatoes and cassava. Like many revolutionary leaders of the time, Cabral was committed to gender equality. Under his leadership, women held important positions in the party organization, and party rules required that at least two of the five members of village councils be women.

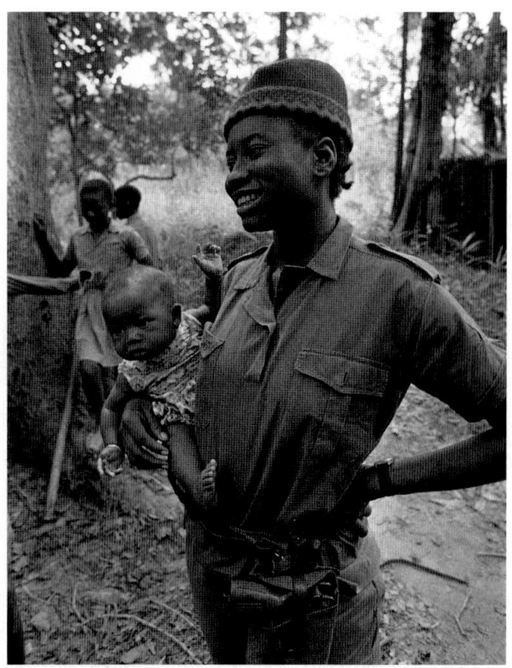

FREEDOM FIGHTER A woman soldier belonging to the African Party for the Independence of Guinea and Cape Verde (PAIGC) poses with a baby during the war for independence in Guinea-Bissau. After this photo was taken in December 1968, years of fighting would be required before Guinea-Bissau received its independence in 1975.

By 1968, two-thirds of Guinea-Bissau was under the military authority of the PAIGC, and by the early 1970s, PAIGC control over the countryside was almost complete. The Portuguese military conducted low-level bombings of villages with napalm and white phosphorus bombs, but seldom ventured out of its defensively oriented garrisons, which were supplied by helicopter because traveling on the roads left it too vulnerable to ambushes. Despite their defensive stance, the Portuguese refused to be driven out, and maintained a total of 30,000 Portuguese soldiers and 18,000 African soldiers guarding the major towns.

The Coming of Independence in Portuguese Africa

In all three Portuguese colonies, even the most successful wars of liberation could not force the Portuguese to withdraw until certain changes had taken place in Portugal itself. The first of these changes came in 1968, when the Portuguese dictator, Antonio Salazar, suffered a brain hemorrhage and was replaced by his associate Marcello Caetano, who continued the policies of the Salazar regime. The second came in 1970, when Portugal received associate membership in the

European Economic Union, which required it to abandon its exclusive trade agreements with its colonies. The result was a dramatic decrease in the economic importance of the colonies to Portugal, as Portuguese trade became more oriented toward Europe.

The most important development, however, was the military coup in Portugal on April 1974, which ended the Salazar-Caetano regime. The coup was, in a large part, a result of the wars Portugal was conducting in the African colonies, and the young military officers who carried out the coup were directly motivated by their weariness of the endless conflict. With as much as 50 percent of Portugal's national budget going to fight colonial wars in Africa, the new leaders sought to bring those wars to an abrupt end by turning the colonies over to their major liberation groups. Guinea-Bissau became independent in September 1974, just 5 months after the coup, while Mozambique and Angola became independent in 1975. In some ways, Portugal's withdrawal from Africa resembled that of the Belgians: both colonial powers refused to recognize even the possibility of eventual independence for their colonies for an extended period, then withdrew precipitously. In Guinea-Bissau, the transition to independence was relatively smooth because the PAIGC already controlled most of the countryside. The transitions were far more difficult, however, in Angola and Mozambique.

Civil War in Angola

On November 10, 1975, the day before Angola was scheduled to gain its independence, it was still not certain which Angolan liberation group would replace the Portuguese. The MPLA held the capital city of Luanda, but FNLA forces, reinforced by Congolese troops and Portuguese mercenaries, were attacking Luanda's northern suburbs. In the meantime, the Zulu Column, a white South African force allied with UNITA, was moving toward the city from the south along the coastal road. To help the MPLA defend Luanda, the communist nation of Cuba—acting independently from Moscow—airlifted 600 elite troops to Luanda just 3 days before Angola's independence. The Cuban troops made all the difference in maintaining the MPLA's hold on Luanda, operating Soviet rocket launchers that nearly annihilated the FNLA attackers and blowing up bridges to halt the advance of the Zulu Column 100 miles short of the city.

In the year following Angola's independence, the Cuban military contingent swelled to 36,000 troops, who helped the MPLA government establish control in all parts of the country. The FNLA retreated to Congo-Kinshasa and never again made a serious attempt to gain control of Angola, but UNITA didn't go away. While the MPLA government and the Cuban soldiers controlled the cities and important towns, UNITA set up headquarters in the extreme southeastern corner of Angola and carried on guerrilla warfare in the countryside. UNITA could not defeat the Cubans, but it could disrupt the roads and stop food from being sent to the cities. Pointing to the large number of Cuban soldiers in Angola, UNITA argued that Cuban colonialism had replaced Portuguese colonialism. By adopting an anticommunist stance, UNITA attracted support from the United States and white-ruled South Africa.

Throughout the 1980s, warfare raged in the Angolan countryside. To cut off supplies that might aid the enemy, both sides laid a total of 9 million land mines around fields and water supplies. The main victims of the mines were not soldiers, but women going to their fields or children going to fetch water. Many of the men were away from the villages, having been conscripted by one army or the other. With agricultural production disrupted, the major source of revenue for the Marxist MPLA government was the offshore oil wells owned by Texas-based Gulf Oil. The Angolan civil war would continue in an off-and-on fashion until 2002, when UNITA leader Jonas Savimbi was killed in battle. By then, the civil war had cost over half a million lives and displaced one-third of Angola's 13 million people.

Counterrevolution in Mozambique

The transition to independence was very different in Mozambique, where FRELIMO took over the government. As Marxists, the FRELIMO leaders saw themselves as modernizers who had a mandate to bring Mozambique rapidly into the modern world. They expanded education and access to modern health care, and they tried to increase agricultural production by setting up state farms on land vacated by Portuguese settlers and by creating rural villages with communal production. At the same time, they attacked traditional institutions that they believed were holding the country back. Chiefs were abolished by law, and former chiefs were barred from holding any public office. Customary practices such as paying a bride-price, polygyny, initiation rites, and rainmaking rituals were repeatedly denounced and sometimes banned by law.

Mozambique shared borders with two countries ruled by white settlers—Zimbabwe to the west and South Africa to the south—whose leaders were worried that Mozambique would provide a base for the liberation movements fighting against them. They therefore sought to disrupt the operations of the FRELIMO government as much as possible. Beginning in 1977, the white settler government of Zimbabwe began to sponsor raids into Mozambique by small groups of ex-FRELIMO soldiers who had turned against the Marxist government. By 1979, this insurgent group, which took the name **Mozambican National Resistance (RENAMO)**, had over a thousand guerrilla fighters operating from bases inside Mozambique.

RENAMO initially recruited fighters from among Mozambicans who had been political prisoners or had been sent to political reeducation camps. It curried favor with local farmers by opposing collective agriculture and supporting the ousted chiefs. Its critiques of the Marxist government were amplified daily by Portuguese-language radio broadcasts from Zimbabwe. When the white settler government in Zimbabwe was ousted in 1980, white-ruled South Africa stepped in to finance and supply RENAMO. After South Africa signed a nonaggression pact with the Mozambican government in 1984, military assistance to RENAMO was reduced to covert aid from South African military intelligence and contributions from third parties. By 1988, RENAMO was operating more or less on its own, capturing weapons and supplies by ambushing government convoys and looting towns.

To supplement its ranks, RENAMO abducted children from schools and villages in a manner reminiscent of nineteenth-century slave raids and took them to camps far away for military training and indoctrination. Up to 40 percent of RENAMO's soldiers were under 18; some were as young as 10. Perhaps their youth and traumatized condition helps to explain why RENAMO soldiers were responsible for numerous incidents of violence and brutality against civilians, including large-scale massacres. When news of RENAMO's brutality came to light, the group developed an international reputation as a terrorist organization. British prime minister Margaret Thatcher once described RENAMO as one of "the most brutal terrorist movements that there is."

With RENAMO operating primarily as a guerrilla military organization that sought to disrupt Mozambique's economic infrastructure and confine the government to the major population centers, about 70 percent of the country was without regular administration. Bandits plagued the countryside, and sometimes it was hard to tell the bandits from the RENAMO fighters. Exhausted by the seemingly endless war, the FRELIMO government signed a peace agreement with RENAMO in 1992, ending 16 years of civil war and paving the way for multiparty elections. In the 1994 parliamentary elections, FRELIMO won 129 seats and RENAMO won 112, suggesting that RENAMO, for all its brutality, nevertheless had strong support in the countryside. The civil war had cost Mozambique between 800,000 and 1,000,000 lives; 2 million people were displaced; and another million became refugees in other countries. Counting the war of liberation and the civil war, Mozambique had been at war for nearly 30 years.

Zimbabwe's War of Liberation

The final war of liberation to be discussed here took place in Zimbabwe, a former British colony that shared a border with Mozambique. Because Zimbabwe had been ruled by a white settler government prior to its 1965 Unilateral Declaration of

Independence from Britain, it was the local white settlers—and not the British—who were seen by the rebels as the enemy. In fact, the rebels hoped that the British would intervene on their behalf against the settlers. During the colonial period, the settlers had confiscated over 50 percent of the land, leaving many African farmers with inadequate land, poor soil, and lack of access to markets. The main issue motivating the rural farmers was recovery of their lost land, not political ideology.

During the early 1960s, two African political parties—the Zimbabwe African National Union (ZANU) and the Zimbabwe African People's Union (ZAPU)—had been formed to agitate for greater African participation in government and against the white settlers. The difference between the two parties was initially based on personalities and tactical disagreements between their leaders, but over time, each party developed an ethnic character, with ZAPU consisting mainly of Ndebele people from the south and ZANU made up largely of Shona people from the north. After the white settler government issued its UDI in 1965, each party created a military wing to fight a guerrilla war. ZAPU got its support from the Soviet Union, which trained its fighters in conventional warfare, while ZANU, which sought to organize the rural peasantry to wage a people's war, was supported by China. The Cold War rivalry between the Soviet Union and China was in full display.

At first, guerrilla incursions by the two liberation organizations were small and sporadic, focusing on sabotage and occasional commando-style raids. In 1972, there were only 300 ZANU and 400 ZAPU guerrilla fighters in Zimbabwe. After the neighboring country of Mozambique became independent in 1975, however, it helped ZANU set up training camps near the border. By 1976, as many as a thousand recruits per week went to Mozambique to join ZANU training camps, and by 1978, ZANU had 10,000 trained guerrilla fighters operating inside Zimbabwe. ZAPU had a similar number of fighters, though many of them were still scattered among training camps around the world. Such was the international dimension of the guerrilla war in Zimbabwe.

Despite the Marxist ideology that was taught in the training camps, the war itself was conducted on a more practical basis, inspired by the history and beliefs of the rural populations themselves. The ZAPU guerrilla fighters reminded villagers that Cecil Rhodes's British South African Company had destroyed the Ndebele Kingdom and seized its land in the 1890s, and they held up the nineteenth-century Ndebele King Lobengula as a folk hero (see chapter 10). ZANU, for its part, pointed to the Shona female spirit medium Nehanda-Charwe, who had been executed by the British for inspiring a rebellion against them in 1898 (see chapter 10).

The ZANU guerrilla fighters began to earn the trust of the Shona farmers when they stopped talking about socialism and began to build relationships with local spirit mediums, men and women who served as important ritual specialists in Shona culture. It was believed that the mediums could channel the spirits of deceased chiefs in order to bring rain and maintain the fertility of the land. During the colonial period, when the chiefs were reduced to low-level colonial bureaucrats by the system of indirect rule, the Shona people began to look to the spirit mediums as their real chiefs. Once the guerrilla fighters won over the spirit mediums to their cause, the support of the local populations followed.

Women as well as men were welcome to join ZANU. Roughly 2,000 women received military training in Mozambique and fought as regular combatants, and ZANU formed a Women's Detachment with its own female commander, who was a member of the military high command. Thousands of other women went to the training camps, where they worked mainly at support tasks such as food production, education, and medical care. Although some women in the camps reported equal treatment with men, others complained of being limited to traditional female roles. Although ZANU's ideology favored gender equality, the practice lagged behind the rhetoric.

By 1979, the white settler government was finding it difficult to provide enough soldiers and finances to maintain the war against the rebels, especially while international sanctions imposed by Britain and the United Nations were taking a toll on Zimbabwe's export economy. Realizing that the war was unsustainable, the government finally entered into negotiations with the two rebel groups at Lancaster House in London in the fall of 1979. In 47 sessions over 3 months, the parties hammered out the **Lancaster House Agreement** for African majority rule along with safety and property guarantees for the white minority. To arrange the transition, Britain took back its former colony for about 4 months, finally granting independence to Zimbabwe on April 18, 1980.

Zimbabwe's struggle for independence differed from that in neighboring Mozambique in two ways: First, the rebels saw their former colonial overlords, the British, as an ally rather than an enemy. Second, Zimbabwe's war of liberation did not try to become a socialist revolution. After their initial attempts to convince the rural farmers to adopt modern socialist ways failed, the rebels often became clients of the traditional spirit mediums. By the time Zimbabwe won its independence in 1980, most of Africa was independent from colonial rule. The exceptions were South Africa, which was independent, but ruled by the white minority, and Namibia, which was South Africa's colony.

THE DECADE OF ECONOMIC DECLINE

Although post-colonial African governments emphasized economic development, most of them were unable to deliver on their promises. In the 1970s, African export commodities such as coffee and copper experienced a sharp drop in prices on the world market. At the same time, there was a sharp rise in the price of imported oil. As a consequence, during the 1980s, countries in sub-Saharan Africa were growing poorer in terms of per capita gross domestic product (GDP). Their economies were growing, but not fast enough to keep up with increases in population. By 1981, 23 countries in sub-Saharan Africa were behind on their debt payments.

Petroleum-producing countries were in a different situation. Libya, a largely desert country with enormous oil reserves and only 6 million people, lived on its petroleum revenue, whereas the other African oil-producing countries, such as Algeria, Angola, and Nigeria, had much larger populations and more diversified economies. Major oil producers have been said to suffer from an "oil curse" because overreliance on oil revenues can lead to currency appreciation and a decline in the competitiveness of other sectors of the economy. Moreover, because oil revenue is easily concentrated in the hands of a few government officials, much of it was stolen by corrupt officials or consumed by expensive projects. In Nigeria, for example, an enormous proportion of the country's oil revenue was poured into the construction of an entirely new capital city, and between 1981 and 1983, Nigeria's international debt actually doubled.

As more and more African countries fell into debt, they turned to the World Bank and the International Monetary Fund (IMF) for help. The World Bank developed a program of **structural adjustment**, which required African governments to privatize key assets, reduce their expenditures, and eliminate certain subsidies and tariffs in return for loans to resolve their debt crises. There were two main problems with these structural adjustment programs: first, the conditions imposed by the World Bank did not yield the promised economic growth because they focused on institutional reforms and not on economic fundamentals; and second, many countries found ways to ignore or work around the conditions. Even so, one analyst has argued that the imposed conditions, however flawed in concept and implementation, helped to curb the worst excesses of some governments and improve the economic stability of others without significantly reducing their national budgets. It is perhaps ironic that the two countries that most conscientiously implemented the World Bank reforms were Ghana and Uganda, both of which had socialist governments. By the end of the 1980s, the IMF and the World Bank were viewed by some critics as the new colonial overlords in many African countries.

CONCLUSION

By the time the Cold War ended in 1991, formal colonial rule had largely disappeared from Africa. The Portuguese colonies of Angola, Mozambique, and Guinea-Bissau had gained their independence in 1975 after fighting wars of liberation lasting a decade or longer, but independence in the first two countries was immediately followed by protracted civil wars fueled by Cold War rivalries. Things went somewhat differently in the former British colony of Zimbabwe, where liberation groups fought for nearly a decade before the white settler regime agreed to a system of majority rule, thus freeing the British to grant independence.

Even after formal decolonization, it was clear that the legacy of colonialism had been woven deeply into the fabric of African political, economic, and cultural life. Independence was less a chance to "start over" than an opportunity to make small adjustments in the institutions bequeathed by decades of colonial rule. Ironies abounded: radical socialist experiments such as *ujamaa* ended up looking remarkably like the peasantries established by the Belgian colonizers, and many independent African countries abolished the last vestiges of the roles of traditional chiefs that the colonial rulers had so carefully preserved.

In the wake of independence, one of the first post-colonial political institutions to go into decline was multiparty electoral democracy, as post-independence rulers proclaimed one-party states and instituted lifetime terms for presidents. In 1989, only three African countries could be considered multiparty electoral democracies, and the majority of Africans were governed by military regimes. Maintaining economies that were competitive in the post-colonial global marketplace was an equally difficult challenge. Manufacturing was limited outside of South Africa, Egypt, and Algeria, and two-thirds of the working population of Africa was still toiling in labor-intensive, low-productivity agriculture. With falling world commodity prices and public pressure on African governments to deliver on promises of economic development, many African governments took out loans from the IMF and the World Bank that required them to restructure their governments under stringent conditions. After the initial enthusiasm and optimism of independence had faded, many Africans viewed their future with a mixture of hope and wariness.

CHAPTER REVIEW

KEY TERMS AND VOCABULARY

Katanga secession

Leopold Senghor

military coup

Idi Amin

ujamaa

Derg

people's war

People's Union for the Liberation of Angola (MPLA)

Front for the Liberation of Mozambique (FRELIMO)

Mozambican National Resistance (RENAMO)

Lancaster House Agreement

structural adjustment

STUDY QUESTIONS

1. Name some ways that the newly independent states in Africa were affected by the Cold War.
2. Why did some African states seek to create a type of African socialism?
3. Assess the results of the major socialist experiments in Africa.
4. Describe the paths by which many African states went from multiparty parliamentary democracy at the time of independence to authoritarian forms of government.
5. How did military coups become the dominant form of regime change in Africa during the 1960s, 1970s, and 1980s?
6. Why was gaining independence so much more difficult for the African states south of the equator than for those north of the equator?
7. What were the effects of white settler populations on African movements for independence or majority rule?

PERSPECTIVES

SOCIALISM AND RURAL DEVELOPMENT

Julius Nyerere, the first president of Tanzania, developed the concept of "African socialism," which he referred to in the Swahili language as ujamaa *(familyhood). In 1967, the government of Tanzania put out a small booklet called* Socialism and Rural Development, *in which President Nyerere outlined his program of African socialism and made the argument that it was based on the same principles that undergirded the traditional African family.*

The traditional African family lived according to the basic principles of *ujamaa*. Its members did this unconsciously, and without any conception of what they were doing in political terms. They lived together and worked together because that was how they understood life, and how they reinforced each other against the difficulties they had to contend with—the uncertainties of weather and sickness, the depredations of wild animals (and sometimes human enemies), and the cycle of life and death.

The results of their joint effort were divided unequally between them, but according to well-understood customs. And the division was always on the basis of the fact that every member of the family had to have enough to eat, some simple covering, and a place to sleep, before any of them (even the head of the family) had anything extra. The family members thought of themselves as one, and all their language and behavior emphasized their unity. They lived together and they worked together; and the result of their joint labor was the property of the family as a whole.

This pattern of living was made possible because of three basic assumptions of traditional life. The first of these basic assumptions was a recognition of mutual involvement in one another. Each member of the family recognized the place and the rights of the other members. The second related to property. It was that all the basic goods were held in common, and shared among all members of the unit. A third principle was that everyone had an obligation to work. These principles were, and are, the foundation of human security, of real practical human equality, and of peace between members of a society. They can also be a basis of economic development if modern knowledge and modern techniques of production are used.

This is the objective of socialism in Tanzania. To build a society in which all members have equal rights and equal opportunities; in which all can live at peace with his neighbors without suffering or imposing injustice, being exploited; or exploiting; and in which all have a gradually increasing basic level of material welfare before any individual lives in luxury. To create this kind of nation we must build on the firm foundations of the three principles of the *ujamaa* family. But we must add to these principles the knowledge and the instruments necessary for the defeat of the poverty which existed in traditional African society. . . .

What is here being proposed is that we in Tanzania should move from being a nation of individual peasant producers who are gradually adopting the incentives and the ethics of the capitalist system. Instead, we should gradually become a nation of *ujamaa* villages where the people cooperate directly in small groups and where these small groups cooperate together for joint enterprises.

---

1. *How convincing is Nyerere's analogy between Tanzanian society and a family?*

2. *According to Nyerere, what were the goals of socialism in Tanzania?*

Source: Julius K. Nyerere, *Socialism and Rural Development* (Dar es Salaam: The government Printer, United Republic of Tanzania), pp. 1–3, 4, 31.

CHILDREN OF THE SOIL

The foremost grievance voiced by the nationalist movement in Zimbabwe was the loss of their land to white settlers. In this excerpt from his memoirs, Ndabaningi Sithole, the founder of the Zimbabwe African National Union (ZANU), explains why the land was so important to the people of Zimbabwe.

"Sons of the Soil" is an English translation of the Shona phrase "*Vana Vevu*" which literally means "Children of the Soil." "*Vana Vevu*" had a special appeal to both young and old, male and female. It was ageless. It was sexless. Both young and old, both male and female, were and are of the Soil. "*Vana Vevu*" was a salutation loaded with deep and stirring emotion. . . .

The black man belonged to the Soil. It claimed him. He and millions of others to come belonged to the Soil which had given birth to millions of his kind stretching back well beyond the human memory and lost in antiquity. The Soil had given birth to thousands of thousands of generations and it had received them back into its bosom after their sojourn on earth. The black man belonged to the Soil by right of birth. He belonged to it by right of death as well.

To deprive him of it was to rob him of his birth-right and his death-right! The Soil possessed him by right of his many ancestors who had lived on it and who had been buried in it. The Soil gave him life, and when that life left him, it claimed him back. He came from it and therefore he belonged to it. No one comes from where he does not belong. At death he returned to it. No one returns where he does not belong. He is of the Soil in life and death—"*Mwana we Vu*," "Child of the Soil."

But it was not only the Soil that possessed the black man, but he, the black man, also possessed it. It was his as much as he was of the Soil. He tilled it to sustain his life. He exploited it in other ways for his own benefit. It supported him. It was his servant, and in a similar capacity it had served countless generations before him, and it would serve countless generations after him. He stood between the long past and the long future guilty before the dead and the unborn that he had allowed this Soil—this God-given Substance of Life—to pass into the grasping hand of the foreigner.

"Children of the Soil" therefore meant those who were possessed by the Soil, and those who possessed it. But under foreign rule the black man lost possession of the Soil. It passed to the foreigner. To retrieve this lost possession was the black man's Problem Number One. The black man's hatred of the white man stemmed from this fact, and the white man's fear of the black man had its origin in the same thing.

1. *What did Ndabaningi Sithole mean by the phrase "children of the Soil"?*
2. *What, according to Sithole, was Problem Number One for the Shona people?*

Source: Ndabaningi Sithole, *Roots of a Revolution: Scenes from Zimbabwe's Struggle* (London: Oxford University Press, 1977), pp. 17–19.

NATIONAL LIBERATION AND CULTURE

Eduardo Mondlane left his job as a professor at Syracuse University in 1963 in order to lead the liberation struggle in Mozambique as president of the Front for the Liberation of Mozambique (FRELIMO). In 1969, he was assassinated by a bomb that exploded when he opened a package. The following year, Syracuse University invited Amilcar Cabral, the founder and leader of the liberation movement in Guinea-Bissau, to give the Eduardo Mondlane Memorial Lecture. Entitling his lecture "National Liberation and Culture," Cabral concluded with a tribute to his fallen comrade.

Ladies and Gentlemen, in celebrating by this ceremony the memory of Dr. Eduardo Mondlane, we pay homage to the politician, to the freedom fighter and, especially to a man of culture. Culture acquired not only during the course of his personal life and in the halls of the university, but culture acquired mainly in the midst of his people, in the course of the struggle for the liberation of his people.

It may be said that Eduardo Mondlane was barbarously assassinated because he was able to identify himself with the culture of his people, with their deepest aspirations, in spite of all the attempts or the temptations to alienate his African and Mozambican personality. Because he forged himself a new culture in the liberation struggle, he fell as a combatant. It is obviously easy to accuse the Portuguese colonialists and the agents of imperialism, their allies, of the abominable crime committed against the person of Eduardo Mondlane, against the people of Mozambique, and against Africa. They were the ones who in cowardly fashion assassinated him.

However, all men of culture, all those who fight for freedom, all spirits afire for peace and progress—all the enemies of colonialism and racism—must have the courage to take upon their shoulders their share of the responsibility for this tragic death. For, if Portuguese colonialism and imperialist agents can still liquidate with impunity a man like Dr. Eduardo Mondlane, it is because there is something rotten in the heart of humanity: *imperialist domination*. It is because men of good will, defenders of the culture of peoples, have not yet accomplished their duty on this planet. In our opinion, this is the measure of the responsibilities of those who listen to us in this temple of culture in relation to the movement for liberation of oppressed peoples.

1. *What did the concept of "culture" mean to Amilcar Cabral?*
2. *According to Cabral, what was the duty of the defenders of culture?*

Source: Amilcar Cabral, "National Liberation and Culture," reprinted in *Ideologies of Liberation in Black Africa, 1856–1970*, edited by J. Ayo Langley (London: Rex Collings, 1979), pp. 720–721.

WANGARI MAATHAI: *UNBOWED*

Wangari Maathai won the Nobel Peace Prize in 2004 for her activities as the founder and leader of the Green Belt Movement, which encouraged Africans to plant trees to counteract environmental degradation. As the first woman to earn a doctorate in East Africa, she became chair of the Department of Veterinary Anatomy at the University of Nairobi before leaving the university to devote her time to the Green Belt Movement. In her memoir, Unbowed, *she recounted how she became an environmental activist.*

I started thinking hard about what the Green Belt Movement could become and the impact it could have if it was nurtured and grew and had sufficient funding and direction. By then I knew that to be successful, an organization and the person heading it had to have plans and carry them out; they could not just talk. You also had to be willing to be something of an activist. . . .

Fortunately, an opportunity presented itself within that year that was to change the course of my life and the future of the Green Belt Movement. Some of the seeds of this were sown earlier. In August 1981, Kenya hosted a UN conference on new and renewable sources of energy. This was an issue high on the international agenda at the time and the Green Belt Movement's work fit well with the conference's goals. For two weeks, government officials and members of environmental, energy, and appropriate technology organizations met and agreed on a plan of action to promote new sources of renewable, "green" energy and good management of forests.

As chair of the local board of the Environment Liaison Centre, I coordinated the efforts of local NGOs [nongovernmental organizations] to prepare for the conference and we formed an umbrella group for all the organizations then dealing with issues of renewable sources of energy. We set up a booth opposite Nairobi's City Hall near where the delegates were meeting at the Kenyatta International Conference Centre and established a woodlot, now called Global Forest, where dignitaries continue to plant trees.

We also organized a march in support of the conference. Hundreds of us wound our way from Uhuru ("Freedom") Park, down Uhuru Highway, past the New Stanley and Hilton hotels, and in front of City Hall, before arriving at the conference center. Many NGOs, both Kenyan and international, participated, including the World Conservation Union, the Chipko movement from India (which had pioneered the hugging of trees to protest rampant logging), and, of course, the Environment Liaison Centre.

I had arranged for a number of children to carry tree seedlings in the march. When we arrived, the children handed their precious packages to the dignitaries who had gathered on the conference center's spacious steps to meet us. It was fantastic to see all these important people from around the world holding tiny trees—and the press was there to cover the entire event.

1. *Why did Wangari Maathai decide to become an activist?*
2. *What concrete actions did she take to gain publicity for her cause?*

Source: Wangari Maathai, *Unbowed: A Memoir* (New York: Anchor Books, 2006), pp. 166–167.

PART 6

AFRICA IN THE AGE OF THE GREAT CONVERGENCE, 1990–2017

The Cold War ended in a process punctuated by the fall of the Berlin Wall in November 1989, the dissolution of the Soviet Communist Party in July 1990, and finally, the official breakup of the Soviet Union on December 31, 1991. At the same time, the Chinese Communist Party was developing a new system of political economy that featured an authoritarian government, a mixed economy with state-directed capitalism, and a welcoming attitude toward foreign corporations and investment. As a result of those transformations, Russia and China no longer supported revolutions around the globe. The world was returning to an older pattern in which each nation pursued its own political, economic, and military interests rather than following a particular political ideology. With Africa no longer caught between competing political and ideological camps, socialist countries such as Tanzania and Mozambique sought loans from the World Bank, in return for which they promised to make certain free-market reforms. In the new world order, each African country followed its own unique path.

In the global economy, there were signs of what some economists have called a Great Convergence, in which the wealth gap between high-income industrialized countries (mainly Western Europe, the United States, Japan, and South Korea) and the rest of the world was shrinking. In 1960, the wealthy countries had accounted for roughly 90 percent of the world's manufacturing, but by 2010, those countries had only 60 percent, while the former low-income countries had 40 percent. The trend lines were converging, but the global shift in manufacturing did not automatically translate into a convergence in overall wealth, because the low-wage workers in the new factories were not the ones who reaped the profits. Nevertheless, the gap in per capita gross domestic product (GDP) between the wealthy and the low-income countries was diminishing: per capita GDP in the wealthy countries was eight times that of the poor countries in the 1980s, but by 2010 it was only five times as much.

Those changes were the result of a number of factors: the deindustrialization of the Western manufacturing countries as they transitioned to more information- and service-oriented economies; the outsourcing of labor-intensive production to lower-wage countries; the rise of multinational corporations that could shift their financial resources from one country to another; and the emergence of petroleum (as opposed to cotton or rubber) as the most sought-after resource. The Great Convergence was most evident in China, India, and Southeast Asia, while it was barely visible in Africa. Nevertheless, its very existence as a global phenomenon meant that the era of the West's stranglehold on wealth and wealth creation was coming to a close, and that new opportunities were opening up for the countries that the West had formerly exploited.

The end of the Cold War allowed African states to form new relationships with a variety of countries around the globe and to develop new forms of political economy that followed neither the European model of parliamentary democracy nor the socialist model of a centrally planned economy. It also allowed some countries to experience what some analysts have called a "second independence" as democracy once again spread across Africa and some economies grew at a pace not seen in decades. After centuries of responding to external challenges such as the Atlantic slave trade, colonialism, and Cold War politics, many of the primary issues facing Africa were now originating in Africa itself. One was the AIDS crisis, which posed serious dangers to economic and human development. Another was the African World War, in which ethnic tensions in one small country in the heart of Africa grew into a war that involved troops from nine different African countries. A third was the Arab Spring, which disrupted and reorganized regimes across North Africa. In these and other areas, Africans were repositioning themselves to define issues in their own terms and create their own paths to the future.

FREE AT LAST! Nelson Mandela, accompanied by his wife Winnie, leaves prison on February 11, 1990. He had been incarcerated for 27 years. After gaining his freedom, he was elected president of the African National Congress (ANC) and led a multiracial delegation to negotiate majority rule for South Africa. After the ANC won nearly two-thirds of the votes in the 1994 elections, the new multiracial National Assembly elected Mandela as the first black president of South Africa.

1990
Benin holds first National Conference in Africa

1994
Nelson Mandela becomes president of South Africa

1996–2003
First and Second Congo Wars

16

AFRICA IN A MULTIPOLAR WORLD, 1990–2017

The end of the Cold War brought new opportunities for African peoples and governments to chart their own course and form external relations with the nations and international organizations of their choosing. In addition to the national governments around the globe that sought to redefine their relations with Africa, a variety of nongovernmental organizations (NGOs) from various parts of the world worked with African governments on cooperative projects ranging from health initiatives to wildlife conservation, while multinational corporations made investments and conducted trade in African countries. Under these altered circumstances, different countries followed different paths of national development and achieved different results.

This chapter explores some of the issues that Africans faced in the new multipolar world and examines some of the paths that they took. Democratic institutions were revived as South Africa achieved majority rule, and numerous countries held multiparty elections in a new trend that some have termed a "second independence." Economic growth returned to many countries as a result of policy changes, technological innovations, and developments in the global economy, most notably as China began to make major investments in Africa. Other trends were more disturbing: AIDS spread across Africa, and the African World War erupted in the heart of the continent. In North Africa, the Arab Spring movements toppled dictators in Tunisia, Egypt, and Libya, but dictatorship quickly reemerged

2000	2002	2011
First China-Africa Cooperation Forum	Anti-AIDS drugs become available	Fall of dictators in Tunisia, Egypt, and Libya

in Egypt, and Libya descended into chaos. The chapter concludes by looking at a unique situation in which past and present collided in the fabled city of Timbuktu.

GROWTH OF DEMOCRACY IN THE 1990s

Africa in the 1990s was a very different place from the continent that was just regaining its independence in the 1960s. One of the biggest changes was in the size of its population. Africa's population was growing at a rate of over 2 percent per year, which made it the fastest-growing continent in the world, while Asia and North America were growing at about 1 percent per year, and Europe's population growth was almost flat. Between 1960 and 1990, the population of Africa had more than doubled, increasing from 287 million to 635 million people. By the year 2000, the population of Africa was over 800 million. A corollary trend was the expansion of cities, which absorbed much of the expanding population from the countryside. The population of Lagos, Nigeria, for example, grew from 76,000 in 1960 to over 5 million in 1990.

In sub-Saharan Africa, political systems were in ferment. Multiparty democracy, which had been in retreat during the 1970s and 1980s, was on the rise in much of sub-Saharan Africa, where there were a total of 55 presidential elections and 85 National Assembly elections between 1990 and 2000, and where South Africa finally gained an elected government that represented the African majority. At the same time, however, the 1990s saw 17 successful military coups, 39 attempted coups, and 22 armed conflicts in the form of civil wars, separatist movements, rebellions, and ethnic warfare.

Freedom in Southern Africa

The collapse of the Soviet Union had significant repercussions at the southern tip of Africa, a region that contained white-ruled South Africa as well as Namibia, a former German colony that the League of Nations had placed under South African administration following World War I. When the United Nations revoked that mandate in 1966, the South African government refused to give up the territory and threatened to incorporate it into South Africa. South Africa's actions sparked an armed struggle for Namibia's independence led by the South-West Africa People's Organization (SWAPO), which was aided by the Cuban soldiers stationed in nearby Angola. After years of fighting, the South African government finally agreed to allow U.N. troops to move in and organize elections, provided that the Cuban troops withdrew to Angola. United Nations–supervised elections were held in November 1989, and Namibia became independent on March 21, 1991.

Equally dramatic events were taking place in South Africa. By 1990, the African National Congress (ANC) had been officially banned for 30 years, and its leader, Nelson Mandela, had been in prison for 26 years. South Africa, with its official policy of apartheid, had become an international pariah state that was increasingly subjected to sanctions, boycotts, and disinvestment by Europe and America. The status quo could not continue indefinitely. The break came when South African president P. W. Botha suffered a stroke in 1989 and was replaced by F. W. de Klerk, a conservative who nevertheless recognized the need to begin negotiations with South Africa's black leaders. On the opening day of the all-white parliament on February 2, 1990, he announced that he was releasing Nelson Mandela from prison and lifting the bans on the ANC and the other anti-apartheid organizations. Nine days later, with the world watching on television, Nelson Mandela walked out of prison.

The South African government had been unyielding in the face of African demands for democratic rights, in part because of its fear of communism. South Africa and Namibia were bordered by Mozambique and Angola to the north, which were both ruled by socialist regimes that were clients of the Soviet Union. Within South Africa itself, the major anti-apartheid organization was the ANC, which received support from the Soviet Union and the South African Communist Party. Moreover, the ANC's military wing, the Spear of the Nation, was being trained and armed by the Soviet Union. Surrounded by socialist regimes and challenged from within by the ANC, the white rulers of South Africa were terrified of being driven out by a communist takeover. The slow collapse of Soviet communism allayed some of those fears and created a space in which the white South African government was finally willing to negotiate with representatives of the black majority.

Negotiations for the future of South Africa began in May 1990, and in August, Mandela called on the Spear of the Nation to end its armed struggle. Even so, political activity during the negotiating process was punctuated by violence as rival African political organizations fought one another in the streets, and as right-wing white groups sought to assassinate President de Klerk and fought street battles to disrupt his speeches. Although the negotiations almost collapsed several times, an interim constitution was approved by December 1993. When South Africa's first multiracial election was held on April 27, 1994, the ANC won 252 seats in the 400-seat National Assembly, while the National Party (which represented most whites) won 82 seats, and smaller parties won the rest. As the leader of the winning party, Nelson Mandela was inaugurated as president of South Africa on May 10, 1994, 4 years and 3 months after his release from prison. The formal decolonization of Africa was finally complete.

The Second Independence in Tropical Africa

In 1989, Botswana and Gambia were the only countries on the African continent that had held regular multiparty elections since gaining their independence. Between 1989 and 2003, however, 44 states held multiparty elections to give democracy a fresh start, and 20 of them completed three successive election cycles. By 2006, no fewer than 18 heads of state had been removed through the ballot box, and by the end of 2007, more than 120 competitive presidential elections had been held in 39 African countries. For this reason, the 1990s became known as the **second independence** in Africa.

How do we explain the return to multiparty democracy at this particular time? For one thing, many of the early nationalist leaders who became the venerated founding fathers of their countries were gone: Kwame Nkrumah had been ousted in Ghana by a military coup; Jomo Kenyatta in Kenya and Ahmed Sékou Touré in Guinea had died; and Julius Nyerere in Tanzania and Leopold Senghor in Senegal had voluntarily retired, handing over their power to hand-picked successors. By the 1990s, a generation of young citizens had grown up without ever experiencing colonialism, and the heroes of anti-colonial struggles held little awe for them. A second reason was that authoritarian presidents, whether in military or civilian regimes, had previously maintained their political base by providing financial support to key persons, interest groups, and organizations in their countries. Budget cuts resulting from economic crises or World Bank structural adjustment policies curtailed the ability of these presidents to keep their supporters happy. A third reason was that with the end of the Cold War, the United States, the Soviet Union, and China had less incentive to provide aid to African regimes, thus further reducing the capacity of authoritarian rulers to reward their supporters.

Despite the dominance of single-party and military regimes in the Cold War era, many religious organizations, labor unions, women's groups, youth groups, university students, and merchants' associations had voiced their opposition to authoritarianism. Although the authoritarian governments tried to control major newspapers and radio and television stations, they could not suppress the private newspapers and foreign shortwave radio broadcasts offering alternative viewpoints. Perhaps the most important way in which people received opposition news was from "sidewalk radio," the colorful term people used for "the word on the street." It was clear that the idea of democracy was still attractive to many people.

National Conferences in Former French Colonies

In the former French colonies, the main vehicle for restoration of democracy was a **National Conference**, in which representatives of various political factions gathered to write a new constitution and organize elections. It was a particularly

French idea, echoing the Estates General meetings that had launched the French Revolution in 1789. The first National Conference in Africa was held in Benin in 1990, at a time when the government was in an economic crisis and unable to pay its employees. The National Conference established an interim government that organized a 1991 election. That election was won by Nicéphore Soglo, a former World Bank official who promised to implement World Bank structural adjustment reforms. Five years later, Soglo was defeated in the 1996 presidential election, in part because the World Bank reforms had failed to yield the promised results.

Benin's decision to restore multiparty democracy through a National Conference was replicated in Mali, Niger, and the Republic of the Congo (the former French Congo, known as Congo-Brazzaville for short) during 1991 and 1992. Mali's National Conference came about as the result of a military coup in which the officers who seized power promised to restore democracy as soon as possible. The election organized by the conference was won by Alpha Konaré, who won reelection in 1997 and retired in 2002 after reaching his constitutional two-term limit. In Niger and in Congo-Brazzaville, however, the multiparty democracies established through National Conferences were short-lived: the government of Congo-Brazzaville was taken over by an armed faction in 1997, and there was a military coup against the elected government in Niger in 1996. In the other former French colonies, National Conferences either failed to take place or did not result in a change of government.

Pressure for Elections in Former British Colonies

Governments in the former British colonies also faced pressure for multiparty elections, but they did not rely on National Conferences. In Zambia, for example, Kenneth Kaunda, who had been president ever since Zambia's independence in 1964, was pressured into calling an election when falling world copper prices pushed the Zambian economy into recession and incited many strikes and demonstrations. He was defeated in that 1991 election by Frederick Chiluba, a trade-union leader. When Kaunda tried to make a comeback in the 1996 election, he was declared ineligible on the grounds that he was not born in Zambia, and leaders of his political party were arrested for treason. As a result, Kaunda's party withdrew from the election, and Chiluba was reelected with little opposition. Chiluba retired at the end of his second term, as the constitution required, and was succeeded by his hand-picked successor, who barely eked out a victory in the 2001 election.

Uganda and Ghana, in contrast, were governed by presidents who had initially resisted elections and gained power by military force. In Uganda, President Yoweri Museveni, who had come to power as the leader of a rebellion, presented a new constitution in 1995 that permitted elections, but not political parties. When no-party elections were finally held in 2001, President Museveni won. In Ghana, Flight Lieutenant Jerry Rawlings, who had come to power in a military coup, at first resisted multiparty elections, but finally agreed to hold elections in 1992. He won with 58 percent of the vote. Tanzania and Kenya, two countries that had been led by a single party since independence, held multiparty elections for the first time in 1995 and 1997, respectively, but in both cases the ruling party won out over the divided opposition.

The Impact of the Elections

Unfortunately, the surge in multiparty elections did not bring an end to military coups. Between 1990 and 2001, there were 50 coup attempts, 13 of which were successful. In many cases, the military coups toppled elected governments. In Guinea-Bissau, for example, the election of 1994 was followed by coups in 1999 and 2003; in the Central African Republic, the president who had been elected in 1993 and reelected in 1999 was overthrown by a military coup in 2003; and in Mauritania, the president won three successive multiparty elections before being ousted by the military.

An alternative pattern emerged in southern Africa, where the former liberation movements maintained uninterrupted power, even though the presidency occasionally changed hands within the ruling party. The most extreme example is Zimbabwe. 93-year-old Robert Mugabe, who had led the country since its independence in 1980, fired his vice president (who had been his right-hand man for nearly 50 years) on November 6, 2017, to clear the way for his 52-year-old wife to become his vice president and designated successor. Mugabe's power grab backfired—the army placed him under house arrest, and the parliament began impeachment proceedings. He resigned on November 21 and was replaced three days later by the recently-fired vice president, Emmerson Mnangagwa, thus continuing the ruling party's grip on power.

THE AIDS CRISIS

At the same time that Africans were struggling to establish functioning democracies, they also faced a very different kind of challenge that was literally a matter of life and death. **AIDS** (Acquired Immune Deficiency Syndrome) destroys the human body's capacity to fight off disease, leaving the affected person vulnerable to death from a variety of common maladies. It is caused by the human immunodeficiency virus (HIV), which is transmitted mostly through unprotected sex, by contaminated hypodermic needles, and from mother to child during pregnancy. Although HIV/AIDS in the United States has often been associated with gay men because of the particular circumstances by which it entered the country, it can just as easily be passed between men and women. People who contract HIV may live for years without knowing they have it before it breaks out into full-blown AIDS. Between 1981, when it first erupted as a pandemic, and 2015, it caused 35 million deaths worldwide, and as of the end of 2015, 37 million people worldwide are living with HIV. Twenty-six million of them live in Africa, which is where two-thirds of the world's new HIV infections are found. AIDS was—and is—in large measure an African tragedy.

The Origin and Spread of AIDS

Although HIV/AIDS was recognized as a disease by the U.S. Centers for Disease Control only in 1981, HIV itself has been present in Africa for a long time. The simian immunodeficiency virus (SIV), which is genetically identical to HIV, lived in the blood of chimpanzees that inhabited the area south of the Sangha River in Cameroon. Because chimpanzees share 98–99 percent of their genome with humans, it was possible for the SIV virus to be transmitted to people who came into contact with chimpanzee blood, such as hunters and cooks. For hundreds of years, such cross-species transmission occurred from time to time and infected isolated individuals, but the virus did not disseminate into larger human populations. Usually, an infected hunter, and perhaps his wife or wives, would die of AIDS without passing the virus on to anybody else.

It was the rise of cities in the colonial period that created the conditions for the widespread dissemination of HIV/AIDS. Researchers have pointed to Brazzaville, the capital of French Equatorial Africa, as the place where HIV is most likely to have first spread to the wider population. During the colonial period, riverboats regularly traveled down the Sangha River, where the infected chimpanzees lived, to the Congo River and on to Brazzaville. At some point in the 1920s, a person identified by scientists as "Patient Zero" is believed to have carried the virus to Brazzaville and infected a local woman, who in turn infected other men. From there, the virus was carried across the Congo River to Kinshasa, the capital of the Belgian Congo, where the demographic predominance of young males had led to a low-level commercial sex trade. In the early 1900s, a typical female sex worker confined her encounters to a small number of regular clients, thus limiting the chain of transmission. By 1930, the total number of infected people was probably less than 100, and it stabilized at a few hundred after that. After Congo-Kinshasa became independent in 1960, however, the colonial restrictions on movement to cities were lifted, and a high-risk commercial sex trade appeared along with the swelling urban population. During the 1970s, the number of infected individuals in Kinshasa rose from 1,400 to 36,000.

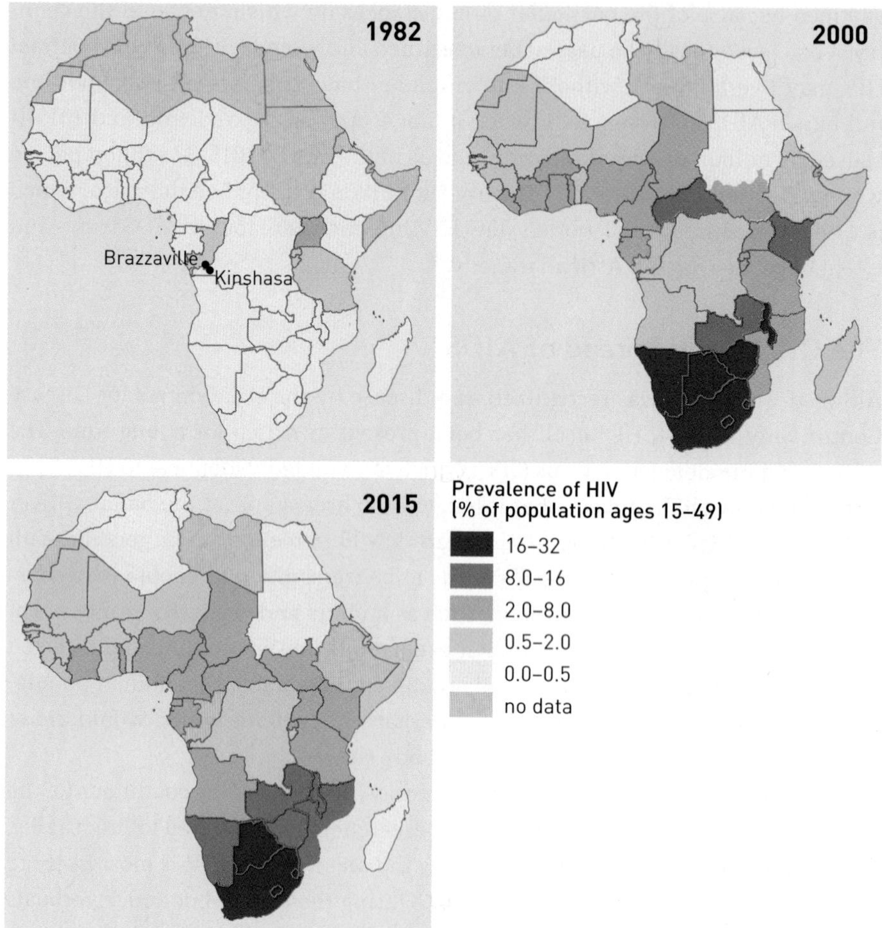

THE RAPID SPREAD OF HIV/AIDS These three maps show the extent of HIV infection in different African countries in 1982, 2000, and 2015. The 1982 map shows the cities of Kinshasa and Brazzaville, where the epidemic is believed to have started. HIV did not spread in a uniform manner. After 2000, the highest rates of infection were found in southern Africa.

HIV/AIDS did not spread in widening circles in the manner of a flu or smallpox epidemic. Instead, it jumped to other cities, carried by infected businessmen or government officials traveling by airplane. From the capital cities, it was carried along the rail lines and along the major roads by infected truck drivers. Because infected persons showed no symptoms during the incubation period, there was no way of knowing who had the virus and who did not, but certainly the unusually large numbers of young, unattached men and women in urban areas made the fast-growing cities incubators of the disease.

The Fight against AIDS

In the early years of the epidemic, government health officials could do little besides advocating condom use or sexual abstinence. By 1996, anti-retroviral drugs (ARVs) that could prevent HIV infection from developing into full-blown AIDS had been discovered, causing a rapid drop in the death rate from AIDS in Europe and North America. But the drugs were prohibitively expensive, costing over $10,000 per year for each patient. A major breakthrough came when a manufacturer of generic drugs in India offered to sell ARVs for $350 per year, a move that forced other pharmaceutical manufacturers to lower their prices. A variety of international agencies and NGOs, such as the World Bank, the United Nations, the U.S. Presidential Emergency Program, and the Bill & Melinda Gates Foundation, contributed funds to make the drugs available in Africa. Botswana launched the first national anti-retroviral project in 2002, and was quickly followed by other African countries in 2004 and 2005. The drugs did not cure the disease, but they could contain it and prevent more fatalities.

Public Pressure in South Africa

The country hit hardest by HIV/AIDS was South Africa, where the first two patients were diagnosed in 1983. The disease entered South Africa along the country's northern border. It initially spread within the dense rural population of KwaZulu-Natal, where there were high rates of migration between the countryside and the port city of Durban, and it also spread to rural areas crossed by major truck routes. By 1993, the virus had spread to a large proportion of the mine workers and commercial sex workers in the region of Johannesburg. Fatalities from AIDS increased from 87,000 in 1998 to 283,000 in 2006—making up 42 percent of all deaths in South Africa. By 2007, more than 5 million South Africans were infected with HIV, more people than in any other country in the world.

As the disease spread across South Africa, the new government launched a major program to distribute condoms, giving out 150 million in 1998 and 310 million in 2003. In 1999, however, Thabo Mbeki, who did not believe that HIV was the sole cause of AIDS and was wary of anti-retroviral drugs, was elected president. It was only after protests by AIDS activists and trade unions and a near revolt by the president's own cabinet that the government agreed to make ARV treatment available to the public. Even then, it moved slowly, and the anti-retroviral program did not really take off until after Mbeki finished his term in 2008. By 2014, some

2.4 million South Africans were being treated with ARVs, and the annual AIDS-related death rate had been cut in half.

Government Activism in Uganda

The most successful government intervention against AIDS was in Uganda, where the first cases occurred in the southwest of the country and in the capital city of Kampala. In the 1970s, bars and brothels that catered to long-haul truckers sprang up along the main roads and developed into a thriving sex trade. In 1979, when the Ugandan rebels and the Tanzanian army that overthrew President Idi Amin passed through that region, their advance was accompanied by the rape of local women and casual sex with multiple partners. All those activities combined to give the region the highest rate of HIV infection in Uganda. At the same time, the rule of Idi Amin had decimated Uganda's health care system. By the mid-1980s, Uganda was experiencing a serious epidemic of HIV/AIDS.

When Yoweri Museveni took power in 1986, he immediately took an interest in combating the AIDS epidemic. A year into his presidency, he announced the first AIDS control program in Africa, which Uganda developed in cooperation with the

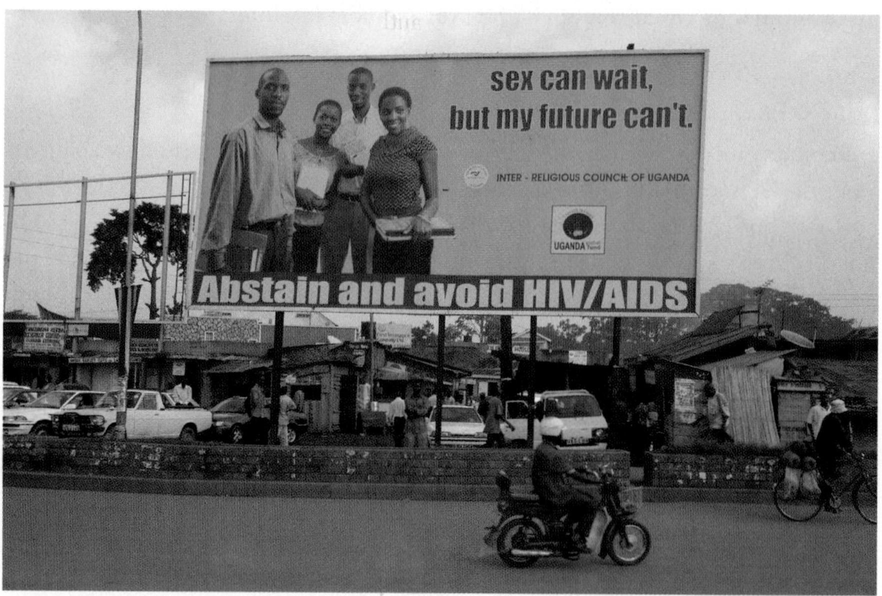

SEX CAN WAIT A billboard in Kampala, Uganda, in May 2006 promotes abstinence among young people as part of the anti-AIDS campaign conducted by the government and the churches of Uganda. With the support of President Yoweri Museveni, Uganda was a leader among African countries in fighting the AIDS epidemic.

World Health Organization. In a speech on World AIDS Day, he promised to expand public health services and urged people to "emulate the social behavior of our ancestors, which forbade immorality and irresponsible communal sexual lifestyles." He initiated a campaign to educate the public all the way down to the village level and made HIV instruction compulsory in all schools. He also welcomed international AIDS organizations, and he initiated a quiet campaign that promoted the use of condoms, a practice opposed by many traditionalists and the Catholic Church.

Studies in Uganda showed a significant drop in new infections during the 1990s. Some health researchers have suggested that it was the result of more restrained sexual behavior among young people, a trend that began in the late 1980s. Other researchers put the emphasis on the distribution of condoms. Surveys revealed a substantial increase in condom use, especially during casual or commercial sex. When anti-retroviral drugs became available, Uganda established one of the most effective treatment programs in Africa, which was reaching 40,000 to 50,000 patients by 2004.

The Political Impact of AIDS

Because the AIDS crisis erupted just as many African countries were experimenting with multiparty elections, some observers worried that the fear, anger, and anxiety provoked by AIDS would favor authoritarian leaders and overwhelm the fledgling steps toward democratization. But their worries proved to be overblown. There is no evidence of significant political fallout from the AIDS crisis, in part because the people realized that there was very little that governments could do prior to the development of ARVs, and in part because subsequent ARV programs were implemented in cooperation with international organizations, so that governments always shared responsibility for the outcomes. President Museveni's leadership in Uganda's fight against AIDS enhanced his popularity, while President Mbeki's reluctance to use ARVs in South Africa provoked resistance from AIDS activists, but in neither case did the AIDS crisis threaten the political system. AIDS was being managed, and lives were being prolonged, but African governments and international organizations made only limited progress in preventing new HIV infections. Living in the presence of AIDS was becoming the new normal.

THE AFRICAN WORLD WAR

In the 1990s, the diffuse challenges of democratization and AIDS were overshadowed by a series of events known as the **African World War**. Most of the fighting took place in Congo-Kinshasa, a country the size of Western Europe located in the center of the continent. Although the warfare did not reach global proportions, it got its name because the antagonists received military and diplomatic support from a number of other African countries. Unlike World War I or World War II, it was not primarily a war between countries, but was instead a war between political regimes and rebel movements. The African World War progressed in three stages: the Rwandan genocide, the First Congo War, and the Second Congo War. In all, more than 5 million Africans died in combat and from massacres, disease, and malnutrition during the war's three stages.

Stage One: Genocide in Rwanda

The African World War began in the tiny country of Rwanda, which is about the size of Massachusetts. Located high in the Virunga Mountains on the western edge of the East African Rift, Rwanda was known as "the land of a thousand hills." In precolonial times, the country was dominated by the Kingdom of Rwanda. The cattle-owning aristocrats who ruled the kingdom were called Tutsi, and the farmers who tilled the rich volcanic soil were called Hutu. To legitimize the Tutsi monopoly on power, the official historians at the Rwandan royal court recounted oral traditions that sought to justify why the Tutsi were the ruling class and the Hutu were left out.

Under the Belgian colonial system of indirect rule, the Kingdom of Rwanda was preserved, and members of the Tutsi minority continued to be the ruling class. Because the Tutsi were in the best position to take advantage of colonial education, they filled the ranks of clerks and low-level administrators in the Belgian colonial government. A Tutsi Catholic priest named Alexis Kagame published embellished versions of the Tutsi oral traditions, which made their way into the schools and spread the idea that the Tutsi were inherently noble while portraying the Hutu as rustic and rude. Beliefs in Tutsi superiority were enhanced and amplified by the Belgian colonial rulers. As the Belgian administrator Pierre Ryckmans wrote, "The Tutsi were meant to rule. Their fine presence is in itself enough to give them great prestige *vis-à-vis* the inferior races."

The notion that Tutsi and Hutu were two different tribes, much less races, is problematic. The Tutsi and Hutu spoke the same language (Kinyarwanda), and each of the 18 clans in the Kingdom of Rwanda had both Tutsi and Hutu members. In keeping with the normal criteria for distinguishing ethno-linguistic groups, it is more accurate to identify their ethnic group as Rwandan (*Banyarwanda* in the Rwandan language), and to see Tutsi and Hutu as hereditary occupational categories within the larger Rwandan ethnic group. Regardless of how their differences are defined, however, there was undeniable inequality and social tension—exacerbated by colonial rule—between the Hutu and Tutsi populations in Rwanda.

The Hutu Majority Takes Control

In the legislative elections of 1961 that preceded Rwandan independence from Belgium, the historical power equation was reversed in favor of the Hutu majority.

The Tutsi candidates got only 17 percent of the vote, while the Hutu candidates got 78 percent. Hutu politicians dominated the newly independent government and dissolved the old Kingdom of Rwanda, causing over 50,000 Tutsi to flee the country. To regain their lost political power, the Tutsi exiles in neighboring Burundi launched a failed invasion of Rwanda in 1963, inciting the Hutu government to retaliate by slaughtering some 10,000 Tutsi and forcing others into exile. Despite the exodus, a substantial number of Tutsi who had never been part of the ruling nobility remained in Rwanda and largely stayed out of politics.

By the late 1970s, over half a million Tutsi refugees were living in neighboring countries such as Uganda, Burundi, Tanzania, and Congo-Kinshasa. They dreamed of returning to Rwanda and reestablishing their former dominance. At the World Congress of Rwandese Refugees held in Washington, D.C., in 1988, they pushed passionately for the "right of return" to Rwanda. The most militant of the refugees were the Tutsi in Uganda, many of whom lived in U.N. refugee camps. They formed the Rwandan Patriotic Front, which crossed the border to wage guerrilla warfare against the Hutu government. By the end of 1992, the Patriotic Front had roughly 12,000 fighters, who were funded in part by Tutsi exile communities in the United States and Canada. With the war causing a strain on the fragile Rwandan economy, the president of Rwanda signed an agreement with the Patriotic Front in August 1993. Known as the Arusha Accords, the agreement called for power sharing between Tutsi and Hutu in government, integration of the army, and the return of exiles. Because the agreement was extremely unpopular among the Hutu majority in Rwanda, the Hutu president kept delaying its implementation.

Planning and Orchestrating the Genocide

Some Hutu extremists believed that the president had betrayed his supporters by signing the Arusha Accords, and they begin to think that slaughtering the Tutsi was the ultimate solution to their fears of Tutsi domination. It was then that the idea of genocide was born. A group of extremist Hutu army officers formed a secret society, called *Amasasu* (Bullets), that had influence over the private youth militias known as *interahamwe*, whose members had been trained and indoctrinated by those officers. Credible reports reached the United Nations in 1993 that the *interahamwe* militias were drawing up lists of Tutsi, although it was not certain whether they were planning isolated massacres or full-scale genocide. Because Hutu and Tutsi spoke the same language and belonged to the same clans, it was often difficult to tell who should be identified with which group, which was why the *interahamwe* militias needed the lists.

In addition to this clandestine activity, a public propaganda campaign against the Tutsi was waged by a new radio station called Thousand Hills Free Radio. The station was cofounded by a Hutu intellectual who held a Ph.D. in history from the University of Paris. Its broadcasts railed against the Arusha Accords and warned darkly that the Tutsi wanted to reestablish the old Kingdom of Rwanda and enslave the Hutu. The anti-Tutsi propaganda turned the old colonial stereotypes on their heads: whereas the Belgian colonizers had claimed that the Tutsi were outsiders in order to emphasize their superiority, the Hutu propaganda campaign used the same claim to argue that the Tutsi were an alien race who did not belong in Rwanda. By 1993–1994, talk of genocide was becoming common; one magazine, for example, published a headline saying, "The Tutsi Race Could Be Extinguished."

Although it was often portrayed in the Western media as a spontaneous eruption of primitive tribal hatred, the **Rwandan genocide** was, in fact, a carefully orchestrated campaign by extremist Hutu intellectuals and military officers. When the president of Rwanda (who was a Hutu) was returning from a trip on April 6, 1994, his presidential plane was shot down by two missiles fired from the perimeter of the Kigali airport. Although the culprits have never been caught, and a gamut of conspiracy theories have been proposed, the timeline of events on April 6 lends support to the view that the plane was shot down by Hutu extremists who felt that their president had betrayed his Hutu supporters. The plane went down at 8:30 p.m., and by 9:15 the *interahamwe* militias had set up roadblocks all over Kigali and had begun searching houses for Tutsi, using their previously prepared lists. Throughout the night, Thousand Hills Free Radio called on people to kill all Tutsi to avenge the death of the president. "Some [Tutsi] are still alive," said one broadcast. "You must go back and finish them off. The graves are not yet full."

Over the next 100 days, the graves were overflowing, as some 800,000 Tutsi and many moderate Hutu were killed. A great many Hutu civilians willingly joined the slaughter under the influence of the incessant radio broadcasts and the *interahamwe* militias, but others did so only out of fear of being killed themselves, and still others worked actively to save Tutsi lives. The killing did not end until the Tutsi rebel army of the Rwandan Patriotic Front captured Rwanda's capital city on July 4, 1994. Fearing revenge, between 1 million and 2 million Hutu fled across the border into Congo-Kinshasa. Among them were many of the military officers and *interahamwe* militia members who had organized and carried out the genocide.

Stage Two: The First Congo War

After 1994, the theater of war shifted from Rwanda to Congo-Kinshasa. With the equator running through its center, much of the Congo is covered with thick tropical rainforests. Eastern Congo, where the war began, is a mountainous region with snowcapped peaks up to 16,700 feet high. The Congo had been ruled since 1965 by

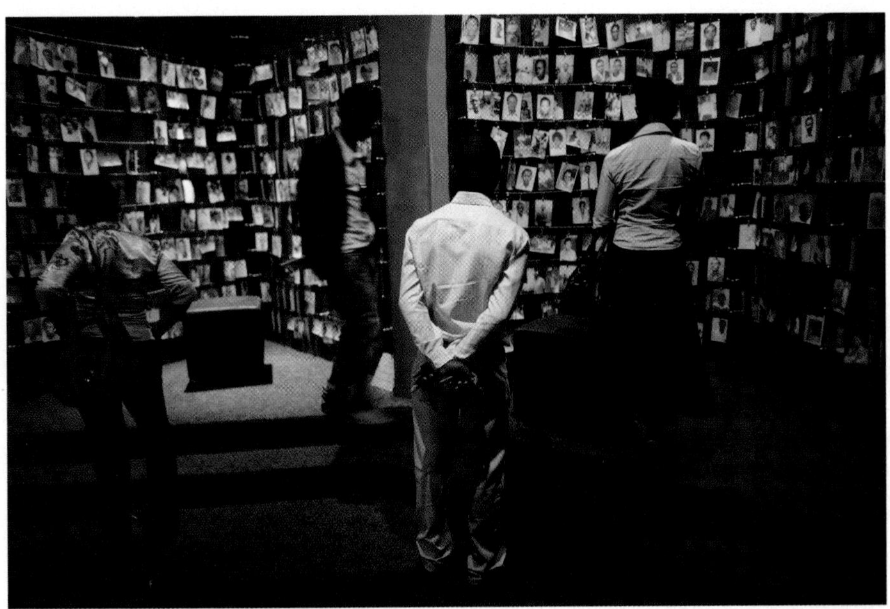

VICTIMS OF GENOCIDE Visitors look over the photos of victims of the 1994 Rwandan genocide at the Kigali Genocide Memorial Centre, in the capital of Rwanda, on April 5, 2014. More than 800,000 Tutsi and moderate Hutu were slaughtered during a 100-day period. The remains of over 250,000 people are buried at the Memorial Centre, which seeks to give comfort to the bereaved.

the authoritarian dictator Mobutu Sese Seko (formerly known as Joseph Mobutu; see chapter 15), who had been strongly supported by the United States during the Cold War despite his corrupt and ineffective governance.

Many of the Hutu living in refugee camps in eastern Congo after the Rwandan genocide created armed militias that planned to invade Rwanda, drive out the new Tutsi government, and retake power. To stop them, the Tutsi government in Rwanda launched attacks on the Hutu refugee camps—attacks that were opposed by the Congolese army of President Mobutu. To increase its military capability in eastern Congo, the Rwandan Tutsi government sought military alliances with Tutsi groups already living in eastern Congo. Wanting to avoid the appearance of waging an ethnic war in the wake of the genocide, the Rwandan government encouraged the Tutsi in eastern Congo to join an anti-Mobutu rebel movement led by Laurent Kabila, a man from southern Congo (and thus neither Hutu nor Tutsi) who was a longtime foe of Congo's President Mobutu.

Strengthened by Rwandan Patriotic Front soldiers and the Tutsi fighters, Kabila's rebel army gained control of eastern Congo by January 1997, and in

REFUGEE CAMP Refugees walk among the tents in a refugee camp in northern Burundi, where some 63,000 Tutsi fled to escape the slaughter in Rwanda. They began to return home only after Tutsi rebel forces took power in Rwanda in July 1994.

February, it began to move westward through the tropical rainforest toward the capital city of Kinshasa, over a thousand miles away. In a bizarre historical irony, the rebel army carried the flag of Belgian king Leopold II's Congo Free State, with its single gold star on a field of blue. On May 17, the rebel army captured Kinshasa, and Laurent Kabila installed himself as head of state. The soldiers had crossed the entire country in only 100 days. Because the core of Kabila's army consisted of Rwandan soldiers, one could say that tiny Rwanda, in effect, had conquered the gigantic Congo. It was a feat akin to Belgium conquering Western Europe. They succeeded because Mobutu's army was a corrupt and undisciplined group that harassed civilians, but sought above all to avoid a real fight.

Stage Three: The Second Congo War

Once Laurent Kabila was in power in Kinshasa, his alliance with the Rwandans began to fray. A little over a year after taking power, he ordered all Rwandan troops to leave the Congo and began to stir up anti-Tutsi sentiment in Kinshasa. The Rwandans now saw Kabila as their enemy, and they moved quickly to take over the major cities in eastern Congo. They also sent a Boeing 707 carrying 180 Rwandan, Ugandan, and Congolese Tutsi soldiers to a military base near Kinshasa to launch an attack on the capital. In response, troops from Zimbabwe, Angola, and Namibia flew to Kinshasa to defend Kabila, while Chad sent troops to aid Kabila in the north. Those alliances contributed to the war's character as an African World War. The Angolan and Zimbabwean troops defended Kinshasa, but by the year 2000, Congolese groups allied with the government of Rwanda controlled most of eastern Congo, while groups allied with the government of Uganda controlled the northern third of the country. Altogether, 140,000 troops representing nine African countries were fighting in the Congo. To these troops would be added 5,500 U.N. peacekeepers, dispatched in 2001 to monitor any cease-fire agreements that might be negotiated.

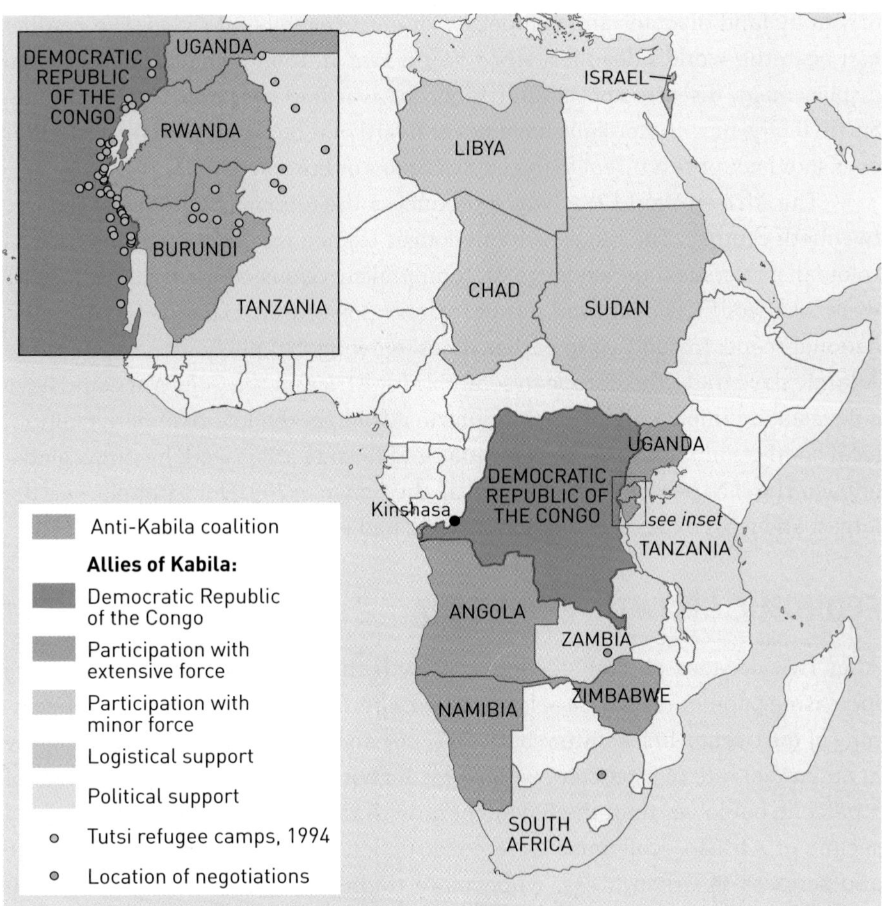

THE INTERNATIONAL DIMENSION OF THE SECOND CONGO WAR This map shows the African countries that were involved in the Second Congo War either as combatants or as providers of logistical or political support. Zimbabwe, Namibia, Angola, Chad, and Sudan provided troops to support the Kabila government, while Rwanda, Burundi, and Uganda supported the anti-Kabila forces. Altogether, 140,000 troops representing nine African countries fought in the Congo.

After numerous attempts to reach a diplomatic solution to the conflict ended in failure, the warring parties signed a treaty in 2003 calling for national elections. United Nations–supervised elections, which were generally deemed to be free and fair, were held in 2006. The African World War was officially over, but fighting among various local factions continued in the mountains of eastern Congo, driven by land disputes and competing claims over mineral rights. The conflict had been the world's deadliest since World War II. If one includes deaths from displacement, disease, and malnutrition, the war had cost over 5 million lives. Surprisingly, most Americans have never heard of it because, with the Cold War over, it did not pose a threat to the United States or Europe.

The African World War was a product of the unique conditions of the late twentieth century. The issues were no longer framed in global dualisms such as colonialism versus independence or communism versus capitalism, but instead were local conflicts over land, property, and power that expanded to an international scope. In contrast to earlier times, when global phenomena such as the Atlantic slave trade, the European scramble for Africa, or the Cold War could have a devastating impact on local situations in Africa, in the late twentieth century, local conflicts amplified by local militias and outside allies were having a global impact. The U.N. peacekeeping mission to the Congo in 2001, for example, was the largest and most expensive mission the U.N. had ever undertaken.

ECONOMIC GROWTH, 2000-2017

After two decades of slow economic growth that could not keep up with its increasing population, Africa at last entered a period of rapid growth at the beginning of the twenty-first century. Between 2001 and 2015, African economies grew at an annual rate of 5 percent, which was higher than the world growth rate of 4 percent, but lower than the 8 percent growth rate in Asia. The fastest-growing sectors of African economies were construction of housing and infrastructure and services in urban areas, while more traditional sectors, such as agriculture and manufacturing, lagged behind. A U.N. report attributed the growth to increased political stability, a high demand for African commodities driven mostly by China, and improved economic policies in African countries. A separate study by the Center for Global Development identified 17 "emerging African countries," with a combined population of 300 million people, that had made dramatic changes in economic growth and poverty rates between 1996 and 2008. The report attributed the renewed growth to five key changes: the rise of more democratic and accountable governments; more sensible economic policies; debt relief extended by international lending agencies; the spread of new technologies; and a new generation of public and private leaders in all sectors of society.

Technological change was led by the explosion of mobile phone use and internet access. Africa had 230 million mobile phone subscriptions in 2007, double the number from just 2 years earlier, making it the fastest-growing phone market in the world. By 2007, mobile phone coverage was available to two-thirds of the population in sub-Saharan Africa. Internet access increased tenfold between

2000 and 2007 to reach 50 million users across the continent, and large cities were dotted with internet cafés that catered to people who could not afford computers of their own. New fiber-optic cables were being installed to increase access and lower costs. In 2009, the new Seacom cable to East Africa provided internet service that was 10 times faster than anywhere else in Africa, and the East African Submarine Cable System, which began operations in 2010, connected 19 different countries with the rest of the world. In West Africa, two fiber-optic cables were laid along the coast. Social impact aside, these technological advances changed the way people did their work. Those in business now had access to up-to-date information on prices and shipment schedules, and health workers could now transmit warnings about disease outbreaks and disseminate treatment information.

CHINA IN AFRICA

The impact of the new, multipolar world could be seen in China's aggressive program of investments in Africa. China itself had entered a period of rapid industrialization in the 1990s that accelerated even more dramatically after 2007, when its industrial output doubled in just 6 years. By 2010, China's industrial output had surpassed that of the United States. This rapid industrialization created a demand for many of Africa's raw materials. During the Cold War, China had supplied arms and training to anti-colonial liberation movements in Africa and given aid to African socialist governments, but it did so mostly for ideological purposes. With a population of over a billion people, an ongoing industrial revolution, and a government dedicated to state-directed capitalism, twenty-first-century China was on the hunt for commodities such as oil, cobalt, nickel, copper, aluminum, bauxite, and iron.

China's new relationship with Africa began in 2000, when it invited government officials from 44 African countries to attend the first meeting of the newly established **China-Africa Cooperation Forum** in Beijing. The second meeting of the forum was held in Ethiopia in 2003. At the third meeting, held in Beijing in 2006, the Chinese government announced that it would double its aid and investment in Africa. Four months later, Chinese president Hu Jintao toured eight African countries, announcing billions of dollars of debt relief along with new investments and low-interest loans. By 2009, China had cancelled more than $10 billion in African debt. These investments paid off in increased trade. By 2012, China's trade with Africa amounted to over $165 billion, far more than the $7 billion of 1999. By then, China was Africa's largest trading partner. By 2014, more than 800 Chinese corporations were doing business with Africa (mostly in the infrastructure, energy, and banking sectors), and an estimated 1 million Chinese citizens were in Africa working for Chinese corporations and projects.

CHINA-AFRICA COOPERATION Chinese president Hu Jintao (center), Ethiopia's prime minister Meles Zenawi (left), and Egypt's president Muhammad Hosni Mubarak (right) read out a declaration at the end of the China-Africa Cooperation Forum held in Beijing on November 5, 2006. Chinese and African leaders ended the forum by signing deals worth $1.9 billion and pledging to boost trade and development between the world's fastest-growing economy and its poorest continent.

China's approach to aid and investment was very different from those of the U.S. Agency for International Development, the International Monetary Fund, and the World Bank. In the first place, those agencies frequently demanded changes in the policies and practices of African governments as a condition for loans. China, in contrast, operated on the principle of noninterference. Because China was itself an authoritarian state, its aid was not accompanied by lectures on democracy and human rights. Second, instead of sponsoring individual projects, as the Western-oriented agencies tended to do, the Chinese preferred complex package deals that included trade, investment, and aid, and they used a combination of grants, loans, debt relief, commercial investment, and trade agreements to gain access to Africa's strategic resources. In 2007, for example, China signed an agreement with Congo-Kinshasa that provided a $6 billion loan for building railroads, roads, and mines in exchange for an equivalent share of the profits from copper mining. Projects built with Chinese grants or loans were usually required to be built mainly by Chinese companies and to use substantial numbers of Chinese workers.

China in Angola, Zambia, and Ethiopia

Examples from Angola, Zambia, and Ethiopia will illustrate different facets of the Chinese approach to aid and cooperation in Africa. In 2005, the Chinese premier visited Angola and signed nine agreements. As Angola is sub-Saharan Africa's second-largest producer of oil, seven of them had to do with Angola's oil industry: China promised to help develop Angola's offshore oil and gas resources, assist its Ministry of Petroleum, and build a new oil refinery; and it signed four agreements with Angola's state-run oil company to guarantee China a long-term supply of oil. In a separate set of agreements, China gave Angola a $2 billion low-interest loan to rehabilitate its infrastructure, which had been badly damaged in its long civil war (see chapter 15). The infrastructure projects included the building of three railroad lines as well as bridges, roads, and airports. The loan agreement stated that 70 percent of the firms doing the work would be Chinese and 30 percent Angolan, but it is unclear how many Angolan companies ever received contracts or how many Angolans were ever employed in the projects. The popular perception in Angola was that most of the loan money went to Chinese contractors, who brought in large numbers of Chinese workers. By 2008, Angola was China's second-largest African trading partner and accounted for 25 percent of China's total trade with Africa.

In Zambia, China's interest was primarily in copper. Between 2000 and 2008, China swallowed up 80 percent of any increase in the world's copper supply. Zambia had been the third-largest copper producer in the world when it gained independence in 1964, but by 2000, low prices and the failure of the state-controlled mining company to invest in maintenance and equipment had diminished its copper production by two-thirds. When the Zambian government put the country's copper mines up for sale in 1998, the China Nonferrous Metal Mining Company, owned by the Chinese government, acquired the Chambishi copper mine for $20 million and pledged to invest $200 million to bring it up to date.

China's role in the Zambian economy became a heated issue during the 2006 presidential election, when the opposition party accused the Chinese mining company of paying low wages and ignoring safety procedures, leading to the deaths of 49 miners in an explosion at the Chambishi mine. They further accused the Chinese of importing cheap goods and driving Zambian traders out of business. The Chinese ambassador to Zambia responded by threatening to pull China's investments out of Zambia if the opposition party won, thus violating China's policy of noninterference. After the Zambian president won reelection, Chinese President Hu Jintao spent 2 days in Zambia during his eight-nation trip to Africa. He promised to invest $800 million in a new multipurpose economic zone near the Chambishi mine, cancel Zambia's debt, and build projects such as a sports stadium, an agricultural technology center, schools, and a hospital. His plan to visit the copper-mining region, however, had to be cancelled for fear of protests by the mine workers.

China's involvement with Ethiopia, a poor country that lacked any valuable minerals, was very different. Ethiopia, with the second-largest population in Africa, offered a ready supply of workers for labor-intensive manufacturing industries. In the 1990s, China's industrial revolution had driven up industrial wages dramatically, and it turned to Ethiopia for cheap labor. In 2014, the average Chinese factory worker made $560 per month, whereas Ethiopian workers in Chinese-owned companies earned a monthly wage of only $30. Some economists predict that as Chinese manufacturing becomes more expensive, China could export as many as 80 million jobs overseas.

In 2014, the Chinese premier announced that China was supporting "Ethiopia's great vision to become Africa's manufacturing powerhouse." To improve

MAKING SHOES IN ETHIOPIA A Chinese supervisor oversees the workers at the Huajian shoe factory in Dukem, Ethiopia, in 2012. The factory employs 2,000 people (1,670 of them Ethiopians), to produce high-quality shoes for the European and Asian markets. It is one of six Chinese factories operating in the Chinese-built Eastern Industry Zone—Ethiopia's first industrial park—which the government hopes will attract private foreign investment and boost the country's manufacturing and export sector.

the country's transportation infrastructure and power grid, China funded a railroad from Ethiopia to the Red Sea and invested in several dams, including the Grand Ethiopian Renaissance Dam, which was expected to increase Ethiopia's electricity supply fivefold by 2020. There was speculation that Ethiopia's combination of low-cost labor and abundant electric power would transform it into a "new China."

Assessing China's Impact

Some African leaders raised the question of whether China's aggressive investments in Africa amounted to a new colonialism. South Africa's president Thabo Mbeki warned in 2006 that Africa risked becoming an economic colony of China. Yet there were clear differences between the nineteenth-century colonialism of Britain, France, and Portugal and the twenty-first-century Chinese initiatives. First, the Chinese were not trying to export Chinese civilization to Africa or to take over African governments. To them, the relationship was strictly business. Second, China did not demand exclusive trade rights, which were a key feature of European colonialism. In Zambia, for example, China owned one of the large copper mines, but the other two large mines were owned by a Swiss and an Indian company, respectively. Third, African countries that accepted aid from China continued to work with Western countries and agencies. Zambia, for example, accepted aid from China, but also from the United States, the World Bank, and the International Monetary Fund, so it could hardly be called a Chinese colony.

A related question was whether African governments would see China as a model to be emulated and would establish politico-economic systems within Africa that mixed authoritarian rule, state-controlled enterprises, and a vigorous capitalist sector welcoming of foreign investment. Political scientist Jeffrey Herbst concluded that African countries were not flocking to the Chinese model, and he pointed to the fact that periodic elections have become entrenched in African countries as part of the political culture, even if those elections are not always free and fair.

Rwanda and Ethiopia, however, did each develop a hybrid form of government that bears some resemblance to the Chinese model. This type of government, which political scientist Hilary Matfess has called **developmental authoritarianism**, emerged in Rwanda in the aftermath of the genocide and in Ethiopia following the overthrow of the Derg. The two countries stand out for their embrace of seemingly opposing traits: free-market ideology along with state intervention in public works and services; formal institutions of democracy along with harsh restrictions on opposition parties; and a welcoming attitude toward foreign investment along with resistance to international human rights organizations. Both countries have experienced rapid economic growth. Between 1990 and

2012, Rwanda nearly doubled its per capita GDP from $353 to $620, while Ethiopia (one of the poorest countries in the world) raised its per capita GDP from $251 to $470. Even though both regimes were juggling elements that seem contradictory, they were among the most stable governments in Africa.

THE ARAB SPRING IN NORTH AFRICA

On December 17, 2010, **Muhammad Bouazizi**, a 26-year-old street vendor in one of Tunisia's smaller cities, who had been continually harassed by the authorities for purportedly selling his vegetables without a license, set himself on fire in front of the police station in protest. Soon, massive anti-government protests erupted all over the country, causing Tunisia's authoritarian regime to fall on January 14, 2011. Less than a month later, the authoritarian regime in Egypt collapsed under the weight of similar protests, and its collapse was followed by that of the Libyan regime on August 23. The unrest then spread to the Arabian Peninsula. In Yemen, the authoritarian government collapsed on November 23, and in Syria, peaceful protests turned into a full-scale rebellion led by a group that called itself the Free Syrian Army. Collectively, these events, which brought about the fall of long-standing authoritarian regimes and held out the promise of democracy, are known as the **Arab Spring**.

Authoritarian Regimes and Their Opponents

At the time the protests began, the five countries of North Africa were each ruled by an authoritarian regime. In Egypt, Hosni Mubarak had been in power for 29 years; in neighboring Libya, Muammar Gaddafi had been in power for 41 years; in Tunisia, Zine El Abidine Ben Ali had ruled for 23 years; and Algeria had been under one-party rule from 1962 to 1989, after which certain small, moderate parties were allowed as long as they did not threaten the dominant party. Only Morocco had maintained a multiparty parliament, but it had little impact because most of the power was held by the monarchy.

Opposition to the authoritarian governments came from two directions. On the one side were secular nationalists. Some of them were socialists and others were liberal democrats, but all of them favored secular laws and government, even though most of them were practicing Muslims themselves. The secular nationalists often found support from groups such as labor unions, student organizations, and women's rights organizations. On the other side were advocates of political Islam, who are often referred to as Islamists. The rise of Islamist politics in North Africa dates from the dissolution of the Ottoman Empire in 1924. Many Muslims saw the Ottoman Empire (or the Ottoman caliphate, as it was sometimes called) as the last embodiment of the Islamic Caliphate that stretched back to the seventh century (see chapter 3). For centuries, the empire had provided the political framework within which most Muslims lived. Politics was not seen as a separate sphere of endeavor; instead, religion and politics were seen as part of a unitary whole under the guidance of the Quran and the discipline of sharia. At its height in the seventeenth century, the Ottoman Empire stretched from Algeria to Iran. Most people living in the empire viewed Islamic law, Islamic rule, and Islamic practice as part of the natural order of things. After the Ottoman Empire was dissolved at the end of World War I, Muslims were faced with the challenge of finding a way to remain faithful to Islam in the political context of modern secular states.

The Muslim Brotherhood in Egypt

One solution came from the **Muslim Brotherhood**, which was founded in Egypt in 1928 by a schoolteacher named Hasan al-Banna. The Brotherhood did not seek to dismantle the modern state, but hoped to harness it for religious ends. Rejecting the passivity and fatalism that was common among the Muslim religious establishment at the time, al-Banna preached that people should fully embrace Islam as a comprehensive way of life in order to create a truly Islamic society. The people would then be able to establish an Islamic state by popular consent. Instead of Islam being taken for granted as part of the natural order of things, al-Banna argued that it had to become a self-conscious and purposeful project in order to counterbalance the corrosive influence of the modern secular state. The Muslim Brotherhood was not trying to foment a political revolution, but sought to gradually transform society and politics from the ground up. By the 1940s, the Muslim Brotherhood had more than half a million members in Egypt.

Despite its focus on personal piety, the Muslim Brotherhood ran afoul of the military government of Gamal Abdel Nasser. The organization was outlawed after a member of the Brotherhood was accused of trying to assassinate Nasser in 1954, and thousands of its members were put in prisons and concentration camps. When Anwar Sadat succeeded Nasser in 1970, he gradually released Muslim Brotherhood members from prison and closed the concentration camps, but the organization itself remained illegal.

When the ban on multiple political parties was loosened in 1977, the Brotherhood sought to get involved in electoral politics. Although it could not legally form a political party, its members ran for parliament as members of other parties or as independents. Their involvement in electoral politics suggests that they accepted the reality of the modern Egyptian state and saw parliamentary democracy as a key to gaining influence.

Al-Nahda (The Renaissance) in Tunisia

The situation in Tunisia was somewhat different. In the mid-1960s, a group of Muslims who felt that Tunisian society had become too secularized and Westernized began meeting in a mosque in Tunis and formed an organization called the Islamic Group. During the 1960s and 1970s, they were largely apolitical and followed the model of the Muslim Brotherhood, which sought to reform Islam from the ground up. In 1981, however, they changed the group's name to the Islamic Tendency Movement and became a formal political organization that called for multiparty elections. Their leadership was quickly arrested and imprisoned.

When multiparty elections in Tunisia were announced for 1989, the group renamed itself *al-Nahda* (the Renaissance) and applied for formal recognition as a political party. The application was rejected. As Tunisian president Ben Ali stated, "We say to those who mix religion and politics that there is no way of allowing them to form a political party." *Al-Nahda* members nevertheless ran as independent candidates in nearly all the electoral districts. The government claimed that they got only 15 percent of the vote, but the Islamists believed that the election had been stolen. When *al-Nahda* activists organized protests at the university and in working-class neighborhoods, the government unleashed late-night raids and house-to-house searches for party activists, some of whom were tortured and tried in military courts. In May 1991, the government announced that it had uncovered a plot to overthrow the regime, and it arrested some 8,000 *al-Nahda* supporters over the next few months, effectively destroying the party.

The Fall of Authoritarian Regimes

The authoritarian governments in North Africa had successfully crushed or co-opted their opponents for many years, but the situation shifted in 2011, when the regimes in Tunisia and Egypt were toppled by massive peaceful protests, and the regime in Libya was overthrown by a combination of protests and armed rebellion. There are three reasons for the successes of the pro-democracy forces: first, in each of these countries, the government had created martyrs that people could rally around; second, there was strong participation by young people and women; and third, the young people used social media to organize protests and recruit demonstrators. Yet each of these countries had its own unique revolution, as a closer look at them will show.

Tunisia

Until 2011, the Ben Ali regime had ruled Tunisia by a mixture of coercion and rewards. There was one uniformed police officer for every 100 people, ordinary citizens were extensively monitored by agents of the ruling party, and political activists were subjected to torture and trial by military courts. On the other hand, there was an implicit "security pact" between the government and the people by which the people gained easy access to credit and consumer goods in return for tolerating the loss of their civil liberties.

The security pact began to unravel after the Tunisian government accepted World Bank recommendations to sell off unprofitable public-sector industries and agricultural cooperatives, leaving workers with few options other than low-paying jobs in resorts and call centers. Nearly half of the young people who had graduated from universities lacked jobs commensurate with their education. Muhammad Bouazizi, the street vendor who set himself on fire, had a university degree.

The uprisings sparked by Muhammad Bouazizi's dramatic protest were originally focused on widespread unemployment and high food prices, but they soon turned against the oppressive president. "Bread, water, yes!" shouted the crowds, "Ben Ali no!" It seemed that people of all generations, social classes, and ideologies were united in demanding the fall of the government. The spread of the protests was aided by electronic media, leading some people to call it the first "Twitter revolution." The Qatar-based satellite-TV channel Al Jazeera broadcast videos and photos sent in by the protesters; other activists used social media to send out the times and locations of upcoming demonstrations and

MARTYR OF THE REVOLUTION Demonstrators gather in the town of Sidi Bouzid in the birthplace of the country's revolution, to protest the visit of Tunisian president Moncef Marzouki on December 17, 2012. The large portrait shows Muhammad Bouazizi, who had set himself on fire in front of the town hall 2 years earlier. He did so after he was publicly slapped and humiliated by a policewoman who reprimanded him for selling vegetables without a license.

report on the movements and activities of the government security organizations. Intense political conversations were held on the streets of the major cities, where people reclaimed their freedom of speech despite the constant threat of attack by the police. Women participated in the street gatherings, a forum that had traditionally been dominated by men. On January 14, 2011, less than a month after the start of the demonstrations, President Ben Ali fled the country.

Egypt

The unrest then spread to Egypt, where structural adjustment programs imposed by the World Bank had created widespread discontent. 40 percent of Egypt's state-owned companies were privatized during the 1990s, which led to stagnant or falling wages and a rise in unemployment. The Egyptian government also cut spending for schools and health care, and it steadily reduced subsidies for bread and fuel. In a country with a severe shortage of agricultural land, large tracts of land were privatized by corporations and wealthy families for industrial agriculture and real estate development.

The rising discontent that resulted created widespread political turmoil in Egypt during the first decade of the twenty-first century. Four independent trade unions were founded, and thousands of wildcat strikes erupted against public and private companies. In addition to workplace protests, there were protests by professional associations, youth groups, and religious groups such as the Muslim Brotherhood, as well as general protests organized by the residents of urban neighborhoods or rural towns. As a result, people in all sectors of Egyptian society gained experience in organizing and carrying out collective action.

Elections for the People's Assembly in November 2010 accelerated the grassroots organizing. The Muslim Brotherhood was still banned, but a variety of small opposition parties organized rallies and demonstrations to drum up support. As the elections approached, the security forces cracked down on the political opposition. Many supporters of the Muslim Brotherhood and other opposition parties were arrested; many candidates were disqualified; and the government worked with internet providers to suppress mass text messaging. After an election marred by violence, intimidation of voters, ballot stuffing, and counting irregularities, the official results gave 420 seats to the ruling party and only 14 to the opposition parties. The opposition parties felt that the election had been rigged, but people who protested the results risked being beaten or arrested.

Tensions were high as the January 25 Police Day holiday approached. Although the holiday was meant as a day of national unity, a variety of opposition groups were planning to protest on that day. The established political parties refused to take part in the demonstrations, so they were organized mainly by youth groups such as the April 6 Youth Movement and *Kefaya* (Enough!). People under 30 years of age made up nearly two-thirds of the Egyptian population, so young people were a powerful political force. Information about the protest was disseminated by Google's Middle East executive, Wael Ghoneim, who started an anti-government website dedicated to Khaled Said, a blogger who was tortured and beaten to death by the police in Alexandria. In symbolic terms, Khaled Said was Egypt's equivalent of Tunisia's martyr, Muhammad Bouazizi.

On Tuesday, January 25, protesters assembled in different parts of Cairo and began moving toward **Tahrir Square**, which was not a square at all, but a large traffic circle where seven roads met. The first group that arrived broke through the police barrier and allowed thousands more to stream in, until there were between 15,000 and 25,000 demonstrators in the square. Over the next 2 days, the crowd in Tahrir Square grew tenfold, and the protests spread to Alexandria, Suez, and other cities. By Friday, the youthful protesters were joined by businessmen, professors,

TAHRIR SQUARE Tahrir Square in Cairo became the focal point of the anti-government protests in January and February 2011. This photo shows Egyptian anti-government protesters praying there on February 4, 2011, during "departure day" demonstrations. These were intended to force President Hosni Mubarak to quit after he said he would like to step down, but feared that chaos would result. Following further protests, Mubarak resigned on February 11.

workers, and even civil servants, as well as the Muslim Brotherhood, which had earlier declined to participate. With the regular security forces failing to maintain order, the government sent in the army with tanks and armored personnel carriers. In contrast to the police, who had attacked the demonstrators with tear gas and water cannons, the soldiers avoided violence. On February 2, they stood aside as police and hired pro-government thugs attacked the demonstrators, killing five and injuring nearly a thousand. The next day, however, the soldiers began to separate the police from the demonstrators in order to protect the demonstrators.

The government had hoped that the demonstrations would die down, but instead they seemed to grow stronger. On February 8, lawyers in black robes joined the demonstrators, doctors marched down the street from Qasr al Aini Hospital, and the transport workers went on strike. On Friday, February 11, millions of people all over the country poured into the streets to demand the resignation of President Mubarak. Then, at 6 p.m., the vice president made an announcement on state television: "President Muhammad Hosni Mubarak has decided to leave his position as president of the Republic, and has entrusted the Supreme Council of the Armed Forces to administer the nation's affairs." By then, Mubarak had boarded a flight to his presidential rest house at the Red Sea resort town of Sharm el Shaykh.

Libya

The next regime to fall to a popular uprising was in Libya, an oil-rich country with a population of only 6 million, sandwiched between Tunisia and Egypt. The government was run by Colonel Muammar Gaddafi, who called himself the "brotherly leader and guide of the revolution" instead of president. After taking power in 1969 in a military coup, Gaddafi had instituted a program of socialism that guaranteed free education and health care to all Libyans and provided office jobs in the burgeoning state sector. Nearly three-quarters of the population worked in government jobs, leaving much of the menial labor for low-wage foreign workers. Libyans paid no taxes, and almost every family had its own car. Gaddafi described his country as a utopia.

Nevertheless, there was a downside to the system. The quality of the education and health care was poor, and the government jobs were often little more than meaningless and redundant busywork. To keep the country's budget from spiraling out of control, Gaddafi froze public-sector wages in 1981 and kept them frozen for nearly 30 years. With a growing population and inflation running as high as 20 percent, people took evening jobs as taxi drivers or engaged in black-market trading just to make ends meet. In addition, Gaddafi's socialism operated through patronage networks that were vulnerable to massive corruption. In 2008,

Gaddafi himself admitted that the government ministries had become centers of graft, mismanagement, and corruption, and he threatened to eliminate them and distribute the funds directly to the people. With the prevailing corruption as well as an unemployment rate that had risen to 30 percent, there was widespread dissatisfaction with the Libyan government.

Gaddafi's Libya was an authoritarian state in which schoolchildren wore military uniforms, the government controlled most outlets for information, and dissent was brutally suppressed. There were no political parties, no independent trade unions, and no civic organizations. Opposition to the government came largely from Islamist groups such as the Muslim Brotherhood, whom Gaddafi dismissed as "mad dogs." In the mid-1990s, he ordered his security forces to deal harshly with the Islamists and authorized collective punishment for the tribes or individuals who harbored them. After executing three prominent Islamist militants in 2000, Gaddafi felt that the Islamist threat had been contained. Another source of opposition was groups of secular nationalists living in exile, who held a meeting in London in 2005 to combine their forces to push for constitutional change. The Muslim Brotherhood was invited to the meeting, but declined because it rejected the secular constitutional agenda of the group.

The first anti-Gaddafi demonstrations broke out in Benghazi (Libya's second-largest city, located in the eastern region of the country) on February 17, 2011, just 24 days after President Mubarak resigned in Egypt. The protesters complained about the lack of housing, jobs, and social services, and they called for the ouster of the Gaddafi regime. Government forces opened fire on the demonstrators, killing 50. The next day, 50 more demonstrators were killed during a funeral procession for the protesters who had died the day before. By the end of February, Benghazi and the other cities in eastern Libya

PROTESTS IN BENGHAZI Women protesters demand the resignation of Libyan leader Muammar Gaddafi during a demonstration in Benghazi, eastern Libya, on March 9, 2011. Many of them were mothers who were still mourning their sons—political prisoners executed in Benghazi by the Gaddafi regime in 1996. Benghazi was the cradle of the anti-Gaddafi revolt, which spread rapidly across the country.

had declared themselves liberated, and a full-scale rebellion was under way. Using weapons they acquired by raiding military depots, the rebels transformed pickup trucks into armored vehicles and built portable rocket launchers out of old pieces of drainpipe. The rebels announced the formation of a National Transition Council (NTC), which pledged to liberate all areas of the country and establish a modern, free, and democratic state. In practice, however, the NTC had no real authority, and each town liberated itself using local resources. As regional rebel groups consolidated their hold over eastern and central Libya, the Berber ethnic minority living in the mountains southwest of Tripoli joined their cause.

The Libyan army, which had initially retreated in the face of the unexpected rebellion, began a counteroffensive that brought it to the outskirts of Benghazi. On March 17, just a month after the initial protests in Benghazi, Gaddafi went on the radio and announced, "I will finish the battle of Benghazi tonight." That same evening, the U.N. Security Council, fearing a bloodbath in Benghazi, imposed a "no-fly zone" over Libya and authorized the use of military action to protect the civilians. Two days later, American, British, and French planes flew sorties over Libya to drive back the government forces. The war then entered a period of stalemate in which towns were taken, lost, and retaken by both sides. By the middle of May, the rebels had captured Misarata, Libya's third-largest city, with the assistance of NATO air strikes. By August, the rebel forces had captured a number of towns in western Libya and had encircled the capital, Tripoli. When they entered Tripoli, the rebels found that Gaddafi's forces had melted away, and Gaddafi was nowhere to be found. He was fleeing with his family to his hometown when rebel forces caught up with him. They found him hiding in a drainpipe that ran under the road, and killed him, on October 20, 2011. The soldier who fired the fatal shot was a teenager.

The Aftermath of the Arab Spring

The optimism felt by the demonstrators when the authoritarian regimes in Tunisia, Egypt, and Libya fell would be short-lived. As African countries south of the Sahara had discovered during the 1960s and 1970s, it was relatively easy to find unity in opposition to an unpopular regime, but much more difficult to agree on a plan going forward. Moreover, the democratic forces operated under heavy constraints: although the authoritarian presidents had fled or been killed, the old military establishments and state bureaucracies remained in place. The only one of these three countries that established a sustainable democratic government was Tunisia.

Egypt

In Egypt, the unity that the protesters displayed in Tahrir Square in January and February 2011 would not last, as different factions began to fight over who would hold power in the new government. The Supreme Council of the Armed Forces, which had been left in charge by the departing Mubarak, issued a statement in November 2011 that it alone was responsible for the "protection of constitutional legality" no matter who dominated the parliament or won the presidency. When elections for the parliament were held, using a complex three-round process, in late 2011 and early 2012, a coalition dominated by the Muslim Brotherhood won 45 percent of the seats, while an additional coalition of Islamist parties gained 25 percent, which gave the Islamists a total of 70 percent of the seats. In the presidential election held in May and June of 2012, 23 candidates campaigned for the position, but it was Muhammad Morsi, the candidate backed by the Muslim Brotherhood, who won the runoff election with 52 percent of the vote. He was the first democratically elected ruler in Egypt's 6,000-year history.

No sooner had Morsi been elected than the Supreme Constitutional Court ruled that the parliamentary elections had been carried out in an unconstitutional manner, and so the parliament itself was illegal. President Morsi quickly issued an order reinstating the parliament. The first job of the parliament was to appoint a 100-person Constituent Assembly to write a new constitution. The Muslim Brotherhood and its allies packed the assembly with Islamists, and the handful of secular nationalists in the group soon resigned in frustration. Stripped of dissenting voices, the assembly quickly produced the draft constitution favored by the Muslim Brotherhood. It was ratified in a December referendum, in spite of 15,000 reports of election fraud. The high-handed tactics of the Islamists caused many of the secular nationalists who had supported the original revolution to come back out into the streets.

On June 30, 2013—exactly a year after President Morsi's inauguration—hundreds of thousands of protesters poured into the streets of Cairo, and Tahrir Square was soon overflowing with people who were calling for a "Second Revolution." This time, the protest was against Muhammad Morsi, the president of Egypt. As the protests continued into the third day, the generals on the Supreme Council of the Armed Forces appeared on TV and announced that they had taken over the government, and that President Morsi had been replaced by the defense minister, Abdul Fatah al-Sisi. The first freely elected president in Egypt's history had lasted for only a year! Tahrir Square erupted in cheers. Two weeks later, the government banned the Muslim Brotherhood, and the army launched a nationwide crackdown, killing over 600 of its members. In November, the government banned all public protests, and it even arrested members of the April 6 Youth Movement who protested the ban. In December 2013, it designated the Muslim Brotherhood a terrorist organization. In Egypt, the Arab Spring was over.

Libya

In Libya, the various rebel brigades that had formed during the fighting did not disband after the death of Gaddafi, and their leaders became the nation's new power brokers. Under these circumstances, the National Transition Council, which was composed mostly of former government bureaucrats, could claim very little legitimacy. Within a year, protests and strikes had become an almost daily occurrence as the promised jobs and improved living standards failed to materialize. In 2012, the NTC was replaced by an elected General National Congress (GNC), which organized elections for a House of Representatives in June 2014. Rather than appeasing the Libyans, the elections split the country in two. Soon, Libya entered a period of low-level civil war, waged primarily through assassinations of prominent members of each opposing side. The conflict represented an ideological battle between Islamists and secular nationalists, but it also reflected competition between regional militias and antipathy between remnants of the Gaddafi regime and former rebels. Despite a U.N. resolution calling for an end to the internal conflict, security conditions deteriorated, and most foreign embassies evacuated the Libyan capital on the grounds that it was too dangerous.

Tunisia

In Tunisia, an election to form a Constituent Assembly was held on October 23, 2011, just 10 months after the fall of the Ben Ali regime. The Islamist *al-Nahda* party was the big winner, capturing 90 of the assembly's 217 seats, but it fell short of a majority, and the next six winners were all secular nationalist parties. The following year, several secular nationalist parties joined together to form the *Nidaa Tounes* (Call for Tunisia) party, which included secular leftists, progressive liberals, and trade unions. When the first parliamentary elections were held under the new constitution, *Nidaa Tounes* won 86 seats, while *al-Nahda* came in second with 69 seats. During the presidential election a month later, the *Nidaa Tounes* candidate won with 56 percent of the vote. Unlike Egypt, which had become a military dictatorship, and Libya, which descended into chaos, Tunisia seemed to be on its way to a more stable form of democratic government in which Islamists and secular nationalists could work together for common goals.

PRESENT MEETS PAST: THE MANUSCRIPTS OF TIMBUKTU

In April 2012, fighters belonging to the National Movement for the Liberation of Azawad drove 80 vehicles flying the tricolor flags of their movement into the city of Timbuktu. They were Tuareg nomads from the Sahara Desert region of northern Mali, who had been fighting off and on for half a century to create an independent Tuareg state called Azawad. Timbuktu, the fabled city at the Niger River bend, had been the location of a Tuareg seasonal camp since its founding in the twelfth century. Over the centuries, it had come under the control of the Mali Empire, the Songhay Empire, and the invading Moroccans before being reclaimed by the Tuareg once again in 1660. Timbuktu was subsequently taken over by the jihadist forces of Umar Tal in 1860 (see chapters 4 and 9), then by the French colonizers, and finally by the independent government of Mali. The Tuareg nationalists wanted their city back, perhaps to make it the capital of their dreamed-of independent state of Azawad.

Soon after the Tuareg fighters moved into Timbuktu in 2012, a rival group arrived. Islamist fighters known as "the bearded ones" entered the city in a convoy of 100 vehicles flying black jihadist flags. They demanded that the Tuareg turn the city over to them. Soon, black jihadist flags replaced the tricolor flags of the secular Tuareg nationalists as the Tuareg withdrew to bases outside the city limits. By August, the jihadists had driven the Tuareg out of those bases and forced them to disperse into the desert. Some of them fled to refugee camps in Mauritania. With the Tuareg nationalists in retreat, the cities at the Niger bend came under the complete control of the jihadists.

The Libraries of Timbuktu

Timbuktu had fallen on hard times since the Moroccan invasion in 1591 (see chapter 4), and in 1837, the French explorer René Caillié had described the city as "nothing but a mass of ill-looking houses." When the jihadists arrived in 2012, the trans-Saharan gold trade that had once made the city wealthy had dried up centuries before, but salt from mines deep in the desert still flowed into Timbuktu, even though most of it now came not by camel caravan, but on all-wheel-drive Mercedes trucks designed for the desert terrain. Timbuktu was no longer a center of higher learning, and students no longer traveled hundreds of miles to study at its mosques, but antique handwritten books on subjects from astronomy to medicine, philosophy, Islamic law, history, and poetry remained in the city as powerful reminders of Timbuktu's glory days. Leo Africanus had written in 1550 that handwritten books were the single most profitable trade item in Timbuktu, and their value had only increased during the years of the city's decline. For many families in Timbuktu, the books were their family treasures.

After the jihad of Umar Tal had pillaged the libraries of Timbuktu in the 1860s and the French had carried a number of precious books off to France following the colonial conquest, many families hid their manuscripts in caves or buried them in metal trunks in their courtyards for safekeeping. It was the mission of the Ahmed Baba Institute, built in 1973 with grants from Kuwait and Iraq, to set about collecting as many books and manuscripts as possible to preserve the great intellectual tradition of Timbuktu. By 2006, it had collected some 25,000 books, which it was repairing and digitizing for better preservation. Prominent Timbuktu families began to bring their manuscripts out of hiding, and by 2010, the city had 45 libraries containing a total of 377,000 books and manuscripts.

Mr. Marlboro Arrives

Mokhtar Belmokhtar, the commander of the jihadist forces that arrived in Timbuktu, wanted to create an Islamic caliphate in the Sahara Desert. Belmokhtar had grown up in the Algerian Sahara and had made his way to an Al Qaeda training camp in Afghanistan, where he lost his left eye in an explosion. After returning to Algeria, he settled in the mountains near its border with Mali. He was so successful at smuggling American cigarettes across the desert to North Africa that he gained the nickname "Mr. Marlboro." Soon he also began smuggling cocaine, which was flown on Boeing 727s from Colombia, South America, to makeshift landing strips deep in the Sahara.

Not forgetting his earlier connections with Al Qaeda, Mokhtar Belmokhtar smuggled weapons into Algeria for a rebel group called Al Qaeda in the Islamic Maghreb (AQIM), which was financing its activities with ransom money acquired by kidnapping foreign tourists and diplomats. AQIM made Belmokhtar an "emir" and put him in command of its activities in Mali. He named his group Al Qaeda in the Islamic Maghreb in Mali (AQIMM). Like its parent organization, his group operated under the authority of Osama bin Laden.

Throughout its storied history, Timbuktu had always promoted a tolerant form of Islam, in which religious and secular knowledge coexisted. Following the tradition of Sufi Islam, Timbuktu was known as the City of 333 Saints, and some of its most revered saints were buried in elaborate tombs that were popularly seen as shrines. The AQIMM commanders, however, wanted to purge Islam of all rites and practices that they viewed as heretical. Claiming that saints are not acceptable in Islam, they began destroying the tombs. They imposed strict dress codes on women, required men to wear beards, and banned music (including musical cell phone ringtones), smoking, and the common practice of setting a TV set outside in the evening so that the neighbors could watch. They also set up sharia courts that imposed harsh sentences, such as amputation of a hand or a foot for thieves, and held public executions. The punishments were publicized worldwide via YouTube videos and Twitter messages.

Saving the Manuscripts

As the religious regulations became more extreme, Abdel Kader Haidara, an employee of the Ahmed Baba Institute who had personally collected over 16,000 manuscripts for its library, began to worry that the jihadists would destroy the books and manuscripts that made up Timbuktu's scholarly heritage. With the help of volunteers all over the city, he accumulated 2,500 metal trunks, which he filled with books and manuscripts from Timbuktu's assorted libraries and dispersed by donkey cart to safe houses all over the city. By the end of July 2012, 95 percent of the 377,000 manuscripts had been distributed to 30 different locations. By late August, however, the librarians began to worry that the safe houses would be discovered, so they began to transport the trunks out of Timbuktu in Toyota Land Cruisers and other four-wheel-drive vehicles. Over the next 3 months, they safely smuggled 270,000 manuscripts to Mali's capital city, Bamako, for safekeeping.

Seeing that the Malian army was no match for the jihadists, Mali's president, Dioncounda Traoré, requested help from the French military. By the end of January 2013, 2,500 French troops had arrived in Mali and were helping to push the jihadists north toward the Niger bend. As the fighting moved toward Timbuktu, the librarians were worried that any remaining manuscripts might be destroyed by vengeful AQIMM fighters or by the rockets and missiles of the French. The roads were unsafe, so they carried trunks filled with manuscripts to the Niger River on donkey carts and loaded them onto wooden boats powered by outboard motors. Traveling in flotillas of up to 20 boats, they brought the trunks to Mopti, which was beyond the fighting zone, and sent them on to Bamako in taxis. On the

LOST TREASURES OF TIMBUKTU Men attempt to recover burnt ancient manuscripts at the Ahmed Baba Institute in Timbuktu, Mali, on January 29, 2013. The previous day, as French-led forces seized the fabled desert city, fleeing jihadist fighters had torched the priceless ancient manuscripts. According to Mali's Ministry of Culture, the Ahmed Baba Institute formerly housed between 60,000 and 100,000 manuscripts.

busiest day of the boatlift, 150 taxis, loaded with three trunks each, drove from Mopti to Bamako to deliver the manuscripts.

On January 25, 2013, as the French forces were closing in on Timbuktu, the AQIMM fighters prepared to evacuate the library of the Ahmed Baba Institute, which they had been using as a barracks. As a final act of vengeance and defiance, they carried over 4,000 manuscripts into the courtyard and burned them, destroying fourteenth- and fifteenth-century works of mathematics, physics, chemistry, and astronomy, among others. The jihadists were unaware that behind a locked door in the basement was a climate-controlled storage room containing over 10,000 more manuscripts. As the fighters retreated into the desert, the French pursued them in planes and helicopters. Many of the jihadists were killed, but Mokhtar Belmokhtar, their commander, escaped to fight another day.

The name of Timbuktu was well known in Europe and America in the nineteenth and twentieth centuries, where it had come to symbolize the most remote place on earth. Yet it was in that very place that some of the greatest glories of Africa's past intersected with the troubles of its present. Al Qaeda, the Arab Spring, drug smugglers, a national government, and a former colonial power all came together in this remote place, in a struggle that raised the question of whether or not history mattered. Would historical documents be destroyed or preserved? Due to the incredible bravery and ingenuity of the librarians of Timbuktu, key artifacts of the history of the West African Sahel have been preserved for future generations. In Timbuktu, history matters.

CHAPTER REVIEW

KEY TERMS AND VOCABULARY

second independence
National Conference
AIDS
African World War
Rwandan genocide
China-Africa Cooperation Forum
developmental authoritarianism
Muhammad Bouazizi
Arab Spring
Muslim Brotherhood
Tahrir Square
Mokhtar Belmokhtar

STUDY QUESTIONS

1. Name some ways in which the end of the Cold War created new possibilities for African states.
2. What factors account for the emergence of African majority rule in South Africa in the 1990s?
3. What was the second independence in Africa in the 1990s? How do you explain this phenomenon?
4. In what ways has the HIV/AIDS epidemic impeded African economic and human development?
5. How did the aftermath of the Rwandan genocide balloon into a kind of world war in the center of Africa?
6. Evaluate the role of young people and new technologies in the Arab Spring uprisings.
7. Why were the inhabitants of Timbuktu willing to take great risks to save the city's ancient manuscripts?

PERSPECTIVES

LIVING IN SOUTH AFRICA WITH AIDS

Puleng was a 29-year-old South African woman living in Alexander Township in Johannesburg who told the story of her illness to the French medical anthropologist Didier Fassin in April 2002. Emaciated by AIDS, she weighed less than eighty pounds. Although antiretroviral drugs were available at private pharmacies, the price was far beyond the means of most sick persons. She died three months after giving this interview.

My name is Puleng. I was born in Baragwanath Hospital in 1973. I grew up in Soweto until the age of seven. Then I came to Alex in this same house where we are now. And this is where I always lived. When I was a child my father went away and my mother raised us alone. She tried so hard. But she drank too much. When she had taken alcohol, we used to sleep in the streets. I have a sister, she was born in 1976. I had a brother also, he was born in 1978, he was my best friend. He died when he was twenty, he was shot by the police, because he was accused of a car theft.

Then came this disease. They told me about it in 1998. I never drank. I never smoked. I never had time to go to casinos. I only had four boyfriends in my whole life. The first one, when I was still in high school, he left me. The second one, I separated from him. The third one, he was married, I could not stay with him. And then the father of my child, I lived ten years with him. He was good to me. But he cheated me. I discovered he had another girlfriend. And his girlfriend died. I said to him: "How could you do that to me? You're killing me now with this disease." When I told him about the disease, he didn't want to believe me. And he lied to me. He said to me he had done the test and when I asked the doctor, because we had the same one, he told me it wasn't true. . . . I'm not willing to have another boyfriend, now. We are living here happy with my child. She's twelve. She goes to school. I want her to be somebody.

So, you see, this is my life. A life of misery. We've been suffering so much. But I was talented. I used to write stories when I was a child. The first one, it was after reading a book on Florence Nightingale. And I liked to write poems. I even got a scholarship to study abroad. But there was a fire in my house and all my documents were burnt. I liked to study. I wanted to be a doctor, because it's nice to heal people. I was so talented. . . . Now, my life is sinking. But I'm very strong, very very strong. And I'll live until God decides I should pass away. I'd like to do many things. I told my family: "On my funeral day, I don't want you to prepare a meal." Because people act like at a party. It costs a lot of money. But what's the use, if I'm dead. It's only to put them in debt. No, I just want them to bury me. . . . But I don't think of that all the time. I thank God to have brought me in this world.

1. *What were Puleng's main talents and ambitions before she contracted AIDS?*
2. *What were her hopes for her daughter?*

Source: Didier Fassin, *When Bodies Remember: Experiences and Politics of AIDS in South Africa*, trans. Amy Jacobs and Gabrielle Varro (Berkeley: University of California Press, 2007), pp. 18–19.

SURVIVING GENOCIDE IN RWANDA

Angelique Mukamanzi is a Tutsi woman who was raised on a farm in the marshy Bugesera region of Rwanda. As a girl, she dreamed of someday becoming a lawyer or a judge. The genocide of 1994 put an end to those dreams as she devoted all of her strength to simply surviving, and later to taking care of eight children who had lost their parents. In the late 1990s, when memories were still fresh, the French journalist Jean Hatzfeld interviewed survivors of the genocide. Here are excerpts from Angelique's story.

Before the war, I studied hard, because I wanted to pass the national exam in Kigali and snag myself a fine career. Boys had a good eye for me, life seemed worthwhile. In school, I had mixed friends, Tutsi and Hutu. The latter never said bad things. I felt the first fears when people began leaving the Bugesera after the clashes in 1992. Our paths then grew loud with more and more evil words. That's another reason why I wanted to turn toward the capital.

Three days after the plane crash [of the President's plane], a small group of us—my family and our neighbors, with bundles of belongings—moved into the church at N'tarama. During the day, the brave among us would venture into the nearby fields to bring back food. When the *interahamwe* surrounded the fences, some men began throwing small rocks to slow down their advance. The women gathered the stones, because they did not want to die just any old way, but this resistance was too weak.

Grenades exploded against the front door. I myself was in the back: for an hour I ran so hard down the slope I don't remember breathing, until I plunged into the *urunfunzo* of the marshes, which I had heard about but never seen before. *Urunfunzo* are the papyrus plants. At the time, of course, I had no idea that for an entire month I would spend my days in the mud from head to toe, at the mercy of mosquitoes.

The killers worked in the marshes from nine to four, four-thirty, while the daylight lasted. They arrived in columns, announcing themselves with whistles and songs. They would beat drums, seeming quite delighted to kill all day long. One morning, they would take one path, and another the next day. When we heard the first whistles, we'd dash in the opposite direction.

In the afternoon they no longer sang, because they were tired, and they would set out for home, chatting as they went. They fortified themselves with drinks and ate the cattle, because they were slaughtering them along with the Tutsis. Truly, these killings were quite coolly done, and well-planned. If the liberators of the RPF [the Tutsi-led Rwandan Patriotic Front] had taken another week to arrive, not one Tutsi in the Bugesera would still be alive. . . .

At the end of the genocide, I was placed for three months in an abandoned hut on a lower slope of Nyamata Hill. I should have been content, but I was still too anxious and exhausted. We felt like strangers in our own skins, if I may put it that way; we had been brought low, and were disturbed by what we had become. I think we didn't believe we would ever be truly safe again.

1. *What survival methods did Angelique Mukamanzi and her family employ?*
2. *What was the attitude of the interahamwe militia members?*

Source: Jean Hatzfeld, *Life Laid Bare: The Survivors in Rwanda Speak* (New York: Other Press, 2006), pp. 81–84.

PERSPECTIVES

THE BIRTH OF A NEW TUNISIA

Ahlem Yazidi is a young Tunisian woman who studied linguistics and literature at the university. After the death of Muhammad Bouazizi, the 26-year-old street vendor who set himself on fire to protest government harassment, she felt that it was her duty as a Tunisian citizen to join the protests. When her parents objected, she left her village and went to Tunis. Here are excerpts from her story.

Thinking back to what happened during the days of the revolution of 2011, I should say that I had not been expecting it, nor had I been ready for it. All I wanted to do when it started was to join the crowds in the streets of the capital, to shout and cheer and to express my anger for the deteriorating and dire situation that my country faced. I have consistently participated in demonstrations and protests organized by the students of my university or those of other, neighboring universities, either to advocate for the Palestinian cause or to condemn the hostility against Iraq.

But when I joined the demonstrations, I found myself, along with other peaceful demonstrators, surrounded and besieged by riot police. We were hit with nightsticks and batons, sprayed with boiling water, and mercilessly tear-gassed. I was shocked by the sheer might of the military arsenal let loose by the government against a peaceful student protest. But we were determined in opposing not only the government and its policies but particularly the corrupt ruling family itself. . . .

On January 13, I went to the streets because I felt that it was the right moment. It was the moment I had been waiting for, for such a long time; it was "now or never." I had to act as a committed Tunisian citizen, choosing to be either a true Tunisian or not. I left the village of Cherifet, where I grew up. Cherifet is close to the city of Soliman, where the demonstrations against the regime began. . . .

When I reached the capital, I was stunned and scared because of the large number of soldiers posted on every street, especially in the public squares. The military presence was strong in Barcelona Square and also in the main street called Habib Bourguiba Avenue. This was ominously accompanied by a complete withdrawal of the policemen who usually handle security issues. I heard people whispering and insisting on the need to go back home out of fear of what might happen next. I was no longer afraid. Deep in my heart I saw my life to be no more valuable than the lives of my fellow Tunisians now filling the streets, which was my answer to my mother when she tried to dissuade me from joining the masses.

1. *Why did Ahlem Yazidi decide to join the demonstrations against the wishes of her mother?*
2. *What shocked her when she joined the demonstrations?*

Source: Asaad al-Saleh, *Voices of the Arab Spring: Personal Stories from the Arab Revolutions* (New York: Columbia University Press, 2015), pp. 25–30.

MAHA HINDAWY'S EGYPTIAN REVOLUTION

Maha Hindawy lived in Cairo, where she worked as a training and development manager at a car company. She had never previously been involved in politics, but the murder of Khaled Said, an anti-government blogger who was tortured and beaten to death by the police, aroused her to action. Note the key role of Facebook posts in recruiting her to join the protests at Tahrir Square. Here are excerpts from her story.

On one night, long before January 25, I saw pictures of Khaled Said on Facebook—I could not sleep at all that night. I joined his support group "We are all Khaled Said" on Facebook. The group started organizing events for which we dressed in black and faced the Nile or the sea for an hour (and in silence) from wherever we were standing. I loved the idea because it allowed me to demonstrate my anger at and condemnation of Khaled's murder in a very civilized way.

On January 25, 2011, the "We are all Khaled Said" Facebook page started promoting the march, which was very well planned in terms of where to meet, what to chant, what to carry and what not to carry, and acceptable types of shoes. Before the morning of January 25, I had never voted in any elections or taken part in any protests, because I always thought both were dangerous in Egypt. I always associated protests with harassment and very violent police reactions. I recall so many pictures of men and women being dragged through the street, and I wanted to avoid becoming one of them—and yet somehow I trusted the Facebook page.

I arrived after Friday prayer and just in time for the protests. There were roughly fifty people in front of the mosque, surrounded by police and soldiers, and even more people watching from nearby. . . . As more and more people joined the protests, we chanted, "*Ya ahalyina domo alayina*" (Our people, join us). Our march reached the borders of Meit Oqba where people had a march of their own. A woman waved a flag to us from her balcony on Arab League Street, and we responded by doing the same. She threw her flag to us, rushed inside her house, and returned waving another. I even saw someone on a three-wheeled bicycle operating the wheels by hand because his feet were damaged. When he joined us, a protester gave him a flag to use as a scarf.

On the street of el-Batal Ahmed Abdel Aziz, I heard not just chanting but roaring. Cars were driving in the opposite direction honking their horns in support, especially when we shouted "*Irhal*" (Leave) in reference to Mubarak and "*Enta la aadly wala habib, irhal ya wazir el-taazeeb*" (You are neither fair nor loved, leave, O minister of torture), which is a reference to the Minister of the Interior's name, which in Arabic means "loved and fair." We clapped for the police, who were very kind and allowed us to march through their barricades and checkpoints. But this sentiment did not last long.

1. *What was the impact of the murder of Khaled Said upon Maha Hindawy's decision to join the demonstrations?*
2. *What was her initial reaction to the police?*

Source: Asaad al-Saleh, *Voices of the Arab Spring: Personal Stories from the Arab Revolutions* (New York: Columbia University Press, 2015), pp. 75–78.

GUIDE TO FURTHER READING

CHAPTER 1. OUT OF AFRICA

Adams, W. M., A. S. Goudie, and A. R. Orme, eds. *The Physical Geography of Africa*. New York: Oxford University Press, 1996.

Barham, Lawrence, and Peter Mitchell. *The First Africans: African Archaeology from the Earliest Tool Makers to Most Recent Foragers*. New York: Cambridge University Press, 2008.

Garlake, Peter. *Early Art and Architecture of Africa*. New York: Oxford University Press, 2002.

Ghazoul, Jaboury, and Douglas Sheil. *Tropical Rain Forest Ecology, Diversity, and Conservation*. New York: Oxford University Press, 2010.

Jablonsky, Nina. *Skin: A Natural History*. Berkeley: University of California Press, 2006.

Newman, James. *The Peopling of Africa: A Geographic Interpretation*. New Haven, CT: Yale University Press, 1995.

Palmer, Douglas. *Origins: Human Evolution Revealed*. London: Mitchell Beazley, 2010.

Tattersall, Ian. *Masters of the Planet: The Search for Our Human Origins*. New York: Palgrave Macmillan, 2012.

Tattersall, Ian, and Rob DeSalle. *Race? Debunking a Scientific Myth*. College Station: Texas A&M University Press, 2011.

United Nations Environment Program. *Africa: Atlas of Our Changing Environment*. Nairobi: UNEP, 2008.

CHAPTER 2. FOOD REVOLUTIONS AND FRONTIER SOCIETIES, 8000 BCE–1000 CE

Barich, Barbara E. *People, Water, and Grain: The Beginnings of Domestication in the Sahara and Nile Valley*. Rome: L'Erma di Bretschneider, 1998.

Bonnet, Charles, and Dominique Valbelle. *The Nubian Pharaohs: Black Kings on the Nile*. New York: American University in Cairo Press, 2006.

Celenko, Theodore, ed. *Egypt in Africa*. Indiana University Press, 1996.

Ehret, Christopher. *An African Classical Age: Eastern and Southern Africa in World History, 1000 B.C. to A.D. 400*. Charlottesville: University of Virginia Press, 1998.

Fisher, Marjorie M., Peter Lacovara, Salima Ikram, and Sue D'Auria, eds. *Ancient Nubia: African Kingdoms on the Nile*. New York: American University in Cairo Press, 2012.

Morkot, Robert G. *The Black Pharaohs: Egypt's Nubian Rulers*. London: Rubicon Press, 2000.

Nurse, Derek, and Gerard Philippson. *The Bantu Languages*. New York: Routledge, 2003.

Phillipson, David W. *Foundations of an African Civilisation: Aksum and the Northern Horn 1000 BC–AD 1300*. Rochester, NY: Boydell & Brewer, 2012.

Redford, Donald B. *From Slave to Pharaoh: The Black Experience in Ancient Egypt*. Baltimore: Johns Hopkins University Press, 2004.

Wilkinson, Toby. *The Rise and Fall of Ancient Egypt*. New York: Random House, 2010.

CHAPTER 3. IMPERIAL POWER AND RELIGIOUS REVOLUTIONS IN THE MEDITERRANEAN WORLD, 800 BCE–1500 CE

Abun-Nasr, Jamil. *A History of the Maghrib in the Islamic Period*. Cambridge: Cambridge University Press, 1987.

Aslan, Reza. *No God but God: The Origins, Evolution, and Future of Islam*. New York: Random House, 2005.

Freeman, Charles. *A New History of Early Christianity*. New Haven, CT: Yale University Press, 2009.

Hoyos, Dexter. *The Carthaginians*. London: Routledge, 2010.

Kennedy, Hugh. *The Great Arab Conquests: How the Spread of Islam Changed the World We Live In*. Philadelphia: Da Capo Press, 2007.

Lancel, Serge. *Carthage: A History*. Oxford: Blackwell, 1995.

McLaughlin, Raoul. *The Roman Empire and the Indian Ocean: Rome's Dealings with the Ancient Kingdoms of Africa, Arabia and India*. Barnsely, UK: Pen & Sword Military, 2014.

Naylor, Philip. *North Africa: A History from Antiquity to the Present*. Austin: University of Texas Press, 2009.

Raven, Susan. *Rome in Africa*, 3rd edition. London: Routledge, 1993.

Watt, William Montgomery. *A Short History of Islam*. Oxford: Oneworld, 1996.

CHAPTER 4. CITIES OF GOLD: THE WEST AFRICAN SAHEL AND THE EAST AFRICAN COAST, 800–1600

Austen, Ralph. *Trans-Saharan Africa in World History*. New York: Oxford University Press: 2010.

Conrad, David C. *Sunjata: A New Prose Version*. Indianapolis, IN: Hackett, 2016.

Dunn, Ross E. *The Adventures of Ibn Battuta, a Muslim Traveler of the 14th Century*, revised edition. Berkeley: University of California Press, 2005.

Horton, Mark, and John Middleton. *The Swahili: The Social Landscape of a Mercantile Society*. Malden, MA: Blackwell, 2000.

Hunwick, John O. *The Hidden Treasures of Timbuktu: Rediscovering Africa's Literary Culture*. New York: Thames and Hudson, 2008.

Levtzion, Nehemia. *Ancient Ghana and Mali*. London: Methuen, 1973.

Levtzion, Nehemia, and Jay Spaulding, eds. *Medieval West Africa: Views from Arab Scholars and Merchants*. Princeton, NJ: Marcus Wiener, 2003.

McIntosh, Roderick J. *The Peoples of the Middle Niger*. Malden, MA: Blackwell, 1998.

Nurse, Derek, and Thomas Spear. *The Swahili: Reconstructing the History and Language of an African Society, 800–1500*. Philadelphia: University of Pennsylvania Press, 1985.

Pikirayi, Innocent. *The Zimbabwe Culture: Origins and Decline in Southern Zambezian States*. Walnut Creek, CA: AltaMira Press, 2001.

CHAPTER 5. ATLANTIC AFRICA AND THE CREATION OF THE ATLANTIC WORLD, 1400–1700

Barry, Boubacar. *Senegambia and the Atlantic Slave Trade*. Cambridge: Cambridge University Press, 1998.

Birmingham, David. *Trade and Conflict in Angola: The Mbundu and Their Neighbours under the Influence of the Portuguese, 1483–1790*. Oxford: Clarendon Press, 1966.

Brooks, George. *Eurafricans in Western Africa*. Athens: Ohio University Press, 2003.

Green, Toby. *The Rise of the Trans-Atlantic Slave Trade in Western Africa, 1300–1859*. New York: Cambridge University Press, 2012.

Heywood, Linda, and John Thornton. *Central Africans, Atlantic Creoles, and the Making of the Foundation of the Americas, 1585–1660*. New York: Cambridge University Press, 2007.

Hilton, Anne. *The Kingdom of Kongo*. Oxford: Clarendon Press, 1985.

Kea, Ray. *Settlements, Trade, and Politics in the Seventeenth-Century Gold Coast*. Baltimore: Johns Hopkins University Press, 1982.

Stilwell, Sean. *Slavery and Slaving in African History*. New York: Cambridge University Press, 2014.

Thornton, John. *The Kongolese Saint Anthony: Dona Beatriz Kimpa Vita and the Antonian movement, 1684–1706*. Cambridge: Cambridge University Press, 1998.

Wilks, Ivor. *Forests of Gold: Essays on the Akan and the Kingdom of Asante*. Athens: Ohio University Press, 1993.

CHAPTER 6. EXPANSIONIST STATES AND DECENTRALIZED POWER IN ATLANTIC AFRICA, 1700–1800

Djata, Sundiata. *The Bamana Empire by the Niger: Kingdom, Jihad, and Colonization, 1712–1920*. Princeton, NJ: Markus Wiener, 1997.

Harms, Robert. *River of Wealth, River of Sorrow: The Central Zaire Basin in the Era of the Slave and Ivory Trade, 1500–1891*. New Haven, CT: Yale University Press, 1981.

Heywood, Linda. *Njinga of Angola: Africa's Warrior Queen*. Cambridge, MA: Harvard University Press, 2017.

Law, Robin. *The Slave Coast of West Africa, 1550–1750: The Impact of the Atlantic Slave Trade on an African Society*. Oxford: Clarendon Press, 1991.

Miller, Joseph C. *Way of Death: Merchant Capitalism and the Angolan Slave Trade, 1730–1830*. Madison: University of Wisconsin Press, 1988.

Northrup, David. *Trade without Rulers: Pre-colonial Economic Development in South-Eastern Nigeria*. Oxford: Clarendon Press, 1978.

Nwokeji, G. Ugo. *The Slave Trade and Culture in the Bight of Biafra: An African Society in the Atlantic World*. New York: Cambridge University Press, 2010.

Roberts, Richard. *Warriors, Merchants, and Slaves: The State and the Economy in the Middle Niger Valley, 1700–1914*. Stanford, CA: Stanford University Press, 1987.

Searing, James. *West African Slavery and Atlantic Commerce: The Senegal River Valley, 1700–1860*. Cambridge: Cambridge University Press, 1993.

Thornton, John. *A Cultural History of the Atlantic World, 1250–1820*. New York: Cambridge University Press, 2012.

CHAPTER 7. THE INDIAN OCEAN AND MEDITERRANEAN SHORES, 1500–1800

Allen, Richard Blair. *Slaves, Freedmen, and Indentured Laborers in Colonial Mauritius*. Cambridge: Cambridge University Press, 1999.

Bradford, Ernie. *The Sultan's Admiral: The Life of Barbarossa*. New York: Harcourt, Brace & World, 1968.

Casale, Giancarlo. *The Ottoman Age of Exploration*. New York: Oxford University Press, 2010.

Coupland, Reginald. *East Africa and Its Invaders, from the Earliest Times to the Death of Seyyid Said in 1856*. New York: Russell & Russell, 1965.

Elphick, Richard, and Herman Gillomee, eds. *The Shaping of South African Society, 1652–1840*. Middletown, CT: Wesleyan University Press, 1988.

Hanna, Nelly. *Ottoman Egypt and the Emergence of the Modern World, 1500–1800*. New York: American University in Cairo Press, 2014.

Isaacman, Allen. *Mozambique: The Africanization of a European Institution; the Zambezi Prazos, 1750–1902*. Madison: University of Wisconsin Press, 1972.

Newitt, Malyn. *A History of Mozambique*. London: Hurst, 1995.

Ross, Robert. *Cape of Torments: Slavery and Resistance in South Africa*. London: Routledge & Kegan Paul, 1983.

Spencer, William. *Algiers in the Age of the Corsairs*. Norman: University of Oklahoma Press, 1976.

CHAPTER 8. ECONOMIC AND POLITICAL UPHEAVALS IN THE NINETEENTH CENTURY

Alpers, Edward A. *Ivory and Slaves: Changing Patterns of International Trade in East Central Africa to the Later Nineteenth Century*. Berkeley: University of California Press, 1975.

Bennett, Norman. *Arab versus European: Diplomacy and War in Nineteenth-Century East Central Africa*. New York: Africana Publishing Company, 1986.

Etherington, Norman. *The Great Treks: The Transformation of Southern Africa, 1815–1854*. Harlow, England: Longman, 2001.

Fahmy, Khaled. *All the Pasha's Men: Mehmed Ali, His Army, and the Making of Modern Egypt*. Cambridge: Cambridge University Press, 1997.

Law, Robin. *Ouidah: The Social History of a West African Slaving Port, 1727–1892*. Athens: Ohio University Press, 2004.

Macola, Giacomo. *The Kingdom of Kazembe: History and Politics in North-Eastern Zambia and Katanga to 1950*. Münster: Lit Verlag, 2002.

Meredith, Martin. *Diamonds, Gold, and War: The Making of South Africa*. New York: Simon & Schuster, 2007.

Ross, Robert. *A Concise History of South Africa*. Cambridge: Cambridge University Press, 2008.

Searing, James F. *"God Alone Is King": Islam and Emancipation in Senegal; The Wolof Kingdoms of Kajoor and Bawol, 1859–1914*. Portsmouth, NH: Heinemann, 2002.

Sheriff, Abdul. *Slaves, Spices, and Ivory in Zanzibar: Integration of an East African Commercial Empire into the World Economy, 1770–1873*. Athens: Ohio University Press, 1987.

CHAPTER 9. RELIGIOUS MOVEMENTS AND STATE-BUILDING STRATEGIES IN THE NINETEENTH CENTURY

Ajayi, J. F. Ade. *A Patriot to the Core: Bishop Ajayi Crowther*. Ibadan, Nigeria: Spectrum Books, 2001.

Hiskett, Mervyn. *The Development of Islam in West Africa*. New York: Longman, 1984.

Holt, P. M. *The Mahdist State in the Sudan, 1881–1898*. Oxford: Clarendon Press, 1970.

Johnson, Charles Spurgeon. *Bitter Canaan: The Story of the Negro Republic*. New Brunswick, NJ: Transaction Books, 1987.

Lovejoy, Paul. *Jihad in West Africa during the Age of Revolution*. Athens: Ohio University Press, 2016.

Omer-Cooper, J. D. *The Zulu Aftermath: A Nineteenth-Century Revolution in Bantu Africa*. London: Longmans, 1966.

Robinson, David. *The Holy War of Umar Tal: The Western Sudan in the Mid-Nineteenth Century*. Oxford: Clarendon Press, 1985.

Sanneh, Lamin. *Abolitionists Abroad: American Blacks and the Making of Modern West Africa*. Cambridge, MA: Harvard University Press, 1999.

Sanneh, Lamin. *Beyond Jihad: The Pacifist Tradition in West African Islam*. New York: Oxford University Press, 2016.

Wright, John. *The Trans-Saharan Slave Trade*. New York: Routledge, 2007.

CHAPTER 10. THE COLONIAL PARTITION OF AFRICA, 1870–1918

Abdulqadir, Abdi. *Divine Madness: Mohammed Abdulle Hassan (1856–1920)*. Atlantic Highlands, NJ: Zed Books, 1993.

Curtin, Philip. *Disease and Empire: The Health of European Troops in the Conquest of Africa*. New York: Cambridge University Press, 1998.

Giblin, James, and Jamie Monson, eds. *Maji Maji: Lifting the Fog of War*. Boston: Brill, 2010.

Headrick, Daniel. *The Tools of Empire: Technology and European Imperialism in the Nineteenth Century*. New York: Oxford University Press, 1981.

Jonas, Raymond. *The Battle of Adwa: African Victory in the Age of Empire*. Cambridge, MA: Harvard University Press, 2011.

Pakenham, Thomas. *The Scramble for Africa, 1876–1912*. London: Weidenfeld and Nicolson, 1991.

Sarkin-Hughes, Jeremy. *Germany's Genocide of the Herero*. Rochester, NY: James Currey, 2011.

Tilley, Helen. *Africa as a Living Laboratory: Empire, Development, and the Problem of Scientific Knowledge, 1850–1950*. Chicago: University of Chicago Press, 2011.

Weiskel, Timothy. *French Colonial Rule and the Baule Peoples: Resistance and Collaboration, 1889–1911*. New York: Oxford University Press, 1980.

Wessling, H. L. *Divide and Rule: The Partition of Africa, 1880–1914*. Translated by Arnold J. Pomerans. Westport, CT: Praeger, 1996.

CHAPTER 11. MAKING COLONIAL STATES, 1914–1940

Allina, Eric. *Slavery by Any Other Name: African Life under Company Rule in Colonial Mozambique*. Charlottesville: University of Virginia Press, 2012.

Bender, Gerald. *Angola under the Portuguese: The Myth and the Reality*. London: Heinemann, 1978.

Conklin, Alice. *A Mission to Civilize: The Republican Idea of Empire in France and West Africa, 1895–1930*. Stanford, CA: Stanford University Press, 1997.

Crush, Jonathan, Alan Jeeves, and David Yudelman. *South Africa's Labor Empire: A History of Black Migrancy to the Gold Mines*. Boulder, CO: Westview Press, 1991.

Isaacman, Allen. *Cotton Is the Mother of Poverty: Peasants, Work, and Rural Struggle in Colonial Mozambique, 1938–1961*. Portsmouth, NH: Heinemann, 1996.

Jeeves, Alan, and Jonathan Crush. *White Farms, Black Labor: The State and Agrarian Change in Southern Africa, 1910–1950*. Portsmouth, NH: Heinemann, 1997.

Likaka, Osumaka. *Rural Society and Cotton in Colonial Zaire*. Madison: University of Wisconsin Press, 1997.

Rupert, Steven. *A Most Promising Weed: A History of Tobacco Farming and Labor in Colonial Zimbabwe, 1890–1945*. Athens: Ohio University Center for International Studies, 1998.

Wilson, Francis. *Labour in the South African Gold Mines, 1911–1969*. Cambridge: Cambridge University Press, 1972.

Young, Crawford. *The African Colonial State in Comparative Perspective*. New Haven, CT: Yale University Press, 1994.

CHAPTER 12. ENCOUNTERS WITH MODERNITY, 1914–1940

Babou, Cheikh Anta. *Fighting the Greater Jihad: Amadu Bamba and the Founding of the Muridiyya of Senegal, 1853–1913*. Athens: University of Ohio Press, 2007.

Echenberg, Myron. *Black Death, White Medicine: Bubonic Plague and the Politics of Public Health in Colonial Senegal, 1914–1945*. Portsmouth, NH: Heinemann, 2002.

Hanretta, Sean. *Islam and Social Change in French West Africa: History of an Emancipatory Community*. New York: Cambridge University Press, 2009.

Klein, Martin A. *Slavery and Colonial Rule in French West Africa*. Cambridge: Cambridge University Press, 1998.

Lovejoy, Paul, and Jan Hogendorn. *Slow Death for Slavery: The Course of Abolition in Northern Nigeria, 1897–1936*. Cambridge: Cambridge University Press, 1993.

Lyons, Maryinez. *The Colonial Disease: A Social History of Sleeping Sickness in Northern Zaire, 1900–1940*. New York: Cambridge University Press, 1992.

Martin, Marie-Louise. *Kimbangu: An African Prophet and His Church*. Oxford: Blackwell, 1975.

Peel, J. D. Y. *Religious Encounter and the Making of the Yoruba*. Bloomington: Indiana University Press, 2000.

Peterson, Brian. *Islamization from Below: The Making of Muslim Communities in Rural French Sudan, 1880–1960*. New Haven, CT: Yale University Press, 2011.

Sivonen, Seppo. *White Collar or Hoe Handle? African Education under British Colonial Policy, 1920–1945*. Helsinki: Suomen Historiallinen Seura, 1995.

CHAPTER 13. LATE COLONIALISM: DEVELOPMENT AND CHANGE, 1935–1965

Anderson, David, and Richard Rathbone. *Africa's Urban Past*. Portsmouth, NH: Heinemann, 2000.

Brennan, James, Andrew Burton, and Yusuf Lawi. *Dar es Salaam: Histories from an Emerging African Metropolis*. Dar es Salaam, Tanzania: Mkuki na Nyota Publishers, 2007.

Byfield, Judith, Carolyn Brown, Timothy Parsons, and Ahmad Sikainga, eds. *Africa and World War II*. New York: Cambridge University Press, 2015.

Colson, Elizabeth. *The Social Consequences of Resettlement: The Impact of the Kariba Resettlement upon the Gwembe Tonga*. Manchester, UK: Manchester University Press, 1971.

Cooper, Frederick. *On the African Waterfront: Urban Disorder and the Transformation of Work in Colonial Mombasa*. New Haven, CT: Yale University Press, 1987.

Echenberg, Myron. *Colonial Conscripts: The Tirailleurs Sénégalais in French West Africa, 1857–1960*. Portsmouth, NH: Heinemann, 1991.

Jeffries, Richard. *Class, Power, and Ideology in Ghana: The Railwaymen of Sekondi*. New York: Cambridge University Press, 1978.

Killingray, David. *Fighting for Britain: African Soldiers during the Second World War*. Rochester, NY: James Currey, 2010.

Martin, Phyllis. *Leisure and Society in Colonial Brazzaville*. New York: Cambridge University Press, 1995.

Throup, David. *Economic and Social Origins of Mau Mau, 1945–53*. London: J. Currey, 1988.

CHAPTER 14. STRUGGLES FOR POLITICAL INDEPENDENCE, 1940–1968

Branch, Daniel. *Defeating Mau Mau, Creating Kenya: Counterinsurgency, Civil War, and Decolonization*. New York: Cambridge University Press, 2009.

Chafer, Tony. *The End of Empire in French West Africa*. New York: Berg, 2002.

Cooper, Frederick. *Decolonization and African Society: The Labor Question in French and British Africa*. New York: Cambridge University Press, 1996.

Elkins, Caroline. *Imperial Reckoning: The Untold Story of Britain's Gulag in Kenya*. New York: Henry Holt, 2005.

Evans, Martin. *Algeria: France's Undeclared War*. Oxford: Oxford University Press, 2012.

Gondola, Ch. Didier. *The History of Congo*. Westport, CT: Greenwood Press, 2003.

Lodge, Tom. *Black Politics in South Africa since 1945*. Johannesburg: Raven Press, 1983.

Schmidt, Elizabeth. *Cold War and Decolonization in Guinea, 1946–1958*. Athens: Ohio University Press, 2007.

Van Reybrouck, David. *Congo: The Epic History of a People*. New York: Ecco, 2014.

Zvobgo, C. J. M. *A History of Zimbabwe, 1890–2000*. Newcastle upon Tyne: Cambridge Scholars, 2009.

CHAPTER 15. AFRICA IN A BIPOLAR WORLD, 1960–1990

Chabal, Patrick. *A History of Postcolonial Lusophone Africa*. London: C. Hurst, 2002.

Emerson, Stephen. *The Battle for Mozambique: The Frelimo-Renamo Struggle, 1977–1992*. Soilhull, West Midlands: Helion, 2014.

Gerard, Emmanuel, and Bruce Kuklick. *Death in the Congo: Murdering Patrice Lumumba*. Cambridge, MA: Harvard University Press, 2015.

Kriger, Norma. *Zimbabwe's Guerrilla War: Peasant Voices*. New York: Cambridge University Press, 1992.

Lal, Priya. *African Socialism in Postcolonial Tanzania: Between the Village and the World*. New York: Cambridge University Press, 2015.

Namikas, Lise A. *Battleground Africa: Cold War in the Congo, 1961–1965*. Stanford, CA: Stanford University Press, 2013.

Nugent, Paul. *Africa since Independence: A Comparative History*, 2nd edition. New York: Palgrave Macmillan, 2012.

Rooney, David. *Kwame Nkrumah: Vision and Tragedy*. Accra, Ghana: Sub-Saharan Publishers, 2007.

Tiruneh, Andargachew. *The Ethiopian Revolution 1974–1987: A Transformation from an Aristocratic to a Totalitarian Aristocracy*. New York: Cambridge University Press, 1993.

Young, Crawford. *The Postcolonial State in Africa: Fifty Years of Independence, 1960–2010*. Madison: University of Wisconsin Press, 2012.

CHAPTER 16. AFRICA IN A MULTIPOLAR WORLD, 1990–2017

Brautigam, Deborah. *The Dragon's Gift: The Real Story of China in Africa*. New York: Oxford University Press, 2009.

Cheeseman, Nicholas. *Democracy in Africa*. New York: Cambridge University Press, 2015.

Cook, Steven A. *The Struggle for Egypt: From Nasser to Tahrir Square*. New York: Oxford University Press, 2011.

Danahar, Paul. *The New Middle East: The World after the Arab Spring*. London: Bloomsbury, 2015.

Hammer, Joshua. *The Bad-Ass Librarians of Timbuktu and their Race to Save the World's Most Precious Manuscripts*. New York: Simon & Schuster, 2016.

Iliffe, John. *The African AIDS Epidemic: A History*. Athens: Ohio University Press, 2006.

Kachiga, Jean. *China in Africa: Articulating China's Africa Policy*. Trenton, NJ: Africa World Press, 2013.

Pepin, Jacques. *The Origin of AIDS*. Cambridge: Cambridge University Press, 2011.

Prunier, Gerard. *The Rwanda Crisis: History of a Genocide*. London: C. Hurst, 1998.

Stearns, Jason. *Dancing in the Glory of Monsters: The Collapse of the Congo and the Great War of Africa*. New York: Public Affairs, 2011.

GLOSSARY

Achimota College—A coeducational secondary school in Accra, Ghana, that opened in 1927. It was modeled after the prestigious private boarding schools in England. Kwame Nkrumah, the first president of independent Ghana, was a graduate of the school, as were four other presidents of Ghana.

African National Congress (ANC)—An organization founded in 1912 to advocate for the rights of black South Africans. During the 1950s, it organized protests across South Africa against the apartheid laws and formed a military wing in 1961. After being banned by the white South African government from 1960 to 1990, it became the dominant political party when South Africa gained majority rule in 1994.

African World War—A name given to the series of wars that began with the Rwandan genocide in 1994 and continued through the First and Second Congo Wars from 1996 to 2003. It is called a world war because many African countries contributed troops on one side or the other. In all, 140,000 troops, representing nine African countries, fought in the Democratic Republic of the Congo (Congo-Kinshasa). The wars left some 5 million people dead from violence, disease, and starvation.

Agaja—King of the small inland kingdom of Dahomey; created a highly disciplined army armed with muskets that he used to conquer nearby coastal kingdoms, giving Dahomey full access to the European trading establishments on the coast. King Agaja used women bodyguards and inserted women into combat, thus inaugurating Dahomey's tradition of female soldiers.

AIDS (Acquired Immune Deficiency Syndrome)—A disease, caused by the human immunodeficiency virus (HIV), that destroys the human body's capacity to fight off other diseases, leaving the infected person open to death from a variety of common maladies. AIDS was first identified in Africa in the 1980s and reached epidemic proportions in the 1990s. By 2007, it was estimated that 15 million Africans had died from AIDS.

Akani—A commercial organization that organized caravans to bring gold to the European forts on the Gold Coast and trade it for European goods. It was based in the tiny kingdom of Assin, which had abundant gold. The Akani organization was destroyed by the army of Denkyira in the 1690s.

Aksum—A powerful kingdom that developed in the Ethiopian highlands in the first seven centuries of the Common Era. It came to dominate the region between the Nile valley and the Red Sea, and its rule extended at times into southern Arabia, to the east, and to Meroe, in the west. Some of the Aksumite rulers erected stelae up to 97 feet high to mark their graves.

Aladura churches—African independent churches that arose in southern Nigeria in the 1920s and 1930s. They differed from missionary churches in their emphasis on the power of prayer and divine healing. Because the Aladura churches included many small independent congregations, they exhibited tremendous variation in their stances on issues such as polygyny, witchcraft, and the validity of certain prophetic visions.

Albion A10 truck—A rugged and reliable truck, built by the Scottish automobile maker Albion, that became the workhorse of colonial Africa during the interwar period. First introduced in 1910, the Albion A10 had a 32-horsepower motor and a carrying capacity of 3 tons.

Almohad Empire—An Islamic state founded in the twelfth century by the Masmuda

Berbers from southern Morocco. The Almohads rejected the legalistic doctrines of the Almoravids and emphasized the transcendental unity of God. At its height around 1200, the empire controlled the entire Maghreb and the southern half of Spain, but it had collapsed by 1269.

Almoravid Empire—An Islamic state created in the eleventh century by the Sanhaja Berbers living in the western part of the Sahara. At its height, it stretched from Awdaghust in the southern Sahara to the middle of Spain. The Almoravids promoted a legalistic interpretation of Islam. They were defeated by the Almohads in 1147.

Al-Zubayr—An ivory trader from Khartoum who created a trading state in present-day southern Sudan that, at its height, was as large as France. In 1873, the khedive of Egypt appointed him district administrator over the lands that he had conquered, but summoned him to Cairo 2 years later and did not allow him to leave.

Amin, Idi—Commander of Uganda's armed forces who became the country's leader after he staged a military coup on January 25, 1971. Although he had originally announced a temporary "caretaker government," he became more and more dictatorial and proclaimed himself "President for Life." He was forced out of office when the Tanzanian army invaded Uganda in 1978.

Anglo-Boer War—The war fought in southern Africa from 1899 to 1902 between Britain and the two Boer republics: the Orange Free State and the South African Republic. It was characterized by Boer guerilla tactics and British use of concentration camps. The British victory led to the creation of the Union of South Africa in 1910.

Angola—A settler colony established by Portuguese settlers in 1575 and taken over by the Portuguese government in 1591. For the first century of its existence, the Portuguese waged war against the neighboring inland kingdoms and exported the resulting captives. Warfare was replaced by a regular trade in slaves after the Portuguese signed a treaty with Queen Njinga in 1681.

apartheid—A system of institutionalized racial segregation and discrimination that was formalized after the National Party came to power in South Africa in 1948. Although discriminatory laws had existed in South Africa prior to 1948, the apartheid laws created a coordinated system of segregation that touched all aspects of South African life.

Arab Spring—The wave of pro-democracy protests, uprisings, and armed rebellions against authoritarian governments in 2011–2012 in Tunisia, Libya, Egypt, Yemen, Bahrain, and Syria. In North Africa, the Arab Spring protests resulted in regime change in Tunisia, Libya, and Egypt, but Libya subsequently descended into chaos, and Egypt experienced a military coup.

Asante Empire—An empire founded after Osei Tutu's Asante coalition defeated the powerful state of Denkyira in 1701. Its political unity was culturally enhanced by the symbol of the Golden Stool and the annual yam harvest festival. By the end of the eighteenth century, the authority of the Asante rulers extended over a territory larger than modern Ghana.

Atlantic Charter—A policy statement issued during World War II and approved by all the Allies that defined Allied goals for the postwar world. Clause no. 3 stated that all peoples have the right to determine their form of government, but the Allies did not apply that principle to the colonized peoples of Africa.

Bamba, Amadu—The founder of the Muslim Muridiyya, or Muride brotherhood, in Senegal. He was feared by French colonial authorities because of his popularity and his refusal to acknowledge French authority. After being sent twice into exile, he reached an accommodation with the French. Members of the Muride brotherhood became known for expanding peanut production in Senegal.

Bantu languages—A group of closely related languages spoken in the southern half of Africa. The name comes from the common Bantu word for "people." Linguists calculate that there are between 440 and 680 Bantu languages spoken in Africa today. The dispersal of the Bantu languages began about 5,000 years ago, when people speaking an ancestral Bantu language moved southward into the tropical African rainforest.

Battle of Adwa—Battle fought in 1896 between the kingdom of Ethiopia and the invading Italians. The Ethiopians defeated the Italians, who withdrew from Ethiopia. As a result, Ethiopia remained an independent kingdom.

Battle of Algiers—A series of bombings and street battles between members of the Algerian National Liberation Front (NLF) and French military units that took place in the city of Algiers in 1956 and 1957. Some 8,000 French paratroopers placed the city in virtual lockdown while searching for the NLF bombers. After the rebels in Algiers were defeated, the war of independence continued in the Algerian countryside.

Beatriz Kimpa Vita, Dona—A young woman of noble Kongolese birth who believed that Saint Anthony had entered her body and that God had given her the mission to end the civil wars and restore the Kongo Kingdom. She succeeded in reoccupying the capital city, but was arrested by members of the Kongolese nobility and burned at the stake as a heretic.

Belmokhtar, Mokhtar—A former cigarette smuggler, known as "Mr. Marlboro," who became the commander of the jihadist group Al Qaeda in the Islamic Maghreb in Mali (AQIMM). The group captured Timbuktu in April 2012 and imposed a strict form of Islamic practice and lifestyle. When the French liberated Timbuktu in January 2013, he fled the city and disappeared into the Sahara Desert.

Berber—A term that refers to the indigenous populations of North Africa and the Sahara Desert who spoke Berber languages. In pre-Roman times, most Berbers were nomadic or seminomadic, although some of them were farmers on the coastal plain of the Maghreb. Following the Islamic conquests of the seventh century, Berbers established the Fatimid, Almoravid, and Almohad empires.

Berlin Conference—Conference held in Berlin from November 1884 to February 1885 in which twelve European nations, plus the United States and Turkey, met to resolve their differences over how to partition Africa among themselves. The most significant decision of the conference was to award most of the vast Congo River basin to King Leopold II of Belgium as his personal property.

bey—A district administrator or low-level military governor in the Ottoman Empire. The exact meaning of the title varied according to time and place. Beys were lower in rank than pashas or deys. The term *bey* was also used as a courtesy title (roughly equivalent to "sir") that was appended after the official's name.

Blyden, Edward Wilmot—Intellectual leader, Liberia; born on the Caribbean island of St. Thomas in 1832; moved to the Republic of Liberia in 1850 after being refused admission to American theological colleges; served as editor of the *Liberia Herald*; later held government and diplomatic positions and served as president of Liberia College. He advocated a synthesis of Africa's "triple heritage"—indigenous, Muslim, and Christian.

Bobangi—An ethnically based trading alliance that controlled the slave and ivory trade along the middle Congo River during the eighteenth and nineteenth centuries. The Bobangi established towns at key points where the Congo River narrowed or received tributaries. Bobangi towns were organized into component villages dominated by rival trading firms, which augmented their capacity through the acquisition of slaves.

Boer—The Dutch word for "farmer," applied to the Dutch immigrants who settled on the Cape Peninsula of southern Africa after 1652. Over time, they developed a unique Dutch dialect known as Afrikaans, whose speakers were called Afrikaners or Boers, regardless of whether or not they farmed.

Boer republics—The Orange Free State and the Transvaal (officially, the South African Republic): two independent, self-governing states that were established by the Trekboers in previously African-held territory during the 1830s and 1840s. They were recognized by Britain as independent states in the 1850s. Each had a constitution and a republican form of government, but Africans were not allowed to vote.

Bouazizi, Muhammad—An unemployed, university-educated street vendor in Tunisia who set himself on fire in front of the police station to protest his harassment by the police for selling vegetables without a license. His fiery suicide set off anti-government demonstrations across the country, leading to the fall of the Tunisian government in January 2011.

Brussels Round Table Conference—A meeting in January and February 1960 that brought nationalist leaders from the Belgian Congo to Brussels to discuss the future of the colony with Belgian government and business leaders. After the Congolese delegates displayed solidarity in demanding immediate independence, the Belgians capitulated and agreed to Congolese independence on June 30, 1960.

canoe house—A form of socioeconomic organization that developed in the Niger Delta in the eighteenth century. A canoe house was a trading corporation capable of manning and maintaining one or more 50-person canoes. Instead of expanding through natural reproduction in the fashion of a traditional lineage, canoe houses expanded through the acquisition of slaves.

Cape Colony—A settler colony founded by the Dutch East India Company in 1652 as a stopover and resupply point for Dutch ships traveling to and from Asia. At first the settlers lived in and around Cape Town, but soon they spread out over the Cape Peninsula and seized territory from the indigenous Khoikhoi cattle herders and San hunters.

Carthage—A city-state on the Mediterranean coast of North Africa that was founded by Phoenicians in 814 BCE. At its height, Carthage dominated a number of other trading towns along the North African coast and controlled the northern half of present-day Tunisia. The Romans destroyed it in 149 BCE, but later rebuilt it as the capital of the Roman province of Africa. In 698, it was destroyed by an invading Arab army and replaced by Tunis.

cheddo—A soldier of slave origin in the service of the one of the rulers of the coastal kingdoms of Senegambia. Unlike the general population, which was predominantly Muslim, the cheddo remained defiantly pagan and flaunted their use of alcohol. By the nineteenth century, cheddo and noble families had become intertwined and formed a ruling aristocracy.

***chibaro* contract**—A forced-labor contract used by the British South Africa Company to recruit workers for the gold mines in colonial Zimbabwe. Company labor recruiters rounded up able-bodied men and forced them to sign 1-year *chibaro* contracts. During the 1920s, about 40,000 men per year worked in the mines on *chibaro* contracts.

China-Africa Cooperation Forum—A series of international meetings between the leaders of China and those of a number of African countries, held in China and Africa beginning in 2000. The meetings produced a variety of trade and cooperation agreements between China and individual African countries and resulted in Chinese pledges of aid to Africa.

Chokwe—An ethnic group living in the hinterland of Angola that had developed a lifestyle based on hunting elephants, gathering beeswax, and warfare. In 1886, after rebellious Lunda chiefs hired Chokwe mercenaries to aid them against the Lunda king, the Chokwe sacked the Lunda capital, thus destroying the Lunda Empire.

Christianity—A monotheistic religion founded by followers of a Jewish preacher named Jesus, who was crucified by the Romans. His followers believed that he was the son of God, and that he had risen from the dead and ascended to heaven. Christianity was spread around the Mediterranean world by evangelists whose religious treatises, written in Greek, were later compiled to create the New Testament.

Cleopatra—The last active ruler of the Ptolemaic dynasty of Egypt (ruled 51–30 BCE). Although of Macedonian Greek descent, she presented herself as a latter-day pharaoh who spoke the Egyptian language and was the reincarnation of the Egyptian goddess Isis. Her involvement in a Roman civil war brought on the Roman invasion of Egypt in 30 BCE, after which Egypt became a province of the Roman Empire.

colonial city—A type of African city that grew up during the colonial period as ports, transportation hubs, commercial centers, or administrative capitals. Colonial cities were inhabited mostly by Africans who came from rural regions. They can be contrasted with the "European cities" built in southern Africa to attract white settlers.

Copperbelt—A copper-rich region now occupying the southern part of the Democratic Republic of the Congo and the northern part of Zambia. Copper mining began in the Congo in 1911 and in Zambia after 1924. During the colonial period, copper became the major export for both colonies.

Coptic Church—The Egyptian Christian Church, so called after it split from the larger Christian world following the Council of Chalcedon in 451. The name comes from its use of Coptic—the ancient Egyptian language written with a modified Greek alphabet—for liturgy and religious texts. The Coptic Church was under the authority of the patriarch of Alexandria.

cordon sanitaire—A French phrase that refers to a boundary line established to stop the spread of infectious diseases. It was usually accomplished by restricting the movement of people within a defined geographical area. The technique was used in the campaigns against the bubonic plague and sleeping sickness in Africa.

corsair—A type of North African pirate operating under the authority of the Ottoman Empire who attacked ships and raided coastal villages to capture slaves and booty. Unlike ordinary pirates, they were protected by the regencies of Algiers, Tripoli, and Tunis, and unlike privateers, who interdicted enemy shipping in times of war, the corsairs would attack any foreign ship at any time.

Crowther, Samuel Ajayi—Religious and intellectual leader; born in 1809 in Yoruba country; enslaved and rescued from a slave ship; settled in Sierra Leone; served as a Christian missionary to the Yoruba and later as the Anglican Church's first bishop of West Africa; sought common ground with Muslims and worked to define a form of religious faith that was both Christian and African.

Dahomey—A small kingdom located inland from the Bight of Benin that expanded militarily in the early eighteenth century by conquering the neighboring coastal kingdoms in order to gain direct access to trade with Europeans. Dahomey's continuing wars provided captives to the British, French, Portuguese, and Dutch during the eighteenth century.

delegalization—The strategy used in British and French colonies to reduce domestic slavery. Instead of formally abolishing slavery and setting all slaves free, colonial administrators "delegalized" slavery by passing laws saying that slave owners had no standing to go to colonial courts to demand the return of slaves who left them. Some slaves left their masters, but others stayed on and renegotiated the terms of their servitude. Instead of ending abruptly, slavery in Africa gradually died out over several decades.

Denkyira—A powerful state in the Akan forest belt of the Gold Coast region that expanded after 1650. Its initial expansion was to the north, but it later moved south to capture the trade routes to the European forts on the coast. It lost its power after being defeated by the Asante coalition in 1701.

Derg—A group of Ethiopian junior military officers who overthrew Emperor Haile Selassie in 1974 and established a Soviet-style communist state. The Derg nationalized all land and announced a plan to move 33 million farmers from their independent homesteads into communal villages. The Derg was toppled from power in 1991 by a coalition of rebel forces.

developmental authoritarianism—A term coined by the political scientist Hilary Matfess to describe the politico-economic philosophy of the governments of Rwanda and Ethiopia. Partially borrowed from China, this seemingly contradictory approach embraces a free-market ideology along with significant state intervention in public works and services, and it supports formal institutions of democracy along with harsh restrictions on opposition parties.

dey—A title given to the rulers of the regencies of Algiers, Tripoli, and Tunis under the Ottoman Empire from 1671 onward. Unlike pashas, who were sent out from Istanbul for 3-year terms, the deys came from the ranks of the permanent Turkish military garrisons and ruled as monarchs with lifetime tenure.

dynasty—A sequence of rulers from the same family who ruled over Egypt. Thirty different dynasties ruled Egypt between its founding by King Narmer and its conquest by Alexander the Great, with an average dynastic reign of a hundred years.

East African Rift System—A series of geological trenches, or rifts, each 20–50 miles wide, that form a shallow arc running roughly parallel to the Indian Ocean coast. The same geological processes that created the rifts pushed up a series of mountain ranges that wall off eastern and northeastern Africa from the climate patterns that prevail elsewhere on the continent, thus creating a unique climate in the region of the rifts.

évolué—An intermediate category for Africans who had attained a certain level of education and adopted Western ways, created by French, Portuguese, and Belgian colonial administrators. Laws and regulations in all African colonies were grounded in a racial distinction between white "Europeans" and black "natives"; *évolués* (also referred to as *assimilés* or *assimilados*, depending on the colony) were exempt from some of the laws that applied to "natives."

Fatimid caliphate—A rival to the Islamic Caliphate that was founded in North Africa in the tenth century. Propelled by Berber armies from the Maghreb, the Fatimid caliphate expanded all across North Africa and into Syria and the Arabian Peninsula.

The Fatimids were followers of Shia Islam who ruled from their capital in Cairo.

Fertile Crescent—A crescent-shaped region, extending from the eastern shore of the Mediterranean Sea to the Persian Gulf, that was an early center for the domestication of many of the crops that feed the world today. It was blessed with a favorable climate as well as wild forms of wheat, barley, rye, peas, and other plants that could be domesticated by farmers.

Firestone Tire and Rubber Company—An American company based in Akron, Ohio, that, in 1926, acquired the rights to lease up to a million acres of land for rubber plantations in Liberia. It established two plantations that together contained 10 million rubber trees. From the beginning, the company found it difficult to recruit labor. In 1929, it was accused of using forced and coerced labor.

Freedom Charter—A document created by the African National Congress in South Africa in 1955 that outlined the organization's goals and principles. The Freedom Charter proclaimed equal status for all national groups and races and guaranteed human rights for all. The multiracial approach of the ANC formed a contrast with the African nationalist approach of the rival Pan-Africanist Congress (PAC).

Free French Forces—The resistance movement against the Germans and their French collaborators during World War II, led by General Charles de Gaulle. The governors of the French colonies in Africa were forced to choose between loyalty to the collaborationist French government at Vichy or the Free French Forces.

Front for the Liberation of Mozambique (FRELIMO)—An anti-colonial liberation movement in Mozambique, organized in Tanzania in 1962 by Mozambican exiles seeking to overthrow Portuguese colonial rule. FRELIMO gained control of the government in 1975, only to find itself opposed by RENAMO.

Fuuta Jaloo—A theocratic Islamic state in the Fuuta Jaloo highlands, founded in 1737 following a jihad waged by cattle-herding Fulbe immigrants against the indigenous Jalonke farmers. The state developed a social system in which the Jalonke lived in servile villages under their own leadership and produced grain for their Fulbe overlords.

germ theory—The guiding theory that underlies modern biomedicine, which states that many diseases are caused by the actions of microorganisms, which can be counteracted by drugs. Germ theory gained gradual acceptance in Europe and the United States from the middle nineteenth century onward and spread to Africa during the colonial period.

Ghana Empire—A large empire in the West African Sahel that was founded between 500 and 700 CE (not to be confused with the modern African nation of Ghana). The key to the empire's prosperity was its middleman position in the gold trade with Morocco. Its prosperity declined after the Almoravids gained control of the trans-Saharan trade routes during the eleventh century.

Gold Coast—The coastal region roughly equivalent to the coast of the modern nation of Ghana (not to be confused with the ancient Ghana Empire). The forest belt inland from the coast contained gold that was mined by digging pits. European trading companies built forts and castles along the coast to carry on the gold trade, but they were later used for slave trading.

Great Trek—The migration of Boer farmers out of the Cape Colony beginning in 1834, after the British had captured the colony from the Dutch in 1806, abolished the Hottentot Code in 1828, and ended slavery in

1833. By 1840, about 10 percent of the white settlers in the Cape Colony had moved north into the interior, where they seized land belonging to Bantu-speaking Africans.

Great Zimbabwe—A city on the Zimbabwe Plateau, containing a great stone palace with walls 35 feet high. Built between the eleventh and fifteenth centuries, it was a center for crafts, industry, and the gold trade, receiving trade goods from as far away as China. For reasons that are not entirely clear, the site was abandoned by 1490.

Hamallah, Amadu—A member of the Tijaniyya who led a religious reform movement in colonial Mali. Hamallah believed that he had received revelations directly from the Prophet Muhammad that guided his reinterpretation of certain Tijaniyya texts. At the urging of Tijaniyya leaders, he was arrested by the French colonial authorities in 1925 and sent into exile in Côte d'Ivoire and France.

Harris, William Wade—A Liberian-born evangelist and healer who spread Christianity in Ghana and Côte d'Ivoire after receiving a vision that he believed came from the angel Gabriel. Preaching an orthodox version of Christianity, he and his followers baptized some 100,000 converts during 1913–1914 before the French arrested him and deported him back to Liberia.

Herero genocide—The German colonial government's brutal repression of the Herero revolt in Namibia between 1904 and 1907, during which over 80 percent of the Herero lost their lives. A United Nations report in 1985 classified the German actions as the first genocide of the twentieth century.

hominin—The biological category that includes modern humans, extinct human species, and the immediate ancestors of humans, but excludes the great apes such as chimpanzees and gorillas. In current usage, hominins make up a subfamily of hominids: a broader category that includes humans, chimpanzees, and gorillas.

Human Genome Project—An international collaborative research program that spent 13 years mapping the human genome (the totality of all our genes) by analyzing human DNA. The results, published in 2003, provided the first complete genetic blueprint for a human being. Genetic mapping of humans has since become common, and scientists even mapped the Neanderthal genome in 2010.

Hut Tax War—A rebellion that broke out in Sierra Leone when the British colonial government tried to impose an annual hut tax on the Africans. It lasted from February to November 1898 and involved some of the "most stubborn fighting" that had been seen in West Africa.

Imbangala—A people living in the hinterland of Angola who had abandoned the agricultural way of life in favor of forming mobile fighting bands. They sometimes joined forces with the Portuguese in their wars against the neighboring kingdoms. They settled down in the seventeenth century to form the kingdom of Kasanje.

indigénat—A law in French colonies that gave French administrators the right to inflict immediate fines or prison time on Africans who challenged their authority or failed to meet their administrative demands. Perhaps the most hated aspect of French colonial rule, the *indigénat* was abolished in 1946.

indirect rule—A system of colonial rule, first formalized by the British, in which African kings and chiefs were allowed to remain in power if they pledged subservience to the colonial administration. Although all colonial powers used chiefs as low-level administrators, indirect rule emphasized the appointment of chiefs who had legitimate traditional authority.

Islam—A monotheistic religion founded in Mecca, on the Arabian Peninsula, in the seventh century by the Prophet Muhammad, who proclaimed "There is no god but God, and Muhammad is God's messenger." After his death, his followers compiled his teachings to create the Quran and developed a uniform set of Islamic religious practices.

Islamic Caliphate—The powerful Islamic state created by conquering Arab armies under the authority of the successors to the Prophet Muhammad. At its height in 750, it stretched from Spain to India. Devoted to Sunni Islam, the Caliphate moved its capital over the years from Medina to Damascus, and finally to Baghdad. It disintegrated in 1258 after a Mongol army from Central Asia sacked Baghdad.

Kariba Dam—A large dam on the Zambezi River constructed between 1955 and 1959 on the border between Zambia and Zimbabwe in order to supply electricity to the Zambian copper mines. It created a lake 170 miles long that displaced many African farmers from the fertile Zambezi valley.

Kasanje—A state in the hinterland of Angola founded in the seventeenth century by the Imbangala war leader Jaga Kasanje, who signed a peace treaty with the Portuguese on the coast in 1683. In the eighteenth century, the market at Kasanje was the key transition point between the Lunda slave caravans coming from the far interior and the caravans going to the coast.

Katanga secession—The declaration of independence by the copper-rich Katanga Province of Congo-Kinshasa on July 11, 1960, just 12 days after the Congo itself gained its independence from Belgium. Katanga remained independent until January 21, 1963, when U.N. troops occupied the province and reintegrated it into the Congo.

Katsina College—A secondary school in northern Nigeria that the British established in 1921 for the training of Muslim students. Located in the capital of the Katsina Emirate, the school took in boys who had come up through the Muslim education system, taught them the skills needed by the British administration, and socialized them to the elite culture of government service.

Kilwa—A Swahili trading town located north of the Mozambique Channel at the southernmost reach of the monsoon winds. Kilwa received gold from the Zimbabwe Plateau via the port of Sofala. In 1500, it had the largest mosque in sub-Saharan Africa.

Kimbangu, Simon—A Baptist lay preacher and faith healer in the Belgian Congo who was arrested by Belgian authorities after only 2 months of ministry and imprisoned for the rest of his life, much of the time in solitary confinement. His followers continued his ministry to form the Church of Jesus Christ on Earth by the Prophet Simon Kimbangu, which claimed over half a million members by the 1960s.

Kongo Kingdom—A powerful kingdom situated south of the mouth of the Congo River. The king proclaimed it a Christian kingdom in the early sixteenth century, and it was recognized as such by the pope in 1596, when the church in the capital was elevated to the status of a cathedral. The Kongo kings provided captives for the slave trade, but they also took measures to safeguard free Kongolese citizens.

lançados—A name given to Portuguese men who left the Cape Verde Islands to live in Africa and conduct trade. Most lançados received permission from a local African chief to settle in a village and set up a trading post. They married African wives, and their descendants have been referred to as Luso-Africans or Eurafricans.

Lancaster House Agreement—The December 21, 1979, agreement that brought majority rule and independence to Zimbabwe, ending Ian Smith's breakaway white government that had controlled the country since 1965. Following the agreement, Britain took back its former colony for about 4 months to arrange the transition and then granted independence to Zimbabwe on April 18, 1980.

Leverville—The headquarters of the Lever Brothers concession in the Belgian Congo, where palm oil was collected for making Sunlight Soap. In 1911, the company received a legal monopoly on all palm fruit within five circles, each one 36 miles in diameter. In 1931, a company drive to forcibly recruit workers triggered a major revolt by the local population.

Liberia, Republic of—A republic on the Atlantic coast of West Africa; originated as a settler colony for free blacks and ex-slaves created by the American Colonization Society in 1821; became the Commonwealth of Liberia in 1839 and an independent republic in 1847.

Lobengula—King of the Ndebele Kingdom on the Zimbabwe Plateau. In 1888, King Lobengula signed a treaty with business associates of Cecil Rhodes allowing for limited gold mining, but the text was manipulated to give the impression that he had signed away his country. The British South Africa Company drove Lobengula out of his capital, Bulawayo, in 1893.

Lucy (*Australopithecus afarensis*)—A well-preserved skeleton of an early hominin female who lived 3.2 million years ago. Her knees and pelvis were completely adapted to walking upright, but she had long arms and curved fingers for climbing trees. She was discovered in the Afar region of Ethiopia in 1974.

Lumumba, Patrice—Leader of the Congolese National Movement, the major national political party involved in the 1960 parliamentary elections leading up to independence for the Belgian Congo. Lumumba became the first prime minister of the Congo, but was targeted for assassination by the American CIA because its members believed that he was a communist. Driven from power by a military coup, he was executed in the breakaway province of Katanga in 1962.

Lunda Empire—An empire founded in the southern savanna roughly halfway between the Atlantic and Indian Oceans. During the eighteenth century, when the empire was expanding rapidly, the Lunda rulers sent caravans of captives toward the Portuguese settlements on the Atlantic coast, making the Lunda Empire the largest single supplier of captives to the Portuguese in Angola in that century.

Luso-tropicalism—A Portuguese theory of imperialism developed by the Brazilian sociologist Gilberto Freyre and adopted by the Portuguese dictator Antonio Salazar in the 1950s. It argued that Portugal had been a multicultural and a multicontinental nation since the fifteenth century, and that the loss of its overseas territories would represent a dismemberment of the Portuguese nation itself.

Mad Mullah—The British nickname for Muhammad Abdullah Hassan, who led a rebellion against the British in Somalia. In 1913, he established the Dervish State, which remained independent until 1920, when the British bombed his capital.

Maghreb—The western half of North Africa; from an Arabic word meaning "land of the sunset." The Maghreb is characterized by a tripartite division of the landscape among the coastal plain, the mountains, and the Sahara Desert. Today, the countries of Morocco, Algeria, and Tunisia make up the Maghreb.

Mahdi, the—The Islamic deliverer who, according to prophecies, would bring justice and equity to the earth at the end of time; also, the title claimed by Muhammad Ahmad, a member of the Sufi Sammaniyya order and leader of a jihad that ousted the Turco-Egyptian regime and established a theocratic state in Sudan.

Maji Maji Rebellion—A rebellion against German colonialism that engulfed the southeastern quarter of Tanganyika from 1905 to 1907. The name comes from the holy water distributed by the African prophet

Kinjikitile to protect people from the bullets of the German soldiers (*maji* is the Swahili word for water).

Mali Empire—A large empire in the West African Sahel that was the successor to the declining Ghana Empire (not to be confused with the modern African nation of Mali). Founded in the thirteenth century, the Mali Empire controlled territory from the Atlantic to the Niger bend. Its fortunes declined in the fifteenth century when many of the trading towns in the Sahel broke away from its control.

Mamari Kulubali—A hunter and charismatic outsider who built up a following among the rebellious and disreputable elements of Bamana society and created a kingdom centered on the trading town of Segu. After his death in 1755, power passed to a former slave soldier named Ngolo Jara, who proclaimed that his troops would live by pillage.

Mamluk—A type of slave soldier who served in the army of a Muslim state. The word *Mamluk* comes from the Turkish term for "owned." Mamluk soldiers seized power in Egypt in 1260 and ruled it until 1517. Although the original Mamluks were enslaved Turks, by the fifteenth century most of them came from the Caucasus Mountains.

Mandela, Nelson—A black South African lawyer and civil rights activist who founded the Youth Wing of the African National Congress in 1943. Mandela played a leading role in organizing the Defiance Campaign in 1952, and he cofounded the armed wing of the ANC in 1961. Mandela was sentenced to life in prison the following year, but was released in 1990. In 1994, he became the first president of majority-ruled South Africa.

Mansa Musa—A Muslim ruler of the Mali Empire who made a pilgrimage to Mecca in 1324, carrying and spending so much gold on his journey that the price of gold in Cairo was depressed for a dozen years. Upon his return to Mali, he ordered the construction of the Great Mosque in Timbuktu.

Marketing Board—A colonial government agency in Britain's African colonies that purchased export commodities from farmers in order to stabilize prices. Marketing Boards generally set their prices so low that they amassed huge surpluses of money that should have gone to the African farmers.

Mascarene Islands—The Indian Ocean islands of Mauritius and Réunion. Located roughly halfway between the southern tip of Africa and the southern tip of India, they served as rest stops and resupply stations for ships crossing the Indian Ocean. Previously uninhabited, they were settled by the Dutch and the French during the seventeenth and eighteenth centuries.

Mau Mau rebellion—An anti-colonial uprising in the central highlands of Kenya between 1952 and 1956. The rebel fighters called themselves the Land and Freedom Army to emphasize their two main grievances. To suppress the rebellion, the British brought in over 10,000 regular army troops to supplement the Kenyan police and Home Guard units. In the wake of the Mau Mau rebellion, the British began negotiations for Kenyan independence.

Maxim gun—The first true machine gun, invented by Hiram Maxim. It was introduced in 1884, just as the scramble for Africa was under way. European armies equipped with Maxim guns could defeat much larger African armies equipped only with muskets.

Memphis—The first capital of Egypt, founded by King Narmer near the point where the Nile valley met the Nile delta, about 15 miles south of modern Cairo. Although Memphis functioned as the capital of Egypt during the Old Kingdom and Middle Kingdom, the capital was moved to Thebes and remained there for much of the New Kingdom and Late Period.

Middle Niger floodplain—A region in West Africa where the Niger River overflowed during the high-water season and irrigated a large region; also known as the inland Niger delta. It was an early center of agriculture, leading to a system of decentralized urbanism characterized by large settlements surrounded by economically specialized satellite villages.

military coup—A takeover of a country's government by military officers. In some military coups that occurred in newly independent African countries, the officers established "caretaker governments" that organized elections and restored civilian rule. In other cases, however, the officers formed a permanent government that ruled until they were overthrown.

Millennium Man (*Orrorin tugenesis*)—An early hominin skeleton discovered in northern Kenya in 2000, dated to about 6 million years ago. Although Millennium Man could function in a mixed environment of trees and open spaces, he was more apelike than human.

monsoon winds—Winds in the Indian Ocean that blow from India to Africa from October to April and then reverse direction from April to October. A sailing ship could therefore make a round trip between Africa and India in a year or less.

Mozambican National Resistance (RENAMO)—An organization originally sponsored by white-ruled Zimbabwe and white-ruled South Africa to carry out military resistance against the Marxist-leaning FRELIMO government of Mozambique. Using guerrilla warfare tactics, RENAMO was known for its violence and brutality against civilians. RENAMO signed a peace agreement with FRELIMO in 1992, calling for multiparty elections and ending 16 years of civil war in Mozambique.

Msiri—A Nyamwezi merchant who pioneered the ivory trade in the region known as Katanga, which was located in the lightly wooded southern savanna roughly halfway between the Atlantic coast and the Indian Ocean coast. In the 1860s, he founded the Yeke Kingdom, which carried on trade with both the eastern and western coasts of Africa.

Muhammad Ali—The Ottoman-appointed governor who became known as the father of modern Egypt. After breaking the Mamluks' hold on the Egyptian administration, he embarked on a series of reforms. During his rule (1805–1848), he improved the irrigation system, encouraged the production of cotton, modernized the army, and extended Egyptian rule over Sudan.

Muslim Brotherhood—A politico-religious organization founded in Egypt in 1928 that did not seek to overthrow the secular government in Egypt, but hoped to harness it for religious purposes in order to transform society and politics from the ground up. The organization was banned by the Egyptian government in 1954, but still retains a great deal of support in Egypt.

Nabta Playa—An archaeological site in Egypt's western desert near the modern border with Sudan that contains prehistoric mounds, stelae, and megalithic structures. About 9,000 years ago, Nabta Playa developed into a settled community where people made their living by hunting, herding cattle, and gathering wild grains. It was especially noteworthy for its role as a regional religious and ceremonial center.

Nasser, Gamal Abdel—An Egyptian army lieutenant who organized a military coup against King Farouk of Egypt in 1952 and was a leading figure on the Revolutionary Command Council that abolished the monarchy, proclaimed Egypt a republic, and secured the departure of British colonial troops. He served as prime minister of Egypt from 1954 to 1956, and as president from 1956 until his death in 1970.

National Conference—A political device for restoring multiparty democracy to a country by calling a conference of all major political factions to write a new constitution and organize multiparty elections. This method was used in the 1990s in former French colonies such as Benin, Mali, Congo-Brazzaville, and Niger.

Native Authority school—A type of primary school in British colonies that were sponsored and financed by local communities. They were especially popular in northern Nigeria, where the Muslim population was hostile to schools sponsored by Christian missions.

native reserve—An area of South Africa reserved for black South Africans under the 1913 Natives Land Act. The law recognized African "tribal" ownership of the land in the native reserves, but would not allow Africans to own land as individuals. In 1913, the reserves contained only 7 percent of the land in South Africa, but the amount was increased to 13 percent in 1936.

Natives Land Act—A law passed by the Union of South Africa in 1913 that reserved 93 percent of the land in South Africa for whites, even though black South Africans made up two-thirds of the population. The law also prohibited blacks from living on white lands as sharecroppers, forcing them to become wage laborers for the white landowners.

Nehanda-Charwe—The woman named Charwe, the most powerful of the Shona spirit mediums in Zimbabwe, who channeled the spirit Nehanda to bring rain and fertility to the land. In 1897, the British executed Nehanda-Charwe on charges of inspiring the Shona people to rebel against the rule of the British South Africa Company.

Ngoni—Collective term for the groups established by generals of the regiments of Zwide's Ndwandwe Kingdom who moved northward after its defeat and disintegration; the Ngoni states conquered and incorporated people from a variety of linguistic and ethnic groups throughout East Central Africa.

Niger scheme—An irrigation scheme along the Niger bend that was created by the French in 1932 to produce cotton. It was officially known as the *Office du Niger*. Plagued by low cotton yields and resistance from tenants, the scheme gradually switched over to rice production.

Nile delta—The triangle-shaped lowland region where the Nile River fanned out to flow into the Mediterranean. Often known as Lower Egypt, the delta measured 100 miles from north to south and 155 miles from east to west. Over the years, the annual floods have deposited a layer of silt between 50 and 75 feet deep on the delta, giving it the richest soil in Africa.

Nile River valley—In the narrowest sense, the floodplain of the Nile River that ran through ancient Egypt from the first cataract in the south to the Nile delta on the Mediterranean coast. In its broader sense, the term can also be applied to Nubia to include the valley of the Nile from the sixth cataract to the first cataract at the southern edge of Egypt, even though fertile floodplains were rare in this region.

Njinga—The sister of the king of Ndongo, who took over the kingdom after her brother's death. After being driven out of her kingdom by a rival claimant to the throne, she joined an Imbangala war band and married its leader. She later led her Imbangala warriors to conquer Matamba and Ndongo, signing a peace treaty with the Portuguese in 1681.

Nkrumah, Kwame—Ghana's first prime minister and later its president. After his studies in Ghana, the United States, and England, Nkrumah founded the Convention People's Party in Ghana in 1949, which demanded immediate self-government. He became prime minister when Ghana gained its independence in 1957. Growing more authoritarian over time, he was overthrown by a military coup in 1966.

Nubia—A general term for the region south of Egypt between the first and the sixth cataracts of the Nile River. The largest single state in Nubia was the kingdom of Kush, which shifted its location southward over the centuries as its capital moved from Kerma to Napata, and finally to Meroe. Egyptian paintings portrayed Nubians as having chocolate-brown or black skin.

Nubian pharaohs—The pharaohs of the Twenty-Fifth Dynasty, which came to power when Piye, the Nubian ruler of Kush, conquered Egypt in 728 BCE; also known as the black pharaohs. Piye and his four dynastic successors ruled Egypt for 71 years. They sought to restore ancient Egyptian culture and the glories of the Old Kingdom. The fall of the Twenty-Fifth Dynasty in 657 BCE ushered in the Late Period in Egyptian history.

Omani Empire—An empire founded by the Arab state of Oman, on the western shore of the Gulf of Oman (at the entrance to the Persian Gulf). After driving the Portuguese out of Mombasa in 1698, it expanded its hegemony over the trading towns of the Swahili Coast. At its height, the Omani Empire controlled the East African coast from present-day Somalia in the north to the Mozambique Channel.

Onitsha market literature—Popular pamphlets that were sold at the large market in Onitsha, Nigeria, in the middle decades of the twentieth century. Over 200 English-language titles by local authors were on sale at the Onitsha market in the postwar years.

Osei Tutu—The ruler of a minor kingdom called Kumasi, who formed a coalition with neighboring kingdoms in the 1690s and founded the Asante Empire. He created a culture of national unity by elevating the Golden Stool of the ruler above the stools of lesser chiefs, and by instituting the annual yam harvest festival, at which he blessed his followers and cursed his enemies.

Ottoman Empire—An empire that originated in Turkey around 1300, then expanded into North Africa, Southwest Asia, and southeastern Europe to become one of the largest and most powerful empires in world history. From their capital in Istanbul, the Ottoman sultans ruled over a mosaic of religious, ethnic, and linguistic communities. The authority of the sultans was supported by an elite group of slave soldiers known as the Janissary Corps.

Out of Africa hypothesis—The hypothesis that all modern humans stem from a single group of *Homo sapiens* who migrated out of Africa some 2,000 generations ago and spread throughout Europe, Asia, and the Americas; currently the dominant model of the geographical origin and early dispersion of modern humans.

patriots—Members of the Ethiopian resistance forces that fought to drive the Italian occupiers out of Ethiopia during World War II. In 1941, Emperor Haile Selassie traveled through the Ethiopian countryside with the British Gideon Force to rally the people to join the patriots and drive out the Italians. Women as well as men joined the patriot forces.

People's Union for the Liberation of Angola (MPLA)—A Marxist-oriented liberation movement in Angola that was founded by educated and mixed-race Angolans based in the capital of Luanda. In 1975, it took over the government of independent Angola, sparking a 10-year civil war with American-backed UNITA.

people's war—A military-political strategy developed by Chinese communist leader Mao Zedong for fighting a war of liberation against a state with a large, well-equipped army. It focused on mobilizing the common people in the countryside. Although Mao successfully carried out this strategy in China, freedom fighters in Angola, Mozambique, and Zimbabwe used this approach with mixed results.

prazo—A type of large feudal estate given to Portuguese settlers in the Zambezi River valley by the Portuguese Crown beginning in the seventeenth century. Prazos were initially granted to Portuguese widows, who passed them down to their female descendants. Over time, many prazos came to be owned by Luso-African women. Using slave labor and private slave armies, the more powerful prazos operated much like the neighboring African chiefdoms.

Rabih Fadlallah—A lieutenant of Al-Zubayr who struck out on his own after his employer was called to Egypt. Continuing Al-Zubayr's pattern of trade and conquest, he established a trading state at Dar al-Kuti and later conquered the kingdom of Bornu.

Red Rubber—The system under which European rubber companies received large concessions of territory in King Leopold II's Congo Free State, which they exploited using brutality and violence. In response to reports of atrocities, the Belgian government took control of the Congo away from the king in 1908.

Rhodes, Cecil—An influential figure in the nineteenth-century history of southern Africa. He was a major investor in diamond and gold mines, the prime minister of the Cape Colony who ordered the disastrous Jameson Raid, and the founder of the British South Africa Company, which orchestrated the European settlement of the Zimbabwe Plateau.

Rwandan genocide—The mass slaughter of members of the Tutsi identity group in Rwanda directed by the Hutu-dominated government and private Hutu militias. The killing spree lasted for 100 days, from April to July 1994, ending when a Tutsi rebel army seized the capital and stopped the killing. Over 800,000 Tutsi and moderate Hutu were killed during the genocide.

Sahara Desert—The largest desert in the world; extends over most of northern Africa. The Sahara is larger than the continent of Australia and almost as large as the United States or China. Although vast plains of sand dunes are typically associated with the Saharan landscape, it also contains mountains that reach 11,000 feet in elevation.

Sahel—An east–west belt of semiarid grassland that forms the transition zone between the Sahara Desert to the north and the grassland savanna to the south. Derived from the Arabic word *sāhil*, which means "shore, coast, or borderland"; *sāhil* can refer to the edge of an ocean or to the edge of a desert.

Samori Touré—A West African kola nut trader who used his profits to buy guns from Sierra Leone and create an army. He conquered a large territory in what is now Guinea and Mali, but lost control of it in 1886 when the populations rebelled against his imposition of Islam. He later built a new empire to the southeast of the old one.

savanna—An environment normally found in broad bands flanking the tropical rainforest. Ecologists distinguish between grassland savanna, which has only scattered trees, and woodland savanna, which has more closely spaced trees, but not a closed canopy. Together, grassland and woodland savannas cover nearly two-thirds of the African continent.

scramble for Africa—The label given to the period between the late 1870s and the late 1890s when Britain, France, Germany, Belgium, Spain, and Portugal laid claim to various parts of Africa and sent armies to occupy the territories that they had claimed. It is called a "scramble" because of its chaotic nature, driven by Great Power rivalries.

second colonial occupation—Intrusions into African life by colonial agricultural agents who arrived in East Africa after World War II to implement terracing campaigns and other agricultural improvement schemes, often by force.

second independence—A loosely defined term that refers to the restoration of multiparty democracy, beginning in the 1990s, in African countries that had fallen under authoritarian rule during the 1960s, 1970s, and 1980s. The term was coined by Nigerian president Olusegun Abasanjo.

Segu—A warlord kingdom in the Middle Niger region founded in 1712 by an outsider, Mamari Kulubali, and his disreputable followers. The group dominated the indigenous Bamana farmers, and they recruited soldiers from among their prisoners of war. By 1796, Segu's territory stretched 700 miles from Timbuktu in the east to Bundu in the west.

Sékou Touré, Ahmed—A trade-union leader in Guinea who became general secretary of Guinea's major political party in 1952. During the 1958 referendum on the new French constitution, Sékou Touré's party, the African Democratic Rally, persuaded the voters in Guinea to reject the French Community and claim immediate independence. He served as president of Guinea from independence in 1958 until his death in a Cleveland, Ohio, heart clinic in 1984.

Selassie, Haile—The emperor of Ethiopia, the only country in Africa that had never been colonized, who was driven into exile by the Italian invasion of 1935. After Ethiopia regained its independence in 1941, he resumed his position as emperor, which he held until he was overthrown in a coup in 1974.

Senegambia—The region near the Atlantic coast between the Senegal River in the north and the Gambia River in the south, located just south of the Sahara Desert. Its inhabitants made their living by farming and herding. After the arrival of Europeans around 1450, the region was at the intersection of the trans-Saharan and trans-Atlantic trading systems.

Senghor, Leopold—A Senegalese poet and statesman who became the first president of independent Senegal in 1960 after his Senegalese Progressive Union won all the legislative seats in the 1959 elections. Although he governed Senegal as a one-party state for several years, he later restored limited multiparty government.

Serengeti—An ecosystem located in northern Tanzania and southwestern Kenya. The name means "endless plain" in the language of the indigenous Maasai people. Vegetation in the Serengeti ranges from treeless grasslands with short grasses to regions with medium-high grasses and thorny acacia trees. It has historically been home to a wide variety of large mammals.

Shaka—Founder of the Zulu Kingdom; known for his innovative military strategies; held power through his adaptations of the traditional age-regiment system of southern Africa and through generous gifts of cattle to subordinates.

***shebeen* queen**—A term that refers to the unattached women who came to the mining areas of South Africa to run unlicensed drinking establishments, called *shebeens*, at which they brewed beer and sold it to the miners, while also avoiding the efforts of the South African police to shut them down.

shifting cultivation—A method of maintaining agricultural production by cultivating a plot of land for 3 or 4 years until the nutrients in the soil are depleted, and then leaving it alone to regenerate for the next 12–20 years. This method was most commonly used in regions with poor tropical soils. It encouraged families and even whole villages to move periodically in search of more fertile soils.

Sierra Leone—The name given by the Portuguese to the stretch of Atlantic coast that encompasses the modern nations of Guinea-Bissau, Guinea, and Sierra Leone. The name came from a mountain that looked like the head of a lion. The coastal region was organized politically into small independent chiefdoms, although there were large states, such as Kaabu and Fuuta Jaloo, in the interior.

Sokoto caliphate—Theocratic Muslim state, established in 1812, with its capital at Sokoto, as a result of the jihad led by Usuman dan Fodio in Hausaland. It continued to expand for much of the nineteenth century.

Songhay Empire—A large empire that arose in the West African Sahel after the decline of the Mali Empire in the fifteenth century. The Songhay Empire controlled the trading cities of the Middle Niger region from Jenne to Gao. During the sixteenth century, the rulers of Songhay gave substantial financial support to Islamic scholars in Timbuktu until the empire fell to the Moroccan invasion in 1591.

Soyo—A province of the Kongo Kingdom bordering on both the Congo River and the Atlantic Ocean. Because of its favorable location, it established independent trade relations with European countries. In 1666, it tried to take over the Kongo Kingdom, thus initiating a long period of civil war.

state—A political entity that controls a defined and sovereign territory. State authorities normally collect taxes, redistribute wealth, and operate military or police forces within their territorial boundaries. In premodern times, states were generally found in areas with settled agricultural populations that were accessible to the authorities for purposes of taxation and control.

structural adjustment—A set of free-market economic policy reforms imposed on developing countries by the World Bank and International Monetary Fund (IMF) as a condition for receipt of loans to help them weather economic crises. Critics saw the programs as a modern form of colonialism.

Sunjata—The thirteenth-century founder of the Mali Empire, whose story has been kept alive over the centuries by Mande bards. According to the epic, Sunjata was a hunter-king who rallied the Mande people to defeat the blacksmith-king of Sosso and establish the core of the Mali Empire.

Swahili—A Bantu language that was spoken along the eastern coast of Africa in the region between Kilwa in the south and Mogadishu in the north. Derived from the Arabic word *sāhil*, the name literally means "the language of the coast." The Swahili speakers developed a distinctive culture characterized by urbanism, maritime orientation, and Islam.

***taarab* band**—A type of musical group that originally performed songs in Arabic, accompanied by Southwest Asian instruments, for the sultan of Zanzibar, but branched out in Tanzania in the 1920s to perform songs in Swahili for popular audiences. Because the bands and their audiences were Muslim, they did not perform in bars, but played at weddings and other festive occasions instead.

Tahrir Square—A traffic circle in downtown Cairo, Egypt, that became the focal point for the 2011 protests against Egyptian president Hosni Mubarak. Some 50,000 protestors occupied the square in the first anti-Mubarak protest on January 25, 2011, and the crowds grew to nearly 300,000 people a week later. The continuing protests convinced President Mubarak to resign on February 11.

10-year plan—A type of plan for developing the economy and infrastructure of an African colony, drawn up by many colonial governments after World War II. The best known of these was the Belgian Congo's 10-year plan, which called for improvements in infrastructure, urban planning, and agriculture and was financed mostly by loans from American banks.

Thebes—City located 400 miles south of Memphis; an important Egyptian religious center and the location of the temple for the creator god Amun. From the Middle Kingdom onward, Thebes periodically served as the capital of Egypt, and it became the regular capital during much of the New Kingdom and the Late Period.

Timbuktu—A city located at the point where the Niger bend approaches the Sahara Desert, a location that made it a key transit point in the trans-Saharan trade. During the sixteenth century, Timbuktu was a major center of Islamic learning and scholarship. It lost much of its luster after being sacked and looted by the Moroccan army in 1593.

Tippu Tip—The nickname of Hamid bin Muhammad el Murjebi, the most successful of the nineteenth-century East African caravan traders. He created a large trading state in the region known as Manyema, located halfway between the Atlantic and the Indian Oceans, which funneled ivory and captives to Zanzibar.

tribe—The intermediate level in a type of political organization, normally found among nomads, by which social units linked by real or fictive genealogical ties can unite or separate according to the needs of the moment. The terminology posits a flexible political structure in which clans make up tribes and tribes make up confederations.

tropical rainforest—A type of tall, dense forest usually found in areas of heavy rainfall near the equator. Tropical rainforests are characterized by a triple-canopy structure that allows very little light to reach the forest floor, and by a high level of biodiversity: up to 480 different species of trees may be found in a single hectare (2.5 acres).

Turkana Boy (*Homo ergaster*)—A hominin skeleton discovered in northern Kenya in 1984 that gives a clear indication of being more human than apelike. Turkana Boy had long legs, body proportions similar to those of modern humans, and a brain that was twice the size of Lucy's. He lived near Lake Turkana about 1.6 million years ago.

ujamaa—The system of African socialism announced in 1967 by Tanzanian president Julius Nyerere. The name *ujamaa*, which means "familyhood" in Swahili, expressed the idea that the citizens of Tanzania should work together like one big family. At the heart of the plan was rural development through the creation of *ujamaa* villages that would engage in collective agriculture. The program was abandoned in 1978.

Umar Tal—Sufi cleric born in the western province of Fuuta Toro, member of the Tijaniyya. He claimed to be a Majaddid (renewer) and to receive messages from God, and led a jihad that established the Tukolor Empire, which stretched more than 900 miles from the middle Senegal River valley to the Niger bend.

Unilateral Declaration of Independence (UDI)—The announcement by the white-dominated government in colonial Zimbabwe on November 11, 1965, that it regarded itself as an independent sovereign state. This unilateral declaration of independence was the first for a British colony since the American Declaration of Independence nearly 200 years earlier. The British and the United Nations refused to accept the 1965 UDI because it did not guarantee the rights of the African population.

Usuman dan Fodio—Fulani cleric born in 1754 in the Hausa kingdom of Gobir who became a member of the Qadiriyya. He launched a successful jihad against the governments of the Hausa kingdoms and founded the Sokoto caliphate.

War of the Marabouts—A peasant rebellion in Senegambia that began in 1672, succeeded for a short time, and was crushed in 1677. It was led by a marabout (itinerant Muslim preacher/teacher) named Nasr al-Din, who mobilized opposition to the kings in the region who enslaved their citizens. After Nasr al-Din was killed in a battle in 1674, his movement lost its unity, allowing the ousted kings to regain their power.

warrant chief—A category of chief created by the British for governing African societies that traditionally had decentralized political systems. In setting up an artificial chiefdom, the British would simply pick a compliant person and give him a warrant that proclaimed him the chief. Because many warrant chiefs abused their authority, Igbo women in southern Nigeria organized a series of protests against them in 1929 that were collectively known as the Women's War.

White Highlands—An area of the highlands of central Kenya where Europeans acquired 99-year leases to large tracts of land to be used for agriculture. The railway to Uganda passed through the region, making it accessible to Europeans. The European settlers did not work the land themselves, but relied on African labor.

William Ponty School—The major secondary school for Africans in French West Africa prior to World War II. Its principal goal was the training of teachers, but students who wanted more technical training could switch to the medical school, the veterinary school, or the school of marine mechanics, all in Dakar. It admitted only about 80 new students per year.

Yoruba Wars—A series of wars that engulfed much of what is now southwestern Nigeria between 1813 and 1893, triggered by destruction of the Oyo Empire by the Sokoto caliphate as smaller Yoruba states fought to succeed the defunct empire.

zariba—A type of fortified trading post that traders from Khartoum established in southern Sudan in the second half of the nineteenth century. The zariba system spread westward across the southern savanna toward Lake Chad, carried by Khartoum traders who had been driven out of Sudan by the Egyptian army.

Zionist churches—The African independent churches founded among the Zulu-speaking people of South Africa in the early twentieth century that traced their roots to a ministry emanating from Zion, Illinois. Zionist churches were characterized by prophetic leaders who claimed direct revelations from God through dreams and visions. In contrast to the missionary churches, they emphasized divine healing, casting out demons, and witch-finding. (The Zionist churches in southern Africa are totally unrelated to the Jewish Zionist movement that was instrumental in founding the state of Israel.)

Zulu Kingdom—Kingdom in the region of southern Africa between the Mkhuze and Thukela Rivers, established by Shaka in 1819.

Zwangendaba—Ngoni leader; in the wake of the disintegration of the Ndwandwe kingdom, he established a migratory state whose regiments moved 2,000 miles northward through present-day southern Mozambique, the Zimbabwe Plateau, and Zambia, conquering and raiding as they traveled. He died near the southern tip of Lake Tanganyika in 1848.

CREDITS

Author Photo Page xxvii: © Richard Castiglione.

CHAPTER 1

Photo Credits Page 2: Peter Chadwick/Getty Images; p. 4: NASA; p. 11: NASA; p. 22: Human Origins Program, Smithsonian Institution; p. 24: Human Origins Program, Smithsonian Institution.

Text Credits Page 36: Erin Biba, "A Superplume is the Reason Africa is Splitting Apart," ScientificAmerican.com, July 15, 2014. Reproduced with permission. Copyright © 2014 Scientific American, a Division of Nature America, Inc. All rights reserved; p. 37: "The Woman Who Shook Up Man's Family Tree," from *Lucy's Legacy: The Quest for Human Origins* by Dr. Donald Johanson, copyright © 2009, 2010 by Donald C. Johanson and Kate Wong. Used by permission of Harmony Books, an imprint of the Crown Publishing Group, a division of Penguin Random House LLC. All rights reserved; p. 38: From *Masters of the Planet: The Search for Our Human Origins*, by Ian Tatersall. © 2012 by Ian Tattersall. Reprinted by permission of St. Martin's Press. All Rights Reserved; p. 39: "Almost all living people outside of Africa trace back to a single migration 50,000 years ago," by Elizabeth Culotta, Ann Gibbons. Sciencemag.org, September 21, 2016. Reprinted with permission from AAAS.

Line Art Credits Page 11: Map: "How Big is Africa?" Reprinted by permission of the Outreach Program, African Studies Center, Boston University, 232 Bay State Rd, Boston, MA 02215, http://www.bu.edu/africa/outreach ©Trustees of Boston University; p. 12: Diagram: Rainforest Strata. © Digital Frog International, Inc. Reprinted with permission.

PART OPENER 1

Photo Credits Page 40: Private Collection/ © Gerard Degeorge/Bridgeman Images; p. 41: © British Library Board. All Rights Reserved/Bridgeman Images.

CHAPTER 2

Photo Credits Page 44: DEA/A. Vergani/ Getty Images; p. 47: Philippe Bourseiller/ Getty Images; p. 48: GNU Free Documentation License/Wikimedia Commons; p. 49: NASA; p. 54: Werner Forman/Universal Images Group/ Getty Images; p. 61: Egyptian National Museum, Cairo, Egypt/Bridgeman Images; p. 62: robert-harding/Alamy Stock Photo; p. 67: GRAY, MARTIN/National Geographic Creative; p. 69: ImageBROKER/Alamy Stock Photo.

Text Credits Page 83: Excerpts from *The Histories*, by Herodotus, translated by Robin Waterfield (Oxford: Oxford University Press, 1998). Translation © Robin Waterfield 1998. By permission of Oxford University Press; p. 85: "Bantu Expansion Shows that Habitat Alters the Route and Pace of Human Dispersal," by Rebecca Grollemund, et. al, *PNAS* Vol. 112, No. 43, October 2015, pp. 13296-13301. Reprinted by permission of PNAS.

CHAPTER 3

Photo Credits Page 86: Moe Zoyari/Redux; p. 89: NASA; p. 95: DEA PICTURE LIBRARY/De Agostini/Getty Images; p. 101: robertharding/Getty Images; p. 102: DEA/G. NIMATALLAH/Getty Images; p. 110: Waj/Shutterstock.

Text Credits Page 120: Excerpts from *Athanasius: The Life of Antony and the Letter to Marcellinus*, from The Classics of Western Spirituality, translated by Robert C. Gregg, Copyright © 1980 by Paulist Press, Inc. New York/Mahwah, N.J. Used with permission of Paulist Press. www.paulistpress.com; p. 121: Book I from *The City of God*, by Saint Augustine, translated by Demetrius B. Zema and Gerald G. Walsh (Washington, DC: The Catholic University of America Press, 1950). © 1950 Catholic University of America Press, Inc. Reprinted by permission of the Catholic University of America Press; p. 122: Excerpts from *Jihad in Mediaeval and Modern Islam*, translated from the Arabic and annotated by Rudolph Peters. © 1977 by E.J. Brill, Leiden, Netherlands. Reprinted by permission of Koninklijke BRILL NV; p. 123: Excerpts from Ibn Khaldûn, *The Muqaddimah: An Introduction to History* Vol. 2, 2nd Ed., translated from the Arabic by Franz Rosenthal (Princeton: Princeton University Press, 1967). © 1967 by Bollingen Foundation. Reprinted by permission of Princeton University Press.

CHAPTER 4

Photo Credits Page 124: Mint Images/Art Wolfe/Getty Images; p. 129: © The Trustees of the British Museum; p. 139: Paris, Bibliotheque Nationale/Getty Images; p. 142: DeAgostini/Getty Images; p. 143: Brent Stirton/Getty Images Reportage; p. 151: Kaku Suzuki/Sebun Photo/Getty Images; p. 152: Nigel Pavitt/Getty Images.

Text Credits Page 158: "Ghana and the customs of its inhabitants," from *Corpus of Early Arabic Sources for West African History*, translated by J.F.P. Hopkins, edited and annotated by N. Levtzion and J.F.P. Hopkins (Cambridge: Cambridge University Press, 1981). © University of Ghana, International Academic Union, Cambridge University Press 1991. Reprinted with the permission of Cambridge University Press; p. 159: "The Kingdom of Mali and what appertains to it," from *Corpus of Early Arabic Sources for West African History*, translated by J.F.P. Hopkins, edited and annotated by N. Levtzion and J.F.P. Hopkins (Cambridge: Cambridge University Press, 1981). © University of Ghana, International Academic Union, Cambridge University Press 1991. Reprinted with the permission of Cambridge University Press; p. 160: Excerpts from *Timbuktu and the Songhay Empire*, translated and edited by John Hunwick. © 1977 by E.J. Brill, Leiden, Netherlands. Reprinted by permission of Koninklijke BRILL NV; p. 161: "Ibn Battuta: A Visit to Zeila, Mogadishu, Mombasa and Kilwa Kisiwani" from *The East African Coast: Select Documents from the First to the Earlier Nineteenth Century*, edited by G.S.P. Freeman-Grenville (Oxford: Clarendon Press, 1962). Reprinted by permission of the Estate of G.S.P. Freeman-Grenville.

PART OPENER 2

Photo Credits Page 162: Indianapolis Museum of Art, USA/The Budd Stalnaker Collection of African Textiles/Bridgeman Images; p. 164: Bodleian Library/Getty Images; p. 165: Wikimedia Commons; p. 166: Wikimedia Commons.

CHAPTER 5

Photo Credits Page 168: Sarin Images/The Granger Collection, NYC. All rights reserved; p. 171: Horacio Villalobos/Corbis via Getty Images; p. 178: General Research Division/New York Public Library; p. 182: General Research Division/New York Public Library; p. 189: Album/Art Resource, NY; p. 190: © The Trustees of the British Museum; p. 194: Dona Beatriz Kimpa Vita (by Fr. Bernardo da Gallo), S.O.C.G. 576, fol. 314. Copyright © Archivio Storico di Propaganda Fide; p. 199: Giovanni Antonio Cavazzi, circa 1665–1668, Araldi Collection, vol. A, book 2. Photo: V. Negro, courtesy of the Araldi Collection, Modena, Italy.

Text Credits Page 205: "The Ladder of Ascent" from *Mi'rāj al-Su'ūd: Aḥmad Bābā's Replies on Slavery* (Rabat, Morocoo: Institute of African Studies, 2000), annotated and translated by John Hunwick and Fatima Harrak. Copyright: Reserve a l'Institut des Etudes Africaines, Rabat, Maroc. Reprinted with permission.

CHAPTER 6

Photo Credits Page 208: © National Maritime Museum, Greenwich, London; p. 218 left: General Research Division/New York Public Library; p. 218 right: General Research Division/New York Public Library; p. 224: Marc DEVILLE/Gamma-Rapho via Getty Images; p. 225: © National Maritime Museum, Greenwich, London 231 British Library, London, UK/© British Library Board. All Rights Reserved/ Bridgeman Images; p. 234: Giovanni Antonio Cavazzi, circa 1665–1668, Araldi Collection, vol. A, book 2. Photo: V. Negro, courtesy of the Araldi Collection, Modena, Italy; p. 236: NASA; p. 240: akg-images/De Agostini/S. Vannini.

Text Credits Page 249: Excerpts from *The Diary of Antera Duke, an Eighteenth-Century African Slave Trader*, edited and annotated by Stephen Behrendt, A.J. H. Latham, and David Northrup (Oxford: Oxford University Press, 2010). © 2010 by Oxford University Press, Inc. By permission of Oxford University Press.

Line Art Credits Pages 210–211: Map 11 from *Atlas of the Transatlantic Slave Trade* by David Eltis and David Richardson (New Have: Yale University Press, 2010). Reprinted by permission of Yale University Press.

CHAPTER 7

Photo Credits Page 250: © National Maritime Museum, Greenwich, London; p. 253: Wikimedia Commons; p. 255: Ulrich Doering/Alamy Stock Photo; p. 256: Ariadne Van Zandbergen/Africa Imagery/African Pictures/ The Image Works; p. 257: Royal Geographical Society, London, UK/Bridgeman Images; p. 261: Wikimedia Commons; p. 263: Royal Geographical Society, London, UK/Bridgeman Images; p. 264: Science & Society Picture Library/Getty Images; p. 266: The Granger Collection, NYC. All rights reserved; p. 271: akg-images/ullstein bild; p. 272: © National Maritime Museum, Greenwich, London.

Text Credits Page 280: "An Arabic History of Kilwa, c. 1520" from *The East African Coast: Select Documents from the First to the Earlier Nineteenth Century*, edited by G.S.P. Freeman-Grenville (Oxford: Clarendon Press, 1962). Reprinted by permission of the Estate of G.S.P. Freeman-Grenville; p. 281: "Father Monclaro: A Journey from Kilwa to Pate in 1569" from *The East African Coast: Select Documents from the First to the Earlier Nineteenth Century*, edited by G.S.P. Freeman-Grenville (Oxford: Clarendon Press, 1962). Reprinted by permission of the Estate of G.S.P. Freeman-Grenville.

PART OPENER 3

Photo Credits Page 282: J. Marshall - Tribaleye Images/Alamy Stock Photo; p. 284: Hulton Archive/Getty Images; p. 285: Ann Ronan Pictures/Print Collector/Getty Images; p. 364: akg-images/Gerard Degeorge.

CHAPTER 8

Photo Credits Page 288: Carl E. Akeley/ National Geographic Creative; p. 290: Print Collector/Getty Image; p. 292: General Research Division/New York Public Library; p. 294: Artokoloro Quint Lox Limited/Alamy Stock Photo; p. 302: Pictures from History/The Granger Collection, NYC. All rights reserved; p. 307: Yale Center for British Art, Paul Mellon Collection; p. 309: Tallandier - Rue des Archives/The Granger Collection, NYC. All rights reserved; p. 312: Wikimedia Commons; p. 313: The Print Collector/Alamy Stock Photo; p. 315: Museum Africa; p. 319: Look and Learn/Bridgeman Images; p. 321: Museum Africa.

Text Credits Page 327: Maisha ya Hamed bin Muhammed el Murjebi, yaani Tippu Tip, Kwa Maneno Yake Mwenyewe [The Story of Hamed bin Muhammed el Murjebi, known as Tippu Tip, in His Own Words], translated by W.H. Whitely (Nairobi: East African Literature Bureau, 1966). First published as a supplement to the *East African Swahili Committee Journals* No. 28/2, July 1958 and No. 29/1, January 1959. Reprinted by permission of the Institute of Kiswahili Studies, University of Dar Es Salaam.

CHAPTER 9

Photo Credits Page 330: DeAgostini/Superstock; p. 333: Quint & Lox Limited/Superstock; p. 334: From: Anthony Karim Kamara, A Concise History of Fourah Bay College, Winnipeg, Manitoba: Anthony Karim Kamara, 2011, p. 5; p. 336: Chronicle/Alamy Stock Photo; p. 338: Library of Congress Prints and Photographs Division; p. 351: Granger, NYC/The Granger Collection, NYC. All rights reserved; p. 357: British Library Board. All Rights Reserved/Bridgeman Images; p. 358: Heritage Image Partnership Ltd/Alamy Stock Photo; p. 364: 1836, William Cornwallis Harris/Wikimedia Commons.

Text Credits Page 369: "Kitab Al-Farq: A Work on the Habe Kingdoms Attributed to 'Uthman Dan Fodio'," by M. Hiskett. *Bulletin of the School of Oriental and African Studies*, Vol. 23, No. 3, (October 1960), pp. 558–579; p. 370: *The Black People and Whence They Came: A Zulu View*, by Magema M. Fuze, translated by H.C. Lugg, edited by A.T. Cope (Pietermaritzburg, South Africa: University of Natal Press and Durban South Africa: Killie Campbell Africana Library, 1979). Reprinted by permission of the University of Natal Press; p. 371: "Grandmother Narwimba" from *Strategies of Slaves and Women: Life Stories from East/Central Africa*, by Marcia Wright (New York: Lillian Barber Press, 1993). © Marcia Wright 1993. Reprinted by permission of the author.

PART OPENER 4

Photo Credits Page 372: akg-images/Gerard Degeorge; p. 375: ILN/Mary Evans/The Image Works; p. 376: Julien-Joseph Virey, Histoire Naturelle de Genre Humain (Paris: Chrocard, 1824); p. 377: Library of Congress Prints and Photographs Division.

CHAPTER 10

Photo Credits Page 378: Art Media/Print Collector/Getty Images; p. 381: Northwestern University Library, Government and Geographic Information and Data Services Collection; p. 389: The Battle of Abu Klea, 17th January 1885, 1896 (oil on canvas), Wollen, William Barnes (1857–1936)/National Army Museum, London/Bridgeman Images; p. 390: Mary Evans Picture Library/The Image Works; p. 392: Jon Bower- art and museums/Alamy Stock Photo; p. 396: Wikimedia Commons The original photo is in the National Archives of Zimbabwe: NAZ/Image 172; p. 398: From Supplement to The Illustrated London News vol. CXV, (28 October 1899), pp. IV–V, Yale Center for British Art; p. 400: The University Library, University of Illinois at Urbana-Champaign; p. 404: This photo from Anti-Slavery International was part of an exhibition on "Congo Dialogues" that was put on by Autograph ABP (a British-based non-profit international photo arts agency) in 2014. Photo courtesy of Anti-Slavery International/ Autograph ABP; p. 410: www.smithsonianmag.com/history/brutal-genocide-colonial-africa-finally-gets-its-deserved-recognition.

Text Credits Page 415: Excerpts from *Records of the Maji Maji Rising, Part One*. Historical Association of Tanzania Paper No. 4, edited by G.C.K. Gwassa and John Iliffe (Nairobi: East African Publishing House, 1968); p. 416:, "Arrivée des Blancs sur les Bords des Rivières Equatoriales," by E. Boelaert, H. Vinck, and Ch. Lonkama. *Annales Aequatoria*, Vol. 16 (1995), pp. 41–43. Translated for this volume by Robert Harms, with permission from Centre Æquatoria; p. 417: "Review of Further Developments in Fields with which the Sub-Commission Has Been Concerned" prepared by B. Whitaker in United Nations Economic and Social Council Commission on Human Rights, Sub-Commission on Prevention of Discrimination and Protection of Minorities, Thirty-eighth session, Item 4. E/CN.4/Sub.2/1985/6. © 1985 United Nations. Reprinted with the permission of the United Nations.

CHAPTER 11

Photo Credits Page 418: Basel Mission Archives/Basel Mission Holdings, ref. no. QD-34.001.0017. Cocoa harvest, Ghana, 1925–1935; p. 434: Eliot Elisofon/The LIFE Picture Collection/Getty Images; p. 439: Wikimedia Commons; p. 443: Nigel Pavitt/Getty Images; p. 446: Bettman/Getty Images; p. 449: Wikimedia Commons; p. 451: The Granger Collection, NYC. All rights reserved; p. 459: Kilo-Moto Mine. Postal Stationery, Belgian Congo, Ruanda, Urundi, 1886–1960, 3rd Series, no. 33. www.congobelge.com.

Text Credits Page 457: Reprinted by permission from "Document 108: The Testimony of Nwanyima," in *The Women's War of 1929: A History of Anti-Colonial Resistance in Eastern Nigeria*, edited by Toyin Falola and Adam Paddock (Durham, NC: Carolina Academic Press, 2011), 597; p. 458: "The Gold Coast Farmers' Hymn," by Joseph Ben Gaisil, *African Morning Post*, February 25, 1938.

CHAPTER 12

Photo Credits Page 460: Campbell Collections of the University of KwaZulu-Natal; p. 461: Special Collections, Yale Divinity School Library; p. 470: Special Collections, Yale Divinity School Library; p. 473: Samuel Ajayi Crowther (New York: 1909), p. 264; p. 476: NNP; p. 479: AFP/Getty Images; p. 485: LitCaf Encyclopedia; p. 487: Extraits de la Prophétie du Grand Prophète Simon Kimbangu, Samedi 10 septembre 1921 à Mbanza-Nsanda, Kongo-Central;

p. 492: Photographie et Fabulation dans le Senegal Urbain, in Anthropologie et Sociétés, vol. 21 (1998), no. 1, pp. 15–40.

Text Credits Page 498: Excerpts from *Ghana: The Autobiography of Kwame Nkrumah* (New York: Thomas Nelson & Sons, 1957). Reprinted by permission of Panaf Books; p. 500: "Bewitching People" from Munzele's *Bakulu beto ye Diela diau*, translated by John M. Janzen and "How Witchcraft Works," from Konda Jean, *Mavanga ma Kindoki*, in *An Anthology of Kongo Religion: Primary Texts from Lower Zaïre*, by John M. Janzen and Wyatt MacGaffey (Lawrence, KS: University of Kansas Publications in Anthropology No. 5, 1974). Reprinted with permission.

PART OPENER 5

Photo Credits Page 502: RMN-Grand Palais/Art Resource, NY.

CHAPTER 13

Photo Credits Page 324: Terrence Spencer/Getty Images; p. 506: AP Photo; p. 510: Corbis via Getty Images; p. 515: SSPL/Getty Images; p. 517: George Arents Collection/NYPL; p. 519: African Studies, Herman B Wells Library/Indiana University Bloomington; p. 524: Keystone Pictures USA/Alamy Stock Photo; p. 537: Jurgen Schadeberg/Getty Images.

Text Credits Page 544: From *An African Soldier Speaks*, by Robert H. Kakembo (London: Livingstone Press, 1947). Reprinted by permission of the Estate of Robert H. Kakembo; p. 546: "Report of the Commission Appointed to Enquire into the Disturbances in the Copperbelt, Northern Rhodesia," in *African History through Sources, Vol. 1*, by Nancy J. Jacobs (Cambridge: Cambridge University Press, 2014), p. 279; p. 547: Excerpts from "Football is King," in *Leisure and Society in Colonial Brazzaville*, by Phyllis M. Martin (Cambridge: Cambridge University Press, 1995), pp. 109–110. © Cambridge University Press 1995.

CHAPTER 14

Photo Credits Page 548: Mark Kauffman/The LIFE Picture Collection/Getty Image; p. 550: Pictures from History/The Granger Collection, NYC. All rights reserved; p. 551: Roger Viollet/Getty Images; p. 558: Stroud/Express/Getty Images; p. 563: Keystone/Hulton Archive/Getty Images; p. 571: AFP/Getty Images; p. 573: Terence Spencer/The LIFE Images Collection/Getty Images; p. 579: Jurgen Schadeberg/Getty Images; p. 580: Universal History Archive/UIG via Getty images.

Text Credits Page 586: From *Mau Mau's Daughter: A Life History*, by Wambui Waiyaki Otieno. Copyright © 1998 by Virginia Edith Wambui Waiyaki Otieno. Reprinted with permission of Lynne Rienner Publishers, Inc; p. 587: 'Future constitutional development in the colonies,' Memorandum for Cabinet Colonial Policy Committee by Sir N. Brook. CAB 134/1556, CPC (57)30, 6 September 1957. Held by The National Archives, Kew. Contains public sector information licensed under the Open Government Licence v3.0; p. 588: "Interview with Bocar Biro Barry, Conakry, 21 Jan. 1991" from *Cold War and Decolonization in Guinea, 1946–1958*, by Elizabeth Schmidt. © 2007 by Ohio University Press. Reprinted by permission of Ohio University Press; p. 589: Excerpts from "I am prepared to die," by Nelson Mandela. Statement from the dock at the opening of the defence case in the Rivonia Trial, Palace of Justice, Pretoria Supreme Court Pretoria South Africa, Monday, April 20, 1984. Reprinted by permission of the Nelson Mandela Foundation.

CHAPTER 15

Photo Credits Page 590: Prensa Latina/Camera Press/Redux; p. 594: Bettman Archive/Getty Images; p. 597: Everett Collection Inc/Alamy Stock Photo; p. 599: Hank Walker/The LIFE Picture Collection/Getty Images; p. 601: Eric Piper/Mirrorpix/Newscom; p. 606: AFP/Getty Images; p. 612: ullstein bild/The Granger Collection, NYC. All rights reserved; p. 613: Keystone Pictures USA/Alamy Stock Photo; p. 615: Immanuel Wallerstein Collection of African Liberation Movement Posters (MS 1865). Manuscripts and Archives, Yale University Library; p. 617: Fondation Gilles CARON/Gamma-Rapho via Getty Images.

Text Credits Page 627: From *Roots of a Revolution: Scenes from Zimbabwe's Struggle*, by Ndabaningi Sithole (Oxford: Oxford University Press, 1977). © Ndabaningi Sithole 1977. Reprinted by permission of the Estate of Ndabaningi Sithole; p. 628: "National Liberation and Culture," February 20, 1970, by Amilcar Cabral. Reprinted in *Return to the Source: Selected Speeches by Amilcar Cabral*, edited by Africa Information Service (New York: Monthly Review Press, 1973). © 1973 by Africa Information Service and the African Party for the Independence of Guinea and the Cape Verde Islands. Reprinted by permission of Monthly Review Press; p. 629: "Seeds of Change" from *Unbowed: A Memoir* by Wangari Maathai, copyright © 2006 by Wangari Muta Maathai. Used by permission of Alfred A. Knopf, an imprint of the Knopf Doubleday Publishing Group, a division of Penguin Random House LLC. All rights reserved. And by permission of the author.

CHAPTER 16

Photo Credits Page 634: AP Photo/Greg English, File; p. 644: Kuenzig/laif/Redux; p. 649: Chip Somodevilla/Getty Images; p. 650: Patrick Robert/Sygma/Corbis/Sygma via Getty Images; p. 654: AP Photo/Ng Han Guan; p. 656: Petterik Wiggers/Panos Pictures; p. 661: AP Photo/Hichem Borni; p. 663: Marco LongariAFP/Getty Images; p. 665: AP Photo/Kevin Frayer; p. 671: Eric Feferberg/AFP/Getty Images.

Text Credits Page 674: Excerpt from "As if Nothing Ever Happened," *When Bodies Remember: Experiences and Politics of AIDS in South Africa*, by Didier Fassin, translated by Amy Jacobs and Gabrielle Varro (Berkeley: University of California Press, 2007). © 2007 by The Regents of the University of California. Reprinted by permission of University of California Press; p. 675: From *Life Laid Bare: The Survivors in Rwanda Speak*, by Jean Hatsfield, translated from the French by Linda Coverdale. Originally published as *Dans Le Nu de La Vie*, © 2000 Éditions du Seuil. Translation © 2006 Linda Coverdale. Reprinted with permission from Other Press; p. 676–677: From *Voices of the Arab Spring: Personal Stories from the Arab Revolutions*, edited by Asaad al-Saleh. Copyright © 2015 Columbia University Press. Reprinted with permission of the publisher.

TEXTILE DESIGN MOTIFS

Pages xix, xxi, xxiii, 2–3, 35–39: Werner Forman Archive/Museum fur Volkerkunde, Berlin/Newscom; pp. 44–45, 81–85, 86–87, 119–123, 124–125, 157–161: Private Collection/© Gerard Degeorge/Bridgeman Images; pp. 164–165, 199–203, 208–209, 245–249, 250–251, 277–281: Indianapolis Museum of Art, USA/The Budd Stalnaker Collection of African Textiles/Bridgeman Images; pp. 288–289, 325–329, 330–331, 367–371: J. Marshall - Tribaleye Images/Alamy Stock Photo; pp. 378–379, 413–417, 418–419, 455–459, 460–461, 497–501: akg-images/Gerard; pp. 502, 506–507, 543–547, 548–549, 585–579, 590–591, 625–629: RMN-Grand Palais/Art Resource, NY; pp. 634–635, 673–677: J. Marshall - Tribaleye Images/Alamy Stock Photo.

INDEX

Italic page references indicate maps or illustrations.